THE LONGMAN READER

TENTH EDITION

Judith Nadell

John Langan

Eliza A. Comodromos

PEARSON

Boston Columbus Indianapolis New York San Francisco Upper Saddle River
Amsterdam Cape Town Dubai London Madrid Milan Munich Paris Montréal Toronto
Delhi Mexico City São Paulo Sydney Hong Kong Seoul Singapore Taipei Tokyo

Senior Editor: Lauren A. Finn
Development Editor: David B. Kear
Development Manager: Mary Ellen Curley
Senior Supplements Editor: Donna Campion
Senior Media Producer: Stefanie Liebman
Senior Marketing Manager: Sandra McGuire
Production Manager: Eric Jorgensen
Project Coordination, Text Design, and Electronic Page Makeup: Integra
Cover Designer/Manager: Wendy Ann Fredericks
Cover Photo: © Don White/SuperStock
Visual Researcher: Rona Tuccillo
Senior Manufacturing Buyer: Dennis J. Para
Printer and Binder: Courier Corporation/Westford
Cover Printer: Moore Langen

Credits and acknowledgments borrowed from other sources and reproduced, with permission, in this textbook appear on the appropriate page within text or on pages 664–666.

Library of Congress Cataloging-in-Publication Data

Nadell, Judith.
The Longman reader/Judith Nadell, John Langan, Eliza A. Comodromos.—10th ed.
p. cm.
ISBN-13: 978-0-205-17289-4
ISBN-10: 0-205-17289-X
1. College readers. 2. English language—Rhetoric—Problems, exercises, etc. 3. Report writing—Problems, exercises, etc. I. Langan, John, 1942- II. Comodromos, Eliza A. III. Title.
PE1417.N33 2012
808'.0427—dc22

2011007703

2 3 4 5 6 7 8 9 10—CRW—14 13

PEARSON

ISBN-13: 978-0-205-17289-4
ISBN-10: 0-205-17289-X

CONTENTS

Suggestions for Using Division-Classification in an Essay 227
Figure 6.1 Development Diagram: Writing a Division-Classification Essay 227
Revision Strategies 230
☑ DIVISION-CLASSIFICATION: A REVISION/PEER REVIEW CHECKLIST 230
Student Essay 231
Commentary 234
Activities: Division-Classification 237

Ann McClintock PROPAGANDA TECHNIQUES IN TODAY'S ADVERTISING 239
Propaganda is not just a tool of totalitarian states. American advertisers also use propaganda to get us to buy their products.
Figure 6.2 Essay Structure Diagram: "Propaganda Techniques in Today's Advertising" by Ann McClintock 245

Stephanie Ericsson THE WAYS WE LIE 247
"You look great!" you tell a friend who resembles something the cat dragged in. "The check's in the mail!" you say, knowing your account is empty as a drum. Stephanie Ericsson explores how, when, and why we lie.

William Zinsser COLLEGE PRESSURES 257
According to Zinsser, many students concentrate almost exclusively on the practical—and miss some of the most important parts of college life.

David Brooks PSST! "HUMAN CAPITAL" 266
Human capital, necessary for a just, prosperous society, is more than skills and knowledge. It includes cultural, social, moral, cognitive, and aspirational capital.

Amy Tan MOTHER TONGUE 270
The author explores the different kinds of English that she uses and how they were shaped by the English her Chinese mother spoke.

Additional Writing Topics 277

7 PROCESS ANALYSIS 279

What Is Process Analysis? 279
How Process Analysis Fits Your Purpose and Audience 280
Suggestions for Using Process Analysis in an Essay 281
Figure 7.1 Development Diagram: Writing a Process Analysis Essay 282
Revision Strategies 286

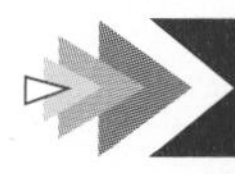

THEMATIC CONTENTS

FAMILY AND CHILDREN

GOVERNMENT AND LAW

HEALTH AND PSYCHOLOGY

HUMAN GROUPS AND SOCIETY

HUMOR AND SATIRE

MEANING IN LIFE

MEDIA AND TECHNOLOGY

MEMORIES AND AUTOBIOGRAPHY

MEN AND WOMEN

NATURE AND SCIENCE

PREFACE

As computers have become firmly established in the lives of students and instructors, the ways in which we acquire information and communicate with one another have been profoundly transformed. Moreover, the ways teachers teach, as well as the ways students learn, have been deeply affected. Perhaps now, more than ever, the need for students to develop sound writing skills has become as essential as it is fundamental. It's to this mission that we continue to be committed.

As in the first nine editions, in this tenth edition we have aimed for a different kind of text—one that would offer fresh examples of professional prose, one that would take a more active role in helping students become stronger readers, thinkers, and writers. *The Longman Reader* continues to include widely read and classic essays, as well as fresh new pieces, such as Chitra Banerjee Divakaruni's "Common Scents" and Alex Wright's "Friending, Ancient or Otherwise." We've been careful to choose selections that range widely in subject matter and approach, from the humorous to the informative, from personal meditation to polemic. We've also made sure that each selection captures students' interest and clearly illustrates a specific pattern of development or a combination of such patterns.

As before, we have also tried to help students bridge the gap between the product and process approaches to reading and writing. Throughout, we describe possible sequences and structures but emphasize that such steps and formats are not meant to be viewed as rigid prescriptions; rather, they are strategies for helping students discover what works best in a particular situation.

WHAT'S NEW IN THE TENTH EDITION OF *THE LONGMAN READER*

In preparing this edition, we looked closely at the reviews completed by instructors using the book. Their comments helped us identify new directions the book might take. Here are some of the new features of this edition of *The Longman Reader*.

- **Fifteen of the fifty-eight selections are new.** Whether written by a journalist such as Barbara Ehrenreich ("Serving in Florida"), an academic writer such as Alexander T. Tabarrok ("A Moral Solution to the Organ Shortage"), or a literary figure such as Amy Tan ("Mother Tongue"), the new selections are bound to stimulate strong writing on a variety of topics—education, technology, interpersonal relationships, gender, and morality, to name a few. When selecting new readings, we took special care to include pieces written from a personal point of view (for example, Riverbend's "Bloggers Without Borders") as well as those citing academic research (for example, Jane S. Shaw's "Nature in the Suburbs"). Finally, honoring the requests of many instructors, we also made an effort to find compelling pieces on technology and contemporary life, such as Alex Wright's "Friending, Ancient or Otherwise"

- **A new discussion on how to read visuals** has been added to Chapter 1 to help students think critically about why and how images as well as visually presented data are used in documents, better preparing them for the sorts of documents they will encounter in other course areas.
- **Appendix A, "A Guide to Using Sources,"** provides new visual instruction and highlighted examples of integrating research using summary, paraphrase, and quotation so that students have more visual and at-a-glance pedagogy available to learn complex academic writing skills.
- **A new pair of pro-con essays** in the argumentation-persuasion chapter further expands coverage of refutation strategies: Alex T. Tabarrock's "A Moral Solution to the Organ Shortage" and Virginia Postrel's "Need Transplant Donors? Pay Them"—two readings that explore the solutions to a shortage of organs for transplant (Ch. 11).

ORGANIZATION OF *THE LONGMAN READER*

Buoyed by compliments about the previous editions' teachability, we haven't tinkered with the book's underlying format. Such a structure, we've been told, does indeed help students read more critically, think more logically, and write more skillfully. Here is the book's basic format.

Chapter 1, "The Reading Process"

Designed to reflect current theories about the interaction of reading, thinking, and writing, this chapter provides guided practice in a three-part process for reading with close attention and a high level of interpretive skill. This step-by-step process sharpens students' understanding of the book's selections and promotes the rigorous thinking needed to write effective essays.

An activity at the end of the chapter gives students a chance to use the three-step process. First, they read an essay by the journalist Ellen Goodman. The essay has been annotated both to show students the reading process in action and to illustrate how close critical reading can pave the way to promising writing topics. Then students respond to sample questions and writing assignments, all similar to those accompanying each of the book's selections. The chapter thus does more than just tell students how to sharpen their reading abilities; it guides them through a clearly sequenced plan for developing critical reading skills.

Chapter 2, "The Writing Process"

As an introduction to essay writing and to make the composing process easier for students to grasp, we provide a separate section for each of the following stages: prewriting, identifying a thesis, supporting the thesis with evidence, organizing the evidence, writing the first draft, revising, and editing and proofreading. The stages are also illustrated in a diagram, "Stages of the Writing Process."

From the start, we point out that the stages are fluid. Indeed, the case history of an evolving student paper illustrates just how recursive and individualized the writing process can be. Guided activities at the end of each section give students practice taking their essays through successive stages in the composing process.

To illustrate the link between reading and writing, the writing chapter presents the progressive stages of a student paper written in response to Ellen Goodman's "Family Counterculture," the selection presented in Chapter 1. An easy-to-spot symbol in the margin makes it possible to locate—at a glance—this evolving student essay. Commentary following the student paper highlights the essay's strengths and points out spots that could use additional work. In short, by the end of the second chapter, the entire reading-writing process has been illustrated, from reading a selection to writing about it.

Chapters 3–11: Patterns of Development

The chapters contain selections grouped according to nine patterns of development: description, narration, exemplification, division-classification, process analysis, comparison-contrast, cause-effect, definition, and argumentation-persuasion. The sequence progresses from the more personal and expressive patterns to the more public and analytic. However, because each chapter is self-contained, the patterns may be covered in any order. Instructors preferring a thematic approach will find the Thematic Contents helpful.

The Longman Reader treats the patterns separately because such an approach helps students grasp the distinctive characteristics of each pattern. At the same time, the book continually shows the way writers usually combine patterns in their work. We also encourage students to view the patterns as strategies for generating and organizing ideas. Writers, we explain, rarely set out to compose an essay in a specific pattern. Rather, they choose a pattern or combination of patterns because it suits their purpose, audience, and subject.

Each of the nine pattern-of-development chapters follows the format below.

1. A **striking visual** opens every pattern-of-development chapter. The photo reappears in thumbnail form following the "How [name of pattern] Fits Your Purpose and Audience" section. There, the image prompts a pattern-related writing activity that encourages students to consider issues of purpose and audience in a piece of real-world writing.
2. **A detailed explanation of the pattern** begins the chapter. The explanation includes (a) a definition of the pattern, (b) a description of the way the pattern helps a writer accommodate his or her purpose and audience, and (c) step-by-step guidelines for using the pattern.
3. **A Development Diagram** in each chapter illustrates how the pattern is expressed in each stage of the writing process.
4. **An annotated student essay** using the pattern appears next. Written in response to one of the professional selections in the chapter, each essay illustrates the characteristic features of the pattern discussed in the chapter.
5. **Commentary** after each student essay points out the blend of patterns in the piece, identifies the paper's strengths, and locates areas needing improvement. "First draft" and "revised" versions of one section of the essay reveal how the student writer went about revising, thus illustrating the relationship between the final draft and the steps taken to produce it.
6. **Professional selections** in the pattern-of-development chapters are accompanied by these items:
   - **An Essay Structure Diagram** for the first essay in each section shows how the essay makes use of patterns of development.
   - **A biographical note** and **Pre-Reading Journal Entry assignment** give students a perspective on the author and create interest in the piece. The journal assignment encourages students to explore—in a loose, unpressured way—their thoughts about an issue that will be raised in the selection. The journal entry thus motivates students to read the piece with extra care, attention, and personal investment.
   - **Questions for Close Reading,** five in all, help students dig into and interpret the selection's content. The first question asks them to identify the selection's thesis; the last provides work on vocabulary development.

- **Questions About the Writer's Craft,** four in all, deal with such matters as purpose, audience, tone, organization, sentence structure, diction, and figures of speech. The first question in the series (labeled "The Pattern") focuses on the distinctive features of the pattern used in the selection. And usually there's another question (labeled "Other Patterns") that asks students to analyze the writer's use of additional patterns in the piece.
- **Writing Assignments,** five in all, follow each selection. Packed with suggestions on how to proceed, the assignments use the selection as a springboard. The first two assignments ask students to write an essay using the same pattern as the one used in the selection; the next two assignments encourage students to experiment with a combination of patterns in their own essay; the last assignment helps students turn the raw material in their pre-reading journal entries into fully considered essays.

  Frequently, the assignments are preceded by the symbol , indicating a cross-reference to at least one other selection in the book. By encouraging students to make connections among readings, such assignments broaden students' perspective and give them additional material to draw on when they write. These "paired assignments" will be especially welcome to instructors stressing recurring ideas and themes. In other cases, assignments are preceded by the symbol , indicating that students might benefit from conducting library and/or Internet research.

7. **Prewriting and revising activities** in shaded boxes at the end of each chapter help students understand the unique demands posed by the pattern being studied.
8. **Two sets of Additional Writing Assignments** close each pattern-of-development chapter: "General Assignments" and "Assignments with a Specific Purpose, Audience, and Point of View." The first set provides open-ended topics that prompt students to discover the best way to use a specific pattern; the second set develops their sensitivity to rhetorical context by asking them to apply the pattern in a real-world situation.

Chapter 12, "Combining the Patterns"

The final chapter offers a sample student essay as well as two essays each by three very different prose stylists. Annotations on the student essay and on one of the professional selections show how writers often blend patterns of development in their work. The chapter also provides guidelines to help students analyze this fusing of patterns.

Appendixes and Glossary

Appendix A, "A Guide to Using Sources," has been extensively rewritten and provides guidelines for evaluating, analyzing, and synthesizing sources; using quotations, summaries, and paraphrases to integrate sources into a paper; and documenting sources following the latest MLA style guidelines. **Appendix B, "Avoiding Ten Common Writing Errors,"** targets common problem areas in student writing and offers quick, accessible solutions for each. The **Glossary** lists and defines all the key terms presented in the text.

SUPPLEMENTS FOR STUDENTS AND INSTRUCTORS

Instructor's Manual

A comprehensive Instructor's Manual contains the following: in-depth answers to the "Questions for Close Reading" and "Questions About the Writer's Craft"; suggested activities; pointers about using the book; a detailed syllabus; and an analysis of the blend of patterns in the selections in the "Combining the Patterns" chapter.

MyCompLab Website

MyCompLab integrates the market-leading instruction, multimedia tutorials, and exercises for writing grammar and research that users have come to identify with the program with a new online composing space and new assessment tools. The result is a revolutionary application that offers a seamless and flexible teaching and learning environment built specifically for writers. Created after years of extensive research and in partnership with composition faculty and students across the country, MyCompLab provides help for writers in the context of their writing, with instructor and peer commenting functionality, proven tutorials and exercises for writing, grammar and research, an e-portfolio, an assignment-builder, a bibliography tool, tutoring services, and a gradebook and course management organization created specifically for writing classes. Visit www.mycomplab.com for more information.

ACKNOWLEDGMENTS

At Pearson, our thanks go to Lauren Finn for her perceptive editorial guidance and enthusiasm for *The Longman Reader*. We're also indebted to Linda Stern and to David Kear, our Development Editor, and to Angela Norris of Integra-Chicago and Eric Jorgensen of Pearson for their skillful handling of the never-ending complexities of the production process.

Over the years, many writing instructors have reviewed *The Longman Reader* and responded to detailed questionnaires about its selections and pedagogy. Their comments have guided our work every step of the way. We are particularly indebted to the following reviewers for the valuable assistance they have provided during the preparation of the tenth edition of *The Longman Reader:* Michael Alleman, Louisiana State University-Eunice; Martha Bachman, Camden County College; Kamala Balasubramanian, Grossmont College; Andrew Ball, Bluegrass Community and Technical College; Samone Polk Brooks, Lane College; Kimberley Browe, University of New Haven; Mary Cantrell, Tulsa Community College; Holly Carey, Lamar University; Patricia Maidei Chogugudza, Langston University; Joseph Couch, Montgomery College; Kathy Daily, Tulsa Community College, Southeast Campus; Darren DeFrain, Wichita State University; Jonathan Fegley, Middle Georgia College; Billy Fontenot, Louisiana State University at Eunice; Hank Galmish, Green River Community College; Barbara Goldstein, Hillsborough Community College; Harold William Halbert, Montgomery County Community College; Lillie Miller Jackson, Southwest Tennessee Community College; Theresa M. Jackson, Western Iowa Tech Community College; Cheryl Johnson, Lamar University; Richard Lee, State University of New York College at Oneonta; Dolores MacNaughton, Umpqua Community College; Raphael Okonkwor, Moraine Park Technical College; Dana Resente, Montgomery County Community College; Mary Simpson, Central Texas College; Charles Snodgrass, Grambling State University; Jean Sorensen, Grayson County College; Alex Tavares; Hillsborough Community College; April Van Camp, Indian River Community College; Deborah LeSure Wilbourn, Northwest Mississippi Community College; and Darcy A. Zabel, Friends University.

Finally, as always, we're thankful to our students. Their reaction to various drafts of material sharpened our thinking and helped focus our work. And we are especially indebted to the eleven students whose essays are included in the book. Their thoughtful, carefully revised papers dramatize the potential of student writing and the power of the composing process.

JUDITH NADELL
JOHN LANGAN
ELIZA A. COMODROMOS

THE READING PROCESS

More than two hundred years ago, essayist Joseph Addison commented, "Of all the diversions of life, there is none so proper to fill up its empty spaces as the reading of useful and entertaining authors." Addison might have added that reading also challenges our beliefs, deepens our awareness, and stimulates our imagination. And the more challenging the material, the more actively involved the reader must be.

The essays in this book, which range from the classic to the contemporary, call for active reading. They contain language that will move you, images that will enlarge your understanding of other people, and ideas that will transform your views on complex issues. They will also help you develop a repertoire of reading skills that will benefit you throughout life.

The novelist Saul Bellow observed, "A writer is a reader moved to emulation." As you become a better reader, your own writing will become more insightful and polished. Increasingly, you'll be able to employ the techniques that professional writers use to express ideas.

The three-stage approach outlined here will help you get the most out of the readings in this book, as well as any other readings, including those with visuals, and ultimately improve your own writing too.

STAGE 1: GET AN OVERVIEW OF THE SELECTION

Ideally, you should get settled in a quiet place that encourages concentration. Once you're settled, it's time to read the selection. To ensure a good first reading, try the following hints.

☑ FIRST READING: A CHECKLIST

- ❑ Get an overview of the essay and its author. Start by reading the biographical note that precedes the selection. By providing background information about the author, the note helps you evaluate the writer's credibility as well as his or her slant on the subject.
- ❑ Do the *Pre-Reading Journal Entry* assignment, which precedes the selection. This assignment "primes" you for the piece by helping you to explore—in an easy, unpressured way—your thoughts about a key point raised in the selection. By preparing the journal entry, you're inspired to read the selection with special care, attention, and personal investment. (For more on pre-reading journal entries, see pages 16–17 and 657.)
- ❑ Consider the selection's title. A good title often expresses the essay's main idea, giving you insight into the selection even before you read it.
- ❑ Read the selection straight through purely for pleasure. Allow yourself to be drawn into the world the author has created. Because you bring your own experiences and viewpoints to the piece, your reading will be unique.
- ❑ If a reading has visuals, ask yourself these questions: Who created the visuals? Is the source reliable? What does the caption say? If the visual is an image, what general mood, feeling, or other impression does it convey? If it is a graphic, is information clearly labeled and presented?
- ❑ After this initial reading of the selection, briefly describe the piece and your reaction to it.

STAGE 2: DEEPEN YOUR SENSE OF THE SELECTION

At this point, you're ready to move more deeply into the selection. A second reading will help you identify the specific features that triggered your initial reaction.

There are a number of techniques you can use during this second, more focused reading. Mortimer Adler, a well-known writer and editor, argued passionately for marking up the material we read. The physical act of annotating, he believed, etches the writer's ideas more sharply in the mind, helping readers grasp and remember those ideas more easily. Adler also described various annotation techniques he used when reading. Several of these techniques, adapted somewhat, are presented in the checklist below.

☑ SECOND READING: A CHECKLIST

Using a pen (or pencil) and highlighter, you might…

- ❑ Underline or highlight the selection's main idea, or thesis, often found near the beginning or end. If the thesis isn't stated explicitly, write down your own version of the selection's main idea.
- ❑ Locate the main supporting evidence used to develop the thesis. Place numbers in the margin to designate the main points that support the thesis.
- ❑ Circle or put an asterisk next to key ideas that are stated more than once.
- ❑ Take a minute to write "Yes," "No," or a brief comment beside points with which you strongly agree or disagree. Your reaction to these points often explains your feelings about the aptness of the selection's ideas.
- ❑ Return to any unclear passages you encountered during the first reading. You may now be able to make sense of initially confusing spots. However, you may discover that the writer's thinking isn't as clear as it could be.
- ❑ Use your dictionary to check the meanings of any unfamiliar words.
- ❑ Take some quick notes about any visuals. What is the author's purpose? Do images such as photos tell a story? Do they make assumptions about viewers' beliefs or knowledge? What elements stand out? How do the colors and composition (arrangement of elements) work to convey an impression? Are any graphs and similar visuals adequately discussed in the text? Is the information up-to-date and presented without distortion? Is it relevant to the text discussion?
- ❑ If your initial impression of the selection has changed in any way, try to determine why you reacted differently on this reading.

STAGE 3: EVALUATE THE SELECTION

Now that you have a good grasp of the selection, you may want to read it a third time, especially if the piece is long or complex. This time, your goal is to make judgments about the essay's effectiveness. Keep in mind, though, that you shouldn't evaluate the selection until after you have a strong hold on it. A negative or even a positive reaction is valid only if it's based on an accurate reading.

To evaluate the essay, ask yourself the following questions.

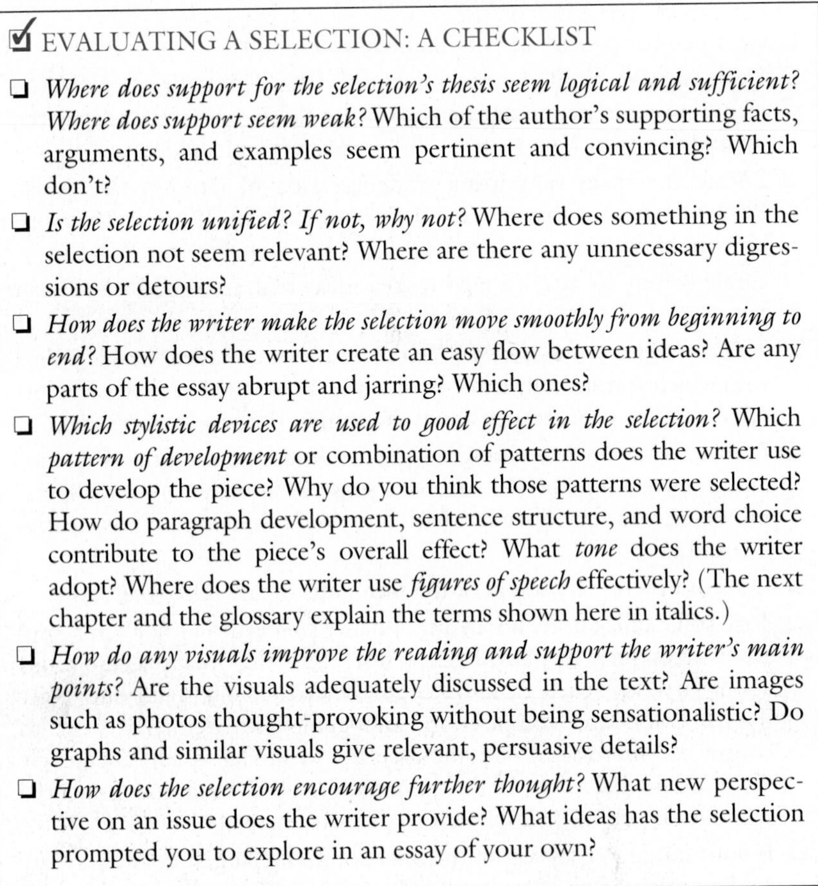

☑ EVALUATING A SELECTION: A CHECKLIST

- ❑ *Where does support for the selection's thesis seem logical and sufficient? Where does support seem weak?* Which of the author's supporting facts, arguments, and examples seem pertinent and convincing? Which don't?
- ❑ *Is the selection unified? If not, why not?* Where does something in the selection not seem relevant? Where are there any unnecessary digressions or detours?
- ❑ *How does the writer make the selection move smoothly from beginning to end?* How does the writer create an easy flow between ideas? Are any parts of the essay abrupt and jarring? Which ones?
- ❑ *Which stylistic devices are used to good effect in the selection?* Which *pattern of development* or combination of patterns does the writer use to develop the piece? Why do you think those patterns were selected? How do paragraph development, sentence structure, and word choice contribute to the piece's overall effect? What *tone* does the writer adopt? Where does the writer use *figures of speech* effectively? (The next chapter and the glossary explain the terms shown here in italics.)
- ❑ *How do any visuals improve the reading and support the writer's main points?* Are the visuals adequately discussed in the text? Are images such as photos thought-provoking without being sensationalistic? Do graphs and similar visuals give relevant, persuasive details?
- ❑ *How does the selection encourage further thought?* What new perspective on an issue does the writer provide? What ideas has the selection prompted you to explore in an essay of your own?

ASSESSING VISUALS IN A READING

Writers may use visuals—images and graphics—to help convey their message. You can incorporate your "reading" of these visuals into the three-stage process you use for reading text: In stage 1, *preview* the visuals at the same time that you get an overview of the text. In stage 2, *analyze and interpret* the visuals as a means of deepening your sense of the reading. Finally, in stage 3, *evaluate* the visuals as part of your evaluation of the entire selection.

Suppose a reading aims to persuade readers that the international community must set up an organization that stands ready to implement an immediate and coordinated response to natural diasters, no matter where they occur. The reading includes a photo (see below) taken in the aftermath of the magnitude 7 earthquake that hit Haiti on January 12, 2010. How can we evaluate this image and its effectiveness for the reader?

1. Previewing the Photo. We see that the photo was found at *Time* magazine online and was taken by a photographer for the Associated Press (AP)—both reliable sources that we can trust. The author of the essay has written a caption that clearly explains the image, and the phrase "Using whatever implements are at their disposal" supports the author's point that an immediate response is needed. We also notice, however, that the caption uses strong language, for example, "catastrophic" and "devastated." Information in the reading will have to support the use of these terms. Still, our first response to the photo would be one of sympathy and perhaps compassion for the people of Haiti.

Using whatever implements are at their disposal, Haitians searched for survivors—and victims—of the catastrophic earthquake that devastated Port-au-Prince and many surrounding areas on January 12, 2010.

Source: "Search and Rescue." *Devastation from the Haiti Earthquake.* Photo essay. *Time.com.* January 2010.

2. Analyzing and Interpreting the Photo. The photo tells a story of people coming together to help one another in the aftermath of the earthquake. The elements in the photo are arranged so that we first see people silhouetted against clouds, working with hand tools. Then we realize the people are standing atop a collapsed building, and we see the startling image of cars crushed beneath that structure. Now we understand the scope of the wreckage. The startling image of the ruined cars and the hopeful brightness of the sky are punctuated by the dark, massive bulk of the collapsed structure. Though we cannot see people's faces, we can imagine their determination. But we can also tell that their tools are unlikely to be adequate for the urgent task of finding those buried in the rubble.

3. Evaluating the Photo. The photo powerfully illustrates the scale of the work facing Haiti and the probable inadequacy of the country's resources. The contrast between the crushed cars and building below and the determined workers above conveys a sense of the hopefulness of the human spirit even in dire situations. So many readers will feel an emotional response to these people, will see that they need help, and will want to help them. The photo and caption together, therefore, successfully support the idea that some countries may not have the means to cope effectively with huge natural disasters. The text of the reading will have to convince the reader that setting up an international organization to coordinate responses to these crises is the right solution.

A MODEL ANNOTATED READING

It takes some work to follow the three-step approach just described, but the selections in *The Longman Reader* are worth the effort. Bear in mind that none of the selections sprang full-blown from the pen of its author. Rather, each essay is the result of hours of work—hours of thinking, writing, rethinking, and revising. As a reader, you should show the same willingness to work with the selections, to read them carefully and thoughtfully.

To illustrate the multi-stage reading process just described, we've annotated the professional essay that follows: "Family Counterculture" by Ellen Goodman. Note that annotations are provided in the margin of the essay as well as at the end of the essay. As you read Goodman's essay, try applying the three-stage sequence. You can measure your ability to dig into the selection by making your own annotations on Goodman's essay and then comparing them to ours. You can also see how well you evaluated the piece by answering the questions in "Evaluating a Selection: A Checklist" and then comparing your responses to ours on pages 10–11.

Ellen Goodman

A recipient of a Pulitzer Prize for Distinguished Commentary, Ellen Goodman (1941–) graduated *cum laude* from Radcliffe College in 1963. She worked for *Newsweek* and the *Detroit Free Press* before joining the staff of *The Boston Globe* in 1967. She began writing a column focused on social change in 1974, and the column has been nationally syndicated by the Washington Post Writers Group since 1976. Her books include *Turning Points* (1979) and, with coauthor Patricia O'Brien, *I Know Just What You Mean: The Power of Friendship in Women's Lives* (2000). She has also published six collections of her columns, including *Value Judgments* (1993), in which the following selection appears.

Pre-Reading Journal Entry

Television is often blamed for having a harmful effect on children. Do you think this criticism is merited? In what ways does TV exert a negative influence on children? In what ways does TV exert a positive influence on youngsters? Take a few minutes to respond to these questions in your journal.

Marginal Annotations

Family Counterculture

Interesting take on the term "counterculture"

Time frame established

Light humor; easy, casual tone

Time frame picked up

Thesis, developed overall by cause-effect pattern

First research-based example to support thesis

Sooner or later, most Americans become card-carrying members of the counterculture. This is not an underground holdout of hippies. No beads are required. All you need to join is a child. 1

At some point between Lamaze and the PTA, it becomes clear that one of your main jobs as a parent is to counter the culture. What the media delivers to children by the masses, you are expected to rebut one at a time. 2

The latest evidence of this frustrating piece of the parenting job description came from pediatricians. This summer, the American Academy of Pediatrics called for a ban on television food ads. Their plea was hard on the heels of a study showing that one Saturday morning of TV cartoons contained 202 junk-food ads. 3

The kids see, want, and nag. That is, after all, the theory behind advertising to children, since few six-year-olds have their own trust funds. The end result, said the pediatricians, is obesity and high cholesterol. 4

Their call for a ban was predictably attacked by the grocers' association. But it was also attacked by people assembled under the umbrella marked "parental responsibility." We don't need bans, said these "PR" people; we need parents who know how to say "no." 5

Relevant paragraph? Identifies Goodman as a parent, but interrupts flow

6 Well, I bow to no one in my capacity for naysaying. I agree that it's a well-honed skill of child raising. By the time my daughter was seven, she qualified as a media critic.

Transition doesn't work but would if ¶6 were cut

7 But it occurs to me now that the call for "parental responsibility" is increasing in direct proportion to the irresponsibility of the marketplace. Parents are expected to protect their children from an increasingly hostile environment.

Series of questions and brief answers consistent with overall casual tone

8 Are the kids being sold junk food? Just say no. Is TV bad? Turn it off. Are there messages about sex, drugs, violence all around? Counter the culture.

Brief real-life examples support thesis

Fragments

9 Mothers and fathers are expected to screen virtually every aspect of their children's lives. To check the ratings on the movies, to read the labels on the CDs, to find out if there's MTV in the house next door. All the while keeping in touch with school and, in their free time, earning a living.

More examples

10 In real life, most parents do a great deal of this monitoring and just-say-no-ing. Any trip to the supermarket produces at least one scene of a child grabbing for something only to have it returned to the shelf by a frazzled parent. An extraordinary number of the family arguments are over the goodies—sneakers, clothes, games—that the young know only because of ads.

Another weak transition—no contrast

Restatement of thesis

11 But at times it seems that the media have become the mainstream culture in children's lives. Parents have become the alternative.

Second research-based example to support thesis

Citing an expert reinforces thesis

12 Barbara Dafoe Whitehead, a research associate at the Institute for American Values, found this out in interviews with middle-class parents. "A common complaint I heard from parents was their sense of being overwhelmed by the culture. They felt their voice was a lot weaker. And they felt relatively more helpless than their parents.

Restatement of thesis

13 "Parents," she notes, "see themselves in a struggle for the hearts and minds of their own children." It isn't that they can't say no. It's that there's so much more to say no to.

14 Without wallowing in false nostalgia, there has been a fundamental shift. Americans once expected parents to raise their children in accordance with the dominant

Comparison-contrast pattern—signaled by "once," "Today," "Once," and "Now"

cultural messages. Today they are expected to raise their children in opposition.

Once the chorus of cultural values was full of ministers, teachers, neighbors, leaders. They demanded more conformity, but offered more support. Now the messengers are Ninja Turtles, Madonna, rap groups, and celebrities pushing sneakers. Parents are considered "responsible" only if they are successful in their resistance. 15

Restatement of thesis

It's what makes child raising harder. It's why parents feel more isolated. It's not just that American families have less time with their kids. It's that we have to spend more of this time doing battle with our own culture. 16

Conveys the challenges that parents face

It's rather like trying to get your kids to eat their green beans after they've been told all day about the wonders of Milky Way. Come to think of it, it's exactly like that. 17

Annotations at End of Selection

Thesis: First stated in paragraph 2 ("... it becomes clear that one of your main jobs as a parent is to counter the culture. What the media delivers to children by the masses, you are expected to rebut one at a time.") and then restated in paragraphs 11 ("the media have become the mainstream culture in children's lives. Parents have become the alternative."); 13 (Parents are frustrated, not because "... they can't say no. It's that there's so much more to say no to."); and 16 ("It's not just that American families have less time with their kids. It's that we have to spend more of this time doing battle with our own culture.").

First reading: A quick take on a serious subject. Informal tone and to-the-point style gets to the heart of the media vs. parenting problem. Easy to relate to.

Second and third readings:

1. Uses the findings of the American Academy of Pediatrics, a statement made by Barbara Dafoe Whitehead, and a number of brief examples to illustrate the relentless work parents must do to counter the culture.
2. Uses cause-effect overall to support thesis and comparison-contrast to show how parenting nowadays is more difficult than it used to be.
3. Not everything works (reference to her daughter as a media critic, repetitive and often inappropriate use of "but" as a transition), but overall the essay succeeds.
4. At first, the ending seems weak. But it feels just right after an additional reading. Shows how parents' attempts to counter the culture are as commonplace as their attempts to get kids to eat vegetables. It's an ongoing and constant battle that makes parenting more difficult than it has to be and less enjoyable than it should be.
5. Possible essay topics: A humorous paper about the strategies kids use to get around their parents' saying "no" or a serious paper on the negative effects on kids of another aspect of television culture (cable television, tabloid-style talk shows, and so on).

The following answers to the questions in "Evaluating a Selection: A Checklist" on page 4 will help crystallize your reaction to Goodman's essay.

1. *Where does support for the selection's thesis seem logical and sufficient? Where does support seem weak?*

   Goodman begins to provide evidence for her thesis when she cites the American Academy of Pediatrics' call for a "ban on television food ads" (paragraphs 3–5). The ban followed a study showing that kids are exposed to 202 junk-food ads during a single Saturday morning of television cartoons. Goodman further buoys her thesis with a list of brief "countering the culture" examples (8–10) and a slightly more detailed example (10) describing the parent-child conflicts that occur on a typical trip to the supermarket. By citing Barbara Dafoe Whitehead's findings later on (12–13), Goodman further reinforces her point that the need for constant rebuttal makes parenting especially frustrating: Because parents have to say "no" to virtually everything, more and more family time ends up being spent "doing battle" with the culture (16).

2. *Is the selection unified? If not, why not?*

   In the first two paragraphs, Goodman identifies the problem and then provides solid evidence of its existence (3–4, 8–10). But Goodman's comments in paragraph 6 about her daughter's skill as a media critic seem distracting. Even so, paragraph 6 serves a purpose because it establishes Goodman's credibility by showing that she, too, is a parent and has been compelled to be a constant naysayer with her child. From paragraph 7 on, the piece stays on course by focusing on the way parents have to compete with the media for control of their children. The concluding paragraphs (16–17) reinforce Goodman's thesis by suggesting that parents' struggle to counteract the media is as common—and as exasperating—as trying to get children to eat their vegetables when all the kids want is to gorge on candy.

3. *How does the writer make the selection move smoothly from beginning to end?*

   The first two paragraphs of Goodman's essay are clearly connected: The phrase "sooner or later" at the beginning of the first paragraph establishes a time frame that is then picked up at the beginning of the second paragraph with the phrase "at some point between Lamaze and the PTA." And Goodman's use in paragraph 3 of the word *this* ("The latest evidence of *this* frustrating piece of the parenting job description...") provides a link to the preceding paragraph. Other connecting strategies can be found in the piece. For example, the words *once, Today, Once,* and *Now* in paragraphs 14–15 provide an easy-to-follow contrast between parenting in earlier times and parenting in this era. However, because paragraph 6 contains a distracting aside, the contrast implied by the word *But* at the beginning of paragraph 7 doesn't work. Nor does Goodman's use of the word *But* at the beginning of paragraph 11 work; the point there emphasizes rather than contrasts with the one made in paragraph 10. From this point on, though, the essay is tightly written and moves smoothly along to its conclusion.

4. *Which stylistic devices are used to good effect in the selection?*

   Goodman uses several patterns of development in her essay. The selection as a whole shows the *effect* of the mass media on kids and their parents. In paragraphs 3 and 12, Goodman provides *examples in the form of research data* to support her thesis, while paragraphs 8–10 provide a series of *brief real-life examples.* Paragraphs 12–15 use *contrast,* and paragraph 17 makes a *comparison* to punctuate Goodman's concluding point. Throughout, Goodman's *informal, conversational tone* draws readers in, and her *no-holds-barred style* drives her point home forcefully. In paragraph 8, she uses a *question-and-answer format* ("Are the kids being sold junk food? Just say no.") and *short sentences* ("Turn it off" and "Counter the culture") to illustrate how pervasive the situation is. And in paragraph 9, she uses *fragments* ("To check the ratings..." and "All the while keeping in touch with school...") to focus attention on the problem. These varied stylistic devices help make the essay a quick, enjoyable read. Finally, although Goodman is concerned about the corrosive effects of the media, she leavens her essay with dashes of *humor.* For example, the image of parents as counterculturists (1) and the comments about green beans and Milky Ways (17) probably elicit smiles or gentle laughter from most readers.

5. *How does the selection encourage further thought?*

   Goodman's essay touches on a problem most parents face at some time or another—having to counter the culture in order to protect their children. Her main concern is how difficult it is for parents to say "no" to virtually every aspect of the culture. Although Goodman offers no immediate solutions, her presentation of the issue urges us to decide for ourselves which aspects of the culture should be countered and which should not.

If, for each essay you read in this book, you consider the preceding questions, you'll be able to respond thoughtfully to the *Questions for Close Reading* and *Questions About the Writer's Craft* presented after each selection. Your responses will, in turn, prepare you for the writing assignments that follow the questions. Interesting and varied, the assignments invite you to examine issues raised by the selections and encourage you to experiment with various writing styles and organizational patterns.

Following are some sample questions and writing assignments based on the Goodman essay; all are similar to the sort that appear later in this book. Note that the final writing assignment paves the way for a student essay, the stages of which are illustrated in Chapter 2.

Questions for Close Reading

1. According to Goodman, what does it mean to "counter the culture"? Why is this harder now than ever before?
2. Which two groups, according to Goodman, protested the American Academy of Pediatrics's ban on television food ads? Which of these two groups does she take more seriously? Why?

Questions About the Writer's Craft

1. What audience do you think Goodman had in mind when she wrote this piece? How do you know? Where does she address this audience directly?
2. What word appears four times in paragraph 16? Why do you think Goodman repeats this word so often? What is the effect of this repetition?

Writing Assignments

1. Goodman believes that parents are forced to say "no" to almost everything the media offer. Write an essay illustrating the idea that not everything the media present is bad for children.
2. Goodman implies that, in some ways, today's world is hostile to children. Do you agree? Drawing upon but not limiting yourself to the material in your pre-reading journal, write an essay in which you support or reject this viewpoint.

The benefits of active reading are many. Books in general and the selections in *The Longman Reader* in particular will bring you face to face with issues that concern all of us. If you study the selections and the questions that follow them, you'll be on the way to discovering ideas for your own papers. Chapter 2, "The Writing Process," offers practical suggestions for turning those ideas into well-organized, thoughtful essays.

THE WRITING PROCESS

Not many people retire at age thirty-eight. But Michel Montaigne, a sixteenth-century French attorney, did exactly that. Montaigne retired at a young age because he wanted to read, think, and write about all the subjects that interested him. After spending years getting his ideas down on paper, Montaigne finally published his short prose pieces. He called them *essais*—French for "trials" or "attempts."

In fact, all writing is an attempt to transform ideas into words, thus giving order and meaning to life. By using the term *essais*—or *essays* in English—Montaigne acknowledged that a written piece is never really finished. Of course, writers have to stop at some point, especially if they have deadlines to meet. But, as all experienced writers know, even after they dot the final *i*, cross the final *t*, and say "That's it," there's always something that could have been explored further or expressed a little better.

Because writing is a process, shaky starts and changes in direction aren't uncommon. Although there's no way to eliminate the work needed to write effectively, certain approaches can make the process more manageable and rewarding. This chapter describes a sequence of steps for writing essays. Familiarity with a specific sequence develops your awareness of strategies and choices, making you feel more confident when it comes time to write. You're less likely to look at a blank piece of paper and think, "Help! Now what do I do?" During the sequence, you do the following:

1. Prewrite.
2. Identify the thesis.
3. Support the thesis with evidence.

4. Organize the evidence.
5. Write the first draft.
6. Revise the essay.
7. Edit and proofread.

We present the sequence as a series of stages, but we urge you not to view it as a formula to be followed rigidly. Most people develop personalized approaches to the writing process. Some writers mull over a topic in their heads and then move quickly into a promising first draft; others outline their essays in detail before beginning to write. Between these two extremes are any number of effective approaches. The sequence here—illustrated in Figure 2.1—can be streamlined or otherwise altered to fit individual writing styles as well as the needs of specific assignments.

FIGURE 2.1
Stages of the Writing Process

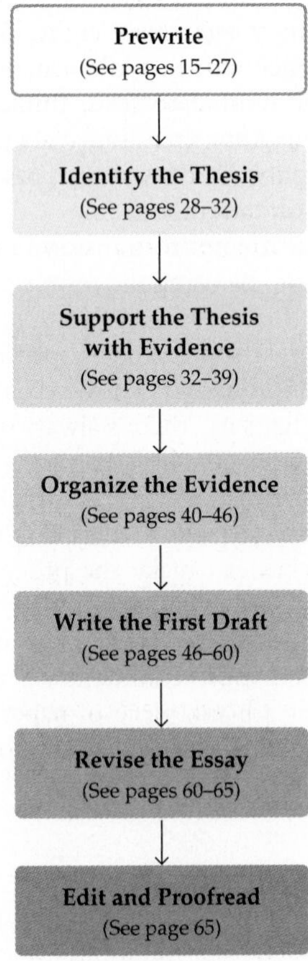

STAGE 1: PREWRITE

Prewriting refers to strategies you can use to generate ideas *before* starting the first draft of a paper. Prewriting techniques are like the warm-ups you do before going out to jog—they loosen you up, get you moving, and help you to develop a sense of well-being and confidence. Since prewriting techniques encourage imaginative exploration, they also help you discover what interests you most about your subject.

During prewriting, you deliberately ignore your internal critic. Your purpose is simply to get ideas down on paper *without evaluating* their effectiveness. Writing without immediately judging what you produce can be liberating. Once you feel less pressure, you'll probably find that you can generate a good deal of material. And that can make your confidence soar.

Keep a Journal

Of all the prewriting techniques, keeping a journal (daily or almost daily) is most likely to make writing a part of your life. Some entries focus on a single theme; others wander from topic to topic. Your starting point may be a dream, a snippet of overheard conversation, a song, a political cartoon, an issue raised in class or in your reading—anything that surprises, interests, angers, depresses, confuses, or amuses you. You may also use a journal to experiment with your writing style—say, to vary your sentence structure if you tend to use predictable patterns.

Here is a fairly focused excerpt from a student's journal:

Today I had to show Paul around school. He and Mom got here by 9. I didn't let on that this was the earliest I've gotten up all semester! He got out of the car looking kind of nervous. Maybe he thought his big brother would be different after a couple of months of college. I walked him around part of the campus and then he went with me to Am. Civ. and then to lunch. He met Greg and some other guys. Everyone seemed to like him. He's got a nice, quiet sense of humor. When I went to Bio., I told him that he could walk around on his own since he wasn't crazy about sitting in on a science class. But he said "I'd rather stick with you." Was he flattering me or was he just scared? Anyway it made me feel good. Later when he was leaving, he told me he's definitely going to apply. I guess that'd be kind of nice, having him here. Mom thinks it's great and she's pushing it. I don't know. I feel kind of like it would invade my privacy. I found this school and have made a life for myself here. Let him find his own school! But it could be great having my kid brother here. I guess this is a classic case of what my psych teacher calls ambivalence. Part of me wants him to come, and part of me doesn't! (November 10)

Although some instructors collect students' journals, you needn't be overly concerned with spelling, grammar, sentence structure, or organization. While journal writing is typically more structured than freewriting (see page 22), you don't have to strive for entries that read like mini-essays. In fact, sometimes you may find it helpful to use a simple list. The important thing is to let your journal writing prompt reflection and new insights, providing you with material to draw upon in your writing. It is, then, a good idea to reread each week's entries to identify recurring themes and concerns. Keep a list of these issues at the back of your journal, under a heading like "Possible Essay Subjects." Here, for instance, are a few topics suggested by the preceding journal entry: deciding which college to attend, leaving home, sibling rivalry. Each of these topics could be developed in a full-length essay.

The pre-reading journal. To reinforce the value of journal writing, we've included a journal assignment before every reading selection in the book. This assignment, called *Pre-Reading Journal Entry*, encourages you to explore—in a tentative fashion—your thoughts about an issue that will be raised in the selection. Here, once again, is the *Pre-Reading Journal Entry* assignment that precedes Ellen Goodman's "Family Counterculture" (page 7):

> Television is often blamed for having a harmful effect on children. Do you think this criticism is merited? In what ways does TV exert a negative influence on children? In what ways does TV exert a positive influence on youngsters? Take a few minutes to respond to these questions in your journal.

The following journal entry shows how one student, Harriet Davids, responded to the journal assignment. A thirty-eight-year-old college student and mother of two young teenagers, Harriet was understandably intrigued by the assignment. As you'll see, Harriet used a listing strategy to prepare her journal entry. She found that lists were perfect for dealing with the essentially "for or against" nature of the journal assignment.

TV's Negative Influence on Kids	TV's Positive Influence on Kids
Teaches negative behaviors (violence, sex, swearing, drugs, alcohol, etc.)	Teaches important educational concepts (*Sesame Street*, shows on The Learning Channel, etc.)
Cuts down on imagination and creativity	Exposes kids to new images and worlds (*Dora the Explorer, Mister Rogers' Neighborhood*)
Cuts down on time spent with parents (talking, reading, playing games together)	Can inspire important discussions (about morals, sexuality, drugs, etc.) between kids and parents

(Continued)

Encourages parents' lack of involvement with kids	Gives parents a needed break from kids
Frightens kids excessively by showing images of real-life violence (terrorist attacks, war, murders, etc.)	Educates kids about the painful realities in the world
Encourages isolation (watching screen rather than interacting with other kids)	Creates common ground among kids, basis of conversations and games
De-emphasizes reading and creates need for constant stimulation	Encourages kids to slow down and read books based on a TV series or show (the *Arthur* and the *Clifford, the Big Red Dog* series, etc.)
Promotes materialism (commercials)	Can be used by parents to teach kids that they can't have everything they see

The journal assignment and subsequent journal entry do more than prepare you to read a selection with extra care and attention; they also pave the way to a full-length essay. Here's how. The final assignment following each selection is called *Writing Assignment Using a Journal Entry as a Starting Point.* This assignment helps you to translate the raw material in your journal entry into a thoughtful, well-considered essay. By the time you get to the assignment, the rough ideas in your journal entry will have been enriched by your reading of the selection. (For an example of a writing assignment that draws upon material in a pre-reading journal entry, turn to page 102.)

As you've just seen, journal writing can stimulate thinking in a loose, unstructured way; it can also prompt the focused thinking required by a specific writing assignment. When you have a specific piece to write, you should approach prewriting in a purposeful, focused manner. You need to:

- Understand the boundaries of the assignment.
- Determine your purpose, audience, and tone.
- Discover your essay's limited subject.
- Generate raw material about your limited subject.
- Organize the raw material.

Understand the Boundaries of the Assignment

Before you start writing a paper, learn what's expected. First, clarify the *kind of paper* the instructor has in mind. Suppose the instructor asks you to discuss the key ideas in an assigned reading. What does the instructor want you to do? Should you include a brief summary of the selection? Should you compare the author's ideas with your own view of the subject? Should you determine if the author's view is supported by valid evidence? If you're not sure about an assignment, ask your instructor to make the requirements clear.

Second, find out *how long* the paper is expected to be. Many instructors will indicate the approximate length of the papers they assign. If no length requirements are provided, discuss with the instructor what you plan to cover and indicate how long you think your paper will be. The instructor will either give you the go-ahead or help you refine the direction and scope of your work.

Determine Your Purpose, Audience, and Tone

Once you understand the requirements for a writing assignment, you're ready to begin thinking about the essay. What is its *purpose?* For what *audience* will it be written? What *tone* will you use? Later on, you may modify your decisions about these issues. That's fine. But you need to understand the way these considerations influence your work in the early phases of the writing process.

Purpose. The papers you write in college are usually meant to *inform* or *explain,* to *convince* or *persuade,* and sometimes to *entertain.* In practice, writing often combines purposes. You might, for example, write an essay trying to *convince* people to support a new trash recycling program in your community. But before you win readers over, you most likely would have to *explain* something about current waste disposal technology.

When purposes blend this way, the predominant one determines the essay's content, organization, emphasis, and choice of words. Assume you're writing about a political campaign. If your primary goal is to *entertain,* to take a gentle poke at two candidates, you might start with several accounts of one candidate's "foot-in-mouth" disease and then describe the attempts of the other candidate, a multimillionaire, to portray himself as an Average Joe. Your language, full of exaggeration, would reflect your objective. But if your primary purpose is to *persuade* readers that the candidates are incompetent and shouldn't be elected, you might adopt a serious, straightforward style. You would use one candidate's gaffes to illustrate her insensitivity to important issues. Similarly, the other candidate's posturing would be presented not as foolish pretension, but as evidence of his lack of judgment.

Audience. To write effectively, you need to identify who your readers are and to take their expectations and needs into account. An essay about the artificial preservatives in the food served by the campus cafeteria would take one form if submitted to your chemistry professor and a very different one if written for the college newspaper. The chemistry paper would probably be formal and technical, complete with chemical formulations and scientific data: "Distillation revealed sodium benzoate particles suspended in a gelatinous medium." But such technical material would be inappropriate in a newspaper column intended for general readers. In this case, you might provide specific examples of cafeteria foods containing additives—"Those deliciously smoky cold cuts are loaded with nitrates and nitrites, both known to cause cancer in laboratory animals"—and suggest ways to eat more healthily: "Pass by the deli counter and fill up instead on vegetarian pizza and fruit juices."

When analyzing your audience, ask yourself the following questions.

☑ ANALYZING YOUR AUDIENCE: A CHECKLIST

- ❑ What are my readers' age, sex, and educational level?
- ❑ What are their political, religious, and other beliefs?
- ❑ What interests and needs motivate my audience?
- ❑ How much do my readers already know about my subject?
- ❑ Do they have any misconceptions?
- ❑ What biases do they have about me, my subject, my opinion?
- ❑ How do my readers expect me to relate to them?
- ❑ What values do I share with my readers that will help me communicate with them?

Tone. Just as a voice projects a range of feelings, writing can convey one or more *tones,* or emotional states: enthusiasm, anger, resignation, and so on. Tone is integral to meaning; it permeates writing and reflects your attitude toward yourself, your purpose, your subject, and your readers. How do you project tone? You pay close attention to sentence structure and word choice.

1. Use appropriate sentence structure. *Sentence structure* refers to the way sentences are shaped. Although the two paragraphs that follow deal with exactly the same subject, note how differences in sentence structure create sharply dissimilar tones:

> During the 1960s, many inner-city minorities considered the police an occupying force and an oppressive agent of control. As a result, violence against police grew in poorer neighborhoods, as did the number of residents killed by police.
>
> An occupying force. An agent of control. An oppressor. That's how many inner-city minorities in the '60s viewed the police. Violence against police soared. Police killings of residents mounted.

Informative in its approach, the first paragraph projects a neutral, almost dispassionate tone. The sentences are fairly long, and clear transitions ("During the 1960s"; "As a result") mark the progression of thought. But the second paragraph, with its dramatic, almost alarmist tone, seems intended to elicit a strong emotional response; its short sentences, fragments, and abrupt transitions reflect the turbulence of those earlier times.

2. Choose effective words. *Word choice* also plays a role in establishing the tone of an essay. Words have *denotations,* neutral dictionary meanings, as well as *connotations,* emotional associations that go beyond the literal meaning. The word *beach,* for instance, is defined in the dictionary as "a nearly level stretch of pebbles and sand beside a body of water." This definition, however, doesn't capture individual responses to the word. For some, *beach* suggests warmth and relaxation; for others, it calls up images of hospital waste and sewage washed up on a once-clean stretch of shoreline.

Since tone and meaning are tightly bound, you must be sensitive to the emotional nuances of words. In a respectful essay about police officers, you wouldn't refer to *cops, narcs,* or *flatfoots;* such terms convey a contempt inconsistent with the tone intended. Your words must also convey tone clearly. Suppose you're writing a satirical piece criticizing a local beauty pageant. Dubbing the participants "livestock on view" leaves no question about your tone. But if you simply referred to the participants as "attractive young women," readers might be unsure of your attitude. Remember, readers can't read your mind, only your paper.

Discover Your Essay's Limited Subject

Because too broad a subject can result in a diffuse, rambling essay, be sure to restrict your general subject before starting to write. The following examples show the difference between general subjects that are too broad for an essay and limited subjects that are appropriate and workable. The examples, of course, represent only a few among many possibilities.

General Subject	Less General	Limited
Education	Computers in education	Computers in elementary school arithmetic classes
	High school education	High school electives
Transportation	Low-cost travel	Hitchhiking
	Getting around a metropolitan area	The transit system in a nearby city
Work	Planning for a career	College internships
	Women in the work force	Women's success as managers

How do you move from a general to a narrow subject? Imagine that you're asked to prepare a straightforward, informative essay for your writing class. Reprinted below is writing assignment 2 from page 12. The assignment, prompted by Ellen Goodman's essay "Family Counterculture," is an extension of the journal-writing assignment on page 7.

> Goodman implies that, in some ways, today's world is hostile to children. Do you agree? Drawing upon but not limiting yourself to the material in your pre-reading journal, write an essay in which you support or reject this viewpoint.

Two techniques—*questioning* and *brainstorming*—can help you limit such a general assignment. While these techniques encourage you to roam freely over a subject, they also help restrict the discussion by revealing which aspects of the subject interest you most.

1. Question the general subject. One way to narrow a subject is to ask a series of *who, how, why, where, when,* and *what* questions. The following example shows how Harriet Davids, the mother of two young teenagers, used this technique to limit the Goodman assignment.

You may recall that, before reading Goodman's essay, Harriet had used her journal to explore TV's effect on children (see page 16). After reading "Family Counterculture," Harriet concluded that she essentially agreed with Goodman; like Goodman, she felt that parents nowadays are indeed forced to raise their kids in an "increasingly hostile environment." She was pleased that the writing assignment gave her an opportunity to expand preliminary ideas she had jotted down in her journal.

Harriet soon realized that she had to narrow the Goodman assignment. She started by asking a number of pointed questions about the general topic. As she proceeded, she was aware that the same questions could have led to different limited subjects—just as other questions would have.

General Subject: We live in a world that is difficult, even hostile to children.

Question	**Limited Subject**
Who is to blame for the difficult conditions under which children grow up?	Parents' casual attitude toward child-rearing
How have schools contributed to the problems children face?	Not enough counseling programs for kids in distress
Why do children feel frightened?	Divorce
Where do kids go to escape?	Television, which makes the world seem even more dangerous

(Continued)

Question	**Limited Subject**
When are children most vulnerable?	The special problems of adolescents
What dangers or fears should parents discuss with their children?	AIDS, drugs, alcohol, war, terrorism

2. Brainstorm the general subject. Another way to focus on a limited subject is to list quickly everything about the general topic that pops into your mind. Just jot down brief words, phrases, and abbreviations to capture your free-floating thoughts. Writing in complete sentences will slow you down. Don't try to organize or censor your ideas. Even the most fleeting, random, or seemingly outrageous thoughts can be productive. An example of brainstorming appears on page 23.

Questioning and brainstorming can suggest many possible limited subjects. To identify especially promising ones, reread your material. What arouses your interest, anger, or curiosity? What themes seem to dominate and cut to the heart of the matter? Star or circle ideas with potential.

After marking the material, write several phrases or sentences summarizing the most promising limited subjects. Here are just a few that emerged from Harriet Davids's prewriting for the Goodman assignment:

- TV partly to blame for children having such a hard time
- Relocation stressful to children
- Schools also at fault
- The special problems that parents face raising children today

Harriet decided to write on the last of these limited subjects—the special problems that parents face raising children today.

Generate Raw Material About Your Limited Subject

When a limited subject strikes you as having possibilities, use these techniques to see if you have enough interesting things to say about the subject to write an effective essay.

1. Freewrite on your limited subject. *Freewriting* means jotting down in rough sentences or phrases everything that comes to mind. To capture this continuous stream of thought, write nonstop for ten minutes or more. Don't censor anything; put down whatever pops into your head. Don't reread, edit, or pay attention to organization, spelling, or grammar. If your mind goes blank, repeat words until another thought emerges.

Here is part of the freewriting that Harriet Davids generated about her limited subject, "The special problems that parents face raising children today":

Parents today have tough problems to face. Lots of dangers. The Internet first and foremost. Also crimes of violence against kids. Parents also have to keep up with cost of living, everything costs more, kids want and expect more. Television? Another thing is *Playboy*, *Penthouse*. Sexy ads and videos on TV, movies deal with sex. Kids grow up too fast, too fast. Kids grow up too fast, too fast. Drugs and alcohol. Witness real-life violence on TV, like terrorist attacks and school shootings. Little kids can't handle knowing too much at an early age. Both parents at work much of the day. Finding good day care a real problem. Lots of latchkey kids. Another problem is getting kids to do homework, lots of other things to do. Especially like going to the mall or chatting with friends online! When I was young, we did homework after dinner, no excuses accepted by my parents.

2. Brainstorm your limited subject. Let your mind wander freely, as you did when using brainstorming to narrow your subject. This time, list every idea, fact, and example that occurs to you about your limited subject. Use brief words and phrases. For now, don't worry whether ideas fit together or whether the points listed make sense.

To gather additional material on her limited subject for the Goodman assignment ("The special problems that parents face raising children today"), Harriet Davids brainstormed the following list:

- Trying to raise kids when both parents work
- Prices of everything outrageous, even when both parents work
- Commercials make everyone want *more* of everything
- Clothes so important
- Day care not always the answer—cases of abuse
- Day care very expensive
- Sex everywhere—TV, movies, magazines, Internet
- Sexy clothes on little kids. Absurd!
- Sexual abuse of kids
- Violence on TV, especially images of real-life terrorist attacks and school shootings—scary for kids!
- Violence against kids when parents abuse drugs
- Meth, Ecstasy, alcohol, heroin, cocaine, AIDS
- Schools have to teach kids about these things
- Schools doing too much—not as good as they used to be
- Not enough homework assigned—kids unprepared
- Distractions from homework—Internet, TV, cell phones, MP3s, computer games

3. Use group brainstorming. Brainstorming can also be conducted as a group activity. Thrashing out ideas with other people stretches the imagination, revealing possibilities you may not have considered on your own.

Group brainstorming doesn't have to be conducted in a formal classroom situation. You can bounce ideas around with friends and family anywhere—over lunch, at the student center, and so on.

4. Map out the limited subject. If you're the kind of person who doodles while thinking, you may want to try *mapping*, sometimes called *diagramming* or *clustering*. Like other prewriting techniques, mapping proceeds rapidly and encourages the free flow of ideas. Begin by expressing your limited subject in a crisp phrase and placing it in the center of a blank sheet of paper. As ideas come to you, put them along lines or in boxes or circles around the limited subject. Draw arrows and lines to show the relationships among ideas. Don't stop there, however. Focus on each idea; as subpoints and details come to you, connect them to their source idea, again using boxes, lines, circles, or arrows to clarify how everything relates.

5. Use the patterns of development. Throughout this book, we show how writers use various patterns of development (narration, process analysis, definition, and so on), singly or in combination, to develop and organize their ideas. Because each pattern has its own distinctive logic, the patterns encourage you, when you prewrite, to think about a subject in different ways, causing insights to surface that might otherwise remain submerged.

The patterns of development are discussed in detail in Chapters 3–11. The following chart shows the way each pattern can generate raw material for a limited subject.

> *Limited Subject:* The special problems that parents face raising children today.

Pattern	**Purpose**	**Raw Material**
Description	To detail what a person, place, or object is like	Detail the sights and sounds of a glitzy mall that attracts kids
Narration	To relate an event	Recount what happened when neighbors tried to forbid their kids from going online
Exemplification	To provide specific instances or examples	Offer examples of family arguments. Will permission be given to go to a party where alcohol will be served? Can parents outlaw certain websites?
Division-classification	To divide something into parts or to group related things in categories	Identify components of a TV commercial that distorts kids' values

(Continued)

		Classify the kinds of commercials that make it difficult to teach kids values
Process analysis	To explain how something happens or how something is done	Explain step by step how family life can disintegrate when parents have to work all the time to make ends meet
Comparison-contrast	To point out similarities and/or dissimilarities	Contrast families today with those of a generation ago
Cause-effect	To analyze reasons and consequences	Explain why parents are not around to be with their kids: Industry's failure to provide day care and its inflexibility about granting time off for parents with sick kids
		Explain the consequences of absentee parents: Kids feel unloved; they spend hours on the Internet; they turn to TV for role models; they're undisciplined; they take on adult responsibility too early
Definition	To explain the meaning of a term or concept	What is meant by "tough love"?
Argumentation-persuasion	To win people over to a point of view	Convince parents that they must work with schools to develop programs that make kids feel safer and more secure

(For more on ways to use the patterns of development in different phases of the writing process, see pages 33, 40–41, and 571–573.)

Conduct research. Depending on your topic, you may find it helpful to visit the library and/or to go online to identify books and articles about your limited subject. At this point, you don't need to read closely the material you find. Just skim and perhaps take a few brief notes on ideas and points that could be useful.

In researching the Goodman assignment, for instance, Harriet Davids could look under such headings and subheadings as the following:

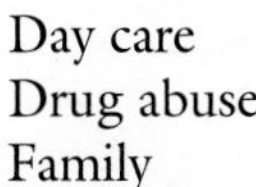

Day care
Drug abuse
Family

Parent-child relationship
- Child abuse
- Children of divorced parents
- Children of working mothers

School and home

Organize the Raw Material

On pages 43–45, we talk about the more formal outline you may need later on in the writing process. However, a *scratch outline* or *scratch list* can be an effective strategy for imposing order on the tentative ideas generated during prewriting.

Reread your exploratory thoughts about the limited subject. Cross out anything not appropriate for your purpose, audience, and tone; add points that didn't originally occur to you. Star or circle compelling items that warrant further development. Then draw arrows between related items, your goal being to group such material under a common heading. Finally, determine what seems to be the best order for those headings.

By giving you a sense of the way your free-form material might fit together, a scratch outline makes the writing process more manageable. You're less likely to feel overwhelmed once you actually start writing because you'll already have some idea about how to shape your material into a meaningful statement. Remember, though, the scratch outline can, and most likely will, be modified along the way.

The following scratch outline shows how Harriet Davids began to shape her brainstorming (page 23) into a more organized format. Note the way she eliminated some items (for example, the points about outrageous prices and about real-life TV violence), added others (for example, the places to go that distract from homework), and grouped the brainstormed items under four main headings, with the appropriate details listed underneath. (If you'd like to see Harriet's more formal outline and her first draft, turn to pages 43–45 and 57–59.)

Limited Subject: The special problems that parents face raising children today.

1. Day care for two-career families
   - Expensive
   - Before-school problems
   - After-school problems
2. Distractions from homework
   - Internet, televisions, cell phones, MP3s
   - Places to go—malls, movies, fast-food restaurants

3. Sexually explicit materials
    - Internet
    - Television shows
    - Movies
    - Magazines
4. Life-threatening dangers
    - Drugs
    - Drinking
    - AIDS
    - Violence against children (by sitters, in day care, etc.)

The prewriting strategies just described provide a solid foundation for the next stages of your work. But invention and imaginative exploration don't end when prewriting is completed. As you'll see, remaining open to new ideas is crucial during all phases of the writing process.

Activities: Prewrite

1. Number the items in each set from 1 (*broadest subject*) to 5 (*most limited subject*):

Set A	**Set B**
Abortion	Business majors
Controversial social issue	Students' majors
Cutting state abortion funds	College students
Federal funding of abortions	Kinds of students on campus
Social issues	Why many students major in business

2. Which of the following topics are too broad for an essay of two to five typewritten pages: soap operas' appeal to college students; day care; trying to "kick" the junk-food habit; male and female relationships; international terrorism?
3. Use the techniques indicated in parentheses to limit each general topic listed below. Then, identify a specific purpose, audience, and tone for the one limited subject you consider most interesting. Next, with the help of the patterns of development, generate raw material about that limited subject. (You may find it helpful to work with others when developing this material.) Finally, shape your raw material into a scratch outline—crossing out, combining, and adding ideas as needed. (Save your scratch outline so you can work with it further after reading about the next stage in the writing process.)

   Friendship *(journal writing)*
   Malls *(mapping)*
   Leisure *(freewriting)*
   Television *(brainstorming)*
   Required courses *(group brainstorming)*
   Manners *(questioning)*

STAGE 2: IDENTIFY THE THESIS

The process of prewriting—discovering a limited subject and generating ideas about it—prepares you for the next stage in writing an essay: identifying the paper's *thesis,* or controlling idea. Presenting your opinion on a subject, the thesis should focus on an interesting and significant issue, one that engages your energies and merits your consideration. You may think of the thesis as the essay's hub—the central point around which all the other material revolves. Your thesis determines what does and does not belong in the essay. The thesis, especially when it occurs early in an essay, also helps focus the reader on the piece's central point.

Sometimes the thesis emerges early in the prewriting stage. Often, though, you'll need to do some work to determine your thesis. For some topics, you may need to do some library research. For others, the best way to identify a promising thesis is to look through your prewriting and ask yourself questions such as these: What statement does all this prewriting support? What aspect of the limited subject is covered in most detail? What is the focus of the most provocative material?

For a look at the process of finding the thesis within prewriting material, glance back at the scratch outline (pages 26–27) that Harriet Davids prepared for the limited subject "The special problems that parents face raising children today." Harriet devised the following thesis to capture the focus of this prewriting: "Being a parent today is much more difficult than it was a generation ago." (The full outline for Harriet's paper appears on pages 43–45; the first draft on pages 57–59; the final draft on pages 66–68.)

Writing an Effective Thesis

Generally expressed in one or two sentences, a thesis statement often has two parts. One part presents the *limited subject;* the other gives your *point of view,* or *attitude,* about that subject. Here are some examples of moving from general subject to limited subject to thesis statement. In each thesis statement, the limited subject is underlined once and the attitude twice.

General Subject	Limited Subject	Thesis
Education	Computers in elementary school arithmetic classes	Computer programs in arithmetic can individualize instruction more effectively than the average elementary school teacher can.

(Continued)

Transportation	A metropolitan transit system	Although the city's transit system still has problems, it has become safer and more efficient in the last two years.
Work	College internships	College internships provide valuable opportunities to students uncertain about what to do after graduation.
Our anti-child world	Special problems that parents face raising children today	Being a parent today is much more difficult than it was a generation ago.

(*Reminder:* The last thesis statement is Harriet Davids's, devised for the essay she planned to write for the assignment on page 12. Harriet's prewriting appears on page 23, and her first draft on pages 57–59.) 

Avoiding Thesis Pitfalls

Because identifying your thesis statement is an important step in writing a sharply focused essay, you need to avoid three common problems that lead to an ineffective thesis.

Don't make an announcement. Some writers use the thesis statement merely to announce the limited subject of their paper and forget to indicate their attitude toward the subject. Such statements are announcements of intent, not thesis statements.

Compare the following three announcements with the thesis statements beside them.

Announcements	Thesis Statements
My essay will discuss whether a student pub should exist on campus.	This college should not allow a student pub on campus.
Handgun legislation is the subject of this paper.	Banning handguns is the first step toward controlling crime in the United States.
I want to discuss cable television.	Cable television has not delivered on its promise to provide an alternative to network programming.

Don't make a factual statement. Your thesis and thus your essay should focus on an issue capable of being developed. If a fact is used as a thesis, you have no place to go; a fact generally doesn't invite much discussion. Notice the difference between these factual statements and thesis statements.

Factual Statements	Thesis Statements
Many businesses pollute the environment.	Tax penalties should be levied against businesses that pollute the environment.
Nowadays, many movies are violent.	Movie violence provides a healthy outlet for aggression.
The population of the United States is growing older.	The aging of the U.S. population will eventually create a crisis in the delivery of health-care services.

Don't make a broad statement. Avoid stating your thesis in vague, general, or sweeping terms. Broad statements make it difficult for readers to grasp your essay's point. Moreover, if you start with a broad thesis, you're saddled with the impossible task of trying to develop a book-length idea in an essay that runs only several pages.

The following examples contrast statements that are too broad with thesis statements that are focused effectively.

Broad Statements	Thesis Statements
Nowadays, high school education is often meaningless.	High school diplomas have been devalued by grade inflation.
Newspapers cater to the taste of the American public.	The success of *USA Today* indicates that people want newspapers that are easy to read and entertaining.
The computer revolution is not all that we have been led to believe it is.	Home computers are still an impractical purchase for many people.

The thesis is often stated near the beginning, but it may be delayed, especially if you need to provide background information before it can be understood. Sometimes the thesis is reiterated—with fresh words—in the essay's conclusion or elsewhere. You may even leave the thesis unstated, relying on strong evidence to convey the essay's central idea.

One final point: Once you start writing your first draft, some feelings, thoughts, and examples may emerge that qualify, even contradict, your initial thesis. Don't resist these new ideas; they frequently move you toward a clearer statement of your main point. Remember, though, your essay must have a thesis. Without this central concept, you have no reason for writing.

Activities: Identify the Thesis

1. For each of the following limited subjects, four possible thesis statements are given. Indicate whether each is an announcement (*A*), a factual statement (*FS*), too broad a statement (*TB*), or an effective thesis (*OK*). Then, for each effective thesis, identify a possible purpose, audience, and tone.

   Limited Subject: The ethics of treating severely handicapped infants

   Some babies born with severe handicaps have been allowed to die.

   There are many serious issues involved in the treatment of handicapped newborns.

   The government should pass legislation requiring medical treatment for handicapped newborns.

   This essay will analyze the controversy surrounding the treatment of severely handicapped babies who would die without medical care.

   Limited Subject: Privacy and computerized records

   Computers raise some significant and crucial questions for all of us.

   Computerized records keep track of consumer spending habits, credit records, travel patterns, and other personal information.

   Computerized records have turned our private lives into public property.

   In this paper, the relationship between computerized records and the right to privacy will be discussed.

2. Each of the following sets lists the key points in an essay. Using the information provided, prepare a possible thesis for each essay.

   Set A
   - One evidence of this growing conservatism is the reemerging popularity of fraternities and sororities.
   - Beauty contests, ROTC training, and corporate recruiting—once rejected by students on many campuses—are again popular.
   - Most important, many students no longer choose risky careers that enable them to contribute to society but select, instead, safe fields with money-making potential.

   Set B
   - We do not know how engineering new forms of life might affect the earth's delicate ecological balance.
   - Another danger of genetic research is its potential for unleashing new forms of disease.
   - Even beneficial attempts to eliminate genetic defects could contribute to the dangerous idea that only perfect individuals are entitled to live.

3. Following are four pairs of general and limited subjects. Generate an appropriate thesis statement for each pair. Select one thesis, and determine which

pattern of development would support it most effectively. Use that pattern to draft a paragraph developing the thesis. (Save the paragraph so you can work with it further after reading about the next stage in the writing process.)

General Subject	**Limited Subject**
Psychology	The power struggles in a classroom
Health	Doctors' attitudes toward patients
U.S. politics	Television's coverage of presidential campaigns
Work	Minimum-wage jobs for young people

4. Return to the scratch outline you prepared for activity 3 on page 27. After examining the outline, identify a thesis that conveys the central idea behind most of the raw material. Then, ask others to evaluate your thesis in light of the material in the outline. Finally, keeping the thesis—as well as your purpose, audience, and tone—in mind, refine the scratch outline by deleting inappropriate items, adding relevant ones, and indicating where more material is needed. (Save your refined scratch outline and thesis so you can work with them further after reading about the next stage in the writing process.)

STAGE 3: SUPPORT THE THESIS WITH EVIDENCE

Supporting material grounds your essay, showing readers you have good reason for feeling as you do about your subject. Your evidence also adds interest and color to your writing. In college essays of five hundred to fifteen hundred words, you usually need at least three major points of evidence to develop your thesis. These major points—each focusing on related but separate aspects of the thesis—eventually become the supporting paragraphs in the body of the essay.

What Is Evidence?

By *evidence,* we mean a number of different kinds of support. *Examples* are just one option. To develop your thesis, you might also include *reasons, facts, details, statistics, anecdotes,* and *quotations from experts.* Imagine you're writing an essay with the thesis "People normally unconcerned about the environment can be galvanized to constructive action if they feel personally affected by an environmental problem." You could support this thesis with any combination of the following types of evidence:

- *Examples* of successful recycling efforts in several neighborhoods.
- *Reasons* why people got involved in a neighborhood recycling effort.
- *Facts* about other residents' efforts to preserve the quality of their well water.

- *Details* about the steps that people can take to get involved in environmental issues.
- *Statistics* showing the number of Americans concerned about the environment.
- An *anecdote* about your involvement in environmental efforts.
- A *quotation* from a well-known scientist about the impact that citizens can have on environmental legislation.

Where Do You Find Evidence?

Where do you find the examples, anecdotes, details, and other types of evidence needed to support your thesis? As you saw when you followed Harriet Davids's strategies for gathering material for an essay (pages 22–26), a good deal of evidence is generated during the prewriting stage. In this phase of the writing process, you tap into your personal experiences, draw upon other people's observations, perhaps interview a person with special knowledge about your subject. The library, with its abundant material, is another rich source of supporting evidence. In addition, the various patterns of development are a valuable source of evidence.

How the Patterns of Development Help Generate Evidence

On pages 24–25, we discussed the way patterns of development help generate material about a limited subject. The same patterns also help develop support for a thesis. The following chart shows how three patterns can generate evidence for this thesis: "To those who haven't done it, babysitting looks easy. In practice, though, babysitting can be difficult, frightening, even dangerous."

Pattern	**Evidence Generated**
Division-classification	A typical babysitting evening divided into stages: playing with the kids; putting them to bed; dealing with their nighttime fears once they're in bed
	Kids' nighttime fears classified by type: monsters under their beds; bad dreams; being abandoned by their parents
Process analysis	Step-by-step account of what a babysitter should do if a child becomes ill or injured
Comparison-contrast	Contrast between two babysitters: one well-prepared, the other unprepared

(For more on ways to use the patterns of development in different phases of the writing process, see pages 24–25, 40–41, and 571–573.)

Characteristics of Evidence

No matter how it is generated, all types of supporting evidence share the characteristics described in the following sections. You should keep these characteristics in mind as you review your thesis and scratch outline. That way, you can make the changes needed to strengthen the evidence gathered earlier. As you'll see shortly, Harriet Davids focused on many of these issues as she worked with the evidence she collected during the prewriting phase.

The evidence is relevant and unified. All the evidence in an essay must clearly support the thesis. It makes no difference how riveting material might be; if it doesn't *relate directly* to the essay's central point, the material should be eliminated. Irrelevant material can weaken your position by implying that no relevant support exists. It also distracts readers from your controlling idea, thus disrupting the paper's overall unity.

The following paragraph, from an essay on changes in Americans' television-viewing habits, focuses on people's reasons for switching from network to cable television. As you'll see, the paragraph lacks unity because it contains points (underlined) unrelated to its main idea. Specifically, the comments about cable's foul language should be deleted. Although these observations bring up interesting points, they shift the paragraph's focus from reasons to objections. If the writer wants to present a balanced view of the pros and cons of cable and network television, these points *should* be covered, but in *another paragraph.*

Nonunified Support

Many people consider cable TV an improvement over network television. For one thing, viewers usually prefer the movies on cable. Unlike network films, cable movies are often only months old, they have not been edited by censors, and they are not interrupted by commercials. Growing numbers of people also feel that cable specials are superior to the ones the networks grind out. Cable viewers may enjoy such pop stars as Billy Joel, Mariah Carey, or Chris Rock in concert, whereas the networks continue to broadcast tired variety shows and boring awards ceremonies. <u>There is, however, one problem with cable comedians. The foul language many of them use makes it hard to watch these cable specials with children. The networks, in contrast, generally present "clean" shows that parents and children can watch together.</u> Then, too, cable TV offers viewers more flexibility since it schedules shows at various times over the month. People working night shifts or attending evening classes can see movies in the afternoon, and viewers missing the first twenty minutes of a show can always catch them later. It's not surprising that cable viewership is growing while network ratings have taken a plunge.

Early in the writing process, Harriet Davids was aware of the importance of relevant evidence. Take a moment to compare Harriet's brainstorming (page 23) and her scratch outline (pages 26–27). Even though Harriet hadn't identified her thesis when she prepared the scratch outline, she realized she should delete a number of items from her brainstorming—for example, the second item and third-to-last item ("prices of everything outrageous" and "schools doing too much"). Harriet eliminated these points because they weren't consistent with the focus of her limited subject.

The evidence is specific. When evidence is vague and general, readers lose interest in what you're saying, become skeptical of your ideas' validity, and feel puzzled about your meaning. In contrast, *specific, concrete evidence* provides sharp *word pictures* that engage your readers, persuade them that your thinking is sound, and clarify meaning.

Consider, for example, the differences between the following two sentences: "The young man had trouble lifting the box out of an old car" and "Joe, only twenty years old but severely weakened by a recent bout with the flu, struggled to lift the heavy wooden crate out of the rusty, dented Chevrolet." The first sentence, filled with generalities, is fuzzy and imprecise while the second sentence, filled with specifics, is crisp and clear.

As the preceding sentences illustrate, three strategies can be used, singly or in combination, to make writing specific. First, you can provide answers to *who, which, what,* and similar *questions.* (The question "How does the car look?" prompts a change in which "an old car" becomes "a rusty, dented Chevrolet.") Second, you can use *vigorous verbs* ("had trouble lifting" becomes "struggled to lift"). Finally, you can replace *vague, abstract* nouns with *vivid, concrete* nouns or phrases ("the young man" becomes "Joe, only twenty years old but severely weakened by a recent bout with the flu").

Following are two versions of a paragraph from an essay about trends in the business community. Although both paragraphs focus on one such trend—flexible working hours—note how the first version's bland language fails to engage the reader and how its vague generalities leave the meaning unclear. What, for example, is meant by the term "flex-time scheduling"? The second paragraph answers this question (as well as several others) with clear specifics; it also uses strong, energetic language. As a result, the second paragraph is more informative and more interesting than the first.

Nonspecific Support

More and more companies have begun to realize that flex-time scheduling offers advantages. Several companies outside Boston have tried flex-time scheduling and are pleased with the way the system reduces the difficulties their employees face getting to work. Studies show that flex-time scheduling also increases productivity, reduces on-the-job conflict, and minimizes work-related accidents.

Specific Support

More and more companies have begun to realize that flex-time scheduling offers advantages over a rigid 9-to-5 routine. Along suburban Boston's Route 128, such companies as Compugraphics and Consolidated Paper now permit employees to schedule their arrival any time between 6 A.M. and 11 A.M. The corporations report that the number of rush-hour jams and accidents has fallen dramatically. As a result, employees no longer arrive at work weighed down by tension induced by choking clouds of exhaust fumes and the blaring horns of gridlocked drivers. Studies sponsored by the journal *Business Quarterly* show that this more mellow state of mind benefits corporations. Traffic-stressed employees begin their workday anxious and exasperated, still grinding their teeth at their fellow commuters, their frustration often spilling over into their performance at work. By contrast, stress-free employees work more productively and take fewer days off. They are more tolerant of coworkers and customers, and less likely to balloon minor irritations into major confrontations. Perhaps most importantly, employees arriving at work relatively free of stress can focus their attention on working safely. They rack up significantly fewer on-the-job accidents, such as falls and injuries resulting from careless handling of dangerous equipment. Flex-time improves employee well-being, and as well-being rises, so do company profits.

At this point, it will be helpful to compare once again Harriet Davids's brainstorming (page 23) and her scratch outline (page 26–27). Note the way she added new details in the outline to make her evidence more specific. For example, to the item "Distractions from homework," she added the new examples "malls," "movies," and "fast-food restaurants." And, as you'll see when you read Harriet's first and final drafts (pages 57–59 and 66–68), she added many more vigorous specifics during later stages of the writing process.

The evidence is adequate. Readers won't automatically accept your thesis; you need to provide *enough specific evidence* to support your viewpoint. On occasion, a single extended example will suffice. Generally, though, you'll need various kinds of evidence: facts, examples, reasons, personal observations, expert opinion, and so on.

Following are two versions of a paragraph from a paper showing how difficult it is to get personal, attentive service nowadays at gas stations, supermarkets, and department stores. Both paragraphs focus on the problem at gas stations, but one paragraph is much more effective. As you'll see, the first paragraph starts with good, specific support, yet fails to provide enough of it. The second paragraph offers additional examples, descriptive details, and dialogue—all of which make the writing stronger and more convincing.

Inadequate Support

Gas stations are a good example of this impersonal attitude. At many stations, attendants have even stopped pumping gas. Motorists pull up to a combination convenience store and gas island where an attendant is enclosed in a glass booth with a tray for taking money. The driver must get out of the car, pump the gas, and walk over to the booth to pay. That's a real inconvenience, especially when compared with the way service stations used to be run.

Adequate Support

Gas stations are a good example of this impersonal attitude. At many stations, attendants have even stopped pumping gas. Motorists pull up to a combination convenience store and gas island where an attendant is enclosed in a glass booth with a tray for taking money. The driver must get out of the car, pump the gas, and walk over to the booth to pay. Even at stations that still have "pump jockeys," employees seldom ask, "Check your oil?" or wash windshields, although they may grudgingly point out the location of the bucket and squeegee. And customers with a balky engine or a nonfunctioning heater are usually out of luck. Why? Many gas stations have eliminated on-duty mechanics. The skillful mechanic who could replace a belt or fix a tire in a few minutes has been replaced by a teenager in a jumpsuit who doesn't know a carburetor from a charge card and couldn't care less.

Now take a final look at Harriet Davids's scratch outline (pages 26–27). Harriet realized she needed more than one block of supporting material to develop her limited subject; that's why she identified four separate blocks of evidence (day care, homework distractions, sexual material, and dangers). When Harriet prepared her first and final drafts (pages 57–59 and 66–68), she decided to eliminate the material about day care. But she added so many more specific and dramatic details that her evidence was more than sufficient.

The evidence is accurate. When you have a strong belief and want readers to see things your way, you may be tempted to overstate or downplay facts, disregard information, misquote, or make up details. Suppose you plan to write an essay making the point that dormitory security is lax. You begin supporting your thesis by narrating the time you were nearly mugged in your dorm hallway. Realizing the essay would be more persuasive if you also mentioned other episodes, you decide to invent some material. Perhaps you describe several supposed burglaries on your dorm floor or exaggerate the amount of time it took campus security to respond to an emergency call from a residence hall. Yes, you've supported your point—but at the expense of truth.

The evidence is representative. Using representative evidence means that you rely on the typical, the usual, to show that your point is valid. Contrary to the maxim, exceptions don't prove the rule. Perhaps you plan to write an essay contending that the value of seat belts has been exaggerated. To support your position, you mention a friend who survived a head-on collision without wearing a seat belt. Such an example isn't representative because the facts and figures on accidents suggest your friend's survival was a fluke.

Borrowed evidence is documented. If you include evidence from outside sources (books, articles, interviews), you need to acknowledge where that information comes from. If you don't, readers may consider your evidence nothing more than your point of view, or they may regard as dishonest your failure to cite your indebtedness to others for ideas that obviously aren't your own.

For help in documenting sources in brief, informal papers, turn to page 482. For information on acknowledging sources in longer, more formal papers, refer to Appendix A (pages 607–638).

Strong supporting evidence is at the heart of effective writing. Without it, essays lack energy and fail to convey the writer's perspective. Such lifeless writing is more apt to put readers to sleep than to engage their interest and convince them that the points being made are valid. Taking the time to accumulate solid supporting material is, then, a critical step in the writing process.

Activities: Support the Thesis with Evidence

1. Each of the following sets includes a thesis statement and four points of support. In each set, identify the one point that is off target.

Set A

Thesis: Colleges should put less emphasis on sports.

Encourages grade fixing
Creates a strong following among former graduates
Distracts from real goals of education
Causes extensive and expensive injuries

Set B

Thesis: The United States is becoming a homogenized country.

Regional accents vanishing
Chain stores blanket country
Americans proud of their ethnic identities
Metropolitan areas almost indistinguishable from one another

2. For each of the following thesis statements, develop three points of relevant support. Then use the patterns of development to generate evidence for each point of support.

Thesis: The trend toward disposable, throwaway products has gone too far.

Thesis: The local (or college) library fails to meet the needs of those it is supposed to serve.

Thesis: Television portrays men as incompetent creatures.

3. Choose one of the following thesis statements. Then identify an appropriate purpose, audience, and tone for an essay with this thesis. Using freewriting, mapping, or the questioning technique, generate at least three supporting points for the thesis. Last, write a paragraph about one of the points, making sure your evidence reflects the characteristics discussed in these pages. Alternatively, you may go ahead and prepare the first draft of an essay having the selected thesis. (If you choose the second option, you may want to turn to page 57 to see a diagram showing how to organize a first draft.) Save whatever you prepare so you can work with it further after reading about the next stage in the writing process.

    - Winning the lottery may not always be a blessing.
    - All of us can take steps to reduce the country's trash crisis.
    - Drug education programs in public schools are (or are not) effective.

4. Select one of the following thesis statements. Then determine your purpose, audience, and tone for an essay with this thesis. Next, use the patterns of development to generate at least three supporting points for the thesis. Finally, write a paragraph about one of the points, making sure that your evidence demonstrates the characteristics discussed in these pages. Alternatively, you may go ahead and prepare a first draft of an essay having the thesis selected. (If you choose the latter option, you may want to turn to page 57 to see a diagram showing how to organize a first draft.) Save whatever you prepare so you can work with it further after reading about the next stage in the writing process.

    - Teenagers should (or should not) be able to obtain birth control devices without their parents' permission.
    - The college's system for awarding student loans needs to be overhauled.
    - E-mail has changed for the worse (or the better) the way Americans communicate with each other.

5. Retrieve the paragraph you wrote in response to activity 3 on pages 31–32. Keeping in mind the characteristics of effective evidence discussed in pages 34–38, make whatever changes are needed to strengthen the paragraph. (Save the paragraph so you can work with it further after reading about the next stage in the writing process.)

6. Look at the thesis and refined scratch outline you prepared in response to activity 4 on page 32. Where do you see gaps in the support for your thesis? By brainstorming with others, generate material to fill these gaps. If some of the new points generated suggest that you should modify your thesis, make the appropriate changes now. (Save this material so you can work with it further after reading about the next stage in the writing process.)

STAGE 4: ORGANIZE THE EVIDENCE

After you've generated supporting evidence, you're ready to *organize* that material. Even highly compelling evidence won't illustrate the validity of your thesis or achieve your purpose if readers have to plow through a maze of chaotic evidence. Some writers can move quickly from generating support to writing a clearly structured first draft. (They usually say they have sequenced their ideas in their heads.) Most, however, need to spend some time sorting out their thoughts on paper before starting the first draft; otherwise, they tend to lose their way in a tangle of ideas.

When moving to the organizing stage, you should have in front of you your scratch outline (see pages 26–27) and thesis plus any supporting material you've accumulated. To find a logical framework for all this material, you'll need to

- Determine which pattern of development is implied in your evidence.
- Select one of four basic approaches for organizing your evidence.
- Outline your evidence.

Use the Patterns of Development

Each pattern of development (see pages 24–25) has its own internal logic that makes it appropriate for some writing purposes but not for others. Once you see which pattern (or combination of patterns) is implied by your purpose, you can block out your paper's general structure. Imagine that you're writing an essay *explaining why* some students drop out of college during the first semester. You might organize the essay around a three-part discussion of the key *causes* contributing to the difficulty that students have adjusting to college: (1) they miss friends and family, (2) they take inappropriate courses, and (3) they experience conflicts with roommates. As you can see, your choice of pattern of development significantly influences your essay's content and organization.

Some essays follow a single pattern, but most blend them, with a predominant pattern providing the piece's organizational framework. In our example essay, you might include a brief *description* of an overwhelmed first-year college student; you might *define* the psychological term "separation anxiety"; you might end the paper by briefly explaining a *process* for making students' adjustment to college easier. Still, the essay's overall organizational pattern would be *cause-effect* since the paper's primary purpose is to explain why students drop out of college. (For more information on the way patterns often blend in writing, see Chapter 12, "Combining the Patterns.")

Although writers often combine the patterns of development, writing an essay organized according to a single pattern can help you understand a particular pattern's unique demands. Keep in mind, though, that most writing begins not with a specific pattern but with a specific *purpose*. The pattern or combination of patterns evolves out of that purpose.

Select an Organizational Approach

No matter which pattern(s) of development you select, you need to know four general approaches for organizing supporting evidence—chronological, spatial, emphatic, and simple-to-complex.

Chronological approach. When an essay is organized *chronologically*, supporting material is arranged in a clear time sequence, usually starting with what happened first and ending with what happened last. Occasionally, chronological sequences can be rearranged to create flashback or flashforward effects, two techniques discussed in Chapter 4 on narration. Essays using narration (for example, an experience with prejudice) or process analysis (for instance, how to deliver an effective speech) are most likely to be organized chronologically. The paper on public speaking might use a time sequence to present its points: how to prepare a few days before the presentation is due; what to do right before the speech; what to concentrate on during the speech itself. (For examples of chronologically arranged student essays, turn to pages 135 and 287.)

Spatial approach. When you arrange supporting evidence *spatially*, you discuss details as they occur in space, or from certain locations. This strategy is particularly appropriate for description. Imagine that you plan to write an essay describing the happy times you spent as a child playing by a towering old oak tree in the neighborhood park. Using spatial organization, you start by describing the rich animal life (the plump earthworms, swarming anthills, and numerous animal tracks) you observed while hunkered down *at the base* of the tree. Next, you re-create the contented feeling you experienced sitting on a branch *in the middle* of the tree. Finally, you end by describing the glorious view of the world you had *from the top* of the tree.

Although spatial arrangement is flexible (you could, for instance, start with a description from the top of the tree), you should always proceed systematically. And once you select a particular spatial order, you should usually maintain that sequence throughout the essay; otherwise, readers may get lost along the way. (A spatially arranged student essay appears on page 80.)

Emphatic approach. In *emphatic* order, the most compelling evidence is saved for last. This arrangement is based on the psychological principle that people remember best what they experience last. Emphatic order has built-in momentum because it starts with the least important point and builds to the most significant. This method is especially effective in argumentation-persuasion essays, in papers developed through examples, and in pieces involving comparison-contrast, division-classification, or causal analysis.

Consider an essay analyzing the negative effect that workaholic parents can have on their children. The paper might start with a brief discussion of relatively minor effects such as the family's eating mostly frozen or takeout foods. Paragraphs on more serious effects might follow: children get no parental help with homework; they try to resolve personal problems without parental advice. Finally, the essay might close with a detailed discussion of the most significant effect—children's lack of self-esteem because they feel unimportant in their parents' lives. (The student essays on pages 183, 344, and 437 all use an emphatic arrangement.)

Simple-to-complex approach. A final way to organize an essay is to proceed from relatively *simple* concepts to more *complex* ones. By starting with easy-to-grasp, generally accepted evidence, you establish rapport with your readers and assure them that the essay is firmly grounded in shared experience. In contrast, if you open with difficult or highly technical material, you risk confusing and alienating your audience.

Assume you plan to write a paper arguing that your college has endangered students' health by not making an all-out effort to remove asbestos from dormitories and classroom buildings. It probably wouldn't be a good idea to begin with a medically sophisticated explanation of precisely how asbestos damages lung tissue. Instead, you might start with an observation that is likely to be familiar to your readers—one that is part of their everyday experience. You could, for example, open with a description of asbestos—as readers might see it—wrapped around air ducts and furnaces or used as electrical insulation and fireproofing material. Having provided a basic, easy-to-visualize description, you could then go on to explain the complicated process by which asbestos can cause chronic lung inflammation. (See page 390 for an example of a student essay using the simple-to-complex arrangement.)

Depending on your purpose, any one of these four organizational approaches might be appropriate. For example, assume that you planned to write an essay developing Harriet Davids's thesis: "Being a parent today is much more difficult than it was a generation ago." To emphasize that the various stages in children's lives present parents with different difficulties, you'd probably select a *chronological* sequence. To show that the challenges that parents face vary depending on whether children are at home, at school, or in the world at large, you'd probably choose a *spatial* sequence. To stress the range of problems that parents face (from less to more serious), you'd probably use an *emphatic* sequence. To illustrate today's confusing array of theories for raising children, you might take a *simple-to-complex* approach, moving from the basic to the most sophisticated theories.

Prepare an Outline

Having an outline—a skeletal version of your paper—*before* you begin the first draft makes the writing process much more manageable. The outline helps you organize your thoughts beforehand, and it guides your writing as you work on the draft. Even though ideas continue to evolve during the draft, an outline clarifies how ideas fit together, which points are major, which should come first, and so on. An outline may also reveal places where evidence is weak, underscoring the need, perhaps, for more prewriting.

Some people prepare highly structured outlines; others make only a few informal jottings. Sometimes outlining will go quickly, with points falling easily into place; at other times you'll have to work hard to figure out how points are related. If that happens, be glad you caught the problem while outlining rather than while writing the first draft.

To prepare an effective outline, you should reread and evaluate your scratch outline and thesis as well as any other evidence you've generated since the prewriting stage. Then decide which pattern of development (description, cause-effect, and so on) seems to be suggested by your evidence. Also determine whether your evidence lends itself to a chronological, a spatial, an emphatic, or a simple-to-complex order. Having done all that, you're ready to identify and sequence your main and supporting points.

The amount of detail in an outline will vary according to the paper's length and the instructor's requirements. A scratch outline (like the one on pages 26–27) is often sufficient, but for longer papers, you'll probably need a more detailed and formal outline. In such cases, the suggestions in the accompanying checklist will help you develop a sound plan. Feel free to modify these guidelines to suit your needs.

☑ OUTLINING: A CHECKLIST

- ❑ Write your purpose, audience, tone, and thesis at the top.
- ❑ Below the thesis, enter the pattern of development you've chosen.
- ❑ Record the organizational approach you've selected.
- ❑ Delete from your supporting material anything that doesn't develop the thesis or that isn't appropriate for your purpose, audience, and tone.
- ❑ Add any new points or material. Group related items together. Give each group a heading that represents a main topic in support of your thesis.
- ❑ Label these main topics with roman numerals (I, II, III, and so on). Let the order of the numerals indicate the best sequence.

- ❑ Identify subtopics and group them under the appropriate main topics. Indent and label these subtopics with capital letters (A, B, C, and so on). Let the order of the letters indicate the best sequence.
- ❑ Identify supporting points (often, reasons and examples) and group them under the appropriate subtopics. Indent and label these supporting points with arabic numbers (1, 2, 3, and so on). Let the numbers indicate the best sequence.
- ❑ Identify specific details (secondary examples, facts, statistics, expert opinions, quotations) and group them under the appropriate supporting points. Indent and label these specific details with lowercase letters (a, b, c, and so on). Let the letters indicate the best sequence.
- ❑ Examine your outline, looking for places where evidence is weak. Where appropriate, add new evidence.
- ❑ Double-check that all main topics, subtopics, supporting points, and specific details develop some aspect of the thesis. Also confirm that all items are arranged in the most logical order.

The sample outline that follows develops the thesis "Being a parent today is much more difficult than it was a generation ago"—the thesis that Harriet Davids devised for the essay she planned to write in response to the assignment on page 12. Harriet's scratch list appears on pages 26–27. When you compare Harriet's scratch list and outline, you'll find some differences. On the whole, the outline contains more specifics, but it doesn't include all the material in the scratch list. For example, after reconsidering her purpose, audience, tone, and thesis, Harriet decided to omit from her outline the section on day care and the point about AIDS.

The plan shown below is called a *topic outline* because it uses phrases, or topics, for each entry. For a lengthier or more complex paper, a *sentence outline* would be more appropriate.

Purpose: To inform

Audience: Instructor as well as class members, most of whom are 18–20 years old

Tone: Serious and straightforward

Thesis: Being a parent today is much more difficult than it was a generation ago.

Pattern of development: Exemplification

Organizational approach: Emphatic order

I. Distractions from homework
  A. At home
    1. MP3 players

    2. Computers—Internet, computer games
    3. Television
  B. Outside home
    1. Malls
    2. Movie theaters
    3. Fast-food restaurants
II. Sexually explicit materials
  A. Internet
    1. Easy-to-access adult chat rooms
    2. Easy-to-access pornographic websites
  B. In print and in movies
    1. Sex magazines
      a. *Playboy*
      b. *Penthouse*
    2. Casual sex
  C. On television
    1. Soap operas
    2. R-rated comedians
    3. R-rated movies on cable
III. Increased dangers
  A. Drugs—peer pressure
  B. Alcohol—peer pressure
  C. Violent crimes against children

(If you'd like to see the first draft that resulted from Harriet's outline, turn to pages 57–59. Hints for moving from an outline to a first draft appear on page 47.)

Before starting to write your first draft, show your outline to several people (your instructor, friends, classmates) for their reactions, especially about areas needing additional work. After making whatever changes are needed, you're in a good position to go ahead and write the first draft of your essay.

Activities: Organize the Evidence

1. The thesis statement below is followed by a scrambled list of supporting points. Prepare an outline for a potential essay, making sure to distinguish between major and secondary points.

   Thesis: Our schools, now in crisis, could be improved in several ways.

   Certification requirements for teachers
   Schedules
   Teachers
   Longer school year
   Merit pay for outstanding teachers
   Curriculum

Better textbooks for classroom use
Longer school days
More challenging content in courses

2. Assume you plan to write an essay based on the following brief outline, which consists of a thesis and several points of support. Determine which pattern of development (page 40) you would probably use for the essay's overall framework. Also identify which organizational approach (pages 41–42) you would most likely adopt to sequence the points of support listed. Then, use one or more patterns of development to generate material to support those points. Having done that, review the material generated, deleting, adding, combining, and arranging ideas in logical order. Finally, make an outline for the body of the essay. (Save your outline so you can work with it further after reading about the next stage in the writing process.)

   Thesis: Friends of the opposite sex fall into one of several categories: the pal, the confidant, or the pest.

   - Frequently, an opposite-sex friend is simply a "pal."
   - Sometimes, though, a pal turns, step by step, into a confidant.
   - If a confidant begins to have romantic thoughts, he or she may become a pest, thus disrupting the friendship.

3. Retrieve the writing you prepared in response to activity 3, 4, or 5 on pages 38–39. As needed, reshape that material, applying the organizational principles discussed in these pages. Be sure, for example, that you select the approach (chronological, spatial, emphatic, or simple-to-complex) that would be most appropriate, given your main idea, purpose, audience, and tone. (Save whatever you prepare so you can work with it further after reading about the next stage in the writing process.)

4. Look again at the thesis and scratch outline you refined and elaborated in response to activity 6 on page 39. Reevaluate this material by deleting, adding, combining, and rearranging ideas as needed. Also, keeping your purpose, audience, and tone in mind, consider whether a chronological, a spatial, an emphatic, or a simple-to-complex approach will be most appropriate. Now prepare an outline of your ideas. Finally, ask at least one person to evaluate your organizational plan. (Save your outline. After reading about the next stage in the writing process, you can use it to write the essay's first draft.)

STAGE 5: WRITE THE FIRST DRAFT

Your *first draft*—a rough, provisional version of your essay—may flow quite smoothly. But don't be discouraged if it doesn't. You may find that your thesis has to be reshaped, that a point no longer fits, that you need to return to a prewriting activity to generate additional material. Such stopping and starting is to be expected. Writing the first draft is a process of discovery, involving the continual clarification and refining of ideas.

How to Proceed

There's no single right way to prepare a first draft. Some writers rely heavily on their scratch lists or outlines; others glance at them only occasionally. Some people write in longhand; others use a computer.

However you choose to proceed, consider the suggestions in the following checklist when moving from an outline or scratch list to a first draft.

☑ TURNING OUTLINE INTO FIRST DRAFT: A CHECKLIST

- ❑ Make the outline's *main topics* (I, II, III) the *topic sentences* of the essay's supporting paragraphs. (Topic sentences are discussed later, on page 48.)
- ❑ Make the outline's *subtopics* (A, B, C) the *subpoints* in each paragraph.
- ❑ Make the outline's *supporting points* (1, 2, 3) the key *examples* and *reasons* in each paragraph.
- ❑ Make the outline's *specific details* (a, b, c) the *secondary examples, facts, statistics, expert opinions,* and *quotations* in each paragraph.

(To see how Harriet Davids moved from outline to first draft, turn to pages 57–59.)

Although outlines and lists are valuable for guiding your work, don't be so dependent on them that you shy away from new ideas that surface during your writing of the first draft. If promising new thoughts pop up, jot them down in the margin. Then, at the appropriate point, go back and evaluate them: Do they support your thesis? Are they appropriate for your essay's purpose, audience, and tone? If so, go ahead and include the material in your draft.

It's easy to get bogged down while preparing the first draft if you try to edit as you write. Remember: A draft isn't intended to be perfect. For the time being, adopt a relaxed, noncritical attitude. Work as quickly as you can, don't stop to check spelling, correct grammar, or refine sentence structure. Save these tasks for later. One good way to help remind you that the first draft is tentative is to write in longhand using scrap paper and pencil. Writing on alternate lines also underscores your intention to revise later on, when the extra space will make it easier to add and delete material. Similarly, writing on only one side of the paper can prove helpful if, during revision, you decide to move a section to another part of the paper.

What should you do if you get stuck while writing your first draft? Stay calm and try to write something—no matter how awkward or imprecise it may seem. Just jot a reminder to yourself in the margin ("Fix this," "Redo," or "Ugh!") to finetune the section later. Or leave a blank space to hold a spot for the right words when they finally break loose. It may also help to reread—out loud is best—what you've already written. Regaining a sense of the larger context is often enough to get you moving again. You might also try talking your way through a troublesome section. By speaking aloud, you tap your natural oral fluency and put it to work in your writing.

If a section of the essay is particularly difficult, don't spend time struggling with it. Move on to an easier section, write that, and then return to the challenging part. If you're still getting nowhere, take a break. Watch television, listen to music, talk with friends. While you're relaxing, your thoughts may loosen up and untangle the knotty section.

Because you read essays from beginning to end, you may assume that writers work the same way, starting with the introduction and going straight through to the conclusion. Often, however, this isn't the case. In fact, since an introduction depends so heavily on everything that follows, it's usually best to write the introduction *after* the essay's body.

When preparing your first draft, you may find it helpful to follow this sequence:

1. Write the supporting paragraphs.
2. Connect ideas in the supporting paragraphs.
3. Write the introduction.
4. Write the conclusion.
5. Write the title.

Write the Supporting Paragraphs

Drawn from the main sections in your outline or scratch list (I, II, III, etc.), each *supporting paragraph* should develop an aspect of your essay's thesis. A strong supporting paragraph is (1) often focused by a topic sentence and (2) organized around one or more patterns of development. As you write, keep in mind that you shouldn't expect your draft paragraphs to be perfect; you'll have a chance to revise them later on.

Use topic sentences. Frequently, a *topic sentence* functions as a kind of mini-thesis for a supporting paragraph. Generally one or two sentences in length, the topic sentence usually appears at or near the beginning of the paragraph. However, it may also appear at the end, in the middle, or—with varied wording—several times within the paragraph.

The topic sentence states the paragraph's main idea while the other sentences in the paragraph provide support for this central point in the form of examples, facts, expert opinion, and so on. Like a thesis statement, the topic sentence *signals the paragraph's subject* and frequently *indicates the writer's attitude* toward that subject. In the topic sentences that follow, the subject of the paragraph is underlined once and the attitude toward that subject is underlined twice:

> Some students select a particular field of study for the wrong reasons.
> The ocean dumping of radioactive waste is a ticking time bomb.
> Several contemporary rock groups show unexpected sensitivity to social issues.
> Political candidates are sold like slickly packaged products.

As you work on the first draft, you may find yourself writing paragraphs without paying too much attention to topic sentences. That's fine, as long as you evaluate the paragraphs later on. When revising, you can provide a topic sentence for a paragraph that needs a sharper focus, recast a topic sentence for a paragraph that ended up taking an unexpected turn, even eliminate a topic sentence altogether if a paragraph's content is sufficiently unified to imply its point.

Use the patterns of development. As you saw on page 40, an entire essay can be organized around one or more patterns of development (narration, process analysis, definition, and so forth). These patterns can also provide the organizational framework for an essay's supporting paragraphs. Assume you're writing an article for your town newspaper with the thesis "Year-round residents of an ocean community must take an active role in safeguarding the seashore environment." Your supporting paragraphs could develop this thesis through a variety of patterns, with each paragraph's topic sentence suggesting a specific pattern or combination of patterns. For example, one paragraph might start with the topic sentence "In a nearby ocean community, signs of environmental danger are everywhere" and go on to *describe* a seaside town with polluted waters, blighted trees, and diseased marine life. The next paragraph might have the topic sentence "Fortunately, not all seaside towns are plagued by such environmental problems" and continue by *contrasting* the troubled community with another, more ecologically sound shore town. A later paragraph, focused by the topic sentence "Residents can get involved in a variety of pro-environment activities," might use *division-classification* to elaborate on activities at the neighborhood, town, and municipal levels.

Connect Ideas in the Supporting Paragraphs

While writing the supporting paragraphs, you can try to smooth out the progression of ideas within and between paragraphs. In a *coherent* essay, the relationship between points is clear; readers can easily follow the development of your thoughts. (Sometimes, working on coherence causes a first draft to get bogged down; if this happens, move on, and wait until the revision stage to focus on such matters.)

The following paragraph lacks coherence for two main reasons. First, it sequences ideas improperly. (The idea about the toll attendants' being cut off from coworkers is introduced, dropped, then picked up again. References to motorists are similarly scattered throughout the paragraph.) Second, it doesn't indicate how individual ideas are related. (What, for example, is the connection between drivers who pass by without saying anything and attendants who have to work at night?)

Incoherent Support

Collecting tolls on the turnpike must be one of the loneliest jobs in the world. Each toll attendant sits in his or her booth, cut off from other attendants. Many drivers pass by each booth. None stays long enough for a brief "hello." Most don't acknowledge the attendant at all. Many toll attendants work at night, pushing them "out of synch" with the rest of the world. And sometimes the attendants have to deal with rude drivers who treat them like non-people, swearing at them for the long lines at the tollgate. Attendants also dislike how cut off they feel from their coworkers. Except for infrequent breaks, they have little chance to chat with each other and swap horror stories—small pleasures that would make their otherwise routine jobs bearable.

Coherent Support

Collecting tolls on the turnpike must be one of the loneliest jobs in the world. First of all, although many drivers pass by the attendants, none stays long enough for more than a brief "hello." Most drivers, in fact, don't acknowledge the toll collectors at all, with the exception of those rude drivers who treat the attendants like non-people, swearing at them for the long lines at the tollgate. Then, too, many toll attendants work at night, pushing them further "out of synch" with the rest of the world. Worst of all, attendants say, is how isolated they feel from their coworkers. Each attendant sits in his or her booth, cut off from other attendants. Except for infrequent breaks, they have little chance to chat with each other and swap horror stories—small pleasures that would make their otherwise routine jobs bearable.

To avoid the kinds of problems found in the incoherent paragraph, use—as the revised version does—two key strategies: (1) a clearly *chronological, spatial, emphatic* ("*Worst of all,* attendants say..."), or *simple-to-complex* approach and

(2) *signal devices* ("*First of all,* although many drivers pass by...") to show how ideas are connected. To review the four organizational approaches, see pages 41–42. The following paragraphs describe signal devices.

Once you determine a logical approach for presenting your points, you need to make sure readers can follow the progression of those points. Signal devices provide readers with cues, reminding them where they have been and indicating where they are going.

Aim to include some signals—however awkward or temporary—in your first draft. If you find you *can't,* that's probably a warning that your ideas may not be arranged logically. A light touch should be your goal with such signals. Too many call attention to themselves, making the essay mechanical and plodding. In any case, here are some signaling devices to consider.

1. Transitions. Words and phrases that ease readers from one idea to another are called transitions. The following list gives a variety of such signals.

Time

first, before, earlier, next, then, now, immediately, at the same time, simultaneously, in the meantime, meanwhile, subsequently, afterward, after, finally, later eventually

Addition (or Sequence)

moreover; also; furthermore; in addition; first,...second,...third; one...another; and; also; too; besides; next; finally; last

Space

above, below, next to, behind

Examples

for instance, for example, to illustrate, specifically, namely

Contrast

but, however, yet, in contrast, on the contrary, although, otherwise, conversely, despite, even though, on the one (other) hand, still, whereas, nevertheless, nonetheless

Comparison

similarly, in the same way, also, likewise, too, in comparison

Cause or Effects

because, as a result, consequently, therefore, then, so, since

Summary or Conclusion

therefore, thus, in short, in conclusion

Here's an earlier paragraph from this chapter. Note how the italicized transitions show readers how ideas fit together.

> *After* you've generated supporting evidence, you're ready to organize that material. Even highly compelling evidence won't illustrate the validity of your thesis or achieve your purpose if the readers have to plow through a maze of chaotic evidence. Some writers can move quickly from generating support to writing a clearly structured first draft. (They usually say they have sequenced their ideas in their heads.) Most, *however,* need to spend some time sorting out their thoughts on paper before starting the first draft; *otherwise,* they tend to lose their way in a tangle of ideas.

2. Bridging sentences. Although bridging sentences may be used within a paragraph, they are more often used to move readers from one paragraph to the next. Look again at the first sentence in the preceding paragraph. Note that the sentence consists of two parts: The first part reminds readers that the previous discussion focused on techniques for generating evidence; the second part tells readers that the focus will now be the organization of such evidence.

3. Repeated words, synonyms, and pronouns. The repetition of important words maintains continuity, reassures readers that they are on the right track, and highlights key ideas. Synonyms—words similar in meaning—also provide coherence, but without unimaginative and tedious repetitions. Finally, pronouns (*he, she, it, they, this, that*) enhance coherence by causing readers to think back to the original word the pronoun replaces (antecedent). When using pronouns, however, be sure there is no ambiguity about antecedents.

Reprinted here is another paragraph from this chapter. Repeated words have been underlined once, synonyms underlined twice, and pronouns printed in italic type to illustrate how these techniques were used to integrate the paragraph's ideas.

> The process of prewriting—discovering a limited subject and generating ideas about *it*—prepares you for the next stage in writing an essay: identifying the paper's <u>thesis</u> or <u>controlling idea.</u> Presenting your opinion on a subject, the <u>thesis</u> should focus on an interesting and significant issue, *one* that engages your energies and merits your consideration. You may think of the <u>thesis</u> as the essay's <u>hub</u>—<u>the central point</u> around which all the other material revolves. Your <u>thesis</u> determines what does and does not belong in the essay. The <u>thesis</u>, especially when *it* occurs early in an essay, also helps focus the reader on the piece's central point.

Write the Introduction

Many writers don't prepare an introduction until they have started to revise; others feel more comfortable if their first draft includes in basic form all parts of the final essay. If that's how you feel, you'll probably write the introduction as you complete your first draft. No matter when you prepare it, keep in mind how crucial the introduction is to your essay's success. Specifically, the introduction serves three distinct functions: It arouses readers' interest, introduces your subject, and presents your thesis.

The length of your introduction will vary according to your paper's scope and purpose. Most essays you write, however, will be served best by a one- or two-paragraph beginning. To write an effective introduction, use any of the following methods, singly or in combination. The thesis statement in each sample introduction is underlined.

Broad Statement Narrowing to a Limited Subject

For generations, morality has been molded primarily by parents, religion, and schools. Children traditionally acquired their ideas about what is right and wrong, which goals are important in life, and how other people should be treated from these three sources collectively. But in the past few decades, a single force—television—has undermined the beneficial influence that parents, religion, and school have on children's moral development. Indeed, television often implants in children negative values about sex, work, and family life.

Brief Anecdote

At a local high school recently, students in a psychology course were given a hint of what it is like to be the parents of a newborn. Each "parent" had to carry a raw egg around at all times to symbolize the responsibilities of parenthood. The egg could not be left alone; it limited the "parents'" activities; it placed a full-time emotional burden on "Mom" and "Dad." This class exercise illustrates a common problem facing the majority of new mothers and fathers. Most people receive little preparation for the job of being parents.

Idea That Is the Opposite of the One Developed

We hear a great deal about divorce's disastrous impact on children. We are deluged with advice on ways to make divorce as painless as possible for youngsters; we listen to heartbreaking stories about the confused, grieving children of divorced parents. Little attention has been paid, however, to a different kind of effect that divorce may have on children. Children from divorced families may become skilled manipulators, playing off one parent against the other, worsening an already painful situation.

Series of Short Questions

What happens if a child is caught vandalizing school property? What happens if a child goes for a joyride in a stolen car and accidentally hits a pedestrian? Should parents be liable for their children's mistakes? Should parents have to pay what might be hundreds of thousands of dollars in damages? Adults have begun to think seriously about such questions because the laws concerning the limits of parental responsibility are changing rapidly. With unfortunate frequency, courts have begun to hold parents legally and financially accountable for their children's misdeeds.

Quotation

Educator Neil Postman believes that television has blurred the line between childhood and adulthood. According to Postman, "All the secrets that a print culture kept from children...are revealed all at once by media that do not, and cannot, exclude any audience." This media barrage of information, once intended only for adults, has changed childhood for the worse.

Refutation of a Common Belief

Adolescents care only about material things; their lives revolve around brand-name sneakers, designer jeans, the latest fad in electronics. They resist education, don't read, barely know who is president, mainline rock 'n' roll, experiment with drugs, and exist on a steady diet of Ring-Dings, nachos, and beer. This is what many adults, including parents, seem to believe about the young. The reality is, however, that young people today show more maturity and common sense than most adults give them credit for.

Dramatic Fact or Statistic

Seventy percent of the respondents in a poll conducted by columnist Ann Landers stated that if they could live their lives over, they would choose not to have children. This startling statistic makes one wonder what these people believed parenthood would be like. Most parents, it seems, have unrealistic expectations about their children. Parents want their children to accept their values, follow their paths, and succeed where they failed.

Introductory paragraphs sometimes end with a *plan of development:* a quick preview of the essay's major points in the order in which those points will be discussed. The plan of development may be part of the thesis (as in the first sample introduction) or it may immediately follow the thesis (as in the last sample introduction). Because the plan of development outlines the essay's organizational structure, it helps prepare the reader for the essay's progression of ideas. In a brief essay, readers can often keep track of the ideas without this extra help. In a longer paper, though, a plan of development can be an effective unifying device since it highlights the main ideas the essay will develop.

Write the Conclusion

You may have come across essays that ended with jarring abruptness because they had no conclusions at all. Other papers may have had conclusions, but they sputtered to a weak close, a sure sign that the writers had run out of steam and wanted to finish as quickly as possible. Just as satisfying closes are an important part of everyday life (we feel cheated if dinner doesn't end with dessert or if a friend leaves without saying goodbye), a strong conclusion is an important part of an effective essay.

Generally one or two paragraphs, the conclusion should give the reader a feeling of completeness and finality. One way to achieve this sense of "rounding off" is to return to an image, idea, or anecdote from the introduction. Because people tend to remember most clearly the points they read last, the conclusion is also a good place to remind readers of your thesis. You may also use the conclusion to make a final point about your subject. Be careful, though, not to open an entirely new line of thought at the essay's close.

Illustrated briefly here are several strategies for writing sound conclusions. These techniques may be used singly or in combination. The first strategy, the summary conclusion, can be especially helpful in long, complex essays since readers may appreciate a review of your points. Tacked onto a short essay, though, a summary conclusion often seems boring and mechanical.

Summary

Contrary to what many adults think, most adolescents are not only aware of the important issues of the times but also deeply concerned about them. They are sensitive to the plight of the homeless, the destruction of the environment, and the pitfalls of rampant materialism. Indeed, today's young people are not less mature and sensible than their parents were. If anything, they are more so.

Prediction

The growing tendency on the part of the judicial system to hold parents responsible for the actions of their wayward children can have a disturbing impact on all of us. Parents will feel bitter toward their own children and cynical about a system that holds them accountable for the actions of minors. Children, continuing to escape the consequences of their actions, will become even more lawless and destructive. Society cannot afford two such possibilities.

Quotation

The comic W. C. Fields is reputed to have said, "Anyone who hates children and dogs can't be all bad." Most people do not share Fields's cynicism. Viewing childhood as a time of purity, they are alarmed at the way television exposes children to the seamy side of life, stripping youngsters of their innocence and giving them a glib sophistication that is a poor substitute for wisdom.

Statistic

Granted, divorce may, in some cases, be the best thing for families torn apart by parents who battle one another. However, in longitudinal studies of children from divorced families, psychologist Judith Wallerstein found that only 10 percent of the youngsters felt relief at their parents' divorce; the remaining 90 percent felt devastated. Such statistics surely call into question parents' claims that they are divorcing for their children's sake.

Recommendation or Call for Action

It is a mistake to leave parenting to instinct. Instead, we should make parenting skills a required course in schools. In addition, a nationwide hotline should be established to help parents deal with crises. Such training and continuing support would help adults deal more effectively with many of the problems they face as parents.

Write the Title

Some writers say that they began a certain piece with only a title in mind. But for most people, writing a title is a finishing touch. Although creating a title for your paper is usually one of the last steps in writing an essay, it shouldn't be done haphazardly. It may take time to write an effective title—one that hints at the essay's thesis and snares the reader's interest.

Good titles may make use of the following techniques: repetition of sounds ("The Border on Our Backs"); questions ("A War Against Boys?"); and humor ("How to Say Nothing in 500 Words"). More often, though, titles are straightforward phrases derived from the essay's subject or thesis: "Shooting an Elephant" and "The Ways We Lie," for example.

Pull It All Together

Now that you know how to prepare a first draft, you might find it helpful to examine Figure 2.2 to see how the different parts of a draft can fit together. Keep in mind that not every essay you write will take this

FIGURE 2.2
Structure of an Essay

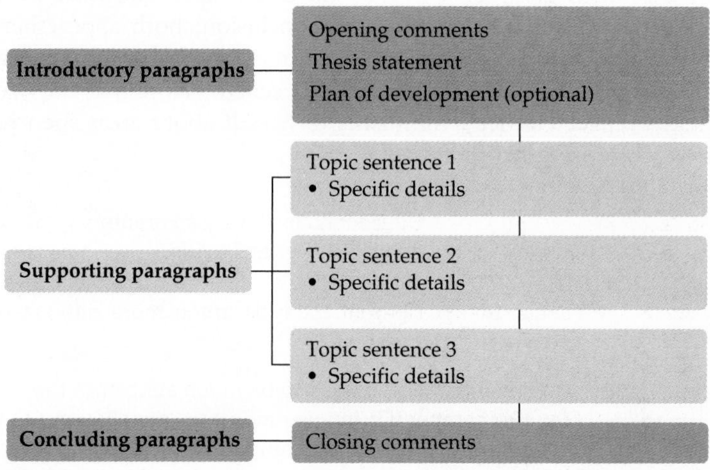

shape. As your purpose, audience, and tone change, so will your essay's structure. An introduction or conclusion, for instance, may be developed in more than one paragraph; the thesis statement may be implied or delayed until the essay's middle or end; not all paragraphs may have topic sentences; and several supporting paragraphs may be needed to develop a single topic sentence. Even so, the basic format presented here offers a strategy for organizing a variety of writing assignments—from term papers to lab reports. Once you feel comfortable with the structure, you have a foundation on which to base your variations. (This book's student and professional essays illustrate some possibilities.) Even when using a specific format, you always have room to give your spirit and imagination free play. The language you use, the details you select, the perspective you offer are uniquely yours. They are what make your essay different from everyone else's.

Sample First Draft

Here is the first draft of Harriet Davids's essay. (The assignment and prewriting for the essay appear on pages 12, 22–23, and 26–27.) Harriet wrote the draft in one sitting. Working at a computer, she started by typing her thesis at the top of the first page. Then, following the guidelines on page 47, she moved the material in her outline (pages 44–45) to her draft. Harriet worked rapidly; she started with the first body paragraph and wrote straight through to the last supporting paragraph.

By moving quickly, Harriet got down her essay's basic text rather easily. Once she felt she had captured in rough form what she wanted to say, she reread her draft to get a sense of how she might open and close the essay. Then she drafted her introduction and conclusion; both appear here, together with the body of the essay. The commentary following the draft will give you a clearer sense of how Harriet proceeded. (Note that the marginal annotations reflect Harriet's comments to herself about areas she needs to address when revising her first draft.)

Challenges for Today's Parents
by Harriet Davids

Thesis: Being a parent today is much more difficult than it was a generation ago.

Raising children used to be much simpler in the '50s and '60s. I remember TV images from that era showing that parenting involved simply teaching kids to clean their rooms, do their homework, and _______. But being a parent today is much more difficult because nowadays parents have to shield/protect kids from lots of things, like distractions from schoolwork, from sexual material, from dangerous situations.

Add specifics

Parents have to control all the new distractions/ temptations that turn kids away from schoolwork. These days many kids have stereos, computers, and televisions in their rooms. Certainly, my girls can't resist the urge to listen to MTV and go online, especially if it's time to do homework. Unfortunately, though, kids aren't assigned much homework and what is assigned too often is busywork. And there are even more distractions outside the home. Teens no longer hang out/congregate on the corner where Dad and Mom can yell to them to come home and do homework. Instead they hang out at the mall, in movie theaters, and fast-food restaurants. Obviously, parents and school can't compete with all this.

Weak trans.

Also parents have to help kids develop responsible sexual values even though sex is everywhere. Kids see sex magazines and dirty paperbacks in the corner store where they used to get candy and comic books. And instead of the artsy nude shots of the past, kids see ronchey, explicit shots in *Playboy* and *Penthouse*. And movies have sexy stuff in them today. Teachers seduce students and people treat sex casually/as a sport. Not exactly traditional values. TV is no better. Kids see soap-opera characters in bed and cable shows full of nudity by just flipping the dial. Even worse is what's on the Internet. Too easy for kids

Sp?

to access chat rooms and websites dealing with adult, sometimes pornographic material. The situation has gotten so out of hand that maybe the government should establish guidelines on what's permissible.

Worst of all are the life-threatening dangers that parents
Awk must help children fend off over the years. With older kids,
Wrong word drugs fall into place as a main concern. Peer pressure to try
drugs is bigger to kids than their parents' warnings. Other
kinds of warnings are common when children are small. Then
Add specifics parents fear violence since news shows constantly report stories of little children being abused. And when kids aren't
much older, they have to resist the pressure to drink. Alcohol
Redo has always attracted kids, but nowadays they are drinking
more and this can be deadly, especially when drinking is combined with driving.

Most adults love their children and want to be good par-
Sp? ents. But it's difficult because the world seems stacked
against young people. Even Holden Caufield had trouble dealing with society's confusing pressures. Parents must give their children some freedom but not so much that the kids lose sight of what's important.

Commentary

As you can see, Harriet's draft is rough. Because she knew she would revise later on (page 60), she "zapped out" the draft in an informal, colloquial style. For example, she occasionally expressed her thoughts in fragments ("Not exactly traditional values"), relied heavily on "and" as a transition, and used slangy expressions such as "kids," "dirty paperbacks," and "lots of things." She also used slashes between alternative word choices and left a blank space when wording just wouldn't come. Then, as Harriet reviewed the printed copy of this rough draft, she made handwritten marginal notes to herself: "Awk" or "Redo" to signal awkward sentences; "Add specifics" to mark overly general statements; "Wrong word" after an imprecise word; "Sp?" to remind herself to check spelling in the dictionary; "Weak trans." to indicate where a stronger signaling device was needed. (Harriet's final draft appears on pages 66–68.)

Writing a first draft may seem like quite a challenge, but the tips offered in these pages should help you proceed with confidence. Indeed, as you work on the draft, you may be surprised how much you enjoy writing. After all, this is your chance to get down on paper something you want to say.

Activities: Write the First Draft

1. Retrieve the writing you prepared in response to activity 3 on page 46. Applying the principles just presented, rework that material. If you wrote a single paragraph earlier, expand the material into a full essay draft. If you prepared an essay, strengthen what you wrote. In both cases, remember to consider your purpose, audience, and tone as you write the body of the essay as well as its introduction and conclusion. (Save your draft so you can rework it even further after reading about the next stage in the writing process.)
2. Referring to the outline you prepared in response to activity 2 or activity 4 on page 46, draft the body of your essay, making your evidence as strong as possible. As you work, keep your purpose, audience, and tone in mind. After reading what you've prepared, go ahead and draft a rough introduction, conclusion, and title. Finally, ask at least one other person to react to your draft by listing its strengths and weaknesses. (Save the draft so you can work with it further after reading about the next stage in the writing process.)

STAGE 6: REVISE THE ESSAY

By now, you've probably abandoned any preconceptions you might have had about good writers sitting down and creating a finished product in one easy step. Alexander Pope's comment that "true ease in writing comes from art, not chance" is as true today as it was more than two hundred years ago. Writing that seems effortlessly clear is often the result of sustained work, not of good luck or even inborn talent. And much of this work takes place during the final stage of the writing process when ideas, paragraphs, sentences, and words are refined and reshaped.

Professional writers—novelists, journalists, textbook authors—seldom submit a piece of writing that hasn't been revised. They recognize that rough, unpolished work doesn't do them justice. What's more, they often look forward to revising. Columnist Ellen Goodman put it this way: "What makes me happy is rewriting. . . . It's like cleaning house, getting rid of all the junk, getting things in the right order, tightening up."

In a sense, revision occurs throughout the writing process: At some earlier stage, you may have dropped an idea, overhauled your thesis, or shifted paragraph order. What, then, is different about the rewriting that occurs in the revision stage? The answer has to do with the literal meaning of the word *revision*—to resee, or to see again. Genuine revision involves casting clear eyes on your work, viewing it as though you're a reader rather than the writer. Revision means that you go through your paper looking for trouble, ready to pick a fight with your own writing. And then you must be willing to sit down and make the changes needed for your writing to be as effective as possible.

Revision is not, as some believe, simply touch-up work—changing a sentence here or a word there, eliminating spelling errors, preparing a neat final copy. Revision means cutting deadwood, rearranging paragraphs, substituting new words for old ones, recasting sentences, improving coherence, even generating new material when appropriate. With experience, you'll learn how to streamline the process so you can focus on the most critical issues for a particular piece of writing. (For advice on correcting some common writing errors, see Appendix B on pages 639–651.)

Five Revision Strategies

Because revision is challenging, you may find yourself unsure about how to proceed. Keep in mind that there are no hard-and-fast rules about the revision process. Even so, the following pointers should help get you going if you balk at or feel overwhelmed by revising.

- *Set your draft aside for a while* before revising. When you pick up your paper again, you'll have a fresh, more objective point of view.
- *Work from printed-out material* whenever possible. Having your essay in neutral typed letters instead of in your own familiar writing helps you see the paper impartially, as if someone else had written it. Each time you make major changes, try to print out a copy of that section so that you can see it anew.
- *Read your draft aloud* as often as you can. Hearing how your writing sounds helps you pick up problems that you passed by before: places where sentences are awkward, meaning is ambiguous, words are imprecise. Even better, have another person read aloud to you what you have written. If the reader slows to a crawl over a murky paragraph or trips over a convoluted sentence, you know where you have to do some rewriting.
- *View revision as a series of steps.* Don't try to tackle all of a draft's problems at once; instead, proceed step by step, starting with the most pressing issues. Although there are bound to be occasions when you have time for only one quick pass over a draft, whenever possible, read your draft several times; each time focus on different matters and ask yourself different questions. Move from a broad view of the draft to an up-close look at its mechanics.
- *Evaluate and respond to instructor feedback.* Often, instructors collect and respond to students' first drafts. Like many students, you may be tempted to look only briefly at your instructor's comments. Perhaps you've "had it" with the essay and don't want to think about revising the paper to reflect the instructor's

remarks. But taking your instructor's comments into account when revising is often what's needed to turn a shaky first draft into a strong final draft.

When an instructor returns a final draft graded, you may think that the grade is all that counts. Remember, though: Grades are important, but comments are even more so. They can help you *improve* your writing—if not in this paper, then in the next one. If you don't understand or agree with the instructor's observations, don't hesitate to request a conference. Getting together gives both you and the instructor a chance to clarify your respective points of view.

Peer Review: An Additional Revision Strategy

Many instructors include in-class or at-home peer review as a regular part of a composition course. Peer review—the critical reading of another person's writing with the intention of suggesting changes—accomplishes several important goals. First, peer review helps you gain a more objective perspective on your work. When you write something, you're often too close to what you've prepared to evaluate it fairly; you may have trouble seeing where the writing is strong and where it needs to be strengthened. Peer review supplies the fresh, neutral perspective you need. Second, reviewing your classmates' work broadens your own composing options. You may be inspired to experiment with a technique you admired in a classmate's writing but wouldn't have thought of on your own. Finally, peer review trains you to be a better reader and critic of your *own* writing. When you get into the habit of critically reading other students' writing, you become more adept at critiquing your own.

The Peer Review/Revision Checklist on the inside front cover of this book will help focus your revision—whether you're reworking your own paper or responding to a peer's. Your instructor may have you respond to all questions on the checklist or to several selected items. What follows is

a peer review worksheet that Harriet Davids's instructor prepared to help students respond to first drafts based on the assignment on page 12. Wanting students to focus on four areas (thesis statement, support for thesis statement, overall organization, and signal devices), the instructor drew upon relevant sections from the Peer Review/Revision Checklist. With this customized worksheet in hand, Harriet's classmate Frank Tejada was able to give Harriet constructive feedback on her first draft (see pages 57–59). (*Note:* Because Harriet didn't want to influence Frank's reaction, the draft she gave him didn't include her marginal notations to herself.)

Peer Review Worksheet

Essay Author's Name: Harriet Davids Reviewer's Name: Frank Tejada

1. What is the essay's thesis? Is it explicit or implied? Does the thesis focus on a limited subject and express the writer's attitude toward that subject?

   Thesis: "Being a parent today is much more difficult [than it used to be]." The thesis is limited and expresses a clear attitude. But the sentence the thesis appears in (last sentence of para. 1) is too long because it also contains the plan of development. Maybe put thesis and plan of development in separate sentences.

2. What are the main points supporting the thesis? List the points. Is each supporting point developed sufficiently? If not, where is more support needed?

   (1) Parents have to control kids' distractions from school.
   (2) Parents have to help kids develop responsible sexual values despite sex being everywhere.
   (3) Parents have to protect kids from life-threatening dangers.

   The supporting points are good and are explained pretty well, except for a few places. The "Unfortunately" sentence in para. 2 is irrelevant. Also, in para. 2, you use the example of your girls, but never again. Either include them throughout or not at all. In para. 3, the final sentence about the government guidelines opens a whole new topic; maybe steer away from this. The items in para. 4 seem vague and need specific examples. In the conclusion, omit Holden Caulfield; since he was from an earlier generation, this example undermines your thesis about parenting today.

3. What overall format (chronological, spatial, emphatic, simple-to-complex) is used to sequence the essay's main points? Does this format work? Why or why not? What organizational format is used in each supporting paragraph? Does the format work? Why or why not?

   The paper's overall emphatic organization seems good. Emphatic order also works in para. 3, and spatial order works well in para. 2. But the sentences in para. 4 need rearranging. Right now, the examples are in mixed-up chronological order, making it hard to follow. Maybe you should reorder the examples from young kids to older kids.

4. What signal devices are used to connect ideas within and between paragraphs? Are there too few signal devices or too many? Where?

The topic sentence of para. 3 needs to be a stronger bridging sentence. Also, too many "and's" in para. 3. Try "in addition" or "another" in some places. I like the "worst of all" transition to para. 4.

As you can see, Frank flagged several areas that Harriet herself also noted needed work. (Turn to pages 58–59 to see Harriet's marginal comments on her draft.) But he also commented on entirely new areas (for example, the sequence problem in paragraph 4), offering Harriet a fresh perspective on what she needed to do to polish her draft. To see which of Frank's suggestions Harriet followed, take a look at her final draft on pages 66–68 and at the "Commentary" following the essay.

Becoming a skilled peer reviewer. Even with the help of a checklist, preparing a helpful peer review is a skill that takes time to develop. At first, you, like many students, may be too easy or too critical. Effective peer review calls for rigor and care; you should give classmates the conscientious feedback that you hope for in return. Peer review also requires tact and kindness; feedback should always be constructive and include observations about what works well in a piece of writing. People have difficulty mustering the energy to revise if they feel there's nothing worth revising.

If your instructor doesn't include peer review, you can set up peer review sessions outside of class, with classmates getting together to respond to each other's drafts. Or you may select non-classmates who are objective (not a love-struck admirer or a doting grandparent) and skilled enough to provide useful commentary.

To focus your readers' comments, you may adapt the Peer Review/Revision Checklist on the inside front cover of this book, or you may develop your own questions. If you prepare the questions yourself, be sure to solicit *specific* observations about what does and doesn't work in your writing. If you simply ask, "How's this?" you may receive a vague comment like "It's not very effective." What you want are concrete observations and suggestions: "I'm confused because what you say in the fifth sentence contradicts what you say in the second." To promote such specific responses, ask your readers targeted (preferably written) questions like "I'm having trouble moving from my second to my third point. How can I make the transition smoother?" Such questions require more than "yes" or "no" responses; they encourage readers to dig into your writing where you sense it needs work. (If it's feasible, encourage readers to *write* their responses to your questions.)

If you and your peer reviewer(s) can't meet in person, e-mail can provide a crucial means of contact. With a couple of clicks, you can simply send each other computer files of your work. You and your reviewer(s) also need to decide exactly how to exchange comments about your drafts. You might conclude, for example, that you'll type your responses, perhaps in bold capitals, into the file itself. Or you might decide to print out the drafts and reply to the comments in writing, later exchanging the annotated drafts in person. No matter what you and your peer(s) decide, you'll probably find e-mail an invaluable tool in the writing process.

Evaluating and responding to peer review. Accepting criticism isn't easy (even if you asked for it), and not all peer reviewers will be diplomatic. Even so, try to listen with an open mind to those giving you feedback. Take notes on their oral observations and/or have them fill out relevant sections from the Peer Review/Revision Checklist (on the inside front cover). Later, when you're ready to revise your paper, reread your notes. Which reviewer remarks seem valid? Which don't? Rank the problems and solutions that your reviewers identified, designating the most critical as number 1. Using the peer feedback, enter your own notes for revising in the margins of a clean copy of your draft. This way, you'll know exactly what changes need to be made in your draft as you proceed. Then, keeping the problems and remedies in mind, start revising. Type in your changes, or handwrite changes directly on the draft above the appropriate line. (Rework extensive sections on a separate piece of paper.) When revising, always keep in mind that you may not agree with every reviewer suggestion. That's fine. It's *your* paper, and it's *your* decision to implement or reject the suggestions made by your peers.

STAGE 7: EDIT AND PROOFREAD

Your essay is not finished until you have dealt with errors in grammar, punctuation, and spelling.

If you are using a computer,

- Use your computer's spelling check program to identify and correct misspelled words.
- Read the screen slowly, looking for wrong words (such as "there" when "their" is meant), errors in proper names, and errors in grammar.
- Format the essay using your instructor's guidelines, and print a copy.
- Proofread the printed paper slowly to catch typos and other mistakes.

If you find just a few errors in the printed paper, you may correct them by hand in dark ink. But if a page starts to look messy, you will need to print a clean, corrected copy to include in your final paper.

STUDENT ESSAY

In this chapter, we've taken you through the various stages in the writing process. You've seen how Harriet Davids used prewriting (pages 22–23 and 26–27) and outlining (pages 44–45) to arrive at her first draft (pages 57–59). You've also seen how Harriet's peer reviewer, Frank Tejada, critiqued her first draft (pages 63–64). In the following pages, you'll look at Harriet's final draft—the paper she submitted to her instructor.

Harriet, a thirty-eight-year-old college student and mother of two teenagers, wanted to write an informative paper with a straightforward, serious tone. While preparing her essay, she kept in mind that her audience would include her course instructor as well as her classmates, many of them considerably younger than she. This is the assignment that prompted Harriet's essay:

> Goodman implies that, in some ways, today's world is hostile to children. Do you agree? Drawing upon but not limiting yourself to the material in your pre-reading journal, write an essay in which you support or reject this viewpoint.

Harriet's essay is annotated so that you can see how it illustrates the essay format described on page 57. As you read her essay, try to determine how well it reflects the principles of effective writing. The commentary following the paper will help you look at the essay more closely and give you some sense of the way Harriet went about revising her first draft.

Challenges for Today's Parents

By Harriet Davids

Introduction

Thesis

Plan of development

1 Reruns of situation comedies from the 1950s and early 1960s dramatize the kinds of problems that parents used to have with their children. On classic television shows such as *Leave It to Beaver*, the Cleavers scold their son Beaver for not washing his hands before dinner; on *Ozzie and Harriet*, the Nelsons dock little Ricky's allowance because he keeps forgetting to clean his room. But times have changed dramatically. Being a parent today is much more difficult than it was a generation ago. Parents nowadays must protect their children from a growing number of distractions, from sexually explicit material, and from life-threatening situations.

First supporting paragraph

Topic sentence

Today's parents must try, first of all, to control all the new distractions that tempt children away from schoolwork. At home, a child may have a room furnished with an MP3 player, television, and computer. Not many young people can resist the urge to listen to music, watch TV, go online, or play computer games and IM their friends—especially if it's time to do schoolwork. Outside the home, the distractions are even more alluring. Children no longer "hang out" on a neighborhood corner within earshot of Mom or Dad's reminder to come in and do homework. Instead, they congregate in vast shopping malls, movie theaters, and gleaming fast-food restaurants. Parents and school assignments have obvious difficulty competing with such enticing alternatives. 2

Second supporting paragraph

Topic sentence with link to previous paragraph

Besides dealing with these distractions, parents have to shield their children from a flood of sexually explicit materials. Today, children can find pornographic websites and chat rooms on the Internet with relative ease. With the click of a mouse, they can be transported, intentionally or unintentionally, to a barrage of explicit images and conversations. Easily obtainable copies of sex magazines can be found at most convenience stores, many times alongside the candy. Children will not see the fuzzily photographed nudes that a previous generation did but will encounter the hard-core raunchiness of *Playboy* or *Penthouse*. Moreover, the movies young people view often focus on highly sexual situations. It is difficult to teach children traditional values when films show young people treating sex as a casual sport. Unfortunately, television, with its often heavily sexual content, is no better. With just a flick of the channel, children can see sexed-up music videos, watch reality-TV stars cavorting in bed, or watch cable programs where nudity is common. 3

Third supporting paragraph

Topic sentence with emphasis signal

Most disturbing to parents today, however, is the increase in life-threatening dangers that face young people. When children are small, parents fear that their youngsters may be victims of violence. Every news program seems to carry a report about a school shooting or child predator who has been released from prison, only to repeat an act of violence against a minor. When children are older, parents begin to worry about their kids' use of drugs. Peer pressure to experiment with drugs is often stronger than parents' warnings. This pressure to experiment can be fatal. Finally, even if young people escape the hazards associated with drugs, they must still resist the pressure to drink. Although 4 alcohol has always held an attraction for teenagers, reports indicate that they are drinking more than ever before. As many parents know, the consequences of this attraction can be deadly—especially when drinking is combined with driving.

Conclusion

References to TV shows recall introduction

Within a generation, the world as a place to raise children 5
has changed dramatically. One wonders how yesterday's parents would have dealt with today's problems. Could the Nelsons have shielded little Ricky from sexually explicit material on the Internet? Could the Cleavers have protected Beaver from drugs and alcohol? Parents must be aware of all these distractions and dangers yet be willing to give their children the freedom they need to become responsible adults. This is not an easy task.

COMMENTARY

Introduction and thesis. The opening paragraph attracts readers' interest by recalling several vintage television shows that have almost become part of our cultural heritage. Harriet begins with these examples from the past because they offer such a sharp contrast to the present, thus underscoring the idea expressed in her *thesis:* "Being a parent today is much more difficult than it was a generation ago." Opening in this way, with material that serves as a striking contrast to what follows, is a common and effective strategy. Note, too, that Harriet's thesis states the paper's subject (being a parent) as well as her attitude toward the subject (the job is more demanding than it was years ago).

Plan of development. Harriet follows her thesis with a *plan of development* that anticipates the three major points to be covered in the essay's supporting paragraphs. When revising her first draft, Harriet followed peer reviewer Frank Tejada's recommendation (page 63–64) to put her thesis and plan of development in separate sentences. Unfortunately, though, her plan of development ends up being somewhat mechanical, with the major points being trotted past the reader in one long, awkward sentence. To deal with the problem, Harriet could have rewritten the sentence or eliminated the plan of development altogether, ending the introduction with her thesis.

Patterns of development. Although Harriet develops her thesis primarily through *examples,* she also draws on two other patterns of development. The whole paper implies a *contrast* between the way life and parenting are now and the way they used to be. The essay also contains an element of *causal analysis* since all the factors that Harriet cites affect children and the way they are raised.

Purpose, audience, and tone. Given the essay's *purpose* and *audience,* Harriet adopts a serious *tone,* providing no-nonsense evidence to support her thesis. But assume she had been asked by her daughters' school newspaper to write a humorous column about the trials and tribulations that parents face raising children. Aiming for a different tone, purpose, and audience, Harriet would have taken another approach. Drawing on her personal experience, she might have confessed how she survives her daughters' nearly nonstop use of the computer, as well as the constant thumping sounds that emanate from the ear buds of their MP3s: She cuts off the electricity and hides the ear buds. This material—with its personalized perspective, exaggeration, and light tone—would be appropriate.

Organization. Structuring the essay around a series of *relevant* and *specific examples,* Harriet uses *emphatic order* to sequence the paper's three main points: that a growing number of distractions, sexually explicit materials, and life-threatening situations make parenting difficult nowadays. The third supporting paragraph begins with the words "Most disturbing to parents today . . . ," signaling that Harriet feels particular concern about the physical dangers children face. Moreover, she uses basic organizational strategies to sequence the supporting examples within each paragraph. The details in the first supporting paragraph are organized *spatially,* starting with distractions at home and moving to those outside the home. The second supporting paragraph arranges examples *emphatically.* Harriet starts with sexually explicit material on the Internet and ends with the "heavily sexual content" on TV. Note that Harriet followed Frank's peer review advice (pages 63–64) about omitting her first-draft observation that kids don't get enough homework—or that they get too much busywork. The third and final supporting paragraph is organized *chronologically;* it begins by discussing dangers to small children and concludes by talking about teenagers. Again, Frank's advice—to use a clearer time sequence in this paragraph (pages 63–64)—was invaluable when Harriet was revising.

The essay also displays Harriet's familiarity with other kinds of organizational strategies. Each supporting paragraph opens with a *topic sentence.* Further, *signal devices* are used throughout the paper to show how ideas are related to one another: *transitions* ("Instead, they congregate in vast shopping malls"; "Moreover, the movies young people attend often focus on highly sexual situations"); *repetition* ("sexual situations" and "sexual content"); *synonyms* ("distractions...enticing alternatives" and "life-threatening...fatal"); *pronouns* ("young people...they"); and *bridging sentences* ("Besides dealing with these distractions, parents have to shield their children from a flood of sexually explicit material").

Two minor problems. Harriet's efforts to write a well-organized essay result in a somewhat predictable structure. It might have been better had she rewritten one of the paragraphs, perhaps embedding the topic sentence in the middle of the paragraph or saving it for the end. Similarly, Harriet's signal devices are a little heavy-handed. Even so, an essay with a sharp focus and clear signals is preferable to one with a confusing or inaccessible structure. As she gains more experience, Harriet can work on making the structure of her essays more subtle.

Conclusion. Following Frank's suggestion, Harriet dropped from the final paragraph the first draft's problematic reference to Holden Caulfield (page 63). Having done that, she's able to bring the essay to a satisfying *close* by reminding readers of the paper's central idea and three main points. The final paragraph also extends the essay's scope by introducing a new but related issue: that parents have to strike a balance between their need to provide limitations and their children's need for freedom. Besides eliminating the distracting reference to Holden Caulfield, she deleted the shopworn opening sentence ("Most adults love their children...") and added references to the vintage TV shows mentioned in the introduction: ("Could the Nelsons...? Could the Cleavers...?"). These questions help unify Harriet's paper and bring it to a rounded close.

These are just a few of the changes Harriet made when reworking her essay. Realizing that writing is a process, she left herself enough time to revise—and to carefully consider Frank Tejada's comments. Early in her composition course, Harriet learned that attention to the various stages in the writing process yields satisfying results, for writer and reader alike.

Activity: Revise the Essay

Return to the draft you wrote in response to either activity 1 or activity 2 on page 60. Also look at any written feedback you received on the draft. To identify any further problems in the draft, get together with several people (classmates, friends, or family members) and request that one of them read the draft aloud to you. Then ask your audience focused questions about the areas you sense need work, or use the checklist on the inside front cover to focus the feedback. In either case, summarize and rank the comments on a feedback chart or in marginal annotations. Then, using the comments as a guide, go ahead and revise the draft. Either type a new version or do your revising by hand, perhaps on a photocopy of the draft. Don't forget to proofread closely before submitting the paper to your instructor.

Rudi Von Briel/PhotoEdit, Inc.

DESCRIPTION

WHAT IS DESCRIPTION?

All of us respond in a strong way to sensory stimulation. The sweet perfume of a candy shop takes us back to childhood; the blank white walls of the campus infirmary remind us of long vigils at a hospital where a grandmother lay dying; the screech of a subway car sets our nerves on edge.

Without any sensory stimulation, we sink into a less-than-human state. Neglected babies, left alone with no human touch, no colors, no lullabies, become withdrawn and unresponsive. And prisoners dread solitary confinement, knowing that the sensory deprivation can be unbearable, even to the point of madness.

Because sensory impressions are so potent, descriptive writing has a unique power and appeal. *Description* can be defined as the expression, in vivid language, of what the five senses experience. A richly rendered description freezes a subject in time, evoking sights, smells, sounds, textures, and tastes in such a way that readers become one with the writer's world.

HOW DESCRIPTION FITS YOUR PURPOSE AND AUDIENCE

Description can be a supportive technique that develops part of an essay, or it can be the dominant technique used throughout an essay. Here are some examples of the way description can help you meet the objective of an essay developed chiefly through another pattern of development:

- In a *causal analysis* showing the *consequences* of pet overpopulation, you might describe the desperate appearance of a pack of starving stray dogs.
- In an *argumentation-persuasion* essay urging more rigorous handgun control, you might start with a description of a violent family confrontation that ended in murder.
- In a *process analysis* explaining the pleasure of making ice cream at home, you might describe the beauty of an old-fashioned, hand-cranked ice-cream maker.
- In a *narrative essay* recounting a day in the life of a street musician, you might describe the musician's energy and the joyous appreciation of passersby.

In each case, the essay's overall purpose would affect the amount of description needed.

Your readers also influence how much description to include. As you write, ask yourself, "What do my particular readers need to know to understand and experience keenly what I'm describing? What descriptive details will they enjoy most?" Your answers to these and similar questions will help you tailor your description to specific readers. Consider an article intended for professional horticulturists; its purpose is to explain a new technique for controlling spider mites. Because of readers' expertise, there would be little need for a lengthy description of the insects. Written for a college newspaper, however, the article would probably provide a detailed description of the mites so student gardeners could distinguish between the pesky parasites and flecks of dust.

While your purpose and audience define *how much* to describe, you have great freedom deciding *what* to describe. Description is especially suited to objects (your car or desk, for example), but you can also describe a person, an animal, a place, a time, and a phenomenon or concept. You might write an effective description of a friend who runs marathons (person), a pair of ducks that return each year to a neighbor's pond (animals), the kitchen of a fast-food restaurant (place), a period when you were unemployed (time), the "fight or flight" response to danger (phenomenon or concept).

Description can be divided into two types: *objective* and *subjective*. In an objective description, you describe the subject in a straightforward and literal way, without revealing your attitude or feelings. Reporters, as well as technical and scientific writers, specialize in objective description;

their jobs depend on their ability to detail experiences without emotional bias. For example, a reporter may write an unemotional account of a township meeting that ended in a fistfight. Or a marine biologist may write a factual report describing the way sea mammals are killed by the plastic refuse (sandwich wrappings, straws, fishing lines) that humans throw into the ocean.

In contrast, when writing a subjective description, you convey a highly personal view of your subject and seek to elicit a strong emotional response from your readers. Such subjective descriptions often take the form of reflective pieces or character studies. For example, in an essay describing the rich plant life in an inner-city garden, you might reflect on people's longing to connect with the soil and express admiration for the gardeners' hard work—an admiration you'd like readers to share. Or, in a character study of your grandfather, you might describe his stern appearance and gentle behavior, hoping that the contradiction will move readers as much as it moves you.

The *tone* of a subjective description is determined by your purpose, your attitude toward the subject, and the reader response you wish to evoke. Consider an essay about a dynamic woman who runs a center for disturbed children. If you want readers to admire the woman, your tone will be serious and appreciative. But if you want to criticize her high-pressure tactics and management style, your tone will be disapproving and severe.

The language of a descriptive piece also depends, to a great extent, on whether your purpose is primarily objective or subjective. If the description is objective, the language is straightforward, precise, and factual. Such *denotative* language consists of neutral dictionary meanings. To describe as dispassionately as possible fans' violent behavior at a football game, you might write about the "large crowd" and its "mass movement onto the field." But for a subjective piece that inspires outrage in readers, you might write about the "swelling mob" and its "rowdy stampede onto the field." In the latter case, the language you used would be *connotative* and emotionally charged so that readers would share your feelings.

Subjective and objective descriptions often overlap. Sometimes a single sentence contains both objective and subjective elements: "Although his hands were large and misshapen by arthritis, they were gentle to the touch, inspiring confidence and trust." Other times, part of an essay may provide a factual description (the physical appearance of a summer cabin your family rented), while another part of the essay may be highly subjective (how you felt in the cabin, sitting in front of a fire on a rainy day).

At this point, you have a good sense of the way writers use description to achieve their purpose and to connect with their readers. Now take a moment to look closely at the photograph at the beginning of this chapter. Imagine you're writing a column, accompanied by the photo, for the local newspaper. Your purpose is to encourage businesspeople to support the city's mural arts program. Jot down some phrases you might use to *describe* the mural and its impact on the community.

SUGGESTIONS FOR USING DESCRIPTION IN AN ESSAY

The suggestions here and in Figure 3.1 on page 76 will be helpful whether you use description as a dominant or a supportive pattern of development.

1. Focus a descriptive essay around a dominant impression. Like other kinds of writing, a descriptive essay must have a thesis, or main point. In a descriptive essay with a subjective slant, the thesis usually centers on the ***dominant impression*** you have about your subject. Suppose you decide to write an essay on your ninth-grade history teacher, Ms. Hazzard. You want the paper to convey how unconventional and flamboyant she was. The essay could, of course, focus on a different dominant impression—how insensitive she could be to students, for example. What's important is that you establish—early in the paper—the dominant impression you intend to convey. Although descriptive essays often imply, rather than explicitly state, the dominant impression, that impression should be unmistakable.

2. Select the details to include. The power of description hinges on your ability to select from all possible details only those that support the dominant impression. All others, no matter how vivid or interesting, must be left out. If you're describing how flamboyant Ms. Hazzard could be, the details in the following paragraph would be appropriate.

A large-boned woman, Ms. Hazzard wore her bright red hair piled on top of her head, where it perched precariously. By the end of class, wayward strands of hair tumbled down and fell into eyes fringed by

FIGURE 3.1
Development Diagram: Writing a Description Essay

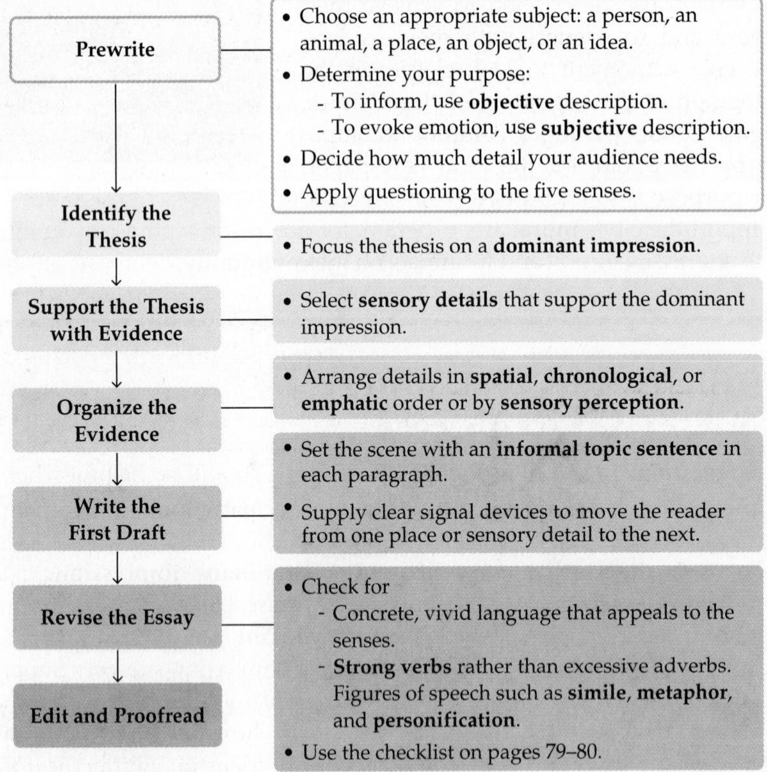

spiky false eyelashes. Ms. Hazzard's nails, filed into crisp points, were painted either bloody burgundy or neon pink. Plastic bangle bracelets, also either burgundy or pink, clattered up and down her ample arms as she scrawled on the board the historical dates that had, she claimed, "changed the world."

Such details—the heavy eye makeup, stiletto nails, gaudy bracelets—contribute to the impression of a flamboyant, unusual person. Even if you remembered times that Ms. Hazzard seemed perfectly conventional and understated, most likely you wouldn't describe those times since they contradict the dominant impression.

You must also be selective in the *number of details* you include. Having a dominant impression helps you eliminate many details gathered during prewriting, but there still will be choices to make. For example, it would be inappropriate to describe in exhaustive detail everything in a messy room:

> The brown desk, made of a grained plastic laminate, is directly under a small window covered by a torn yellow-and-gold plaid curtain. In the left corner of the desk are four crumbled balls of blue-lined yellow paper, three red markers, two fine-point blue pens, an ink eraser, and four letters, two bearing special wildlife stamps. A green down-filled vest and a red cable-knit sweater are thrown over the back of the bright blue metal bridge chair pushed under the desk. Under the chair is an oval braided rug, its once brilliant blues and greens spotted by old coffee stains.

Readers will be reluctant to wade through such undifferentiated specifics. Even more important, such excessive detailing dilutes the focus of the essay. You end up with a seemingly endless list of specifics rather than with a carefully crafted picture in words. In this regard, sculptors and writers are similar—what they take away is as important as what they leave in.

Perhaps you're wondering how to generate the details that support your dominant impression. As you can imagine, you have to develop heightened powers of observation and recall. To sharpen these key faculties, it can be helpful to make up a chart with separate columns for each of the five senses. If you can observe your subject directly, enter in the appropriate columns what you see, hear, taste, and so on. If you're attempting to remember something from the past, try to recollect details under each of these sense headings. Ask yourself questions ("How did it smell? What did I hear?") and list each memory recaptured. You'll be surprised how this simple technique can tune you in to your experiences and help uncover the specific details needed to develop your dominant impression.

3. Organize the descriptive details. Select the organizational pattern (or combination of patterns) that best supports your dominant impression. The paragraphs in a descriptive essay are usually sequenced *spatially* (from top to bottom, interior to exterior, near to far) or *chronologically* (as the subject is experienced in time). But the paragraphs can also be ordered *emphatically* (ending with your subject's most striking elements) or by *sensory impression* (first smell, then taste, then touch, and so on).

You might, for instance, use a *spatial* pattern to organize a description of a large city as you viewed it from the air, a taxi, and a subway car. A description of your first day on a new job might move *chronologically*, starting with how you felt the first hour on the job and proceeding through the rest of the day. In a paper describing a bout with the flu, you might arrange details *emphatically*, beginning with a description of your low-level aches and pains and concluding with an account of your raging fever. An essay about a neighborhood garbage dump, euphemistically called an "ecology landfill" by its owners, could be organized by *sensory impressions:* the sights of the dump, its smells, its sounds. Regardless of the organizational pattern you use, provide enough *signal devices* (for example, *about, next, worst of all*) so that readers can follow the description easily.

Finally, although descriptive essays don't always have conventional topic sentences, each descriptive paragraph should have a clear focus. Often this focus is indicated by a sentence early in the paragraph that names the scene, object, or individual to be described. Such a sentence functions as a kind of *informal topic sentence;* the paragraph's descriptive details then develop that topic sentence.

4. Use vivid sensory language and varied sentence structure. The connotative language typical of subjective description should be richly evocative. The words you select must etch in readers' minds the same picture that you have in yours. For this reason, rather than relying on vague generalities, you must use language that involves readers' senses. Consider the difference between the following paired descriptions.

Vague	Vivid
The food was unappetizing.	The stew congealed into an oval pool of milky-brown fat.
The toothpaste was refreshing.	The toothpaste, tasting minty sweet, felt good against slippery teeth, free finally from braces.
Filled with passengers and baggage, the car moved slowly down the road.	Burdened with its load of clamoring children and well-worn suitcases, the car labored down the interstate on bald tires and worn shocks, emitting puffs of blue exhaust and an occasional backfire.

Unlike the *concrete, sensory-packed* sentences on the right, the sentences on the left fail to create vivid word pictures that engage readers. While all good writing blends abstract and concrete language, descriptive writing demands an abundance of specific sensory language.

Keep in mind, too, that *verbs pack more of a wallop* than adverbs. The following sentence has to rely on adverbs (italicized) because its verbs are so weak: "She walked *casually* into the room and *deliberately* tried not to pay much attention to their stares." Rewritten, so that verbs (italicized), not adverbs, do the bulk of the work, the sentence becomes more powerful: "She *strolled* into the room and *ignored* their stares."

Figures of speech—nonliteral, imaginative comparisons between two basically dissimilar things—are another way to enliven descriptive writing. *Similes* use the words *like* or *as* when comparing; *metaphors* state or imply that two things being compared are alike; and *personification* attributes human characteristics to inanimate things.

The examples that follow show how effective figurative language can be in descriptive writing.

> Moving as jerkily as a marionette on strings, the old man picked himself up off the sidewalk and staggered down the street. (*simile*)
>
> Stalking their prey, the hall monitors remained hidden in the corridors, motionless and ready to spring on any unsuspecting student who dared to sneak into class late. (*metaphor*)
>
> The scoop of vanilla ice cream, plain and unadorned, cried out for hot-fudge sauce and a sprinkling of sliced pecans. (*personification*)

Finally, when writing descriptive passages, you need to *vary sentence structure.* Don't use the same subject-verb pattern in all sentences. The second example above, for instance, could have been written as follows: "The hall monitors stalked their prey. They hid in the corridors. They remained motionless and ready to spring on any unsuspecting student who tried to sneak into class late." But the sentence is richer and more interesting when the descriptive elements are embedded, eliminating what would otherwise have been a clipped and predictable subject-verb pattern.

REVISION STRATEGIES

Once you have a draft of the essay, you're ready to revise. The following checklist will help you and those giving you feedback apply to description some of the revision techniques discussed on pages 60–62.

☑ DESCRIPTION: A REVISION/PEER REVIEW CHECKLIST

Revise Overall Meaning and Structure

- ❑ What dominant impression does the essay convey? Is the dominant impression stated or implied? Where? Should it be made more obvious or more subtle?
- ❑ Is the essay primarily objective or subjective? Should the essay be more emotionally charged or less so?
- ❑ Which descriptive details don't support the dominant impression? Should they be deleted, or should the dominant impression be adjusted to encompass the details?

Revise Paragraph Development

- ❑ How are the essay's descriptive paragraphs organized—spatially, chronologically, emphatically, or by sensory impression? Would another organizational pattern be more effective? Which one(s)?
- ❑ Which paragraphs lack a distinctive focus?
- ❑ Which descriptive paragraphs are mere lists of sensory impressions?
- ❑ Which descriptive paragraphs fail to engage the reader's senses? How could they be made more concrete?

Revise Sentences and Words

- ❑ What signal devices guide readers through the description? Are there enough signals? Too many?
- ❑ Where should sentence structure be varied to make it less predictable?
- ❑ Which sentences should include more sensory images?
- ❑ Which flat verbs should be replaced with vigorous verbs?
- ❑ Where should there be more or fewer adjectives?
- ❑ Do any figures of speech seem contrived or trite? Which ones?

STUDENT ESSAY

The following student essay was written by Marie Martinez in response to this assignment:

> The essay "Flavio's Home" is a poignant piece about the slums of Rio de Janeiro. Write an essay about a place that holds rich significance for you, centering the description on a dominant impression.

While reading Marie's paper, try to determine how well it applies the principles of description. The annotations on Marie's paper and the commentary following it will help you look at the essay more closely.

Salt Marsh
by Marie Martinez

Introduction

In one of his journals, Thoreau told of the difficulty he had escaping the obligations and cares of society: "It sometimes happens that I cannot easily shake off the village. The thought of some work will run in my head and I am not where my body is—I am out of my senses. In my walks I... return to my senses." All of us feel out of our senses at times. Overwhelmed 1

Dominant impression (thesis)

by problems or everyday annoyances, we lose touch with sensory pleasures as we spend our days in noisy cities and stuffy classrooms. Just as Thoreau walked in the woods to return to his senses, I have a special place where I return to mine: the salt marsh behind my grandparents' house.

Informal topic sentences: Definition paragraph

My grandparents live on the East Coast, a mile or so inland from the sea. Between the ocean and the mainland is a wide fringe of salt marsh. A salt marsh is not a swamp, but an expanse of dark, spongy soil threaded with saltwater creeks and clothed in a kind of grass called salt meadow hay. All the water in the marsh rises and falls daily with the ocean tides, an endless cycle that changes the look of the marsh—partly flooded or mostly dry—as the day progresses. 2

Informal topic sentence: First paragraph in a four-part spatial sequence

Heading out to the marsh from my grandparents' house, I follow a short path through the woods. As I walk along, a sharp smell of salt mixed with the rich aroma of peaty soil fills my nostrils. I am always amazed by the way the path changes with the seasons. Sometimes I walk in the brilliant green of spring, sometimes in the tawny gold of autumn, sometimes in the grayish tan of winter. No matter the season, the grass flanking the trail is often flattened into swirls, like thick Van Gogh brush strokes that curve and recurve in circular patterns. No people come here. The peacefulness heals me like a soothing drug. 3

Simile

Informal topic sentence: Second paragraph in the spatial sequence

After a few minutes, the trail suddenly opens up to a view that calms me no matter how upset or discouraged I might be: a line of tall waving reeds bordering and nearly hiding the salt marsh creek. To get to the creek, I part the reeds. 4

Informal topic sentence: Third paragraph in the spatial sequence

The creek is a narrow body of water no more than fifteen feet wide, and it ebbs and flows as the ocean currents sweep toward the land or rush back toward the sea. The creek winds in a sinuous pattern so that I cannot see its beginning or end, the places where it trickles into the marsh or spills into the open ocean. Little brown birds dip in and out of the reeds on the far shore of the creek, making a special "tweep-tweep" sound peculiar to the marsh. When I stand at low tide on the shore of the creek, I am on a miniature cliff, for the bank of the creek falls abruptly and steeply into the water. Below me, green grasses wave and shimmer under the water while tiny minnows flash their silvery sides as they dart through the underwater tangles. 5

Informal topic sentence: Last paragraph in the spatial sequence

The creek water is often much warmer than the ocean, so I can swim there in three seasons. Sitting on the edge of the creek, I scoop some water into my hand, rub my face and neck, then ease into the water. Where the creek is shallow, my feet sink into a foot of muck that feels like mashed potatoes mixed with motor oil. But once I become accustomed to it, I enjoy 6

Simile

squishing the slimy mud through my toes. Sometimes I feel brushing past my legs the blue crabs that live in the creek. Other times, I hear the splash of a turtle or an otter as it slips from the shore into the water. Otherwise, it is silent. The salty water is buoyant and lifts my spirits as I stroke through it to reach the middle of the creek. There in the center, I float weightlessly, surrounded by tall reeds that reduce the world to water and sky. I am at peace.

Conclusion

The salt marsh is not the kind of dramatic landscape found on picture postcards. There are no soaring mountains, sandy beaches, or lush valleys. The marsh is a flat world that some consider dull and uninviting. I am glad most people do not respond to the marsh's subtle beauty because that means I can be alone there. Just as the rising tide sweeps over the marsh, floating debris out to the ocean, the marsh washes away my concerns and restores me to my senses. 7

Echo of idea in introduction

COMMENTARY

The dominant impression. Marie responded to the assignment by writing a moving tribute to a place having special meaning for her—the salt marsh near her grandparents' home. Like most descriptive pieces, Marie's essay is organized around a *dominant impression:* the marsh's peaceful solitude and gentle, natural beauty. The essay's introduction provides a context for the dominant impression by comparing the pleasure Marie experiences in the marsh to the happiness Thoreau felt in his walks around Walden Pond.

Combining patterns of development. Before developing the essay's dominant impression, Marie uses the second paragraph to *define* a salt marsh. An *objective description,* the definition clarifies that a salt marsh—with its spongy soil, haylike grass, and ebbing tides—is not to be confused with a swamp. Because Marie offers such a factual definition, readers have the background needed to enjoy the personalized view that follows.

Besides the definition paragraph and the comparison in the opening paragraph, the essay contains a strong element of *causal analysis:* Throughout, Marie describes the marsh's effect on her.

Sensory language. At times, Marie develops the essay's dominant impression explicitly, as when she writes "No people come here" (paragraph 3) and "I am at peace" (6). But Marie generally uses the more subtle techniques characteristic of *subjective description* to convey the dominant impression. First of all, she fills the essay with strong *connotative language,* rich with *sensory images.* The third paragraph describes what she smells (the "sharp smell of salt mixed with the rich aroma of peaty soil") and what she sees ("brilliant green," "tawny gold," and "grayish tan"). In the fifth paragraph, she tells us that she hears the chirping sounds of small birds. And the sixth paragraph includes vigorous descriptions of how the marsh feels to Marie's touch. She splashes water on her face and neck; she digs her toes into the mud at the bottom of the creek; she delights in the delicate brushing of crabs against her legs.

Figurative language, vigorous verbs, and varied sentence structure. You might also have noted that *figurative language, energetic verbs,* and *varied sentence patterns* contribute to the essay's descriptive power. Marie develops a *simile* in the third paragraph when she compares the flattened swirls of swamp grass to the brush strokes in a painting by Van Gogh. Later she uses another simile when she writes that the creek's thick mud feels "like mashed potatoes mixed with motor oil." Moreover, throughout the essay, she uses lively verbs ("shimmer," "flash") to capture the marsh's magical quality. Similarly, Marie enhances descriptive passages by varying the length of her sentences. Long, fairly elaborate sentences are interspersed with short, dramatic statements. In the third paragraph, for example, the long sentence describing the circular swirls of swamp grass is followed by the brief statement "No people come here." And the sixth paragraph uses two short sentences ("Otherwise, it is silent" and "I am at peace") to punctuate the paragraph's longer sentences.

Organization. We can follow Marie's journey through the marsh because she uses an easy-to-follow combination of *spatial, chronological,* and *emphatic* patterns to sequence her experience. The essay relies primarily on a spatial arrangement since the four body paragraphs focus on the different spots that Marie reaches: first, the path behind her grandparents' house (paragraph 3); then the area bordering the creek (4); next, her view of the creek (5); last, the creek itself (6). Each stage of her walk is signaled by an *informal topic sentence* near the start of each paragraph. Furthermore, *signal devices* (marked by italics here) indicate not only her location but also the chronological passage of time: "*As* I walk along, a sharp smell . . . fills my nostrils" (3); "*After* a few minutes, the trail suddenly opens up . . ." (4); "*Below* me, green grasses wave . . ." (5). And to call attention to the creek's serene beauty, Marie saves for last the description of the peace she feels while floating in the creek.

An inappropriate figure of speech. Although the four body paragraphs focus on the distinctive qualities of each location, Marie runs into a minor problem in the third paragraph. Take a moment to reread that paragraph's last sentence. Comparing the peace of the marsh to the effect of a "soothing drug" is jarring. The effectiveness of Marie's essay hinges on her ability to create a picture of a pure, natural world. A reference to drugs is inappropriate. Now, reread the paragraph aloud, stopping after "No people come here." Note how much more in keeping with the essay's dominant impression the paragraph is when the reference to drugs is omitted.

Conclusion. The concluding paragraph brings the essay to a graceful close. The powerful *simile* found in the last sentence contains an implied reference to Thoreau and to Marie's earlier statement about the joy to be found in special places having restorative powers. Such an allusion echoes, with good effect, the paper's opening comments.

Revising the first draft. When Marie met with some classmates during a peer review session, the students agreed that Marie's first draft was strong and moving. But they also said that they had difficulty following her route through the marsh; they found her third paragraph especially confusing. Marie kept track of her classmates' comments on a separate piece of paper and then entered them, numbered in order of importance, in the margin of her first draft. Following is the first-draft version of Marie's third paragraph.

Original Version of the Third Paragraph

As I head out to the marsh from the house, I follow a short trail through the woods. A smell of salt mixed with the aroma of soil fills my nostrils. The end of the trail suddenly opens up to a view that calms me no matter how upset or discouraged I might be: a line of tall waving reeds bordering the salt marsh creek. Civilization seems far away as I walk the path of flattened grass and finally reach my goal, the salt marsh creek hidden behind the tall waving reeds. The path changes with the seasons; sometimes I walk in the brilliant green of spring, sometimes in the tawny gold of autumn, sometimes in the quiet grayish tan of winter. In some areas, the grass is flattened into swirls that make the marsh resemble one of those paintings by Van Gogh. No people come here. The peacefulness heals me like a soothing drug. The path stops at the line of tall waving reeds, standing upright at the border of the creek. I part the reeds to get to the creek.

When Marie looked more carefully at the paragraph, she agreed it was confusing. For one thing, the paragraph's third and fourth sentences indicated that she had come to the path's end and had reached the reeds bordering the creek. In the following sentences, however, she was on the path again. Then, at the end, she was back at the creek, as if she had just arrived there. Marie resolved this confusion by breaking the single paragraph into two separate ones—the first describing the walk along the path, the second describing her arrival at the creek. This restructuring, especially when combined with clearer transitions, eliminated the confusion.

While revising her essay, Marie also intensified the sensory images in her original paragraph. She changed the "smell of salt and soil" to the "sharp smell of salt mixed with the rich aroma of peaty soil." And when she added the phrase "thick Van Gogh brush strokes that curve and recurve in circular patterns," she made the comparison between the marsh grass and a Van Gogh painting more vivid.

These are just some of the changes Marie made while rewriting her paper. Her skillful revisions provided the polish needed to make an already strong essay even more evocative.

Activities: Description

Prewriting Activities

1. Imagine you're writing two essays: One explains the *process* by which students get "burned out"; the other *argues* that being a spendthrift is better (or worse) than being frugal. Jot down ways you might use description in each essay.

2. Go to a place on campus where students congregate. In preparation for an *objective* description of this place, make notes of various sights, sounds, smells, and textures, as well as the overall "feel" of the place. Then, in preparation for a *subjective* description, observe and take notes on another sheet of paper. Compare the two sets of material. What differences do you see in word choice and selection of details?

Revising Activities

3. Revise each of the following sentence sets twice. The first time, create an unmistakable mood; the second time, create a sharply contrasting mood. To convey atmosphere, vary sentence structure, use vigorous verbs, provide rich sensory details, and pay special attention to words' connotations.

   a. The card players sat around the table. The table was old. The players were, too.
   b. A long line formed outside the movie theater. People didn't want to miss the show. The movie had received a lot of attention recently.
   c. A girl walked down the street in her first pair of high heels. This was a new experience for her.

4. The following descriptive paragraph is from the first draft of an essay showing that personal growth may result when romanticized notions and reality collide. How effective is the paragraph in illustrating the essay's thesis? Which details are powerful? Which could be more concrete? Which should be deleted? Where should sentence structure be more varied? How could the description be made more coherent? Revise the paragraph, correcting any problems you discover and adding whatever sensory details are needed to enliven the description. Feel free to break the paragraph into two or more separate ones.

As a child, I was intrigued by stories about the farm in Harrison County, Maine, where my father spent his teens. Being raised on a farm seemed more interesting than growing up in the suburbs. So about a year ago, I decided to see for myself what the farm was like. I got there by driving on Route 334, a surprisingly easy-to-drive, four-lane highway that had recently been built with matching state and federal funds. I turned into the dirt road leading to the farm and got out of my car. It had been washed and waxed for the occasion. Then I headed for a dirt-colored barn. Its roof was full of huge, rotted holes. As I rounded the bushes, I saw the house. It too was dirt-colored. Its paint must have worn off decades ago. A couple of dead-looking old cars were sprawled in front of the barn. They were dented and windowless. Also by the barn was an ancient refrigerator, crushed like a discarded accordion. The porch steps to the house were slanted and wobbly. Through the open windows came a stale smell and the sound of television. Looking in the front door screen, I could see two chickens jumping around inside. Everything looked dirty both inside and out. Secretly grateful that no one answered my knock, I bolted down the stairs, got into my clean, shiny car, and drove away.

Maya Angelou

Born Marguerite Johnson in 1928, Maya Angelou spent her childhood in Stamps, Arkansas, with her brother, Bailey, and her grandmother, "Momma." Although her youth was difficult—she was raped at age eight and became a mother at sixteen—Angelou somehow managed to thrive. Multi-talented, she later worked as a professional dancer, starred in an off-Broadway play, appeared in the television miniseries *Roots,* served as a coordinator for the Southern Christian Leadership Conference, and wrote several well-received volumes of poetry—among them *Oh Pray My Wings Are Gonna Fit Me Well* (1975) and *Still I Rise* (1996). She has also written essay collections, such as *Even the Stars Look Lonesome* (1997), and children's books, including *My Painted House, My Friendly Chicken, and Me* (1994), and *Kofi and His Magic* (1996). A professor at Wake Forest University since 1981, Angelou delivered at the 1993 presidential inauguration a stirring poem written for the occasion. The recipient of numerous honorary doctorates, Angelou is best known for her series of six autobiographical books, starting with *I Know Why the Caged Bird Sings* (1970) and concluding with *A Song Flung Up to Heaven* (2002). The following essay is taken from *I Know Why the Caged Bird Sings.*

For ideas about how this description essay is organized, see Figure 3.2 on page 92.

Pre-Reading Journal Entry

Growing up isn't easy. In your journal, list several challenges you've had to face in your life. In each case, was there someone who served as a "lifeline," providing you with crucial guidance and support? Who was that individual? How did this person steer you through the difficulty?

Sister Flowers

1 For nearly a year [after I was raped], I sopped around the house, the Store, the school and the church, like an old biscuit, dirty and inedible. Then I met, or rather got to know, the lady who threw me my first life line.

2 Mrs. Bertha Flowers was the aristocrat of Black Stamps. She had the grace of control to appear warm in the coldest weather, and on the Arkansas summer days it seemed she had a private breeze which swirled around, cooling her. She was thin without the taut look of wiry people, and her printed voile dresses and flowered hats were as right for her as denim overalls for a farmer. She was our side's answer to the richest white woman in town.

3 Her skin was a rich black that would have peeled like a plum if snagged, but then no one would have thought of getting close enough to Mrs. Flowers to ruffle her dress, let alone snag her skin. She didn't encourage familiarity. She wore gloves too.

I don't think I ever saw Mrs. Flowers laugh, but she smiled often. A slow 4
widening of her thin black lips to show even, small white teeth, then the slow effortless closing. When she chose to smile on me, I always wanted to thank her. The action was so graceful and inclusively benign.

She was one of the few gentlewomen I have ever known, and has remained 5
throughout my life the measure of what a human being can be.

Momma had a strange relationship with her. Most often when she passed 6
on the road in front of the Store, she spoke to Momma in that soft yet carrying voice, "Good day, Mrs. Henderson." Momma responded with "How you, Sister Flowers?"

Mrs. Flowers didn't belong to our church, nor was she Momma's familiar. 7
Why on earth did she insist on calling her Sister Flowers? Shame made me want to hide my face. Mrs. Flowers deserved better than to be called Sister. Then, Momma left out the verb. Why not ask, "How *are* you, *Mrs.* Flowers?" With the unbalanced passion of the young, I hated her for showing her ignorance to Mrs. Flowers. It didn't occur to me for many years that they were as alike as sisters, separated only by formal education.

Although I was upset, neither of the women was in the least shaken by 8
what I thought an unceremonious greeting. Mrs. Flowers would continue her easy gait up the hill to her little bungalow, and Momma kept on shelling peas or doing whatever had brought her to the front porch.

Occasionally, though, Mrs. Flowers would drift off the road and down 9
to the Store and Momma would say to me, "Sister, you go on and play." As she left I would hear the beginning of an intimate conversation. Momma persistently using the wrong verb, or none at all.

"Brother and Sister Wilcox is sho'ly the meanest—" "Is," Momma? 10
"Is"? Oh, please, not "is," Momma, for two or more. But they talked, and from the side of the building where I waited for the ground to open up and swallow me, I heard the soft-voiced Mrs. Flowers and the textured voice of my grandmother merging and melting. They were interrupted from time to time by giggles that must have come from Mrs. Flowers (Momma never giggled in her life). Then she was gone.

She appealed to me because she was like people I had never met per- 11
sonally. Like women in English novels who walked the moors (whatever they were) with their loyal dogs racing at a respectful distance. Like the women who sat in front of roaring fireplaces, drinking tea incessantly from silver trays full of scones and crumpets. Women who walked over the "heath" and read morocco-bound books and had two last names divided by a hyphen. It would be safe to say that she made me proud to be Negro, just by being herself.

She acted just as refined as whitefolks in the movies and books and she 12
was more beautiful, for none of them could have come near that warm color without looking gray by comparison.

It was fortunate that I never saw her in the company of powhitefolks. 13
For since they tend to think of their whiteness as an evenizer, I'm certain that I would have had to hear her spoken to commonly as Bertha, and my image of her would have been shattered like the unmendable Humpty-Dumpty.

One summer afternoon, sweet-milk fresh in my memory, she stopped 14
at the Store to buy provisions. Another Negro woman of her health and age would have been expected to carry the paper sacks home in one hand, but Momma said, "Sister Flowers, I'll send Bailey up to your house with these things."

She smiled that slow dragging smile, "Thank you, Mrs. Henderson. I'd 15
prefer Marguerite, though." My name was beautiful when she said it. "I've been meaning to talk to her, anyway." They gave each other age-group looks.

Momma said, "Well, that's all right then. Sister, go and change your 16
dress. You going to Sister Flowers's."

The chifforobe was a maze. What on earth did one put on to go to 17
Mrs. Flowers's house? I knew I shouldn't put on a Sunday dress. It might be sacrilegious. Certainly not a house dress, since I was already wearing a fresh one. I chose a school dress, naturally. It was formal without suggesting that going to Mrs. Flowers's house was equivalent to attending church.

I trusted myself back into the Store. 18

"Now, don't you look nice." I had chosen the right thing, for once.... 19

There was a little path beside the rocky road, and Mrs. Flowers walked 20
in front swinging her arms and picking her way over the stones.

She said, without turning her head, to me, "I hear you're doing very 21
good school work, Marguerite, but that it's all written. The teachers report that they have trouble getting you to talk in class." We passed the triangular farm on our left and the path widened to allow us to walk together. I hung back in the separate unasked and unanswerable questions.

"Come and walk along with me, Marguerite." I couldn't have refused 22
even if I wanted to. She pronounced my name so nicely. Or more correctly, she spoke each word with such clarity that I was certain a foreigner who didn't understand English could have understood her.

"Now no one is going to make you talk—possibly no one can. But bear 23
in mind, language is man's way of communicating with his fellow man and it is language alone which separates him from the lower animals." That was a totally new idea to me, and I would need time to think about it.

"Your grandmother says you read a lot. Every chance you get. That's good, 24
but not good enough. Words mean more than what is set down on paper. It takes the human voice to infuse them with the shades of deeper meaning."

I memorized the part about the human voice infusing words. It seemed 25
so valid and poetic.

She said she was going to give me some books and that I not only 26
must read them, I must read them aloud. She suggested that I try to make a sentence sound in as many different ways as possible.

"I'll accept no excuse if you return a book to me that has been badly 27
handled." My imagination boggled at the punishment I would deserve if in fact I did abuse a book of Mrs. Flowers's. Death would be too kind and brief.

The odors in the house surprised me. Somehow I had never connected 28
Mrs. Flowers with food or eating or any other common experience of common people. There must have been an outhouse, too, but my mind never recorded it.

The sweet scent of vanilla had met us as she opened the door. 29

"I made tea cookies this morning. You see, I had planned to invite you 30
for cookies and lemonade so we could have this little chat. The lemonade is in the icebox."

It followed that Mrs. Flowers would have ice on an ordinary day, when 31
most families in our town bought ice late on Saturdays only a few times during the summer to be used in the wooden ice-cream freezers.

She took the bags from me and disappeared through the kitchen door. 32
I looked around the room that I had never in my wildest fantasies imagined I would see. Browned photographs leered or threatened from the walls and the white, freshly done curtains pushed against themselves and against the wind. I wanted to gobble up the room entire and take it to Bailey, who would help me analyze and enjoy it.

"Have a seat, Marguerite. Over there by the table." She carried a platter 33
covered with a tea towel. Although she warned that she hadn't tried her hand at baking sweets for some time, I was certain that like everything else about her the cookies would be perfect.

They were flat round wafers, slightly browned on the edges and butter- 34
yellow in the center. With the cold lemonade they were sufficient for childhood's lifelong diet. Remembering my manners, I took nice little lady-like bites off the edges. She said she had made them expressly for me and that she had a few in the kitchen that I could take home to my brother. So I jammed one whole cake in my mouth and the rough crumbs scratched the insides of my jaws, and if I hadn't had to swallow, it would have been a dream come true.

As I ate she began the first of what we later called "my lessons in liv- 35
ing." She said that I must always be intolerant of ignorance but understanding of illiteracy. That some people, unable to go to school, were more educated and even more intelligent than college professors. She encouraged me to listen carefully to what country people called mother wit. That in those homely sayings was couched the collective wisdom of generations.

36 When I finished the cookies she brushed off the table and brought a thick, small book from the bookcase. I had read *A Tale of Two Cities* and found it up to my standards as a romantic novel. She opened the first page and I heard poetry for the first time in my life.

37 "It was the best of times and the worst of times..." Her voice slid in and curved down through and over the words. She was nearly singing. I wanted to look at the pages. Were they the same that I had read? Or were there notes, music, lined on the pages, as in a hymn book? Her sounds began cascading gently. I knew from listening to a thousand preachers that she was nearing the end of her reading, and I hadn't really heard, heard to understand, a single word.

38 "How do you like that?"

39 It occurred to me that she expected a response. The sweet vanilla flavor was still on my tongue and her reading was a wonder in my ears. I had to speak.

40 I said, "Yes, ma'am." It was the least I could do, but it was the most also.

41 "There's one more thing. Take this book of poems and memorize one for me. Next time you pay me a visit, I want you to recite."

42 I have tried often to search behind the sophistication of years for the enchantment I so easily found in those gifts. The essence escapes but its aura remains. To be allowed, no, invited, into the private lives of strangers, and to share their joys and fears, was a chance to exchange the Southern bitter wormwood for a cup of mead with Beowulf[1] or a hot cup of tea and milk with Oliver Twist.[2] When I said aloud, "It is a far, far better thing that I do, than I have ever done..."[3] tears of love filled my eyes at my selflessness.

43 On that first day, I ran down the hill and into the road (few cars ever came along it) and had the good sense to stop running before I reached the Store.

44 I was liked, and what a difference it made. I was respected not as Mrs. Henderson's grandchild or Bailey's sister but for just being Marguerite Johnson.

45 Childhood's logic never asks to be proved (all conclusions are absolute). I didn't question why Mrs. Flowers had singled me out for attention, nor did it occur to me that Momma might have asked her to give me a little talking to. All I cared about was that she had made tea cookies for *me* and read to *me* from her favorite book. It was enough to prove that she liked me.

---

[1] The hero of an Old English epic poem dating from the eighth century (editors' note).
[2] The main character in Charles Dickens's novel *Oliver Twist* (1837) (editors' note).
[3] The last words of Sydney Carton, the selfless hero of Charles Dickens's novel *A Tale of Two Cities* (1859) (editors' note).

FIGURE 3.2
Essay Structure Diagram: "Sister Flowers" by Maya Angelou

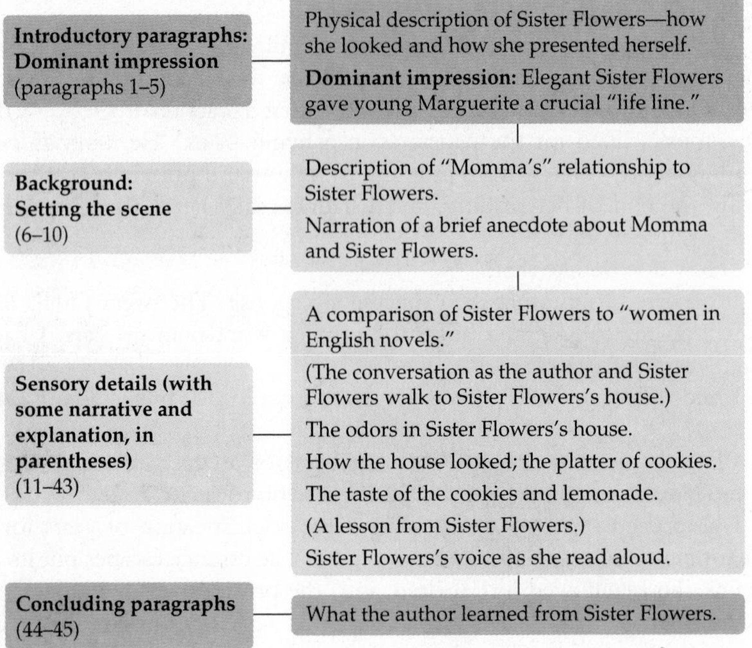

Introductory paragraphs: Dominant impression (paragraphs 1–5)
Physical description of Sister Flowers—how she looked and how she presented herself.
Dominant impression: Elegant Sister Flowers gave young Marguerite a crucial "life line."
Background: Setting the scene (6–10)
Description of "Momma's" relationship to Sister Flowers.
Narration of a brief anecdote about Momma and Sister Flowers.
Sensory details (with some narrative and explanation, in parentheses) (11–43)
A comparison of Sister Flowers to "women in English novels."
(The conversation as the author and Sister Flowers walk to Sister Flowers's house.)
The odors in Sister Flowers's house.
How the house looked; the platter of cookies.
The taste of the cookies and lemonade.
(A lesson from Sister Flowers.)
Sister Flowers's voice as she read aloud.
Concluding paragraphs (44–45)
What the author learned from Sister Flowers.

Questions for Close Reading

1. What is the selection's thesis (or dominant impression)? Locate the sentence(s) in which Angelou states her main idea. If she doesn't state the thesis explicitly, express it in your own words.
2. Angelou states that Mrs. Flowers "has remained throughout my life the measure of what a human being can be" (paragraph 5). What does Angelou admire about Mrs. Flowers?
3. Why is young Angelou so ashamed of Momma when Mrs. Flowers is around? How do Momma and Mrs. Flowers behave with each other?
4. What are the "lessons in living" that Angelou receives from Mrs. Flowers during their first visit? How do you think these lessons might have subsequently influenced Angelou?
5. Refer to your dictionary as needed to define the following words used in the selection: *taut* (paragraph 2), *voile* (2), *benign* (4), *unceremonious* (8), *gait* (8), *moors* (11), *incessantly* (11), *scones* (11), *crumpets* (11), *heath* (11), *chifforobe* (17), *sacrilegious* (17), *infuse* (24), *couched* (35), and *aura* (42).

Questions About the Writer's Craft

1. **The pattern.** Reread the essay, focusing on the descriptive passages first of Mrs. Flowers and then of Angelou's visit to Mrs. Flowers's house. To what senses does Angelou appeal in these passages? What method of organization (see pages 41–42) does she use to order these sensory details?
2. To enrich the description of her eventful encounter with Mrs. Flowers, Angelou draws upon figures of speech (see pages 78–79). Consider, for example, the similes in paragraphs 1 and 11. How do these figures of speech contribute to the essay's dominant impression?
3. **Other patterns.** Because Angelou's description has a strong *narrative* component, it isn't surprising that there's a considerable amount of dialogue in the selection. For example, in paragraphs 7 and 10, Angelou quotes Momma's incorrect grammar. She then provides an imagined conversation in which the young Angelou scolds Momma and corrects her speech. What do these imagined scoldings of Momma reveal about young Angelou? How do they relate to Mrs. Flowers's subsequent "lessons in life"?
4. Although it's not the focus of this selection, the issue of race remains in the background of Angelou's portrait of Mrs. Flowers. Where in the selection does Angelou imply that race was a fact of life in her town? How does this specter of racism help Angelou underscore the significance of her encounter with Mrs. Flowers?

Writing Assignments Using Description as a Pattern of Development

1. At one time or another, just about all of us have met someone who taught us to see ourselves more clearly and helped us understand what we wanted from life. Write an essay describing such a person. Focus on the individual's personal qualities, as a way of depicting the role he or she played in your life. Be sure not to limit yourself to an objective description. Subjective description, filled with lively language and figures of speech, will serve you well as you provide a portrait of this special person. Read Amy Tan's "Mother Tongue" (page 270) to see how another author writes about a person who influenced her.
2. Thrilled by the spectacle of Mrs. Flowers's interesting home, Angelou says she wanted to "gobble up the room entire" and share it with her brother. Write an essay describing in detail a place that vividly survives in your memory. You may describe a setting that you visited only once or a familiar setting that holds a special place in your heart. Before you write, list the qualities and sensory impressions you associate with this special place; then refine the list so that all details support your dominant impression.

Writing Assignments Combining Patterns of Development

3. When the young Angelou discovers, thanks to Mrs. Flowers, the thrill of acceptance, she experiences a kind of *epiphany*—a moment of enlightenment. Write an essay about an event in your life that represented a kind of epiphany. You might

write about a positive discovery, such as when you realized you had a special talent for something, or about a negative discovery, such as when you realized that a beloved family member had a serious flaw. To make the point that the moment was a turning point in your life, start by *describing* what kind of person you were before the discovery. Then *narrate* the actual incident, using vivid details and dialogue to make the event come alive. End by discussing the importance of this epiphany in your life. For additional accounts of personal epiphanies, you might read Audre Lorde's "The Fourth of July" (page 140), Langston Hughes's "Salvation" (page 158), and Beth Johnson's "Bombs Bursting in Air" (page 211).

4. Think of an activity that engages you completely, one that provides—as reading does for Angelou—an opportunity for growth and expansion. Possibilities include reading, writing, playing an instrument, doing crafts, dancing, hiking, playing a sport, cooking, or traveling. Write an essay in which you *argue* the merits of your chosen pastime. Assume that some of your readers are highly skeptical. To win them over, you'll need to provide convincing *examples* that demonstrate the pleasure and benefits you have discovered in the activity.

Writing Assignment Using a Journal Entry as a Starting Point

5. Write an essay about a time when someone threw you a much-needed "lifeline" at a challenging time. Review your pre-reading journal entry, selecting *one* time when a person's encouragement and support made a great difference in your life. Be sure to describe the challenge you faced before recounting the specific details of the person's help. Dialogue and descriptive details will help you recreate the power of the experience. You should consider reading "Showing What Is Possible" (page 402), in which Jacques D'Amboise shows how a "wise" teacher made a world of difference in his life.

Gordon Parks

The son of deeply religious tenant farmers, Gordon Parks (1912–2006) grew up in Kansas knowing both the comforts of familial love and the torments of poverty and racism. Sent as a teenager to live with his sister in Minnesota after his mother's death, Parks was thrown out on his own in a frigid winter by his brother-in-law. To support himself, Parks worked as a janitor in a flophouse and as a piano player in a bordello. These and other odd jobs gave Parks the means to buy his first camera. Fascinated by photographic images, Parks studied the masters and eventually developed his own powers as a photographer. So evocative were his photographic studies that both *Life* and *Vogue* brought him on staff, the first black photographer to be hired by the two magazines. Parks's prodigious creativity has found expression in filmmaking (*Shaft* in 1971), musical composition (both classical and jazz), fiction, nonfiction, and poetry. Titles include *The Learning Tree, A Choice of Weapons, To Smile in Autumn, Arias in Silence, Glimpses Toward Infinity, A Star for Noon,* and *The Sun Stalker,* published, respectively, in 1986, 1987, 1988, 1994, 1996, 2000, and 2003. But it is Parks's photographic essays, covering five decades of American life, that brought him the most acclaim. In the following essay, taken from his 1990 autobiography, *Voices in the Mirror,* Parks tells the story behind one of his most memorable photographic works—that of a twelve-year-old boy and his family, living in the slums of Rio de Janeiro.

Pre-Reading Journal Entry

The problem of poverty has provoked a wide array of proposed solutions. One controversial proposal argues that the government should pay poor women financial incentives to use birth control. What do you think of this proposal? Why is such a policy controversial? Use your journal to explore your thinking on this issue.

Flavio's Home

I've never lost my fierce grudge against poverty. It is the most savage of all human afflictions, claiming victims who can't mobilize their efforts against it, who often lack strength to digest what little food they scrounge up to survive. It keeps growing, multiplying, spreading like a cancer. In my wanderings I attack it wherever I can—in barrios, slums and favelas. 1

Catacumba was the name of the favela[1] where I found Flavio da Silva. 2
It was wickedly hot. The noon sun baked the mud-rot of the wet mountainside. Garbage and human excrement clogged the open sewers snaking down the slopes. José Gallo, a *Life* reporter, and I rested in the shade of a jacaranda tree halfway up Rio de Janeiro's most infamous deathtrap. Below and above

[1]Slums on the outskirts of Rio de Janeiro, Brazil, inhabited by seven hundred thousand people (editors' note).

us were a maze of shacks, but in the distance alongside the beach stood the gleaming white homes of the rich.

Breathing hard, balancing a tin of water on his head, a small boy climbed 3
toward us. He was miserably thin, naked but for filthy denim shorts. His legs resembled sticks covered with skin and screwed into his feet. Death was all over him, in his sunken eyes, cheeks and jaundiced coloring. He stopped for breath, coughing, his chest heaving as water slopped over his bony shoulders. Then jerking sideways like a mechanical toy, he smiled a smile I will never forget. Turning, he went on up the mountainside.

The detailed *Life* assignment in my back pocket was to find an impov- 4
erished father with a family, to examine his earnings, political leanings, religion, friends, dreams and frustrations. I had been sent to do an essay on poverty. This frail boy bent under his load said more to me about poverty than a dozen poor fathers. I touched Gallo, and we got up and followed the boy to where he entered a shack near the top of the mountainside. It was a leaning crumpled place of old plankings with a rusted tin roof. From inside we heard the babblings of several children. José knocked. The door opened and the boy stood smiling with a bawling naked baby in his arms.

Still smiling, he whacked the baby's rump, invited us in and offered us a 5
box to sit on. The only other recognizable furniture was a sagging bed and a broken baby's crib. Flavio was twelve, and with Gallo acting as interpreter, he introduced his younger brothers and sisters: "Mario, the bad one; Baptista, the good one; Albia, Isabel and the baby Zacarias." Two other girls burst into the shack, screaming and pounding on one another. Flavio jumped in and parted them. "Shut up, you two." He pointed at the older girl. "That's Maria, the nasty one." She spit in his face. He smacked her and pointed to the smaller sister. "That's Luzia. She thinks she's pretty."

Having finished the introductions, he went to build a fire under the 6
stove—a rusted, bent top of an old gas range resting on several bricks. Beneath it was a piece of tin that caught the hot coals. The shack was about six by ten feet. Its grimy walls were a patchwork of misshapen boards with large gaps between them, revealing other shacks below stilted against the slopes. The floor, rotting under layers of grease and dirt, caught shafts of light slanting down through spaces in the roof. A large hole in the far corner served as a toilet. Beneath that hole was the sloping mountainside. Pockets of poverty in New York's Harlem, on Chicago's south side, in Puerto Rico's infamous El Fungito seemed pale by comparison. None of them had prepared me for this one in the favela of Catacumba.

Flavio washed rice in a large dishpan, then washed Zacarias's feet in the 7
same water. But even that dirty water wasn't to be wasted. He tossed in a chunk of lye soap and ordered each child to wash up. When they were finished he splashed the water over the dirty floor, and, dropping to his knees,

he scrubbed the planks until the black suds sank in. Just before sundown he put beans on the stove to warm, then left, saying he would be back shortly. "Don't let them burn," he cautioned Maria. "If they do and Poppa beats me, you'll get it later." Maria, happy to get at the licking spoon, switched over and began to stir the beans. Then slyly she dipped out a spoonful and swallowed them. Luzia eyed her. "I see you. I'm going to tell on you for stealing our supper."

Maria's eyes flashed anger. "You do and I'll beat you, you little bitch." 8
Luzia threw a stick at Maria and fled out the door. Zacarias dropped off to sleep. Mario, the bad one, slouched in a corner and sucked his thumb. Isabel and Albia sat on the floor clinging to each other with a strange tenderness. Isabel held onto Albia's hair and Albia clutched at Isabel's neck. They appeared frozen in an act of quiet violence.

Flavio returned with wood, dumped it beside the stove and sat down 9
to rest for a few minutes, then went down the mountain for more water. It was dark when he finally came back, his body sagging from exhaustion. No longer smiling, he suddenly had the look of an old man and by now we could see that he kept the family going. In the closed torment of that pitiful shack, he was waging a hopeless battle against starvation. The da Silva children were living in a coffin.

When at last the parents came in, Gallo and I seemed to be part of the 10
family. Flavio had already told them we were there. "Gordunn Americano!" Luzia said, pointing at me. José, the father, viewed us with skepticism. Nair, his pregnant wife, seemed tired beyond speaking. Hardly acknowledging our presence, she picked up Zacarias, placed him on her shoulder and gently patted his behind. Flavio scurried about like a frightened rat, his silence plainly expressing the fear he held of his father. Impatiently, José da Silva waited for Flavio to serve dinner. He sat in the center of the bed with his legs crossed beneath him, frowning, waiting. There were only three tin plates. Flavio filled them with black beans and rice, then placed them before his father. José da Silva tasted them, chewed for several moments, then nodded his approval for the others to start. Only he and Nair had spoons; the children ate with their fingers. Flavio ate off the top of a coffee can. Afraid to offer us food, he edged his rice and beans toward us, gesturing for us to take some. We refused. He smiled, knowing we understood.

Later, when we got down to the difficult business of obtaining permis- 11
sion from José da Silva to photograph his family, he hemmed and hawed, wallowing in the pleasant authority of the decision maker. He finally gave in, but his manner told us that he expected something in return. As we were saying good night Flavio began to cough violently. For a few moments his lungs seemed to be tearing apart. I wanted to get away as quickly as possible. It was cowardly of me, but the bluish cast of his skin beneath the sweat, the choking and spitting were suddenly unbearable.

Gallo and I moved cautiously down through the darkness trying not to 12
appear as strangers. The Catacumba was no place for strangers after sundown. Desperate criminals hid out there. To hunt them out, the police came in packs, but only in daylight. Gallo cautioned me. "If you get caught up here after dark it's best to stay at the da Silvas' until morning." As we drove toward the city the large white buildings of the rich loomed up. The world behind us seemed like a bad dream. I had already decided to get the boy Flavio to a doctor, and as quickly as possible.

The plush lobby of my hotel on the Copacabana waterfront was crammed 13
with people in formal attire. With the stink of the favela in my clothes, I hurried to the elevator hoping no passengers would be aboard. But as the door was closing a beautiful girl in a white lace gown stepped in. I moved as far away as possible. Her escort entered behind her, swept her into his arms and they indulged in a kiss that lasted until they exited on the next floor. Neither of them seemed to realize that I was there. The room I returned to seemed to be oversized; the da Silva shack would have fit into one corner of it. The steak dinner I had would have fed the da Silvas for three days.

Billowing clouds blanketed Mount Corcovado as we approached the 14
favela the following morning. Suddenly the sun burst through, silhouetting Cristo Redentor, the towering sculpture of Christ with arms extended, its back turned against the slopes of Catacumba. The square at the entrance to the favela bustled with hundreds of favelados. Long lines waited at the sole water spigot. Others waited at the only toilet on the entire mountainside. Women, unable to pay for soap, beat dirt from their wash at laundry tubs. Men, burdened with lumber, picks and shovels and tools important to their existence threaded their way through the noisy throngs. Dogs snarled, barked and fought. Woodsmoke mixed with the stench of rotting things. In the mist curling over the higher paths, columns of favelados climbed like ants with wood and water cans on their heads.

We came upon Nair bent over her tub of wash. She wiped away sweat 15
with her apron and managed a smile. We asked for her husband and she pointed to a tiny shack off to her right. This was José's store, where he sold kerosene and bleach. He was sitting on a box, dozing. Sensing our presence, he awoke and commenced complaining about his back. "It kills me. The doctors don't help because I have no money. Always talk and a little pink pill that does no good. Ah, what is to become of me?" A woman came to buy bleach. He filled her bottle. She dropped a few coins and as she walked away his eyes stayed on her backside until she was out of sight. Then he was complaining about his back again.

"How much do you earn a day?" Gallo asked. 16

"Seventy-five cents. On a good day maybe a dollar." 17

"Why aren't the kids in school?" 18

"I don't have money for the clothes they need to go to school." 19

"Has Flavio seen a doctor?" 20

He pointed to a one-story wooden building. "That's the clinic right there. They're mad because I built my store in front of their place. I won't tear it down so they won't help my kids. Talk, talk, talk and pink pills." We bid him good-bye and started climbing, following mud trails, jutting rock, slime-filled holes and shack after shack propped against the slopes on shaky pilings. We sidestepped a dead cat covered with maggots. I held my breath for an instant, only to inhale the stench of human excrement and garbage. Bare feet and legs with open sores climbed above us—evils of the terrible soil they trod every day, and there were seven hundred thousand or more afflicted people in favelas around Rio alone. Touching me, Gallo pointed to Flavio climbing ahead of us carrying firewood. He stopped to glance at a man descending with a small coffin on his shoulder. A woman and a small child followed him. When I lifted my camera, grumbling erupted from a group of men sharing beer beneath a tree. 21

"They're threatening," Gallo said. "Keep moving. They fear cameras. Think they're evil eyes bringing bad luck." Turning to watch the funeral procession, Flavio caught sight of us and waited. When we took the wood from him he protested, saying he was used to carrying it. He gave in when I hung my camera around his neck. Then, beaming, he climbed on ahead of us. 22

The fog had lifted and in the crisp morning light the shack looked more squalid. Inside the kids seemed even noisier. Flavio smiled and spoke above their racket. "Someday I want to live in a real house on a real street with good pots and pans and a bed with sheets." He lit the fire to warm leftovers from the night before. Stale rice and beans—for breakfast and supper. No lunch; midday eating was out of the question. Smoke rose and curled up through the ceiling's cracks. An air current forced it back, filling the place and Flavio's lungs with fumes. A coughing spasm doubled him up, turned his skin blue under viscous sweat. I handed him a cup of water, but he waved it away. His stomach tightened as he dropped to his knees. His veins throbbed as if they would burst. Frustrated, we could only watch; there was nothing we could do to help. Strangely, none of his brothers or sisters appeared to notice. None of them stopped doing whatever they were doing. Perhaps they had seen it too often. After five interminable minutes it was over, and he got to his feet, smiling as though it had all been a joke. "Maria, it's time for Zacarias to be washed!" 23

"But there's rice in the pan!" 24

"Dump it in another pan—and don't spill water!" 25

Maria picked up Zacarias, who screamed, not wanting to be washed. Irritated, Maria gave him a solid smack on his bare bottom. Flavio stepped over and gave her the same, then a free-for-all started with Flavio, Maria and 26

Mario slinging fists at one another. Mario got one in the eye and fled the shack calling Flavio a dirty son-of-a-bitch. Zacarias wound up on the floor sucking his thumb and escaping his washing. The black bean and rice breakfast helped to get things back to normal. Now it was time to get Flavio to the doctor.

The clinic was crowded with patients—mothers and children covered with open sores, a paralytic teenager, a man with an ear in a state of decay, an aged blind couple holding hands in doubled darkness. Throughout the place came wailings of hunger and hurt. Flavio sat nervously between Gallo and me. "What will the doctor do to me?" he kept asking. 27

"We'll see. We'll wait and see." 28

In all, there were over fifty people. Finally, after two hours, it was Flavio's turn and he broke out in a sweat, though he smiled at the nurse as he passed through the door to the doctor's office. The nurse ignored it; in this place of misery, smiles were unexpected. 29

The doctor, a large, beady-eyed man with a crew cut, had an air of impatience. Hardly acknowledging our presence, he began to examine the frightened Flavio. "Open your mouth. Say 'Ah.' Jump up and down. Breathe out. Take off those pants. Bend over. Stand up. Cough. Cough louder. Louder." He did it all with such cold efficiency. Then he spoke to us in English so Flavio wouldn't understand. "This little chap has just about had it." My heart sank. Flavio was smiling, happy to be over with the examination. He was handed a bottle of cough medicine and a small box of pink pills, then asked to step outside and wait. 30

"This the da Silva kid?" 31

"Yes." 32

"What's your interest in him?" 33

"We want to help in some way." 34

"I'm afraid you're too late. He's wasted with bronchial asthma, malnutrition and, I suspect, tuberculosis. His heart, lungs and teeth are all bad." He paused and wearily rubbed his forehead. "All that at the ripe old age of twelve. And these hills are packed with other kids just as bad off. Last year ten thousand died from dysentery alone. But what can we do? You saw what's waiting outside. It's like this every day. There's hardly enough money to buy aspirin. A few wealthy people who care help keep us going." He was quiet for a moment. "Maybe the right climate, the right diet, and constant medical care might..." He stopped and shook his head. "Naw. That poor lad's finished. He might last another year—maybe not." We thanked him and left. 35

"What did he say?" Flavio asked as we scaled the hill. 36

"Everything's going to be all right, Flav. There's nothing to worry about." 37

It had clouded over again by the time we reached the top. The rain swept in, clearing the mountain of Corcovado. The huge Christ figure loomed up 38 again with clouds swirling around it. And to it I said a quick prayer for the boy walking beside us. He smiled as if he had read my thoughts. "Papa says 'El Cristo' has turned his back on the favela."

"You're going to be all right, Flavio." 39

"I'm not scared of death. It's my brothers and sisters I worry about. What would they do?" 40

"You'll be all right, Flavio."[2] 41

---

[2]Parks's photo-essay on Flavio generated an unprecedented response from *Life* readers. Indeed, they sent so much money to the da Silvas that the family was able to leave the *favela* for better living conditions. Parks brought Flavio to the United States for medical treatment, and the boy's health was restored. However, Flavio's story didn't have an unqualifiedly happy ending. Although he overcame his illness and later married and had a family, Flavio continuously fantasized about returning to the United States, convinced that only by returning to America could he improve his life. His obsession eventually eroded the promise of his life in Brazil (editors' note).

Questions for Close Reading

1. What is the selection's thesis (or dominant impression)? Locate the sentence(s) in which Parks states his main idea. If he doesn't state the thesis explicitly, express it in your own words.
2. What is Flavio's family like? Why does Flavio have so much responsibility in the household?
3. What are some of the distinctive characteristics of Flavio's neighborhood and home?
4. What seems to be the basis of Flavio's fear of giving food to Parks and Gallo? What did Parks and Gallo understand that led them to refuse?
5. Refer to your dictionary as needed to define the following words used in the selection: *barrios* (paragraph 1), *jacaranda* (2), *jaundiced* (3), and *spigot* (14).

Questions About the Writer's Craft

1. **The pattern.** Without stating it explicitly, Parks conveys a dominant impression about Flavio. What is that impression? What details create it?
2. **Other patterns.** When relating how Flavio performs numerous household tasks, Parks describes several *processes*. How do these step-by-step explanations reinforce Parks's dominant impression of Flavio?
3. Parks provides numerous sensory specifics to depict Flavio's home. Look closely, for example, at the description in paragraph 6. Which words and phrases convey strong sensory images? How does Parks use transitions to help the reader move from one sensory image to another?
4. Paragraph 13 includes a scene that occurs in Parks's hotel. What's the effect of this scene? What does it contribute to the essay that the most detailed description of the *favela* could not?

Writing Assignments Using Description as a Pattern of Development

1. Parks paints a wrenching portrait of a person who remains vibrant and hopeful even though he is suffering greatly—from physical illness, poverty, overwork, and worry. Write a description about someone you know who has shown courage or other positive qualities during a time of personal trouble. Include, as Parks does, plentiful details about the person's appearance and behavior so that you don't have to state directly what you admire about the person. Maya Angelou's "Sister Flowers" (page 87) shows how one writer conveys the special quality of an admirable individual.
2. Parks presents an unforgettable description of the *favela* and the living conditions there. Write an essay about a region, city, neighborhood, or building that also projects an overwhelming negative feeling. Include only those details that convey your dominant impression, and provide—as Parks does—vivid sensory language to convey your attitude toward your subject.

Writing Assignments Combining Patterns of Development

3. The doctor reports that a few wealthy people contribute to the clinic, but the reader can tell from the scene in Parks's hotel that most people are insensitive to those less fortunate. Write an essay *describing* a specific situation that you feel reflects people's tendency to ignore the difficulties of others. Analyze why people distance themselves from the problem; then present specific *steps* that could be taken to sensitize them to the situation. John M. Darley and Bibb Latané's "When Will People Help in a Crisis?" (page 415), and Mark Twain's "The Damned Human Race" (page 525) will provide some perspective on the way people harden themselves to the pain of others.
4. Although Parks celebrates Flavio's generosity of spirit, the writer also *illustrates* the brutalizing effect of an impoverished environment. Prepare an essay in which you also show that setting, architecture, even furnishings can influence mood and behavior. You may, as Parks does, focus on the corrosive effect of a negative environment, or you may write about the nurturing effect of a positive environment. Either way, provide vivid *descriptive* details of the environment you're considering. Possible subjects include a park in the middle of a city, a bus terminal, and a college library.

Writing Assignment Using a Journal Entry as a Starting Point

5. Write an essay explaining why you think impoverished women should—or should not—be paid financial incentives to practice birth control. To help define your position, review your pre-reading journal entry, and interview classmates, friends, and family members to get their opinions. Consider supplementing this informal research with material gathered in the library and/or on the Internet. Weigh all the evidence carefully before formulating your position.

David Helvarg

David Helvarg is a journalist and environmental activist. Born in 1951, he started his career as a freelance journalist and then became a war correspondent. Today he writes primarily about politics, AIDS, and marine life. Helvarg is also the founder and president of Blue Frontier Campaign, a marine conservation lobbying group that was inspired by his book about the world's oceans, *Blue Frontier*. Helvarg's lobbying on environmental issues grows out of his experiences covering war, political conflict, and marine biology. This article, about the aftermath of Hurricane Katrina, which devastated New Orleans and the Gulf Coast in 2005, is excerpted from the September/October 2005 issue of *Multinational Monitor*, a magazine that examines multinational corporations and also covers issues relating to the environment and development.

Pre-Reading Journal Entry

Although humans have shaped the environment in many ways, we are still at the mercy of nature at times. Recall a hurricane, tornado, thunderstorm, windstorm, mudslide, earthquake, volcanic eruption, tsunami, drought, flood, or other natural event that affected you and your community. What was the event? What was the experience like? Use your journal to answer these questions.

The Storm This Time

Urban Floodplain

I arrive in Baton Rouge with a planeload of relief workers, FEMA functionaries and crew cut contractors, all working their cell phones and BlackBerrys. After renting a car and making my way through the daily traffic jam (Baton Rouge's population has exploded since the storm) I head south on Interstate 10, tuning into the United Radio Broadcasters of New Orleans, a consortium of local stations playing 24/7 information and call-in reports on Katrina's aftermath. 1

A police spokesperson assures listeners there are still 20 to 30 roadblocks around New Orleans and 11,000 guardsmen in the city. The mayor wants to open the city back up to residents but the approach of Hurricane Rita has forced him to postpone his plan. 2

Around the New Orleans airport in Jefferson Parish, I begin to see box stores, warehouses and motels with their roofs ripped off or caved in, downed trees and broken street signs, house roofs covered in blue tarps and high-rises with glass windows popped out like broken eyes. I hit a traffic jam and follow an SUV across the median strip to an exit where I stop to take a picture of a small office complex with its second story front and roof gone. Rain-soaked cardboard boxes fill the exposed floor above a CPA's office. 3

I talk to a carpet-store owner removing samples. He helps me locate where we are on a map. I get a call from a contact at the New Orleans Aquarium. They lost most of their fish when the pumps failed but managed to evacuate the penguins and sea otters to Monterey. I get on a wide boulevard that leads to a roadblock where a police officer checks my press identification. "This is only for emergency vehicles, but go ahead," she says.

I drive into Lakeview, one of the large sections of the city that sat under- 4
water for two weeks and will likely have to be bulldozed. It reminds me of war zones I've been in after heavy street fighting. There are trees and power poles down, electric lines hanging, metal sheets and street signs on mud-caked pavement, smashed cars, boats on sidewalks and torn-open houses, all colored in sepia tones of gray and brown. Unable to drive far in the debris chocked streets, I get out of my car, half expecting the sweet, rotting smell of death. Instead, I'm confronted with an equally noxious odor. It's what I'll come to think of as the smell of a dead city, like dried cow pies and mold with a stinging chemical aftertaste. Fine yellow dust starts rising up from under my boots and infiltrating the car. I retreat. The I-10 exit is barricaded, forcing me north again. I do a U-turn at a major roadblock and get chased down by some angry cops. I explain that I'm just following another cop's helpful directions and soon find myself speeding along a near-empty freeway bridge approaching downtown.

The rusted ruined roof of the Superdome inspires me to choose an exit 5
and, after getting turned around at a friendly National Guard checkpoint, I'm soon in the deserted streets of the central business district, checking out the rubble piles and empty highrises. A big wind-damaged 'Doubletree' hotel sign reads D UL EE. The French Quarter is still intact with even a few bars open for soldiers, FBI agents and fire fighters. On Canal Street, it looks like a Woodstock for first responders with Red Cross and media satellite trucks, tents and RVs pulled up on the central streetcar median by the Sheraton. Red-bereted troops from the 82nd Airborne cruise by in open-sided trucks, M-4s at the ready in case the undead should appear at sunset. Uptown, some boats lie in the middle of the street, along with cars crushed by a falling wall and a pharmacy trashed by looters. Further on are the smashed homes and muddied boulevards and still-flooded underpasses and cemeteries, abandoned cars and broken levees of an eerily hollow city.

In the coming days. I'll travel across this new urban landscape, tracing 6
the brown floodwater line that marks tens of thousands of homes, schools, offices, banks, churches, grocery stores and other ruined structures, including the main sewage plant. I'll cross paths with animal rescue crews, military patrols, utility crews from New York and Pennsylvania, and body recovery search teams with K-9 dogs using orange spray paint to mark the doors of still unexamined buildings, writing the date and adding a zero for no bodies or numbers where bodies have been found....

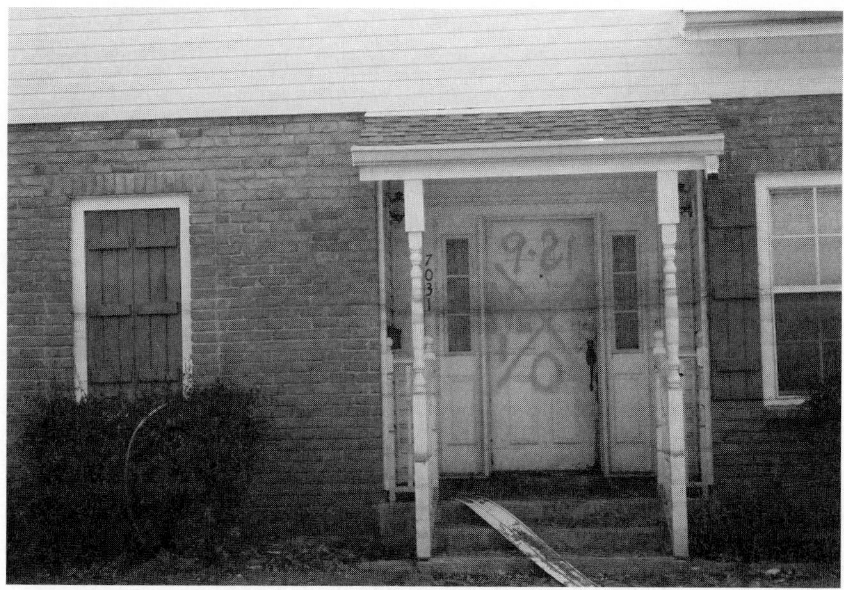

New Orleans house showing flood line and searcher's graffiti. The zero indicates that no bodies were found in the house. (*©David Helvarg*)

Life After Katrina

I put up with an AP colleague in the less damaged Algiers Point section 7
of the city just across the Mississippi from where the helicopter assault ship Iwo Jima and Carnival Cruise Line ship Ecstasy are being used to house city employees and relief workers. Blackhawk helicopters fly overhead at sunset while a Red Cross truck down the street offers hot food to the handful of residents still here.

Back in Lakeview, I encounter Bob Chick. Bob snuck past the check- 8
points to see if he can salvage anything from his green Cajun Cottage near where the 17th Street floodwall breached.

He hasn't had much luck, "just some tools that might be OK," he says. "I 9
left all my photos on top of a chest of drawers thinking the water wouldn't get that high. They say if you have more than five inches of water in your house for five days it's a loss. We had eight feet for two weeks." He's found one of his cats dead but thinks the other two might have escaped. He invites me to look inside. From the door it's a jumble of furniture, including a sofa, table, twisted carpet, lamps and wooden pieces all covered in black and gray gunk, reeking of mold and rotted cat food. I try not to breathe too deeply. "I had a collection of Jazz Fest T shirts going back to '79 but they're gone." He's wearing a mask, rubber boots and gloves, but still manages to give an expressive shrug of resignation

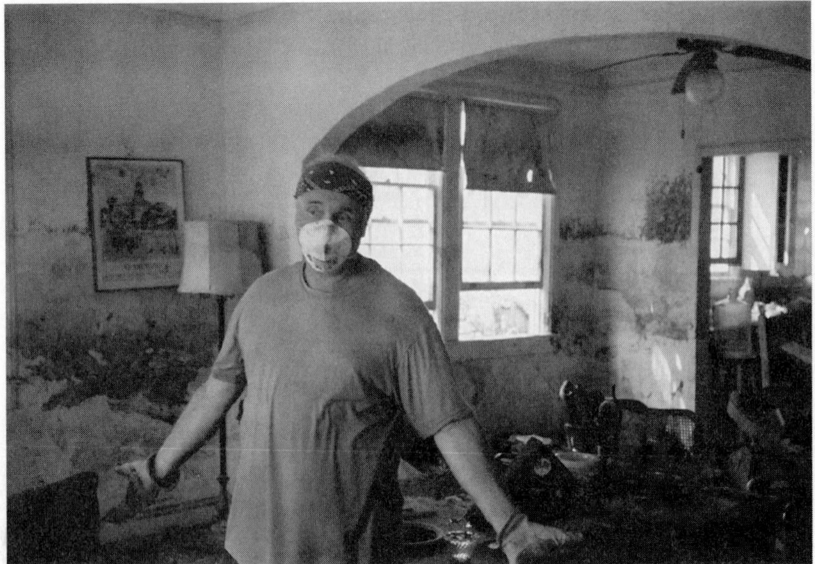

Bob Chick examines his flood-ruined house in the Lakeview section of New Orleans. (*©David Helvarg*)

when I take his picture. "I lived in this house 16 years. We'd have been fine if the levee hadn't broke. We'd be moving back right now."...

A Disappeared Town

I catch a ride along the west bank of the Mississippi in Plaquemines Parish south of New Orleans with deputy Sheriff Ken Harvey. This is where towns of several thousand, like Empire and Buras, got washed away and some oil tank farms ruptured. Where the road's cut by water, we drive up on the eroded levee and keep going. There are boats on the land, and houses in the water or washed onto the road or turned into woodpiles. At one point where the levee broke and the water poured through, there's nothing but a field where Diamond, an unincorporated town of about 300 including many trailer-park residents, stood. Those folks never seem to catch a break. 10

I take a picture of an antebellum white mansion in the water along with a floating pickup, a larger truck hanging off a tree, a semi-trailer cab under the bottom of an uplifted house, a speedboat through a picture window, the Buras water tower collapsed next to a wrecked store, shrimp boats on the levee, on the road and in the bushes with military patrols passing by. We stop and stare in awe at a 200-foot barge tossed atop the levee like a bath toy on a tub rim. 11

Approaching the Empire Bridge, I note the white church facing north towards us is still intact and suggest that's a hopeful sign. "It used to face the road," Ken points out.... 12

Unfortunately, as I drive east through Mississippi and Alabama I find most of [the] coastal trees and wetlands festooned with plastic like Tibetan prayer flags (as if monks were praying over dead turtles and seabirds). In Biloxi, along with smashed casinos, historic homes and neighborhoods, I find miles of beachfront covered in plastic buckets and insulation, mattresses, furniture, chunks of drywall and Styrofoam pellets that the seabirds are eyeing as potential snack food. I wave down a truck marked "Department of Natural Resources," but the guys inside are from Indiana. 13

I feel like an eco-geek being more concerned about the gulls and wetlands than the lost revenue from the casinos that everyone else seems to be obsessing on. The waterside wing of the new Hard Rock Casino is now a smashed tangle of twisted girders and concrete. I pull over by an 8,000 ton, 600-foot-long casino barge that was pushed half a mile by the storm, landing on Beach Drive. Somewhere underneath its barnacle-encrusted black hull is a historic mansion. Nearby, the Grand Casino barge has taken out much of the stately facade of the six story yellow brick Biloxi Yacht Club before grounding next to it. Another barge landed on the Holiday Inn, where more than 25 people may have been trying to ride out the hurricane. No one's been able to do a body-recovery there yet. 14

Because Southern Baptist and other religious conservatives objected to "land-based" gambling in Mississippi, much of Biloxi's wetlands were torn up to make way for these floating casinos. 15

I talk with Phil Sturgeon, a Harrah's security agent hanging out with some cops from Winter Park, Florida. He's in jeans and a gray shirt with a toothbrush and pen sticking out the pocket. He tells me the storm surge crested at about 35 feet, at least five feet higher than Camille in '69. 16

In Waveland, I drive over twisted railroad tracks where the eye of Katrina passed into neighborhoods of jagged wooden debris. A middle-aged couple is trying to clear the drive to the lot where their home once stood. A surfboard leans up against one of the live oaks that seem to have fared better then the houses in between them. 17

"Are you an adjuster," the woman asks. 18

"No, a reporter." 19

"Good, because we don't like adjusters. Nationwide was not on our side." 20

Apparently they've been offered $1,700 on their $422,000 home. 21

"At least you've got your surfboard," I tell John, her husband, "Oh, that's not my surfboard," he grins, pointing around. "And that's not my boat, and that's not my Corvette (buried to its hood in the rubble), and that's not our roof. We think it might belong to the house at the end of the street."... 22

Starting Again

I'm back in New Orleans on Canal Street, where the Salvation Army offers me cold water, a baloney sandwich (I decline) and a fruit cocktail. It's been a long day with the Army Corps of Engineers, who've leased helicopters that are dropping 3,000 and 7,000 pound sandbags on the latest breach in the Industrial Canal which has reflooded the Lower Ninth Ward. I enter the Sheraton after getting cleared by muscular Blackwater Security guys in tan and khaki tee shirts and shorts with Glocks on their hips. Another one sits by the elevators checking room IDs. I wonder if being a professional mercenary is good training for concierge duty. I sit by the Pelican bar in the lobby looking out the big three-story glass window at the media RVs and SUVs on the street—feeling as if I've been in this hotel before in various war zones and Third World capitals like Managua, Tegucigalpa, and Suva. 23

The Gulf region is now very much like a war zone, only with fewer deaths (about 1,200 bodies recovered at the time of my visit) and far more extensive damage. It also offers many of the same ironies and bizarre moments. Unity Radio announces that if you're going to tonight's Louisiana State University football game in Baton Rouge you can return after curfew provided you show your game stubs to the deputies at the roadblocks. 24

Three years ago I made a decision. I'd lost a key person in my life and was trying to decide what to do next. I was considering either going back to war reporting, as George Bush was clearly planning a pre-emptive invasion of Iraq, or turning from journalism to ocean advocacy.... Finally, I decided that while we'll probably always have wars, we may not always have living reefs, wild fish or protective coastal wetlands. 25

What we know we are going to have are more environmental disasters like the Hurricane Season of '05 linked to fossil-fuel-fired climate change and bad coastal policies driven by saltwater special interests. 26

Still, destruction on a biblical scale also offers Noah-like opportunities for restoration after the flood. There are practical solutions to the dangers we confront, along with models of how to live safely by the sea. Things can be done right in terms of building wisely along the coasts, and advancing social and environmental equity. But it will take a new wave of citizen activism to avoid repetition of old mistakes, with even more dire consequences. 27

Questions for Close Reading

1. What is the selection's thesis? Locate the sentence(s) in which Helvarg states his main idea. If he doesn't state his thesis explicitly, express it in your own words.
2. Helvarg uses headings to divide his essay into sections. What is the subject of the section entitled "Urban Floodplain"? How does this section frame the remainder of the essay?

3. Most of the details in Helvarg's essay focus on the destruction caused by the hurricane and the recovery effort. However, he does give a description of an activity that shows life going on as normal. What is it? Why does Helvarg include this description?
4. Some words are so new they are not yet in dictionaries. Helvarg uses such a word when he describes himself as an "eco-geek" in paragraph 14. Given the context, and the meanings of the root *eco* and the word *geek,* how would you define this word?
5. Refer to your dictionary as needed to define the following words used in the selection: *consortium* (paragraph 1), *infiltrating* (4), *Woodstock* (5), *salvage* (8), *ruptured* (10), *antebellum* (11), *festooned* (13), *storm surge* (16), *adjuster* (18), and *mercenary* (23).

Questions About the Writer's Craft

1. **The pattern.** How does Helvarg organize his points in this essay? What transitional words and phrases does he use to keep the reader oriented as his essay progresses?
2. Most of the description in this essay focuses on visual details, but Helvarg also describes some other sensations. Find the passages in which Helvarg describes something other than the sights of the post-Katrina landscape, and evaluate their vividness. What do these passages contribute to the essay?
3. In paragraphs 4 and 24, to what does Helvarg compare the post-Katrina Gulf Coast? How does this analogy help the reader envision the destruction? How does it help express the dominant impression of the essay?
4. Helvarg took the photographs that accompany this essay. Compare the photograph of the marked door on page 105 with the author's description of it in paragraph 6. Does this photograph add to the description in the essay, or is the author's description so vivid that the photograph is unnecessary? Now compare the photograph of Bob Chick on page 106 with the author's description of him in paragraph 9. Does this photograph add to the description of Bob in the essay, or is the author's description so vivid that the photograph is unnecessary? If you were writing this essay, would you include the photographs? If so, how would they affect the way you wrote the essay?

Writing Assignments Using Description as a Pattern of Development

1. One reason Helvarg's essay has such an impact is that destruction of the normal Gulf Coast environment was sudden as well as devastating. Not all environmental destruction is so dramatic, however. Find something in your own environment—your home, neighborhood, city, or region—that has been damaged or destroyed by gradual overuse or neglect. For example, your home may have a shabby room, or part of your yard may be overgrown. Or your neighborhood may have a run-down playground or park, or roads full of potholes, or an abandoned building. Select a location that has been neglected or overused, and write an essay in which you describe this damaged environment.

2. Although severe weather, like Hurricane Katrina, provides good subject matter for description, so does more common, less destructive weather. Think of a day on which the weather was important to you but turned out badly. For example, you might have planned an outdoor event and it rained, or you might have scheduled a trip and it snowed, or you might have worn great new clothes and been too hot or too cold. Write an essay in which you describe this uncooperative weather. Use sensory details and figures of speech to convey your feelings about this day.

Writing Assignments Combining Patterns of Development

3. In "The Storm This Time," the environmental devastation was caused by a natural event. However, much destruction of the environment is caused by people rather than by weather or other natural disasters. Select a place you know that has changed for the worse through human use. For example, you might choose an industrial site, a polluted river or lake, or a park. *Compare* and *contrast* the place as it once was and as it is now. Provide vivid *descriptions* of how the place has changed.
4. The Gulf Coast has a lot of experience with hurricanes; Katrina was just the most destructive one in recent years. Other areas are prone to other types of natural disasters. Research the destructive weather and other natural events that your area typically experiences. Good places to start are the websites of the Federal Emergency Management Agency (www.fema.gov) and the National Oceanic and Atmospheric Administration (www.noaa.gov). You might also read Tim Folger's "Waves of Destruction" (page 295) for ideas. Then write an essay in which you *classify* the natural disasters that occur in your area and *describe* each type, giving specific *examples* where possible.

Writing Assignment Using a Journal Entry as a Starting Point

5. Review your pre-reading journal entry about the natural disaster or event that you experienced. Write an essay in which you *describe* its aftermath. How did it *affect* you and others in your community? How did the event change your attitude toward nature? How did it *affect* the way you prepare for future natural emergencies? You might first read Joan Didion's "The Santa Ana" (page 601), an essay about a recurring hot wind that affects southern California.

Riverbend

The author known by the pseudonym, or fictitious name, Riverbend is an Iraqi woman in her twenties. In 2003, she began writing a blog, *Baghdad Burning*, in which she described her personal experiences of the U.S. invasion and occupation of Iraq. The blog entries have been collected in two books—*Baghdad Burning: Girl Blog from Iraq* (2005) and *Baghdad Burning II: More Girl Blog from Iraq* (2006)—published by The Feminist Press. "Bloggers Without Borders..." is Riverbend's last blog entry, posted on October 22, 2007.

Pre-Reading Journal Entry

Can you remember a time you endured a frustrating situation? Maybe you were appealing a ticket in traffic court or waiting to board an airplane. In your journal, jot down what you recall about the scene. What was the setting like? Who else was present? Why was the situation frustrating? How else did you feel in the situation?

Bloggers Without Borders...

Syria is a beautiful country—at least I think it is. I say "I think" because while I perceive it to be beautiful, I sometimes wonder if I mistake safety, security and normalcy for 'beauty'. In so many ways, Damascus is like Baghdad before the war—bustling streets, occasional traffic jams, markets seemingly always full of shoppers... And in so many ways it's different. The buildings are higher, the streets are generally narrower and there's a mountain, Qasiyoun, that looms in the distance. 1

The mountain distracts me, as it does many Iraqis—especially those from Baghdad. Northern Iraq is full of mountains, but the rest of Iraq is quite flat. At night, Qasiyoun blends into the black sky and the only indication of its presence is a multitude of little, glimmering spots of light—houses and restaurants built right up there on the mountain. Every time I take a picture, I try to work Qasiyoun into it—I try to position the person so that Qasiyoun is in the background. 2

The first weeks here were something of a cultural shock. It has taken me these last three months to work away certain habits I'd acquired in Iraq after the war. It's funny how you learn to act a certain way and don't even know you're doing strange things—like avoiding people's eyes in the street or crazily murmuring prayers to yourself when stuck in traffic. It took me at least three weeks to teach myself to walk properly again—with head lifted, not constantly looking behind me. 3

It is estimated that there are at least 1.5 million Iraqis in Syria today. I believe it. Walking down the streets of Damascus, you can hear the Iraqi accent everywhere. There are areas like Geramana and Qudsiya that are 4 packed full of Iraqi refugees. Syrians are few and far between in these areas. Even the public schools in the areas are full of Iraqi children. A cousin of mine is now attending a school in Qudsiya and his class is composed of 26 Iraqi children, and 5 Syrian children. It's beyond belief sometimes. Most of the families have nothing to live on beyond their savings which are quickly being depleted with rent and the costs of living.

Within a month of our being here, we began hearing talk about Syria 5
requiring visas from Iraqis, like most other countries. Apparently, our esteemed puppets in power met with Syrian and Jordanian authorities and decided they wanted to take away the last two safe havens remaining for Iraqis—Damascus and Amman. The talk began in late August and was only talk until recently—early October. Iraqis entering Syria now need a visa from the Syrian consulate or embassy in the country they are currently in. In the case of Iraqis still in Iraq, it is said that an approval from the Ministry of Interior is also required (which kind of makes it difficult for people running away from militias OF the Ministry of Interior…). Today, there's talk of a possible fifty dollar visa at the border.

Iraqis who entered Syria before the visa was implemented were getting 6
a one month visitation visa at the border. As soon as that month was over, you could take your passport and visit the local immigration bureau. If you were lucky, they would give you an additional month or two. When talk about visas from the Syrian embassy began, they stopped giving an extension on the initial border visa. We, as a family, had a brilliant idea. Before the commotion of visas began, and before we started needing a renewal, we decided to go to one of the border crossings, cross into Iraq, and come back into Syria—everyone was doing it. It would buy us some time—at least 2 months.

We chose a hot day in early September and drove the six hours to 7
Kameshli, a border town in northern Syria. My aunt and her son came with us—they also needed an extension on their visa. There is a border crossing in Kameshli called Yaarubiya. It's one of the simpler crossings because the Iraqi and Syrian borders are only a matter of several meters. You walk out of Syrian territory and then walk into Iraqi territory—simple and safe.

When we got to the Yaarubiya border patrol, it hit us that thousands 8
of Iraqis had had our brilliant idea simultaneously—the lines to the border patrol office were endless. Hundreds of Iraqis stood in a long line waiting to have their passports stamped with an exit visa. We joined the line of people and waited. And waited. And waited…

It took four hours to leave the Syrian border after which came the lines 9
of the Iraqi border post. Those were even longer. We joined one of the lines of weary, impatient Iraqis. "It's looking like a gasoline line…" My younger cousin joked. That was the beginning of another four hours of waiting under the sun, taking baby steps, moving forward ever so slowly. The line kept

getting longer. At one point, we could see neither the beginning of the line, where passports were being stamped to enter Iraq, nor the end. Running up and down the line were little boys selling glasses of water, chewing gum and cigarettes. My aunt caught one of them by the arm as he zipped past us, "How many people are in front of us?" He whistled and took a few steps back to assess the situation, "A hundred! A thousand!" He was almost gleeful as he ran off to make business.

I had such mixed feelings standing in that line. I was caught between a 10
feeling of yearning, a certain homesickness that sometimes catches me at the oddest moments, and a heavy feeling of dread. What if they didn't agree to let us out again? It wasn't really possible, but what if it happened? What if this was the last time I'd see the Iraqi border? What if we were no longer allowed to enter Iraq for some reason? What if we were never allowed to leave?

We spent the four hours standing, crouching, sitting and leaning in the 11
line. The sun beat down on everyone equally—Sunnis, Shia and Kurds alike. E. tried to convince the aunt to faint so it would speed the process up for the family, but she just gave us a withering look and stood straighter. People just stood there, chatting, cursing or silent. It was yet another gathering of Iraqis—the perfect opportunity to swap sad stories and ask about distant relations or acquaintances.

We met two families we knew while waiting for our turn. We greeted 12
each other like long lost friends and exchanged phone numbers and addresses in Damascus, promising to visit. I noticed the 23-year-old son, K., from one of the families was missing. I beat down my curiosity and refused to ask where he was. The mother was looking older than I remembered and the father looked constantly lost in thought, or maybe it was grief. I didn't want to know if K. was dead or alive. I'd just have to believe he was alive and thriving somewhere, not worrying about borders or visas. Ignorance really is bliss sometimes...

Back at the Syrian border, we waited in a large group, tired and hungry, 13
having handed over our passports for a stamp. The Syrian immigration man sifting through dozens of passports called out names and looked at faces as he handed over the passports patiently, "Stand back please—stand back". There was a general cry towards the back of the crowded hall where we were standing as someone collapsed—as they lifted him I recognized an old man who was there with his family being chaperoned by his sons, leaning on a walking stick.

By the time we had reentered the Syrian border and were headed back 14
to the cab ready to take us into Kameshli, I had resigned myself to the fact that we were refugees. I read about refugees on the Internet daily... in the newspapers... hear about them on TV. I hear about the estimated 1.5 million plus Iraqi refugees in Syria and shake my head, never really

considering myself or my family as one of them. After all, refugees are people who sleep in tents and have no potable water or plumbing, right? Refugees carry their belongings in bags instead of suitcases and they don't have cell phones or Internet access, right? Grasping my passport in my hand like my life depended on it, with two extra months in Syria stamped inside, it hit me how wrong I was. We were all refugees. I was suddenly a number. No matter how wealthy or educated or comfortable, a refugee is a refugee. A refugee is someone who isn't really welcome in any country—including their own . . . especially their own.

We live in an apartment building where two other Iraqis are renting. 15
The people in the floor above us are a Christian family from northern Iraq who got chased out of their village by Peshmerga and the family on our floor is a Kurdish family who lost their home in Baghdad to militias and were waiting for immigration to Sweden or Switzerland or some such European refugee haven.

The first evening we arrived, exhausted, dragging suitcases behind us, 16
morale a little bit bruised, the Kurdish family sent over their representative—a 9 year old boy missing two front teeth, holding a lopsided cake, "We're Abu Mohammed's house—across from you—mama says if you need anything, just ask—this is our number. Abu Dalia's family live upstairs, this is their number. We're all Iraqi too . . . Welcome to the building."

I cried that night because for the first time in a long time, so far away 17
from home, I felt the unity that had been stolen from us in 2003.

Questions for Close Reading

1. What is the selection's thesis (or dominant impression)? Locate the sentence(s) in which Riverbend states her main idea. If she doesn't state her thesis explicitly, express it in your own words.
2. At the start of the reading, the author compares Damascus, the capital of Syria, with her native Baghdad. How do the cities seem the same? How do they seem different? Why do you think the author is "distracted" by the mountain Qasiyoun?
3. The author uses two numerical examples. What are they? What are the sources for these examples? How do the examples contribute to the dominant impression of the reading?
4. For much of the selection, the author describes the scene as she and her family cross the border into Iraq and then immediately cross back into Syria. Why have they decided to take these actions? What realization does the author have as a result?
5. Refer to your dictionary as needed to define the following words used in the selection: *normalcy* (paragraph 1), *cultural shock* (3), *depleted* (4), *visas* (5), *esteemed* (5), *puppets* (5), *havens* (5), *militias* (5), *implemented* (6), *immigration* (6), *simultaneously* (8), *withering* (11), *chaperoned* (13), *refugees* (14), *potable* (14), and *morale* (16).

Questions About the Writer's Craft

1. **The pattern.** How does the author use description in the selection? What phrases convey the physical discomfort of the border-crossing experience? Why does the author spend so much of the selection describing the experience?
2. At times, the selection expresses an ironic or humorously sardonic tone. Which specific sentences does the author use to achieve this tone? What is the effect of the selection's tone for the reader?
3. **Other patterns.** The author *compares* Damascus to Baghdad at the start of the reading and then *narrates* the story of the border crossing. In addition, the author gives at least four personal *ancedotes* from the border crossing and afterward. What are these anecdotes, and what do they illustrate for the reader?
4. What is the significance of the selection's title, "Blogging Without Borders..."? Is the title effective?

Writing Assignments Using Description as a Pattern of Development

1. The author uses the phrase "Ignorance is bliss" to underscore that she would rather continue imagining a young family friend as "alive and thriving somewhere" than risk finding out for sure that he was dead or missing. Like the author, we may suddenly find ourselves reminded of the possibility of death. For example, we may hear about a friend's serious accident or illness. Write an essay in which you *describe* your thoughts and feelings in response to such a reminder. Did you feel sad, afraid, angry, vulnerable, or lucky? How were you affected by the experience? To see how another writer handles the idea of mortality, read Beth Johnson's "Bombs Bursting in Air" (page 211).
2. Riverbend describes the "culture shock" she experiences in Damascus. Have you ever spent time in a place that is very different from your home? For example, if you live in the city, have you ever spent a summer on a farm? Or if you live in a warm region, have you spent a winter holiday in a cold climate? In an essay, *describe* your experience in that strange place. Use colorful details to tell readers about the environment, food, customs, and other aspects of the place and its inhabitants.

Writing Assignments Combining Patterns of Development

3. As the author discovers, sometimes an experience can turn out to be different than expected. Think about a time you were pleasantly or unpleasantly surprised by a journey that you took or an event you attended. You might have gone to a much-anticipated concert and been disappointed, or you might have dreaded attending a family reunion but ended up having a good time. Why were you surprised? *Narrate* the story of your experience in an essay, taking care to *describe* the place or event, including the setting, your own expectations, and the people involved. Give details to support your ideas. You might read Audre Lorde's "The

Fourth of July" (page 140) to learn about another writer's disappointment in a journey taken.

4. The author implies that Syria imposed new visa requirements in an attempt to control the number of Iraqi refugees. Immigration is a contentious issue in many countries, whether refugees are seeking safety, freedom from oppression, or economic betterment. Do some research into conditions for Iraqi refugees and their host countries—primarily Syria, Jordan, Egypt, and the United States. In an essay, ***argue*** for or against the policies of one host country, using your researched evidence to support your view. For insight into arguments for and against immigration, read Roberto Rodriguez's "The Border on Our Backs" (page 559) and Star Parker's "*Se Habla* Entitlement" (page 564).

Writing Assignment Using a Journal Entry as a Starting Point

5. Review your pre-reading journal entry, in which you wrote about a frustrating situation and your reaction to it. Write an essay in which you *describe* the progressive *stages* of frustration in such a situation. For example, you might say that your feelings started out as curiosity, and then progressed to boredom, anger, and finally apathy or resignation. Remember to give details about what you were thinking or imagining at each stage. The tone of your essay can be serious or humorous.

Judith Ortiz Cofer

Born in Puerto Rico, raised both on her native island and in the United States, and educated in sites that included Oxford University in England, Judith Ortiz Cofer (1952–) knows what it is to move between cultures, absorbing from each while keeping mindful of her own heritage. Cofer earned a master's degree in English from the University of Florida before spending a year in graduate study at Oxford. Following a stint as a bilingual teacher, Cofer taught English at several colleges and universities and currently teaches Creative Writing at the University of Georgia. She has published collections of poetry, including *Peregrine* (1986), *Terms of Survival* (1995), *Reaching for the Mainland and Selected New Poems* (1995), and *A Love Story Beginning in Spanish* (2005); novels, *The Line of the Sun* (1989), *The Meaning of Consuelo* (2003), and *Call Me Maria* (2004); and four books of essays, *Silent Dancing: A Partial Remembrance of a Puerto Rican Childhood* (1990), *The Latin Deli: Telling the Lives of Barrio Women* (1993), *An Island Like You: Stories of the Barrio* (1995), and *Woman in Front of the Sun* (2000). The following essay is taken from *Silent Dancing.*

Pre-Reading Journal Entry

Everyone loves a good story. But stories do more than merely entertain us. Use your journal to reflect on two or more stories that adults told you in your childhood as a way to teach an important lesson about life. In addition to sketching out the stories themselves, outline the circumstances of hearing the stories: who told them, where you were when you heard the stories, why the stories were recounted.

A Partial Remembrance of a Puerto Rican Childhood

At three or four o'clock in the afternoon, the hour of *café con leche,*[1] the women of my family gathered in Mamá's living room to speak of important things and retell familiar stories meant to be overheard by us young girls, their daughters. In Mamá's house (everyone called my grandmother Mamá) was a large parlor built by my grandfather to his wife's exact specifications so that it was always cool, facing away from the sun. The doorway was on the side of the house so no one could walk directly into her living room. First they had to take a little stroll through and around her beautiful garden where prize-winning orchids grew in the trunk of an ancient tree she had hollowed out for that purpose. This room was furnished with several mahogany rocking chairs, acquired at the births of her children, and one intricately carved rocker that had passed down to Mamá at the death of her own mother. 1

[1]Spanish for "coffee with milk" (editors' note).

It was on these rockers that my mother, her sisters, and my grandmother sat on these afternoons of my childhood to tell their stories, teaching each other, and my cousin and me, what it was like to be a woman, more specifically, a Puerto Rican woman. They talked about life on the island, and life in *Los Nueva Yores,* their way of referring to the United States from New York City to California: the other place, not home, all the same. They told real-life stories though, as I later learned, always embellishing them with a little or a lot of dramatic detail. And they told *cuentos,* the morality and cautionary tales told by the women in our family for generations: stories that became a part of my subconscious as I grew up in two worlds, the tropical island and the cold city, and that would later surface in my dreams and in my poetry. 2

One of these tales was about the woman who was left at the altar. Mamá liked to tell that one with histrionic intensity. I remember the rise and fall of her voice, the sighs, and her constantly gesturing hands, like two birds swooping through her words. This particular story usually would come up in a conversation as a result of someone mentioning a forthcoming engagement or wedding. The first time I remember hearing it, I was sitting on the floor at Mamá's feet, pretending to read a comic book. I may have been eleven or twelve years old, at that difficult age when a girl was no longer a child who could be ordered to leave the room if the women wanted freedom to take their talk into forbidden zones, nor really old enough to be considered a part of their conclave. I could only sit quietly, pretending to be in another world, while absorbing it all in a sort of unspoken agreement of my status as silent auditor. On this day, Mamá had taken my long, tangled mane of hair into her ever-busy hands. Without looking down at me and with no interruption of her flow of words, she began braiding my hair, working at it with the quickness and determination that characterized all her actions. My mother was watching us impassively from her rocker across the room. On her lips played a little ironic smile. I would never sit still for *her* ministrations, but even then, I instinctively knew that she did not possess Mamá's matriarchal power to command and keep everyone's attention. This was never more evident than in the spell she cast when telling a story. 3

"It is not like it used to be when I was a girl," Mamá announced. "Then, a man could leave a girl standing at the church altar with a bouquet of fresh flowers in her hands and disappear off the face of the earth. No way to track him down if he was from another town. He could be a married man, with maybe even two or three families all over the island. There was no way to know. And there were men who did this. *Hombres*[2] with the devil in their flesh who would come to a *pueblo,*[3] like this one, take a job at one of the *haciendas,*[4] never meaning to stay, only to have a good time and to seduce the women." 4

[2]Spanish for "men" (editors' note).

[3]Spanish for "community" (editors' note).

[4]Spanish for "large estate" or "ranch" (editors' note).

The whole time she was speaking, Mamá would be weaving my hair into a flat plait that required pulling apart the two sections of hair with little jerks that made my eyes water; but knowing how grandmother detested whining and *boba* (sissy) tears, as she called them, I just sat up as straight and stiff as I did at La Escuela San Jose, where the nuns enforced good posture with a flexible plastic ruler they bounced off of slumped shoulders and heads. As Mamá's story progressed, I noticed how my young Aunt Laura lowered her eyes, refusing to meet Mamá's meaningful gaze. Laura was seventeen, in her last year of high school, and already engaged to a boy from another town who had staked his claim with a tiny diamond ring, then left for Los Nueva Yores to make his fortune. They were planning to get married in a year. Mamá had expressed serious doubts that the wedding would ever take place. In Mamá's eyes, a man set free without a legal contract was a man lost. She believed that marriage was not something men desired, but simply the price they had to pay for the privilege of children and, of course, for what no decent (synonymous with "smart") woman would give away for free. 5

"María La Loca was only seventeen when *it* happened to her." I listened closely at the mention of this name. María was a town character, a fat middle-aged woman who lived with her old mother on the outskirts of town. She was to be seen around the pueblo delivering the meat pies the two women made for a living. The most peculiar thing about María, in my eyes, was that she walked and moved like a little girl though she had the thick body and wrinkled face of an old woman. She would swing her hips in an exaggerated, clownish way, and sometimes even hop and skip up to someone's house. She spoke to no one. Even if you asked her a question, she would just look at you and smile, showing her yellow teeth. But I had heard that if you got close enough, you could hear her humming a tune without words. The kids yelled out nasty things at her, calling her *La Loca,*[5] and the men who hung out at the *bodega*[6] playing dominoes sometimes whistled mockingly as she passed by with her funny, outlandish walk. But María seemed impervious to it all, carrying her basket of *pasteles*[7] like a grotesque Little Red Riding Hood through the forest. 6

María La Loca interested me, as did all the eccentrics and crazies of our pueblo. Their weirdness was a measuring stick I used in my serious quest for a definition of normal. As a Navy brat shuttling between New Jersey and the pueblo, I was constantly made to feel like an oddball by my peers, who made fun of my two-way accent: a Spanish accent when I spoke English, and when I spoke Spanish I was told that I sounded like a *Gringa.*[8] Being the outsider had already turned my brother and me into cultural chameleons. We developed 7

[5]Spanish for "crazy one" (editors' note).

[6]Spanish for a neighborhood grocery store (editors' note).

[7]Spanish for "pastries" (editors' note).

[8]A negatively charged Latin American slang expression for a female foreigner (editors' note).

early on the ability to blend into a crowd, to sit and read quietly in a fifth story apartment building for days and days when it was too bitterly cold to play outside, or, set free, to run wild in Mamá's realm, where she took charge of our lives, releasing Mother for a while from the intense fear for our safety that our father's absences instilled in her. In order to keep us from harm when Father was away, Mother kept us under strict surveillance. She even walked us to and from Public School No. 11, which we attended during the months we lived in Paterson, New Jersey, our home base in the States. Mamá freed all three of us like pigeons from a cage. I saw her as my liberator and my model. Her stories were parables from which to glean the *Truth*.

"María La Loca was once a beautiful girl. Everyone thought she would marry the Méndez boy." As everyone knew, Rogelio Méndez was the richest man in town. "But," Mamá continued, knitting my hair with the same intensity she was putting into her story, "this *macho* made a fool out of her and ruined her life." She paused for the effect of her use of the word "macho," which at that time had not yet become a popular epithet for an unliberated man. This word had for us the crude and comical connotation of "male of the species," stud; a *macho* was what you put in a pen to increase your stock. 8

I peeked over my comic book at my mother. She too was under Mamá's spell, smiling conspiratorially at this little swipe at men. She was safe from Mamá's contempt in this area. Married at an early age, an unspotted lamb, she had been accepted by a good family of strict Spaniards whose name was old and respected, though their fortune had been lost long before my birth. In a rocker Papá had painted sky blue sat Mamá's oldest child, Aunt Nena. Mother of three children, stepmother of two more, she was a quiet woman who liked books but had married an ignorant and abusive widower whose main interest in life was accumulating wealth. He too was in the mainland working on his dream of returning home rich and triumphant to buy the *finca*[9] of his dreams. She was waiting for him to send for her. She would leave her children with Mamá for several years while the two of them slaved away in factories. He would one day be a rich man, and she a sadder woman. Even now her life-light was dimming. She spoke little, an aberration in Mamá's house, and she read avidly, as if storing up spiritual food for the long winters that awaited her in Los Nueva Yores without her family. But even Aunt Nena came alive to Mamá's words, rocking gently, her hands over a thick book in her lap. 9

Her daughter, my cousin Sara, played jacks by herself on the tile porch outside the room where we sat. She was a year older than I. We shared a bed and all our family's secrets. Collaborators in search of answers, Sara and I discussed everything we heard the women say, trying to fit it all 10

[9]Spanish for "farm" or "ranch" (editors' note).

together like a puzzle that, once assembled, would reveal life's mysteries to us. Though she and I still enjoyed taking part in boys' games—chase, volleyball, and even *vaqueros,* the island version of cowboys and Indians involving cap-gun battles and violent shoot-outs under the mango tree in Mamá's backyard—we loved best the quiet hours in the afternoon when the men were still at work, and the boys had gone to play serious baseball at the park. Then Mamá's house belonged only to us women. The aroma of coffee perking in the kitchen, the mesmerizing creaks and groans of the rockers, and the women telling their lives in *cuentos* are forever woven into the fabric of my imagination, braided like my hair that day I felt my grandmother's hands teaching me about strength, her voice convincing me of the power of storytelling.

That day Mamá told how the beautiful María had fallen prey to a 11 man whose name was never the same in subsequent versions of the story; it was Juan one time, José, Rafael, Diego, another. We understood that neither the name or any of the *facts* were important, only that a woman had allowed love to defeat her. Mamá put each of us in María's place by describing her wedding dress in loving detail: how she looked like a princess in her lace as she waited at the altar. Then, as Mamá approached the tragic denouement of her story, I was distracted by the sound of my Aunt Laura's violent rocking. She seemed on the verge of tears. She knew the fable was intended for her. That week she was going to have her wedding gown fitted, though no firm date had been set for the marriage. Mamá ignored Laura's obvious discomfort, digging out a ribbon from the sewing basket she kept by her rocker while describing María's long illness, "a fever that would not break for days." She spoke of a mother's despair: "that woman climbed the church steps on her knees every morning, wore only black as a *promesa* to the Holy Virgin in exchange for her daughter's health." By the time María returned from her honeymoon with death, she was ravished, no longer young or sane. "As you can see, she is almost as old as her mother already," Mamá lamented while tying the ribbon to the ends of my hair, pulling it back with such force that I just knew I would never be able to close my eyes completely again.

"That María's getting crazier every day." Mamá's voice would take a 12 lighter tone now, expressing satisfaction, either for the perfection of my braid, or for a story well told—it was hard to tell. "You know that tune María is always humming?" Carried away by her enthusiasm, I tried to nod, but Mamá still had me pinned between her knees.

"Well, that's the wedding march." Surprising us all, Mamá sang out, 13 "Da, da, dara... da, da, dara." Then lifting me off the floor by my skinny shoulders, she would lead me around the room in an impromptu waltz—another session ending with the laughter of women, all of us caught up in the infectious joke of our lives.

Questions for Close Reading

1. What is the selection's thesis (or dominant impression)? Locate the sentence(s) in which Cofer states her main idea. If she doesn't state the thesis explicitly, express it in your own words.
2. Who are the women who participate in the storytelling sessions? Why is Cofer allowed to join them? Why aren't men or boys part of the group?
3. What lessons about men and women does Mamá intend the story of María La Loca to teach?
4. What information does Cofer provide about her aunts and her mother? What similarities and/or differences are there between each of their lives and the story of María La Loca?
5. Refer to your dictionary as needed to define the following words used in the selection: *intricately* (paragraph 1), *embellishing* (2), *cautionary* (2), *histrionic* (3), *conclave* (3), *auditor* (3), *impassively* (3), *ministrations* (3), *matriarchal* (3), *quest* (7), *chameleons* (7), *surveillance* (7), *conspiratorially* (9), *aberration* (9), *mesmerizing* (10), *denouement* (11), *ravished* (11), and *impromptu* (13).

Questions About the Writer's Craft

1. **The pattern.** Of all the women mentioned in the essay, only María La Loca is described in detail. What descriptive details does Cofer offer about her? Why do you suppose Cofer provides so much description about this particular woman?
2. In paragraph 7, Cofer provides some specifics about her childhood as a "Navy brat." What would have been lost if Cofer hadn't included this material?
3. **Other patterns.** Reread paragraphs 4, 6, 8, and 11–13, where Cofer *recounts* her grandmother's story. Why do you think Cofer doesn't tell the story straight through, without interruptions? What purpose do the interruptions serve? How does Cofer signal when she is moving away from the story or back to it?
4. Why might Cofer have mentioned in several spots the braiding of her hair, which goes on the whole time Mamá tells María's story? What similarities are there between the braiding and the storytelling session? What similarities are there between the braiding and Cofer's descriptive style (consider especially the last sentence of paragraph 10)?

Writing Assignments Using Description as a Pattern of Development

1. Cofer paints a vivid picture of a childhood ritual: the telling of stories among the women in her family. Think of a specific scene, event, or ritual from your own childhood or youth that has special meaning for you. Then write a descriptive essay conveying the distinctive flavor of that occasion. Draw upon vivid sensory language to capture your dominant impression of that time. Consider using dialogue, as Cofer does, to add texture to your description and reveal character.
2. To Cofer, Mamá was a "liberator" and a "model." Think of a person in your life who served as a role model or opened doors for you, and write an essay describing that person. Like Cofer, place the person in a characteristic setting and supply

vigorous details about the person's actions, speech, looks, and so forth. Make sure that all the descriptive details reinforce your dominant impression of the individual. You may want to read Maya Angelou's "Sister Flowers" (page 87) or Amy Tan's "Mother Tongue" (page 270) to see how an especially skilled writer describes a powerful, influential person.

Writing Assignments Combining Patterns of Development

3. Cofer's family is close-knit, but family life nowadays is more likely to be fragmented, with everyone going separate ways. Write an essay explaining what *steps* families could take to offset this tendency toward fragmentation. You might want to focus on a particular area of family life, such as mealtimes, after-supper hours, or vacations. Be sure to spend some time discussing the expected *outcomes* of the steps you propose. You might benefit from conducting research in the library and/or on the Internet into how to increase the quality and quantity of family time.

4. The stories Cofer heard taught her "what it was like to be a woman." What information and experiences shaped your understanding of your gender? Write an essay showing how your perception of your gender identity was *influenced* by what you heard, witnessed, and experienced as a child. Along the way, you might briefly *narrate* one or more of these gender-shaping interactions. Before writing your paper, you may wish to read the following essays, each of which provides insight into gender expectations:, Ann Sutherland's "What Shamu Taught Me About a Happy Marriage" (page 308) and Dave Barry's "Beauty and the Beast" (page 368).

Writing Assignment Using a Journal Entry as a Starting Point

5. Write an essay narrating an experience that put to the test the moral of a story you were told when you were young. Select from your pre-reading journal entry the *one* story whose "truth" was most memorably validated *or* discredited by an experience later in your life. Your tone might be serious or humorous. In either case, be sure to make clear how you felt about the truth of the story after it was "tested" by experience.

Additional Writing Topics

DESCRIPTION

General Assignments

Write an essay using description to develop any of the following topics. Remember that an effective description focuses on a dominant impression and arranges details in a way that best supports that impression. Your details—vivid and appealing to the senses—should be carefully chosen so that the essay isn't overburdened with material of secondary importance. When writing, keep in mind that varied sentence structure and imaginative figures of speech are ways to make a descriptive piece compelling.

1. A favorite item of clothing
2. A school as a young child might see it
3. A hospital room you visited or stayed in
4. An individualist's appearance
5. A coffee shop, a bus shelter, a newsstand, or some other small place
6. A parade or victory celebration
7. A banana, a squash, or another fruit or vegetable
8. A particular drawer in a desk or bureau
9. A houseplant
10. A "media event"
11. A dorm room
12. An elderly person
13. An attractive man or woman
14. A prosthetic device or wheelchair
15. A TV, film, or music celebrity
16. A student lounge
17. A once-in-a-lifetime event
18. The inside of something, such as a cave, boat, car, shed, or machine
19. A friend, a roommate, or another person you know well
20. An essential gadget or a useless gadget

Assignments with a Specific Purpose, Audience, and Point of View

On Campus

1. For an audience of incoming first-year students, prepare a speech describing registration day at your college. Use specific details to help prepare students for the actual event. Choose an adjective that represents your dominant impression of the experience, and keep that word in mind as you write.

2. Your college has decided to replace an old campus structure (for example, a dorm or dining hall) with a new version. Write the administration a letter of protest describing the place so vividly and appealingly that its value and need for preservation are unquestionable.
3. As a staff member of the campus newspaper, you have been asked to write a weekly column of social news and gossip. For your first column, you plan to describe a recent campus event—a dance, party, or concert, or other social activity. With a straightforward or tongue-in-cheek tone, describe where the event was held, the appearance of the people who attended, and so on.

At Home or in the Community

4. As a subscriber to a community-wide dating service, you've been asked to submit a description of the kind of person you'd like to meet. Describe your ideal date. Focus on specifics about physical appearance, personal habits, character traits, and interests.
5. As a resident of a particular town, you're angered by the appearance of a certain spot and by the activities that take place there. Write the town council a letter describing in detail the undesirable nature of this place (a video arcade, an adult bookstore, a bar, a bus station, a neglected park or beach). End with some suggestions about ways to improve the situation.

On the Job

6. You've noticed a recurring problem in your workplace, and you want to bring it to the attention of your boss, who is typically inattentive. Write a letter to your boss describing the problem. Your goal is not to provide solutions, but rather, to provide vivid description—complete with sensory details—so that your boss can no longer deny the problem.

NARRATION

WHAT IS NARRATION?

Human beings are instinctively storytellers. In prehistoric times, our ancestors huddled around campfires to hear tales of hunting and magic. In ancient times, warriors gathered in halls to listen to bards praise in song the exploits of epic heroes. Things are no different today. Boisterous children invariably settle down to listen when their parents read to them; millions of people tune in day after day to the ongoing drama of their favorite soap operas; vacationers sit motionless on the beach, caught up in the latest best-sellers; and all of us enjoy saying, "Just listen to what happened to me today." Our hunger for storytelling is a basic part of us.

Narration means telling a single story or several related stories. The story can be a way to support a main idea or thesis. For instance, to demonstrate that television has become the constant companion of many children, you might narrate a typical child's day in front of the television—from frantic cartoons in the morning to dizzy situation comedies at night.

Narration is powerful. Every public speaker, from politician to classroom teacher, knows that stories capture the attention of listeners as nothing else can. Narration speaks to us strongly because it is about us; we want to know what happened to others, not simply because we're curious, but because their experiences shed light on the nature of our own lives. Narration lends force to opinions, triggers the flow of memory, and evokes places and times in ways that are compelling and affecting.

HOW NARRATION FITS YOUR PURPOSE AND AUDIENCE

Narration can appear in essays as a supplemental pattern of development. For example, if your purpose in a paper is to *persuade* apathetic readers that airport security regulations must be followed strictly, you might lead off with a brief account of a friend who inadvertently tried to board a plane with a pocket knife in his backpack. In a paper *defining* good teaching, you might keep readers engaged by including satirical anecdotes about one hapless instructor, the antithesis of an effective teacher. An essay on the *effects* of an overburdened judicial system might provide a dramatic account of the way one clearly guilty murderer plea-bargained his way to freedom.

Narration can also serve as an essay's dominant pattern of development. You might choose to narrate the events of a day spent with your three-year-old nephew as a way of revealing how you rediscovered the importance of family life. Or you might relate the story of your roommate's mugging, evoking the powerlessness and terror of being a victim. Any story can form the basis for a narrative essay as long as you convey the essence of the experience and evoke its meaning.

At this point, you have a good sense of the way writers use narration to achieve their purpose and to connect with their readers. Now take a moment to look closely at the photograph at the beginning of this chapter. Imagine you're writing a "Recent Events" update, accompanied by the photo, for the website of an organization that supports (*or* opposes) the wars in Iraq and Afghanistan. Your purpose is to recount what happened at the protest in a way that supports the website's position. Jot down some phrases you might use when *narrating* the events of the day.

SUGGESTIONS FOR USING NARRATION IN AN ESSAY

The suggestions here and in Figure 4.1 on page 128 will be helpful whether you use narration as a dominant or a supportive pattern of development.

1. Identify the conflict in the event. The power of many narratives is rooted in a special kind of tension that "hooks" readers and makes them want

FIGURE 4.1
Development Diagram: Writing a Narration Essay

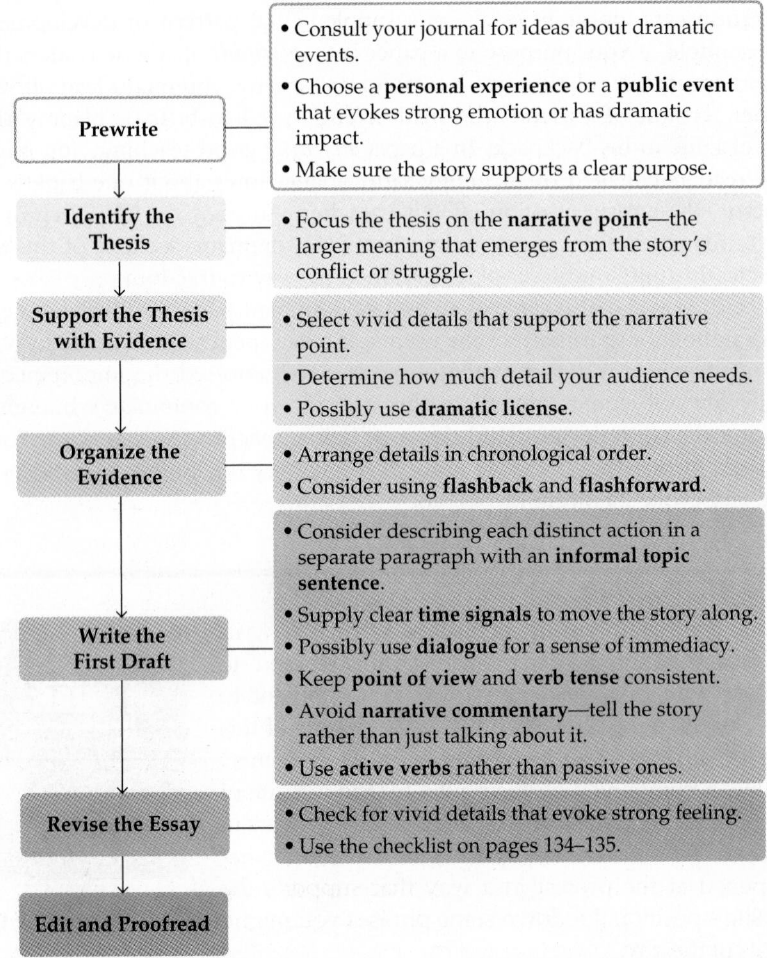

to follow the story to its end. This narrative tension is often a by-product of some form of *conflict* within the story. Many narratives revolve around an internal conflict experienced by a key person in the story. Or the conflict may be between people in the story or between a pivotal character and some social institution or natural phenomenon.

Prewrite
• Consult your journal for ideas about dramatic events.
• Choose a personal experience or a public event that evokes strong emotion or has dramatic impact.
• Make sure the story supports a clear purpose.
Identify the Thesis
• Focus the thesis on the narrative point—the larger meaning that emerges from the story's conflict or struggle.
Support the Thesis with Evidence
• Select vivid details that support the narrative point.
• Determine how much detail your audience needs.
• Possibly use dramatic license.
Organize the Evidence
• Arrange details in chronological order.
• Consider using flashback and flashforward.
Write the First Draft
• Consider describing each distinct action in a separate paragraph with an informal topic sentence.
• Supply clear time signals to move the story along.
• Possibly use dialogue for a sense of immediacy.
• Keep point of view and verb tense consistent.
• Avoid narrative commentary—tell the story rather than just talking about it.
• Use active verbs rather than passive ones.
Revise the Essay
• Check for vivid details that evoke strong feeling.
• Use the checklist on pages 134–135.
Edit and Proofread

2. Identify the point of the narrative. In *The Adventures of Huckleberry Finn,* Mark Twain warned: "Persons attempting to find a motive in this narrative will be prosecuted; persons attempting to find a moral in it will be banished; persons attempting to find a plot in it will be shot." Twain was, of course, being ironic; his novel's richness lies in its "motives" and "morals." Similarly, when you recount a narrative, it's your responsibility to convey the event's *significance* or *meaning.* In other words, be sure readers are clear about your *narrative point,* or thesis.

Suppose you decide to write about the time you got locked in a mall late at night. Your narrative might focus on the way the mall looked after hours and the way you struggled with mounting terror. But you would also use the narrative to make a point. Perhaps you want to emphasize that fear can be instructive. Or your point might be that malls have a disturbing, surreal underside. You could state this thesis explicitly. ("After hours, the mall shed its cheerful daytime demeanor and took on a more sinister quality.") Or you could rely on your details and language to convey the point of the narrative: "The mannequins stared at me with glazed eyes and frozen smiles" and "The steel grates pulled over each store's entrance glinted in the cold light, making each shop look like a prison cell."

3. Develop only those details that advance the narrative point. You know from experience that nothing is more boring than a storyteller who gets sidetracked and drags out a story with nonessential details. If a friend started to tell about the time his car broke down in the middle of an expressway—but interrupted his story to complain at length about the slipshod work done by his auto repair shop—you might become annoyed, wishing your friend would get back to the interesting part of the story.

Brainstorming ("What happened? When? Where? Who was involved? Why did it happen?") can be valuable for helping you amass narrative details. Then, after generating the specifics, you cull the nonessential and devote your energies to the key specifics needed to advance your narrative point. When telling a story, you maintain an effective narrative pace by focusing on that point and eliminating details that don't support it. A good narrative depends not only on what is included, but also on what has been left out.

But how do you determine which specifics to omit, which to treat briefly, and which to emphasize? Having a clear sense of your narrative point and knowing your audience are crucial. Assume you're writing a narrative about a disastrous get-acquainted dance sponsored by your college the first week of the academic year. In addition to telling what happened, you want to make a point; perhaps you want to emphasize that, despite the college's good intentions, such official events actually make it difficult to meet people. So you might write about how stiff and unnatural students seemed, all dressed up in their best clothes; you might narrate snatches of strained conversation; you might describe the way males gathered on one side of the room, females on the other—reverting to behaviors supposedly abandoned in fifth grade. All these details would support your narrative point.

Because you don't want to get away from that point, you would leave out details about the topnotch band and the appetizing refreshments. The music and food may have been surprisingly good, but since these details don't advance the point you want to make, they should be omitted.

You also need to keep your audience in mind when selecting narrative details. If the audience consists of your instructor and other students—all of them familiar with the new student center where the dance was held—specific details about the center probably wouldn't have to be provided. But imagine that the essay is going to appear in the quarterly magazine published by the college's community relations office. Many of the magazine's readers are former graduates who haven't been on campus for several years. They may need some additional specifics about the student center: its location, how many people it holds, how it is furnished.

As you write, keep asking yourself, "Is this detail or character or snippet of conversation essential? Does my audience need this detail to understand the conflict in the situation? Does this detail advance or intensify the narrative action?" Summarize details that have some importance but do not deserve lengthy treatment ("Two hours went by..."). And try to limit *narrative commentary*—statements that tell rather than show what happened—since such remarks interrupt the narrative flow. Focus instead on the specifics that propel action forward in a vigorous way.

Sometimes, especially if the narrative re-creates an event from the past, you won't be able to remember what happened detail for detail. In such a case, you should take advantage of what is called *dramatic license*. Using as a guide your powers of recall as well as the perspective you now have of that particular time, feel free to reshape events to suit your narrative point.

4. Organize the narrative sequence. Every narrative begins somewhere, presents a span of time, and ends at a certain point. Frequently, you'll want to use a straightforward time order, following the event *chronologically* from beginning to end: first this happened, next this happened, finally this happened.

But sometimes a strict chronological recounting may not be effective—especially if the high point of the narrative gets lost somewhere in the middle of the time sequence. To avoid that possibility, you may want to disrupt chronology, plunge the reader into the middle of the story, and then return in a *flashback* to the beginning of the tale. You're probably familiar with the way flashback is used on television and in film. You see someone appealing to the main character for financial help, then return to an earlier time when both were students in the same class, before learning how the rest of the story unfolds. Narratives can also use *flashforward*. You give readers a glimpse of the future (the main character being jailed) before the story continues in the present (the events leading to the arrest). These techniques shift the story onto several planes and keep it from becoming a step-by-step, predictable account. Reserve flashforwards and flashbacks, however, for crucial incidents only, since breaking out of chronological order acts as emphasis. Here are examples of how flashback and flashforward can be used:

Flashback

Standing behind the wooden counter, Greg wielded his knife expertly as he shucked clams—one every ten seconds—with practiced ease. The scene contrasted sharply with his first day on the job, when his hands broke out in blisters and when splitting each shell was like prying open a safe.

Flashforward

Rushing to move my car from the no-parking zone, I waved a quick goodbye to Karen as she climbed the steps to the bus. I didn't know then that by the time I picked her up at the bus station later that day, she had made a decision that would affect both our lives.

Whether or not you choose to include flashbacks or flashforwards in an essay, remember to limit the time span covered by the narrative. Otherwise, you will have trouble generating the details needed to give the story depth and meaning. Also, regardless of the time sequence you select, organize the tale so that it drives toward a strong finish. Be careful that your story doesn't trail off into minor, anticlimactic details.

5. Make the narrative easy to follow. Describing each distinct action in a separate paragraph helps readers grasp the flow of events. Although narrative essays don't always have conventional topic sentences, each narrative paragraph should have a clear focus. Often this focus is indicated by a sentence early in the paragraph that directs attention to the action taking place. Such a sentence functions as a kind of *informal topic sentence;* the rest of the paragraph then develops that topic sentence. You should also be sure to use time signals when narrating a story. Words like *now, then, next, after,* and *later* ensure that your reader won't get lost as the story progresses.

6. Make the narrative vigorous and immediate. A compelling narrative provides an abundance of specific details, making readers feel as if they're experiencing the story being told. Readers must be able to see, hear, touch, smell, and taste the event you're narrating. *Vivid sensory description* is, therefore, an essential part of an effective narrative. Not only do specific sensory details make writing a pleasure to read—we all enjoy learning the particulars about people, places, and things—but they also give the narrative the stamp of reality. The specifics convince the reader that the event actually did, or could, occur.

Compare the following excerpts from a narrative essay. The first version is lifeless and dull; the revised version, packed with sensory images, grabs readers with its sense of foreboding:

That eventful day started out like every other summer day. My sister Tricia and I made several elaborate mud pies, which we decorated with care. A little later on, as we were spraying each other with the garden hose, we heard my father walk up the path.

That sad summer day started out uneventfully enough. My sister Tricia and I spent a few hours mixing and decorating mud pies. Our hands caked with dry mud, we sprinkled each lopsided pie with alternating rows of dandelion and clover petals. Later when the sun got hotter, we tossed our white T-shirts over the red picket fence–forgetting my grandmother's frequent warnings to be more ladylike. Our sweaty backs bared to the sun, we doused each other with icy sprays from the garden hose. Caught up in the primitive pleasure of it all, we barely heard my father as he walked up the garden path, the gravel crunching under his heavy work boots.

A caution: Sensory language enlivens narration, but it also slows the pace. Be sure that the slower pace suits your purpose. For example, a lengthy description fits an account of a leisurely summer vacation but is inappropriate in a tale about a frantic search for a misplaced wallet.

Another way to create an aura of narrative immediacy is to use ***dialogue.*** Our sense of other people comes, in part, from what they say and how they sound. Dialogue allows the reader to experience characters directly. Compare the following fragments of a narrative, one with dialogue and one without, noting how much more energetic the second version is.

When I finally found my way back to the campsite, the trail guide commented on my disheveled appearance.

When I finally found my way back to the campsite, the trail guide took one look at me and drawled, "What on earth happened to you, Daniel Boone? You look as though you've been dragged through a haystack backwards."

"I'd look a lot worse if I hadn't run back here. When a bullet whizzes by me, I don't stick around to see who's doing the shooting."

When using dialogue, begin a new paragraph to indicate a shift from one person's speech to another's (as in the second example above).

Using *varied sentence structure* is another strategy for making narratives lively and vigorous. Sentences that plod along predictably (subject-verb, subject-verb) put readers to sleep. Experiment with your sentences by juggling length and sentence type; mix long and short sentences, simple and complex. Compare the following original and revised versions to get an idea of how effective varied sentence rhythm can be in narrative writing.

Original

The store manager went to the walk-in refrigerator every day. The heavy metal door clanged shut behind her. I had visions of her freezing to death among the hanging carcasses. The shiny door finally swung open. She waddled out.

Revised

Each time the store manager went to the walk-in refrigerator, the heavy metal door clanged shut behind her. Visions of her freezing to death among the hanging carcasses crept into my mind until the shiny door finally swung open and she waddled out.

Original

The yellow-and-blue-striped fish struggled on the line. Its scales shimmered in the sunlight. Its tail waved frantically. I saw its desire to live. I decided to let it go.

Revised

Scales shimmering in the sunlight, tail waving frantically, the yellow-and-blue-striped fish struggled on the line. Seeing its desire to live, I let it go.

Finally, *vigorous verbs* lend energy to narratives. Use active verb forms ("The boss *yelled at* him") rather than passive ones ("He *was yelled at* by the boss"), and try to replace anemic *to be* verbs ("She *was* a good basketball player") with more dynamic constructions ("She *played* basketball well").

7. Keep your point of view and verb tense consistent. All stories have a *narrator,* the person who tells the story. If you, as narrator, tell a story as you experienced it, the story is written in the *first-person point of view* ("*I* saw the dog pull loose"). But if you observed the event (or heard about it from others) and want to tell how someone else experienced the incident, you would use the *third-person point of view* ("*Anne* saw the dog pull loose"). Each point of view has advantages and limitations. First person allows you to express ordinarily private thoughts and to re-create an event as you actually experienced it. This point of view is limited, though, in its ability to depict the inner thoughts of other people involved in the event. By way of contrast, third person makes it easier to provide insight into the thoughts of all the participants. However, its objective, broad perspective may undercut some of the subjective immediacy of the "I was there" point of view. No matter which you select, stay with that vantage point throughout the narrative.

Knowing whether to use the *past* or *present tense* ("I *strolled* into the room" as opposed to "I *stroll* into the room") is important. In most narrations, the past tense predominates, enabling the writer to span a considerable period of time. Although more rarely used, the present tense can be powerful for events of short duration—a wrestling match or a medical emergency, for instance. A narrative in the present tense prolongs each moment, intensifying the reader's sense of participation. Be careful, though; unless the event is intense and fast-paced, the present tense can seem contrived. Whichever tense you choose, avoid shifting midstream—starting, let's say, in the past tense ("she skated") and switching to the present ("she runs").

REVISION STRATEGIES

Once you have a draft of the essay, you're ready to revise. The following checklist will help you and those giving you feedback apply to narration some of the revision techniques discussed on pages 60–62.

☑ NARRATION: A REVISION/PEER REVIEW CHECKLIST

Revise Overall Meaning and Structure

- ❑ What is the essay's main point? Is it stated explicitly or is it implied? Where? Could the point be conveyed more clearly? How?
- ❑ What is the narrative's conflict? Is it stated explicitly or is it implied? Where? Could the conflict be made more dramatic? How?
- ❑ From what point of view is the narrative told? Is it the most effective point of view for this essay? Why or why not?

Revise Paragraph Development

- ❑ Which paragraphs fail to advance the action, reveal character, or contribute to the story's mood? Should these sections be condensed or eliminated?
- ❑ Where should the narrative pace be slowed down or quickened?
- ❑ Where is it difficult to follow the chronology of events? Should the order of paragraphs be changed? How? Where would additional time signals help?
- ❑ How could flashback or flashforward paragraphs be used to highlight key events?
- ❑ Would dramatic dialogue or mood-setting description help make the essay's opening paragraph more compelling?

- ❑ What could be done to make the essay's closing paragraph more effective? Should the essay end earlier? Should it close by echoing an idea or image from the opening?

Revise Sentences and Words

- ❑ Where is sentence structure monotonous? Where would combining sentences, mixing sentence types, and alternating sentence length help?
- ❑ Where could dialogue replace commentary to convey character and propel the story forward?
- ❑ Which sentences and words are inconsistent with the essay's tone?
- ❑ Where do vigorous verbs convey action? Where could active verbs replace passive ones? Where could dull *to be* verbs be converted to more dynamic forms?
- ❑ Where are there inappropriate shifts in point of view or verb tense?

STUDENT ESSAY

The following student essay was written by Paul Monahan in response to this assignment:

> In "Shooting an Elephant," George Orwell tells about an incident that forced him to act in a manner that ran counter to his better instincts. Write a narrative about a time when you faced a disturbing conflict and ended up doing something you later regretted.

While reading Paul's paper, try to determine how well it applies the principles of narration. The annotations on Paul's paper and the commentary following it will help you look at the essay more closely.

If Only
by Paul Monahan

Introduction

Narrative point (thesis)

Having worked at a 7-Eleven store for two years, I thought I had become successful at what our manager calls "customer relations." I firmly believed that a friendly smile and an automatic "sir," "ma'am," and "thank you" would see me through any situation that might arise, from soothing impatient or unpleasant people to apologizing for giving out the wrong change. But the other night an old woman shattered 1 my belief that a glib response could smooth over the rough spots of dealing with other human beings.

Informal topic sentence — The moment she entered, the woman presented a sharp contrast to our shiny store with its bright lighting and neatly arranged shelves. Walking as if each step were painful, she slowly pushed open the glass door and hobbled down the nearest aisle. She coughed dryly, wheezing with each breath. On a forty-degree night, she was wearing only a faded print dress, a thin, light beige sweater too small to button, and black vinyl slippers with the backs cut out to expose calloused heels. There were no stockings or socks on her splotchy, blue-veined legs. 2

Sensory details

After strolling around the store for several minutes, the old woman stopped in front of the rows of canned vegetables. She picked up some corn niblets and stared with a strange intensity at the label. At that point, I decided to be a good, courteous employee and asked her if she needed help. As I stood close to her, my smile became harder to maintain; her red-rimmed eyes were partially closed by yellowish crusts; her hands were covered with layer upon layer of grime; and the stale smell of sweat rose in a thick vaporous cloud from her clothes. 3

Informal topic sentence

Sensory details

Start of dialogue — "I need some food," she muttered in reply to my bright "Can I help you?" 4

"Are you looking for corn, ma'am?" 5

"I need some food," she repeated. "Any kind." 6

"Well, the corn is ninety-five cents," I said in my most helpful voice. "Or, if you like, we have a special on bologna today." 7

"I can't pay," she said. 8

Conflict established — For a second, I was tempted to say, "Take the corn." But the employee rules flooded into my mind: Remain polite, but do not let customers get the best of you. Let them know that you are in control. For a moment, I even entertained the idea that this was some sort of test, and that this woman was someone from the head office, testing my loyalty. I responded dutifully, "I'm sorry, ma'am, but I can't give away anything free." 9

Informal topic sentence — The old woman's face collapsed a bit more, if that were possible, and her hands trembled as she put the can back on the shelf. She shuffled past me toward the door, her torn and dirty clothing barely covering her bent back. 10

Conclusion

Moments after she left, I rushed out the door with the can of corn, but she was nowhere in sight. For the rest of my shift, the image of the woman haunted me. I had been young, healthy, and smug. She had been old, sick, and desperate. Wishing with all my heart that I had acted like a human being rather than a robot, I was saddened to realize how fragile a hold we have on our better instincts. 11

Echoing of narrative point in the introduction

COMMENTARY

Point of view, tense, and conflict. Paul chose to write "If Only" from the *first-person point of view,* a logical choice because he appears as a main character in his own story. Using the *past tense,* Paul recounts an incident filled with *conflicts*—between him and the woman and between his fear of breaking the rules and his human instinct to help someone in need.

Narrative point. It isn't always necessary to state the *narrative point* of an essay; it can be implied. But Paul decided to express the controlling idea of his narrative in two places—in the introduction ("But the other night an old woman shattered my belief that a glib response could smooth over the rough spots of dealing with other human beings") and again in the conclusion, where he expands his idea about rote responses overriding impulses of independent judgment and compassion. All of the essay's *narrative details* contribute to the point of the piece; Paul does not include any extraneous information that would detract from the central idea he wants to convey.

Organization. The narrative is *organized chronologically,* from the moment the woman enters the store to Paul's reaction after she leaves. Paul limits the narrative's time span. The entire incident probably occurs in under ten minutes, yet the introduction serves as a kind of *flashback* by providing some necessary background about Paul's past experiences. To help the reader follow the course of the narrative, Paul uses *time signals: "The moment* she entered, the woman presented a sharp contrast" (paragraph 2); "*At that point,* I decided to be a good, courteous employee" (3); "*For the rest of my shift,* the image of the woman haunted me" (11).

The paragraphs (except for those consisting solely of dialogue) also contain *informal topic sentences* that direct attention to the specific stage of action being narrated. Indeed, each paragraph focuses on a distinct event: the elderly woman's actions when she first enters the store, the encounter between Paul and the woman, Paul's resulting inner conflict, the woman's subsequent response, and Paul's delayed reaction.

Combining patterns of development. This chronological chain of events, with one action leading to another, illustrates that the *cause-effect* pattern underlies the basic structure of Paul's essay. And by means of another pattern—*description*—Paul gives dramatic immediacy to the events being recounted. Throughout, he provides rich sensory details to engage the reader's interest. For instance, the sentence "her red-rimmed eyes were partially closed by yellowish crusts" (3) vividly re-creates the woman's appearance while also suggesting Paul's inner reaction to the woman.

Dialogue and sentence structure. Paul dramatizes the conflict through *dialogue* that crackles with tension. And he achieves a vigorous narrative pace by *varying the length and structure of his sentences.* In the second paragraph, a short sentence ("There were no stockings or socks on her splotchy, blue-veined legs") alternates with a longer one ("On a forty-degree night, she was wearing only a faded print dress, a thin, light beige sweater too small to button, and black vinyl slippers with the backs cut out to expose calloused heels"). Some sentences open with a subject and verb ("She coughed dryly"), while others start with dependent clauses or participial phrases ("As I stood close to her, my smile became harder to maintain"; "Walking as if each step were painful, she slowly pushed open the glass door") or with a prepositional phrase ("For a second, I was tempted").

Revising the first draft. Comparing the final version of the essay's third paragraph with the following preliminary version reveals some of the changes Paul made while revising the essay.

Original Version of the Third Paragraph

After sneezing and hacking her way around the store, the old woman stopped in front of the vegetable shelves. She picked up a can of corn and stared at the label. She stayed like this for several minutes. Then I walked over to her and asked if I could be of help.

After putting the original draft aside for a while, Paul reread his paper aloud and realized the third paragraph especially lacked power. So he decided to add compelling descriptive details about the woman ("the stale smell of sweat," for example). Also, by expanding and combining sentences, he gave the paragraph an easier, more graceful rhythm. Much of the time, revision involves paring down excess material. In this case, though, Paul made the right decision to elaborate his sentences. Furthermore, he added the following comment to the third paragraph: "I decided to be a good, courteous employee." These few words introduce an appropriate note of irony and serve to echo the essay's controlling idea.

Finally, Paul decided to omit the words "sneezing and hacking" because he realized they were too comic or light for his subject. Still, the first sentence in the revised paragraph is somewhat jarring. The word *strolling* isn't quite appropriate since it implies a leisurely grace inconsistent with the impression he wants to convey. Replacing *strolling* with, say, *shuffling* would bring the image more into line with the essay's overall mood.

Despite this slight problem, Paul's revisions are right on the mark. The changes he made strengthened his essay, turning it into a more evocative, more polished piece of narrative writing.

Activities: Narration

Prewriting Activities

1. Imagine you're writing two essays: One analyzes the *effect* of insensitive teachers on young children; the other *argues* the importance of family traditions. With the help of your journal or freewriting, identify different narratives you could use to open each essay.

2. For each of the situations below, identify two different conflicts that would make a story worth relating. Then prepare six to ten lines of natural-sounding dialogue for each potential conflict in *one* of the situations.
   a. Going to the supermarket with a friend
   b. Telling your parents which college you've decided to attend
   c. Participating in a demonstration
   d. Preparing for an exam in a difficult course

Revising Activities

1. Revise each of the following narrative sentence groups twice: once with words that carry negative connotations, and again with words that carry positive connotations. Use varied sentence structure, sensory details, and vigorous verbs to convey mood.
   a. The bell rang. It rang loudly. Students knew the last day of class was over.
   b. Last weekend, our neighbors burned leaves in their yard. We went over to speak with them.
   c. The sun shone in through my bedroom window. It made me sit up in bed. Daylight was finally here, I told myself.

2. The following paragraph is the introduction from the first draft of an essay proposing harsher penalties for drunk drivers. Revise this narrative paragraph to make it more effective. How can you make sentence structure less predictable? Which details should you delete? As you revise, provide language that conveys the event's sights, smells, and sounds. Also, clarify the chronological sequence.

   As I drove down the street in my bright blue sports car, I saw a car coming rapidly around the curve. The car didn't slow down as it headed toward the traffic light. The light turned yellow and then red. A young couple, dressed like models, started crossing the street. When the woman saw the car, she called out to her husband. He jumped onto the shoulder. The man wasn't hurt but, seconds later, it was clear the woman was. I ran to a nearby emergency phone and called the police. The ambulance arrived, but the woman was already dead. The driver, who looked terrible, failed the sobriety test, and the police found out that he had two previous offenses. It's apparent that better ways have to be found for getting drunk drivers off the road.

Audre Lorde

Named poet laureate of the state of New York in 1991, Audre Lorde (1934–92) was a New Yorker born of African-Caribbean parents. After earning degrees at Hunter College and Columbia University, Lorde held numerous teaching positions throughout the New York City area. She later toured the world as a lecturer, forming women's rights coalitions in the Caribbean, Africa, and Europe. Best known as a feminist theorist, Lorde combined social criticism and personal revelation in her writing on such topics as race, gender relations, and sexuality. Her numerous poems and nonfiction pieces were published in a variety of magazines and literary journals. Her books include *The Black Unicorn: Poems* (1978), *Sister Outsider: Essays and Speeches* (1984), and *A Burst of Light* (1988). The following selection is an excerpt from her autobiography, *Zami: A New Spelling of My Name* (1982).

For ideas about how this narration essay is organized, see Figure 4.2 on page 144.

Pre-Reading Journal Entry

When you were a child, what beliefs about the United States did you have? List these beliefs. For each, indicate whether subsequent experience maintained or shattered your childhood understanding of these beliefs. Take a little time to explore these issues in your journal.

The Fourth of July

The first time I went to Washington, D.C., was on the edge of the summer when I was supposed to stop being a child. At least that's what they said to us all at graduation from the eighth grade. My sister Phyllis graduated at the same time from high school. I don't know what she was supposed to stop being. But as graduation presents for us both, the whole family took a Fourth of July trip to Washington, D.C., the fabled and famous capital of our country. 1

It was the first time I'd ever been on a railroad train during the day. When I was little, and we used to go to the Connecticut shore, we always went at night on the milk train, because it was cheaper. 2

Preparations were in the air around our house before school was even over. We packed for a week. There were two very large suitcases that my father carried, and a box filled with food. In fact, my first trip to Washington was a mobile feast; I started eating as soon as we were comfortably ensconced in our seats, and did not stop until somewhere after Philadelphia. I remember it was Philadelphia because I was disappointed not to have passed by the Liberty Bell. 3

My mother had roasted two chickens and cut them up into dainty bite-size pieces. She packed slices of brown bread and butter and green pepper 4 and carrot sticks. There were little violently yellow iced cakes with scalloped edges called "marigolds," that came from Cushman's Bakery. There was a spice bun and rock-cakes from Newton's, the West Indian bakery across Lenox Avenue from St. Mark's School, and iced tea in a wrapped mayonnaise jar. There were sweet pickles for us and dill pickles for my father, and peaches with the fuzz still on them, individually wrapped to keep them from bruising. And, for neatness, there were piles of napkins and a little tin box with a washcloth dampened with rosewater and glycerine for wiping sticky mouths.

I wanted to eat in the dining car because I had read all about them, but my mother reminded me for the umpteenth time that dining car food always costs too much money and besides, you never could tell whose hands had been playing all over that food, nor where those same hands had been just before. My mother never mentioned that Black people were not allowed into railroad dining cars headed south in 1947. As usual, whatever my mother did not like and could not change, she ignored. Perhaps it would go away, deprived of her attention. 5

I learned later that Phyllis's high school senior class trip had been to Washington, but the nuns had given her back her deposit in private, explaining to her that the class, all of whom were white, except Phyllis, would be staying in a hotel where Phyllis "would not be happy," meaning, Daddy explained to her, also in private, that they did not rent rooms to Negroes. "We will take you to Washington, ourselves," my father had avowed, "and not just for an overnight in some measly fleabag hotel." 6

American racism was a new and crushing reality that my parents had to deal with every day of their lives once they came to this country. They handled it as a private woe. My mother and father believed that they could best protect their children from the realities of race in america and the fact of american racism by never giving them name, much less discussing their nature. We were told we must never trust white people, but *why* was never explained, nor the nature of their ill will. Like so many other vital pieces of information in my childhood, I was supposed to know without being told. It always seemed like a very strange injunction coming from my mother, who looked so much like one of those people we were never supposed to trust. But something always warned me not to ask my mother why she wasn't white, and why Auntie Lillah and Auntie Etta weren't, even though they were all that same problematic color so different from my father and me, even from my sisters, who were somewhere in-between. 7

In Washington, D.C., we had one large room with two double beds and an extra cot for me. It was a back-street hotel that belonged to a friend of my father's who was in real estate, and I spent the whole next day after Mass 8 squinting up at the Lincoln Memorial where Marian Anderson[1] had sung after the D.A.R.[2] refused to allow her to sing in their auditorium because she was Black. Or because she was "Colored," my father said as he told us the story. Except that what he probably said was "Negro," because for his time, my father was quite progressive.

I was squinting because I was in that silent agony that characterized all of my childhood summers, from the time school let out in June to the end of July, brought about by my dilated and vulnerable eyes exposed to the summer brightness. 9

I viewed Julys through an agonizing corolla of dazzling whiteness and I always hated the Fourth of July, even before I came to realize the travesty such a celebration was for Black people in this country. 10

My parents did not approve of sunglasses, nor of their expense. 11

I spent the afternoon squinting up at monuments to freedom and past presidencies and democracy, and wondering why the light and heat were both so much stronger in Washington, D.C., than back home in New York City. Even the pavement on the streets was a shade lighter in color than back home. 12

Late that Washington afternoon my family and I walked back down Pennsylvania Avenue. We were a proper caravan, mother bright and father brown, the three of us girls step-standards in-between. Moved by our historical surroundings and the heat of the early evening, my father decreed yet another treat. He had a great sense of history, a flair for the quietly dramatic and the sense of specialness of an occasion and a trip. 13

"Shall we stop and have a little something to cool off, Lin?" 14

Two blocks away from our hotel, the family stopped for a dish of vanilla ice cream at a Breyer's ice cream and soda fountain. Indoors, the soda fountain was dim and fan-cooled, deliciously relieving to my scorched eyes. 15

Corded and crisp and pinafored, the five of us seated ourselves one by one at the counter. There was I between my mother and father, and my two sisters on the other side of my mother. We settled ourselves along the white mottled marble counter, and when the waitress spoke at first no one understood what she was saying, and so the five of us just sat there. 16

The waitress moved along the line of us closer to my father and spoke again. "I said I kin give you to take out, but you can't eat here. Sorry." Then she dropped her eyes looking very embarrassed, and suddenly we heard what it was she was saying all at the same time, loud and clear. 17

[1]Acclaimed African-American opera singer (1902–93), famed for her renderings of Black spirituals (editors' note).

[2]Daughters of the American Revolution. A society, founded in 1890, for women who can prove direct lineage to soldiers or others who aided in winning American independence from Great Britain during the Revolutionary War (1775–83) (editors' note).

Straight-backed and indignant, one by one, my family and I got down from the counter stools and turned around and marched out of the store, quiet and outraged, as if we had never been Black before. No one would answer my emphatic questions with anything other than a guilty silence. "But we hadn't done anything!" This wasn't right or fair! Hadn't I written poems about Bataan and freedom and democracy for all? 18

My parents wouldn't speak of this injustice, not because they had contributed to it, but because they felt they should have anticipated it and avoided it. This made me even angrier. My fury was not going to be acknowledged by a like fury. Even my two sisters copied my parents' pretense that nothing unusual and anti-american had occurred. I was left to write my angry letter to the president of the united states all by myself, although my father did promise I could type it out on the office typewriter next week, after I showed it to him in my copybook diary. 19

The waitress was white, and the counter was white, and the ice cream I never ate in Washington, D.C., that summer I left childhood was white, and the white heat and the white pavement and the white stone monuments of my first Washington summer made me sick to my stomach for the whole rest of that trip and it wasn't much of a graduation present after all. 20

Questions for Close Reading

1. What is the selection's thesis (or narrative point)? Locate the sentence(s) in which Lorde states her main idea. If she doesn't state the thesis explicitly, express it in your own words.
2. In paragraph 4, Lorde describes the elaborate picnic her mother prepared for the trip to Washington, D.C. Why did Lorde's mother make such elaborate preparations? What do these preparations tell us about Lorde's mother?
3. Why does Lorde have trouble understanding her parents' dictate that she "never trust white people" (paragraph 7)?
4. In general, how do Lorde's parents handle racism? How does the family as a whole deal with the racism they encounter in the ice-cream parlor? How does the family's reaction to the ice-cream parlor incident make Lorde feel?
5. Refer to your dictionary as needed to define the following words used in the selection: *fabled* (paragraph 1), *injunction* (7), *progressive* (8), *dilated* (9), *vulnerable* (9), *travesty* (10), *decreed* (13), and *pretense* (19).

Questions About the Writer's Craft

1. **The pattern.** What techniques does Lorde use to help readers follow the unfolding of the story as it occurs in both time and space?
2. When telling a story, skilled writers limit narrative commentary—statements that tell rather than show what happened—because it tends to interrupt the narrative flow. Lorde, however, provides narrative commentary in several spots. Find these instances. How is the information she provides essential to her narrative?

FIGURE 4.2
Essay Structure Diagram: "The Fourth of July" by Audre Lorde

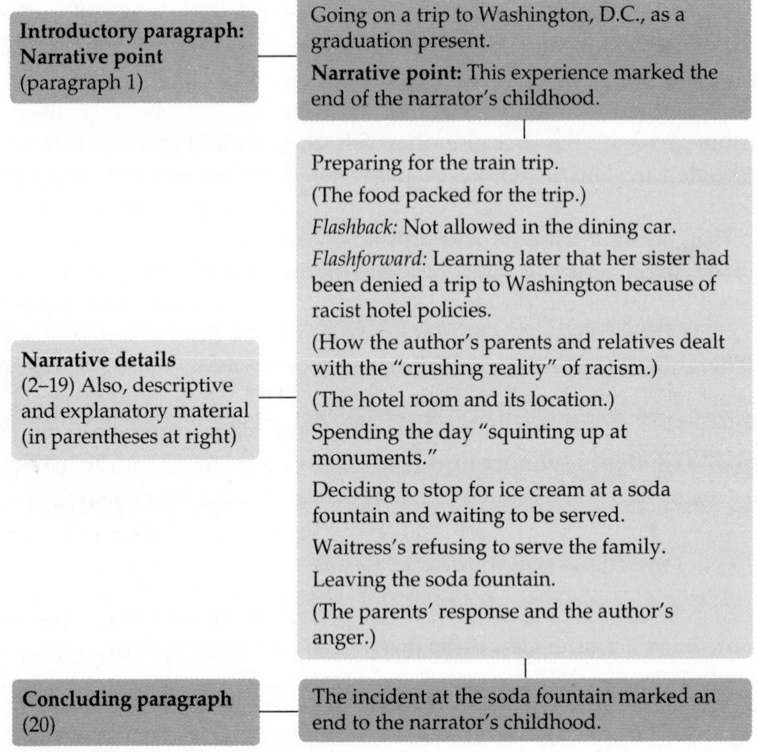

Introductory paragraph: Narrative point (paragraph 1)
Going on a trip to Washington, D.C., as a graduation present.
Narrative point: This experience marked the end of the narrator's childhood.
Narrative details (2–19) Also, descriptive and explanatory material (in parentheses at right)
Preparing for the train trip.
(The food packed for the trip.)
Flashback: Not allowed in the dining car.
Flashforward: Learning later that her sister had been denied a trip to Washington because of racist hotel policies.
(How the author's parents and relatives dealt with the "crushing reality" of racism.)
(The hotel room and its location.)
Spending the day "squinting up at monuments."
Deciding to stop for ice cream at a soda fountain and waiting to be served.
Waitress's refusing to serve the family.
Leaving the soda fountain.
(The parents' response and the author's anger.)
Concluding paragraph (20)
The incident at the soda fountain marked an end to the narrator's childhood.

3. In paragraphs 7 and 19, Lorde uses all lowercase letters for *America, American,* and *President of the United States.* Why do you suppose she doesn't follow the rules of capitalization? In what ways does her rejection of these rules reinforce what she is trying to convey through the essay's title?
4. What key word does Lorde repeat in paragraph 20? What effect do you think she hopes the repetition will have on readers?

Writing Assignments Using Narration as a Pattern of Development

1. Lorde recounts an incident during which she was treated unfairly. Write a narrative about a time when either you were treated unjustly or you treated someone else in an unfair manner. Like Lorde, use vivid details to make the incident come alive and to convey how it affected you. George Orwell's "Shooting an Elephant" (page 146) and Barbara Ehrenreich's "Serving in Florida" (page 162) will prompt some ideas worth exploring.

2. Write a narrative about an experience that dramatically changed your view of the world. The experience might have been jarring and painful, or it may have been positive and uplifting. In either case, recount the incident with compelling narrative details. To illustrate the shift in your perspective, begin with a brief statement of the way you viewed the world before the experience. The following essays provide insight into the way a single experience can alter one's understanding of the world: Maya Angelou's "Sister Flowers" (page 87) Langston Hughes's "Salvation" (page 158).

Writing Assignments Combining Patterns of Development

3. Lorde suggests that her parents use the coping mechanism of denial to deal with life's harsh realities, writing that whatever her mother "did not like and could not change, she ignored." Refer to a psychology textbook to learn more about denial. When is it productive? Counterproductive? Drawing upon your own experiences as well as those of friends, family, and classmates, write an essay *contrasting* effective and ineffective uses of denial. Near the end of the paper, present brief *guidelines* that will help readers identify when denial may be detrimental.
4. In her essay, Lorde decries and by implication takes a strong stance against racial discrimination. Brainstorm with friends, family members, and classmates to identify other injustices in American society. You might begin by considering attitudes toward the elderly, the overweight, the physically disabled; the funding of schools in poor and affluent neighborhoods; the portrayal of a specific ethnic group on television; and so on. Focusing on *one* such injustice, write an essay *arguing* that such an injustice indeed exists. To document the nature and extent of the injustice, use the library and/or Internet research. You should also consider *recounting* your own and other people's experiences. Acknowledge and, when you can, dismantle the views of those who think there isn't a problem.

Writing Assignment Using a Journal Entry as a Starting Point

5. Write an essay comparing and/or contrasting the beliefs you had about the United States as a child with those you have as an adult. Review your prereading journal entry, and select *one* American belief to focus on. Provide strong, dramatic examples that show why your childhood belief in this concept has been strengthened or weakened. Before writing, you should consider reading Juan Williams's "The Ruling That Changed America" (page 408), about the impact of desegregation, and Stanley Fish's "Free-Speech Follies" (page 509), a strongly argued examination of rights covered by the First Amendment of the Constitution.

George Orwell

Born Eric Blair in the former British colony of India, George Orwell (1903–50) is probably best known for his two novels, *Animal Farm* (1946) and *1984* (1949), both searing depictions of totalitarian societies. Orwell was also the author of numerous books and essays, many based on his diverse life experiences. He served with the Indian imperial police in Burma, worked at various jobs in London and Paris, and fought in the Spanish Civil War. His experiences in Burma provide the basis for the following essay, which is taken from his collection, *Shooting an Elephant and Other Essays* (1950).

Pre-Reading Journal Entry

Think of times when you were keenly aware of institutional injustice—an action, law, or regulation that was legally in the right but that you felt was wrong. In your journal, record several such examples. Why do you consider them wrong? Have you always felt that way? If not, what changed your opinion?

Shooting an Elephant

In Moulmein, in Lower Burma, I was hated by large numbers of people—the only time in my life that I have been important enough for this to happen to me. I was sub-divisional police officer of the town, and in an aimless, petty kind of way anti-European feeling was very bitter. No one had the guts to raise a riot, but if a European woman went through the bazaars alone somebody would probably spit betel juice over her dress. As a police officer I was an obvious target and was baited whenever it seemed safe to do so. When a nimble Burman tripped me up on the football field and the referee (another Burman) looked the other way, the crowd yelled with hideous laughter. This happened more than once. In the end the sneering yellow faces of young men that met me everywhere, the insults hooted after me when I was at a safe distance, got badly on my nerves. The young Buddhist priests were the worst of all. There were several thousand of them in the town and none of them seemed to have anything to do except stand on street corners and jeer at Europeans. 1

All this was perplexing and upsetting. For at that time I had already made up my mind that imperialism was an evil thing and the sooner I chucked up my job and got out of it the better. Theoretically—and secretly, of course—I was all for the Burmese and all against their oppressors, the British. As for the job I was doing, I hated it more bitterly than I can perhaps make clear. In a job like that you see the dirty work of Empire at close quarters. The wretched prisoners huddling in the stinking cages of the lock-ups, the grey, 2 cowed faces of the long-term convicts, the scarred buttocks of the men who had been flogged with bamboos—all these oppressed me with an intolerable sense of guilt. But I could get nothing into perspective. I was young and ill-educated and I had had to think out my problems in the utter silence that is imposed on every Englishman in the East. I did not even know that the British Empire is dying, still less did I know that it is a great deal better than the younger empires that are going to supplant it. All I knew was that I was stuck between my hatred of the empire I served and my rage against the evil-spirited little beasts who tried to make my job impossible. With one part of my mind I thought of the British Raj as an unbreakable tyranny, as something clamped down, in *saecula saeculorum,*[1] upon the will of prostrate peoples; with another part I thought that the greatest joy in the world would be to drive a bayonet into a Buddhist priest's guts. Feelings like these are the normal by-products of imperialism; ask any Anglo-Indian official, if you can catch him off duty.

One day something happened which in a roundabout way was enlightening. It was a tiny incident in itself, but it gave me a better glimpse than I had had before of the real nature of imperialism—the real motives for which despotic governments act. Early one morning the sub-inspector at a police station at the other end of the town rang me up on the 'phone and said that an elephant was ravaging the bazaar. Would I please come and do something about it? I did not know what I could do, but I wanted to see what was happening and I got onto a pony and started out. I took my rifle, an old .44 Winchester and much too small to kill an elephant, but I thought the noise might be useful *in terrorem.*[2] Various Burmans stopped me on the way and told me about the elephant's doings. It was not, of course, a wild elephant, but a tame one which had gone "must." It had been chained up, as tame elephants always are when their attack of "must" is due, but on the previous night it had broken its chain and escaped. Its mahout, the only person who could manage it when it was in that state, had set out in pursuit, but had taken the wrong direction and was now twelve hours' journey away, and in the morning the elephant had suddenly reappeared in the town. The Burmese population had no weapons and were quite helpless against it. It had already destroyed somebody's bamboo hut, killed a cow and raided some fruit-stalls and devoured the stock; also it had met the municipal rubbish van and, when the driver jumped out and took to his heels, had turned the van over and inflicted violence upon it. 3

The Burmese sub-inspector and some Indian constables were waiting for me in the quarter where the elephant had been seen. It was a very poor quarter, a labyrinth of squalid bamboo huts, thatched with palm-leaf, winding all over a steep hillside. I remember that it was a cloudy, stuffy morning 4

[1]For ever and ever (editors' note).
[2]As a warning (editors' note).

at the beginning of the rains. We began questioning the people as to where the elephant had gone and, as usual, failed to get any definite information. That is invariably the case in the East; a story always sounds clear enough at a distance, but the nearer you get to the scene of events the vaguer it becomes. Some of the people said that the elephant had gone in one direction, some said that he had gone in another, some professed not even to have heard of any elephant. I had almost made up my mind that the whole story was a pack of lies, when we heard yells a little distance away. There was a loud, scandalized cry of "Go away, child! Go away this instant!" and an old woman with a switch in her hand came round the corner of a hut, violently shooing away a crowd of naked children. Some more women followed, clicking their tongues and exclaiming; evidently there was something that the children ought not to have seen. I rounded the hut and saw a man's dead body sprawling in the mud. He was an Indian, a black Dravidian coolie, almost naked, and he could not have been dead many minutes. The people said that the elephant had come suddenly upon him round the corner of the hut, caught him with its trunk, put its foot on his back and ground him into the earth. This was the rainy season and the ground was soft, and his face had scored a trench a foot deep and a couple of yards long. He was lying on his belly with arms crucified and head sharply twisted to one side. His face was coated with mud, the eyes wide open, the teeth bared and grinning with an expression of unendurable agony. (Never tell me, by the way, that the dead look peaceful. Most of the corpses I have seen looked devilish.) The friction of the great beast's foot had stripped the skin from his back as neatly as one skins a rabbit. As soon as I saw the dead man I sent an orderly to a friend's house nearby to borrow an elephant rifle. I had already sent back the pony, not wanting it to go mad with fright and throw me if it smelt the elephant.

5 The orderly came back in a few minutes with a rifle and five cartridges, and meanwhile some Burmans had arrived and told us that the elephant was in the paddy fields below, only a few hundred yards away. As I started forward practically the whole population of the quarter flocked out of the houses and followed me. They had seen the rifle and were all shouting excitedly that I was going to shoot the elephant. They had not shown much interest in the elephant when he was merely ravaging their homes, but it was different now that he was going to be shot. It was a bit of fun to them, as it would be to an English crowd; besides they wanted the meat. It made me vaguely uneasy. I had no intention of shooting the elephant—I had merely sent for the rifle to defend myself if necessary—and it is always unnerving to have a crowd following you. I marched down the hill, looking and feeling a fool, with the rifle over my shoulder and an ever-growing army of people jostling at my heels. At the bottom, when you got away from the huts, there was a metalled road and beyond that a miry waste of paddy fields a thousand yards across, not yet ploughed but soggy from the first rains and dotted with

coarse grass. The elephant was standing eight yards from the road, his left side towards us. He took not the slightest notice of the crowd's approach. He was tearing up bunches of grass, beating them against his knees to clean them and stuffing them into his mouth.

I had halted on the road. As soon as I saw the elephant I knew with perfect certainty that I ought not to shoot him. It is a serious matter to shoot a working elephant—it is comparable to destroying a huge and costly piece of machinery—and obviously one ought not to do it if it can possibly be avoided. And at that distance, peacefully eating, the elephant looked no more dangerous than a cow. I thought then and I think now that his attack of "must" was already passing off; in which case he would merely wander harmlessly about until the mahout came back and caught him. Moreover, I did not in the least want to shoot him. I decided that I would watch him for a little while to make sure that he did not turn savage again, and then go home. 6

But at that moment I glanced round at the crowd that had followed me. It was an immense crowd, two thousand at the least and growing every minute. It blocked the road for a long distance on either side. I looked at the sea of yellow faces above the garish clothes—faces all happy and excited over this bit of fun, all certain that the elephant was going to be shot. They were watching me as they would watch a conjurer about to perform a trick. They did not like me, but with the magical rifle in my hands I was momentarily worth watching. And suddenly I realized that I should have to shoot the elephant after all. The people expected it of me and I had got to do it; I could feel their two thousand wills pressing me forward, irresistibly. And it was at this moment, as I stood there with the rifle in my hands, that I first grasped the hollowness, the futility of the white man's dominion in the East. Here was I, the white man with his gun, standing in front of the unarmed native crowd—seemingly the leading actor of the piece; but in reality I was only an absurd puppet pushed to and fro by the will of those yellow faces behind. I perceived in this moment that when the white man turns tyrant it is his own freedom that he destroys. He becomes a sort of hollow, posing dummy, the conventionalized figure of a sahib. For it is the condition of his rule that he shall spend his life in trying to impress the "natives," and so in every crisis he has got to do what the "natives" expect of him. He wears a mask, and his face grows to fit it. I had got to shoot the elephant. I had committed myself to doing it when I sent for the rifle. A sahib has got to act like a sahib; he has got to appear resolute, to know his own mind and do definite things. To come all that way, rifle in hand, with two thousand people marching at my heels, and then to trail feebly away, having done nothing—no, that was impossible. The crowd would laugh at me. And my whole life, every white man's life in the East, was one long struggle not to be laughed at. 7

But I did not want to shoot the elephant. I watched him beating his bunch of grass against his knees, with that preoccupied grandmotherly air 8 that elephants have. It seemed to me that it would be murder to shoot him. At that age I was not squeamish about killing animals, but I had never shot an elephant and never wanted to. (Somehow it always seems worse to kill a *large* animal.) Besides, there was the beast's owner to be considered. Alive, the elephant was worth at least a hundred pounds; dead, he would only be worth the value of his tusks, five pounds, possibly. But I had got to act quickly. I turned to some experienced-looking Burmans who had been there when we arrived, and asked them how the elephant had been behaving. They all said the same thing: he took no notice of you if you left him alone, but he might charge if you went too close to him.

It was perfectly clear to me what I ought to do. I ought to walk up to 9
within, say, twenty-five yards of the elephant and test his behavior. If he charged, I could shoot; if he took no notice of me, it would be safe to leave him until the mahout came back. But also I knew that I was going to do no such thing. I was a poor shot with a rifle and the ground was soft mud into which one would sink at every step. If the elephant charged and I missed him, I should have about as much chance as a toad under a steam-roller. But even then I was not thinking particularly of my own skin, only of the watchful yellow faces behind. For at that moment, with the crowd watching me, I was not afraid in the ordinary sense, as I would have been if I had been alone. A white man mustn't be frightened in front of "natives"; and so, in general, he isn't frightened. The sole thought in my mind was that if anything went wrong those two thousand Burmans would see me pursued, caught, trampled on and reduced to a grinning corpse like that Indian up the hill. And if that happened it was quite probable that some of them would laugh. That would never do. There was only one alternative. I shoved the cartridges into the magazine and lay down on the road to get a better aim.

The crowd grew very still, and a deep, low, happy sigh, as of people who 10
see the theatre curtain go up at last, breathed from innumerable throats. They were going to have their bit of fun after all. The rifle was a beautiful German thing with cross-hair sights. I did not then know that in shooting an elephant one would shoot to cut an imaginary bar running from ear-hole to ear-hole. I ought, therefore, as the elephant was sideway on, to have aimed straight at his ear-hole; actually I aimed several inches in front of this, thinking the brain would be further forward.

When I pulled the trigger I did not hear the bang or feel the kick—one 11
never does when a shot goes home—but I heard the devilish roar of glee that went up from the crowd. In that instant, in too short a time, one would have thought, even for the bullet to get there, a mysterious, terrible change had come over the elephant. He neither stirred nor fell, but every line of his body had altered. He looked suddenly stricken, shrunken, immensely old, as though the frightful impact of the bullet had paralyzed him without knocking him down. At last, after what seemed a long time—it might have been

five seconds, I dare say—he sagged flabbily to his knees. His mouth slobbered. An enormous senility seemed to have settled upon him. One could have imagined him thousands of years old. I fired again into the same spot. At the second shot he did not collapse but climbed with desperate slowness to his feet and stood weakly upright, with legs sagging and head drooping. I fired a third time. That was the shot that did for him. You could see the agony of it jolt his whole body and knock the last remnant of strength from his legs. But in falling he seemed for a moment to rise, for as his hind legs collapsed beneath him he seemed to tower upward like a huge rock toppling, his trunk reaching skywards like a tree. He trumpeted, for the first and only time. And then down he came, his belly towards me, with a crash that seemed to shake the ground even where I lay.

I got up. The Burmans were already racing past me across the mud. 12
It was obvious that the elephant would never rise again, but he was not dead. He was breathing very rhythmically with long rattling gasps, his great mound of a side painfully rising and falling. His mouth was wide open—I could see far down into caverns of pale pink throat. I waited a long time for him to die, but his breathing did not weaken. Finally I fired my two remaining shots into the spot where I thought his heart must be. The thick blood welled out of him like red velvet, but still he did not die. His body did not even jerk when the shots hit him, the tortured breathing continued without a pause. He was dying, very slowly and in great agony, but in some world remote from me where not even a bullet could damage him further. I felt that I had got to put an end to that dreadful noise. It seemed dreadful to see the great beast lying there, powerless to move and yet powerless to die, and not even to be able to finish him. I sent back for my small rifle and poured shot after shot into his heart and down his throat. They seemed to make no impression. The tortured gasps continued as steadily as the ticking of a clock.

In the end I could not stand it any longer and went away. I heard later 13
that it took him half an hour to die. Burmans were bringing dahs and baskets even before I left, and I was told they had stripped the body almost to the bones by the afternoon.

Afterwards, of course, there were endless discussions about the shooting 14
of the elephant. The owner was furious, but he was only an Indian and could do nothing. Besides, legally I had done the right thing, for a mad elephant has to be killed, like a mad dog, if its owner fails to control it. Among the Europeans opinion was divided. The older men said I was right, the younger men said it was a damn shame to shoot an elephant for killing a coolie, because an elephant was worth more than any damn Coringhee coolie. And afterwards I was very glad that the coolie had been killed; it put me legally in the right and it gave me a sufficient pretext for shooting the elephant. I often wondered whether any of the others grasped that I had done it solely to avoid looking a fool.

Questions for Close Reading

1. What is the selection's thesis (or narrative point)? Locate the sentence(s) in which Orwell states his main idea. If he doesn't state the thesis explicitly, express it in your own words.
2. How does Orwell feel about the Burmans? What words does he use to describe them?
3. What reasons does Orwell give for shooting the elephant?
4. In paragraph 3, Orwell says that the elephant incident gave him a better understanding of "the real motives for which despotic governments act." What do you think he means? Before you answer, reread paragraph 7 carefully.
5. Refer to your dictionary as needed to define the following words used in the selection: *imperialism* (paragraph 2), *prostrate* (2), *despotic* (3), *mahout* (3), *miry* (5), *conjurer* (7), *futility* (7), and *sahib* (7).

Questions About the Writer's Craft

1. **The pattern.** Most effective narratives encompass a restricted time span. How much time elapses from the moment Orwell gets his gun to the death of the elephant? What time signals does Orwell provide to help the reader follow the sequence of events in this limited time span?
2. Orwell doesn't actually begin his narrative until the third paragraph. What purposes do the first two paragraphs serve?
3. **Other patterns.** In paragraph 6, Orwell says that shooting a working elephant "is comparable to destroying a huge and costly piece of machinery." This kind of *comparison* is called an *analogy*—describing something unfamiliar, often abstract, in terms of something more familiar and concrete. Find at least three additional analogies in Orwell's essay. What effect do they have?
4. **Other patterns.** Much of the power of Orwell's narrative comes from his ability to convey sensory impressions—what he saw, heard, smelled. Orwell's *description* becomes most vivid when he writes about the death of the elephant in paragraphs 11 and 12. Find some evocative words and phrases that give the description its power.

Writing Assignments Using Narration as a Pattern of Development

1. Orwell recounts a time he acted under great pressure. Write a narrative about an action you once took simply because you felt pressured. Perhaps you were attempting to avoid ridicule or to fulfill someone else's expectations. Like Orwell, use vivid details to bring the incident to life and to convey its effect on you. Langston Hughes's "Salvation" (page 158) may lead you to some insights about the way stress influences behavior.
2. Write a narrative essay about an experience that gave you, like Orwell, a deeper insight into your own nature. You may have discovered, for instance, that you can be surprisingly naive, compassionate, petty, brave, rebellious, or good at something. Consider first reading David Helvarg's "The Storm This Time" (page 103),

Joan Murray's "Someone's Mother" (page 154), and Barbara Ehrenreich's "Serving in Florida" (page 162), essays showing how the authors' responses to a challenge revealed much about their character.

Writing Assignments Combining Patterns of Development

3. Was Orwell justified in shooting the elephant? Write an essay *arguing* that Orwell was either justified *or* not justified. To develop your thesis, cite several specific reasons, each supported by *examples* drawn from the essay. Here are some points you might consider: the legality of Orwell's act, the elephant's temperament, the crowd's presence, the aftermath of the elephant's death, the death itself.

4. Orwell's essay concerns, in part, the tendency to conceal indecision and confusion behind a facade of authority. Focusing on one or two groups of people (parents, teachers, doctors, politicians, and so on), write an essay *arguing* that people in authority sometimes *pretend* to know what they're doing so that subordinates won't suspect their insecurity or incompetence. Part of your essay should focus on the *consequences* of such behaviors.

Writing Assignment Using a Journal Entry as a Starting Point

5. Review your pre-reading journal entry, and select *one* action, law, or regulation that you consider indefensible. Interview friends, family, and classmates in an effort to gather views on all sides of the issue. Also consider supplementing this informal research with information gathered in the library and/or on the Internet. After weighing all your material, formulate a thesis; then write an essay convincing readers of the validity of your position.

Joan Murray

Joan Murray—a poet, writer, editor, and playwright—was born in New York City in 1945. She attended Hunter College and New York University, and published her first volume of poetry, which she also illustrated, in 1975. Three of her poetry books—*Queen of the Mist, Looking for the Parade,* and *The Same Water*—have won prizes. Her most recent volume of poetry is *Dancing on the Edge*, published in 2002. This essay appeared in the "Lives" section of the weekly *New York Times Magazine* on May 13, 2007.

Pre-Reading Journal Entry

We are used to having our mothers care for us, but sometimes we have to care for our mothers. Reflect on an occasion when you had to do something important for your mother or other caregiver. What was the situation? How did you help? How did you feel about helping someone who normally helped you? Use your journal to respond to these questions.

Someone's Mother

Hitchhiking is generally illegal where I live in upstate New York, but it's not unusual to see someone along Route 20 with an outstretched thumb or a handmade sign saying "Boston." This hitchhiker, though, was waving both arms in the air and grinning like a president boarding Air Force One. 1

I was doing 60—eager to get home after a dental appointment in Albany—and I was a mile past the hitchhiker before something made me turn back. I couldn't say if the hitchhiker was a man or a woman. All I knew was that the hitchhiker was old. 2

As I drove back up the hill, I eyed the hitchhiker in the distance: dark blue raincoat, jaunty black beret. Thin arms waving, spine a little bent. Wisps of white hair lilting as the trucks whizzed by. I made a U-turn and pulled up on the gravel, face to face with an eager old woman who kept waving till I stopped. I saw no broken-down vehicle. There was no vehicle at all. She wore the same broad grin I noticed when I passed her. 3

I rolled my window down. "Can I call someone for you?" 4

"No, I'm fine—I just need a ride." 5

"Where are you going?" 6

"Nassau." 7

That was three miles away. "Are you going there to shop?" 8

"No. I live there." 9

"What are you doing here?" I asked with a tone I hadn't used since my son was a teenager. 10

"I was out for a walk." 11

I glanced down the road: Jet's Autobody. Copeland Coating. Thoma Tire Company. And the half-mile hill outside Nassau—so steep that there's a second lane for trucks. She must have climbed the shoulder of that hill. And the next one. And the next. Until something made her stop and throw her hands in the air. 12

"Did you get lost?" I asked, trying to conceal my alarm. 13

"It was a nice day," she said with a little cry. "Can't an old lady go for a walk on a nice day and get lost?" 14

It wasn't a question meant to be answered. She came around to the passenger side, opened the door and sat down. On our way to Nassau, she admitted to being 92. Though she ducked my questions about her name, her address and her family. "Just leave me at the drugstore," she said. 15

"I'll take you home," I said. "Then you can call someone." 16

"Please," she said, "just leave me at the drugstore." 17

"I can't leave you there," I replied just as firmly. "I'm going to take you to your house. Or else to the police station." 18

"No, no," she begged. She was agitated now. "If my son finds out, he'll put me in a home." 19

Already I was seeing my own mother, who's 90. A few years ago, she was living in her house on Long Island, surrounded by her neighbors, her bird feeders, her azaleas. Then one morning she phoned my brother to say she didn't remember how to get dressed anymore. A few weeks later, with sorrow and worry, we arranged her move to a nursing home. 20

I noticed that the hitchhiker had a white dove pinned to her collar. "Do you belong to a church?" I tried. "Yes," she said. She was grinning. "I'd like to take you there," I said. "No, please," she said again. "My son will find out." 21

Things were getting clearer. "You've gotten lost before?" 22

"A few times," she shrugged. "But I always find my way home. Just take me to the drugstore." 23

As we drove, I kept thinking about my mother, watched over and cared for in a bright, clean place. I also thought about her empty bird feeders, her azaleas blooming for no one, the way she whispers on the phone, "I don't know anyone here." 24

When I pulled into the parking strip beside the drugstore, the hitchhiker let herself out. "I just need to sit on the step for a while," she said before closing the door. I stepped out after her. "Can't I take you home?" I asked as gently as I could. 25

She looked into my eyes for a moment. "I don't know where I live," she said in the tiniest voice. "But someone will come along who knows me. They always do." 26

I watched as she sat herself down on the step. Already she had dismissed me from her service. She was staring ahead with her grin intact, waiting for the next person who would aid her. 27

I should call the police, I thought. But then surely her son would be told. I should speak with the pharmacists. Surely they might know her—though they might know her son as well. Yet who was I to keep this incident from him? And yet how could I help him put the hitchhiker in a home? 28

"Promise me you'll tell the druggist if no one comes soon," I said to her with great seriousness. 29

"I promise," she said with a cheerful little wave. 30

Questions for Close Reading

1. What is the selection's thesis? Locate the sentence(s) in which Murray states her main idea. If she doesn't state her thesis explicitly, express it in your own words.
2. What is the external conflict Murray experiences in this essay? What is the internal conflict?
3. In paragraph 22, the author says "Things were getting clearer." What does she mean by this?
4. Why does Murray finally go along with the hitchhiker's wishes?
5. Refer to your dictionary as needed to define the following words used in the selection: *jaunty* (paragraph 3), *beret* (3), *lilting* (3), *shoulder* (12), *agitated* (19), and *azaleas* (20).

Questions About the Writer's Craft

1. **The pattern.** How does Murray organize the events in this essay? How does she keep the reader oriented as her story progresses?
2. **Other patterns.** In some passages, Murray *describes* the hitchhiker's appearance. What do these descriptions contribute to the narrative?
3. In paragraphs 12, 20, 24, and 28, Murray tells us her thoughts. What effect do these sections have on the pace of the narrative? How do they affect our understanding of what is happening?
4. Murray uses a lot of dialogue in this essay. Explain why the use of dialogue is (or is not) effective. What function does the dialogue have?

Writing Assignments Using Narration as a Pattern of Development

1. Murray's encounter with the hitchhiker happens as she is driving home. Recall a time when you were traveling in a car, bus, or other vehicle and something surprising occurred. Were you frightened, puzzled, amused? Did you learn something about people or about yourself? Tell the story using first-person narration, being sure to include your thoughts as well as your actions and the actions of others.
2. Write a narrative about an incident in your life in which a stranger helped you, and explain how this made you feel. The experience might have made you grateful, resentful, or anxious like the hitchhiker. Use either flashback or flashforward to emphasize an event in your narrative. To read an essay that uses flashback, see Audre Lorde's "The Fourth of July" (page 140) and Beth Johnson's "Bombs Bursting in Air" (page 211).

Writing Assignments Combining Patterns of Development

3. Did Murray do the right thing when she left the elderly woman sitting in front of the drugstore? Write an essay in which you *argue* that Murray did or did not act properly. You can support your argument using *examples* from the essay showing the hitchhiker's state of mental and physical health. You can also support your argument by presenting the possible positive or negative effects of Murray's action, depending on your point of view.

4. Murray is concerned that the hitchhiker, like Murray's own mother, may not be able to take care of herself sufficiently. Do some research on the Internet or in the library about options available for elderly people who can no longer live alone. Write an essay in which you give *examples* of these options and *compare* them in terms of price, services, and quality of life.

Writing Assignment Using a Journal Entry as a Starting Point

5. Review your pre-reading journal entry in which you described a time when you had to help your mother or other caregiver. Compare your experience to those of Joan Murray, who helped her own mother as well as the hitchhiker, who was "someone's mother." How did your experience differ from hers? How was it similar? If you were to do it again, would you do so the same way, or would you do it differently? Why? Consider reading Amy Tan's "Mother Tongue" (page 270) for an author's description of helping her mother.

Langston Hughes

One of the foremost members of the 1920s literary movement known as the Harlem Renaissance, Langston Hughes (1902–67) committed himself to portraying the richness of Black life in the United States. A poet and a writer of short stories, Hughes was greatly influenced by the rhythms of blues and jazz. In his later years, he published two autobiographical works, *The Big Sea* (1940) and *I Wonder as I Wander* (1956), and he wrote a history of the National Association for the Advancement of Colored People (NAACP). The following selection is from *The Big Sea*.

Pre-Reading Journal Entry

Young people often feel pressured by family and community to adopt certain values, beliefs, or traditions. In your journal, reflect on some of the pressures that you've experienced. What was your response to these pressures? What have been the consequences of your response? Do you think your experience with these family or community pressures was unique or fairly common?

Salvation

I was saved from sin when I was going on thirteen. But not really saved. It happened like this. There was a big revival at my Auntie Reed's church. Every night for weeks there had been much preaching, singing, praying, and shouting, and some very hardened sinners had been brought to Christ, and the membership of the church had grown by leaps and bounds. Then just before the revival ended, they held a special meeting for children, "to bring the young lambs to the fold." My aunt spoke of it for days ahead. That night I was escorted to the front row and placed on the mourners' bench with all the other young sinners, who had not yet been brought to Jesus. 1

My aunt told me that when you were saved you saw a light, and something happened to you inside! And Jesus came into your life! And God was with you from then on! She said you could see and hear and feel Jesus in your soul. I believed her. I had heard a great many old people say the same thing and it seemed to me they ought to know. So I sat there calmly in the hot, crowded church, waiting for Jesus to come to me. 2

The preacher preached a wonderful rhythmical sermon, all moans and shouts and lonely cries and dire pictures of hell, and then he sang a song about the ninety and nine safe in the fold, but one little lamb was left out in the cold. Then he said: "Won't you come? Won't you come to Jesus? Young lambs, won't you come?" And he held out his arms to all us young sinners there on the mourners' bench. And the little girls cried. And some of them jumped up and went to Jesus right away. But most of us just sat there. 3

A great many older people came and knelt around us and prayed, old women with jet-black faces and braided hair, old men with work-gnarled hands. And the church sang a song about the lower lights are burning, some poor sinners to be saved. And the whole building rocked with prayer and song. 4

Still I kept waiting to *see* Jesus. 5

Finally all the young people had gone to the altar and were saved, but one boy and me. He was a rounder's son named Westley. Westley and I were surrounded by sisters and deacons praying. It was very hot in the church, and getting late now. Finally Westley said to me in a whisper: "God damn! I'm tired o' sitting here. Let's get up and be saved." So he got up and was saved. 6

Then I was left all alone on the mourners' bench. My aunt came and knelt at my knees and cried, while prayers and songs swirled all around me in the little church. The whole congregation prayed for me alone, in a mighty wail of moans and voices. And I kept waiting serenely for Jesus, waiting, waiting—but he didn't come. I wanted to see him, but nothing happened to me. Nothing! I wanted something to happen to me, but nothing happened. 7

I heard the songs and the minister saying: "Why don't you come? My dear child, why don't you come to Jesus? Jesus is waiting for you. He wants you. Why don't you come? Sister Reed, what is this child's name?" 8

"Langston," my aunt sobbed. 9

"Langston, why don't you come? Why don't you come and be saved? Oh, Lamb of God! Why don't you come?" 10

Now it was really getting late. I began to be ashamed of myself, holding everything up so long. I began to wonder what God thought about Westley, who certainly hadn't seen Jesus either, but who was now sitting proudly on the platform, swinging his knickerbockered legs and grinning down at me, surrounded by deacons and old women on their knees praying. God had not struck Westley dead for taking his name in vain or for lying in the temple. So I decided that maybe to save further trouble, I'd better lie, too, and say that Jesus had come, and get up and be saved. 11

So I got up. 12

Suddenly the whole room broke into a sea of shouting, as they saw me rise. Waves of rejoicing swept the place. Women leaped in the air. My aunt threw her arms around me. The minister took me by the hand and led me to the platform. 13

When things quieted down, in a hushed silence, punctuated by a few ecstatic "Amens," all the new young lambs were blessed in the name of God. Then joyous singing filled the room. 14

That night, for the last time in my life but one—for I was a big boy twelve years old—I cried. I cried, in bed alone, and couldn't stop. I buried my head under the quilts, but my aunt heard me. She woke up and told 15 my uncle I was crying because the Holy Ghost had come into my life, and because I had seen Jesus. But I was really crying because I couldn't bear to tell her that I had lied, that I had deceived everybody in the church, and I hadn't seen Jesus, and that now I didn't believe there was a Jesus any more, since he didn't come to help me.

Questions for Close Reading

1. What is the selection's thesis (or narrative point)? Locate the sentence(s) in which Hughes states his main idea. If Hughes doesn't state the thesis explicitly, express it in your own words.
2. During the revival meeting, what pressures are put on the young Langston to get up and be saved?
3. How does Westley's attitude differ from Hughes's?
4. Does the narrator's Auntie Reed really understand him? Why can't he tell her the truth about his experience in the church?
5. Refer to your dictionary as needed to define the following words used in the selection: *revival* (paragraph 1), *knickerbockered* (11), *punctuated* (14), and *ecstatic* (14).

Questions About the Writer's Craft

1. **The pattern.** A narrative's power can often be traced to a conflict within the event being recounted. What conflict does the narrator of "Salvation" experience? How does Hughes create tension about this conflict?
2. What key role does Westley serve in the resolution of the narrator's dilemma? How does Hughes's inclusion of Westley in the story help us to understand the narrator better?
3. **Other patterns.** The thirteenth paragraph presents a *metaphor* of the church as an ocean. What images develop this metaphor? What does the metaphor tell us about Hughes's feelings and those of the church people?
4. The singing of hymns is a major part of this religious service. Why do you think Hughes has the narrator reveal the subjects and even the lyrics of some of the hymns?

Writing Assignments Using Narration as a Pattern of Development

1. Like Hughes, we sometimes believe that deception is our best alternative. Write a narrative about a time you felt deception was the best way either to protect those you care about or to maintain the respect of those important to you.
2. Write a narrative essay about a chain of events that caused you to become disillusioned about a person or institution you had previously regarded highly. Begin as Hughes does by presenting your initial beliefs. Relate the sequence of events that changed your evaluation of the person or organization. In the conclusion, explain the short- and long-term effects of the incident. For more accounts of childhood disillusionment, read Audre Lorde's "The Fourth of July" (page 140) and Beth Johnson's "Bombs Bursting in Air" (page 211).

Writing Assignments Combining Patterns of Development

3. Hughes writes, "My aunt told me that when you were saved, you saw a light, and something happened to you inside! And Jesus came into your life!" What *causes* people to change their beliefs? Do such changes come from waiting calmly, as Hughes tried to do in church, or must they come from a more active process? Write an essay explaining your viewpoint. You may use *process analysis, causal analysis,* or some other organizational pattern to develop your thesis. Be sure to include specific examples to support your understanding of the way beliefs change.
4. Write a *persuasive* essay *arguing* either that lying is sometimes right or that lying is always wrong. Apply your thesis to particular situations and show how lying is or is not the right course of action. Be sure to keep your *narration* of these situations brief and focused on your point. Remember to acknowledge the opposing viewpoint. Charles Sykes's "The 'Values' Wasteland" (page 198) may help you define your position. You might even mention this author's perspective in your essay.

Writing Assignment Using a Journal Entry as a Starting Point

5. Review your pre-reading journal entry, and select *one* family or community pressure with which you've had to contend. Then write an essay examining the effect that this pressure has had on you. Refer to your journal as you prepare to explain the values, beliefs, or traditions that you were expected to adopt. Discuss your response to this pressure and how your reaction has affected you.

Barbara Ehrenreich

Barbara Ehrenreich was born in Montana in 1941. Early on, she studied science, earning a Ph.D. in cell biology from Rockefeller University. But her interest soon turned to social issues, and she became an activist for peace, women's rights, health care, and economic justice. Ehrenreich has published articles in *Time, Mother Jones, The Nation,* and the *New York Times.* Her books include *For Her Own Good: Two Centuries of the Experts' Advice to Women* (2005), *Bait and Switch: The (Futile) Pursuit of the American Dream* (2006), and most recently *Bright-Sided: How the Relentless Promotion of Positive Thinking Has Undermined America* (2009). The following excerpt is from her book *Nickel and Dimed: On (Not) Getting By in America* (2001), in which she chronicles her experiences as a worker in low-wage, blue collar jobs.

Pre-Reading Journal Entry

Ehrenreich says that her experience as a server changed her, but not necessarily in a good way. Think of experiences that you feel have changed you for the better—perhaps made you more thoughtful, serious, optimistic, helpful, or caring. Was the change gradual or sudden? Write some notes in your journal.

Serving in Florida

Picture a fat person's hell, and I don't mean a place with no food. Instead 1
there is everything you might eat if eating had no bodily consequences—the cheese fries, the chicken-fried steaks, the fudge-laden desserts—only here every bite must be paid for, one way or another, in human discomfort. The kitchen is a cavern, a stomach leading to the lower intestine that is the garbage and dishwashing area, from which issue bizarre smells combining the edible and the offal: creamy carrion, pizza barf, and that unique and enigmatic Jerry's[1] scent, citrus fart. The floor is slick with spills, forcing us to walk through the kitchen with tiny steps, like Susan McDougal[2] in leg irons. Sinks everywhere are clogged with scraps of lettuce, decomposing lemon wedges, water-logged toast crusts. Put your hand down on any counter and you risk being stuck to it by the film of ancient syrup spills, and this is unfortunate because hands are utensils here, used for scooping up lettuce onto the salad plates, lifting out pie slices, and even moving hash browns from one plate to another. The regulation poster in the single unisex rest room admonishes us to wash our hands thoroughly, and even offers instructions for doing so, but there is always some vital substance missing—soap, paper towels, toilet

[1]"Jerry's" is the fictitious name for the "national chain" where the author worked (editors' note).

[2]Susan McDougal was imprisoned for refusing to testify against President Bill Clinton and Hillary Clinton before the 1996 Whitewater grand jury (editors' note).

paper—and I never found all three at once. You learn to stuff your pockets with napkins before going in there, and too bad about the customers, who must eat, although they don't realize it, almost literally out of our hands.

The break room summarizes the whole situation: there is none, because there are no breaks at Jerry's. For six to eight hours in a row, you never sit except to pee. Actually, there are three folding chairs at a table immediately adjacent to the bathroom, but hardly anyone ever sits in this, the very rectum of the gastroarchitectural system. Rather, the function of the peri-toilet area is to house the ashtrays in which servers and dishwashers leave their cigarettes burning at all times, like votive candles, so they don't have to waste time lighting up again when they dash back here for a puff. Almost everyone smokes as if their pulmonary well-being depended on it—the multinational mélange of cooks; the dishwashers, who are all Czechs here; the servers, who are American natives—creating an atmosphere in which oxygen is only an occasional pollutant. My first morning at Jerry's, when the hypoglycemic shakes set in, I complain to one of my fellow servers that I don't understand how she can go so long without food. "Well, I don't understand how *you* can go so long without a cigarette," she responds in a tone of reproach. Because work is what you do for others; smoking is what you do for yourself. I don't know why the antismoking crusaders have never grasped the element of defiant self-nurturance that makes the habit so endearing to its victims—as if, in the American workplace, the only thing people have to call their own is the tumors they are nourishing and the spare moments they devote to feeding them. 2

Now, the Industrial Revolution[3] is not an easy transition, especially, in my experience, when you have to zip through it in just a couple of days. I have gone from craft work straight into the factory, from the air-conditioned morgue of the Hearthside[4] directly into the flames. Customers arrive in human waves, sometimes disgorged fifty at a time from their tour buses, puckish and whiny. Instead of two "girls" on the floor at once, there can be as many as six of us running around in our brilliant pink-and-orange Hawaiian shirts. Conversations, either with customers or with fellow employees, seldom last more than twenty seconds at a time. On my first day, in fact, I am hurt by my sister servers' coldness. My mentor for the day is a supremely competent, emotionally uninflected twenty-three-year-old, and the others, who gossip a little among themselves about the real reason someone is out sick today and the size of the bail bond someone else has had 3

[3]"Industrial Revolution" refers to the rapid social and economic change occurring when machine-made production is introduced into a society, as in England in the late eighteenth century (editors' note).

[4]"Hearthside" is the fictitious name for the other restaurant where the author worked (editors' note).

to pay, ignore me completely. On my second day, I find out why. "Well, it's good to see *you* again," one of them says in greeting. "Hardly anyone comes back after the first day." I feel powerfully vindicated—a survivor—but it would take a long time, probably months, before I could hope to be accepted into this sorority.

I start out with the beautiful, heroic idea of handling the two jobs at once, and for two days I almost do it: working the breakfast/lunch shift at Jerry's from 8:00 till 2:00, arriving at the Hearthside a few minutes late, at 2:10, and attempting to hold out until 10:00. In the few minutes I have between jobs, I pick up a spicy chicken sandwich at the Wendy's drive-through window, gobble it down in the car, and change from khaki slacks to black, from Hawaiian to rust-colored polo. There is a problem, though. When, during the 3:00-4:00 o'clock dead time, I finally sit down to wrap silver, my flesh seems to bond to the seat. I try to refuel with a purloined cup of clam chowder, as I've seen Gail[5] and Joan do dozens of times, but Stu catches me and hisses "No *eating!*" although there's not a customer around to be offended by the sight of food making contact with a server's lips. So I tell Gail I'm going to quit, and she hugs me and says she might just follow me to Jerry's herself. 4

But the chances of this are minuscule. She has left the flophouse and her annoying roommate and is back to living in her truck. But, guess what, she reports to me excitedly later that evening, Phillip has given her permission to park overnight in the hotel parking lot, as long as she keeps out of sight, and the parking lot should be totally safe since it's patrolled by a hotel security guard! With the Hearthside offering benefits like that, how could anyone think of leaving? This must be Phillip's theory, anyway. He accepts my resignation with a shrug, his main concern being that I return my two polo shirts and aprons. 5

Gail would have triumphed at Jerry's, I'm sure, but for me it's a crash course in exhaustion management. Years ago, the kindly fry cook who trained me to waitress at a Los Angeles truck stop used to say: Never make an unnecessary trip; if you don't have to walk fast, walk slow; if you don't have to walk, stand. But at Jerry's the effort of distinguishing necessary from unnecessary and urgent from whenever would itself be too much of an energy drain. The only thing to do is to treat each shift as a one-time-only emergency: you've got fifty starving people out there, lying scattered on the battlefield, so get out there and feed them! Forget that you will have to do this again tomorrow, forget that you will have to be alert enough to dodge the drunks on the drive home tonight—just burn, burn, burn! Ideally, at some point you enter what servers call a "rhythm" and psychologists term a "flow state," where signals pass from the sense organs 6

[5]Gail, Joan, Stu, and Phillip (in the next paragraph) work at the Hearthside (editors' note).

directly to the muscles, bypassing the cerebral cortex, and a Zen-like emptiness sets in. I'm on a 2:00-10:00 P.M. shift now, and a male server from the morning shift tells me about the time he "pulled a triple"—three shifts in a row, all the way around the clock—and then got off and had a drink and met this girl, and maybe he shouldn't tell me this, but they had sex right then and there and it was like *beautiful*.

But there's another capacity of the neuromuscular system, which is pain. 7
I start tossing back drugstore-brand ibuprofens as if they were vitamin C, four before each shift, because an old mouse-related repetitive-stress injury in my upper back has come back to full-spasm strength, thanks to the tray carrying. In my ordinary life, this level of disability might justify a day of ice packs and stretching. Here I comfort myself with the Aleve commercial where the cute blue-collar guy asks: If you quit after working four hours, what would your boss say? And the not-so-cute blue-collar guy, who's lugging a metal beam on his back, answers: He'd fire me, that's what. But fortunately, the commercial tells us, we workers can exert the same kind of authority over our painkillers that our bosses exert over us. If Tylenol doesn't want to work for more than four hours, you just fire its ass and switch to Aleve.

True, I take occasional breaks from this life, going home now and 8
then to catch up on e-mail and for conjugal visits (though I am careful to "pay" for everything I eat here, at $5 for a dinner, which I put in a jar), seeing *The Truman Show*[6] with friends and letting them buy my ticket. And I still have those what-am-I-doing-here moments at work, when I get so homesick for the printed word that I obsessively reread the six-page menu. But as the days go by, my old life is beginning to look exceedingly strange. The e-mails and phone messages addressed to my former self come from a distant race of people with exotic concerns and far too much time on their hands. The neighborly market I used to cruise for produce now looks forbiddingly like a Manhattan yuppie emporium. And when I sit down one morning in my real home to pay bills from my past life, I am dazzled by the two- and three-figure sums owed to outfits like Club Body Tech and Amazon.com.

Management at Jerry's is generally calmer and more "professional" 9
than at the Hearthside, with two exceptions. One is Joy, a plump, blowsy woman in her early thirties who once kindly devoted several minutes of her time to instructing me in the correct one-handed method of tray carrying but whose moods change disconcertingly from shift to shift and even within one. The other is B.J., aka B.J. the Bitch, whose contribution is to stand by the kitchen counter and yell, "Nita, your order's up, move it!" or "Barbara, didn't you see you've got another table out there? Come *on*,

[6]In *The Truman Show*, a 1998 movie, a man discovers he has lived his whole life as a kind of reality television show (editors' note).

girl!" Among other things, she is hated for having replaced the whipped cream squirt cans with big plastic whipped-cream-filled baggies that have to be squeezed with both hands—because, reportedly, she saw or thought she saw employees trying to inhale the propellant gas from the squirt cans, in the hope that it might be nitrous oxide. On my third night, she pulls me aside abruptly and brings her face so close that it looks like she's planning to butt me with her forehead. But instead of saying "You're fired," she says, "You're doing fine." The only trouble is I'm spending time chatting with customers: "That's how they're getting you." Furthermore I am letting them "run me," which means harassment by sequential demands: you bring the catsup and they decide they want extra Thousand Island; you bring that and they announce they now need a side of fries, and so on into distraction. Finally she tells me not to take her wrong. She tries to say things in a nice way, but "you get into a mode, you know, because everything has to move so fast."[7]

I mumble thanks for the advice, feeling like I've just been stripped 10
naked by the crazed enforcer of some ancient sumptuary law:[8] No chatting for *you,* girl. No fancy service ethic allowed for the serfs: Chatting with customers is for the good-looking young college-educated servers in the downtown carpaccio and ceviche joints, the kids who can make $70–$100 a night. What had I been thinking? My job is to move orders from tables to kitchen and then trays from kitchen to tables. Customers are in fact the major obstacle to the smooth transformation of information into food and food into money—they are, in short, the enemy. And the painful thing is that I'm beginning to see it this way myself. There are the traditional asshole types—frat boys who down multiple Buds and then make a fuss because the steaks are so emaciated and the fries so sparse—as well as the variously impaired—due to age, diabetes, or literacy issues—who require patient nutritional counseling. The worst, for some reason, are the Visible Christians—like the ten-person table, all jolly and sanctified after Sunday night service, who run me mercilessly and then leave me $1 on a $92 bill. Or the guy with the crucifixion T-shirt (SOMEONE TO LOOK UP TO) who complains that his baked potato is too hard and his iced tea too icy (I cheerfully fix both) and leaves no tip at all. As a general rule, people wearing crosses or WWJD? ("What Would Jesus Do?") buttons look at us

[7]In *Workers in a Lean World: Unions in the International Economy* (Verso, 1997), Kim Moody cites studies finding an increase in stress-related workplace injuries and illness between the mid-1980s and the early 1990s. He argues that rising stress levels reflect a new system of "management by stress" in which workers in a variety of industries are being squeezed to extract maximum productivity, to the detriment of their health (author's note).

[8]A sumptuary law regulates personal habits, especially regarding food and dress, on the basis of a community's moral or religious beliefs (editors' note).

disapprovingly no matter what we do, as if they were confusing waitressing with Mary Magdalene's original profession.

I make friends, over time, with the other "girls" who work my shift: Nita, the tattooed twenty-something who taunts us by going around saying brightly, "Have we started making money yet?" Ellen, whose teenage son cooks on the graveyard shift and who once managed a restaurant in Massachusetts but won't try out for management here because she prefers being a "common worker" and not "ordering people around." Easygoing fiftyish Lucy, with the raucous laugh, who limps toward the end of the shift because of something that has gone wrong with her leg, the exact nature of which cannot be determined without health insurance. We talk about the usual girl things—men, children, and the sinister allure of Jerry's chocolate peanut-butter cream pie—though no one, I notice, ever brings up anything potentially expensive, like shopping or movies. As at the Hearthside, the only recreation ever referred to is partying, which requires little more than some beer, a joint, and a few close friends. Still, no one is homeless, or cops to it anyway, thanks usually to a working husband or boyfriend. All in all, we form a reliable mutual-support group: if one of us is feeling sick or overwhelmed, another one will "bev" a table or even carry trays for her. If one of us is off sneaking a cigarette or a pee, the others will do their best to conceal her absence from the enforcers of corporate rationality.[9] 11

But my saving human connection—my oxytocin receptor, as it were—is George, the nineteen-year-old Czech dishwasher who has been in this country exactly one week. We get talking when he asks me, tortuously, how much cigarettes cost at Jerry's. I do my best to explain that they cost over a dollar more here than at a regular store and suggest that he just take one from the half-filled packs that are always lying around on the break table. But that would be unthinkable. Except for the one tiny earring signaling his allegiance to some vaguely alternative point of view, George is a perfect straight arrow—crew-cut, hardworking, and hungry for eye contact. "Czech Republic," I ask, "or Slovakia?" and he seems delighted that I know the 12

[9]Until April 1998, there was no federally mandated right to bathroom breaks. According to Marc Linder and Ingrid Nygaard, authors of *Void Where Prohibited: Rest Breaks and the Right to Urinate on Company Time* (Cornell University Press, 1997), "The right to rest and void at work is not high on the list of social or political causes supported by professional or executive employees, who enjoy personal workplace liberties that millions of factory workers can only dream about.... While we were dismayed to discover that workers lacked an acknowledged right to void at work, [the workers] were amazed by outsiders' naïve belief that their employers would permit them to perform this basic bodily function when necessary.... A factory worker, not allowed a break for six-hour stretches, voided into pads worn inside her uniform; and a kindergarten teacher in a school without aides had to take all twenty children with her to the bathroom and line them up outside the stall door while she voided" (author's note).

difference. "Vaclav Havel."[10] I try, "Velvet Revolution, Frank Zappa?" "Yes, yes, 1989," he says, and I realize that for him this is already history.

My project is to teach George English. "How are you today, George?" I say at the start of each shift. "I am good, and how are you today, Barbara?" I learn that he is not paid by Jerry's but by the "agent" who shipped him over—$5 an hour, with the agent getting the dollar or so difference between that and what Jerry's pays dishwashers. I learn also that he shares an apartment with a crowd of other Czech "dishers," as he calls them, and that he cannot sleep until one of them goes off for his shift, leaving a vacant bed. We are having one of our ESL sessions late one afternoon when B.J. catches us at it and orders "Joseph" to take up the rubber mats on the floor near the dishwashing sinks and mop underneath. "I thought your name was George," I say loud enough for B.J. to hear as she strides off back to the counter. Is she embarrassed? Maybe a little, because she greets me back at the counter with "George, Joseph—there are so many of them!" I say nothing, neither nodding nor smiling, and for this I am punished later, when I think I am ready to go and she announces that I need to roll fifty more sets of silverware, and isn't it time I mixed up a fresh four-gallon batch of blue-cheese dressing? May you grow old in this place, B.J., is the curse I beam out at her when I am finally permitted to leave. May the syrup spills glue your feet to the floor.... 13

In line with my reduced living conditions, a new form of ugliness arises at Jerry's. First we are confronted—via an announcement on the computers through which we input orders—with the new rule that the hotel bar, the Driftwood, is henceforth off-limits to restaurant employees. The culprit, I learn through the grapevine, is the ultraefficient twenty-three-year-old who trained me—another trailer home dweller and a mother of three. Something had set her off one morning, so she slipped out for a nip and returned to the floor impaired. The restriction mostly hurts Ellen, whose habit it is to free her hair from its rubber band and drop by the Driftwood for a couple of Zins before heading home at the end of her shift, but all of us feel the chill. Then the next day, when I go for straws, I find the dry-storage room locked. It's never been locked before; we go in and out of it all day—for napkins, jelly containers, Styrofoam cups for takeout. Vic, the portly assistant manager who opens it for me, explains that he caught one of the dishwashers attempting to steal something and, unfortunately, the miscreant will be with us until a replacement can be found—hence the locked door. I neglect to ask what he had been trying to steal but Vic tells me who he is—the kid with the buzz cut and the earning, you know, he's back there right now. 14

[10]Vaclav Havel, a writer and dissident, became the first president of the Czech Republic, which was established after the 1989 Velvet Revolution, a nonviolent revolution that ended communism in Czechoslovakia (editors' note).

I wish I could say I rushed back and confronted George to get his side of the story. I wish I could say I stood up to Vic and insisted that George be given a translator and allowed to defend himself or announced that I'd find a lawyer who'd handle the case pro bono. At the very least I should have testified as to the kid's honesty. The mystery to me is that there's not much worth stealing in the dry-storage room, at least not in any fenceable quantity: "Is Gyorgi here, and am having 200—maybe 250—catsup packets. What do you say?" My guess is that he had taken—if he had taken anything at all—some Saltines or a can of cherry pie mix and that the motive for taking it was hunger. 15

So why didn't I intervene? Certainly not because I was held back by the kind of moral paralysis that can mask as journalistic objectivity. On the contrary, something new—something loathsome and servile—had infected me, along with the kitchen odors that I could still sniff on my bra when I finally undressed at night. In real life I am moderately brave, but plenty of brave people shed their courage in POW camps, and maybe something similar goes on in the infinitely more congenial milieu of the low-wage American workplace. Maybe, in a month or two more at Jerry's, I might have regained my crusading spirit. Then again, in a month or two I might have turned into a different person altogether—say, the kind of person who would have turned George in.... 16

I can do this two-job thing, is my theory, if I can drink enough caffeine and avoid getting distracted by George's ever more obvious suffering.[11] The first few days after the alleged theft, he seemed not to understand the trouble he was in, and our chirpy little conversations had continued. But the last couple of shifts he's been listless and unshaven, and tonight he looks like the ghost we all know him to be, with dark half-moons hanging from his eyes. At one point, when I am briefly immobilized by the task of filling little paper cups with sour cream for baked potatoes, he comes over and looks as if he'd like to explore the limits of our shared vocabulary, but I am called to the floor for a table. I resolve to give him all my tips that night, and to hell with the experiment in low-wage money management. At eight, Ellen and I grab a snack together standing at the mephitic end of the kitchen counter, but I can only manage two or three mozzarella sticks, and lunch had been a mere handful of McNuggets. I am not tired at all, I assure myself, though it may be that there is simply no more "I" left to do the tiredness monitoring. What I would see if I were more alert to the situation is that the forces of destruction are already massing against me. There is only one cook on duty, a young man named Jesus ("Hay-Sue," that is), and he is new to the job. And there is Joy, who shows up 17

[11]In 1996 the number of persons holding two or more jobs averaged 7.8 million, or 6.2 percent of the workforce. It was about the same rate for men and women (6.1 versus 6.2). About two-thirds of multiple jobholders work one job full-time and the other part-time. Only a heroic minority—4 percent of men and 2 percent of women—work two full-time jobs simultaneously (John F. Stinson Jr., "New Data on Multiple Jobholding Available from the CPS," *Monthly Labor Review*, March 1997) (author's note).

to take over in the middle of the shift dressed in high heels and a long, clingy white dress and fuming as if she'd just been stood up in some cocktail bar.

Then it comes, the perfect storm. Four of my tables fill up at once. 18
Four tables is nothing for me now, but only so long as they are obligingly staggered. As I bev table 27, tables 25, 28, and 24 are watching enviously. As I bev 25, 24 glowers because their bevs haven't even been ordered. Twenty-eight is four yuppyish types, meaning everything on the side and agonizing instructions as to the chicken Caesars. Twenty-five is a middle-aged black couple who complain, with some justice, that the iced tea isn't fresh and the tabletop is sticky. But table 24 is the meteorological event of the century: ten British tourists who seem to have made the decision to absorb the American experience entirely by mouth. Here everyone has at least two drinks—iced tea *and* milk shake, Michelob *and* water (with lemon slice in the water, please)—and a huge, promiscuous orgy of breakfast specials, mozz sticks, chicken strips, quesadillas, burgers with cheese and without, sides of hash browns with cheddar, with onions, with gravy, seasoned fries, plain fries, banana splits. Poor Jesus! Poor me! Because when I arrive with their first tray of food—after three prior trips just to refill bevs—Princess Di refuses to eat her chicken strips with her pancake and sausage special since, as she now reveals, the strips were meant to be an appetizer. Maybe the others would have accepted their meals, but Di, who is deep into her third Michelob, insists that everything else go back while they work on their starters. Meanwhile, the yuppies are waving me down for more decaf and the black couple looks ready to summon the NAACP.

Much of what happens next is lost in the fog of war. Jesus starts going 19
under. The little printer in front of him is spewing out orders faster than he can rip them off, much less produce the meals. A menacing restlessness rises from the tables, all of which are full. Even the invincible Ellen is ashen from stress. I take table 24 their reheated main courses, which they immediately reject as either too cold or fossilized by the microwave. When I return to the kitchen with their trays (three trays in three trips) Joy confronts me with arms akimbo: "What *is* this?" She means the food—the plates of rejected pancakes, hash browns in assorted flavors, toasts, burgers, sausages, eggs. "Uh, scrambled with cheddar," I try, "and that's—" "*No*," she screams in my face, "is it a traditional, a super-scramble, an eye-opener?" I pretend to study my check for a clue, but entropy has been up to its tricks, not only on the plates but in my head, and I have to admit that the original order is beyond reconstruction. "You don't know an eye-opener from a traditional?" she demands in outrage. All I know, in fact, is that my legs have lost interest in the current venture and have announced their intention to fold. I am saved by a yuppie (mercifully not one of mine) who chooses this moment to charge into the kitchen to bellow that his food is twenty-five minutes late. Joy screams at him to get the hell out of her kitchen, *please*, and then turns on Jesus in a fury, hurling an empty tray across the room for emphasis.

I leave. I don't walk out, I just leave. I don't finish my side work or pick up my credit card tips, if any, at the cash register or, of course, ask Joy's permission to go. And the surprising thing is that you *can* walk out without permission, that the door opens, that the thick tropical night air parts to let me pass, that my car is still parked where I left it. There is no vindication in this exit, no fuck-you surge of relief, just an overwhelming dank sense of failure pressing down on me and the entire parking lot. I had gone into this venture in the spirit of science, to test a mathematical proposition, but somewhere along the line, in the tunnel vision imposed by long shifts and relentless concentration, it became a test of myself, and clearly I have failed. Not only had I flamed out as a housekeeper/server, I had forgotten to give George my tips, and, for reasons perhaps best known to hardworking, generous people like Gail and Ellen, this hurts. I don't cry, but I am in a position to realize, for the first time in many years, that the tear ducts are still there and still capable of doing their job. 20

When I moved out of the trailer park, I gave the key to number 46 to Gail and arranged for my deposit to be transferred to her. She told me that Joan was still living in her van and that Stu had been fired from the Hearthside. According to the most up-to-date rumors, the drug he ordered from the restaurant was crack and he was caught dipping into the cash register to pay for it. I never found out what happened to George. 21

Questions for Close Reading

1. What is the selection's thesis? Locate the sentence(s) in which Ehrenreich states her main idea. If she doesn't state her thesis explicitly, express it in your own words.
2. What sort of restaurant is Jerry's? What happens to the author's plan to work two jobs? Why?
3. The author describes several people that she works with at Jerry's. Who are these people? Who becomes her "saving human connection"? Why?
4. What factors contribute to the author's leaving her job at Jerry's? How does her relationship with George change? What is the "perfect storm"? Why does the author feel she has "failed" a test?
5. Refer to your dictionary as needed to define the following words used in the selection: *offal* (1), *mélange* (2), *hypoglycemic* (2), *reproach* (2), *disgorged* (3), *puckish* (3), *uninflected* (3), *purloined* (4), *cerebral cortex* (5), *conjugal* (8), *blowsy* (9), *disconcertingly* (9), *nitrous oxide* (9), *raucous* (11), *tortuously* (12), *miscreant* (14), *pro bono* (15), *mephitic* (17), and *entropy* (19).

Questions About the Writer's Craft

1. **The pattern.** How strong is the narrative focus? What narrative techniques does the author use to keep the story compelling for the reader? Give some examples.
2. **Other patterns.** The selection opens, in paragraphs 1 and 2, with a *description* of Jerry's. What do you think is the author's purpose? Is she successful?

3. Throughout the selection, Ehrenreich uses a wide-ranging vocabulary, from formal language, to conversational language, to slang and even vulgarities. Find some examples of the different types of language used. What is the effect of this type of diction?
4. Ehrenreich uses comparisons in several places. For example, in paragraph 1, she compares the kitchen to a "stomach leading to a lower intestine that is the garbage and dishwashing area." Find at least two other comparisons the author makes. How effective are these comparisons?

Writing Assignments Using Narration as a Pattern of Development

1. Ehrenreich is unprepared for the exhaustion and hard work involved in waitressing at Jerry's. Think of a situation in which you expected a task—for example, caring for a friend's pet or throwing a surprise party—to be easier than it turned out to be. Write an essay in which you *narrate* what happened. Be sure to use time signals to keep the story focused. Your essay may be serious or humorous in tone. For inspiration, you might read another selection about an unexpected outcome, for example, "Bloggers Without Borders" by Riverbend (page 111), "The Fourth of July" by Audre Lorde (page 140), or "What Shamu Taught Me About a Happy Marriage" by Amy Sutherland (page 308).
2. The author gives a lot of detail about the beginning of her job at Jerry's. Think of your own experience with starting a new job, attending classes at a new school, taking a vacation to a new place, or some similar situation. How helpful were the people you encountered? In an essay, *tell* the story of what happened on your first day. Use present tense verbs, and include dialogue.

Writing Assignments Combining Patterns of Development

3. Research the job of server in your state. How much do servers earn? What labor regulations apply to them? What employment benefits do serving jobs typically offer? If possible, interview a waiter about what he or she likes about the job. Write an essay in which you *compare* the pros and cons of working as a server. Use facts from your research to *illustrate* your ideas.
4. Ehrenreich writes about her lack of courage in the incident with George, though she describes herself as usually "moderately brave." Select a term that describes character, such as *bravery, courage,* or *loyalty,* and write an essay in which you define the term. Use examples from history, the news, and your own experience to *illustrate* your ideas.

Writing Assignment Using a Journal Entry as a Starting Point

Think about the change you wrote about in your journal. Was this a minor adjustment or a major transformation for you? Write an essay in which you compare how you were before and after this change occurred. Use personal anecdotes to illustrate your evolution.

Additional Writing Topics

NARRATION

General Assignments

Prepare an essay on any of the following topics, using narration as the paper's dominant method of development. Be sure to select details that advance the essay's narrative purpose; you may even want to experiment with flashback or flashforward. In any case, keep the sequence of events clear by using transitional cues. Within the limited time span covered, use vigorous details and varied sentence structure to enliven the narrative. Tell the story from a consistent point of view.

1. An emergency that brought out the best or worst in you
2. The hazards of taking children out to eat
3. An incident that made you believe in fate
4. Your best or worst day at school or work
5. A major decision
6. An encounter with a machine
7. An important learning experience
8. A narrow escape
9. Your first date, first day on the job, or first anything
10. A memorable childhood experience
11. A fairy tale the way you would like to hear it told
12. A painful moment
13. An incredible but true story
14. A significant family event
15. An experience in which a certain emotion (pride, anger, regret, or some other) was dominant
16. A surprising coincidence
17. An act of heroism
18. An unpleasant confrontation
19. A cherished family story
20. An imagined meeting with an admired celebrity or historical figure

Assignments with a Specific Purpose, Audience, and Point of View

On Campus

1. Write an article for your old high school newspaper. The article will be read primarily by seniors who are planning to go away to college next year. In the article, narrate a story that points to some truth about the "breaking away" stage of life.
2. A friend of yours has seen someone cheat on a test, plagiarize an entire paper, or seriously violate some other academic policy. In a letter, convince this friend

to inform the instructor or a campus administrator by narrating an incident in which a witness did (or did not) speak up in such a situation. Tell what happened as a result.

At Home or in the Community

3. You have had a disturbing encounter with one of the people who seems to have "fallen through the cracks" of society—a homeless person, an unwanted child, or anyone else who is alone and abandoned. Write a letter to the local newspaper describing this encounter. Your purpose is to arouse people's indignation and compassion and to get help for such unfortunates.
4. Your younger brother, sister, relative, or neighborhood friend can't wait to be your age. Write a letter in which you narrate a dramatic story that shows the young person that your age isn't as wonderful as he or she thinks. Be sure to select a story that the person can understand and appreciate.

On the Job

5. As fund-raiser for a particular organization (for example, the Red Cross, the SPCA, Big Brothers/Big Sisters), you're sending a newsletter to contributors. Support your cause by telling the story of a time when your organization made all the difference—the blood donation that saved a life, the animal that was rescued from abuse, and so on.
6. A customer has written a letter to you (or your boss) telling about a bad experience that he or she had with someone in your workplace. On the basis of that single experience, the customer now regards your company and its employees with great suspicion. It's your responsibility to respond to this complaint. Write a letter to the customer balancing his or her negative picture by narrating a story that shows the "flip side" of your company and its employees.

Bill Arnon/PhotoEdit, Inc.

EXEMPLIFICATION

WHAT IS EXEMPLIFICATION?

If someone asked you, "Have you been to any good restaurants lately?" you probably wouldn't answer "Yes" and then immediately change the subject. Most likely, you would go on to illustrate with *examples.* Perhaps you'd give the names of restaurants you've enjoyed and talk briefly about the specific things you liked: the attractive prices, the tasty main courses, the pleasant service, the tempting desserts. Such examples and details are needed to convince others that your opinion—in this or any matter—is valid. Similarly, when you talk about larger and more important issues, people won't pay much attention to your opinion if all you do is string together vague generalizations: "We have to do something about acid rain. It's had disastrous consequences for the environment. Its negative effects increase every year. Action must be taken to control the problem." To be taken seriously and to convince others that your point is well-founded, you must provide specific supporting examples: "The forests in the Adirondacks are dying"; "Yesterday's rainfall was fifty times more acidic than normal"; "Pine Lake, in the northern part of the state, was once a great fishing spot but now has no fish population."

Examples are equally important when you write an essay. It's not fuzzy generalities and highfalutin abstractions that make writing impressive. Just the opposite is true. Facts, anecdotes, statistics, details, opinions, and observations are at the heart of effective writing, giving your work substance and solidity.

HOW EXEMPLIFICATION FITS YOUR PURPOSE AND AUDIENCE

The wording of assignments and essay exam questions may signal the need for specific examples:

> Soap operas, whether shown during the day or in the evening, are among the most popular television programs. Why do you think this is so? Provide specific examples to support your position.
>
> Some observers claim that college students are less interested in learning than in getting ahead in their careers. Cite evidence to support or refute this claim.
>
> A growing number of people feel that parents should not allow young children to participate in highly competitive team sports. Basing your conclusion on your own experiences and observations, indicate whether you think this point of view is reasonable.

Such phrases as "Provide specific examples," "Cite evidence," and "Basing your conclusion on your own experiences and observations" signal that each essay should be developed through examples.

Usually, though, you won't be told so explicitly to provide examples. Instead, as you think about the best way to achieve your essay's purpose, you'll see the need for illustrative details—no matter which patterns of development you use. For instance, to *persuade* skeptical readers of the value of the Patient Protection and Affordable Care Act of 2010, you might mention specific cases—such as a family bankrupted by medical bills or a chronically ill person denied insurance because of a pre-existing condition—and explain how the law would ameliorate these situations. Similarly, you would supply examples in a *causal analysis* speculating on the likely impact of a proposed tuition hike at your college. To convince the college administration of the probable negative effects of such a hike, you might cite the following examples: articles reporting a nationwide upswing in student transfers to less expensive schools; statistics indicating a significant drop in grades among already employed students forced to work more hours to pay increased tuition costs; interviews with students too financially strapped to continue their college education.

Examples make writing *interesting*. Assume you're writing an essay showing that television commercials are biased against women. Your essay would be lifeless and boring if all it did was repeat, in a general way, that commercials present stereotyped views of women.

> An anti-female bias is rampant in television commercials. It is very much alive, yet most viewers seem to take it all in stride. Few people protest the obviously sexist characters and statements in such commercials. Surely, these commercials misrepresent the way most of us live.

Without interesting particulars, readers may respond, "Who cares?" But if you provide specific examples, you'll attract your readers' attention:

> Sexism is rampant in television commercials. Although millions of women hold responsible jobs outside the home, commercials continue to portray women as simple creatures who spend most of their time thinking about wax buildup, cottony-soft bathroom tissue, and static-free clothes. Men, apparently, have better things to do than fret over such mundane household matters. How many commercials can you recall that depict men proclaiming the virtues of squeaky-clean dishes or sparkling bathrooms? Not many.

Examples also make writing *persuasive*. Most writing conveys a point, but many readers are reluctant to accept someone else's point of view unless evidence demonstrates its validity. Imagine you're writing an essay showing that latchkey children are more self-sufficient and emotionally secure than children who return to a home where a parent awaits them. Without specific examples—from your own experience, personal observations, or research studies—your readers would undoubtedly question your position's validity.

Further, examples *help explain* difficult, abstract, or unusual ideas. Suppose you're assigned an essay on a complex subject such as inflation, zero population growth, or radiation exposure. As a writer, you have a responsibility to your readers to make these difficult concepts concrete and understandable. If writing an essay on radiation exposure in everyday life, you might start by providing specific examples of home appliances that emit radiation—color televisions, computers, and microwave ovens—and tell exactly how much radiation we absorb in a typical day from such equipment.

Finally, examples *help prevent unintended ambiguity*. All of us have experienced the frustration of having someone misinterpret what we say.

At this point, you have a good sense of the way writers use exemplification to achieve their purposes and to connect with their readers. Now take a moment to look closely at the advertisement at the beginning of this chapter. Imagine you're taking part in a "focus group" assembled by the advertiser of this product. Your task is to rate the ad on a scale of 1 (negative) to 10 (positive) on the basis of the images it promotes. To support your rating, jot down some phrases that express the values that you believe are *illustrated* by the ad.

In face-to-face communication, we can provide on-the-spot clarification. In writing, however, instantaneous feedback isn't available, so it's crucial that meaning be as unambiguous as possible. Examples will help.

SUGGESTIONS FOR USING EXEMPLIFICATION IN AN ESSAY

The suggestions here and in Figure 5.1 will be helpful whether you use examples as a dominant or a supportive pattern of development.

FIGURE 5.1
Development Diagram: Writing an Exemplification Essay

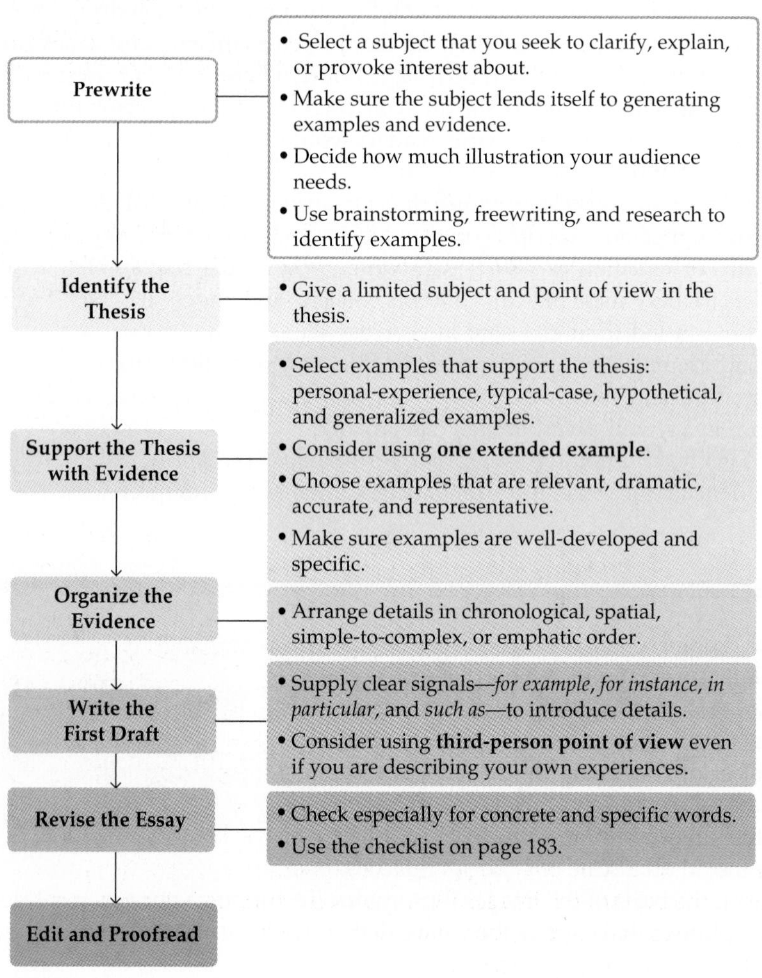

Prewrite
• Select a subject that you seek to clarify, explain, or provoke interest about.
• Make sure the subject lends itself to generating examples and evidence.
• Decide how much illustration your audience needs.
• Use brainstorming, freewriting, and research to identify examples.
Identify the Thesis
• Give a limited subject and point of view in the thesis.
Support the Thesis with Evidence
• Select examples that support the thesis: personal-experience, typical-case, hypothetical, and generalized examples.
• Consider using **one extended example**.
• Choose examples that are relevant, dramatic, accurate, and representative.
• Make sure examples are well-developed and specific.
Organize the Evidence
• Arrange details in chronological, spatial, simple-to-complex, or emphatic order.
Write the First Draft
• Supply clear signals—*for example, for instance, in particular*, and *such as*—to introduce details.
• Consider using **third-person point of view** even if you are describing your own experiences.
Revise the Essay
• Check especially for concrete and specific words.
• Use the checklist on page 183.
Edit and Proofread

1. Generate examples. The first batch of examples is generated during the prewriting stage. With your purpose and thesis in mind, you make a broad sweep for examples, using brainstorming, freewriting, the mapping technique—whichever prewriting technique you prefer. You may also read through your journal for relevant specifics, interview other people, or conduct library research.

Examples can take several forms, including specific names (of people, places, products, and so on), anecdotes, personal observations, expert opinion, as well as facts, statistics, and case studies gathered through research. While prewriting, try to generate more examples than you think you'll need. Starting with abundance—and then picking out the strongest examples—will give you a firm base on which to build the essay. If you have a great deal of trouble finding examples to support your thesis, you may need to revise the thesis. On the other hand, while prewriting, you may unearth numerous examples but find that many of them contradict the point you started out to support. If that happens, don't hesitate to recast your central point.

2. Select the examples to include. Once you've used prewriting to generate as many examples as possible, you're ready to limit your examples to the strongest ones. Keeping your purpose, thesis, and audience in mind, ask yourself several key questions: "Which examples support my thesis? Which do not? Which are most convincing? Which are most likely to interest readers and clarify meaning?"

You may include several brief examples within a single sentence:

> The French people's fascination with some American literary figures, such as Poe and Hawthorne, is understandable, but their great respect for "artists" like comedian Jerry Lewis is a mystery.

Or you may develop a paragraph with a number of "for instances":

> A uniquely American style of movie-acting reached its peak in the 1950s. Certain charismatic actors completely abandoned the stage techniques and tradition that had been the foundation of acting up to that time. Instead of articulating their lines clearly, the actors mumbled; instead of making firm eye contact with their colleagues, they hung their heads, shifted their eyes, even talked with their eyes closed. Marlon Brando, Montgomery Clift, and James Dean were three actors who exemplified this new trend.

As the preceding paragraph shows, *several examples* are usually needed to make a point. An essay with the thesis "Rock videos are dangerously violent" wouldn't be convincing if you gave only one example of a violent rock video. Several strong examples would be needed for readers to feel you had illustrated your point sufficiently.

As a general rule, you should strive for variety in the kinds of examples you include. For instance, you might choose a *personal-experience example* drawn from your own life or from the life of someone you know. Such examples pack the wallop of personal authority and lend drama to writing. Or you might include a *typical-case example,* an actual event or situation that did occur—but not to you or to anyone you know. The objective nature of such cases makes them especially convincing. You might also include a speculative or *hypothetical example* ("Imagine how difficult it must be for an elderly person to carry bags of groceries from the market to a bus stop several blocks away"). You'll find that hypothetical cases are effective for clarifying and dramatizing key points, but be sure to acknowledge that the example is indeed invented. Finally, you might create a *generalized example*—one that is a composite of the typical or usual. Such generalized examples are often signaled by words that involve the reader ("*All of us,* at one time or another, have been driven to distraction by a trivial annoyance like the buzzing of a fly or the sting of a paper cut"), or they may refer to humanity in general ("When *most people* get a compliment, they perk up, preen, and think the praise-giver is blessed with astute powers of observation").

Occasionally, *one extended example,* fully developed with many details, can support an essay. It might be possible, for instance, to support the thesis "States should raise the legal driving age to eighteen" with a single compelling, highly detailed example of the effects of one sixteen-year-old's high-speed driving spree.

The examples you choose must also be *relevant;* that is, they must have direct bearing on the point you want to make. You would have a hard time convincing readers that Americans have callous attitudes toward the elderly if you described the wide range of new programs, all staffed by volunteers, at a well-financed center for senior citizens. Because these examples *contradict,* rather than support, your thesis, readers are apt to dismiss what you have to say.

Make certain, too, that your examples are *accurate.* Exercise special caution when using statistics. An old saying warns that there are lies, damned lies, and statistics—meaning that statistics can be misleading. A commercial may claim, "In a taste test, 80 percent of those questioned indicated that they preferred Fizzy Cola." Impressed? Don't be—at least, not until you find out how the test was conducted.

Finally, select *representative* examples. Picking the oddball, one-in-a-million example to support a point—and passing it off as typical—is dishonest. Consider an essay with the thesis "Part-time jobs contribute to academic success." Citing only one example of a student who works at a job twenty-five hours a week while earning straight A's isn't playing fair. Why not? You've made a *hasty generalization* based on only one case. To be convincing, you need to show how holding down a job affects *most* students' academic performance. (For more on hasty generalizations, see pages 487–488.)

3. Develop your examples sufficiently. To ensure that you get your ideas across, your examples must be *specific.* An essay on the types of heroes in American movies wouldn't succeed if you simply strung together a series of undeveloped examples in paragraphs like this one:

> Heroes in American movies usually fall into types. One kind of hero is the tight-lipped loner, men like Clint Eastwood and Humphrey Bogart. Another movie hero is the quiet, shy, or fumbling type who has appeared in movies since the beginning. The main characteristic of this hero is lovableness, as seen in actors like Jimmy Stewart. Perhaps the most one-dimensional and predictable hero is the superman who battles tough odds. This kind of hero is best illustrated by Sylvester Stallone as Rocky and Rambo.

If you developed the essay in this way—if you moved from one undeveloped example to another—you would be doing little more than making a list. To be effective, key examples must be expanded in sufficient detail. The examples in the preceding paragraph could be developed in paragraphs of their own. You could, for instance, develop the first example this way:

> Heroes can be tight-lipped loners who appear out of nowhere, form no permanent attachments, and walk, drive, or ride off into the sunset. In many of his westerns, from the low-budget "spaghetti westerns" of the 1960s to *Unforgiven* in 1992, Clint Eastwood personifies this kind of hero. He is remote, mysterious, and not talkative. Yet he guns down an evil sheriff, runs other villains out of town, and helps a handicapped girl—acts that cement his heroic status. The loner might also be Sam Spade as played by Humphrey Bogart. Spade solves the crime and sends the guilty off to jail, yet he holds his emotions in check and has no permanent ties beyond his faithful secretary and shabby office. One gets the feeling that he could walk away from these, too, if necessary. Even in *The Right Stuff,* an account of the United States' early astronauts, the scriptwriters mold Chuck Yeager, the man who broke the sound barrier, into a classic loner. Yeager, portrayed by the aloof Sam Shepard, has a wife, but he is nevertheless insular. Taking mute pride in his ability to distance himself from politicians, bureaucrats, even colleagues, he soars into space, dignified and detached.

(For hints on ways to make writing specific, see pages 35–36.)

4. Organize the examples. If, as is usually the case, several examples support your point, be sure that you present the examples in an *organized* manner. Often you'll find that other patterns of development (cause-effect, comparison-contrast, definition, and so on) suggest ways to sequence examples. Let's say you're writing an essay showing that stay-at-home vacations offer numerous opportunities to relax. You might begin the essay with examples that *contrast* stay-at-home and get-away vacations. Then you might move to a *process analysis* that illustrates different techniques for unwinding at home. The essay might end with examples showing the *effect* of such leisurely at-home breaks.

Finally, you need to select an *organizational approach consistent* with your *purpose* and *thesis.* Imagine you're writing an essay about students' adjustment during the first months of college. The supporting examples could be arranged *chronologically.* You might start by illustrating the ambivalence many students feel the first day of college when their parents leave for home; you might then offer an anecdote or two about students' frequent calls to Mom and Dad during the opening weeks of the semester; the essay might close with an account of students' reluctance to leave campus at the midyear break.

Similarly, an essay demonstrating that a room often reflects the character of its occupant might be organized *spatially:* from the empty soda cans on the floor to the spitballs on the ceiling. In an essay illustrating the kinds of skills taught in a composition course, you might move from *simple* to *complex* examples: starting with relatively matter-of-fact skills such as spelling and punctuation and ending with more conceptually difficult skills such as formulating a thesis and organizing an essay. Last, the *emphatic sequence*—in which you lead from your first example to your final, most significant one—is another effective way to organize an essay with many examples.

5. Choose a point of view. Many essays developed by illustration place the subject in the foreground and the writer in the background. Such an approach calls for the *third-person point of view.* For example, even if you draw examples from your own personal experience, you can present them without using the *first-person* "I." You might convert such personal material into generalized examples (see page 179), or you might describe the personal experience as if it happened to someone else. Of course, you may use the first person if the use of "I" will make the example more believable and dramatic. But remember: Just because an event happened to you personally doesn't mean you have to use the first-person point of view.

REVISION STRATEGIES

Once you have a draft of the essay, you're ready to revise. The following checklist will help you and those giving you feedback apply to exemplification some of the revision techniques discussed on pages 60–62.

☑ EXEMPLIFICATION: A REVISION/PEER REVIEW CHECKLIST

Revise Overall Meaning and Structure

- ❑ What thesis is being advanced? Which examples don't support the thesis? Should these examples be deleted, or should the thesis be reshaped to fit the examples? Why?
- ❑ Which patterns of development and methods of organization (chronological, spatial, simple-to-complex, emphatic) provide the essay's framework? Would other ordering principles be more effective? If so, which ones?

Revise Paragraph Development

- ❑ Which paragraphs contain too many or too few examples? Which contain examples that are too brief or too extended? Which include insufficiently or overly detailed examples?
- ❑ Which paragraphs contain examples that could be made more compelling?
- ❑ Which paragraphs include examples that are atypical or incorrect?

Revise Sentences and Words

- ❑ What signal devices introduce examples and clarify the line of thought? Where are there too many or too few of these devices?
- ❑ Where would more varied sentence structure heighten the essay's illustrations?
- ❑ Where would more concrete and specific words make the examples more effective?

STUDENT ESSAY

The following student essay was written by Michael Pagano in response to this assignment:

> One implication in Beth Johnson's "Bombs Bursting in Air" is that, given life's unanticipated tragedies, people need to focus on what's really important rather than on trivial complications and distractions. Observe closely the way you and others conduct your daily lives. Use your observations for an essay that supports or refutes Johnson's point of view.

While reading Michael's paper, try to determine how effectively it applies the principles of exemplification. The annotations on Michael's paper and the commentary following it will help you look at the essay more closely.

Pursuit of Possessions
by Michael Pagano

Introduction

Thesis

Plan of development

In the essay "Bombs Bursting in Air," Beth Johnson develops the extended metaphor of bombs exploding unexpectedly to represent the tragedies that occur without warning in our daily lives. Herself a survivor of innumerable life bombs, Johnson suggests that in light of life's fragility, we need to remember and appreciate what's really important to us. But very often, we lose sight of what truly matters in our lives, instead occupying ourselves with trivial distractions. In particular, many of us choose to spend our lives in pursuit of material possessions. Much of our time goes into buying new things, dealing with the complications they create, and working madly to buy more things or pay for the things we already have. 1

Topic sentence

The first of three paragraph in a chronological sequence

We devote a great deal of our lives to acquiring the material goods we imagine are essential to our well-being. Hours are spent planning and thinking about our future purchases. We window-shop for designer jogging shoes; we leaf through magazines looking at ads for new sound equipment; we research back issues of *Consumer Reports* to find out about recent developments in exercise equipment. Moreover, once we find what we are looking for, more time is taken up when we decide to actually buy the items. How do we find this time? That's easy. We turn evenings, weekends, and holidays—time that used to be set aside for family and friends—into shopping expeditions. No wonder family life is deteriorating and children spend so much time in front of television sets. Their parents are seldom around. 2

Topic sentence

The second paragraph in the chronological sequence

A paragraph with many specific examples

As soon as we take our new purchases home, they begin to complicate our lives. A sleek new sports car has to be washed, waxed, and vacuumed. A fashionable pair of overpriced dress pants can't be thrown in the washing machine but must be taken to the dry cleaner. New sound equipment has to be connected with a tangled network of cables to the TV, computer, and speakers. Eventually, of course, the inevitable happens. Our indispensable possessions break down and need to be repaired. The home computer starts to lose data, the microwave has to have its temperature controls adjusted, and the DVD player has to be serviced when a disc becomes jammed in the machine. 3

Topic sentence

The third paragraph in the chronological sequence

After more time has gone by, we sometimes discover that our purchases don't suit us anymore, and so we decide to replace them. Before making our replacement purchases, though, we have to find ways to get rid of the old items. If we want to replace our "small" 19-inch television set with a 35-inch flat-screen, we have to find time to put an ad in the classified section of the paper. Then we have to handle phone calls and set up times people can come to look at the TV. We could store the set in the basement—if we are lucky enough to find a spot that isn't already filled with other discarded purchases. 4

Topic sentence with emphasis signal

Worst of all, this mania for possessions often influences our approach to work. It is not unusual for people to take a second or even a third job to pay off the debt they fall into because they have overbought. After paying for food, clothing, and shelter, many people see the rest of their paycheck go to Visa, MasterCard, department store charge accounts, and time payments. Panic sets in when they realize there simply is not enough money to cover all their expenses. Just to stay afloat, people may have to work overtime or take on additional jobs. 5

Conclusion

It is clear that many of us have allowed the pursuit of possessions to dominate our lives. We are so busy buying, maintaining, and paying for our worldly goods that we do not have much time to think about what is really important. We should try to step back from our compulsive need for more of everything and get in touch with the basic values that are the real point of our lives. 6

COMMENTARY

Thesis, combining patterns of development, and plan of development. In "Pursuit of Possessions," Michael analyzes the mania for acquiring material goods that permeates our society. He begins by addressing an implication conveyed in Beth Johnson's "Bombs Bursting in Air"—that life's fragility dictates that we need to focus on what really matters in our lives. This reference to Johnson gives Michael a chance to *contrast* the reflective way she suggests we should live with the acquisitive and frenzied way many people lead their lives. This contrast leads to the essay's *thesis:* "[M]any of us choose to spend our lives in pursuit of material possessions."

Besides introducing the basic contrast at the heart of the essay, Michael's opening paragraph helps readers see that the essay contains an element of *causal analysis.* The final sentence of the introductory paragraph lays out the effects of our possession obsession. This sentence also serves as the essay's *plan of development* and reveals that Michael feels the pursuit of possessions negatively affects our lives in three key ways.

Evidence. Support for the thesis consists of numerous examples presented in the *first-person-plural point of view* ("*[W]e* lose sight of...," "*We* devote a great deal of our lives...," and so on). Many of these examples seem drawn from Michael's, his friends', or his family's experiences; however, to emphasize the events' universality, Michael converts these essentially personal examples into generalized ones that "we" all experience.

These examples, in turn, are organized around the three major points signaled by the plan of development. Michael uses one paragraph to develop his first and third points and two paragraphs to develop his second point. Each of the four supporting paragraphs is focused by a *topic sentence* that appears at the start of the paragraph. The transitional phrase "Worst of all" (paragraph 5) signals that Michael has sequenced his major points *emphatically,* saving for last the issue he considers most significant: how the "mania for possessions... influences our approach to work."

Organizational strategies. Emphatic order isn't Michael's only organizational technique. When reading the paper, you probably felt that there was an easy flow from one supporting paragraph to the next. How does Michael achieve such *coherence between paragraphs?* For one thing, he sequences paragraphs 2–4 *chronologically:* what happens before a purchase is made; what happens afterward. Secondly, topic sentences in paragraphs 3 and 4 include *signal devices* that indicate this passage of time. The topic sentences also strengthen coherence by *linking back* to the preceding paragraph: "*As soon as we take our new purchases home,* they... complicate our lives" and "*After more time has gone by,* we... discover that our purchases don't suit us anymore."

The same organizing strategies are used *within paragraphs* to make the essay coherent. Details in paragraphs 2 through 4 are sequenced chronologically, and to help readers follow the chronology, Michael uses *signal devices:* "*Moreover, once* we find what we are looking for, more time is taken up..." (2); "*Eventually,* of course, the inevitable happens" (3); "*Then* we have to handle phone calls..." (4).

Problems with paragraph development. You probably recall that an essay developed primarily through exemplification must include examples that are *relevant, interesting, convincing, representative, accurate,* and *specific.* On the whole, Michael's examples meet these requirements. The third and fourth paragraphs, especially, include vigorous details that show how our mania for buying things can govern our lives. We may even laugh with self-recognition when reading about "overpriced dress pants [that] can't be thrown in the washing machine" or a basement "filled with other discarded purchases."

The fifth paragraph, however, is underdeveloped. We know that this paragraph presents what Michael considers his most significant point, but the paragraph's examples are rather *flat* and *unconvincing.* To make this final section more compelling, Michael could mention specific people who overspend, revealing how much they are in debt and how much they have to work to become solvent again. Or he could cite a television documentary or magazine article dealing with the issue of consumer debt. Such specifics would give the paragraph the solidity it now lacks.

Shift in tone. The fifth paragraph has a second, more subtle problem; *a shift in tone.* Although Michael has, up to this point, been critical of our possession-mad culture, he has poked fun at our obsession and kept his tone conversational and gently satiric. In this paragraph, though, he adopts a serious tone and, in the next paragraph, his tone becomes even weightier, almost preachy. It is, of course, legitimate to have a serious message in a lightly satiric piece. In fact, most satiric writing has such an additional layer of meaning. But because Michael has trouble blending these two moods, there's a jarring shift in the essay.

Shift in focus. The second paragraph shows another kind of shift—in *focus.* The paragraph's controlling idea is that too much time is spent acquiring possessions. However, starting with "No wonder family life is deteriorating," Michael includes two sentences that introduce a complex issue beyond the scope of the essay. Since these last two sentences disrupt the paragraph's unity, they should be deleted.

Revising the first draft. Although the final version of the essay needs work in spots, it's much stronger than Michael's first draft. To see how Michael went about revising the draft, compare his paper's second and third supporting paragraphs with his draft version reprinted here.

Original Version of the Second Paragraph

Our lives are spent not only buying things but in dealing with the inevitable complications that are created by our newly acquired possessions. First, we have to find places to put all the objects we bring home. More clothes demand more closets; a second car demands more garage space; a home entertainment center requires elaborate shelving. We shouldn't be surprised that the average American family moves once every three years. A good many families move simply because they need more space to store all the things they buy. In addition, our possessions demand maintenance time. A person who gets a new car will spend hours washing it, waxing it, and vacuuming it. A new pair of pants has to go to the dry cleaners. New sound systems have to be connected to already existing equipment. Eventually, of course, the inevitable happens. Our new items need to be repaired. Or we get sick of them and decide to replace them. Before making our replacement purchases, though, we have to get rid of the old items. That can be a real inconvenience.

When Michael looked more closely at this paragraph, he realized it rambled and lacked energy. He started to revise the paragraph by tightening the first sentence, making it more focused and less awkward. Certainly, the revised sentence ("As soon as we take our new purchases home, they begin to complicate our lives") is crisper than the original. Next, he decided to omit the discussion about finding places to put new possessions; these sentences about inadequate closet, garage, and shelf space were so exaggerated that they undercut the valid point he wanted to make. He also chose to eliminate the sentences about the mobility of American families. This was, he felt, an interesting point, but it introduced an issue too complex to be included in the paragraph.

Michael strengthened the rest of the paragraph by making his examples more specific. A "new car" became a "sleek new sports car," and a "pair of pants" became a "fashionable pair of overpriced dress pants." Michael also realized he had to do more than merely write, "Eventually,... our new items need to be repaired." This point had to be dramatized by sharp, convincing details. Therefore, Michael added lively examples to describe how high-tech possessions—microwaves, home computers, DVD players—break down. Similarly, Michael realized it wasn't enough simply to say, as he had in the original, that we run into problems when we try to replace out-of-favor purchases. Vigorous details were again needed to illustrate the point. Michael thus used a typical "replaceable" (a "small" 19-inch TV set) as his key example and showed the annoyance involved in handling phone calls and setting up appointments so people could see the TV.

After adding these specifics, Michael realized he had enough material to devote a separate paragraph to the problems associated with replacing old purchases. By dividing his original paragraph, Michael ended up with two well-focused paragraphs, neither of which has the rambling quality found in the original.

In short, Michael strengthened his essay through substantial revision. Another round of rewriting would have made the essay stronger still. Even without this additional work, Michael's essay provides an interesting perspective on an American preoccupation.

Activities: Exemplification

Prewriting Activities

1. Imagine you're writing two essays: One is a serious paper analyzing the factors that *cause* large numbers of public school teachers to leave the profession each year; the other is a light essay *defining* "preppie," "head banger," or some other slang term used to describe a kind of person. Jot down ways you might use examples in each essay.

2. Use mapping or another prewriting technique to gather examples illustrating the truth of *one* of the following familiar sayings. Then, using the same or a different prewriting technique, accumulate examples that counter the saying. Weigh both sets of examples to determine the saying's validity. After developing an appropriate thesis, decide which examples you would elaborate in an essay.
   a. Haste makes waste.
   b. There's no use crying over spilled milk.
   c. A bird in the hand is worth two in the bush.

Revising Activities

3. The following paragraph is from the first draft of an essay about the decline of small-town shopping districts. The paragraph is meant to show what small towns can do to revitalize business. Revise the paragraph, strengthening it with specific and convincing examples.

   A small town can compete with a large new mall for shoppers. But merchants must work together, modernizing the stores and making the town's main street pleasant, even fun, to walk. They should also copy the malls' example by including attention-getting events as often as possible.

4. Reprinted here is a paragraph from the first draft of a light-spirited essay showing that Americans' pursuit of change for change's sake has drawbacks. The paragraph is meant to illustrate that infatuation with newness costs consumers money yet leads to no improvement in product quality. How effective is the paragraph? Which examples are specific and convincing? Which are not? Do any seem nonrepresentative, offensive, or sexist? How could the paragraph's organization be improved? Consider these questions as you rewrite the paragraph. Add specific examples where needed. Depending on the way you revise, you may want to break this one paragraph into several.

   We end up paying for our passion for the new and improved. Trendy clothing styles convince us that last year's outfits are outdated, even though our old clothes are fine. Women are especially vulnerable in this regard. What, though, about items that have to be replaced periodically, like shampoo? Even slight changes lead to new formulations requiring retooling of the production process. That means increased manufacturing costs per item–all of which get passed on to us, the consumer. Then there are those items that tout new, trendsetting features that make earlier versions supposedly obsolete. Some manufacturers, for example, boast that their sound systems transmit an expanded-frequency range. The problem is that humans can't even hear such frequencies. But the high-tech feature dazzles men who are too naive to realize they're being hoodwinked.

Kay S. Hymowitz

A senior fellow at the Manhattan Institute and a contributing editor of the urban-policy magazine *City Journal,* Kay S. Hymowitz (1948–) writes on education and childhood in America. A native of Philadelphia, Hymowitz received graduate degrees from Tufts University and Columbia University. She has taught English literature and composition at Brooklyn College and at Parsons School of Design. Hymowitz is the author of *Liberation's Children: Parents and Kids in a Postmodern Age* (2003) and *Ready or Not: Why Treating Our Children as Small Adults Endangers Their Future and Ours* (1999) and is a principal contributor to *Modern Sex: Liberation and Its Discontents* (2001). In 2006, she published *Marriage and Caste in America: Separate and Unequal Families in a Post-Marital Age,* a collection of her *City Journal* essays. Her latest book is *Manning Up: How the Rise of Women Is Turning Men into Boys* (2011). Her work has appeared in publications including *The New York Times, The Washington Post,* and *The New Republic.* The following essay appeared in the Autumn 1998 issue of *City Journal.*

For ideas about how this exemplification essay is organized, see Figure 5.2 page 195.

Pre-Reading Journal Entry

Think back on your childhood. What were some possessions and activities that you cherished and enjoyed? Freewrite for a few moments in your pre-reading journal about these beloved objects and/or pastimes. What exactly were they? Why did you enjoy them so much? Did your feelings about them change as you matured into adolescence?

Tweens: Ten Going On Sixteen

During the past year my youngest morphed from child to teenager. Down came the posters of adorable puppies and the drawings from art class; up went the airbrushed faces of Leonardo di Caprio and Kate Winslet. CDs of Le Ann Rimes and Paula Cole appeared mysteriously, along with teen fan magazines featuring glowering movie and rock-and-roll hunks.... She started reading the newspaper—or at least the movie ads—with all the intensity of a Talmudic scholar, scanning for glimpses of her beloved Leo or, failing that, Matt Damon. As spring approached and younger children skipped past our house on their way to the park, she swigged from a designer water bottle, wearing the obligatory tank top and denim shorts as she whispered on the phone to friends about games of Truth or Dare. The last rites for her childhood came when, embarrassed at reminders of her foolish past, she pulled a sheet over her years-in-the-making American Girl doll collection, now dead to the world. 1

So what's new in this dog-bites-man story? Well, as all this was going on, my daughter was ten years old and in the fourth grade. 2

Those who remember their own teenybopper infatuation with Elvis or the Beatles might be inclined to shrug their shoulders as if to say, "It was ever thus." But this is different. Across class lines and throughout the country, elementary and middle-school principals and teachers, child psychologists and psychiatrists, marketing and demographic researchers all confirm the pronouncement of Henry Trevor, middle-school director of the Berkeley Carroll School in Brooklyn, New York: "There is no such thing as preadolescence anymore. Kids are teenagers at ten." 3

Marketers have a term for this new social animal, kids between eight and 12: they call them "tweens." The name captures the ambiguous reality: though chronologically midway between early childhood and adolescence, this group is leaning more and more toward teen styles, teen attitudes, and, sadly, teen behavior at its most troubling. 4

The tween phenomenon grows out of a complicated mixture of biology, demography, and the predictable assortment of Bad Ideas. But putting aside its causes for a moment, the emergence of tweendom carries risks for both young people and society. Eight- to 12-year-olds have an even more wobbly sense of themselves than adolescents; they rely more heavily on others to tell them how to understand the world and how to place themselves in it. Now, for both pragmatic and ideological reasons, they are being increasingly "empowered" to do this on their own, which leaves them highly vulnerable both to a vulgar and sensation-driven marketplace and to the crass authority of their immature peers. In tweens, we can see the future of our society taking shape, and it's not at all clear how it's going to work. 5

Perhaps the most striking evidence for the tweening of children comes from market researchers. "There's no question there's a deep trend, not a passing fad, toward kids getting older younger," says research psychologist Michael Cohen of Arc Consulting, a public policy, education, and marketing research firm in New York. "This is not just on the coasts. There are no real differences geographically." It seems my daughter's last rites for her American Girl dolls were a perfect symbol not just for her own childhood but for childhood, period. The Toy Manufacturers of America Factbook states that, where once the industry could count on kids between birth and 14 as their target market, today it is only birth to ten. "In the last ten years we've seen a rapid development of upper-age children," says Bruce Friend, vice president of worldwide research and planning for Nickelodeon, a cable channel aimed at kids. "The 12- to 14-year-olds of yesterday are the ten to 12s of today." The rise of the preteen teen is "the biggest trend we've seen." 6

Scorning any symbols of their immaturity, tweens now cultivate a self-image that emphasizes sophistication. The Nickelodeon-Yankelovich Youth Monitor found that by the time they are 12, children describe themselves as "flirtatious, sexy, trendy, athletic, cool." Nickelodeon's Bruce Friend reports that by 11, children in focus groups say they no longer even think of themselves as children. 7

They're very concerned with their "look," Friend says, even more so than older teens. Sprouting up everywhere are clothing stores like the chain Limited Too and the catalog company Delia, geared toward tween girls who scorn old-fashioned, little-girl flowers, ruffles, white socks, and Mary Janes[1] in favor of the cool—black mini-dresses and platform shoes.... Teachers complain of ten- or 11-year-old girls arriving at school looking like madams, in full cosmetic regalia, with streaked hair, platform shoes, and midriff-revealing shirts. Barbara Kapetanakes, a psychologist at a conservative Jewish day school in New York, describes her students' skirts as being about "the size of a belt." Kapetanakes says she was told to dress respectfully on Fridays, the eve of the Jewish Sabbath, which she did by donning a long skirt and a modest blouse. Her students, on the other hand, showed their respect by looking "like they should be hanging around the West Side Highway," where prostitutes ply their trade. 8

Lottie Sims, a computer teacher in a Miami middle school, says that the hooker look for tweens is fanning strong support for uniforms in her district. But uniforms and tank-top bans won't solve the problem of painted young ladies. "You can count on one hand the girls not wearing makeup," Sims says. "Their parents don't even know. They arrive at school with huge bags of lipstick and hair spray, and head straight to the girls' room." 9

Though the tweening of youth affects girls more visibly than boys, especially since boys mature more slowly, boys are by no means immune to these obsessions. Once upon a time, about ten years ago, fifth- and sixth-grade boys were about as fashion-conscious as their pet hamsters. But a growing minority have begun trading in their baseball cards for hair mousse and baggy jeans. In some places, \$200 jackets, emblazoned with sports logos like the warm-up gear of professional athletes, are *de rigueur;* in others, the preppy look is popular among the majority, while the more daring go for the hipper style of pierced ears, fade haircuts, or ponytails. Often these tween peacocks strut through their middle-school hallways taunting those who have yet to catch on to the cool look.... 10

Those who seek comfort in the idea that the tweening of childhood is merely a matter of fashion—who maybe even find their lip-synching, hip-swaying little boy or girl kind of cute—might want to think twice. There are disturbing signs that tweens are not only eschewing the goody-goody childhood image but its substance as well.... 11

The clearest evidence of tweendom's darker side concerns crime. Although children under 15 still represent a minority of juvenile arrests, their numbers grew disproportionately in the past 20 years. According to a report by the Office of Juvenile Justice and Delinquency Prevention, "offenders under age 12

[1]Trademark name of patent-leather shoes for girls, usually having a low heel and a strap that fastens at the side (editors' note).

15 represent the leading edge of the juvenile crime problem, and their numbers are growing." Moreover, the crimes committed by younger teens and preteens are growing in severity. "Person offenses,[2] which once constituted 16 percent of the total court cases for this age group," continues the report, "now constitute 25 percent." Headline grabbers—like Nathaniel Abraham of Pontiac, Michigan, an 11-year-old who stole a rifle from a neighbor's garage and went on a shooting spree in October 1997, randomly killing a teenager coming out of a store; and 11-year-old Andrew Golden, who, with his 13-year-old partner, killed four children and one teacher at his middle school in Jonesboro, Arkansas—are extreme, exceptional cases, but alas, they are part of a growing trend toward preteen violent crime....

The evidence on tween sex presents a troubling picture, too. Despite a 13
decrease among older teens for the first time since records have been kept, sexual activity among tweens increased during that period. It seems that kids who are having sex are doing so at earlier ages. Between 1988 and 1995, the proportion of girls saying they began sex before 15 rose from 11 percent to 19 percent. (For boys, the number remained stable, at 21 percent.) This means that approximately one in five middle-school kids is sexually active. Christie Hogan, a middle-school counselor for 20 years in Louisville, Kentucky, says: "We're beginning to see a few pregnant sixth-graders." Many of the principals and counselors I spoke with reported a small but striking minority of sexually active seventh-graders....

Certainly the days of the tentative and giggly preadolescent seem to 14
be passing. Middle-school principals report having to deal with miniskirted 12-year-olds "draping themselves over boys" or patting their behinds in the hallways, while 11-year-old boys taunt girls about their breasts and rumors about their own and even their parents' sexual proclivities. Tweens have even given new connotations to the word "playground": one fifth-grade teacher from southwestern Ohio told me of two youngsters discovered in the bushes during recess.

Drugs and alcohol are also seeping into tween culture. The past six years 15
have seen more than a doubling of the number of eighth-graders who smoke marijuana (10 percent today) and those who no longer see it as dangerous. "The stigma isn't there the way it was ten years ago," says Dan Kindlon, assistant professor of psychiatry at Harvard Medical School and co-author with Michael Thompson of *Raising Cain*. "Then it was the fringe group smoking pot. You were looked at strangely. Now the fringe group is using LSD."

Aside from sex, drugs, and rock and roll, another teen problem—eating 16
disorders—is also beginning to affect younger kids. This behavior grows out of premature fashion-consciousness, which has an even more pernicious effect on tweens than on teens, because, by definition, younger kids have a more

[2]Crimes against a person. They include assault, robbery, rape, and homicide (editors' note).

vulnerable and insecure self-image. Therapists say they are seeing a growing number of anorexics and obsessive dieters even among late-elementary-school girls. "You go on Internet chat rooms and find ten- and 11-year-olds who know every [fashion] model and every statistic about them," says Nancy Kolodny, a Connecticut-based therapist and author of *When Food's a Foe: How You Can Confront and Conquer Your Eating Disorder*. "Kate Moss is their god. They can tell if she's lost a few pounds or gained a few. If a powerful kid is talking about this stuff at school, it has a big effect."

What change in our social ecology has led to the emergence of tweens? Many note that kids are reaching puberty at earlier ages, but while earlier physical maturation may play a small role in defining adolescence down, its importance tends to be overstated. True, the average age at which girls begin to menstruate has fallen from 13 to between 11 and 12½ today, but the very gradualness of this change means that 12-year-olds have been living inside near-adult bodies for many decades without feeling impelled to build up a cosmetics arsenal or head for the bushes at recess. In fact, some experts believe that the very years that have witnessed the rise of the tween have also seen the age of first menstruation stabilize. Further, teachers and principals on the front lines see no clear correlation between physical and social maturation. Plenty of budding girls and bulking boys have not put away childish things, while an abundance of girls with flat chests and boys with squeaky voices ape the body language and fashions of their older siblings.... 17

Of course, the causes are complex, and most people working with tweens know it. In my conversations with educators and child psychologists who work primarily with middle-class kids nationwide, two major and fairly predictable themes emerged: a sexualized and glitzy media-driven marketplace and absentee parents. What has been less commonly recognized is that at this age, the two causes combine to augment the authority of the peer group, which in turn both weakens the influence of parents and reinforces the power of the media. Taken together, parental absence, the market, and the peer group form a vicious circle that works to distort the development of youngsters.... 18

Questions for Close Reading

1. What is the selection's thesis? Locate the sentence(s) in which Hymowitz states her main idea. If she doesn't state the thesis explicitly, express it in your own words.
2. According to Hymowitz, what self-image do tweens cultivate? How do they "project" this image to others?
3. What physically dangerous behavioral trends does Hymowitz link to the tween phenomenon?
4. According to Hymowitz, what are the primary causes of the tween phenomenon?
5. Refer to your dictionary as needed to define the following words used in the selection: *glowering* (paragraph 1), *Talmudic* (1), *rites* (1), *demographic* (3), *pragmatic* (5), *ideological* (5), *regalia* (8), *donning* (8), *ply* (8), *emblazoned* (10), *de rigueur* (10),

eschewing (11), *tentative* (14), *proclivities* (14), *connotations* (14), *stigma* (15), *pernicious* (16), *correlation* (17), and *augment* (18).

Questions About the Writer's Craft

1. **The pattern.** Hymowitz opens her essay with an anecdotal example of tweenhood—her daughter's. What does this example add to her essay?
2. **The pattern.** What types of examples does Hymowitz provide in her essay? (See pages 179–181 for a discussion of the various forms that examples can take.) Cite at least one example of each type. How does each type of example contribute to her thesis?
3. How would you characterize Hymowitz's tone in the selection? Cite vocabulary that conveys this tone.
4. **Other patterns.** In paragraph 8, Hymowitz uses clothing as a means of presenting an important *contrast.* What does she contrast in these paragraphs? How does this contribute to her thesis?

FIGURE 5.2
Essay Structure Diagram: "Tweens: Ten Going On Sixteen" by Kay S. Hymowitz

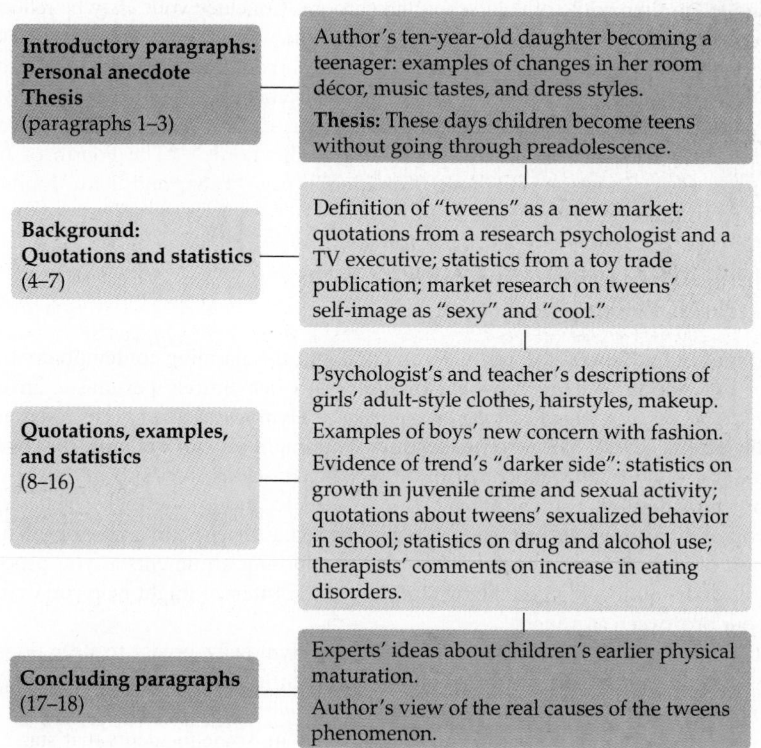

Introductory paragraphs: Personal anecdote Thesis (paragraphs 1–3)
Author's ten-year-old daughter becoming a teenager: examples of changes in her room décor, music tastes, and dress styles.
Thesis: These days children become teens without going through preadolescence.
Background: Quotations and statistics (4–7)
Definition of "tweens" as a new market: quotations from a research psychologist and a TV executive; statistics from a toy trade publication; market research on tweens' self-image as "sexy" and "cool."
Quotations, examples, and statistics (8–16)
Psychologist's and teacher's descriptions of girls' adult-style clothes, hairstyles, makeup.
Examples of boys' new concern with fashion.
Evidence of trend's "darker side": statistics on growth in juvenile crime and sexual activity; quotations about tweens' sexualized behavior in school; statistics on drug and alcohol use; therapists' comments on increase in eating disorders.
Concluding paragraphs (17–18)
Experts' ideas about children's earlier physical maturation.
Author's view of the real causes of the tweens phenomenon.

Writing Assignments Using Exemplification as a Pattern of Development

1. Hymowitz is troubled and perplexed by her daughter's behavior. Think about an older person, such as a parent or another relative, who finds *your* behavior troubling and perplexing. Write an essay in which you illustrate why your behavior distresses this person. (Or, conversely, think of an elder whose behavior *you* find problematic, and write an essay illustrating why that person evokes this response in you.) You might structure your essay by picking the two or three most irksome characteristics or habits and developing supporting paragraphs around each of them. However you choose to organize your essay, be sure to provide abundant examples throughout.
2. The cultivation of a sophisticated self-image is, according to Hymowitz, a hallmark of tweenhood. Think back to when you were around that age. What was your self-image at that time? Did you think of yourself as worldly or inexperienced? Cool or awkward? Attractive or unappealing? In your journal, freewrite about the traits that you would have identified in yourself as either a tween or an adolescent. Write an essay in which you illustrate your self-image at that age, focusing on two to three dominant characteristics you associated with yourself. It's important that you illustrate each trait with examples of when and how you displayed it. For example, if you saw yourself as "dorky," you might recall an embarrassing time when you tripped and fell in the middle of your school lunchroom. Conclude your essay by reflecting on whether the way you saw yourself at the time was accurate, and whether your feelings about yourself have changed since then. You'd also benefit from reading any of the following authors' musings on their childhood self-perceptions: Maya Angelou's "Sister Flowers" (page 87), Judith Ortiz Cofer's "A Partial Remembrance of a Puerto Rican Childhood" (page 117), Audre Lorde's "The Fourth of July" (page 140), Langston Hughes's "Salvation" (page 158), and Beth Johnson's "Bombs Bursting in Air" (page 211).

Writing Assignments Combining Patterns of Development

3. Hymowitz advances a powerful argument about the alarming contemporary trend of tweenhood. But many would disagree with her entirely pessimistic analysis. Write an essay in which you *argue*, contrary to Hymowitz, that tweens today actually exhibit several *positive* characteristics. You might say, for example, that tweens today are more independent or more socially conscious than kids in the past. In order to develop your argument, you'll need to show how each characteristic you're discussing *contrasts* favorably with that characteristic in a previous generation of kids. Be sure, too, to acknowledge opposing arguments as you proceed. Research conducted in the library and/or on the Internet might help you develop your pro-tween argument.
4. Though she doesn't use the term explicitly, Hymowitz points to peer pressure as a significant factor in tweens' premature maturity. In your journal, take a few moments to reflect on your own experiences with peer pressure, whether as a pre-teen or teen, or even into adulthood. What are some incidents that stand out

in your memory? Write an essay *narrating* a particularly memorable incident of peer pressure in which you were involved. You may have been the object of the pressure, or even perhaps the source. What were the circumstances? Who was involved? How did you respond at the time? How did the episode *affect* you? In retrospect, how do you feel about the incident today? Be sure to use dialogue as well as *descriptive* language in order to make the episode come alive.

Writing Assignment Using a Journal Entry as a Starting Point

5. As a way of illustrating her daughter's evolving tween tastes, Hymowitz cites the "years-in-the-making American Girl doll collection" over which her disaffected daughter has now drawn a sheet. Reviewing what you wrote in your pre-reading journal entry, identify some once-loved childhood items or activities that you distanced yourself from as you got older. Write an essay in which you exemplify your growth into adolescence by identifying two or three childhood possessions or activities that you cast off. You might, for example, discuss building up a beloved rock collection or playing with action figures. As you introduce these items, be sure to describe them and to explain the significance they once held for you, as well as your reasons for leaving them behind. Conclude your essay by offering some reflections on whether you currently regard the childhood items with the same distaste or disinterest you felt as a teen.

Charles Sykes

A journalist whose work has appeared in the *The New York Times, The Wall Street Journal,* and other leading newspapers, Charles Sykes (1954–) usually writes about education issues. His books include *ProfScam: Professors and the Demise of Higher Education* (1988), *The Hollow Men: Politics and Corruption in Higher Education* (1990), *A Nation of Victims: The Decay of the American Character* (1992), *The End of Privacy* (1999), and *50 Rules Kids Won't Learn in School* (2007). A senior fellow at the Wisconsin Policy Research Institute and host of a popular Milwaukee radio show, Sykes lectures widely on topics having to do with what he sees as the collapse of standards in American culture. The following excerpt is from Sykes's 1995 book, *Dumbing Down Our Kids: Why America's Children Feel Good About Themselves but Can't Read, Write, or Add.*

Pre-Reading Journal Entry

Studies reveal that sexual misbehavior, drug use, shoplifting, and cheating are common among some young people. In your journal, explore your thinking about young people's misconduct in two of these (or other) areas. Why do you think young people engage in such risky behavior?

The "Values" Wasteland

Eric Richardson was a seventeen-year-old member of the Spur Posse, a group of boys accused of raping girls as young as ten years old. After their arrests, the posse members reportedly returned to school as heroes, applauded for their exploits by their fellow students. In talk show appearances and media interviews, the boys were unrepentant. "They pass out condoms, teach sex education and pregnancy this and pregnancy that," Eric said after polishing off a Nacho Supreme and necking with his girlfriend in a booth at the Taco Bell. "But they don't teach us any rules."[1] His response was too glib and too convenient; it wasn't our fault, he was saying, you taught us to be like this. No school, however misguided, can ever be blamed for a piece of work like Eric Richardson. Even so, the evidence suggests that his ethical compass is not an isolated aberration. 1

A 1988 study of more than 2,000 Rhode Island students in grades six through nine found that two-thirds of the boys and half of the girls thought that "it was acceptable for a man to force sex on a woman" if they had been dating six months or more.[2] A write-in survey of 126,000 teenagers found 2

[1]Jane Gross, "Where 'Boys will be Boys,' And Adults Are Bewildered," *New York Times,* 29 March 1993.

[2]J. Kikuchi, "Rhode Island Develops Successful Intervention Program for Adolescents," *National Coalition Against Sexual Assault Newsletter,* Fall 1988.

that 25 to 40 percent of teens see nothing wrong with cheating on exams, stealing from employers, or keeping money that wasn't theirs. A seventeen-year-old high school senior explained: "A lot of it is a gray area. It's everybody doing their own thing."[3]

A 1992 survey by the Josephson Institute for Ethics of nearly 7,000 high school and college students, most of them from middle- and upper middle-class backgrounds, found the equivalent of a "hole in the moral ozone" among American youth. 3

- A third of high school students and 16 percent of college students said they have shoplifted in the last year. Nearly the same number (33 percent of high school students and 11 percent of college students) said they have stolen from their parents or relatives at least once.[4]
- One in eight college students admitted to committing an act of fraud, including borrowing money they did not intend to repay, and lying on financial aid or insurance forms.
- A third of high school and college students said they would lie to get a job. One in six said they have already done so at least once.
- More than 60 percent of high school students said they had cheated at least once on an exam.
- Forty percent of the high school students who participated in this survey admitted that they "were not completely honest" on at least one or two questions—meaning that they may have lied on a survey about lying.[5]

"I think it's very easy to get through high school and college these days and hardly ever hear, 'That's wrong,'" commented Patrick McCarthy of Pasadena's Jefferson Center for Character Education. Michael Josephson, the president of the Josephson Institute of Ethics, describes a large and growing population as the "I-Deserve-Its," or IDIs. "Their IDI-ology is exceptionally and dangerously self-centered, preoccupied with personal needs, wants, don't-wants and rights." In pursuit of success, or comfort, or self-gratification, the IDIs are blithely willing to jettison traditional ethical restraints, and as a result "IDIs are more likely to lie, cheat and engage in irresponsible behavior when it suits their purposes. IDIs act as if they need whatever they want and deserve whatever they need...."[6] American youth's culture of entitlement cannot, of course, be laid solely at the feet of the schools. If there has been an ethical meltdown among young Americans we need to look first to their parents, 4

[3] *USA Weekend*, 21–22 August 1992.
[4] Gary Abrams, "Youth Gets Bad Marks in Morality," *Los Angeles Times*, 12 November 1992.
[5] Ibid.
[6] Michael Josephson, "Young America Is Looking Out for No. 1," *Los Angeles Times*, 16 October 1990.

communities, the media, and even the churches for explanations. Society's shift from a culture of self-control to one of self-gratification, self-actualization, and self-realization, and its changing norms regarding personal responsibility and character, was not restricted to the arena of public education. Even so, the ethical state of America's young people may, at least in part, have something to do with the way our schools teach them about right and wrong.

At one time, American students used to study historical role models like 5
Benjamin Franklin, Florence Nightingale, Thomas Edison, Madame Curie, Abraham Lincoln, and George Washington—whose stories were used to provide object lessons in inventiveness, character, compassion, curiosity, and truthfulness. Following Aristotle, ethicists recognized that humanity does not become virtuous simply by precept, but by "nature, habit, rational principle." "We become just by the practice of just actions," Aristotle observed, "self-controlled by exercising self-control." This process was most effectively begun by placing examples of such virtues in front of young people for them to emulate. But while Asian children continue to read about stories of perseverance, hard work, loyalty, duty, prudence, heroism, and honesty, [educational researcher] Harold Stevenson finds that "For the most part, such cultural models have been displaced in the United States today."[7] In its place, we provide children a jumbled smorgasbord of moral choices.

How Do You *Feel* About Cheating?

The course is officially about "citizenship," but the subject is values.[8] 6
Specially prepared for students in the fourth to sixth grades, the class is designed to help students clarify and discover their own values on issues like lying and cheating. As a group or by secret ballot, the fourth, fifth, and sixth graders are asked: "How many of you . . .

Think children should have to work for their allowances?
Think most rules are dumb?
Think that there are times when cheating is ok?
Wish you didn't have grades in school?
Think prizes should be awarded for everything?"

The section on cheating asks students: "What are your attitudes toward cheating?" They are asked to complete the following statements:

Tests are ______________
Grades are ______________

[7]Harold W. Stevenson and James W. Stigler, *The Learning Gap* (New York: Summit Books, 1992), pp. 85–86.
[8]"Citizenship: 4th–6th Grade," xeroxed worksheets, undated. Several copies were provided to me by parents whose children had been given the assignment during class.

The bad thing about cheating is ______________
The good thing about cheating is ______________
If there were no such things as grades, would your attitude toward cheating change?
Is school the only place cheating takes place? Where else does cheating take place?
Is it ever OK to cheat? When?

It is not clear whether there are ever any right and wrong answers to these questions. The class takes a similar approach to lying. Students are asked, "Lying, What's Your View?"...Children in the class are...presented with a series of ethical problems. They are not asked to define right and wrong or moral or immoral. Instead, they are asked to say which actions are "acceptable...and...which are...unacceptable. Do any of the situations involve lying?" 7

A factory worker oversleeps and is late for work. He tells his supervisor that he was involved in a minor traffic accident.
Janine just can't face a big history exam for which she hasn't studied. She convinces her mother that she has a terrible sore throat and must stay home.
Bill runs into a friend he hasn't seen in months. The friend asks how he is. Bill smiles and answers "great!" even though his dog just died, he's flunking English, and he just broke up with his girlfriend....

Such nonjudgmentalism is a feature of the approach known as "values clarification," in which, as [journalist] William Kirk Kilpatrick writes, classroom discussions are turned into "'bull sessions' where opinions go back and forth but conclusions are never reached."...Many of these classes seem to be based on the rather fantastic notion that since none of the civilizations anywhere in the world throughout the entire sweep of human history has been able to work out a moral code of conduct worthy of being passed on, we should therefore leave it to fourth graders to work out questions of right and wrong on their own. 8

The Values Clarifiers

The developers of Values Clarification and other nonjudgmental approaches to moral decision making often claimed to be value-free, but their agenda was quite specific. Their bête noir was "moralizing" in any form. "Moralizing," the authors of *Values Clarification: A Handbook of Practical Strategies for Teachers and Students* wrote in 1978, "is the direct, although sometimes subtle inculcation of the adults' values upon the young."[9] For the authors of the new curriculum, this was not merely authoritarian and 9

[9]Sidney B. Simon, Leland W. Howe, and Howard Kirschenbaum, *Values Clarification: A Handbook of Practical Strategies for Teachers and Students* (New York: Hart Publishing, 1972), p. 15.

stifling, but also dangerous to the ethical health of children. By passing on a set of moral values, they argued, parents were hampering the ability of children to come up with their own values. "Young people brought up by moralizing adults are not prepared to make their own responsible choices," they warned.[10] In any case, moralizing was no longer practical. Children were bombarded with so many different sets of values and parents were only some of the many voices they heard. In the end, they argue, every child had to make his own choices. That, of course, is true—making choices is the essence of free will. But where values clarification departed from older moral philosophies was in its contention that children do not need to be grounded in value systems or provided with moral road maps before they are asked to make such choices. Values clarifiers also did not care what values the child chose to follow. Specifically, values clarification did not concern itself with inculcating values such as self-control, honesty, responsibility, loyalty, prudence, duty, or justice. In its purest form, values clarification did not even argue that these virtues were superior or preferable to their opposites and had little to say about concepts of right and wrong. The goal of values clarification was not to create a virtuous young person, or young adult with character or probity; its goal was empowering youngsters to make their own decisions, *whatever those decisions were....*

The assumption behind such programs was that children had the capacity to develop character on their own; that students as young as third grade had the knowledge, insight, and cognitive abilities to wrestle through difficult dilemmas and thorny moral paradoxes without the benefit of a moral compass, either from parents or teachers.... 10

At the heart of the values clarification program was the effort to have students develop an individual identity. One exercise was "Are You Someone Who..." followed by a long list of options, including: "is likely to marry someone of another religion?"; "is likely to grow a beard?"; "would consider joining the John Birch Society?"; "is apt to go out of your way to have a black (white) neighbor?"; "will subscribe to *Playboy* magazine?"; will change your religion?"; "will be likely to win a Nobel Peace Prize?"; "is apt to experiment with pot?"; "would get therapy on your own initiative?"; "will make a faithless husband? wife?" 11

The authors explain that such questions will cause students "to consider more thoughtfully what they value, what they want out of life and what type of persons they want to become."[11] But the questions send another message as well by treating the various options simply as different choices of apparently equal weight, like choices on a personality buffet line: Will you win the Nobel 12

[10]Ibid., p. 16.
[11]Ibid., p. 366.

Prize or experiment with pot? Subscribe to *Playboy* or change your religion? There is no suggestion that growing a beard or cheating on your wife might be decisions that carry rather different moral weights.

Ultimately, the values clarification approach reduces moral choice to a matter of personal taste with no more basis in objective reality than a preference for a red car rather than a blue one. There is no right or wrong answer and no real ground to regard your own choice either as better or more valid than any other. 13

But is this really a process of working out moral values or is it simply a process of rationalization? Humans rationalize because it is convenient and it suits our interests. If we choose, we can shape morality to meet our inclinations and impulses, rather than try to shape our inclinations to accord with moral law. Moral reasoning, in contrast, involves asking whether an act is good, whether it is made with right intent, and examining the act's circumstances. To make such judgments requires an understanding of what the moral law might be, not simply how we feel about the act. But to take the subjective state of mind and make it the sole test of morality is to rationalize and call it moral reasoning. Checking one's inclinations is not the same as examining one's conscience, precisely because the conscience needs to be educated. 14

One would never get that idea from watching a values clarification "simulation" of a moral choice. In one popular exercise, students have to imagine that their class has been trapped in a cave-in. In the exercise, students are asked to imagine that they have to form a single line to work their way out of the cave. At any moment, another rock slide may close the way out. Those at the head of the line are therefore the most likely to survive. In the class exercise, each member of the class must give the reason he or she should be at the head of the line. The teacher tells them: "Your reasons can be of two kinds. You can tell us what you want to live for or what you have yet to get out of life that is important to you. Or you can talk about what you have to contribute to others in the world that would justify your being near the front of the line." After hearing all of the pleas, the class then decides the order in which they will file out of the cave.[12] 15

Like other values clarification chestnuts, youngsters are asked to make life-and-death decisions. But what are the practical implications? Do students emerge from the class more empathetic? More willing to sacrifice for others? Are they likely to treat their peers with more respect? Show more self-restraint in the presence of their parents? Or are they likely to have a keener sense of their own egos?.... 16

[12]Ibid., p. 288.

Other exercises ask students to choose who should be allowed to stay in a fallout shelter (and who should be left to die) during a nuclear attack; to decide whether it is morally permissible for a poor man to steal a drug that his desperately ill wife needs; to work through the dilemma of trapped settlers who must decide whether to turn to cannibalism or starve to death; to put themselves in the place of a mother who must choose which of her two children she will save; and consider the ethical dilemma of a doctor who must decide to operate on an injured child despite the religious objections of the parents. "Like a roller-coaster ride," William Kilpatrick writes, "the dilemma approach can leave its passengers a bit breathless. That is one of its attractions. But like a roller-coaster ride, it may also leave them a bit disoriented—or more than a bit."[13] As entertaining as such problems may be, they are hardly a guide for developing a moral code; morality is more than solving a complex and perhaps even unsolvable puzzle. Take the case of the man whose wife is dying of an incurable illness and who needs a rare and expensive drug. Kilpatrick wonders whether youngsters who spend a diverting and lively class period debating whether stealing is right or wrong in this case would be less likely to steal themselves? Or lie? Or cheat? Or will they come to the conclusion that moral questions are inevitably so complicated, so fraught with doubt, that no one answer is necessarily ever any better than any other and that all moral questions come down in the end simply to a matter of opinion? Or will they get the idea that it is less important whether one steals or not than that one has developed a system of "valuing" with which one is comfortable? 17

One of the striking things about spending time with high school students is the near universality of this notion that values are something they work out on their own. One frequent speaker on ethical issues recounts his experience with high school students in which he presents them with a typical values clarification dilemma. They must imagine that they are on a lifeboat with another person and their family dog; the students can save only one, so they must choose either the human being, who is a complete stranger, or the beloved and cherished family dog. Typically, some of the students choose to save the dog and allow the man to die; most students choose to save the human being. But then the speaker asks them what they thought of their classmates who had opted for the dog over the man. Almost never, says the speaker, do students say that those choices were "wrong" or morally objectionable.[14] Even for those who made the correct moral choice, it was merely a matter of personal opinion, and they refuse to be judgmental toward those who put the dog's life ahead of the human being's. The concept that there might be universal and objective moral principles at stake is completely alien to these youngsters. 18

[13]William Kirk Kilpatrick, *Why Johnny Can't Tell Right from Wrong* (New York: Simon & Schuster, 1992), p. 84.

[14]Dennis Prager, conversation with author.

Questions for Close Reading

1. What is the selection's thesis? Locate the sentence(s) in which Sykes states his main idea. If he doesn't state it directly, express it in your own words.
2. What, according to Sykes, is the difference between contemporary American education and American education in the past?
3. What group of people does Sykes blame for the erosion of morality in American education? What justification do these people provide for their approach?
4. Reread paragraphs 15 and 18. In each, Sykes describes a classroom exercise in "values clarification." What is the educational intent of the two exercises? How are they similar? How do they differ? What is Sykes's opinion of the two exercises?
5. Refer to your dictionary as needed to define the following words used in the selection: *unrepentant* (paragraph 1), *self-actualization* (4), *precept* (5), *emulate* (5), *perseverance* (5), *smorgasbord* (5), *bête noir* (9), *moralizing* (9), *cognitive* (10), *rationalization* (14), and *fraught* (17).

Questions About the Writer's Craft

1. **The pattern.** In the first three paragraphs of his essay, Sykes provides numerous examples to illustrate what he considers the moral looseness of young people. Why do you think he starts with the example of the seventeen-year-old rapist? In what ways is this example different from the examples he provides in paragraphs 2 and 3?
2. Why do you suppose Sykes entitles his essay "The 'Values' Wasteland"? Consider what each word means. Why do you think he puts quotation marks around the word "Values"?
3. In paragraphs 2 and 3, Sykes makes heavy use of statistics. Why do you suppose he cites statistics only in the beginning of the essay?
4. **Other patterns.** How would you characterize Sykes's tone? How does this tone reinforce his *argument?*

Writing Assignments Using Exemplification as a Pattern of Development

1. Sykes contends that modern education fails to teach morality. Do you agree? Write an essay illustrating the point that contemporary schooling blunts *or* enhances young people's moral sense. In either case, offer convincing examples from your own and other people's schooling to support your point of view. Consider opening your essay, as Sykes does, with a highly dramatic example.
2. Sykes believes that the moral fiber of young people has deteriorated. Interview classmates, friends, and family members of varying ages to see if they think that young people today are less moral than they were in earlier times. Ask each person to supply at least one example to illustrate his or her opinion. Review the examples, and decide whether you agree with or reject Sykes's position. Then write an essay in which you support your opinion, using the most compelling examples from your interviews as well as your own experiences and observations.

Writing Assignments Combining Patterns of Development

3. Sykes believes that there are "universal and objective moral principles." Write an essay *narrating* a time when you faced a moral dilemma but knew deep down that there was only one moral way to act—even though such an action might have been to your personal disadvantage. *Describe* the situation, the conflict you experienced, and how you resolved the conflict. You might also conclude by briefly reflecting on the *results* of your actions. Before writing, read one or more of the following essays for insight into humans' moral impulse: George Orwell's "Shooting an Elephant" (page 146), Joan Murray's "Someone's Mother" (page 154), Langston Hughes's "Salvation" (page 158), Stephanie Ericsson's "The Ways We Lie" (page 247), and Stephen Chapman's "The Prisoner's Dilemma" (page 372).
4. Sykes writes that "we need to look first to...parents, communities, the media, and even the churches" to explain the "ethical meltdown" in young people. Focus on *one* of these forces, and write an essay analyzing the positive and negative *effects* it can have on young people's moral sense. To support your analysis, draw upon *examples* from your own observations as well as those of friends, classmates, and family members. Reading Kay S. Hymowitz's "Tweens: Ten Going On Sixteen" (page 190) might give you further perspective on how social influences can have a detrimental impact on children.

Writing Assignment Using a Journal Entry as a Starting Point

5. Reread your pre-reading journal entry, and decide which *one* type of misconduct you think is most prevalent among young people nowadays. Then write an essay in which you illustrate the extent of the impropriety, using several persuasive examples to make your point. One section of the essay should explore causes of the misbehavior; another should discuss consequences. Brainstorming with others will help you identify examples, causes, and effects of the misbehavior. At the end of your essay, you might suggest steps that could be taken to set young people in the right direction. Also, consider supplementing your observations with information about your topic gathered in the library and/or on the Internet.

Brent Staples

After earning a Ph.D. in psychology from the University of Chicago, Brent Staples (1951–) soon became a nationally recognized essayist. He has worked on numerous newspapers and is now an Editorial Board member of *The New York Times.* Staples's autobiography, *Parallel Time: Growing Up in Black and White*, was published in 1995. This selection first appeared in slightly different form in *Ms.* magazine (1986) and then in *Harper's* (1987).

Pre-Reading Journal Entry

In recent years, racial profiling—targeting people for investigation based on their race or ethnicity—has become a controversial issue. What is your opinion of this practice? Is racial profiling ever acceptable? Freewrite on these questions in your journal.

Black Men and Public Space

My first victim was a woman—white, well dressed, probably in her early twenties. I came upon her late one evening on a deserted street in Hyde Park, a relatively affluent neighborhood in an otherwise mean, impoverished section of Chicago. As I swung onto the avenue behind her, there seemed to be a discreet, uninflammatory distance between us. Not so. She cast back a worried glance. To her, the youngish black man—a broad six feet two inches with a beard and billowing hair, both hands shoved into the pockets of a bulky military jacket—seemed menacingly close. After a few more quick glimpses, she picked up her pace and was soon running in earnest. Within seconds she disappeared into a cross street. 1

That was more than a decade ago. I was twenty-two years old, a graduate student newly arrived at the University of Chicago. It was in the echo of that terrified woman's footfalls that I first began to know the unwieldy inheritance I'd come into—the ability to alter public space in ugly ways. It was clear that she thought herself the quarry of a mugger, a rapist, or worse. Suffering a bout of insomnia, however, I was stalking sleep, not defenseless wayfarers. As a softy who is scarcely able to take a knife to a raw chicken—let alone hold one to a person's throat—I was surprised, embarrassed, and dismayed all at once. Her flight made me feel like an accomplice in tyranny. It also made it clear that I was indistinguishable from the muggers who occasionally seeped into the area from the surrounding ghetto. That first encounter, and those that followed, signified that a vast, unnerving gulf lay between nighttime pedestrians—particularly women—and me. And I soon gathered that being perceived as dangerous is a hazard in itself. I only needed to turn a corner into a dicey situation, or crowd some frightened, armed person in a foyer somewhere, or make an errant move after being 2 pulled over by a policeman. Where fear and weapons meet—and they often do in urban America—there is always the possibility of death.

In that first year, my first away from my hometown, I was to become thoroughly familiar with the language of fear. At dark, shadowy intersections, I could cross in front of a car stopped at a traffic light and elicit the *thunk, thunk, thunk, thunk* of the driver—black, white, male, or female—hammering down the door locks. On less traveled streets after dark, I grew accustomed to but never comfortable with people crossing to the other side of the street rather than pass me. Then there were the standard unpleasantries with policemen, doormen, bouncers, cabdrivers, and others whose business it is to screen out troublesome individuals *before* there is any nastiness. 3

I moved to New York nearly two years ago and I have remained an avid night walker. In central Manhattan, the near-constant crowd cover minimizes tense one-on-one street encounters. Elsewhere—in SoHo, for example, where sidewalks are narrow and tightly spaced buildings shut out the sky—things can get very taut indeed. 4

After dark, on the warrenlike streets of Brooklyn where I live, I often see women who fear the worst from me. They seem to have set their faces on neutral, and with their purse straps strung across their chests bandolier-style, they forge ahead as though bracing themselves against being tackled. I understand, of course, that the danger they perceive is not a hallucination. Women are particularly vulnerable to street violence, and young black males are drastically overrepresented among the perpetrators of that violence. Yet these truths are no solace against the kind of alienation that comes of being ever the suspect, a fearsome entity with whom pedestrians avoid making eye contact. 5

It is not altogether clear to me how I reached the ripe old age of twenty-two without being conscious of the lethality nighttime pedestrians attributed to me. Perhaps it was because in Chester, Pennsylvania, the small, angry industrial town where I came of age in the 1960s, I was scarcely noticeable against a backdrop of gang warfare, street knifings, and murders. I grew up one of the good boys, had perhaps a half-dozen fistfights. In retrospect, my shyness of combat has clear sources. 6

As a boy, I saw countless tough guys locked away; I have since buried several, too. They were babies, really—a teenage cousin, a brother of twenty-two, a childhood friend in his mid-twenties—all gone down in episodes of bravado played out in the streets. I came to doubt the virtues of intimidation early on. I chose, perhaps unconsciously, to remain a shadow—timid, but a survivor. 7

The fearsomeness mistakenly attributed to me in public places often has a perilous flavor. The most frightening of these confusions occurred in the late 1970s and early 1980s, when I worked as a journalist in Chicago. One day, rushing into the office of a magazine I was writing for with a deadline story in hand, I was mistaken for a burglar. The office manager called security and, with an ad hoc posse, pursued me through the labyrinthine halls, 8 nearly to my editor's door. I had no way of proving who I was. I could only move briskly toward the company of someone who knew me.

Another time I was on assignment for a local paper and killing time before an interview. I entered a jewelry store on the city's affluent Near North Side. The proprietor excused herself and returned with an enormous red Doberman pinscher straining at the end of a leash. She stood, the dog extended toward me, silent to my questions, her eyes bulging nearly out of her head. I took a cursory look around, nodded, and bade her good night. 9

Relatively speaking, however, I never fared as badly as another black male journalist. He went to nearby Waukegan, Illinois, a couple of summers ago to work on a story about a murderer who was born there. Mistaking the reporter for the killer, police officers hauled him from his car at gunpoint and but for his press credentials would probably have tried to book him. Such episodes are not uncommon. Black men trade tales like this all the time. 10

Over the years, I learned to smother the rage I felt at so often being taken for a criminal. Not to do so would surely have led to madness. I now take precautions to make myself less threatening. I move about with care, particularly late in the evening. I give a wide berth to nervous people on subway platforms during the wee hours, particularly when I have exchanged business clothes for jeans. If I happen to be entering a building behind some people who appear skittish, I may walk by, letting them clear the lobby before I return, so as not to seem to be following them. I have been calm and extremely congenial on those rare occasions when I've been pulled over by the police. 11

And on late-evening constitutionals I employ what has proved to be an excellent tension-reducing measure: I whistle melodies from Beethoven and Vivaldi and the more popular classical composers. Even steely New Yorkers hunching toward nighttime destinations seem to relax, and occasionally they even join in the tune. Virtually everybody seems to sense that a mugger wouldn't be warbling bright, sunny selections from Vivaldi's *Four Seasons.* It is my equivalent of the cowbell that hikers wear when they know they are in bear country. 12

Questions for Close Reading

1. What is the selection's thesis? Locate the sentence(s) in which Staples states his main idea. If he doesn't state the thesis explicitly, express it in your own words.
2. How did Staples first learn that he was considered a threat by many people? How did this discovery make him feel?
3. What are some of the dangers that Staples has encountered because of his race? How has he handled each dangerous situation?
4. What "precautions" does Staples take to appear nonthreatening to others? Why do these precautions work?
5. Refer to your dictionary as needed to define the following words used in the selection: *uninflammatory* (paragraph 1), *dicey* (2), *bandolier* (5), *lethality* (6), *bravado* (7), *berth* (11), and *constitutionals* (12).

Questions About the Writer's Craft

1. **The pattern.** Brent Staples reveals both causes and effects of people's reacting with fear to a Black male. Does the essay end with a discussion of causes or of effects? Why do you suppose Staples concludes the essay as he does?
2. **Other patterns.** Why do you think Staples opens the piece with such a dramatic, yet intentionally misleading, *narrative*? What *effect* does he achieve?
3. Is Staples writing primarily for whites, Blacks, or both? How do you know?
4. What is Staples's tone? Why do you think he chose this tone?

Writing Assignments Using Cause-Effect as a Pattern of Development

1. Write an essay showing how your or someone else's entry into a specific public space influenced other people's behavior. Identify the possible reasons that others reacted as they did, and explain how their reactions, in turn, affected the newcomer. Use your analysis to reach some conclusions about human nature. For another example of an uncomfortable cultural intersection, read Audre Lorde's "The Fourth of July" (page 140), Joan Murray's "Someone's Mother" (page 154), and Amy Tan's "Mother Tongue" (page 270).
2. Staples describes circumstances that often result in fear. Focusing on a more positive emotion, like admiration or contentment, illustrate the situations that tend to elicit that emotion in you. Discuss why these circumstances have the effect they do.

Writing Assignments Combining Patterns of Development

3. Staples describes how others' expectations oblige him to alter his behavior. *Narrate* an event during which you felt forced to conform to what others expected. What did you learn as a *result* of the experience? Audre Lorde's "The Fourth of July" (page 140), George Orwell's "Shooting an Elephant" (page 146), and Anna Quindlen's "Driving to the Funeral" (page 532) may prompt some interesting thoughts on the issue of conformity.
4. When he encounters a startled pedestrian, Staples feels some fear but manages to control it. Write an essay showing the *steps* you took one time when you felt afraid but, like Staples, remained in control and got through safely. *Illustrate* your initial fear, your later relief, and any self-discovery that *resulted* from the experience.

Writing Assignment Using a Journal Entry as a Starting Point

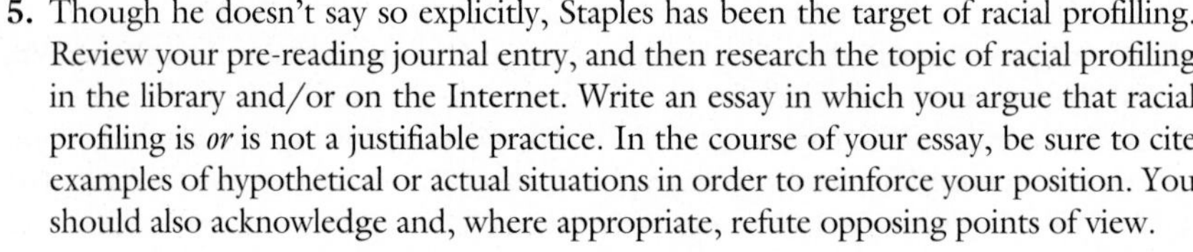

5. Though he doesn't say so explicitly, Staples has been the target of racial profilling. Review your pre-reading journal entry, and then research the topic of racial profiling in the library and/or on the Internet. Write an essay in which you argue that racial profiling is *or* is not a justifiable practice. In the course of your essay, be sure to cite examples of hypothetical or actual situations in order to reinforce your position. You should also acknowledge and, where appropriate, refute opposing points of view.

Beth Johnson

Beth Johnson (1956–) is a writer, occasional college teacher, and freelance editor. A graduate of Goshen College and Syracuse University, Johnson is the author of numerous inspirational real-life accounts, including *Facing Addiction* (2006) and *Surviving Abuse* (2006) as well as several college texts, including *Everyday Heroes* (1996) and *Reading Changed My Life* (2003); she also coauthored *Voices and Values* (2002) and *English Essentials* (2004). Containing profiles of men and women who have triumphed over obstacles to achieve personal and academic success, the books have provided a motivational boost to college students nationwide. She lives with her husband and three children in Lederach, Pennsylvania. The following piece is one of several that Johnson has written about the complexities and wonders of life.

Pre-Reading Journal Entry

When you were young, did adults acknowledge the existence of life's tragedies, or did they deny such harsh truths? In your journal, list several difficult events that you observed or experienced firsthand as a child. How did the adults in your life explain these hardships? In each case, do you think the adults acted appropriately? If not, how should they have responded?

Bombs Bursting in Air

It's Friday night and we're at the Olympics, the Junior Olympics, that is. My son is on a relay-race team competing against fourth-graders from all over the school district. His little sister and I sit high in the stands, trying to pick Isaac out from the crowd of figures milling around on the field during these moments of pre-game confusion. The public address system sputters to life and summons our attention. "And now," the tinny voice rings out, "please join together in the singing of our national anthem." 1

"Oh saaay can you seeeeee," we begin. My arm rests around Maddie's shoulders. I am touching her a lot today, and she notices. "Mom, you're *squishing* me," she chides, wriggling from my grip. I content myself with stroking her hair. News that reached me today makes me need to feel her near. We pipe along, squeaking out the impossibly high note of "land of the freeeeeeeee." Maddie clowns, half-singing, half-shouting the lyrics, hitting the "b's" explosively on "bombs bursting in air." 2

Bombs indeed, I think, replaying the sound of my friend's voice over the phone that afternoon: "Bumped her head sledding. Took her in for an x-ray, just to make sure. There was something strange, so they did more tests... a brain tumor... Children's Hospital in Boston Tuesday... surgery, yes, right away...." Maddie's playmate Shannon, only five years old. We'd last seen her at Halloween, dressed in her blue princess costume, and we'd talked of 3

Furby and Scooby-Doo and Tootsie Rolls. Now her parents were hurriedly learning a new vocabulary—CAT scans, glioma, pediatric neurosurgery, and frontal lobe.[1] A bomb had exploded in their midst, and, like troops under attack, they were rallying in response.

The games over, the children and I edge our way out of the school parking lot, bumper to bumper with other parents ferrying their families home. I tell the kids as casually as I can about Shannon. "She'll have to have an operation. It's lucky, really, that they found it by accident this way while it's small." 4

"I want to send her a present," Maddie announces. "That'd be nice," I say, glad to keep the conversation on a positive note. 5

But my older son is with us now. Sam, who is thirteen, says, "She'll be OK, though, right?" It's not a question, really; it's a statement that I must either agree with or contradict. I want to say yes. I want to say of course she'll be all right. I want them to inhabit a world where five-year-olds do not develop silent, mysterious growths in their brains, where "malignancy" and "seizure" are words for *New York Times* crossword puzzles, not for little girls. They would accept my assurance; they would believe me and sleep well tonight. But I can't; the bomb that exploded in Shannon's home has sent splinters of shrapnel into ours as well, and they cannot be ignored or lied away. "We hope she'll be just fine," I finally say. "She has very good doctors. She has wonderful parents who are doing everything they can. The tumor is small. Shannon's strong and healthy." 6

"*She'll* be OK," says Maddie matter-of-factly. "In school we read about a little boy who had something wrong with his leg and he had an operation and got better. Can we go to Dairy Queen?" 7

Bombs on the horizon don't faze Maddie. Not yet. I can just barely remember from my own childhood the sense that still surrounds her, that feeling of being cocooned within reassuring walls of security and order. Back then, Monday meant gym, Tuesday was pizza in the cafeteria, Wednesday brought clarinet lessons. Teachers stood in their familiar spots in the classrooms, telling us with reassuring simplicity that World War II happened because Hitler, a very bad man, invaded Poland. Midterms and report cards, summer vacations and new notebooks in September gave a steady rhythm to the world. It wasn't all necessarily happy—through the years there were poor grades, grouchy teachers, exclusion from the desired social group, dateless weekends when it seemed the rest of the world was paired off—but it was familiar territory where we felt walled off from the really bad things that happened to other people. 8

[1]A CAT scan is a computerized cross-sectional image of an internal body structure; a glioma is a tumor in the brain or spinal cord; pediatric neurosurgery is surgery performed on the nerves, brain, or spinal cord of a child; the frontal lobe is the largest section of the brain (editors' note).

There were hints of them, though, even then. Looking back, I recall 9
the tiny shock waves, the tremors from far-off explosions that occasionally rattled our shelter. There was the little girl who was absent for a week and when she returned wasn't living with her mother and stepfather anymore. There was a big girl who threw up in the bathroom every morning and then disappeared from school. A playful, friendly custodian was suddenly fired, and it had something to do with an angry parent. A teacher's husband had a heart attack and died. These were interesting tidbits to report to our families over dinner, mostly out of morbid interest in seeing our parents bite their lips and exchange glances.

As we got older, the bombs dropped closer. A friend's sister was arrested 10
for selling drugs; we saw her mother in tears at church that Sunday. A boy I thought I knew, a school clown with a sweet crooked grin, shot himself in the woods behind his house. A car full of senior boys, going home from a dance where I'd been sent into ecstasy when the cutest of them all greeted me by name, rounded a curve too fast and crashed, killing them. We wept and hugged each other in the halls. Our teachers listened to us grieve and tried to comfort us, but their words came out impatient and almost angry. I realize now that what sounded like anger was a helplessness to teach us lessons we were still too young or too ignorant to learn. For although our sorrow was real, we still had some sense of a protective curtain between us and the bombs. If only, we said. If only she hadn't used drugs. If only he'd told someone how depressed he was. If only they'd been more careful. *We* weren't like them; we were careful. Like magical incantations, we recited the things that we would or wouldn't do in order to protect ourselves from such sad, unnecessary fates.

And then my best friend, a beautiful girl of sixteen, went to sleep one 11
January night and never woke up. I found myself shaken to the core of my being. My grief at the loss of my vibrant, laughing friend was great. But what really tilted my universe was the nakedness of my realization that there was no "if only." There were no drugs, no careless action, no crime, no accident, nothing I could focus on to explain away what had happened. She had simply died. Which could only mean that there was no magic barrier separating me and my loved ones from the bombs. We were as vulnerable as everyone else. For months the shock stayed with me. I sat in class watching my teachers draw diagrams of Saturn, talk about Watergate,[2] multiply fractions, and wondered at their apparent cheer and normalcy. Didn't they ***know***

[2]In June 1972, supporters of Republican President Richard Nixon were caught breaking into the Democratic campaign headquarters in the Watergate office complex in Washington, D.C. The resulting investigation of the White House connection to the break-in led to President Nixon's eventual resignation in August 1974 (editors' note).

we were all doomed? Didn't they know it was only a matter of time until one of us took a direct hit? What was the point of anything?

But time moved on, and I moved with it. College came and went, graduate school, adulthood, middle age. My heightened sense of vulnerability began to subside, though I could never again slip fully into the soothing security of my younger days. I became more aware of the intertwining threads of joy, pain, and occasional tragedy that weave through all our lives. College was stimulating, exciting, full of friendship and challenge. I fell in love for the first time, reveled in its sweetness, then learned the painful lesson that love comes with no guarantee. A beloved professor lost two children to leukemia, but continued with skill and passion to introduce students to the riches of literature. My father grew ill, but the last day of his life, when I sat by his bed holding his hand, remains one of my sweetest memories. The marriage I'd entered into with optimism ended in bitter divorce, but produced three children whose existence is my daily delight. At every step along the way, I've seen that the most rewarding chapters of my life have contained parts that I not only would not have chosen, but would have given much to avoid. But selecting just the good parts is not an option we are given. 12

The price of allowing ourselves to truly live, to love and be loved, is (and it's the ultimate irony) the knowledge that the greater our investment in life, the larger the target we create. Of course, it is within our power to refuse friendship, shrink from love, live in isolation, and thus create for ourselves a nearly impenetrable bomb shelter. There are those among us who choose such an existence, the price of intimacy being too high. Looking about me, however, I see few such examples. Instead, I am moved by the courage with which most of us, ordinary folks, continue soldiering on. We fall in love, we bring our children into the world, we forge our friendships, we give our hearts, knowing with increasing certainty that we do so at our own risk. Still we move ahead with open arms, saying yes, yes to life. 13

Shannon's surgery is behind her; the prognosis is good. Her mother reports that the family is returning to its normal routines, laughing again and talking of ordinary things, even while they step more gently, speak more quietly, are more aware of the precious fragility of life and of the blessing of every day that passes without explosion. 14

Bombs bursting in air. They can blind us, like fireworks at the moment of explosion. If we close our eyes and turn away, all we see is their fiery image. But if we have the courage to keep our eyes open and welcoming, even bombs finally fade against the vastness of the starry sky. 15

Questions for Close Reading

1. What is the selection's thesis? Locate the sentence(s) in which Johnson states her main idea. If she doesn't state the thesis explicitly, express it in your own words.
2. In paragraph 2, Johnson describes her "need to feel her [daughter] near." What compels her to want to be physically close to her daughter? Why do you think Johnson responds this way?
3. In describing her family's responses to Shannon's illness, Johnson presents three reactions: Maddie's, Sam's, and her own. How do these responses differ? In what ways do Maddie's, Sam's, and Johnson's reactions typify the age groups to which they belong?
4. In paragraph 13, Johnson describes two basic ways people respond to life's inevitable "bombs." What are these ways? Which response does Johnson endorse?
5. Refer to your dictionary as needed to define the following words used in the selection: *ferrying* (paragraph 4), *shrapnel* (6), *faze* (8), *cocooned* (8), *tremors* (9), *incantations* (10), *vulnerable* (11), *intertwining* (12), *impenetrable* (13), *soldiering on* (13), *prognosis* (14), and *fragility* (14).

Questions About the Writer's Craft

1. **The pattern.** Although Johnson provides many examples of life's "bombs," she gives more weight to some examples than to others. Which examples does she emphasize? Which ones receive less attention? Why?
2. **Other patterns.** What important *contrast* does Johnson develop in paragraph 6? How does this contrast reinforce the essay's main idea?
3. Writers generally vary sentence structure in an effort to add interest to their work. But in paragraphs 9 and 10, Johnson employs a repetitive sentence structure. Where is the repetition in these two paragraphs? Why do you think she uses this technique?
4. Johnson develops her essay by means of an extended metaphor (see page 79), using bombs as her central image. Identify all the places where Johnson draws upon language and imagery related to bombs and battles. What do you think Johnson hopes to achieve with this sustained metaphor?

Writing Assignments Using Exemplification as a Pattern of Development

1. In paragraphs 9 and 10, Johnson catalogues a number of events that made her increasingly aware of life's bombs. Write an essay of your own, illustrating how you came to recognize the inevitability of painful life events. Start by listing the difficult events you've encountered. Select the three most compelling occurrences, and do some freewriting to generate details about each. Before writing, decide whether you will order your examples chronologically or emphatically; use whichever illustrates more effectively your dawning realization of life's complexity. End with some conclusions about your ability to cope with difficult times.
2. Johnson describes her evolving understanding of life. In an essay of your own, show the way several events combined to change your understanding of a specific aspect of your life. Perhaps a number of incidents prompted you to reconsider career 
of your life. Perhaps a number of incidents prompted you to reconsider career

choices, end a relationship, or appreciate the importance of family. Cite only those events that illustrate your emerging understanding. Your decision to use either chronological or emphatic sequence depends on which illustrates more dramatically the change in your perception. To see how other writers describe their journeys of self-discovery, read Maya Angelou's "Sister Flowers" (page 87), Riverbend's "Bloggers Without Borders" (page 111), Amy Tan's "Mother Tongue" (page 270), Richard Rodriguez's "Workers" (page 361), and Jacques D'Amboise's "Showing What Is Possible" (page 402).

Writing Assignments Combining Patterns of Development

3. Johnson explores the lasting impact the death of her friend had on her life. Write an essay about the *effect* of a *single* "bomb" on your life. You might *recount* getting left back in school, losing a loved one, seeing the dark side of someone you admired, and so on. Your causal analysis should make clear how the event affected your life. Perhaps the event had painful short-term consequences but positive long-term repercussions. Langston Hughes's "Salvation" (page 158) and Jacques D'Amboise's "Showing What Is Possible" (page 402) provide helpful models for examining the effects of a life-changing event.

4. In an essay, offer readers a *guide* to surviving a specific life calamity. You might, for instance, explain how to survive a pet's death, a painful breakup, a financial hardship. Consider doing some library and/or Internet research on your subject. Combining your own insights with any material gathered through research, *describe* fully the *steps* readers should take to recover from the devastating events.

Writing Assignment Using a Journal Entry as a Starting Point

5. Johnson asserts that painful truths shouldn't "be ignored or lied away" by adults. Do you agree? Write an essay explaining why you think adults should protect children from harsh realities—or why they should present the whole truth, even when it's painful. Review your pre-reading journal entry, searching for strong examples to support your position. Discussing this topic with others will also help you shape your point of view, as will reading Audre Lorde's "The Fourth of July" (page 140).

Chitra Banerjee Divakaruni

Chitra Banerjee Divakaruni was born in Calcutta, India, in 1956. After getting a B.A. from the University of Calcutta, she came to the United States, earning a master's degree in English from Wright State University and, in 1976, a Ph.D. from the University of California at Berkeley. Divakaruni currently teaches in the creative writing program at the University of Houston. Her work is widely published, including in *The New Yorker* and the *Atlantic Monthly*, and she has won an American Book Award for her short story collection *Arranged Marriage* (1995), as well as other awards. In addition to stories, young adult fiction, and poetry, Divakaruni has published several novels, including *The Mistress of Spices* (1997), *Sister of My Heart* (1999), *Queen of Dreams* (2004), and most recently *One Amazing Thing* (2010). The following essay appeared in *Salon.com* on June 26, 1997.

Pre-Reading Journal Entry

Like distinctive smells, other sensory experiences can also evoke specific memories or feelings. For example, a particular song might remind you of a past romance. Do some freewriting in your journal about sensory experiences that evoke strong memories or feelings for you.

Common Scents: The Smell of Childhood Never Fades

It's a cool December morning halfway across the world in Gurap, a little village outside Calcutta where we've come to visit my mother. I sit on the veranda and watch my little boys, Anand and Abhay, as they play on the dirt road. They have a new cricket bat and ball, a gift from their grandma, but soon they abandon these to feed mango leaves to the neighbor's goat, which has wandered over. Abhay, who is 2, wants to climb onto the goat's back. Anand, who is 5 and very much the big brother, tells him it's not a good idea, but Abhay doesn't listen. 1

Behind me the door opens. Even before I hear the flap-flap of her leather chappals,[1] I know who it is. My mother, fresh from her bath, heralded by the scent of the sandalwood soap she has been using ever since I can remember. Its clean, familiar smell pulls me back effortlessly into my childhood. 2

When I was young, my mother and I had a ritual every evening. She would comb my hair, rub in hibiscus oil and braid it into thick double plaits. It took a long time—there were a lot of knots to work through. But I was rarely impatient. I loved the sleepy fragrance of the oil (the same oil she used, which she sometimes let me rub into her hair). I loved, too, the 3

[1]Sandals (editors' note).

rhythm of her hands, and the stories (each with its not-so-subtle moral) that she told me as she combed. The tale of Sukhu and Dukhu, the two sisters. The kind one gets the prince, the greedy one is eaten up by a serpent. Or the tale of the little cowherd boy who outwits the evil witch. Size and strength, after all, are no match for intelligence.

What is it about smells that lingers in our subconscious, comforting and giving joy, making real what would otherwise be wooden and wordy? I'm not sure. But I do know this: Every lesson that I remember from my childhood, from my mother, has a smell at its center. 4

The smell of turmeric, which she made into a paste with milk and rubbed into my skin to take away blemishes, reminds me to take pride in my appearance, to make the best of what nature has given me. 5

The smell of the rosewater-scented rice pudding she always made for New Year is the smell of hope. It reminds me to never give up. Who knows—something marvelous may be waiting just around the bend. 6

Even the smell of the iodine she dabbed on my scraped knees and elbows, which I so hated then, is one I now recall with wry gratitude. Its stinging, bitter-brown odor is that of love, love that sometimes hurts while it's doing its job. 7

Let me not mislead you. I wasn't always so positively inclined toward my mother's lessons—or the smells that accompanied them. When I first moved to the United States, I wanted to change myself, completely. I washed every last drop of hibiscus oil from my hair with Vidal Sassoon shampoo. I traded in my saris for Levis and tank tops. I danced the night away in discos and returned home in the bleary-eyed morning smelling of vodka and sweat and cigarettes, the perfume of young America. 8

But when Anand was born, something changed. They say you begin to understand your mother only when you become a mother yourself. Only then do you appreciate all the little things about her that you took for granted. Maybe that's true. Otherwise, that morning in the hospital, looking down at Anand's fuzzy head, why did I ask my husband to make a trip to the Indian store and bring me back a bar of sandalwood soap? 9

I have my own rituals now, with my boys, my own special smells that are quite different. (I learned early that we can't be our mothers. Most times, it's better to not even try.) 10

On weekends I make a big chicken curry with turmeric and cloves. Anand helps me cut up the tomatoes into uneven wedges; Abhay finger-shreds the cilantro with great glee. As the smell of spices fills the house, we sing. Sometimes it's a song from India: *Ay, ay, Chanda mama*—Come to me, Uncle Moon. Sometimes it's "Old MacDonald Had a Farm." 11

When the children are sick, I sprinkle lavender water on a handkerchief and lay it on their foreheads to fend off that other smell, hot and metallic: the smell of fever and fear. 12

If I have a special event coming up, I open the suitcase my mother gave me at my wedding and let them pick out an outfit for me, maybe a gold-embroidered kurta[2] or a silk shawl. The suitcase smells of rose potpourri. The boys burrow into it and take deep, noisy breaths. 13

Am I creating memories for them? Things that will comfort them in the dark, sour moments that must come to us all at some time? Who knows—there is so much out of my own childhood that I've forgotten that I can only hope so. 14

"Watch out!" says my mother now, but it's too late. The goat, having eaten enough mango leaves, has decided to move on. He gives a great shrug, and Abhay comes tumbling off his back. He lies on the dirt for a moment, his mouth a perfect O of surprise, then runs crying to me. A twinge goes through me even as I hide my smile. A new lesson, this, since motherhood: how you can feel someone else's pain so sharply, like needles, in your own bones. 15

When I pick him up, Abhay buries his face in my neck and stays there a long time, even after the tears have stopped. Is he taking in the smell of my body? Is he going to remember the fragrance of the jabakusum[3] oil that I asked my mother to rub into my hair last night, for old time's sake? I'm not sure. But I do know this—I've just gained something new, something to add to my scent-shop of memories: the dusty, hot smell of his hair, his hands pungent with the odor of freshly-torn mango leaves. 16

Questions for Close Reading

1. What is the selection's thesis? Locate the sentence(s) in which Divakaruni states her main idea. If she doesn't state her thesis explicitly, express it in your own words.
2. Identify the author's initial inspiration for her main idea. What specific life lessons does the author say she learned from her mother?
3. What two occurrences prompt reversals in the author's feelings about her mother? Describe the two scents the author associates with these reversals.
4. What scent-memories does the author hope to pass along to her own children? How does the meaning of these scent-memories differ from the meaning of memories she has of her mother?
5. Refer to your dictionary as needed to define the following words used in the selection: *veranda* (paragraph 1), *heralded* (2), *subconscious* (4), *turmeric* (5), *iodine* (7), *fend off* (12), and *pungent* (16).

Questions About the Writer's Craft

1. **The pattern.** What kind of examples does the author mostly give—personal experience, typical-case, hypothetical, or generalized? Is her choice effective in supporting her main point? What other types of evidence might she have included?

[2]A long shirt or blouse that is worn over pants (editors' note).
[3]Hibiscus (editors' note).

2. **Other patterns.** In what way does the author use *narrative* devices to draw in the reader? Explain.
3. **Other patterns.** In what way does the author use *description* to draw in the reader? Gives some examples of descriptive language. What tone does the description give to the essay?
4. The author uses a number of Hindi (or Hindi-derived) terms (*chappals, kurta, jabakusum*) that she does not define, and she refers to children's songs and stories that American audiences may not know. What effect does this produce?

Writing Assignments Using Exemplification as a Pattern of Development

1. Divakaruni gives a number of life lessons she learned from her mother. Think of positive life lessons that you learned from your parents, grandparents, or other people you admire. Choose one or two lessons and give *examples* of how those teachings influenced your behavior or the choices you have made in your life.
2. In the essay, *veranda* is an example of a Hindi word that has become a common English word. Research some other terms that have come into English from Hindi or another Indian language. Write an essay in which you give *examples* of some words, including if possible how their meanings have changed. Explain whether you think the effect of that language on English is beneficial, detrimental, or neutral.

Writing Assignments Combining Patterns of Development

3. As the author learned, people often find it hard to maintain their family's values in a new culture. Think of a situation in which you or someone you know had to adapt to a new cultural norm. *Describe* the situation, *comparing* the previous cultural experience with the new one. To see how others have written about different cultural experiences and expectations, read "Bloggers Without Borders" by Riverbend (page 111), "A Partial Remembrance of a Puerto Rican Childhood" by Judith Ortiz Cofer (page 117), "Serving in Florida" by Barbara Ehrenreich (page 162), "Mother Tongue" by Amy Tan (page 270), or "Workers" by Richard Rodriguez (page 361).
4. Do you think parents can deliberately create good memories for their children, or do you think it's impossible to predict which experiences will give children their most cherished memories? Write an essay in which you *argue* for one side or the other. Remember to give *examples* from your own experience or from the experiences of people you know.

Writing Assignment Using a Journal Entry as a Starting Point

5. From the notes in your journal, select a sense other than smell—sight, hearing, touch, or taste. Write an essay in which you explore the power of that sense. What meaningful memories or feelings can it trigger in you? Give examples from your own experience. You might also explore whether you think this particular sense is more or less effective than the sense of smell at evoking strong memories.

Additional Writing Topics

EXEMPLIFICATION

General Assignments

Use examples to develop any one of the following topics into a well-organized essay. When writing the paper, choose enough relevant examples to support your thesis. Organize the material into a sequence that most effectively illustrates the thesis, keeping in mind that emphatic order is often the most compelling way to present specifics.

1. Many of today's drivers have dangerous habits.
2. Drug and alcohol abuse is (or is not) a serious problem among many young people.
3. One rule of restaurant dining is "Management often seems oblivious to problems that are perfectly obvious to customers."
4. Children today are not encouraged to use their imaginations.
5. The worst kind of hypocrite is a religious hypocrite.
6. The best things in life are definitely not free.
7. A part-time job is an important experience that every college student should have.
8. The Internet has resulted in a generation of lazy young people.
9. ___________ (name someone you know well) is a ___________ (use a quality: open-minded, dishonest, compulsive, reliable, gentle, and so on) person.
10. Television commercials stereotype the elderly (or another minority group).
11. Today, salespeople act as if they're doing you a favor by taking your money.
12. Most people behave decently in their daily interactions with each other.
13. Pettiness, jealousy, and selfishness abound in our daily interactions with each other.
14. You can tell a lot about people by observing what they wear and eat.
15. Too many Americans are overly concerned/completely unconcerned with being physically fit.
16. There are several study techniques that will help a student learn more efficiently.
17. Some teachers seem to enjoy turning tests into ordeals.
18. "How to avoid bad eating habits" is one course all college students should take.
19. More needs to be done to eliminate obstacles faced by the physically disabled.
20. Some of the best presents are those that cost the least.

Assignments with a Specific Purpose, Audience, and Point of View

On Campus

1. Lately, many people at your college have been experiencing stress. As a member of the Student Life Committee, you've been asked to prepare a pamphlet illustrating strategies for reducing different kinds of stress. Decide which stresses to discuss, and explain coping strategies for each, providing helpful examples as you go.

2. A friend of yours will be going away to college in an unfamiliar environment—in a bustling urban setting or in a quiet rural one. To help your friend prepare for this new environment, write a letter giving examples of what life on an urban or a rural campus is like. You might focus on the benefits and dangers with which your friend is unlikely to be familiar.

At Home or in the Community

3. Shopping for a new car, you become annoyed at how many safety features are available only as expensive options. Write a letter of complaint to the auto manufacturer, citing at least three examples of such options. Avoid sounding hostile.
4. A pet food company is having an annual contest to choose a new animal to feature in its advertising. To win the contest, you must convince the company that your pet is personable, playful, and unique. Write an essay giving examples of your pet's special qualities.

On the Job

5. Assume that you're an elementary school principal planning to give a speech in which you'll try to convince parents that television distorts children's perceptions of reality. Write the speech, illustrating your point with vivid examples.
6. The online publication you work for has asked you to write an article on what you consider to be the "three best consumer products of the past twenty-five years." Support your opinion with lively, engaging specifics that are consistent with the website's offbeat and slightly ironic tone.

6

DIVISION-CLASSIFICATION

WHAT IS DIVISION-CLASSIFICATION?

Imagine what life would be like if this is how an average day unfolded:

> You go to the supermarket for only five items, but your marketing takes over an hour because all the items in the store are jumbled together. Clerks put new shipments anywhere they please; the milk might be with the vegetables on Monday but with hair products on Thursday. Next, you go to the drugstore to pick up photos you left to be developed. You don't have time, though, to wait while the cashier roots through the large carton into which all the pickup envelopes have been thrown. You leave to go visit a friend in the hospital with the flu. There you find your friend in a room with three other patients: a middle-aged man with a heart problem, a young boy ready to have his tonsils removed, and a woman in labor.

Such a muddled world, lacking the most basic forms of organization, would make daily life chaotic. All of us instinctively look for ways to order our environment. Without sorting mechanisms, we'd be overwhelmed by life's complexity. An organization such as a university, for example, is made manageable by being divided into various schools (Liberal Arts, Performing Arts, Engineering, and so on). The schools are then separated into departments (English, History, Political Science), and each department's offerings are grouped into categories—English, for instance, into Literature and Composition—before being further divided into specific courses.

The kind of ordering system we've been discussing is called *division-classification,* a logical way of thinking that allows us to make sense of a complex world. Division and classification, though separate processes, are often used together as complementary techniques. *Division* involves taking a single unit or concept, breaking the unit down into its parts, and then analyzing the connections among the parts and between the parts and the whole. For instance, if we wanted to organize the chaotic hospital described at the start of the chapter, we might think about how the single concept "a hospital" could be broken down into its components. We might come up with the following breakdown: pediatric wing, cardiac wing, maternity wing, and so on.

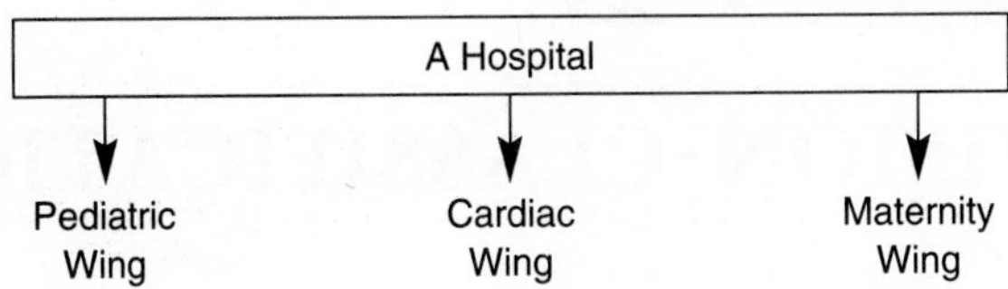

What we have just done involves division: We've taken a single entity (a hospital) and divided it into some of its component parts (wings), each with its own facilities and patients.

In contrast, *classification* brings two or more related items together and categorizes them according to type or kind. If the disorganized supermarket described earlier were to be restructured, the clerks would have to classify the separate items arriving at the loading dock. Cartons of lettuce, tomatoes, cucumbers, butter, yogurt, milk, shampoo, conditioner, and styling gel would be assigned to the appropriate categories:

HOW DIVISION-CLASSIFICATION FITS YOUR PURPOSE AND AUDIENCE

The reorganized hospital and supermarket show the way division and classification work in everyday life. But division and classification also come into play during the writing process. Because division involves breaking a subject into parts, it can be a helpful strategy during prewriting, especially if you're analyzing a broad, complex subject: the structure of a film; the motivation of a character in a novel; the problem your community has with vandalism; the controversy surrounding school prayer.

Classification can be useful for imposing order on ideas generated during prewriting. You examine that material to see which of your rough ideas are alike, so that you can cluster related items in the same category. You might, for instance, use classification in a paper showing that Americans are undermining their health through their obsessive pursuit of various diets. Perhaps you begin by brainstorming all the diets that have gained popularity in recent years (Atkins, South Beach, Zone, whatever). Then you categorize the diets according to type: high-fiber, low-protein, high-carbohydrate, and so on. Once the diets are grouped, you can discuss the problems within each category, demonstrating to readers why some of the diets may not be safe or effective.

Division-classification can be crucial when responding to college assignments like the following:

> From your observations, what kinds of appeals do television advertisers use when selling automobiles? In your view, are any of these appeals morally irresponsible?
>
> Analyze the components of effective parenting. Indicate those you consider most vital for raising confident, well-adjusted children.
>
> Describe the hierarchy of the typical high school clique, identifying the various parts of the hierarchy. Use your analysis to support or refute the view that adolescence is a period of rigid conformity.
>
> Many social commentators have observed that discourtesy is on the rise. Indicate whether you think this is a valid observation by characterizing the types of everyday encounters you have with people.

These assignments suggest division-classification through the use of such words as *kinds, components, parts,* and *types.* Generally, though, you won't receive such clear signals to use division-classification. Instead, the broad purpose of the essay—and the point you want to make—will lead you to the analytical thinking characteristic of division-classification.

Sometimes division-classification will be the dominant technique for structuring an essay; other times it will be used as a supplemental pattern in an essay organized primarily according to another pattern of development. Say you want to write a paper *explaining a process.* You could *divide* the process into parts or stages, showing, for instance, that the Heimlich maneuver is an easily mastered skill that readers should acquire. Or perhaps you plan to write a light-spirited essay analyzing the *effect* that increased awareness of sexual stereotypes has had on college students' social lives. In such a case, you might use *classification*. To show readers that shifting gender roles make young men and women comically self-conscious, you could categorize the places where students scout each other out: in class, at the library, at parties, in dorms. You could then show how students—not wishing to be macho or coyly feminine—approach each other with laughable tentativeness in these four environments.

Now imagine that you're writing an *argumentation-persuasion* essay urging that the federal government prohibit the use of growth-inducing antibiotics in livestock feed. The paper could begin by *dividing* the antibiotics cycle into stages: the effects of antibiotics on livestock; the short-term effects on humans who consume the animals; the possible long-term effects of consuming antibiotic-tainted meat. To increase readers' understanding of the problem, you might also discuss the antibiotics controversy in terms of an even larger issue: the dangerous ways food is treated before being consumed. In this case, you would consider the various procedures (use of additives, preservatives, artificial colors, and so on), *classifying* these treatments into several types—from least harmful (some additives or artificial colors, perhaps) to most harmful (you might slot the antibiotics here). Such an essay would be developed using both division *and* classification: first, the division of the antibiotics cycle and then the classification of the various food treatments. Frequently, this interdependence will be reversed, and classification will precede rather than follow division.

At this point, you have a good sense of the way writers use division-classification to achieve their purpose and to connect with their readers. Now take a moment to look closely at the photograph at the beginning of this chapter. Imagine you're writing an article, accompanied by the photo, for a parenting magazine. Your purpose is twofold: to alert parents to the danger of pushing young children to achieve, and to help parents foster in children healthy attitudes toward achievement. Jot down some ideas you might include when *dividing* and/or *classifying* things parents should and shouldn't do to foster a balanced view of accomplishment and success in youngsters.

SUGGESTIONS FOR USING DIVISION-CLASSIFICATION IN AN ESSAY

The suggestions here and in Figure 6.1 will be helpful whether you use division-classification as a dominant or a supportive pattern of development.

1. Select a principle of division-classification consistent with your purpose. Most subjects can be divided or classified according to a *number*

FIGURE 6.1

Development Diagram: Writing a Division-Classification Essay

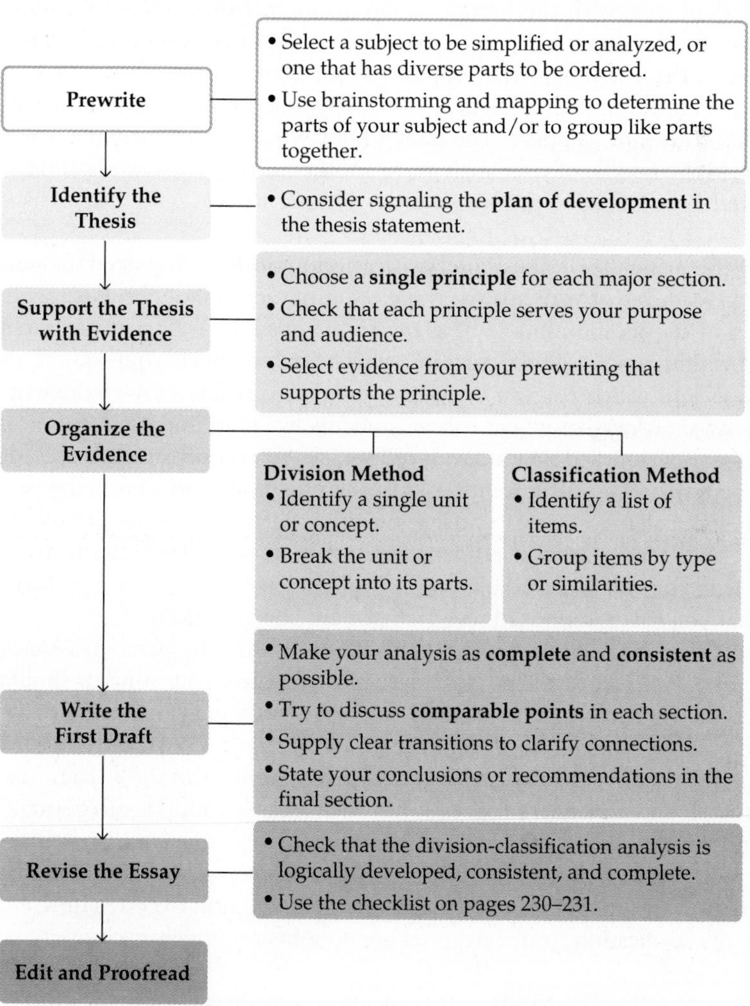
Prewrite
• Select a subject to be simplified or analyzed, or one that has diverse parts to be ordered.
• Use brainstorming and mapping to determine the parts of your subject and/or to group like parts together.
Identify the Thesis
• Consider signaling the plan of development in the thesis statement.
Support the Thesis with Evidence
• Choose a single principle for each major section.
• Check that each principle serves your purpose and audience.
• Select evidence from your prewriting that supports the principle.
Organize the Evidence
Division Method
• Identify a single unit or concept.
• Break the unit or concept into its parts.
Classification Method
• Identify a list of items.
• Group items by type or similarities.
Write the First Draft
• Make your analysis as complete and consistent as possible.
• Try to discuss comparable points in each section.
• Supply clear transitions to clarify connections.
• State your conclusions or recommendations in the final section.
Revise the Essay
• Check that the division-classification analysis is logically developed, consistent, and complete.
• Use the checklist on pages 230–231.
Edit and Proofread

of different principles. For example, when writing about an ideal vacation, you could divide your subject according to any of these principles: location, cost, recreation available. Similarly, when analyzing students at your college, you could base your classification on a variety of principles: students' majors, their racial or ethnic background, whether they belong to a fraternity or sorority. In all cases, though, the principle of division-classification must help you meet your overall purpose and reinforce your central point.

When you write an essay that uses division-classification as its primary method of development, a *single principle* of division-classification provides the foundation for each major section of the paper. Imagine you're writing an essay showing that the success of contemporary music groups has less to do with talent than with the groups' ability to market themselves to distinct audiences. To develop your point, you might categorize several performers according to the age ranges they appeal to (preteens, adolescents, people in their late twenties) and then analyze the marketing strategies the musicians use to gain their fans' support. The essay's logic would be undermined if you switched, in the middle of your analysis, to another principle of classification—say, the influence of earlier groups on today's music scene.

2. Apply the principle of division-classification logically. You need to demonstrate to readers that your analysis is the result of careful thought. First of all, your division-classification should be as *complete* as possible. Your analysis should include—within reason—all the parts into which you can divide your subject, or all the types into which you can categorize your subjects. Let's say you're writing an essay showing that where college students live is an important factor in determining how satisfied they are with college life. You classify students according to where they live: with parents, in dorms, in fraternity and sorority houses. But what about all the students who live in rented apartments, houses, or rooms off campus? If these places of residence are ignored, your classification won't be complete; you will lose credibility with your readers because they'll probably realize that you have overlooked several important considerations.

Your division-classification should also be *consistent:* The parts into which you break your subject or the groups into which you place your subjects should be as mutually exclusive as possible. The parts or categories should not be mixed, nor should they overlap. Assume you're writing an essay describing the animals at the zoo in a nearby city. You decide to describe the zoo's mammals, reptiles, birds, and endangered species. But such a classification is inconsistent. You begin by categorizing the animals according to scientific class (mammals, birds, reptiles), then switch to another principle when you classify some animals according to whether they are endangered. Because you drift over to a different principle of classification, your categories are no longer mutually exclusive.

3. Prepare an effective thesis. If your essay uses division-classification as its dominant method of development, it might be helpful to prepare a thesis that does more than signal the paper's subject and suggest your attitude toward that general subject. You might also want the thesis to state the principle of division-classification at the heart of the essay. Furthermore, you might want the thesis to reveal which part or category you regard as most important.

Consider the two thesis statements that follow:

> As the observant beachcomber moves from the tidal area to the upper beach to the sandy dunes, rich variations in marine life become apparent.

> Although most people focus on the dangers associated with the disposal of toxic waste in the land and ocean, the incineration of toxic matter may pose an even more serious threat to human life.

The first thesis statement makes clear that the writer will organize the paper by classifying forms of marine life according to location. Because the purpose of the essay is to inform as objectively as possible, the thesis doesn't suggest the writer's opinion about which category is most significant.

The second thesis signals that the essay will divide the issue of toxic waste by methods of disposal. Moreover, because the paper takes a stance on a controversial subject, the thesis is worded to reveal which aspect of the topic the writer considers most important. Such a clear statement of the writer's position is an effective strategy in an essay of this kind.

You may have noted that each thesis statement also signals the paper's plan of development. The first essay, for example, will use specific facts, examples, and details to describe the kinds of marine life found in the tidal area, upper beach, and dunes. However, thesis statements in papers developed primarily through division-classification don't have to be so structured. If a paper is well written, your principle of division-classification, your opinion about which part or category is most important, and the essay's plan of development will become apparent as the essay unfolds.

4. Organize the paper logically. Whether your paper is developed wholly or in part by division-classification, it should have a logical structure. As much as possible, try to discuss *comparable points* in each section of the paper. In the essay on seashore life, for example, you might describe life in the tidal area by discussing the mollusks, crustaceans, birds, and amphibians that live or feed there. You would then follow through, as much as you could, with this arrangement in the paper's other sections (upper beach and dune). Not describing the bird life thriving in the dunes, especially when you had discussed bird life in the tidal and upper-beach areas, would compromise the paper's structure. Of course, perfect parallelism is not always possible—there are no mollusks in the dunes, for instance.

You should also use *signal devices* to connect various parts of the paper: "*Another* characteristic of marine life battered by the tides"; "A *final* important trait of both tidal and upper-beach crustaceans"; "*Unlike* the creatures of the tidal area and the upper beach." Such signals clarify the connections among the essay's ideas.

5. State any conclusions or recommendations in the paper's final section. The analytic thinking that occurs during division-classification often leads to surprising insights. Such insights may be introduced early on, or they may be reserved for the end, where they are stated as conclusions or recommendations. A paper might categorize different kinds of coaches—from inspiring to incompetent—and make the point that athletes learn a great deal about human relations simply by having to get along with their coaches, regardless of the coaches' skills. Such a paper might conclude that participation in a team sport teaches more about human nature than several courses in psychology. Or the essay might end with a proposal: Rookies and seasoned team members should be paired so that novice players can get advice on dealing with coaching eccentricities.

REVISION STRATEGIES

Once you have a draft of the essay, you're ready to revise. The following checklist will help you and those giving you feedback apply to division-classification some of the revision techniques discussed on pages 60–62.

☑ DIVISION-CLASSIFICATION: A REVISION/PEER REVIEW CHECKLIST

Revise Overall Meaning and Structure

- ❑ What is the principle of division-classification at the heart of the essay? How does this principle contribute to the essay's overall purpose and thesis?
- ❑ Does the thesis state the essay's principle of division-classification? Should it? Does the thesis signal which part or category is most important? Should it? Does the thesis reveal the essay's plan of development? Should it?
- ❑ Is the essay organized primarily through division, classification, or a blend of both?
- ❑ If the essay is organized mainly through division, is the subject sufficiently complex to be broken down into parts? What are the parts?

- ❑ If the essay is organized mainly through classification, what are the categories? How does this categorizing reveal similarities and/or differences that would otherwise not be apparent?

Revise Paragraph Development

- ❑ Are comparable points discussed in each of the paper's sections? What are these points?
- ❑ In which paragraphs does the division-classification seem illogical, incomplete, or inconsistent? In which paragraphs are parts or categories not clearly explained?
- ❑ Are the subject's different parts or categories discussed in separate paragraphs? Is there any overlap among categories?

Revise Sentences and Words

- ❑ What signal devices help integrate the paper? Are there enough signals? Too many?
- ❑ Where should sentences and words be made more specific in order to clarify the parts and categories being discussed?

STUDENT ESSAY

The following student essay was written by Gail Oremland in response to this assignment:

> In "Propaganda Techniques in Today's Advertising," Ann McClintock describes the flaws in many of the persuasive strategies used by advertisers. Choose another group of people whose job is also to communicate—for example, parents, bosses, teachers. Then, in an essay of your own, divide the group into types according to the flaws they make when communicating.

While reading Gail's paper, try to determine how effectively it applies the principles of division-classification. The annotations on Gail's paper and the commentary following it will help you look at the essay more closely.

The Truth About College Teachers
by Gail Oremland

Introduction

1 A recent TV news story told about a group of college professors from a nearby university who were hired by a local school system to help upgrade the teaching in the community's

public schools. The professors were to visit classrooms, analyze teachers' skills, and then conduct workshops to help the teachers become more effective at their jobs. But after the first round of workshops, the superintendent of schools decided to cancel the whole project. He fired the learned professors and sent them back to their ivory tower. Why did the project fall apart? There was a simple reason. The college professors, who were supposedly going to show the public school teachers how to be more effective, were themselves poor teachers. Many college students could have predicted such a disastrous outcome. They know, firsthand, that college teachers are strange. They know that professors often exhibit bizarre behaviors, relating to students in ways that make it difficult for students to stay awake, or—if awake—to learn.

Thesis

2 One type of professor assumes, legitimately enough, that her function is to pass on to students the vast store of knowledge she has acquired. But because the "Knowledgeable One" regards herself as an expert and her students as the ignorant masses, she adopts an elitist approach that sabotages learning. The Knowledgeable One enters a lecture hall with a self-important air, walks to the podium, places her yellowed-with-age notes on the stand, and begins her lecture at the exact second the class is officially scheduled to begin. There can be a blizzard or hurricane raging outside the lecture hall; students can be running through freezing sleet and howling winds to get to class on time. Will the Knowledgeable One wait for them to arrive before beginning her lecture? Probably not. The Knowledgeable One's time is precious. She's there, set to begin, and that's what matters.

Topic sentence

The first of three paragraphs on the first category of teacher

The first paragraph in a three-part chronological sequence: What happens *before* class

3 Once the monologue begins, the Knowledgeable One drones on and on. The Knowledgeable One is a fact person. She may be the history prof who knows the death toll of every Civil War battle, the biology prof who can diagram all the common biological molecules, the accounting prof who enumerates every clause of the federal tax form. Oblivious to students' glazed eyes and stifled yawns, the Knowledgeable One delivers her monologue, dispensing one dry fact after another. The only advantage to being on the receiving end of this boring monologue is that students do not have to worry about being called on to question a point or provide an opinion; the Knowledgeable One is not willing to relinquish one minute of her time by giving students a voice. Assume for one improbable moment that a student actually manages to stay awake during the monologue and is brave enough to ask a question. In such a case, the Knowledgeable One will address the questioning student as "Mr." or "Miss." This formality does not, as some students mistakenly suppose, indicate respect for the student as a fledgling member of the

Topic sentence

The second paragraph on the first category of teacher

The second paragraph in the chronological sequence: What happens *during* class academic community. Not at all. This impersonality represents the Knowledgeable One's desire to keep as wide a distance as possible between her and her students.

Topic sentence

The third paragraph on the first category of teacher

The final paragraph in the chronological sequence: What happens *after* class

The Knowledgeable One's monologue always comes to a 4
close at the precise second the class is scheduled to end. No sooner has she delivered her last forgettable word than the Knowledgeable One packs up her notes and shoots out the door, heading back to the privacy of her office, where she can pursue her specialized academic interests—free of any possible interruption from students. The Knowledgeable One's hasty departure from the lecture hall makes it clear she has no desire to talk with students. In her eyes, she has met her obligations; she has taken time away from her research to transmit to students what she knows. Any closer contact might mean she would risk contagion from students, that great unwashed mass. Such a danger is to be avoided at all costs.

Topic sentence

Paragraph on the second category of teacher

Unlike the Knowledgeable One, the "Leader of Intellectual 5
Discussion" seems to respect students. Emphasizing class discussion, the Leader encourages students to confront ideas ("What is Twain's view of morality?" "Was our intervention in Iraq justified?" "Should big business be given tax breaks?") and discover their own truths. Then, about three weeks into the semester, it becomes clear that the Leader wants students to discover *his* version of the truth. Behind the Leader's democratic guise lurks a dictator. When a student voices an opinion that the Leader accepts, the student is rewarded by hearty nods of approval and "Good point, good point." But if a student is rash enough to advance a conflicting viewpoint, the Leader responds with killing politeness: "Well, yes, that's an interesting perspective. But don't you think that...?" Grade-conscious students soon learn not to chime in with their viewpoint. They know that when the Leader, with seeming honesty, says, "I'd be interested in hearing what you think. Let's open this up for discussion," they had better figure out what the Leader wants to hear before advancing their own theories. "Me-tooism" rather than independent thinking, they discover, guarantees good grades in the Leader's class.

Topic sentence

Paragraph on the third category of teacher

Then there is the professor who comes across as the stu- 6
dents' "Buddy." This kind of professor does not see himself as an imparter of knowledge or a leader of discussion but as a pal, just one in a community of equals. The Buddy may start his course this way. "All of us know that this college stuff—grades, degrees, exams, required reading—is a game. So let's not play it, okay?" Dressed in jeans, sweatshirt, and scuffed sneakers, the Buddy projects a relaxed, casual attitude. He arranges the class seats in a circle (he would never take a position in front of the room) and insists that students call him by his

first name. He uses no syllabus and gives few tests, believing that such constraints keep students from directing their own learning. A free spirit, the Buddy often teaches courses like "The Psychology of Interpersonal Relations" or "The Social Dynamics of the Family." If students choose to use class time to discuss the course material, that's fine. If they want to discuss something else, that's fine, too. It's the self-expression, the honest dialogue, that counts. In fact, the Buddy seems especially fond of digressions from academic subjects. By talking about his political views, his marital problems, his tendency to drink one too many beers, the Buddy lets students see that he is a regular guy—just like them. At first, students look forward to classes with the Buddy. They enjoy the informality, the chitchat, the lack of pressure. But after a while, they wonder why they are paying for a course where they learn nothing. They might as well stay home and watch the soaps.

Conclusion

Echoes opening anecdote

Obviously, some college professors are excellent. They are learned, hardworking, and imaginative; they enjoy their work and like being with students. On the whole, though, college professors are a strange lot. Despite their advanced degrees and their own exposure to many different kinds of teachers, they do not seem to understand how to relate to students. Rather than being hired as consultants to help others upgrade their teaching skills, college professors should themselves hire consultants to tell them what they are doing wrong and how they can improve. Who should these consultants be? That's easy: the people who know them best—their students. 7

COMMENTARY

Introduction and thesis. After years of being graded by teachers, Gail took special pleasure in writing an essay that gave her a chance to evaluate her teachers—in this case, her college professors. Even the essay's title, "The Truth About College Teachers," implies that Gail is going to have fun knocking profs down from their ivory towers. To introduce her subject, she uses a timely news story. This brief anecdote leads directly to the essay's *thesis:* "[P]rofessors often exhibit bizarre behaviors, relating to students in ways that make it difficult for students to stay awake, or—if awake—to learn." Note that Gail's thesis isn't highly structured; it doesn't, for example, name the specific categories to be discussed. Still, her thesis suggests that the essay is going to *categorize* a range of teaching behaviors, using as a *principle of classification* the strange ways that college profs relate to students.

Purpose. As with all good papers developed through division-classification, Gail's essay doesn't use classification as an end in itself. Gail uses classification because it helps her achieve a broader *purpose*. She wants to *convince* readers—without moralizing or abandoning her humorous tone—that such teaching styles inhibit learning. In other words, there's a serious underside to her essay. This additional layer of meaning is characteristic of satiric writing.

Categories and topic sentences. The essay's body, consisting of five paragraphs, presents the three categories that make up Gail's analysis. According to Gail, college teachers can be categorized as the Knowledgeable One (paragraphs 2–4), the Leader of Intellectual Discussion (5), or the Buddy (6). Obviously, there are other ways professors might be classified. But given Gail's purpose, audience, tone, and point of view, her categories are appropriate; they are reasonably *complete, consistent,* and *mutually exclusive*. Note, too, that Gail uses *topic sentences* near the beginning of each category to help readers see which professorial type she's discussing.

Overall organization and paragraph structure. Gail is able to shift smoothly and easily from one category to the next. How does she achieve such graceful transitions? Take a moment to reread the sentences that introduce her second and third categories (paragraphs 5 and 6). Look at the way each sentence's beginning (in italics here) links back to the preceding category or categories: "*Unlike the Knowledgeable One,* the 'Leader of Intellectual Discussion' seems to respect students"; and "[the Buddy]...*does not see himself as an imparter of knowledge or a leader of discussion* but as a pal...."

Gail is equally careful about providing an easy-to-follow structure within each section. She uses a *chronological sequence* to organize her three-paragraph discussion of the Knowledgeable One. The first paragraph deals with the beginning of the Knowledgeable One's lecture; the second, with the lecture itself; the third, with the end of the lecture. And the paragraphs' *topic sentences* clearly indicate this passage of time. Similarly, *transitions* are used in the paragraphs on the Leader of Intellectual Discussion and the Buddy to ensure a logical progression of points: "*Then,* about three weeks into the semester, it becomes clear that the Leader wants students to discover *his* version of the truth" (5) and "*At first,* students look forward to classes with the Buddy.... But *after a while,* they wonder why they are paying for a course where they learn nothing" (6).

Tone. The essay's unity can also be traced to Gail's skill in sustaining her satiric tone. Throughout the essay, Gail selects details that fit her gently mocking attitude. She depicts the Knowledgeable One lecturing from "yellowed-with-age notes..., oblivious to students' glazed eyes and stifled yawns," unwilling to wait for students who "run...through freezing sleet and howling winds to get to class on time." Then she presents another tongue-in-cheek description, this one focusing on the way the Leader of

Intellectual Discussion conducts class: "Good point, good point.... Well, yes, that's an interesting perspective. But don't you think that...?" Finally, with similar killing accuracy, Gail portrays the Buddy, democratically garbed in "jeans, sweatshirt, and scuffed sneakers."

Combining patterns of development. Gail's satiric depiction of her three professorial types employs a number of techniques associated with *narrative* and *descriptive writing*: vigorous images, highly connotative language, and dialogue. *Definition, exemplification, causal analysis,* and *comparison-contrast* also come into play. Gail defines the characteristics of each type of professor; she provides numerous examples to support her categories; she explains the effects of the different teaching styles on students; and, in her description of the Leader of Intellectual Discussion, she contrasts the appearance of democracy with the dictatorial reality.

Unequal development of categories. Although Gail's essay is unified, organized, and well-developed, you may have felt that the first category outweighs the other two. There is, of course, no need to balance the categories exactly. But Gail's extended treatment of the first category sets up an expectation that the others will be treated as fully. One way to remedy this problem would be to delete some material from the discussion of the Knowledgeable One. Gail might, for instance, omit the last five sentences in the third paragraph (about the professor's habit of addressing students as "Mr." or "Miss"). Such a change could be made without taking the bite out of her portrayal. Even better, Gail could simply switch the order of her sections, putting the portrait of the Knowledgeable One at the essay's end. Here, the extended discussion wouldn't seem out of proportion. Instead, the sections would appear in *emphatic order,* with the most detailed category saved for last.

Revising the first draft. It's apparent that an essay as engaging as Gail's must have undergone a good deal of revising. That was in fact the case. Gail made many changes in the body of the essay, but it's particularly interesting to review what happened to the introduction as she revised the paper. Printed here is Gail's original introduction.

Original Version of the Introduction

Despite their high IQs, advanced degrees, and published papers, some college professors just don't know how to teach. Found in almost any department, in tenured and untenured positions, they prompt student apathy. They fail to convey ideas effectively and to challenge or inspire students. Students thus finish their courses having learned very little. Contrary to popular opinion, these professors' ineptitude is not simply a matter of delivering boring lectures or not caring about students. Many of them care a great deal. Their failure actually stems from their unrealistic perceptions of what a teacher should be.

Specifically, they adopt teaching styles or roles that alienate students and undermine learning. Three of the most common ones are "The Knowledgeable One," "The Leader of Intellectual Discussion," and "The Buddy."

When Gail showed the first draft of the essay to her composition instructor, he laughed—and occasionally squirmed—as he read what she had prepared. He was enthusiastic about the paper but felt that there was a problem with the introduction's tone; it was too serious when compared to the playful, lightly satiric mood of the rest of the essay. When Gail reread the paragraph, she agreed, but she was uncertain about the best way to remedy the problem. After revising other sections of the essay, she decided to let the paper sit for a while before going back to rewrite the introduction.

In the meantime, Gail switched on the TV. The timing couldn't have been better: She tuned into a news story about several supposedly learned professors who had been fired from a consulting job because they had turned out to know so little about teaching. This was exactly the kind of item Gail needed to start her essay. Now she was able to prepare a completely new introduction, making it consistent in spirit with the rest of the paper.

With this stronger introduction and the rest of the essay well in hand, Gail was ready to write a conclusion. Now, as she worked on the concluding paragraph, she deliberately shaped it to recall the story about the fired consultants. By echoing the opening anecdote in her conclusion, Gail was able to end the paper with another poke at professors—a perfect way to close her clever and insightful essay.

Activities: Division-Classification

Prewriting Activities

1. Imagine you're writing two essays: One is a humorous paper outlining a *process* for impressing college instructors; the other is a serious essay examining the *causes* of the recent rise in volunteerism. What about the topics might you divide and/or classify?

2. Use group brainstorming to identify three principles of division for *one* of the topics in Set A below. Focusing on one of the principles, decide what your thesis might be if you were writing an essay. That done, use group brainstorming to identify three principles of classification that might provide the structure for *one* of the topics in Set B. Focusing on one of the principles, decide what your thesis might be if you were writing an essay.

Set A	Set B
• Rock music	• Why people get addicted to computers
• A shopping mall	• How fast-food restaurants affect family life
• A good horror movie	• Why long-term relationships break up

Revising Activities

3. Following is a scratch outline for an essay developed through division-classification. On what principle of division-classification is the essay based? What problem do you see in the way the principle is applied? How could the problem be remedied?

   Thesis: The same experience often teaches opposite things to different people.

   - What working as a fast-food cook teaches: Some learn responsibility; others learn to take a "quick and dirty" approach.
   - What a negative experience teaches optimists: Some learn from their mistakes; others continue to maintain a positive outlook.
   - What a difficult course teaches: Some learn to study hard; others learn to avoid demanding courses.
   - What the breakup of a close relationship teaches: Some learn how to negotiate differences; others learn to avoid intimacy.

4. Following is a paragraph from the first draft of an essay urging that day-care centers adopt play programs tailored to children's developmental needs. What principle of division-classification focuses the paragraph? Is the principle applied consistently and logically? Are parts/categories developed sufficiently? Revise the paragraph, eliminating any problems you discover and adding specific details where needed.

   Within a few years, preschool children move from self-absorbed to interactive play. Babies and toddlers engage in solitary play. Although they sometimes prefer being near other children, they focus primarily on their own actions. This is very different from the highly interactive play of the elementary school years. Sometime in children's second year, solitary play is replaced by parallel play, during which children engage in similar activities near one another. However, they interact only occasionally. By age three, most children show at least some cooperative play, a form that involves interaction and cooperative role-taking. Such role-taking can be found in the "pretend" games that children play to explore adult relationships (games of "Mommy and Daddy") and anatomy (games of "Doctor"). Additional signs of youngsters' growing awareness of peers can be seen at about age four. At this age, many children begin showing a special devotion to one other child and may want to play only with that child. During this time, children also begin to take special delight in physical activities such as running and jumping, often going off by themselves to expend their abundant physical energy.

Ann McClintock

Ann McClintock (1946–) was educated at Temple University in Philadelphia and later earned an advanced degree from the University of Pennsylvania. Formerly director of occupational therapy at Ancora State Hospital in New Jersey, she has also worked as a freelance editor and writer. A frequent speaker before community groups, McClintock is especially interested in the effects of advertising on American life. The following selection, revised for this text, is part of a work in progress on the way propaganda techniques are used to sell products and political candidates.

For ideas on how this division-classification essay is organized, see Figure 6.2 on page 245.

Pre-Reading Journal Entry

How susceptible are you to ads and commercials? Do you consider yourself an easy target, or are you a "hard sell"? Have you purchased any products simply because you were won over by effective advertising strategies? What products have you not purchased because you deliberately didn't let yourself be swayed by advertisers' tactics? In your journal, reflect on these questions.

Propaganda Techniques in Today's Advertising

Americans, adults and children alike, are being seduced. They are being brainwashed. And few of us protest. Why? Because the seducers and the brainwashers are the advertisers we willingly invite into our homes. We are victims, content—even eager—to be victimized. We read advertisers' propaganda messages in newspapers and magazines; we watch their alluring images on television. We absorb their messages and images into our subconscious. We all do it—even those of us who claim to see through advertisers' tricks and therefore feel immune to advertising's charm. Advertisers lean heavily on propaganda to sell products, whether the "products" are a brand of toothpaste, a candidate for office, or a particular political viewpoint. 1

Propaganda is a systematic effort to influence people's opinions, to win them over to a certain view or side. Propaganda is not necessarily concerned with what is true or false, good or bad. Propagandists simply want people to believe the messages being sent. Often, propagandists will use outright lies or more subtle deceptions to sway people's opinions. In a propaganda war, any tactic is considered fair. 2

When we hear the word "propaganda," we usually think of a foreign menace: anti-American radio programs broadcast by a totalitarian regime or brainwashing tactics practiced on hostages. Although propaganda may seem 3 relevant only in the political arena, the concept can be applied fruitfully to the way products and ideas are sold in advertising. Indeed, the vast majority of us are targets in advertisers' propaganda war. Every day, we are bombarded with slogans, print and Internet pop-up ads, commercials, packaging claims, billboards, trademarks, logos, and designer brands—all forms of propaganda. One study reports that each of us, during an average day, is exposed to over *five hundred* advertising claims of various types. This saturation may even increase in the future since current trends include ads on movie screens, shopping carts, videocassettes, even public television.

What kind of propaganda techniques do advertisers use? There are seven basic types: 4

1. *Name Calling* Name calling is a propaganda tactic in which negatively charged names are hurled against the opposing side or competitor. By using such names, propagandists try to arouse feelings of mistrust, fear, and hate in their audiences. For example, a political advertisement may label an opposing candidate a "loser," "fence-sitter," or "warmonger." Depending on the advertiser's target market, labels such as "a friend of big business" or "a dues-paying member of the party in power" can be the epithets that damage an opponent. Ads for products may also use name calling. An American manufacturer may refer, for instance, to a "foreign car" in its commercial—not an "imported" one. The label of foreignness will have unpleasant connotations in many people's minds. A childhood rhyme claims that "names can never hurt me," but name calling is an effective way to damage the opposition, whether it is another car maker or a congressional candidate. 5

2. *Glittering Generalities* Using glittering generalities is the opposite of name calling. In this case, advertisers surround their products with attractive—and slippery—words and phrases. They use vague terms that are difficult to define and that may have different meanings to different people: *freedom, democratic, all-American, progressive, Christian,* and *justice.* Many such words have strong, affirmative overtones. This kind of language stirs positive feelings in people, feelings that may spill over to the product or idea being pitched. As with name calling, the emotional response may overwhelm logic. Target audiences accept the product without thinking very much about what the glittering generalities mean—or whether they even apply to the product. After all, how can anyone oppose "truth, justice, and the American way"? 6

The ads for politicians and political causes often use glittering generalities because such "buzz words" can influence votes. Election slogans include high-sounding but basically empty phrases like the following: 7

"He cares about people." (That's nice, but is he a better candidate than his opponent?)

"Vote for progress." (Progress by *whose* standards?)

"They'll make this country great again." (What does "great" mean? Does "great" mean the same thing to others as it does to me?)
"Vote for the future." (What kind of future?)
"If you love America, vote for Phyllis Smith." (If I don't vote for Smith, does that mean I don't love America?)

Ads for consumer goods are also sprinkled with glittering generalities. Product names, for instance, are supposed to evoke good feelings: *Luvs* diapers, *Stayfree* feminine hygiene products, *Joy* liquid detergent, *Loving Care* hair color, *Almost Home* cookies, *Yankee Doodle* pastries. Product slogans lean heavily on vague but comforting phrases: Sears is "Good life. Great price," General Electric "brings good things to life," and Dow Chemical "lets you do great things." Chevrolet, we are told, is the "heartbeat of America," and Chrysler boasts cars that are "built by Americans for Americans." 8

3. *Transfer* In transfer, advertisers try to improve the image of a product by associating it with a symbol most people respect, like the American flag or Uncle Sam. The advertisers hope that the prestige attached to the symbol will carry over to the product. Many companies use transfer devices to identify their products: Lincoln Insurance shows a profile of the president; Continental Insurance portrays a Revolutionary War minuteman; Amtrak's logo is red, white, and blue; Liberty Mutual's corporate symbol is the Statue of Liberty; Allstate's name is cradled by a pair of protective, fatherly hands. 9

Corporations also use the transfer technique when they sponsor prestigious shows on radio and television. These shows function as symbols of dignity and class. Kraft Corporation, for instance, sponsored a "Leonard Bernstein Conducts Beethoven" concert, while Gulf Oil is the sponsor of *National Geographic* specials and Mobil supports public television's *Masterpiece Theater*. In this way, corporations can reach an educated, influential audience and, perhaps, improve their public image by associating themselves with quality programming. 10

Political ads, of course, practically wrap themselves in the flag. Ads for a political candidate often show either the Washington Monument, a Fourth of July parade, the Stars and Stripes, a bald eagle soaring over the mountains, or a white-steepled church on the village green. The national anthem or "America the Beautiful" may play softly in the background. Such appeals to Americans' love of country can surround the candidate with an aura of patriotism and integrity. 11

4. *Testimonial* The testimonial is one of advertisers' most-loved and most-used propaganda techniques. Similar to the transfer device, the testimonial capitalizes on the admiration people have for a celebrity to make the product shine more brightly—even though the celebrity is not an expert on the product being sold. 12

Print and television ads offer a nonstop parade of testimonials: here's William Shatner for Priceline.com; here's basketball star Michael Jordan eating Wheaties; a slew of well-known people (including pop star Madonna) advertise clothing from the Gap; and Jerry Seinfeld assures us he never goes anywhere without his American Express card. Testimonials can sell movies, too; newspaper ads for films often feature favorable comments by well-known reviewers. And, in recent years, testimonials have played an important role in pitching books; the backs of paperbacks frequently list complimentary blurbs by celebrities. 13

Political candidates, as well as their ad agencies, know the value of testimonials. Barbra Streisand lent her star appeal to the presidential campaign of Bill Clinton, while Arnold Schwarzenegger endorsed George H. W. Bush. Even controversial social issues are debated by celebrities. The nuclear-freeze debate, for instance, starred Paul Newman for the pro side and Charlton Heston for the con. 14

As illogical as testimonials sometimes are (Pepsi's Michael Jackson, for instance, is a health-food adherent who does not drink soft drinks), they are effective propaganda. We like the *person* so much that we like the *product* too. 15

5. *Plain Folks* The plain folks approach says, in effect, "Buy me or vote for me. I'm just like you." Regular folks will surely like Bob Evans's Down on the Farm Country Sausage or good old-fashioned Countrytime Lemonade. Some ads emphasize the idea that "we're all in the same boat." We see people making long-distance calls for just the reasons we do—to put the baby on the phone to Grandma or to tell Mom we love her. And how do these folksy, warmhearted (usually saccharine) scenes affect us? They're supposed to make us feel that AT&T—the multinational corporate giant—has the same values we do. Similarly, we are introduced to the little people at Ford, the ordinary folks who work on the assembly line, not to bigwigs in their executive offices. What's the purpose of such an approach? To encourage us to buy a car built by these honest, hardworking "everyday Joes" who care about quality as much as we do. 16

Political advertisements make almost as much use of the "plain folks" appeal as they do of transfer devices. Candidates wear hard hats, farmers' caps, and assembly-line coveralls. They jog around the block and carry their own luggage through the airport. The idea is to convince voters that the candidates are average people, not the elite—not wealthy lawyers or executives but common citizens. 17

6. *Card Stacking* When people say that "the cards were stacked against me," they mean that they were never given a fair chance. Applied to propaganda, card stacking means that one side may suppress or distort evidence, tell half-truths, oversimplify the facts, or set up a "straw man"—a false target—to divert attention from the issue at hand. Card stacking is a difficult form of propaganda both to detect and to combat. When a candidate claims 18

that an opponent has "changed his mind five times on this important issue," we tend to accept the claim without investigating whether the candidate had good reasons for changing his mind. Many people are simply swayed by the distorted claim that the candidate is "waffling" on the issue.

Advertisers often stack the cards in favor of the products they are pushing. 19
They may, for instance, use what are called "weasel words." These are small words that usually slip right past us, but that make the difference between reality and illusion. The weasel words are underlined in the following claims:

> "Helps control dandruff symptoms." (The audience usually interprets this as *stops* dandruff.)
>
> "Most dentists surveyed recommend sugarless gum for their patients who chew gum." (We hear the "most dentists" and "for their patients," but we don't think about how many were surveyed or whether the dentists first recommended that the patients not chew gum at all.)
>
> "Sticker price $1,000 lower than most comparable cars." (How many is "most"? What car does the advertiser consider "comparable"?)

Advertisers also use a card stacking trick when they make an unfinished 20
claim. For example, they will say that their product has "twice as much pain reliever." We are left with a favorable impression. We don't usually ask, "Twice as much pain reliever as what?" Or advertisers may make extremely vague claims that sound alluring but have no substance: Toyota's "Oh, what a feeling!"; Vantage cigarettes' "The taste of success"; "The spirit of Marlboro"; Coke's "the real thing." Another way to stack the cards in favor of a certain product is to use scientific-sounding claims that are not supported by sound research. When Ford claimed that its LTD model was "400% quieter," many people assumed that the LTD must be quieter than all other cars. When taken to court, however, Ford admitted that the phrase referred to the difference between the noise level inside and outside the LTD. Other scientific-sounding claims use mysterious ingredients that are never explained as selling points: "Retsyn," "special whitening agents," "the ingredient doctors recommend."

7. *Bandwagon* In the bandwagon technique, advertisers pressure, 21
"Everyone's doing it. Why don't you?" This kind of propaganda often succeeds because many people have a deep desire not to be different. Political ads tell us to vote for the "winning candidate." Advertisers know we tend to feel comfortable doing what others do; we want to be on the winning team. Or ads show a series of people proclaiming, "I'm voting for the Senator. I don't know why anyone wouldn't." Again, the audience feels under pressure to conform.

In the marketplace, the bandwagon approach lures buyers. Ads tell us 22
that "nobody doesn't like Sara Lee" (the message is that you must be weird if you don't). They tell us that "most people prefer Brand X two to one over

other leading brands" (to be like the majority, we should buy Brand X). If we don't drink Pepsi, we're left out of "the Pepsi generation." To take part in "America's favorite health kick," the National Dairy Council asks us, "Got Milk?" And Honda motorcycle ads, praising the virtues of being a follower, tell us, "Follow the leader. He's on a Honda."

Why do these propaganda techniques work? Why do so many of us buy the products, viewpoints, and candidates urged on us by propaganda messages? They work because they appeal to our emotions, not to our minds. Often, in fact, they capitalize on our prejudices and biases. For example, if we are convinced that environmentalists are radicals who want to destroy America's record of industrial growth and progress, then we will applaud the candidate who refers to them as "treehuggers." Clear thinking requires hard work: analyzing a claim, researching the facts, examining both sides of an issue, using logic to see the flaws in an argument. Many of us would rather let the propagandists do our thinking for us. 23

Because propaganda is so effective, it is important to detect it and understand how it is used. We may conclude, after close examination, that some propaganda sends a truthful, worthwhile message. Some advertising, for instance, urges us not to drive drunk, to become volunteers, to contribute to charity. Even so, we must be aware that propaganda is being used. Otherwise, we have consented to handing over to others our independence of thought and action. 24

Questions for Close Reading

1. What is the selection's thesis? Locate the sentence(s) in which McClintock states her main idea. If she doesn't state the thesis explicitly, express it in your own words.
2. What is *propaganda?* What mistaken associations do we have with this term?
3. What are "weasel words"? How do they trick listeners?
4. Why does McClintock believe we should know about propaganda techniques?
5. Refer to your dictionary as needed to define the following words used in the selection: *seduced* (paragraph 1), *warmonger* (5), and *elite* (17).

Questions About the Writer's Craft

1. **The pattern and other patterns.** Before explaining the categories into which propaganda techniques can be grouped, McClintock provides a *definition* of propaganda. Is the definition purely informative, or does it have a larger objective? If you think the latter, what is the definition's broader purpose?
2. In her introduction, McClintock uses loaded words such as *seduced* and *brainwashed.* What effect do these words have on the reader?
3. Locate places in the essay where McClintock uses questions. Which are rhetorical and which are genuine queries?
4. What kind of conclusion does McClintock provide for the essay?

FIGURE 6.2
Essay Structure Diagram: "Propaganda Techniques in Today's Advertising" by Ann McClintock

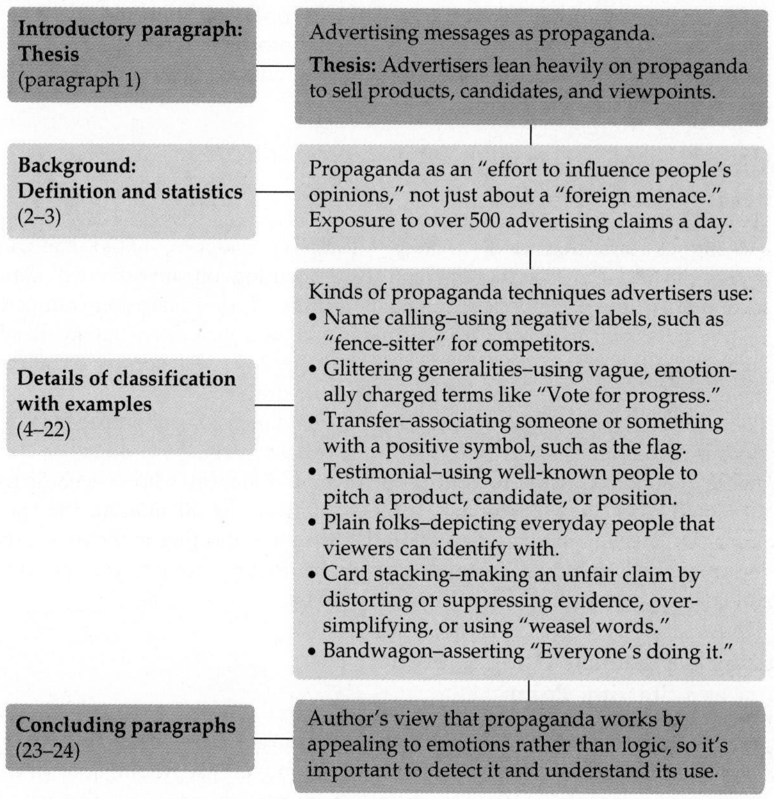
Introductory paragraph: Thesis
(paragraph 1)
Advertising messages as propaganda.
Thesis: Advertisers lean heavily on propaganda to sell products, candidates, and viewpoints.
Background: Definition and statistics
(2–3)
Propaganda as an "effort to influence people's opinions," not just about a "foreign menace." Exposure to over 500 advertising claims a day.
Details of classification with examples
(4–22)
Kinds of propaganda techniques advertisers use:
• Name calling–using negative labels, such as "fence-sitter" for competitors.
• Glittering generalities–using vague, emotionally charged terms like "Vote for progress."
• Transfer–associating someone or something with a positive symbol, such as the flag.
• Testimonial–using well-known people to pitch a product, candidate, or position.
• Plain folks–depicting everyday people that viewers can identify with.
• Card stacking–making an unfair claim by distorting or suppressing evidence, oversimplifying, or using "weasel words."
• Bandwagon–asserting "Everyone's doing it."
Concluding paragraphs
(23–24)
Author's view that propaganda works by appealing to emotions rather than logic, so it's important to detect it and understand its use.

Writing Assignments Using Division-Classification as a Pattern of Development

1. McClintock cautions us to be sensitive to propaganda in advertising. Young children, however, aren't capable of this kind of awareness. With pen or pencil in hand, watch some commercials aimed at children, such as those for toys, cereals, and fast food. Then analyze the use of propaganda techniques in these commercials. Using division-classification, write an essay describing the main propaganda techniques you observed. Support your analysis with examples drawn from the commercials. Remember to provide a thesis that indicates your opinion of the advertising techniques. For additional insight into this issue, read Ellen Goodman's "Family Counterculture" (page 7) and Kay S. Hymowitz's "Tweens: Ten Going On Sixteen" (page 190).

2. Like advertising techniques, television shows can be classified. Avoiding the obvious system of classifying according to game shows, detective shows, and situation comedies, come up with your own original division-classification principle. Possibilities include how family life is depicted, the way work is presented, how male-female relationships are portrayed. Using one such principle, write an essay in which you categorize popular TV shows into three types. Refer to specific shows to support your classification system. Your attitude toward the shows being discussed should be made clear.

Writing Assignments Combining Patterns of Development

3. McClintock says that card stacking "distort[s] evidence, tell[s] half-truths, oversimpli[fies] the facts" (paragraph 18). Focusing on an extended *example* such as an editorial, a political campaign, a print ad, or a television commercial, analyze the extent to which card stacking is used as a *persuasive* strategy. Reading Stephanie Ericsson's "The Ways We Lie" (page 247) will deepen your understanding of the extent to which the truth can be distorted.
4. To increase further your sensitivity to the moral dimensions of propaganda, write a proposal outlining an ad campaign for a real or imaginary product or elected official. The introduction to your proposal should identify who or what is to be promoted, and the thesis or plan of development should indicate the specific propaganda techniques you suggest. In the paper's supporting paragraphs, explain the *process* by which these techniques would be used to promote your product or candidate and what their desired *effects* would be.

Writing Assignment Using a Journal Entry as a Starting Point

5. Write an essay showing that, on the whole, you are fairly susceptible to *or* are fairly immune to advertising ploys. Drawing upon your pre-reading journal entry, illustrate your position with lively details of advertising campaigns that won you over—or that failed to sway you. Use some of McClintock's terminology when describing advertisers' techniques. Your essay may be serious or playful.

Stephanie Ericsson

Stephanie Ericsson (1953–) is a writer, screenwriter, and ad copywriter who often uses her own life experiences as starting points for her deeply personal work. She wrote *Companion Through the Darkness: Inner Dialogues on Grief* (1993) in response to her husband's sudden death while she was pregnant, and she chronicled her struggles with substance abuse in both *Shamefaced* (1985) and *Women of AA: Recovering Together* (1986). Ericsson's latest book is *Companion into the Dawn: Inner Dialogues on Loving* (1994). A frequent speaker on the subject of loss, she lives in Minneapolis, Minnesota. "The Ways We Lie" was originally published in the *Utne Reader* in 1992.

Pre-Reading Journal Entry

Something that everyone is guilty of, but may not want to admit to, is lying. Think for a moment about times when you told a lie. In your pre-reading journal, begin by listing any episodes of lying you can recall. Then go back and freewrite to a greater extent about these incidents. In each case, why did you tell the lie—what were the circumstances? What was the outcome? Do you now regret having lied, or are you thankful you did it?

The Ways We Lie

The bank called today and I told them my deposit was in the mail, even though I hadn't written a check yet. It'd been a rough day. The baby I'm pregnant with decided to do aerobics on my lungs for two hours, our three-year-old daughter painted the living room couch with lipstick, the IRS put me on hold for an hour, and I was late to a business meeting because I was tired. 1

I told my client that traffic had been bad. When my partner came home, his haggard face told me his day hadn't gone any better than mine, so when he asked, "How was your day?" I said, "Oh, fine," knowing that one more straw might break his back. A friend called and wanted to take me to lunch. I said I was busy. Four lies in the course of a day, none of which I felt the least bit guilty about. 2

We lie. We all do. We exaggerate, we minimize, we avoid confrontation, we spare people's feelings, we conveniently forget, we keep secrets, we justify lying to the big-guy institutions. Like most people, I indulge in small falsehoods and still think of myself as an honest person. Sure I lie, but it doesn't hurt anything. Or does it? 3

I once tried going a whole week without telling a lie, and it was paralyzing. I discovered that telling the truth all the time is nearly impossible. It means living with some serious consequences: The bank charges me $60 in 4 overdraft fees, my partner keels over when I tell him about my travails, my client fires me for telling her I didn't feel like being on time, and my friend takes it personally when I say I'm not hungry. There must be some merit to lying.

But if I justify lying, what makes me any different from slick politicians or the corporate robbers who raided the S&L industry?[1] Saying it's okay to lie one way and not another is hedging. I cannot seem to escape the voice deep inside me that tells me: When someone lies, someone loses. 5

What far-reaching consequences will I, or others, pay as a result of my lie? Will someone's trust be destroyed? Will someone else pay *my* penance because I ducked out? We must consider the *meaning of our actions.* Deception, lies, capital crimes, and misdemeanors all carry meanings. *Webster's* definition of *lie* is specific: 6

> 1: a false statement or action especially made with the intent to deceive; 2: anything that gives or is meant to give a false impression.

A definition like this implies that there are many, many ways to tell a lie. Here are just a few. 7

The White Lie

A man who won't lie to a woman has very little consideration for her feelings.

—Bergen Evans

The white lie assumes that the truth will cause more damage than a simple, harmless untruth. Telling a friend he looks great when he looks like hell can be based on a decision that the friend needs a compliment more than a frank opinion. But, in effect, it is the liar deciding what is best for the lied to. Ultimately, it is a vote of no confidence. It is an act of subtle arrogance for anyone to decide what is best for someone else. 8

Yet not all circumstances are quite so cut-and-dried. Take, for instance, the sergeant in Vietnam who knew one of his men was killed in action but listed him as missing so that the man's family would receive indefinite compensation instead of the lump-sum pittance the military gives widows and children. His intent was honorable. Yet for twenty years this family kept their hopes alive, unable to move on to a new life. 9

[1]Reference to the savings and loan scandal of the 1980s, in which corrupt owners of bank-like institutions defrauded the federal government of vast amounts of money (editors' note).

Façades

Et tu, Brute?

—Caesar

We all put up façades to one degree or another. When I put on a suit to go to see a client, I feel as though I am putting on another face, obeying the expectation that serious businesspeople wear suits rather than sweatpants. But I'm a writer. Normally, I get up, get the kid off to school, and sit at my computer in my pajamas until four in the afternoon. When I answer the phone, the caller thinks I'm wearing a suit (though the UPS man knows better). 10

But façades can be destructive because they are used to seduce others into an illusion. For instance, I recently realized that a former friend was a liar. He presented himself with all the right looks and the right words and offered lots of new consciousness theories, fabulous books to read, and fascinating insights. Then I did some business with him, and the time came for him to pay me. He turned out to be all talk and no walk. I heard a plethora of reasonable excuses, including in-depth descriptions of the big break around the corner. In six months of work, I saw less than a hundred bucks. When I confronted him, he raised both eyebrows and tried to convince me that I'd heard him wrong, that he'd made no commitment to me. A simple investigation into his past revealed a crowded graveyard of disenchanted former friends. 11

Ignoring the Plain Facts

Well, you must understand that Father Porter is only human....

—A Massachusetts priest

In the '60s, the Catholic Church in Massachusetts began hearing complaints that Father James Porter was sexually molesting children. Rather than relieving him of his duties, the ecclesiastical authorities simply moved him from one parish to another between 1960 and 1967, actually providing him with a fresh supply of unsuspecting families and innocent children to abuse. After treatment in 1967 for pedophilia, he went back to work, this time in Minnesota. The new diocese was aware of Father Porter's obsession with children, but they needed priests and recklessly believed treatment had cured him. More children were abused until he was relieved of his duties a year later. By his own admission, Porter may have abused as many as a hundred children. 12

Ignoring the facts may not in and of itself be a form of lying, but consider the context of this situation. If a lie is *a false action done with the intent to deceive,* then the Catholic Church's conscious covering for Porter created irreparable consequences. The church became a co-perpetrator with Porter. 13

Deflecting

When you have no basis for an argument, abuse the plaintiff.

—Cicero

I've discovered that I can keep anyone from seeing the true me by being selectively blatant. I set a precedent of being up-front about intimate issues, but I never bring up the things I truly want to hide; I just let people assume I'm revealing everything. It's an effective way of hiding. 14

Any good liar knows that the way to perpetuate an untruth is to deflect attention from it. When Clarence Thomas[2] exploded with accusations that the Senate hearings were a "high-tech lynching," he simple switched the focus from a highly charged subject to a radioactive subject. Rather than defending himself, he took the offensive and accused the country of racism. It was a brilliant maneuver. Racism is now politically incorrect in official circles—unlike sexual harassment, which still rewards those who can get away with it. 15

Some of the most skillful deflectors are passive-aggressive[3] people who, when accused of inappropriate behavior, refuse to respond to the accusations. This you-don't-exist stance infuriates the accuser, who, understandably, screams something obscene out of frustration. The trap is sprung and the act of deflection successful, because now the passive-aggressive person can indignantly say, "Who can talk to someone as unreasonable as you?" The real issue is forgotten and the sins of the original victim become the focus. Feeling guilty of name-calling, the victim is fully tamed and crawls into a hole, ashamed. I have watched this fighting technique work thousands of times in disputes between men and women, and what I've learned is that the real culprit is not necessarily the one who swears the loudest. 16

Omission

The cruelest lies are often told in silence.

—R. L. Stevenson

Omission involves telling most of the truth minus one or two key facts whose absence changes the story completely. You break a pair of glasses that are guaranteed under normal use and get a new pair, without mentioning that the first pair broke during a rowdy game of basketball. Who hasn't tried 17

[2]Nominated to the Supreme Court in 1993, Clarence Thomas, an African American jurist, was accused by former colleague Anita Hill of sexual harassment. Much of Thomas's confirmation hearing, televised nationwide, focused on this issue (editors' note).

[3]A psychological pattern in which hostility is expressed through an infuriating detachment and nonresponsiveness (editors' note).

something like that? But what about omission of information that could make a difference in how a person lives his or her life?

For instance, one day I found out that rabbinical legends tell of another woman in the Garden of Eden before Eve. I was stunned. The omission of the Sumerian goddess Lilith from Genesis—as well as her demonization by ancient misogynists as an embodiment of female evil—felt like spiritual robbery. I felt like I'd just found out my mother was really my stepmother. To take seriously the tradition that Adam was created out of the same mud as his equal counterpart, Lilith, redefines all of Judeo-Christian history. 18

Some renegade Catholic feminists introduced me to a view of Lilith that had been suppressed during many centuries when this strong goddess was seen only as a spirit of evil. Lilith was a proud goddess who defied Adam's need to control her, attempted negotiations, and when this failed, said adios and left the Garden of Eden. 19

This omission of Lilith from the Bible was a patriarchal strategy to keep women weak. Omitting the strong-woman archetype of Lilith from Western religions and starting the story with Eve the Rib has helped keep Christian and Jewish women believing they were the lesser sex for thousands of years. 20

Stereotypes and Clichés

Where opinion does not exist, the status quo becomes stereotyped and all originality is discouraged.

—Bertrand Russell

Stereotype and cliché serve a purpose as a form of shorthand. Our need for vast amounts of information in nanoseconds has made the stereotype vital to modern communication. Unfortunately, it often shuts down original thinking, giving those hungry for the truth a candy bar of misinformation instead of a balanced meal. The stereotype explains a situation with just enough truth to seem unquestionable. 21

All the "isms"—racism, sexism, ageism, et al.—are founded on and fueled by the stereotype and the cliché, which are lies of exaggeration, omission, and ignorance. They are always dangerous. They take a single tree and make it a landscape. They destroy curiosity. They close minds and separate people. The single mother on welfare is assumed to be cheating. Any black male could tell you how much of his identity is obliterated daily by stereotypes. Fat people, ugly people, beautiful people, old people, large-breasted women, short men, the mentally ill, and the homeless all could tell you how much more they are like us than we want to think. I once admitted to a group of people that I had a mouth like a truck driver. Much to my surprise, a man stood up and said, "I'm a truck driver, and I never cuss." Needless to say, I was humbled. 22

Groupthink

Who is more foolish, the child afraid of the dark,
or the man afraid of the light?

—Maurice Freehill

Irving Janis, in *Victims of Group Think,* defines this sort of lie as a psychological phenomenon within decision-making groups in which loyalty to the group has become more important than any other value, with the result that dissent and the appraisal of alternatives are suppressed. If you've ever worked on a committee or in a corporation, you've encountered groupthink. It requires a combination of other forms of lying—ignoring facts, selective memory, omission, and denial, to name a few. 23

The textbook example of groupthink came on December 7, 1941. From as early as the fall of 1941, the warnings came in, one after another, that Japan was preparing for a massive military operation. The Navy command in Hawaii assumed Pearl Harbor was invulnerable—the Japanese weren't stupid enough to attack the United States' most important base. On the other hand, racist stereotypes said the Japanese weren't smart enough to invent a torpedo effective in less than 60 feet of water (the fleet was docked in 30 feet); after all, U.S. technology hadn't been able to do it. 24

On Friday, December 5, normal weekend leave was granted to all the commanders at Pearl Harbor, even though the Japanese consulate in Hawaii was busy burning papers. Within the tight, good-ole-boy cohesiveness of the U.S. command in Hawaii, the myth of invulnerability stayed well entrenched. No one in the group considered the alternatives. The rest is history. 25

Out-and-Out Lies

The only form of lying that is beyond reproach is lying for its own sake.

—Oscar Wilde

Of all the ways to lie, I like this one the best, probably because I get tired of trying to figure out the real meanings behind things. At least I can trust the bald-faced lie. I once asked my five-year-old nephew, "Who broke the fence?" (I had seen him do it.) He answered, "The murderers." Who could argue? 26

At least when this sort of lie is told it can be easily confronted. As the person who is lied to, I know where I stand. The bald-faced lie doesn't toy with my perceptions—it argues with them. It doesn't try to refashion reality, it tries to refute it. *Read my lips*... No sleight of hand.[4] No guessing. If this 27

[4]A phrase used by presidential candidate George H. W. Bush during the 1988 campaign (and often parodied thereafter): "Read my lips.... No new taxes" (editors' note).

were the only form of lying, there would be no such things as floating anxiety[5] or the adult, children-of-alcoholics movement.

Dismissal

Pay no attention to that man behind the curtain! I am the Great Oz!

—The Wizard of Oz

Dismissal is perhaps the slipperiest of all lies. Dismissing feelings, perceptions, or even the raw facts of a situation ranks as a kind of lie that can do as much damage to a person as any other kind of lie. 28

The roots of many mental disorders can be traced back to the dismissal of reality. Imagine that a person is told from the time she is a tot that her perceptions are inaccurate. *"Mommy, I'm scared."* "No you're not, darling." *"I don't like that man next door, he makes me feel icky."* "Johnny, that's a terrible thing to say, of course you like him. You go over there right now and be nice to him." 29

I've often mused over the idea that madness is actually a sane reaction to an insane world. Psychologist R. D. Laing supports this hypothesis in *Sanity, Madness and the Family,* an account of his investigations into the families of schizophrenics. The common thread that ran through all of the families he studied was a deliberate, staunch dismissal of the patient's perceptions from a very early age. Each of the patients started out with an accurate grasp of reality, which, through meticulous and methodical dismissal, was demolished until the only reality the patient could trust was catatonia. 30

Dismissal runs the gamut. Mild dismissal can be quite handy for forgiving the foibles of others in our day-to-day lives. Toddlers who have just learned to manipulate their parents' attention sometimes are dismissed out of necessity. Absolute attention from the parents would require so much energy that no one would get to eat dinner. But we must be careful and attentive about how far we take our "necessary" dismissals. Dismissal is a dangerous tool, because it's nothing less than a lie. 31

Delusion

We lie loudest when we lie to ourselves.

—Eric Hoffer

I could write the book on this one. Delusion, a cousin of dismissal, is the tendency to see excuses as facts. It's a powerful lying tool because it filters out information that contradicts what we want to believe. Alcoholics 32

[5]A psychological condition in which a person feels generalized anxiety for no specific reason (editors' note).

who believe that the problems in their lives are legitimate reasons for drinking rather than results of the drinking offer the classic example of deluded thinking. Delusion uses the mind's ability to see things in myriad ways to support what it wants to be the truth.

But delusion is also a survival mechanism we all use. If we were to fully contemplate the consequences of our stockpiles of nuclear weapons or global warming, we could hardly function on a day-to-day level. We don't want to incorporate that much reality into our lives because to do so would be paralyzing. 33

Delusion acts as an adhesive to keep the status quo intact. It shamelessly employs dismissal, omission, and amnesia, among other sorts of lies. Its most cunning defense is that it cannot see itself. 34

• • •

The liar's punishment... is that he cannot believe anyone else.

—George Bernard Shaw

These are only a few of the ways we lie. Or are lied to. As I said earlier, it's not easy to entirely eliminate lies from our lives. No matter how pious we may try to be, we will still embellish, hedge, and omit to lubricate the daily machinery of living. But there is a world of difference between telling functional lies and living a lie. Martin Buber[6] once said, "The lie is the spirit committing treason against itself." Our acceptance of lies becomes a cultural cancer that eventually shrouds and reorders reality until moral garbage becomes as invisible to us as water is to a fish. 35

How much do we tolerate before we become sick and tired of being sick and tired? When will we stand up and declare our *right* to trust? When do we stop accepting that the real truth is in the fine print? Whose lips do we read this year when we vote for president? When will we stop being so reticent about making judgments? When do we stop turning over our personal power and responsibility to liars? 36

Maybe if I don't tell the bank the check's in the mail I'll be less tolerant of the lies told me every day. A country song I once heard said it all for me: "You've got to stand for something or you'll fall for anything." 37

---

[6]A German Jewish scholar and philosopher (1878–1965) (editors' note).

Questions for Close Reading

1. What is the selection's thesis? Locate the sentence(s) in which Ericsson states her main idea. If she doesn't state the thesis explicitly, express it in your own words.
2. What did Ericsson discover when she tried to go a whole week without lying?

3. Ericsson classifies as "lies" some behaviors not always considered dishonest. How can "ignoring the plain facts," "deflecting," and "omission" be types of lies? How do "stereotypes and clichés" and "groupthink" qualify as lies?
4. Why doesn't Ericsson easily accept the fact that lies are a necessary part of her life and that of most people?
5. Refer to your dictionary as needed to define the following words used in the selection: *travails* (paragraph 4), *hedging* (5), *penance* (6), *pittance* (9), *façades* (10), *plethora* (11), *disenchanted* (11), *ecclesiastical* (12), *pedophilia* (12), *irreparable* (13), *blatant* (14), *demonization* (18), *misogynists* (18), *embodiment* (18), *archetype* (20), *obliterated* (22), *dissent* (23), *cohesiveness* (25), *invulnerability* (25), *entrenched* (25), *catatonia* (30), and *gamut* (31).

Questions About the Writer's Craft

1. **The pattern.** In paragraph 6, Ericsson asserts that we "must consider the *meaning of our actions*" when deciding whether or not we have lied. How does this principle of classification help her show that each category of behavior discussed is a type of lying?
2. **Other patterns.** In the body of her essay, Ericsson draws upon both personal experience and third-person material to make her point. Her introduction, though, includes only a first-person *narrative.* Why do you suppose Ericsson decided to open the essay with this brief first-person account?
3. Despite the seriousness of her subject, Ericsson's overall tone is informal—almost conversational. Identify at least five instances of this informality. Why do you suppose Ericsson adopted such a tone?
4. **Other patterns.** In her concluding paragraphs (35–37), Ericsson *contrasts* two broad types of lies, saying that "there is a world of difference between telling functional lies and living a lie." How does this contrast help her sum up the essay?

Writing Assignments Using Division-Classification as a Pattern of Development

1. Ericsson takes an often used, seemingly simple word and, by categorizing its various manifestations, shows that it represents a complex phenomenon. Choose another frequently used word—such as *loyalty, excellence, arrogance,* or *hypocrisy*—and show its complexity by categorizing its different types. Before presenting your categories, offer a definition, either yours or the dictionary's, of the word; then provide dramatic examples to illustrate the various categories.
2. In paragraph 23, Ericsson cites Irving Janus's definition of "groupthink." Using this definition as a starting point, analyze several situations involving groupthink that you have observed or heard about. Classify the kinds of groupthink that are revealed in these situations, illustrating each type with at least one vivid example. To deepen your understanding of groupthink, read the following essays before writing your paper: George Orwell's "Shooting an Elephant" (page 146), Langston Hughes's "Salvation" (page 158), and John M. Darley and Bibb Latané's "When Will People Help in a Crisis?" (page 415).

Writing Assignments Combining Patterns of Development

3. Stereotypes, Ericsson writes, "explain a situation with just enough truth to seem unquestionable." Write a *narrative* about a specific time that you or someone you know either falsely stereotyped a person or reacted stereotypically to a situation. Include only those details and *examples* that dramatize your narrative point. Before writing, you'll find it helpful to read one of the following essays, which show how pervasive and corrosive stereotypes can be: Audre Lorde's "The Fourth of July" (page 140), Brent Staples's "Black Men and Public Space" (page 207), or William Raspberry's "The Handicap of Definition" (page 468).
4. Many social commentators call attention, as Ericsson does in paragraph 15, to the growing tendency of individuals to absolve themselves from responsibility for something they've done by claiming that *they* are actually the victims. Gain some background on the issue of victimization by brainstorming with others and locating relevant material in the library and/or on the Internet. (You might find articles and books by Charles Sykes, David Brooks, William Raspberry, and Stanley Fish especially helpful.) Then write an essay *arguing* that we are or are not becoming a nation of victims and crybabies. Discredit the opposing viewpoint as much as possible by drawing upon your own and other people's experiences, as well as the outside sources you've read. And, in the course of your essay, speculate about the *causes* of the behavior you have identified.

Writing Assignment Using a Journal Entry as a Starting Point

5. At the beginning of her essay, Ericsson says that "there are many, many ways to tell a lie." Refer to your pre-reading journal entry, and select *one* memorable incident in which you lied, making sure the incident you select is substantial enough to support an entire essay. Then review Ericsson's ten categories of lying and determine which one best applies to the lie in question. Write an essay in which you *narrate* your episode of lying as a way of *illustrating* that particular category. Be sure, at the beginning of your essay, to briefly cite Ericsson's explanation of the category. As you narrate the incident involving your lie, point out the ways in which it illustrates that category. In addition, you should conclude with some commentary on whether lying was justified in the circumstances. You might benefit, too, from reading Langston Hughes's "Salvation" (page 158), a compelling account of telling a childhood, but not a *childish*, lie.

William Zinsser

Currently on the faculty of the Columbia University Graduate School of Journalism, and the New School in New York City, William Zinsser has written news journalism, drama criticism, magazine columns, a memoir, and several books on U.S. culture. Born in 1922 in New York, Zinsser worked for *The New York Herald Tribune* and *Life*. In 1970, Zinsser designed a course in nonfiction writing for Yale University. Using what he learned at Yale about the way college students approach the writing process, Zinsser wrote the popular guide *On Writing Well* (1976), now in its seventh edition. His other books include *The City Dwellers* (1962), *Pop Goes America* (1966), *The Lunacy Boom* (1970), *Writing with a Word Processor* (1982), *American Places: A Writer's Pilgrimage to 15 of This Country's Most Visited and Cherished Sites* (1992), *Speaking of Journalism* (1994), and *Writing About Your Life* (2004). He also edited seven books on writing, including *Inventing the Truth: The Art & Craft of Memoir* (1995). The following essay first appeared in the magazine *Country Journal* in 1979.

Pre-Reading Journal Entry

Many students feel pressured by college graduation requirements. Do you? What courses are you required to take that you wouldn't ordinarily choose? What courses would you like to take but don't have time for? Should colleges require students to take courses that aren't part of their majors? Why or why not? Use your journal to respond to these questions.

College Pressures

Dear Carlos: I desperately need a dean's excuse for my chem midterm which will begin in about 1 hour. All I can say is that I totally blew it this week. I've fallen incredibly, inconceivably behind.

Carlos: Help! I'm anxious to hear from you. I'll be in my room and won't leave it until I hear from you. Tomorrow is the last day for...

Carlos: I left town because I started bugging out again. I stayed up all night to finish a take-home make-up exam & am typing it to hand in on the 10th. It was due on the 5th. P.S. I'm going to the dentist. Pain is pretty bad.

Carlos: Probably by Friday I'll be able to get back to my studies. Right now I'm going to take a long walk. This whole thing has taken a lot out of me.

Carlos: I'm really up the proverbial creek. The problem is I really *bombed* the history final. Since I need that course for my major I...

Carlos: Here follows a tale of woe. I went home this weekend, had to help my Mom, & caught a fever so didn't have much time to study. My professor...

Carlos: Aargh! Trouble. Nothing original but everything's piling up at once. To be brief, my job interview...

Hey Carlos, good news! I've got mononucleosis.

Who are these wretched supplicants, scribbling notes so laden with anxiety, seeking such miracles of postponement and balm? They are men and women who belong to Branford College, one of the twelve residential colleges at Yale University, and the messages are just a few of the hundreds that they left for their dean, Carlos Hortas—often slipped under his door at 4 A.M.—last year. 1

But students like the ones who wrote those notes can also be found on campuses from coast to coast—especially in New England and at many other private colleges across the country that have high academic standards and highly motivated students. Nobody could doubt that the notes are real. In their urgency and their gallows humor they are authentic voices of a generation that is panicky to succeed. 2

My own connection with the message writers is that I am master of Branford College. I live in its Gothic quadrangle and know the students well. (We have 485 of them.) I am privy to their hopes and fears—and also to their stereo music and their piercing cries in the dead of the night ("Does anybody *ca-a-are*?"). If they went to Carlos to ask how to get through tomorrow, they come to me to ask how to get through the rest of their lives. 3

Mainly I try to remind them that the road ahead is a long one and that it will have more unexpected turns than they think. There will be plenty of time to change jobs, change careers, change whole attitudes and approaches. They don't want to hear such liberating news. They want a map—right now—that they can follow unswervingly to career security, financial security, Social Security and, presumably, a prepaid grave. 4

What I wish for all students is some release from the clammy grip of the future. I wish them a chance to savor each segment of their education as an experience in itself and not as a grim preparation for the next step. I wish them the right to experiment, to trip and fall, to learn that defeat is as instructive as victory and is not the end of the world. 5

My wish, of course, is naïve. One of the few rights that America does not proclaim is the right to fail. Achievement is the national god, venerated in 6 our media—the million-dollar athlete, the wealthy executive—and glorified in our praise of possessions. In the presence of such a potent state religion, the young are growing up old.

I see four kinds of pressure working on college students today: economic pressure, parental pressure, peer pressure, and self-induced pressure. It is easy to look around for villains—to blame the colleges for charging too much money, the professors for assigning too much work, the parents for pushing their children too far, the students for driving themselves too hard. But there are no villains; only victims. 7

"In the late 1960s," one dean told me, "the typical question that I got from students was 'Why is there so much suffering in the world?' or 'How can I make a contribution?' Today it's 'Do you think it would look better for getting into law school if I did a double major in history and political science, or just majored in one of them?'" Many other deans confirmed this pattern. One said: "They're trying to find an edge—the intangible something that will look better on paper if two students are about equal." 8

Note the emphasis on looking better. The transcript has become a sacred document, the passport to security. How one appears on paper is more important than how one appears in person. *A* is for Admirable and *B* is for Borderline, even though, in Yale's official system of grading, *A* means "excellent" and *B* means "very good." Today, looking very good is no longer good enough, especially for students who hope to go on to law school or medical school. They know that entrance into the better schools will be an entrance into the better law firms and better medical practices where they will make a lot of money. They also know that the odds are harsh. Yale Law School, for instance, matriculates 170 students from an applicant pool of 3,700; Harvard enrolls 550 from a pool of 7,000. 9

It's all very well for those of us who write letters of recommendation for our students to stress the qualities of humanity that will make them good lawyers or doctors. And it's nice to think that admission officers are really reading our letters and looking for the extra dimension of commitment or concern. Still, it would be hard for a student not to visualize these officers shuffling so many transcripts studded with *A*s that they regard a *B* as positively shameful. 10

The pressure is almost as heavy on students who just want to graduate and get a job. Long gone are the days of the "gentleman's *C*," when students journeyed through college with a certain relaxation, sampling a wide variety of courses—music, art, philosophy, classics, anthropology, poetry, religion—that would send them out as liberally educated men and women. If I were an employer I would rather employ graduates who have this range and curiosity than those who narrowly pursued safe subjects and high grades. I know countless students whose inquiring minds exhilarate me. I like to hear the play of their ideas. I don't know if they are getting *A*s or *C*s, 11 and I don't care. I also like them as people. The country needs them, and they will find satisfying jobs. I tell them to relax. They can't.

Nor can I blame them. They live in a brutal economy. Tuition, room, and board at most private colleges now comes to at least $7,000 [in 1979], not counting books and fees. This might seem to suggest that the colleges are getting rich. But they are equally battered by inflation. Tuition covers only 60 percent of what it costs to educate a student, and ordinarily the remainder comes from what colleges receive in endowments, grants, and gifts. Now the remainder keeps being swallowed by the cruel costs—higher every year—of just opening the doors. Heating oil is up. Insurance is up. Postage is up. Health-premium costs are up. Everything is up. Deficits are up. We are witnessing in America the creation of a brotherhood of paupers—colleges, parents, and students, joined by the common bond of debt. 12

Today it is not unusual for a student, even if he works part time at college and full time during the summer, to accrue $5,000 in loans after four years—loans that he must start to repay within one year after graduation. Exhorted at commencement to go forth into the world, he is already behind as he goes forth. How could he not feel under pressure throughout college to prepare for this day of reckoning? I have used "he," incidentally, only for brevity. Women at Yale are under no less pressure to justify their expensive education to themselves, their parents, and society. In fact, they are probably under more pressure. For although they leave college superbly equipped to bring fresh leadership to traditionally male jobs, society hasn't yet caught up with this fact. 13

Along with economic pressure goes parental pressure. Inevitably, the two are deeply intertwined. 14

I see many students taking pre-medical courses with joyless tenacity. They go off to their labs as if they were going to the dentist. It saddens me because I know them in other corners of their life as cheerful people. 15

"Do you want to go to medical school?" I ask them. 16

"I guess so," they say, without conviction, or "Not really." 17

"Then why are you going?" 18

"Well, my parents want me to be a doctor. They're paying all this money and..." 19

Poor students, poor parents. They are caught in one of the oldest webs of love and duty and guilt. The parents mean well; they are trying to steer their sons and daughters toward a secure future. But the sons and daughters want to major in history or classics or philosophy—subjects with no "practical" value. Where's the payoff on the humanities? It's not easy to persuade such loving parents that the humanities do indeed pay off. The intellectual faculties developed by studying subjects like history and classics—an ability to synthesize and relate, to weigh cause and effect, to see events in perspective—are just the faculties that make creative leaders in business or 20 almost any general field. Still, many fathers would rather put their money on courses that point toward a specific profession—courses that are pre-law, pre-medical, pre-business, or, as I sometimes heard it put, "pre-rich."

But the pressure on students is severe. They are truly torn. One part of them feels obligated to fulfill their parents' expectations; after all, their parents are older and presumably wiser. Another part tells them that the expectations that are right for their parents are not right for them. 21

I know a student who wants to be an artist. She is very obviously an artist and will be a good one—she has already had several modest local exhibits. Meanwhile she is growing as a well-rounded person and taking humanistic subjects that will enrich the inner resources out of which her art will grow. But her father is strongly opposed. He thinks that an artist is a "dumb" thing to be. The student vacillates and tries to please everybody. She keeps up with her art somewhat furtively and takes some of the "dumb" courses her father wants her to take—at least they are dumb courses for her. She is a free spirit on a campus of tense students—no small achievement in itself—and she deserves to follow her muse. 22

Peer pressure and self-induced pressure are also intertwined, and they begin almost at the beginning of freshman year. 23

"I had a freshman student I'll call Linda," one dean told me, "who came in and said she was under terrible pressure because her roommate, Barbara, was much brighter and studied all the time. I couldn't tell her that Barbara had come in two hours earlier to say the same thing about Linda." 24

The story is almost funny—except that it's not. It's symptomatic of all the pressures put together. When every student thinks every other student is working harder and doing better, the only solution is to study harder still. I see students going off to the library every night after dinner and coming back when it closes at midnight. I wish they would sometimes forget about their peers and go to a movie. I hear the clacking of typewriters in the hours before dawn. I see the tension in their eyes when exams are approaching and papers are due: *"Will I get everything done?"* 25

Probably they won't. They will get sick. They will get "blocked." They will sleep. They will oversleep. They will bug out. *Hey, Carlos, help!* 26

Part of the problem is that they do more than they are expected to do. A professor will assign five-page papers. Several students will start writing ten-page papers to impress him. Then more students will write ten-page papers, and a few will raise the ante to fifteen. Pity the poor student who is still just doing the assignment. 27

"Once you have twenty or thirty percent of the student population deliberately overexerting," one dean points out, "it's bad for everybody. When a teacher gets more and more effort from his class, the student who is doing normal work can be perceived as not doing well. The tactic works, psychologically." 28

Why can't the professor just cut back and not accept longer papers? He can, and he probably will. But by then the term will be half over and the damage done. Grade fever is highly contagious and not easily reversed. Besides, the professor's main concern is with his course. He knows his students only in relation to the course and doesn't know that they are also overexerting in their other courses. Nor is it really his business. He didn't sign up for dealing with the student as a whole person and with all the emotional baggage the student brought along from home. That's what deans, masters, chaplains, and psychiatrists are for. 29

To some extent this is nothing new: a certain number of professors have always been self-contained islands of scholarship and shyness, more comfortable with books than with people. But the new pauperism has widened the gap still further, for professors who actually like to spend time with students don't have as much time to spend. They are also overexerting. If they are young, they are busy trying to publish in order not to perish, hanging by their fingernails onto a shrinking profession. If they are old and tenured, they are buried under the duties of administering departments—as departmental chairmen or members of committees—that have been thinned out by the budgetary axe. 30

Ultimately it will be the students' own business to break the circles in which they are trapped. They are too young to be prisoners of their parents' dreams and their classmates' fears. They must be jolted into believing in themselves as unique men and women who have the power to shape their own future. 31

"Violence is being done to the undergraduate experience," says Carlos Hortas. "College should be open-ended: at the end it should open many, many roads. Instead, students are choosing their goal in advance, and their choices narrow as they go along. It's almost as if they think that the country has been codified in the type of jobs that exist—that they've got to fit into certain slots. Therefore, fit into the best-paying slot. 32

"They ought to take chances. Not taking chances will lead to a life of colorless mediocrity. They'll be comfortable. But something in the spirit will be missing." 33

I have painted too drab a portrait of today's students, making them seem a solemn lot. That is only half of their story; if they were so dreary I wouldn't so thoroughly enjoy their company. The other half is that they are easy to like. They are quick to laugh and to offer friendship. They are not introverts. They are unusually kind and are more considerate of one another than any student generation I have known. 34

Nor are they so obsessed with their studies that they avoid sports and extracurricular activities. On the contrary, they juggle their crowded hours to play on a variety of teams, perform with musical and dramatic groups, and write for campus publications. But this in turn is one more cause of anxiety. There are too many choices. Academically, they have 1,300 courses to select 35 from; outside class they have to decide how much spare time they can spare and how to spend it.

This means that they engage in fewer extracurricular pursuits than their predecessors did. If they want to row on the crew and play in the symphony they will eliminate one; in the '60s they would have done both. They also tend to choose activities that are self-limiting. Drama, for instance, is flourishing in all twelve of Yale's residential colleges as it never has before. Students hurl themselves into these productions—as actors, directors, carpenters, and technicians—with a dedication to create the best possible play, knowing that the day will come when the run will end and they can get back to their studies. 36

They also can't afford to be the willing slave of organizations like the *Yale Daily News*.... At the one-hundredth anniversary banquet of that paper—whose past chairmen include such once and future kings as Potter Stewart, Kingman Brewster, and William F. Buckley, Jr.—much was made of the fact that the editorial staff used to be small and totally committed and that "newsies" routinely worked fifty hours a week. In effect they belonged to a club; Newsies is how they defined themselves at Yale. Today's student will write one or two articles a week, when he can, and he defines himself as a student. I've never heard the word Newsie except at the banquet. 37

If I have described the modern undergraduate primarily as a driven creature who is largely ignoring the blithe spirit inside who keeps trying to come out and play, it's because that's where the crunch is, not only at Yale but throughout American education. It's why I think we should all be worried about the values that are nurturing a generation so fearful of risk and so goal-obsessed at such an early age. 38

I tell students that there is no one "right" way to get ahead—that each of them is a different person, starting from a different point and bound for a different destination. I tell them that change is a tonic and that all the slots are not codified nor the frontiers closed. One of my ways of telling them is to invite men and women who have achieved success outside the academic world to come and talk informally with my students during the year. They are heads of companies or ad agencies, editors of magazines, politicians, public officials, television magnates, labor leaders, business executives, Broadway producers, artists, writers, economists, photographers, scientists, historians—a mixed bag of achievers. 39

I ask them to say a few words about how they got started. The students assume that they started in their present profession and knew all along that it was what they wanted to do. Luckily for me, most of them got into their field by a circuitous route, to their surprise, after many detours. The students are startled. They can hardly conceive of a career that was not pre-planned. They can hardly imagine allowing the hand of God or chance to nudge them down some unforeseen trail. 40

Questions for Close Reading

1. What is the selection's thesis? Locate the sentence(s) in which Zinsser states his main idea. If he doesn't state the thesis explicitly, express it in your own words.
2. According to Zinsser, why are the pressures on college students so harmful?
3. Zinsser says that some of the pressures are "intertwined." What does he mean? Give examples from the essay.
4. What actions or attitudes on the part of students can help free them from the pressures that Zinsser describes?
5. Refer to your dictionary as needed to define the following words used in the selection: *privy* (paragraph 3), *venerated* (6), *exhorted* (13), *tenacity* (15), *vacillates* (22), *furtively* (22), and *circuitous* (40).

Questions About the Writer's Craft

1. **The pattern.** When analyzing a subject, writers usually try to identify divisions and classifications that are—within reason—mutually exclusive. But Zinsser acknowledges that the four pressures he discusses can be seen as two distinct pairs, with each pair consisting of two "deeply intertwined" pressures. How does this overlapping of categories help Zinsser make his point?
2. **Other patterns.** In addition to using classification in this essay, what other pattern of development does Zinsser use? How does this additional pattern help him make his point?
3. Why do you suppose Zinsser uses the notes to Carlos as his essay's introduction? What profile of college students does the reader get from these notes?
4. In paragraph 4, the author writes that students want a map "they can follow unswervingly to career security, financial security, Social Security and, presumably, a prepaid grave." What tone is Zinsser using here? Where else does he use this tone?

Writing Assignments Using Division-Classification as a Pattern of Development

1. Zinsser writes as if all students are the same—panicky, overwrought, and materialistic. Take a position counter to his, and write an essay explaining that campuses contain many students different from those Zinsser writes about. To support your point, categorize students into types, giving examples of what each type is like. Be sure that the categories you identify refute Zinsser's analysis of the typical student. The tone of your essay may be serious or playful.
2. Is economic security the only kind of satisfaction that college students should pursue? Write an essay classifying the various kinds of satisfactions that students could aim for. At the end of the paper, include brief recommendations about ways that students could best spend their time preparing for these different kinds of satisfactions. David Brooks's "Psst! Human Capital" (page 266), Jacques D'Amboise's "Showing What Is Possible" (page 402), Gerry Garibaldi's "How the Schools Shortchange Boys" (page 536), and Michael Kimmel's "A War Against Boys?" (page 543) might offer you further perspectives on education.

Writing Assignments Combining Patterns of Development

3. Using Zinsser's analysis of the pressures on college students, write an essay explaining how these pressures can be reduced or eliminated. Give ***practical suggestions*** showing how students can avoid or get around the pressures. Also, indicate what society, parents, and college staff can do to help ease students' anxieties. You might benefit from gathering ***examples*** of and information on this topic in the library and/or on the Internet before writing.

4. Zinsser's essay indicates that today's students are "slotting" themselves into preordained careers and not leaving themselves open to later opportunities. Write an essay ***arguing*** that this tendency to specialize early in college is either beneficial *or* disastrous for students. Consider such issues as individual freedom, career confusion, changing job markets, changes in society, and the like. In making your argument, consider the *effects* on students of earlier specialization.

Writing Assignment Using a Journal Entry as a Starting Point

5. Write an essay arguing in favor of *or* against the policy of requiring college students to take courses outside their major field. Take the ideas in your pre-reading journal entry and shape them into a convincing argument, remembering to cite the opposing point of view. To gain insight into the complexity of this issue, interview a variety of people having a broad range of viewpoints.

David Brooks

David Brooks is a syndicated columnist whose work appears in newspapers throughout the nation. Born in 1961, Brooks began his journalism career as a police reporter for the City News Bureau in Chicago and then spent nine years at *The Wall Street Journal* as a critic, foreign correspondent, and op-ed page editor. In 1995 he joined *The Weekly Standard* at its inception, and in 2003 he began to write a regular column for *The New York Times.* Brooks is interested in cultural as well as political issues. He often is on National Public Radio, including *The Diane Rehm Show,* as an analyst and is a commentator on the *PBS NewsHour* (Public Broadcasting Service). He has written three books, *Bobos in Paradise: The New Upper Class and How They Got There* (2000), *On Paradise Drive: How We Live Now (and Always Have) in the Future Tense* (2004), and *The Social Animal: The Hidden Sources of Love, Character, and Achievement* (2011). He is editor of the anthology *Backward and Upward: The New Conservative Writing.* This column was published in *The New York Times* on November 13, 2005.

Pre-Reading Journal Entry

When you are a student, it's natural to think of success and failure simply in terms of grades. However, academic accomplishment is not the only measure of success in one's life. What are your own strengths and successes in life, beyond what you may have achieved in school? Who or what has inspired you to undertake each of these pursuits? Take a few minutes to respond to these questions in your journal.

Psst! "Human Capital"

Help! I'm turning into the "plastics" guy from *The Graduate.*[1] I'm pulling people aside at parties and whispering that if they want to understand the future, it's just two words: "Human Capital." 1

If we want to keep up with the Chinese and the Indians, we've got to develop our Human Capital. If we want to remain a just, fluid society: Human Capital. If we want to head off underclass riots: Human Capital. 2

As people drift away from me at these parties by pretending to recognize long-lost friends across the room, I'm convinced that they don't really understand what human capital is. 3

Most people think of human capital the way economists and policy makers do—as the skills and knowledge people need to get jobs and thrive 4

[1]Refers to an oft-cited scene in the 1967 film, *The Graduate.* The main character, Benjamin Braddock, has just graduated college and feels adrift about the future. At a family party, the character of Mr. McGuire cryptically "tips off" Benjamin about the plastics industry. He says, "There's a great future in plastics. Think about it. Will you think about it?...Shh! Enough said." (editors' note).

in a modern economy. When President [George W.] Bush proposed his big education reform, he insisted on tests to measure skills and knowledge. When commissions issue reports, they call for longer school years, revamped curriculums and more funds so teachers can transmit skills and knowledge.

But skills and knowledge—the stuff you can measure with tests—is only 5
the most superficial component of human capital. U.S. education reforms have generally failed because they try to improve the skills of students without addressing the underlying components of human capital.

These underlying components are hard to measure and uncomfortable 6
to talk about, but they are the foundation of everything that follows.

There's cultural capital: the habits, assumptions, emotional dispositions 7
and linguistic capacities we unconsciously pick up from families, neighbors and ethnic groups—usually by age 3. In a classic study, James S. Coleman found that what happens in the family shapes a child's educational achievement more than what happens in school. In more recent research, James Heckman and Pedro Carneiro found that "most of the gaps in college attendance and delay are determined by early family factors."

There's social capital: the knowledge of how to behave in groups and 8
within institutions. This can mean, for example, knowing what to do if your community college loses your transcript. Or it can mean knowing the basic rules of politeness. The University of North Carolina now offers seminars to poorer students so they'll know how to behave in restaurants.

There's moral capital: the ability to be trustworthy. Students who drop 9
out of high school, but take the G.E.D. exam, tend to be smarter than high school dropouts. But their lifetime wages tend to be no higher than they are for those with no high school diplomas. That's because many people who pass the G.E.D. are less organized and less dependable than their less educated peers—as employers soon discover. Brains and skills don't matter if you don't show up on time.

There's cognitive capital. This can mean pure, inherited brainpower. But 10
important cognitive skills are not measured by IQ tests and are not fixed. Some people know how to evaluate themselves and their abilities, while others with higher IQ's are clueless. Some low-IQ people can sense what others are feeling, while brainier peers cannot. Such skills can be improved over a lifetime.

Then there's aspirational capital: the fire-in-the-belly ambition to 11
achieve. In his book *The Millionaire Mind,* Thomas J. Stanley reports that the average millionaire had a B-minus collegiate G.P.A.—not very good. But millionaires often had this experience: People told them they were too stupid to achieve something, so they set out to prove the naysayers wrong.

Over the past quarter-century, researchers have done a lot of work trying 12
to understand the different parts of human capital. Their work has been almost completely ignored by policy makers, who continue to treat human capital as just skills and knowledge. The result? A series of expensive policy failures.

We now spend more per capita on education than just about any other country on earth, and the results are mediocre. No Child Left Behind treats students as skill-acquiring cogs in an economic wheel, and the results have been disappointing. We pour money into Title 1 and Head Start, but the long-term gains are insignificant. 13

These programs are not designed for the way people really are. The only things that work are local, human-to-human immersions that transform the students down to their very beings. Extraordinary schools, which create intense cultures of achievement, work. Extraordinary teachers, who inspire students to transform their lives, work. The programs that work touch all the components of human capital. 14

There's a great future in Human Capital, buddy. Enough said. 15

Questions for Close Reading

1. What is the selection's thesis? Locate the sentence(s) in which Brooks states his main idea. If he doesn't state his thesis explicitly, express it in your own words.
2. According to Brooks, why do policies that focus on teaching children skills and knowledge ultimately fail to develop human capital? What policies does he use as examples of such failure?
3. In Brooks's view, what role does the family play in the development of human capital?
4. What type of human capital do many millionaires possess, and how did they acquire it?
5. Refer to your dictionary as needed to define the following words used in the selection: *capital* (paragraph 1), *revamped* (4), *cognitive* (10), *aspirational* (11), *naysayers* (11), *per capita* (13), and *immersions* (14).

Questions About the Writer's Craft

1. Brooks opens this essay by comparing himself to a character in the 1967 movie *The Graduate*. What are the benefits and risks of using such a reference to frame the contents of an essay? In your opinion, is this a successful opening? Why or why not?
2. **The pattern.** How does Brooks organize his explanation of what human capital really consists of? What cues guide the reader in following Brooks's discussion?
3. **Other patterns.** In paragraphs 7 through 11, Brooks develops his ideas about the components of human capital. What patterns does he use in each of these paragraphs?
4. This essay was published as a newspaper op-ed column, a type of writing that is relatively short—about 750 words. How does the limited length of the piece affect the development of Brooks's ideas and evidence? If the piece were longer, how could Brooks strengthen its argument?

Writing Assignments Using Division-Classification as a Pattern of Development

1. Choose one of the elements of human capital that Brooks describes, and write an essay in which you analyze it further into its component parts. For example, if you choose cognitive capital, you can write about specific cognitive skills such as memorizing, learning, problem solving, and creativity.
2. According to economists, capital is any human-made resource used to produce goods and services. For example, capital includes buildings, factories, machinery, equipment, parts, tools, roads, and railroads. Do some research on the concept of capital as used by economists, and write an essay explaining how economists categorize various types of capital, including the human capital Brooks discusses in his essay.

Writing Assignments Combining Patterns of Development

3. Brooks indicates that the results of the government programs No Child Left Behind, Title I, and Head Start fail to improve human capital. Select one of these programs, and do some research on it at the library or on the Internet. Write an essay that *explains* how aspects of the program are designed to solve specific problems. *Compare* and *contrast* the goals of the program with its actual *effects*.
4. Brooks's concept of moral capital is closely tied to the moral values that society holds important and that children learn from their families and others with whom they interact. Write an essay in which you *narrate* the story of a moral issue you have faced, *comparing* and *contrasting* the choices you had. Explain the *process* you went through to resolve the problem.

Writing Assignment Using a Journal Entry as a Starting Point

5. Review your pre-reading journal entry about your successes and strengths beyond what you may have achieved in school. Select the two or three most significant ones, and write an essay in which you divide and classify these achievements. Are these achievements athletic, artistic, or service- or family-oriented—or do they belong to some other category? As you write about each achievement, consider who or what has *caused* or inspired you to strive for that accomplishment. To see how three writers address the issue of how children's character can be influenced, read Ellen Goodman's "Family Counterculture" (page 7), Gordon Parks's "Flavio's Home" (page 95), and Judith Ortiz Cofer's "Remembrance of a Puerto Rican Childhood" (page 117).

Amy Tan

The American writer Amy Tan was born in 1952, a few years after her parents had emigrated from China. Tan grew up in California and Switzerland, and she earned a master's degree in linguistics from San José State University. Her first novel, *The Joy Luck Club* (1987), won a National Book Award. Her other novels include *The Kitchen God's Wife* (1991), *The Bonesetter's Daughter* (2000), and *Saving Fish from Drowning* (2005). The following essay, first published in *The Threepenny Review*, is from her memoir *The Opposite of Fate: A Book of Musings* (2003).

Pre-Reading Journal Entry

Most people have different ways of speaking in different situations. Think of how you talk to your parents and other relatives; to children; to friends; to colleagues at work; to professors, doctors, and other professionals; and to your spouse or partner. Write down in your journal some examples of how you speak in various situations.

Mother Tongue

I am not a scholar of English or literature. I cannot give you much more than personal opinions of the English language and its variations in this country or others. 1

I am a writer. And by that definition, I am someone who has always loved language. I am fascinated by language in daily life. I spend a great deal of my time thinking about the power of language—the way it can evoke an emotion, a visual image, a complex idea, or a simple truth. Language is the tool of my trade. And I use them all—all the Englishes I grew up with. 2

Recently, I was made keenly aware of the different Englishes I do use. I was giving a talk to a large group of people, the same talk I had already given to half a dozen other groups. The nature of the talk was about my writing, my life, and my book, *The Joy Luck Club.* The talk was going along well enough, until I remembered one major difference that made the whole talk sound wrong. My mother was in the room. And it was perhaps the first time she had heard me give a lengthy speech, using the kind of English I have never used with her. I was saying things like, "The intersection of memory upon imagination" and "There is an aspect of my fiction that relates to thus-and-thus"—a speech filled with carefully wrought grammatical phrases, burdened, it suddenly seemed to me, with nominalized forms, past perfect tenses, conditional phrases, all the forms of standard English that I had learned in school and through books, the forms of English I did not use at home with my mother. 3

Just last week, I was walking down the street with my mother, and I again found myself conscious of the English I was using, and the English 4

I do use with her. We were talking about the price of new and used furniture and I heard myself saying this: "Not waste money that way." My husband was with us as well, and he didn't notice any switch in my English. And then I realized why. It's because over the twenty years we've been together I've often used the same kind of English with him, and sometimes he even uses it with me. It has become our language of intimacy, a different sort of English that relates to family talk, the language I grew up with.

So you'll have some idea of what this family talk I heard sounds like, I'll quote what my mother said during a recent conversation which I videotaped and then transcribed. During this conversation, my mother was talking about a political gangster in Shanghai who had the same last name as her family's, Du, and how the gangster in his early years wanted to be adopted by her family, which was rich by comparison. Later, the gangster became more powerful, far richer than my mother's family, and one day showed up at my mother's wedding to pay his respects. Here's what she said in part: 5

> "Du Yusong having business like fruit stand. Like off the street kind. He is Du like Du Zong—but not Tsung-ming Island people. The local people call putong, the river east side, he belong to that side local people. The man want to ask Du Zong father take him in like become own family. Du Zong father wasn't look down on him, but didn't take seriously, until the man big like become a mafia. Now important person, very hard to inviting him. Chinese way, came only to show respect, don't stay for dinner. Respect for making big celebration, he shows up. Mean gives lots of respect. Chinese custom. Chinese social life that way. If too important won't have to stay too long. He come to my wedding. I didn't see, I heard it. I gone to boy's side, they have YMCA dinner. Chinese age I was nineteen." 6

You should know that my mother's expressive command of English belies how much she actually understands. She reads the Forbes report, listens to *Wall Street Week*, converses daily with her stockbroker, reads all of Shirley MacLaine's books with ease—all kinds of things I can't begin to understand. Yet some of my friends tell me they understand 50 percent of what my mother says. Some say they understand 80 to 90 percent. Some say they understand none of it, as if she were speaking pure Chinese. But to me, my mother's English is perfectly clear, perfectly natural It's my mother tongue. Her language, as I hear it, vivid, direct, full of observation and imagery. That was the language that helped shape the way I saw things expressed things, made sense of the world. 7

Lately, I've been giving more thought to the kind of English my mother speaks. Like others, I have described it to people as "broken" or "fractured" English. But I wince when I say that. It has always bothered me that I can 8 think of no way to describe it other than "broken," as if it were damaged and needed to be fixed, as if it lacked a certain wholeness and soundness. I've heard other terms used, "limited English," for example. But they seem just as bad, as if everything is limited, including people's perceptions of the limited English speaker.

I know this for a fact, because when I was growing up, my mother's "limited" English limited *my* perception of her. I was ashamed of her English. I believed that her English reflected the quality of what she had to say. That is, because she expressed them imperfectly her thoughts were imperfect. And I had plenty of empirical evidence to support me: the fact that people in department stores, at banks, and at restaurants did not take her seriously, did not give her good service, pretended not to understand her, or even acted as if they did not hear her. 9

My mother has long realized the limitations of her English as well. When I was fifteen, she used to have me call people on the phone to pretend I was she. In this guise, I was forced to ask for information or even to complain and yell at people who had been rude to her. One time it was a call to her stockbroker in New York. She had cashed out her small portfolio and it just so happened we were going to go to New York the next week, our very first trip outside California. I had to get on the phone and say in an adolescent voice that was not very convincing, "This is Mrs. Tan." 10

And my mother was standing in back whispering loudly, "Why he don't send me check, already two weeks late. So mad he lie to me, losing me money." 11

And then I said in perfect English, "Yes, I'm getting rather concerned. You had agreed to send the check two weeks ago, but it hasn't arrived." 12

Then she began to talk more loudly. "What he want, I come to New York tell him front of his boss, you cheating me?" And I was trying to calm her down, make her be quiet, while telling the stockbroker, "I can't tolerate any more excuses. If I don't receive the check immediately, I am going to have to speak to your manager when I'm in New York next week." And sure enough, the following week there we were in front of this astonished stockbroker, and I was sitting there red-faced and quiet, and my mother, the real Mrs. Tan, was shouting at his boss in her impeccable broken English. 13

We used a similar routine just five days ago, for a situation that was far less humorous. My mother had gone to the hospital for an appointment, to find out about a benign brain tumor a CAT scan had revealed a month ago. She said she had spoken very good English, her best English, no mistakes. Still, she said, the hospital did not apologize when they said they had lost the CAT scan and she had come for nothing. She said they did not seem to have any sympathy when she told them she was anxious to know the exact diagnosis, since her husband and son had both died of brain tumors. She said they would not give her any more information until the next time and she would have to make another appointment for that. So she said she 14 would not leave until the doctor called her daughter. She wouldn't budge. And when the doctor finally called her daughter, me, who spoke in perfect English—lo and behold—we had assurances the CAT scan would be found, promises that a conference call on Monday would be held, and apologies for any suffering my mother had gone through for a most regrettable mistake.

15 I think my mother's English almost had an effect on limiting my possibilities in life as well. Sociologists and linguists probably will tell you that a person's developing language skills are more influenced by peers. But I do think that the language spoken in the family, especially in immigrant families which are more insular, plays a large role in shaping the language of the child. And I believe that it affected my results on achievement tests, IQ tests, and the SAT. While my English skills were never judged as poor, compared to math, English could not be considered my strong suit. In grade school I did moderately well, getting perhaps B's, sometimes B-pluses, in English and scoring perhaps in the sixtieth or seventieth percentile on achievement tests. But those scores were not good enough to override the opinion that my true abilities lay in math and science, because in those areas I achieved A's and scored in the ninetieth percentile or higher.

16 This was understandable. Math is precise; there is only one correct answer. Whereas, for me at least, the answers on English tests were always a judgment call, a matter of opinion and personal experience. Those tests were constructed around items like fill-in-the-blank sentence completion, such as, "Even though Tom was ______, Mary thought he was ______." And the correct answer always seemed to be the most bland combinations of thoughts, for example, "Even though Tom was shy, Mary thought he was charming," with the grammatical structure "even though" limiting the correct answer to some sort of semantic opposites, so you wouldn't get answers like, "Even though Tom was foolish, Mary thought he was ridiculous." Well, according to my mother, there were very few limitations as to what Tom could have been and what Mary might have thought of him. So I never did well on tests like that.

17 The same was true with word analogies, pairs of words in which you were supposed to find some sort of logical, semantic relationship—for example, "*Sunset* is to *nightfall* as ______ is to ______." And here you would be presented with a list of four possible pairs, one of which showed the same kind of relationship: *red* is to *stoplight*, *bus* is to *arrival*, *chills* is to *fever*, *yawn* is to *boring*. Well, I could never think that way. I knew what the tests were asking, but I could not block out of my mind the images already created by the first pair, "*sunset* is to *nightfull*"—and I would see a burst of colors against a darkening sky, the moon rising, the lowering of a curtain of stars. And all the other pairs of words—red, bus, stoplight, boring—just threw up a mess of confusing images, making it impossible for me to sort out something as logical as saying: "A sunset precedes nightfall" is the same as "a chill precedes a fever." The

only way I would have gotten that answer right would have been to imagine an associative situation, for example, my being disobedient and staying out past sunset, catching a chill at night, which turns into feverish pneumonia as punishment, which indeed did happen to me.

I have been thinking about all this lately, about my mother's English, about achievement tests. Because lately I've been asked, as a writer, why there are not more Asian Americans represented in American literature. Why are there few Asian Americans enrolled in creative writing programs? Why do so many Chinese students go into engineering? Well, these are broad sociological questions I can't begin to answer. But I have noticed in surveys—in fact, just last week—that Asian students, as a whole, always do significantly better on math achievement tests than in English. And this makes me think that there are other Asian-American students whose English spoken in the home might also be described as "broken" or "limited." And perhaps they also have teachers who are steering them away from writing and into math and science, which is what happened to me. 18

Fortunately, I happen to be rebellious in nature and enjoy the challenge of disproving assumptions made about me. I became an English major my first year in college, after being enrolled as pre-med. I started writing nonfiction as a freelancer the week after I was told by my former boss that writing was my worst skill and I should hone my talents toward account management. 19

But it wasn't until 1985 that I finally began to write fiction. And at first I wrote using what I thought would be wittily crafted sentences, sentences that would finally prove I had mastery over the English language. Here's an example from the first draft of a story that later made its way into *The Joy Luck Club,* but without this line: "That was my mental quandary in the nascent state." A terrible line, which I can barely pronounce. 20

Fortunately, for reasons I won't get into today, I later decided I should envision a reader for the stories I would write. And the reader I decided upon was my mother, because these were stories about mothers. So with this reader in mind—and in fact she did read my early drafts—I began to write stories using all the Englishes I grew up with: the English I spoke to my mother, which for lack of a better term might be described as "simple"; the English she used with me, which for lack of a better term might be described as "broken"; my translation of her Chinese, which could certainly be described as "watered down"; and what I imagined to be her translation of her Chinese if she could speak in perfect English, her internal language, and for that I sought to preserve the essence, but neither an English nor a Chinese structure. I wanted to capture what language ability tests can never reveal: her intent, her passion, her imagery, the rhythms of her speech and the nature of her thoughts. 21

Apart from what any critic had to say about my writing, I knew I had succeeded where it counted when my mother finished reading my book and gave me her verdict: "So easy to read." 22

Questions for Close Reading

1. What is the selection's thesis? Locate the sentence(s) in which Tan states her main idea. If she doesn't state her thesis explicitly, express it in your own words.
2. Describe the particular event that prompted the author to think about her use of language. What does she mean by "different Englishes"? What are these "different Englishes"?
3. What questions has Tan been asked "as a writer"? What survey information does she use in formulating her response? Is the survey information valid? How does Tan use it to support personal information she gives in the essay?
4. How have Tan's feelings about her mother's command of English changed over the years?
5. Refer to your dictionary as needed to define the following words used in the selection: *intersection* (paragraph 3), *nominalized* (3), *transcribed* (5), *belies* (7), *fractured* (8), *empirical* (9), *guise* (10), *portfolio* (10), *impeccable* (13), *benign* (14), *CAT scan* (14), *diagnosis* (14), *sociologists* (15), *linguists* (15), *insular* (15), *percentile* (15), *semantic* (16), *analogies* (17), *associative* (17), *hone* (19), *quandary* (20), and *nascent* (20).

Questions About the Writer's Craft

1. **The pattern.** What principle of classification does the author use to identify the "different Englishes" she describes? How is that principle reflected in the different types of English Tan mentions?
2. In paragraph 6, the author gives an extended example of her mother's speech. Why does she do this? What is the effect of having this quotation in the essay? How easy do you think it is to follow Tan's mother's speech?
3. **Other patterns.** The author uses personal anecdotes about her relationship with her mother to illustrate some important points. Identify at least two anecdotes. What points do they support? How effective are they? Why?
4. In paragraph 20, the author quotes a line that she wrote but ultimately did not include in the final version of her novel. Why does she call it a "terrible line," and why do you think she included it? How does the English in that line compare with the English in the excerpt of her mother's speech?

Writing Assignments Using Classification-Division as a Pattern of Development

1. Like the author, you probably do different kinds of writing. You might write e-mails at work, academic papers in class, text messages to friends, and journal or diary entries. You might also compose song lyrics, poems, or other kinds of creative writing. Write an essay in which you classify the types of writing you do. Choose an appropriate principle of classification, and then show how the types of writing are similar and dissimilar. Use examples, including excerpts from your writing, to illustrate the points you make. For insight into how others write about writing, read one or more of the following: Ann McClintock's "Propaganda Techniques in Today's Advertising" (page 239), David Shipley's "Talk About Editing" (page 303), Paul 

Roberts's "How to Say Nothing in 500 Words" (page 314), Caroline Rego's "The Fine Art of Complaining" (page 327), Eric Weiner's "Euromail and Amerimail" (page 350), or Stanley Fish's "Free-Speech Follies" (page 509).

2. Tan classifies types of English, but there are other types of expression that can be classified. For example, you can classify manners, modes of dress, facial expressions, and kinds of greetings. Choose one of these topics or another such subject, and write an essay in which you classify types in this group. Decide whether you wish to inform or entertain, and develop a principle of classification that suits your purpose. Remember to include relevant examples.

Writing Assignments Combining Patterns of Development

3. You may know someone who, like the author's mother, has struggled to learn English, or you may yourself have tried to learn a language different from your "mother tongue." Brainstorm a list of steps a person could take to improve his or her language skills. Then write a *process* essay explaining at least four such steps. Give examples to *illustrate* each step.
4. The author mentions surveys showing how Asian Americans perform on standardized tests, such as the SAT. Proponents of standardized tests believe the tests hold all students to the same objective standard. Opponents believe some tests are unintentionally biased against one or more groups of students. Do some research on one standardized test. Develop a position about the test, and *argue* your position in an essay. Include the results of *relevant studies* and the opinions of *experts* as evidence for your views.

Writing Assignment Using a Journal Entry as a Starting Point

5. Reread the notes in your journal. Choose at least four kinds of speech—for example, slang, profanity, baby talk, and technical jargon—that you use. Write an essay in which you *describe* situations in which you might use each *type* of speech. Use personal examples and ancedotes to illustrate when you used, or heard, inappropriate speech. The tone of your essay can be serious or humorous.

Additional Writing Topics

DIVISION-CLASSIFICATION

General Assignments

Choose one of the following subjects and write an essay developed wholly or in part through division-classification. Start by determining the purpose of the essay. Do you want to inform, compare and contrast, or persuade? Apply a single, significant principle of division or classification to your subject. Don't switch the principle midway through your analysis. Also, be sure that the types or categories you create are as complete and mutually exclusive as possible.

Division

1. A shopping mall
2. A video and/or sound system
3. A fruit, such as a pineapple, an orange, or a banana
4. A tax dollar
5. A particular kind of team
6. A word-processing system
7. A human hand
8. A meal
9. A meeting
10. A favorite poem, story, or play
11. A favorite restaurant
12. A school library
13. A basement
14. A playground, gym, or other recreational area
15. A church service
16. A wedding or funeral
17. An eventful week in your life
18. A college campus
19. A television show or movie
20. A homecoming or other special weekend

Classification

1. People in a waiting room
2. Holidays
3. Closets
4. Roommates
5. Salad bars
6. Divorces
7. Beds
8. Students in a class
9. Shoes

10. Summer movies
11. Teachers
12. Neighbors
13. College courses
14. Bosses
15. Computer/Internet users
16. Mothers or fathers
17. Commercials
18. Vacations
19. Trash
20. Relatives

Assignments with a Specific Purpose, Audience, and Point of View

On Campus

1. You're a dorm counselor. During orientation week, you'll be talking to students on your floor about the different kinds of problems they may have with roommates. Write your talk, describing each kind of problem and explaining how to cope with it.
2. As your college newspaper's TV critic, you plan to write a review of the fall shows, most of which—in your opinion—lack originality. To show how stereotypical the programs are, select one type (for example, situation-comedies or crime dramas). Then use a specific division-classification principle to illustrate that the same stale formulas are trotted out from show to show.
3. Asked to write an editorial for the campus paper, you decide to do a half-serious piece on taking "mental health" days off from classes. Structure your essay around three kinds of occasions when "playing hooky" is essential for maintaining sanity.

At Home or in the Community

4. Your favorite magazine runs an editorial asking readers to send in what they think are the main challenges facing their particular gender group. Write a letter to the editor in which you identify at least three categories of problems that your sex faces. Be sure to provide lively, specific examples to illustrate each category. In your letter, you may adopt a serious or lighthearted tone, depending on your overall subject matter.

On the Job

5. As a driving instructor, you decide to prepare a lecture on the types of drivers that your students are likely to encounter on the road. In your lecture, categorize drivers according to a specific principle and show the behaviors of each type.
6. A seasoned camp counselor, you've been asked to prepare, for new counselors, an informational sheet on children's emotional needs. Categorizing those needs into types, explain what counselors can do to nurture youngsters emotionally.

PROCESS ANALYSIS

WHAT IS PROCESS ANALYSIS?

We spend a good deal of our lives learning—everything from speaking our first word to balancing our first bank statement. Indeed, the milestones in our lives are often linked to the processes we have mastered: how to cross the street alone; how to drive a car; how to make a speech without being paralyzed by fear.

Process analysis, a technique that explains the steps or sequence involved in doing something, satisfies our need to learn as well as our curiosity about how the world works. All the self-help books continually flooding the market are examples of process analysis. The instructions on the federal tax form and the recipes in a cookbook are also process analyses. Several television shows also capitalize on our desire to learn how things happen: *Nature* shows how animals and ecosystems survive, and *CSI: Crime Scene Investigation* details how investigators gather evidence and use crime lab techniques to catch criminals. Process analysis can be more than merely interesting or entertaining, though; it can be of critical importance. Consider a waiter hurriedly skimming the "Choking Aid" instructions posted on a restaurant wall or an air-traffic controller following emergency procedures in an effort to prevent a midair collision. In these last examples, the consequences could be fatal if the process analyses were slipshod, inaccurate, or confusing.

Undoubtedly, all of us have experienced less dramatic effects of poorly written process analyses. Perhaps you've tried to assemble a bicycle and spent hours sorting through a stack of parts, only to end up with one or two extra pieces never mentioned in the instructions. No wonder many people stay clear of anything that actually admits "assembly required."

HOW PROCESS ANALYSIS FITS YOUR PURPOSE AND AUDIENCE

You will use process analysis in two types of writing situations: (1) when you want to give step-by-step instructions to readers showing how they can do something, or (2) when you want readers to understand how something happens even though they won't actually follow the steps outlined. The first kind of process analysis is *directional;* the second is *informational.*

Process analysis, both directional and informational, is often appropriate in *problem-solving situations.* In such cases, you say, "Here's the problem and here's what should be done to solve the problem." Indeed, college assignments frequently take the form of problem-solving process analyses. Consider these examples:

> Community officials have been accused of mismanaging recent unrest over the public housing ordinance. Describe the steps the officials took, indicating why you think their strategy was unwise. Then explain how you think the situation should have been handled.
>
> Over the years, there have been many reports citing the abuse of small children in day-care centers. What can parents do to guard against the mistreatment of their children?
>
> Because many colleges have changed the eligibility requirements for financial aid, fewer students can depend on loans or scholarships. How can students cope with the rising costs of higher education?

Note that the first assignment asks students to explain what's wrong with the current approach before they present their own step-by-step solution. Problem-solving process analyses are often organized in this way. You may also have noted that none of the assignments explicitly requires an essay response using process analysis. However, the wording of the assignments—"*Describe* the *steps,*" "*What* can parents *do,*" "*How* can students *cope,*"—suggests that process analysis would be an appropriate strategy for developing the responses.

Assignments don't always signal the use of process analysis so clearly. But during the prewriting stage, you'll often realize that you can best achieve your purpose by developing the essay using process analysis. Sometimes process analysis will be the primary strategy for organizing an essay; other times it will help make a point in an essay organized according to another pattern of development. Let's look at process analysis as a supporting strategy.

Assume that you're writing a *causal analysis* examining the impact of television commercials on people's buying behavior. To help readers see that commercials create a need where none existed before, you might describe the various stages of an advertising campaign to pitch a new, completely frivolous product. In an essay *defining* a good boss, you could convey the point that effective managers must be skilled at settling disputes by explaining the steps your boss took to resolve a heated disagreement between two employees. If you write an *argumentation-persuasion* paper urging the funding of programs to ease the plight of the homeless, to dramatize the tragedy of these people's lives, you could explain how the typical street person goes about the desperate jobs of finding a place to sleep and getting food to eat.

At this point, you have a good sense of the way writers use process analysis to achieve their purpose and to connect with their readers. Now take a moment to look closely at the photograph of the brand-new mall at the beginning of this chapter. Imagine you're writing an article, accompanied by the photo, for a local newspaper. Your purpose is to suggest to local store owners, who are losing business to the new mall, ways they might attract more customers to the area's downtown shopping district. Jot down some ideas you might include in a *process analysis* explaining the steps the business owners should take.

SUGGESTIONS FOR USING PROCESS ANALYSIS IN AN ESSAY

The suggestions here and in Figure 7.1 (page 282) will be helpful whether you use process analysis as a dominant or a supportive pattern of development.

1. Identify the desired outcome of the process analysis. Many papers developed primarily through process analysis have a clear-cut purpose—simply to *inform* readers as objectively as possible about a process: "Here's a way of making french fries at home that will surpass the best served in your favorite fast-food restaurant." But a process analysis essay may also have a *persuasive* edge, with the writer advocating a point of view about the process, perhaps even urging a course of action: "If you don't want your arguments to deteriorate into ugly battles, you should follow a series of foolproof steps for having disagreements that leave friendships intact." Before starting to write, you need to decide if the essay is to be purely factual or if it will include this kind of persuasive dimension.

FIGURE 7.1
Development Diagram: Writing a Process Analysis Essay

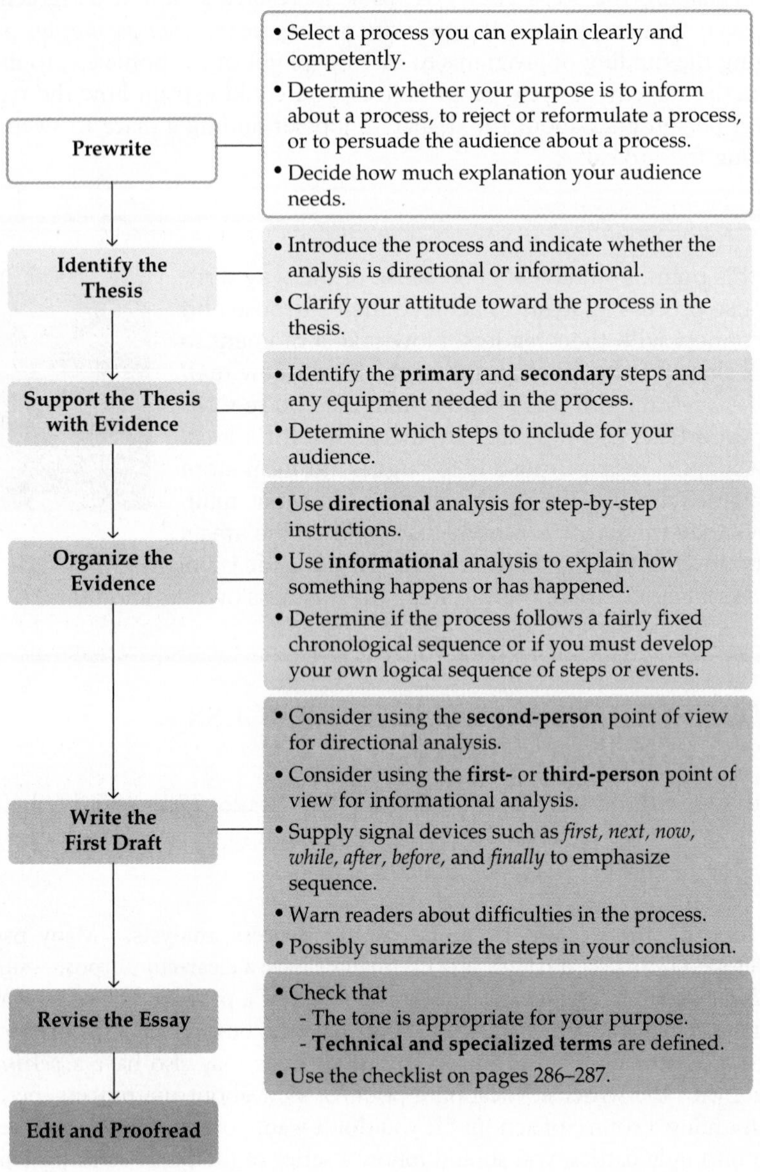

Prewrite
• Select a process you can explain clearly and competently.
• Determine whether your purpose is to inform about a process, to reject or reformulate a process, or to persuade the audience about a process.
• Decide how much explanation your audience needs.
Identify the Thesis
• Introduce the process and indicate whether the analysis is directional or informational.
• Clarify your attitude toward the process in the thesis.
Support the Thesis with Evidence
• Identify the primary and secondary steps and any equipment needed in the process.
• Determine which steps to include for your audience.
Organize the Evidence
• Use directional analysis for step-by-step instructions.
• Use informational analysis to explain how something happens or has happened.
• Determine if the process follows a fairly fixed chronological sequence or if you must develop your own logical sequence of steps or events.
Write the First Draft
• Consider using the second-person point of view for directional analysis.
• Consider using the first- or third-person point of view for informational analysis.
• Supply signal devices such as first, next, now, while, after, before, and finally to emphasize sequence.
• Warn readers about difficulties in the process.
• Possibly summarize the steps in your conclusion.
Revise the Essay
• Check that
- The tone is appropriate for your purpose.
- Technical and specialized terms are defined.
• Use the checklist on pages 286–287.
Edit and Proofread

2. Formulate a thesis that clarifies your attitude toward the process. Like the thesis in any other paper, the thesis in a process analysis should do more than announce your subject. ("Here's how the college's work-study program operates.") It should also state or imply your attitude toward the process: "Enrolling in the college's work-study program has become unnecessarily complicated. The procedure could be simplified if the college adopted the helpful guidelines prepared by the Student Senate."

3. Keep your audience in mind. Suppose you've been asked to write an article informing students of the best way to use the university computer center. The article will be published in a newsletter for computer science majors. You would seriously misjudge your audience—and probably put them to sleep—if you explained in detail how to transfer material from disk to disk or how to delete information from a file. However, an article on the same topic prepared for a general audience—your composition class, for instance—might require such detailed instructions.

To determine how much explanation is needed, put yourself in your readers' shoes. Don't assume readers will know something just because you do. Ask questions such as these about your audience: "Will my readers need some background about the process before I describe it in depth?" "Are there technical terms I should define?" "If my essay is directional, should I specify near the beginning the ingredients, materials, and equipment needed to perform the process?" (For more help in analyzing your audience, see the checklist on page 19.)

4. Use prewriting to identify the steps in the process. To explain a sequence to your readers, you need to think through the process thoroughly, identifying its major parts and subparts, locating possible missteps or trouble spots. With your purpose, thesis, and audience in mind, use the appropriate prewriting techniques (brainstorming and mapping should be especially helpful) to break down the process into its component parts. In prewriting, it's a good idea to start by generating more material than you expect to use. Then the raw material can be shaped and pruned to fit your purpose and the needs of your audience.

5. Identify the directional and informational aspects of the process analysis. Directional and informational process analyses are not always distinct. In fact, they may be complementary. Your prewriting may reveal that you'll need to provide background information about a process before outlining its steps. For example, in a paper describing a step-by-step approach for losing weight, you might first need to explain how the body burns calories.

The kind of process analysis chosen has implications for the way you will relate to your reader. When the process analysis is *directional,* the reader is addressed in the *second person:* "You should first rinse the residue from the radiator by...," or "Wrap the injured person in a blanket and then...." (In the second example, the pronoun *you* is implied.)

If the process analysis has an *informational* purpose, you won't address the reader directly but will choose from a number of other options. For example, you might use the *first-person* point of view. In a humorous essay explaining how not to prepare for finals, you could cite your own disastrous study habits: "Filled with good intentions, I sit on my bed, pick up a pencil, open my notebook, and promptly fall asleep." The *third-person singular or plural* can also be used in informational process essays: "The door-to-door salesperson walks up the front walk, heart pounding, more than a bit nervous, but also challenged by the prospect of striking a deal." Whether you use the first, second, or third person, avoid shifting point of view midstream.

6. Explain the process, one step at a time. At times your purpose will be to explain a process with a *fairly fixed chronological sequence:* how to make pizza, how to pot a plant, how to change a tire. In such cases, you should include all necessary steps, in the correct chronological order. However, if a strict chronological ordering of steps means that a particularly important part of the sequence gets buried in the middle, the sequence probably should be juggled so that the crucial step receives the attention it deserves.

Other times your goal will be to describe a process having *no commonly accepted sequence.* For example, in an essay explaining how to discipline a child or how to pull yourself out of a blue mood, you will have to come up with your own definition of the key steps and then arrange those steps in some logical order. You may also use process analyses to *reject* or *reformulate* a traditional sequence. In this case, you would propose a more logical series of steps: "Our system for electing congressional representatives is inefficient and undemocratic; it should be reformed in the following ways."

Whether the essay describes a generally agreed-on process or one that is not commonly accepted, you must provide all the details needed to explain the process. Your readers should be able to understand, even visualize, the process. There should be no fuzzy patches or confusing cuts from one step to another.

It's not unusual, especially in less defined sequences, for some steps in a process to occur simultaneously and overlap. When this happens, you should present the steps in the most logical order, being sure to tell your readers that several steps are not perfectly distinct and may merge.

7. Provide readers with the help they need to follow the sequence. As you move through the steps of a process analysis, don't forget to *warn readers* *about difficulties* they might encounter. For example, when writing a paper on the artistry involved in butterflying a shrimp, you might say something like this:

> Next, make a shallow cut with your sharpened knife along the convex curve of the shrimp's intestinal tract. The tract, usually a thin black line along the outside curve of the shrimp, is faintly visible beneath the translucent flesh. But some shrimp have a thick orange, blue, or gray line instead of a thin black one. In all cases, be careful not to slice too deeply, or you will end up with two shrimp halves instead of one butterflied shrimp.

Transitional words and phrases are also critical in helping readers understand the order of the steps being described. Time signals such as *first, next, now, while, after, before,* and *finally* provide readers with a clear sense of the sequence. Entire sentences can also be used to link parts of the process, reminding your audience of what has already been discussed and indicating what will now be explained: "Once the panel of experts finishes its evaluation of the exam questions, randomly selected items are field-tested in schools throughout the country."

8. Maintain an appropriate tone. When writing a process analysis essay, be sure your tone is consistent with your purpose, your attitude toward your subject, and the effect you want to have on the reader. When explaining how fraternities and sororities recruit new members, do you want to use an objective, nonjudgmental tone? To decide, take into account readers' attitudes toward your subject. Does your audience have a financial or emotional investment in the process being described? Does your own interest in the process coincide or conflict with that of your audience? Awareness of your readers' stance can be crucial. Consider another example: Assume you're writing a letter to the director of the student health center proposing a new system to replace the currently chaotic one. You'd do well to be tactful in your criticisms. Offend your reader, and your cause is lost. If, however, the letter is slated for the college newspaper and directed primarily to other students, you could adopt a more pointed, even sarcastic tone. Readers, you would assume, will probably share your view and favor change.

Once you settle on the essay's tone, maintain it throughout. If you're writing a light piece on the way computers are taking over our lives, you wouldn't include a grim step-by-step analysis of the way confidential computerized medical records may become public.

9. Open and close the process analysis effectively. A paper developed primarily through process analysis should have a strong beginning. The introduction should state the process to be described and imply whether the essay has an informational or directional intent.

If you suspect readers are indifferent to your subject, use the introduction to motivate them, telling them how important the subject is:

> Do you enjoy the salad bars found in many restaurants? If you do, you probably have noticed that the vegetables are always crisp and fresh—no matter how many hours they have been exposed to the air. What are the restaurants doing to make the vegetables look so inviting? There's a simple answer. Many restaurants spray the vegetables with, or dip them into, potent chemicals to make them appetizing.

If you think your audience may be intimidated by your subject (perhaps because it's complex or relatively obscure), the introduction is the perfect spot to reassure them that the process being described is not beyond their grasp:

> Studies show that many people willingly accept a defective product just so they won't have to deal with the uncomfortable process of making a complaint. But once a few easy-to-learn basics are mastered, anyone can register a complaint that gets results.

Most process analysis essays don't end as soon as the last step in the sequence is explained. Instead, they usually include some brief final comments that round out the piece and bring it to a satisfying close. This final section of the essay may summarize the main steps in the process—not by repeating the steps verbatim but by rephrasing and condensing them in several concise sentences. The conclusion can also be an effective spot to underscore the significance of the process, recalling what may have been said in the introduction about the subject's importance. Or the essay can end by echoing the note of reassurance that may have been included at the start.

REVISION STRATEGIES

Once you have a draft of the essay, you're ready to revise. The following checklist will help you and those giving you feedback apply to process analysis some of the revision techniques discussed on pages 60–62.

☑ PROCESS ANALYSIS: A REVISION/PEER REVIEW CHECKLIST

Revise Overall Meaning and Structure

- ❑ What purpose does the process analysis serve—to inform, to persuade, or to do both?
- ❑ Is the process analysis primarily *directional* or *informational*? How can you tell?

- ❑ Where does the process seem confusing? Where have steps been left out? Which steps need simplifying?
- ❑ What is the essay's tone? Is the tone appropriate for the essay's purpose and readers? Where are there distracting shifts in tone?

Revise Paragraph Development

- ❑ Does the introduction specify the process to be described? Does it provide an overview? Should it?
- ❑ Which paragraphs are difficult to follow? Have any steps or materials been omitted or explained in too much or too little detail? Which paragraphs should warn readers about potential trouble spots or overlapping steps?
- ❑ Where are additional time signals needed to clarify the sequence within and between paragraphs? Where does overreliance on time signals make the sequence awkward and mechanical?
- ❑ Which paragraph describes the most crucial step in the sequence? How has the step been highlighted?
- ❑ How could the conclusion be more effective?

Revise Sentences and Words

- ❑ What technical or specialized terms appear in the essay? Have they been sufficiently explained? Where could simpler, less technical language be used?
- ❑ Are there any places where the essay's point of view awkwardly shifts? How could this problem be corrected?
- ❑ Does the essay use correct verb tenses—the past tense for completed events, the present tense for habitual or ongoing actions?
- ❑ Where does the essay use the passive voice ("The hole is dug")? Would the active voice ("You dig the hole") be more effective?

STUDENT ESSAY

The following student essay was written by Robert Barry in response to this assignment:

> In "How to Say Nothing in 500 Words," Paul Roberts makes fun of college students' addiction to an inflated, padded writing style. By observing people, identify another example of an obsessive behavior that borders on the addictive. Then write a light-spirited

essay explaining the various stages in the addiction. Since your essay is humorous in tone, be sure to describe an addiction that doesn't have serious consequences.

While reading Robert's paper, try to determine how effectively it applies the principles of process analysis. The annotations on Robert's paper and the commentary following it will help you look at the essay more closely.

Becoming a Recordoholic
by Robert Barry

Introduction

As a technological breakthrough, the DVR (digital video recorder) has been an enormous success—almost as popular as television itself. Not only can you watch TV while you record other programs, but you can pause and rewind live TV. Better yet, you can program the DVR to record a roster of programs—even entire seasons—with a simple push of a button. No consumer warning labels are attached to this ingenious invention, DVRs, but there should be. DVRs can be dangerous. Barely aware of what is happening, a person can turn into a compulsive recorder. The descent from innocent hobby to full-blown addiction takes place in several stages. 1

Start of two-sentence thesis

Topic sentence

First stage in process (DVR addiction)

In the first innocent stage, the unsuspecting person buys a DVR for occasional use. I was at this stage when I asked my parents if they would buy me a DVR as a birthday gift. With the DVR, I could record reruns of *Seinfeld* and new episodes of *The Simpsons* while watching *Grey's Anatomy.* The DVR was perfect. I hooked it up to the TV in my bedroom and recorded the antics of Jerry, Elaine, George, and Kramer and the adventures of my favorite cartoon family, while watching the residents of Seattle Grace save lives and make utter fools of themselves. Occasionally, I'd DVR a movie, which my friends and I watched over the weekend. I recorded only a few shows, and after I watched those shows, I'd delete them from the DVR. In these early days, my use of the DVR was the equivalent of light social drinking. 2

Beginning of analogy to alcoholism

Topic sentence

Second stage in process

In the second phase on the road to recordoholism, an individual uses the DVR more frequently and begins to stockpile recordings rather than watch them. My troubles began in July when my family and I went to the shore for two weeks of vacation. I set my DVR to record all five episodes of *Seinfeld* and *The Sopranos,* and two episodes each of *Heroes, The Simpsons,* and *Grey's Anatomy,* while I was at the beach working on my tan. Even I, an avid TV viewer, didn't have time to sit and watch all those shows. The DVR continued to record these programs, but there weren't enough hours 3 in the day to watch everything and do my schoolwork, so the programs piled up in my DVR queue. How did I resolve this problem? Very easily. I set my DVR to record episodes of *Seinfeld* three days a week, rather than five. However, with this notion that I had such control with my DVR, I began to realize that there were probably other shows out there that I could record and watch whenever I desired. I could DVR classics like *Law & Order* and *Buffy the Vampire Slayer*. Very quickly, I accumulated six *Seinfelds*, four *Law & Orders*, and three *Buffys*. Then a friend—who shall go nameless—told me that only 144 episodes of *Buffy* were ever made. Excited by the thought that I could acquire as impressive a collection of episodes as a Hollywood executive, I continued recording *Buffy*, even recording shows while I watched them. Clearly, my once innocent hobby was getting out of control. I was now using the DVR on a regular basis—the equivalent of several stiff drinks a day.

Continuation of analogy

Topic sentence

Third stage in process

4 In the third stage of recordoholism, the amount of recording increases significantly, leading to an even more irrational stockpiling of programs in the DVR queue. The catalyst that propelled me into this third stage was my parents' decision to get a premium movie package added to their cable. Selfless guy that I am, I volunteered to move my DVR into the living room, where the connection was located. Now I could record all the most recent movies and specials. I began to record a couple of other shows every day. I also went movie-crazy and taped *Gangs of New York, Barbershop 2,* and *The Godfather I, II,* and *III.* I recorded an HBO comedy special with Chris Rock and an MTV concert featuring Radiohead. Where did I get time to watch all these shows? I didn't. Using the DVR was more satisfying than watching. Reason and common sense were abandoned. Getting things on the DVR had become an obsession, and I was setting the DVR to record programs all the time.

Continuation of analogy

Topic sentence

Fourth stage in process

5 In the fourth stage, recordoholism creeps into other parts of the addict's life, influencing behavior in strange ways. Secrecy becomes commonplace. One day, my mother came into my room and asked about a recent test I had taken. What she didn't know was that the night before the exam, I had checked my DVR recording list and found that I had run out of storage space. For three hours after everyone went to bed, I watched episodes of *The Sopranos* so I could delete them and record a movie on Showtime. I was so tired the next morning that I wound up getting a bad grade on my biology exam. "Robert," my mother exclaimed, "isn't this getting a bit out of hand?" I assured her it was just a hobby, but I continued to sneak downstairs in the middle of the night to watch recorded

Continuation of analogy

shows, removing any trace of my presence from the living room when I was finished. Also, denial is not unusual during this stage of DVR addiction. At the dinner table, when my younger sister commented, "Robert records all the time," I laughingly told everyone—including myself—that the recording was no big deal. I was getting bored with it and was going to stop any day, I assured my family. Obsessive behavior also characterizes the fourth stage of recordoholism. Each week, I pulled out the TV magazine from the Sunday paper and went through it carefully, circling in red all the shows I wanted to record. Another sign of addiction was the secret calender I kept in my desk drawer. With more diligence than I ever had for any term paper, I would log in each program I recorded and plan for the coming week's recording schedule.

Topic sentence

Continuation of analogy

Final stage in process

6 In the final stage of an addiction, the individual either succumbs completely to the addiction or is able to break away from the habit. I broke my addiction, and I broke it cold turkey. This total withdrawal occurred when I went off to college. There was no point in taking my DVR to school because TVs were not allowed in the freshman dorms. Even though there were many things to occupy my time during the school week, cold sweats overcame me whenever I thought about everything on TV I was not recording. I even considered calling home and asking members of my family to record things for me, but I knew they would think I was crazy. At the beginning of the semester, I also had to resist the overwhelming desire to travel the three hours home every weekend so I could get my fix. But after a while, the urgent need to record subsided. Now, months later, as I write this, I feel detached and sober.

Conclusion

Final references to analogy

7 I have no illusions, though. I know that once a recordoholic, always a recordoholic. Soon I will return home for the holidays, which, as everyone knows, can be a time for excess eating—and recording. But I will cope with the pressure. I will take each day one at a time. I plan to watch what I'm able to, and no more. And if I feel myself succumbing to the temptations of recording, I will pick up the telephone and dial the recordoholics' hot line: 1-800-DVR-STOP. I will win the battle.

COMMENTARY

Purpose, thesis, and tone. Robert's essay is an example of *informational process analysis;* his purpose is to describe—rather than teach—the process of becoming a "recordoholic." The title, with its coined term *recordoholic,* tips us off that the essay is going to be entertaining. And the introductory paragraph clearly establishes the essay's playful, mock-serious tone. The tone established, Robert briefly defines the term *recordoholic* as a "compulsive recorder" and then moves to the essay's *thesis:* "Barely aware of what is happening, a person can turn into a compulsive recorder. The descent from innocent hobby to full-blown addiction takes place in several stages."

Throughout the essay, Robert sustains the introduction's humor by mocking his own motivations and poking fun at his quirks: "Selfless guy that I am, I volunteered to move my DVR" (paragraph 4), and "With more diligence than I ever had for any term paper, I would log in each program I recorded and plan for the coming week's recording schedule" (5). Robert probably uses a bit of *dramatic license* when reporting some of his obsessive behavior, and we, as readers, understand that he's exaggerating for comic effect. Most likely, he didn't break out in a cold sweat at the thought of the TV shows he was unable to record. Nevertheless, this tinkering with the truth is legitimate because it allows Robert to create material that fits the essay's lightly satiric tone.

Organization and topic sentences. To meet the requirements of the assignment, Robert needed to provide a *step-by-step* explanation of a process. And because he invented the term *recordoholism,* Robert also needed to invent the stages in the progression of his addiction. During his prewriting, Robert discovered five stages in his recordoholism. Presented *chronologically,* these stages provide the organizing focus for his paper. Specifically, each supporting paragraph is devoted to one stage, with the *topic sentence* for each paragraph indicating the stage's distinctive characteristics.

Transitions. Although Robert's essay is playful, it is nonetheless a process analysis and so must have an easy-to-follow structure. Keeping this in mind, Robert wisely includes *transitions* to signal what happened at each stage of his recordoholism: "*However* with this notion that I had such control" (paragraph 3); "*Now,* I could record all the most recent movies and specials." (4); "*One day,* my mother came into my room" (5); and "*But after a while,* the urgent need to record subsided" (6). In addition to such transitions, Robert uses crisp questions to move from idea to idea within a paragraph: "How did I resolve this problem? Very easily. I set my DVR to record episodes of *Seinfeld* three days a week, rather than five" (3), and "Where did I get time to watch all these shows? I didn't" (4).

Combining patterns of development. Even though Robert's essay is a process analysis, it contains elements of other patterns of development. For example, his paper is unified by an *analogy*—a sustained *comparison* between Robert's recording addiction and the obviously more serious addiction to alcohol. Handled incorrectly, the analogy could have been offensive, but Robert makes the comparison work to his advantage. The analogy is stated specifically in several spots: "In these early days, my use of the DVR was the equivalent of light social drinking" (2); "I was now using the DVR on a regular basis—the equivalent of several stiff drinks a day" (3). Finally, he generates numerous lively details or *examples* to illustrate the different stages in his addiction.

Two unnecessary sentences. Perhaps you noticed that Robert runs into a minor problem at the end of the fourth paragraph. Starting with the sentence, "Reason and common sense were abandoned," he begins to ramble and repeat himself. The paragraph's last two sentences fail to add anything substantial. Take a moment to read paragraph 4 aloud, omitting the last two sentences. Note how much sharper the new conclusion is: "Where did I get time to watch all these tapes? I didn't. Using the DVR was more satisfying than watching." This new ending says all that needs to be said.

Revising the first draft. When it was time to revise, Robert—in spite of his apprehension—showed his paper to his roommate and asked him to read it out loud. Robert knew this strategy would provide a more objective point of view on his work. His roommate, at first an unwilling recruit, nonetheless laughed as he read the essay aloud. That was just the response Robert wanted. But when his roommate got to the conclusion, Robert heard that the closing paragraph was flat and anticlimactic. His roommate agreed, so the two of them brainstormed ways to make the conclusion livelier and more in spirit with the rest of the essay. Printed here is Robert's original conclusion.

Original Version of the Conclusion

I have no illusions, though, that I am over my recordoholism. Soon I will be returning home for the holidays, which can be a time for excess recording. All I can do is watch what I'm able to and not use the DVR. After that, I will hope for the best.

Robert and his roommate brainstormed ways to make the conclusion livelier and more in spirit with the rest of the essay. They decided that the best approach would be to reinforce the playful, mock-serious tone that characterized earlier parts of the essay. Robert thus made three major changes to his conclusion. First, he tightened the first sentence of the paragraph ("I have no illusions, though, that I am over my recordoholism"), making it crisper and more dramatic: "I have no illusions, though." Second, he added a few sentences to sustain the light, self-deprecating tone he had used earlier: "I know that once a recordoholic, always a recordoholic"; "But I will cope with the pressure"; "I will win the battle." Third, and perhaps most important, he returned to the alcoholism analogy: "I will take each day one at a time.... And if I feel myself succumbing to the temptations of recording, I will pick up the telephone and dial the recordoholics' hotline..."

These weren't the only changes Robert made while reworking his paper, but they help illustrate how sensitive he was to the effect he wanted to achieve. Certainly, the recasting of the conclusion was critical to the overall success of this amusing essay.

Activities: Process Analysis

Prewriting Activities

1. Imagine you're writing two essays: One *defines* the term "comparison shopping"; the other *contrasts* two different teaching styles. Jot down ways you might use process analysis in each essay.

2. Select *one* of the essay topics that follow and determine what your purpose, tone, and point of view would be for each audience indicated in parentheses. Then use brainstorming, questioning, mapping, or another prewriting technique to identify the points you'd cover for each audience. Finally, organize the raw material, noting the differences in emphasis and sequence for each group of readers.

   a. How to buy a car (*young people who have just gotten a driver's license; established professionals*)
   b. How children acquire their values (*first-time parents; elementary school teachers*)
   c. How to manage money (*grade school children; college students*)
   d. How loans or scholarships are awarded to incoming students on your campus (*high school graduates applying for financial aid; high school guidance counselors*)
   e. How arguments can strengthen relationships (*preteen children; young adults*)
   f. How to relax (*college students; parents with young children*)

Revising Activities

1. Below is the brainstorming for a brief essay that describes the steps involved in making a telephone sales call. The paper has the following thesis: "Establishing rapport with customers is the most challenging and the most important part of phone sales." Revise the brainstormed material by deleting anything that undermines the paper's unity and organizing the steps in a logical sequence.

   - Keep customers on the phone as long as possible to learn what they need
   - The more you know about customers' needs, the better
   - The tone of the opening comments is very important
   - Gently introduce the product
   - Use a friendly tone in opening comments
   - End on a friendly tone, too
   - Don't introduce the product right away
   - Growing rudeness in society. Some people hang up right away. Very upsetting.
   - Try in a friendly way to keep the person on the phone

- Many people are so lonely they don't mind staying on the phone so they can talk to someone—anyone
- How sad that there's so much loneliness in the world
- Describe the product's advantages—price, convenience, installment plan
- If person is not interested, try in a friendly way to find out why
- Don't tell people that their reasons for not being interested are silly
- Don't push people if they're not interested
- Encourage credit card payment—the product will arrive earlier
- Explain payment—check, money order, or credit card payment

2. Reprinted here is a paragraph from the first draft of a humorous essay advising shy college students how to get through a typical day. Written as a process analysis, the paragraph outlines techniques for surviving class. Revise the paragraph, deleting digressions that disrupt the paragraph's unity, eliminating unnecessary repetition, and sequencing the steps in the proper order. Also correct inappropriate shifts in person and add transitions where needed. Feel free to add any telling details.

Simply attending class can be stressful for shy people. Several strategies, though, can lessen the trauma. Shy students should time their arrival to coincide with that of most other class members—about two minutes before the class is scheduled to begin. If you arrive too early, you may be seen sitting alone, or, even worse, may actually be forced to talk with another early arrival. If you arrive late, all eyes will be upon you. Before heading to class, the shy student should dress in the least conspicuous manner possible—say, in the blue jeans, sweatshirt, and sneakers that 99.9 percent of your classmates wear. That way you won't stand out from everyone else. Take a seat near the back of the room. Don't, however, sit at the very back since professors often take sadistic pleasure in calling on students back there, assuming they chose those seats because they didn't want to be called on. A friend of mine who is far from shy uses just the opposite ploy. In an attempt to get in good with her professors, she sits in the front row and, incredibly enough, volunteers to participate. However, since shy people don't want to call attention to themselves, they should stifle any urge to sneeze or cough. You run the risk of having people look at you or offer you a tissue or cough drop. And of course, never, ever volunteer to answer. Such a display of intelligence is sure to focus all eyes on you. In other words, make yourself as inconspicuous as possible. How, you might wonder, can you be inconspicuous if you're blessed (or cursed) with great looks? Well, . . . have you ever considered earning your degree through the mail?

Tim Folger

Currently a resident of northern New Mexico, Tim Folger, born in 1954, holds a bachelor's degree in physics from the University of California at Santa Cruz and a master's degree in science journalism from New York University. He is the series editor of *The Best American Science and Nature Writing*, an annual anthology, as well as a contributing editor at *Discover* magazine. He has written numerous science articles for such publications as *The New York Times, Popular Science, OnEarth,* and *National Geographic.* In 2007, Folger won the American Institute of Physics Science Writing Award in the Journalist category for an article entitled "If an Electron Can Be in Two Places at Once, Why Can't You?" The following selection is excerpted from an article that first appeared in the May 1994 issue of *Discover.*

Pre-Reading Journal Entry

You may have thought about processes that you see happen all around you. For example, you might wonder how dough becomes bread, how bicycle gears work, or how animals migrate in the fall or spring. List two or three processes that pique your interest, and jot down a few ideas about each.

Waves of Destruction

Like most people in Nicaragua, Chris Terry didn't feel the mild earthquake that shook the country at about 8 p.m. on September 1, 1992. He didn't notice anything out of the ordinary until some minutes later. Terry and his friend Scott Willson, both expatriate Americans, run a charter fishing business in San Juan del Sur, a sleepy village on Nicaragua's Pacific coast. On the evening of the earthquake they were aboard their boat in San Juan del Sur's harbor. 1

"We were down below," says Terry. "We heard a slam." The sound came from the keel of their boat, which had just scraped bottom in a harbor normally more than 20 feet deep. Somehow the harbor had drained as abruptly as if someone had pulled a giant plug. 2

Terry and Willson didn't have much time to contemplate the novelty of a waterless harbor. Within seconds they were lifted back up by a powerful wave. "Suddenly the boat whipped around very, very fast," says Terry. "It was dark. We had no idea what had happened." 3

The confusion was just beginning. As Willson and Terry struggled to their feet, the boat began dropping once again, this time into the trough of a large wave. Willson was the first to get out to the deck. There he found himself staring into the back side of a hill of water rushing toward the shore. "He was seeing the lights of the city through the water," says Terry. "And then the swell hit, and the lights went out, and we could hear people screaming." 4

One of those on the shore was Inez Ortega, the owner of a small beachfront restaurant. She hadn't noticed the earthquake either. While preparing dinner she glanced out at the harbor and noticed that the water seemed unusually low. "I didn't pay much attention at the time," she says. But when she looked up again a swell of water at least five feet high was racing up the beach toward her restaurant. 5

"I started running, but I didn't even get out of the restaurant when the wave hit," she says. Ortega and several of her customers spent about half an hour swimming in a debris-filled stew before they managed to drag themselves out of the water. 6

Ortega and everyone else in San Juan del Sur looked about themselves in stunned silence. The waves had swept away restaurants and bars lining the beach, as well as homes and cars—and people—hundreds of yards inland. Terry and Willson managed to ride out the disaster on their boat. Still reeling, they witnessed the receding wake of the last wave. 7

"When the wave came back out, it was like being in a blender," says Terry. Collapsed homes bobbed in the water around their boat. 8

Terry, Willson, and Ortega had survived a tsunami, a devastating wave triggered by an undersea earthquake. Although the waves that hit San Juan del Sur were extremely powerful, they rose only 5 to 6 feet high. Other parts of Nicaragua weren't so lucky. All told, the offshore earthquake sent tsunamis crashing along a 200-mile stretch of the coast, and newspapers reported 65-foot waves in some places (though seismologists consider that figure unlikely; a more realistic wave height might be about 30 feet). The waves killed about 170 people, mostly children who were sleeping when the waves came. More than 13,000 Nicaraguans were left homeless. 9

Destructive tsunamis strike somewhere in the world an average of once a year. But the period from September 1992, the time of the Nicaraguan tsunami, through last July was unusually grim, with three major tsunamis. In December 1992 an earthquake off Flores Island in Indonesia hurled deadly waves against the shore, killing more than 1,000 people. Entire villages washed out to sea. And in July 1993 an earthquake in the Sea of Japan generated one of the largest tsunamis ever to hit Japan, with waves washing over areas 97 feet above sea level; 120 people drowned or were crushed to death. 10

In Japanese *tsunami* literally means "harbor wave." In English the phenomenon is often called a tidal wave, but in truth tsunamis have nothing to do with the tame cycle of tides. While volcanic eruptions and undersea landslides can launch tsunamis, earthquakes are responsible for most of them. And most tsunami-spawning earthquakes occur around the Pacific rim in areas geologists call subduction zones, where the dense crust of the ocean floor dives beneath the edge of the lighter continental crust and sinks down into Earth's mantle. The west coasts of North and South America and the coasts of Japan, East Asia, and many Pacific island chains border subduction 11 zones. There is also a subduction zone in the Caribbean, and tsunamis have occurred there, but the Atlantic is seismically quiet compared with the restless Pacific.

More often than not, the ocean crust does not go gentle into that good mantle. As it descends, typically at a rate of a few inches a year, an oceanic plate can snag like a Velcro strip against the overlying continent. Strain builds, sometimes for centuries, until finally the plates spasmodically jerk free in an earthquake. As the two crustal plates lumber past each other into a new locked embrace, they sometimes permanently raise or lower parts of the seafloor above. A 1960 earthquake off Chile, for example, took only minutes to elevate a California-size chunk of real estate by about 30 feet. In some earthquakes, one stretch of the sea bottom may rise while an adjoining piece drops. Generally, only earthquakes that directly raise or lower the seafloor cause tsunamis. Along other types of faults—for example, the San Andreas, which runs under California and into the ocean—crustal plates don't move up and down but instead scrape horizontally past each other, usually without ruffling the ocean. 12

Seismologists believe the sudden change in the seafloor terrain is what triggers a tsunami. When the seafloor rapidly sinks—or jumps—during an earthquake, it lowers (or raises) an enormous mountain of water, stretching from the seafloor all the way to the surface. "Whatever happens on the seafloor is reflected on the surface," says Eddie Bernard, an oceanographer with the National Oceanic and Atmospheric Administration (NOAA). "So if you imagine the kind of deformation where a portion of the ocean floor is uplifted and a portion subsides, then you'd have—on the ocean surface—a hump and a valley of water simultaneously, because the water follows the seafloor changes." 13

One major difference between the seafloor and the ocean surface, however, is that when the seafloor shifts, it stays put, at least until the next earthquake. But the mound of water thrust above normal sea level quickly succumbs to the downward pull of gravity. The vast swell, which may cover up to 10,000 square miles depending on the area uplifted on the ocean floor, collapses. Then the water all around the sinking mound gets pushed up, just as a balloon bulges out around a point where it's pressed. This alternating swell and collapse spreads out in concentric rings, like the ripples in a pond disturbed by a tossed stone. 14

Although you might think a tsunami spreading across the ocean would be about as inconspicuous as a tarantula walking on your pillow, the wave is, in fact, essentially invisible in deep ocean water. On the open sea, a tsunami might be only ten feet high, while its wavelength—the distance from one tsunami crest to another—can be up to 600 miles. The tsunami slopes very gently, becoming steeper only by an inch or so every mile. The waves so feared on land are at sea much flatter than the most innocuous bunny-run 15 ski slope; they wouldn't disturb a cruise ship's shuffleboard game. Normal surface waves hide tsunamis. But that placid surface belies the power surging through the water. Unlike wind-driven waves, which wrinkle only the upper few feet of the ocean, a tsunami extends for thousands of fathoms, all the way to the ocean bottom.

Tsunamis and surface waves differ in another crucial respect: tsunamis can cross oceans, traveling for thousands of miles without dissipating, whereas normal waves run out of steam after a few miles at most. Tsunamis are so persistent that they can reverberate through an ocean for days, bouncing back and forth between continents. The 1960 Chilean earthquake created tsunamis that registered on tide gauges around the Pacific for more than a week. 16

"You've got to remember how much energy is involved here," says Bernard. "Look at the size of these earthquakes. The generating mechanism is like a huge number of atomic bombs going off simultaneously, and a good portion of that energy is transferred into the water column." 17

The reason for tsunamis' remarkable endurance lies in their unusually long wavelengths—a reflection of the vast quantity of water set in motion. Normal surface waves typically crest every few feet and move up and down every few seconds. Spanning an ocean thus involves millions of wavelengths. In a tsunami, on the other hand, each watery surge and collapse occurs over perhaps 100 miles in a matter of minutes. For a large subduction-zone earthquake—magnitude 8 or more—the earthquake's impulse can be powerful enough to send tsunamis traveling across the Pacific—from the Chilean coast to Japan, Australia, Alaska, and all the islands en route as well. 18

For much the same reason, tsunamis can race through the ocean at jetliner speeds—typically 500 miles an hour. To span a sea, they need travel a distance equal to just a few dozen of their own wavelengths, a few swells and collapses. That means the wave only has to rise and fall a handful of times before the surge reaches its destination. The outsize scale of a tsunami makes an ocean seem like a pond. 19

As a tsunami speeds on its covert way, undersea mountains and valleys may alter its course. During the 1992 Indonesian earthquake, villages on the south side of Babi Island were the hardest hit, even though the source of the tsunami was to the north of the island. Seismologists believe that the underwater terrain sluiced the tsunami around and back toward the islands south coast. 20

Only when a tsunami nears land does it reveal its true, terrible nature. When the wave reaches the shallow water above a continental shelf, friction with the shelf slows the front of the wave. As the tsunami approaches shore, the trailing waves in the train pile onto the waves in front of them, like a rug crumpled against a wall. The resulting wave may rear up to 30 feet before hitting the shore. Although greatly slowed, a tsunami still bursts onto land at freeway speeds, with enough momentum to flatten buildings and trees and to carry ships miles inland. For every five-foot stretch of coastline, a large 21 tsunami can deliver more than 100,000 tons of water. Chances are if you are close enough to see a tsunami, you wont be able to outrun it.

As Inez Ortega and Chris Terry witnessed in San Juan del Sur, the first sign of a tsunami's approach is often not an immense wave but the sudden emptying of a harbor. This strange phenomenon results from a tremendous magnification of normal wave motion. In most waves, the water within the crest is actually moving in a circular path; a wave is like a wheel rolling toward the shore, with only the top half of the wheel visible. When that wave is 100 miles long, the water in the crest moves in long, squashed ellipses rather than in circles. Near the front and bottom of the wave, water is actually on the part of the elliptical "wheel" moving backward—toward the wave and out to sea. If you've ever floated in front of a wave, you've probably felt the pull of the wave as water sloshes back toward the crest. With a tsunami, that seaward pull reaches out over tens of miles, sometimes with tragic results: when an earthquake and tsunami struck Lisbon in 1755, exposing the bottom of the city's harbor, the bizarre sight drew curious crowds who drowned when the tsunami rushed in a few minutes later. Many people died in the same way when a tsunami hit Hawaii in 1946. 22

Although seismologists and oceanographers understand in broad terms how tsunamis form and speed across oceans, they are still grappling with some nagging fundamental questions. One of the major mysteries is why sometimes relatively small earthquakes generate outlandishly large waves. Such deceptive earthquakes can be particularly devastating because they may be ignored by civil agencies that are charged with issuing tsunami warnings. 23

The Nicaraguan earthquake is a case in point. By conventional measures, it shouldn't have produced a tsunami at all. The earthquake registered magnitude 7.0 on the Richter scale, not puny by any means, but not large enough, seismologists believed, to pose much of a tsunami risk. The quake's epicenter was 60 miles offshore, distant enough to dampen the tremors on land. Yet people who had not even felt the quake found themselves swept out to sea minutes later.... 24

Questions for Close Reading

1. What is the selection's thesis? Locate the sentence(s) in which Folger states his main idea. If he doesn't state his thesis explicitly, express it in your own words.
2. The first nine paragraphs describe a tsunami that hit Nicaragua on September 1, 1992. How many witnesses does Folger quote? Who are they? What do they describe? What additional evidence does Folger give to show the destructiveness of the tsunami?
3. In which paragraphs does the author describe how tsunamis are formed? What kinds of earthquakes cause tsunamis? Why? Where do most tsunamis start?
4. Folger lists several characteristics of tsunamis that make them difficult to detect. What are those characteristics?

5. Refer to your dictionary as needed to define the following words used in the selection: *keel* (paragraph 2), *trough* (4), *seismologists* (9), *geologists* (11), *subduction* (11), *crust* (11), *mantle* (11), *seismically* (11), *plate* (12), *faults* (12), *oceanographer* (13), *wavelength* (15), *innocuous* (15), *fathoms* (15), *reverberate* (16), *covert* (20), *sluiced* (20), *continental shelf* (21), *ellipses* [sing. *ellipse*] (22), *Richter scale* (24), and *epicenter* (24).

Questions About the Writer's Craft

1. **The pattern.** Does the author use directional or informational process analysis? Who is the audience for this essay? Why do you think the author expects that readers will be interested in this subject? What clues in the essay tell us how familiar the audience is with geology, seismology, and oceanography?
2. **Other patterns.** What do you think the author hopes to achieve by starting the essay with a detailed narrative about the 1992 Nicaraguan tsunami? Is he successful? What role does cause and effect analysis play in the essay?
3. The author uses figures of speech to illustrate the nature of some phenomena he describes. List at least four such figures of speech. How effective are they?
4. Expert opinion and statistics are two kinds of evidence the author uses. What are some examples of these? How effective are they?

Writing Assignments Using Process Analysis as a Pattern of Development

1. Folger's essay is about the process behind a natural phenomenon. Think of a human-caused event and the process involved. For example, you might consider how a workout or team practice session unfolds or how a person learns to drive or gets a driver's license. Decide whether to write an informational or a directional process analysis. Then write an essay in which you give the various stages in the process. Remember to use sufficient details and examples.
2. By the time people see a tsunami approaching, Folger says, it is too late to escape to safety. However, people can take steps to prepare for many other natural events. Think of a common encounter with nature, for example, hiking in the woods or driving in a snowstorm. Write a directional essay in which you give the steps people should take to prepare for and protect themselves in the situation. For insight into how others have written about encounters with the natural world, read David Helvarg's "The Storm This Time" (page 103), George Orwell's "Shooting an Elephant" (page 146), Amy Sutherland's "What Shamu Taught Me About a Happy Marriage" (page 308), Natalie Angier's "The Cute Factor" (page 461), or Joan Didion's "The Santa Ana" (page 601).

Writing Assignments Combining Patterns of Development

3. Folger creates lively images to describe how one crustal plate acts against another. For example, he writes that "the plates spasmodically jerk free" of each other. Choose two common natural phenomena you have experienced, and write an

FIGURE 7.2
Essay Structure Diagram: "Waves of Destruction" by Tim Folger

Introductory paragraphs: Anecdotes (paragraphs 1–8)	Story of Terry and Willson on a boat during the Nicaraguan tsunami, Sept. 1, 1992. Story of Inez Ortega in her beachfront restaurant during the same tsunami.
Background: Definition Statistics (9–10)	Definition of *tsunami.* Statistics for 1992 Nicaraguan tsunami. Statistics for tsunamis worldwide.
Informational process analysis **Causes and effects** **Definitions** **Examples** **Expert opinion** (11–14)	Tsunami-causing earthquakes occur in Pacific rim subduction zones. (Definition of *subduction zone*) **Stage 1:** Ocean crust descends under earth's mantle. Strain can cause an earthquake that raises or lowers a section of the seafloor. (Examples and figures of speech) **Stage 2:** Change in the seafloor causes a mountain of water to rise and fall. (Expert opinion) **Stage 3:** Swell and collapse of water spreads out in concentric circles, forming tsunami.
Causes and effects (15–21)	Effects of the great wavelength of tsunamis: • Tsunamis are unnoticeable on the open seas. • They can reverberate for days without losing force. (Expert opinion) • They can travel far and fast undetected. By the time people take notice, it's too late to escape. Tsunami pathways are affected by undersea terrain so landing spots are not predictable.
Concluding paragraphs **Reference to opening anecdotes** **Thesis** (implied) (22–24)	Tsunamis will cause the sudden emptying of a harbor noticed by Terry, Willson, and Ortega. Despite low Richter scores, some earthquakes can still cause devastating tsunamis. **Thesis:** Though scientists know earthquakes can cause tsunamis, several characteristics of tsunamis make it hard to predict with timely accuracy which earthquakes will result in devastating tsunamis.

essay in which you *compare* and *contrast* them. You might compare a sunrise with a sunset, or a small creek with a large river. Use colorful language to *describe* the scenes and the feelings or ideas each evokes in you.

4. After a natural disaster occurs, many victims of property loss turn to their governments for help. While some citizens think that government compensation is appropriate or even say that governments don't help enough, others argue that people should minimize their own risk by, for example, not building homes in areas prone to flooding. Do some research on disaster management and humanitarian intervention. Write an essay in which you *argue* one approach or another for dealing with victims of natural disasters. Be sure to include *examples* of recent natural disasters and government responses to them. You might also read "The Storm This Time" by David Helvarg (page 103) about the disaster caused by Hurricane Katrina in 2005.

Writing Assignment Using a Journal Entry as a Starting Point

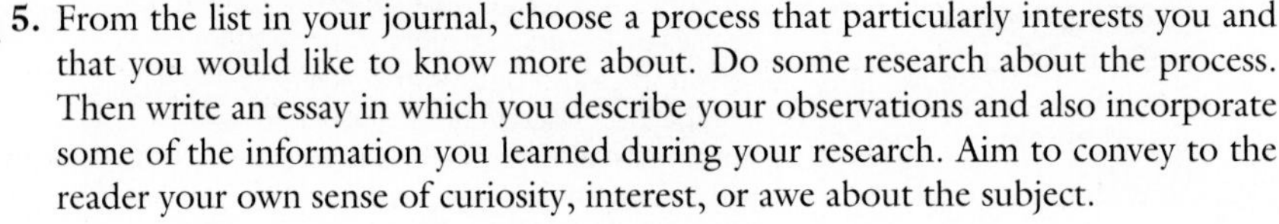

5. From the list in your journal, choose a process that particularly interests you and that you would like to know more about. Do some research about the process. Then write an essay in which you describe your observations and also incorporate some of the information you learned during your research. Aim to convey to the reader your own sense of curiosity, interest, or awe about the subject.

David Shipley

David Shipley is the editor of *The New York Times*'s op-ed page, on which opinion pieces by *Times* columnists and others are published. He was born in Portland, Oregon, in 1963 and graduated with a degree in English from Williams College in 1985. Shipley won a Thomas J. Watson Fellowship for 1985–1986, which allowed him to spend a year traveling to do independent study. From 1993 to 1995 he was executive editor of *The New Republic,* and from 1995 to 1997 he was a special assistant and senior speechwriter for President Bill Clinton. Shipley joined *The New York Times* in 1998 and was deputy editor of the Sunday *New York Times Magazine*'s millennium issues, senior editor of the magazine, and enterprise editor of the national desk before moving to his present position as op-ed editor. With coauthor Will Schwalbe, Shipley wrote a book about e-mail entitled *Send.* It was published in 2007 and revised in 2008. This essay, originally entitled "What We Talk About When We Talk About Editing," appeared in *The New York Times* on July 31, 2005.

Pre-Reading Journal Entry

People often seek advice and help from others to help them do a job or improve their performance. For example, if you were writing your résumé, you might ask a friend to edit and proofread it. Or if you were trying out for a sports team, you might ask a coach for feedback and advice. Think of some occasions in the past when you asked others for help with your work or gave help to someone else when asked. What was the task? What was your goal in helping or being helped? Did the assistance actually improve the end product, or was it useless? Use your journal to answer these questions.

Talk About Editing

. . . Not surprisingly, readers have lots of questions about the editing that goes on [on the *New York Times* op-ed page]. What kind of changes do we suggest—and why? What kind of changes do we insist on—and why? When do we stay out of the way? And the hardy perennial: do we edit articles to make them adhere to a particular point of view? I thought I'd try to provide a few answers. 1

Just like Times news articles and editorials, Op-Ed essays are edited. Before something appears in our pages, you can bet that questions have been asked, arguments have been clarified, cuts have been suggested—as have additions—and factual, typographical and grammatical errors have been caught. (We hope.) 2

Our most important rule, however, is that nothing is published on the Op-Ed page unless it has been approved by its author. Articles go to press only after the person under whose name the article appears has explicitly O.K.'d the editing. 3

While it's important to know that we edit, it's also important to know how we edit. The best way to explain this is to take a walk through the process. 4

Say you send us an article by regular mail, e-mail, fax or, this summer at least, owl post[1]—and it's accepted. You'll be told that we'll contact you once your article is scheduled for publication. That could be days, weeks or even months away. 5

When your article does move into the on-deck circle, you'll be sent a contract, and one of the several editors here will get to work. 6

Here are the clear-cut things the editor will do: 7

- Correct grammatical and typographical errors. 8
- Make sure that the article conforms to *The New York Times Manual of Style and Usage*. Courtesy titles, for example, will miraculously appear if they weren't there before; expletives will be deleted; some words will be capitalized, others lowercased. 9
- See to it that the article fits our allotted space. With staff columnists, advertisements and illustrations, there's a limit to the number of words we can squeeze onto the page. 10
- Fact-check the article. While it is the author's responsibility to ensure that everything written for us is accurate, we still check facts—names, dates, places, quotations. 11

We also check assertions. If news articles—from The Times and other publications—are at odds with a point or an example in an essay, we need to resolve whatever discrepancy exists. 12

For instance, an Op-Ed article critical of newly aggressive police tactics in Town X can't flatly say the police have no reason to change their strategy if there have been news reports that violence in the town is rising. This doesn't mean the writer can't still argue that there are other ways to deal with Town X's crime problem—he just can't say that the force's decision to change came out of the blue. 13

How would we resolve the Town X issue? Well, we'd discuss it with the writer—generally by telephone or e-mail—and we'd try to find a solution that preserves the writer's argument while also adhering to the facts. 14

Now to some people, this may sound surprising, as if we're putting words in people's mouths. But there's a crucial distinction to be made between changing a writer's argument—and suggesting language that will help a writer make his point more effectively. 15

Besides grammar and accuracy, we're also concerned about readability. Our editors try to approach articles as average readers who know nothing 16

[1]In J. K. Rowling's Harry Potter books, mail is delivered each morning to Hogwarts, Harry's school, by owls (editors' note).

about the subject. They may ask if a point is clear, if a writer needs transitional language to bridge the gap between two seemingly separate points, if a leap of logic has been made without sufficient explanation.

To make a piece as clear and accessible as possible, the editor may add a transition, cut a section that goes off point or move a paragraph. If a description is highly technical, the editor may suggest language that lay readers will understand. If it isn't clear what a writer is trying to say, the editor may take a guess, based on what he knows from the author, and suggest more precise language. (There are also times when we do precious little.) 17

The editor will then send the edited version of the article to the writer. The changes will often be highlighted to make it easy for the author to see what's been done. (I tend to mark edits I've made with an //ok?//.) If a proposed revision is significant, the editor will often write a few sentences to describe the reasoning behind the suggestion. 18

Every change is a suggestion, not a demand. If a solution offered by an editor doesn't work for a writer, the two work together to find an answer to the problem. Editing is not bullying. 19

Of course, it's not always warm and cuddly, either. The people who write for Op-Ed have a responsibility to be forthright and specific in their arguments. There's no room on the page for articles that are opaque or written in code. 20

What our editors expressly do not do is change a point of view. If you've written an article on why New York's street fairs should be abolished, we will not ask you to change your mind and endorse them. We're going to help you make the best case you can. If you followed this page carefully in the run-up to the Iraq war, for example, you saw arguments both for and against the invasion—all made with equal force. 21

Editing is a human enterprise. Like writing, it is by nature subjective. Sometimes an editor will think a writer is saying something that she isn't. But our editing process gives writer and editor plenty of time to sort out any misunderstandings before the article goes to press. And if a mistake gets through, we do our best to correct it as quickly as possible. 22

The Op-Ed page is a venue for people with a wide range of perspectives, experiences and talents. Some of the people who appear in this space have written a lot; others haven't. If we published only people who needed no editing, we'd wind up relying on only a very narrow range of professional writers, and the page would be much the worse for it. 23

So what's the agenda? A lively page of clashing opinions, one where as many people as possible have the opportunity to make the best arguments they can. 24

And just so you know, this article has been edited. Changes have been suggested—and gratefully accepted. Well, most of them. 25

Questions for Close Reading

1. What is the selection's thesis? Locate the sentence(s) in which Shipley states his main idea. If he doesn't state his thesis explicitly, express it in your own words.
2. What tasks are involved in editing an op-ed piece for *The New York Times*? Of these, which does Shipley seem to think need the most explanation?
3. In paragraphs 18 through 22, Shipley describes the relationship between the editor and writer of an op-ed piece. What is the nature of this relationship?
4. In paragraph 22, Shipley says that "Editing is a human enterprise." What does he mean by this?
5. Refer to your dictionary as needed to define the following words used in the selection: *hardy* (paragraph 1), *perennial* (1), *on-deck circle* (6), *expletives* (9), *assertions* (12), *adhering* (14), *readability* (16), and *venue* (23).

Questions About the Writer's Craft

1. **The pattern.** Who is the audience for Shipley's essay? Why would this audience be interested in this topic? What type of process analysis does Shipley use?
2. **Other patterns.** Shipley *divides* the editing process into three main types of tasks and covers each type in its own section. Identify the main editing tasks and the paragraph(s) that introduce each type. Why does he break down the process this way rather than deal with the editing process as a whole?
3. In paragraphs 13 and 14, Shipley uses an example to clarify what he means by checking "assertions." Why does he provide an example here? Is the example effective?
4. Shipley concludes this essay with some mild humor. What is the joke? What does this use of humor contribute to the point he has been making in his essay?

Writing Assignments Using Process Analysis as a Pattern of Development

1. Shipley describes the process involved in editing opinion pieces, or arguments, that appear in a newspaper with national circulation. However, many other types of works are edited. For example, news articles, news broadcasts, documentaries, movies, commercials, advertisements, novels, and comic strips are all edited. Select one of these media and do research on the tasks involved in editing it. Write an essay in which you analyze the editing process and explain why it is important.
2. Before a piece can be edited, it must be written. Examine the process involved in producing an essay from the writer's rather than the editor's point of view. What process do you use when you write an essay in your English course? Write an essay in which you analyze your own writing process. For inspiration, you might want to read "How to Say Nothing in 500 Words" by Paul Roberts (page 314) and "Euromail and Amerimail" by Eric Weiner (page 350).

Writing Assignments Combining Patterns of Development

3. Op-ed pieces are usually arguments about current issues; in contrast, news articles are more objective, describing or narrating events. From *The New York Times* or your local newspaper, select one op-ed page essay and one news article on a related topic, if possible. *Compare* and *contrast* the two pieces, analyzing their purpose and content. What patterns of development are used in each piece? Give *examples* to support your analysis.

4. A process analysis essay describes a general procedure, such as how to make chili, whereas a narrative presents a specific story, for example, a story about the time you dropped a pot of chili right before your guests arrived for dinner. Write an essay in which you blend a *process analysis* with a *specific narrative*. You can emphasize either the process analysis or the narrative, whichever seems more effective. Your essay can be humorous, serious, fantastical, or ironic.

Writing Assignment Using a Journal Entry as a Starting Point

5. Review your pre-reading journal entry and select one of the occasions on which you helped someone or were helped to perform a task. First, identify the steps in the process and any missteps or problems. Second, decide whether the process lends itself to an informative or a directional process analysis, or some combination of the two. Finally, write an essay in which you describe the process. To add interest to your essay, you might want to use humor, describe interpersonal conflicts, give examples, or focus on problem areas. Be sure—perhaps in your conclusion—to indicate whether the assistance you gave or received was effective in getting the task done.

Amy Sutherland

Amy Sutherland was born in 1959 and grew up in suburban Cincinnati, Ohio. She has a B.A. in art history from the University of Cincinnati, and an M.S.J. from the Medill School of Journalism at Northwestern University. After thirteen years as an arts and features reporter for newspapers in Vermont and Maine, Sutherland accompanied a Maine resident to the 2000 Pillsbury Bake-off in San Francisco, an assignment that turned into a book, *Cookoff: Recipe Fever in America* (2003). Her next book, *Kicked, Bitten, and Scratched: Life and Lessons at the Premier School for Exotic Animal Trainers,* was published in 2006 and inspired the essay that follows, which appeared in *The New York Times.* In turn, the essay led to another book, *What Shamu Taught Me About Life, Love, and Marriage* (2008) as well as a movie. In addition to writing, Sutherland teaches journalism at Boston University.

Pre-Reading Journal Entry

All of us have habits—patterns of behavior that we repeat, sometimes even without being aware that we are performing them. Reflect on your own habits, good and bad, past and present. In your journal, list some of your habits, and describe the situations in which they arise and the patterns of behavior that characterize them.

What Shamu Taught Me About a Happy Marriage

As I wash dishes at the kitchen sink, my husband paces behind me, irritated. "Have you seen my keys?" he snarls, then huffs out a loud sigh and stomps from the room with our dog, Dixie, at his heels, anxious over her favorite human's upset. 1

In the past I would have been right behind Dixie. I would have turned off the faucet and joined the hunt while trying to soothe my husband with bromides like, "Don't worry, they'll turn up." But that only made him angrier, and a simple case of missing keys soon would become a full-blown angst-ridden drama starring the two of us and our poor nervous dog. 2

Now, I focus on the wet dish in my hands. I don't turn around. I don't say a word. I'm using a technique I learned from a dolphin trainer. 3

I love my husband. He's well read, adventurous and does a hysterical rendition of a northern Vermont accent that still cracks me up after 12 years of marriage. 4

But he also tends to be forgetful, and is often tardy and mercurial. He hovers around me in the kitchen asking if I read this or that piece in *The New Yorker* when I'm trying to concentrate on the simmering pans. He leaves wadded tissues in his wake. He suffers from serious bouts of spousal deafness 5 but never fails to hear me when I mutter to myself on the other side of the house. "What did you say?" he'll shout.

These minor annoyances are not the stuff of separation and divorce, but in sum they began to dull my love for Scott. I wanted—needed—to nudge him a little closer to perfect, to make him into a mate who might annoy me a little less, who wouldn't keep me waiting at restaurants, a mate who would be easier to love. 6

So, like many wives before me, I ignored a library of advice books and set about improving him. By nagging, of course, which only made his behavior worse: he'd drive faster instead of slower; shave less frequently, not more; and leave his reeking bike garb on the bedroom floor longer than ever. 7

We went to a counselor to smooth the edges off our marriage. She didn't understand what we were doing there and complimented us repeatedly on how well we communicated. I gave up. I guessed she was right—our union was better than most—and resigned myself to stretches of slow-boil resentment and occasional sarcasm. 8

Then something magical happened. For a book I was writing about a school for exotic animal trainers, I started commuting from Maine to California, where I spent my days watching students do the seemingly impossible: teaching hyenas to pirouette on command, cougars to offer their paws for a nail clipping, and baboons to skateboard. 9

I listened, rapt, as professional trainers explained how they taught dolphins to flip and elephants to paint. Eventually it hit me that the same techniques might work on that stubborn but lovable species, the American husband. 10

The central lesson I learned from exotic animal trainers is that I should reward behavior I like and ignore behavior I don't. After all, you don't get a sea lion to balance a ball on the end of its nose by nagging. The same goes for the American husband. 11

Back in Maine, I began thanking Scott if he threw one dirty shirt into the hamper. If he threw in two, I'd kiss him. Meanwhile, I would step over any soiled clothes on the floor without one sharp word, though I did sometimes kick them under the bed. But as he basked in my appreciation, the piles became smaller. 12

I was using what trainers call "approximations," rewarding the small steps toward learning a whole new behavior. You can't expect a baboon to learn to flip on command in one session, just as you can't expect an American husband to begin regularly picking up his dirty socks by praising him once for picking up a single sock. With the baboon you first reward a hop, then a bigger hop, then an even bigger hop. With Scott the husband, I began to praise every small act every time: if he drove just a mile an hour slower, tossed one pair of shorts into the hamper, or was on time for anything. 13

I also began to analyze my husband the way a trainer considers an exotic animal. Enlightened trainers learn all they can about a species, from anatomy 14 to social structure, to understand how it thinks, what it likes and dislikes, what comes easily to it and what doesn't. For example, an elephant is a herd animal, so it responds to hierarchy. It cannot jump, but can stand on its head. It is a vegetarian.

The exotic animal known as Scott is a loner, but an alpha male. So hierarchy matters, but being in a group doesn't so much. He has the balance of a gymnast, but moves slowly, especially when getting dressed. Skiing comes naturally, but being on time does not. He's an omnivore, and what a trainer would call food-driven. 15

Once I started thinking this way, I couldn't stop. At the school in California, I'd be scribbling notes on how to walk an emu or have a wolf accept you as a pack member, but I'd be thinking, "I can't wait to try this on Scott." 16

On a field trip with the students, I listened to a professional trainer describe how he had taught African crested cranes to stop landing on his head and shoulders. He did this by training the leggy birds to land on mats on the ground. This, he explained, is what is called an "incompatible behavior," a simple but brilliant concept. 17

Rather than teach the cranes to stop landing on him, the trainer taught the birds something else, a behavior that would make the undesirable behavior impossible. The birds couldn't alight on the mats and his head simultaneously. 18

At home, I came up with incompatible behaviors for Scott to keep him from crowding me while I cooked. To lure him away from the stove, I piled up parsley for him to chop or cheese for him to grate at the other end of the kitchen island. Or I'd set out a bowl of chips and salsa across the room. Soon I'd done it: no more Scott hovering around me while I cooked. 19

I followed the students to SeaWorld San Diego, where a dolphin trainer introduced me to least reinforcing syndrome (L. R. S.). When a dolphin does something wrong, the trainer doesn't respond in any way. He stands still for a few beats, careful not to look at the dolphin, and then returns to work. The idea is that any response, positive or negative, fuels a behavior. If a behavior provokes no response, it typically dies away. 20

In the margins of my notes I wrote, "Try on Scott!" 21

It was only a matter of time before he was again tearing around the house searching for his keys, at which point I said nothing and kept at what I was doing. It took a lot of discipline to maintain my calm, but results were immediate and stunning. His temper fell far shy of its usual pitch and then waned like a fast-moving storm. I felt as if I should throw him a mackerel. 22

Now he's at it again; I hear him banging a closet door shut, rustling through papers on a chest in the front hall and thumping upstairs. At the sink, I hold steady. Then, sure enough, all goes quiet. A moment later, he walks into the kitchen, keys in hand, and says calmly, "Found them." 23

Without turning, I call out, "Great, see you later." 24

Off he goes with our much-calmed pup. 25

After two years of exotic animal training, my marriage is far smoother, my husband much easier to love. I used to take his faults personally; his dirty clothes on the floor were an affront, a symbol of how he didn't care enough about me. But thinking of my husband as an exotic species gave me the distance I needed to consider our differences more objectively. 26

I adopted the trainers' motto: "It's never the animal's fault." When my training attempts failed, I didn't blame Scott. Rather, I brainstormed new strategies, thought up more incompatible behaviors and used smaller approximations. I dissected my own behavior, considered how my actions might inadvertently fuel his. I also accepted that some behaviors were too entrenched, too instinctive to train away. You can't stop a badger from digging, and you can't stop my husband from losing his wallet and keys. 27

Professionals talk of animals that understand training so well they eventually use it back on the trainer. My animal did the same. When the training techniques worked so beautifully, I couldn't resist telling my husband what I was up to. He wasn't offended, just amused. As I explained the techniques and terminology, he soaked it up. Far more than I realized. 28

Last fall, firmly in middle age, I learned that I needed braces. They were not only humiliating, but also excruciating. For weeks my gums, teeth, jaw and sinuses throbbed. I complained frequently and loudly. Scott assured me that I would become used to all the metal in my mouth. I did not. 29

One morning, as I launched into yet another tirade about how uncomfortable I was, Scott just looked at me blankly. He didn't say a word or acknowledge my rant in any way, not even with a nod. 30

I quickly ran out of steam and started to walk away. Then I realized what was happening, and I turned and asked, "Are you giving me an L.R.S.?" Silence. "You are, aren't you?" 31

He finally smiled, but his L.R.S. has already done the trick. He'd begun to train me, the American wife. 32

Questions for Close Reading

1. What is the selection's thesis? Locate the sentence(s) in which Sutherland states her main idea. If she doesn't state her thesis explicitly, express it in your own words.
2. Sutherland tries a couple of solutions to her problems with her husband before she starts using the behavioral techniques that are the main focus of the essay. What were these initial solutions, and why did they fail to improve her relationship with her husband?
3. What techniques for changing behavior did Sutherland learn from the animal trainers? How did she apply each of these techniques to her husband Scott's behavior?

4. Why did changing her husband's behavior improve Sutherland's marriage?
5. Refer to your dictionary as needed to define the following words used in the selection: *bromides* (paragraph 2), *angst* (2), *mercurial* (5), *reeking* (7), *pirouette* (9), *basked* (12), *hierarchy* (14), *alpha male* (15), *omnivore* (15), *emu* (16), *incompatible* (17), *provokes* (20), *affront* (26), *inadvertently* (27), and *tirade* (30).

Questions About the Writer's Craft

1. **The pattern.** What type of process analysis does Sutherland use in this essay? How does the first-person point of view support the pattern of development?
2. What is the tone of Sutherland's essay? What contributes to the tone?
3. **Other patterns.** What pattern of development, besides process analysis, helps organize this essay? What does the other pattern contribute to the essay?
4. Is Sutherland's conclusion effective? How does her conclusion change your response to the essay?

Writing Assignments Using Process Analysis as a Pattern of Development

1. In this essay, Sutherland describes how animal trainers teach cranes, dolphins, and other animals to behave in certain ways. Imagine turning this scenario around, and thinking of animals teaching their human masters how to behave. For example, a cat might train its owner to feed it at 5:00 a.m. by ceasing to howl the second her bowl of food is set on the floor. Write an essay from an animal's point of view in which you explain how the animal trains its human "master" to meet its needs.
2. The animal-training techniques Sutherland describes in this essay are similar to behavioral therapies used by psychologists and other mental health professionals to treat people for phobias, anxiety, and other disorders, and to change specific behaviors, like smoking and other undesirable habits. Do some research in the library and on the Internet about behavioral therapies. Select one type of behavioral therapy and write an essay explaining how it works. Give examples of its use in your essay.

Writing Assignments Combining Patterns of Development

3. Recent television shows have been devoted to showing viewers how to train animals—and even children. *Dog Whisperer,* starring Cesar Millan, and *Supernanny,* starring Jo Frost, are two examples of shows that feature an "expert" working with ordinary people who have agreed to be filmed. The point of these shows is to (entertainingly) train the adults as well as their pets and children. Watch one of these shows or video clips (you can do so on their websites), or another similar show of your choosing, and write an essay in which you explain the *processes* used to train the animals and their owners or the children and their parents. Then evaluate the show's techniques, and *argue* that the show does (or does not) present effective and humane methods of changing behaviors.

4. Sutherland's essay shows how irritating even the people we love can sometimes be. Select one of your own close relationships, and write an essay in which you *describe* what you find annoying about the other person. Give *examples* of the person's behavior to illustrate your points. What *effects* do this person's annoying traits have on the relationship as a whole? How would you change this person if you could? If you choose to write about a friend, read Alex Wright's "Friending, Ancient and Otherwise" (page 356) for some perspectives on friendship.

Writing Assignment Using a Journal Entry as a Starting Point

5. Review your pre-reading journal entry in which you listed and described some of your own habits. Choose one habit that you tried to break, successfully or not, and write an essay describing the habit and the steps you took to change your behavior. Before you write, decide on your purpose. For example, is your main purpose to inform others about a useful technique to change behavior or to entertain readers with a humorous narrative of your attempts to break a habit?

Paul Roberts

Paul Roberts (1917–67) was a scholar of linguistics and a respected teacher whose textbooks helped scores of high school and college students become better writers. Roberts's works include *English Syntax* (1954) and *Patterns of English* (1956). The following selection is from his best-known book, *Understanding English* (1958).

Pre-Reading Journal Entry

Many educators argue that first-year college students write bland essays because their high school English classes didn't teach them how to think clearly and creatively. Do you agree? Take some time to reflect in your journal about your best and worst high school English classes. For each class, focus on teaching style, classroom atmosphere, assignments, activities, and so on.

How to Say Nothing in 500 Words

Nothing About Something

1 It's Friday afternoon, and you have almost survived another week of classes. You are just looking forward dreamily to the weekend when the English instructor says: "For Monday you will turn in a five-hundred-word composition on college football."

2 Well, that puts a good big hole in the weekend. You don't have any strong views on college football one way or the other. You get rather excited during the season and go to all the home games and find it rather more fun than not. On the other hand, the class has been reading Robert Hutchins in the anthology and perhaps Shaw's "Eighty-Yard Run," and from the class discussion you have got the idea that the instructor thinks college football is for the birds. You are no fool, you. You can figure out what side to take.

3 After dinner you get out the portable typewriter that you got for high school graduation. You might as well get it over with and enjoy Saturday and Sunday. Five hundred words is about two double-spaced pages with normal margins. You put in a sheet of paper, think up a title, and you're off:

Why College Football Should Be Abolished

> 4 College football should be abolished because it's bad for the school and also bad for the players. The players are so busy practicing that they don't have any time for their studies.

5 This, you feel, is a mighty good start. The only trouble is that it's only thirty-two words. You still have four hundred and sixty-eight to go, and you've pretty well exhausted the subject. It comes to you that you do your

best thinking in the morning, so you put away the typewriter and go to the movies. But the next morning you have to do your washing and some math problems, and in the afternoon you go to the game. The English instructor turns up too, and you wonder if you've taken the right side after all. Saturday night you have a date, and Sunday morning you have to go to church. (You shouldn't let English assignments interfere with your religion.) What with one thing and another, it's ten o'clock Sunday night before you get out the typewriter again. You make a pot of coffee and start to fill out your views on college football. Put a little meat on the bones.

Why College Football Should Be Abolished

In my opinion, it seems to me that college football should be abolished. The reason why I think this to be true is because I feel that football is bad for the colleges in nearly every respect. As Robert Hutchins says in his article in our anthology in which he discusses college football, it would be better if the colleges had race horses and had races with one another, because then the horses would not have to attend classes. I firmly agree with Mr. Hutchins on this point, and I am sure that many other students would agree too. 6

One reason why it seems to me that college football is bad is that it has become too commercial. In the olden times when people played football just for the fun of it, maybe college football was all right, but they do not play football just for the fun of it now as they used to in the old days. Nowadays college football is what you might call a big business. Maybe this is not true at all schools, and I don't think it is especially true here at State, but certainly this is the case at most colleges and universities in America nowadays, as Mr. Hutchins points out in his very interesting article. Actually the coaches and alumni go around to the high schools and offer the high school stars large salaries to come to their colleges and play football for them. There was one case where a high school star was offered a convertible if he would play football for a certain college. 7

Another reason for abolishing college football is that it is bad for the players. They do not have time to get a college education, because they are so busy playing football. A football player has to practice every afternoon from three to six, and then he is so tired that he can't concentrate on his studies. He just feels like dropping off to sleep after dinner, and then the next day he goes to his classes without having studied and maybe he fails the test. 8

(Good ripe stuff so far, but you're still a hundred and fifty-one words from home. One more push.)

> Also I think college football is bad for the colleges and the universities because not very many students get to participate in it. Out of a college of ten thousand students only seventy-five or a hundred play football, if that many. Football is what you might call a spectator sport. That means that most people go to watch it but do not play it themselves. 9

(Four hundred and fifteen. Well, you still have the conclusion, and when you retype it, you can make the margins a little wider.)

> These are the reasons why I agree with Mr. Hutchins that college football should be abolished in American colleges and universities. 10

On Monday you turn it in, moderately hopeful, and on Friday it comes back marked "weak in content" and sporting a big "D." 11

This essay is exaggerated a little, not much. The English instructor will recognize it as reasonably typical of what an assignment on college football will bring in. He knows that nearly half of the class will contrive in five hundred words to say that college football is too commercial and bad for the players. Most of the other half will inform him that college football builds character and prepares one for life and brings prestige to the school. As he reads paper after paper all saying the same thing in almost the same words, all bloodless, five hundred words dripping out of nothing, he wonders how he allowed himself to get trapped into teaching English when he might have had a happy and interesting life as an electrician or a confidence man. 12

Well, you may ask, what can you do about it? The subject is one on which you have few convictions and little information. Can you be expected to make a dull subject interesting? As a matter of fact, this is precisely what you are expected to do. This is the writer's essential task. All subjects, except sex, are dull until somebody makes them interesting. The writer's job is to find the argument, the approach, the angle, the wording that will take the reader with him. This is seldom easy, and it is particularly hard in subjects that have been much discussed: College Football, Fraternities, Popular Music, Is Chivalry Dead?, and the like. You will feel that there is nothing you can do with such subjects except repeat the old bromides. But there are some things you can do which will make your papers, if not throbbingly alive, at least less insufferably tedious than they might otherwise be. 13

Avoid the Obvious Content

Say the assignment is college football. Say that you've decided to be against it. Begin by putting down the arguments that come to your mind: it is too commercial, it takes the students' minds off their studies, it is hard on 14 the players, it makes the university a kind of circus instead of an intellectual center, for most schools it is financially ruinous. Can you think of any more arguments just off hand? All right. Now when you write your paper, *make sure that you don't use any of the material on this list.* If these are the points that leap to your mind, they will leap to everyone else's too, and whether you get a "C" or a "D" may depend on whether the instructor reads your paper early when he is fresh and tolerant or late, when the sentence "In my opinion, college football has become too commercial," inexorably repeated, has brought him to the brink of lunacy.

Be against college football for some reason or reasons of your own. 15
If they are keen and perceptive ones, that's splendid. But even if they are trivial or foolish or indefensible, you are still ahead so long as they are not everybody else's reasons too. Be against it because the colleges don't spend enough money on it to make it worth while, because it is bad for the characters of the spectators, because the players are forced to attend classes, because the football stars hog all the beautiful women, because it competes with baseball and is therefore un-American and possibly Communist inspired. There are lots of more or less unused reasons for being against college football.

Sometimes it is a good idea to sum up and dispose of the trite and con- 16
ventional points before going on to your own. This has the advantage of indicating to the reader that you are going to be neither trite nor conventional. Something like this:

> We are often told that college football should be abolished because 17
> it has become too commercial or because it is bad for the players. These arguments are no doubt very cogent, but they don't really go to the heart of the matter.

Then you go to the heart of the matter.

Take the Less Usual Side

One rather simple way of getting interest into your paper is to take 18
the side of the argument that most of the citizens will want to avoid. If the assignment is an essay on dogs, you can, if you choose, explain that dogs are faithful and lovable companions, intelligent, useful as guardians of the house and protectors of children, indispensable in police work—in short, when all is said and done, man's best friends. Or you can suggest that those big brown eyes conceal, more often than not, a vacuity of mind and an inconstancy of purpose; that the dogs you have known most intimately have been mangy, ill-tempered brutes, incapable of instruction; and that only your nobility of mind and fear of arrest prevent you from kicking the flea-ridden animals when you pass them on the street.

Naturally, personal convictions will sometimes dictate your approach. If the assigned subject is "Is Methodism Rewarding to the Individual?" and you are a pious Methodist, you have really no choice. But few assigned subjects, if any, will fall in this category. Most of them will lie in broad areas of discussion with much to be said on both sides. They are intellectual exercises and it is legitimate to argue now one way and now another, as debaters do in similar circumstances. Always take the side that looks to you hardest, least defensible. It will almost always turn out to be easier to write interestingly on that side. 19

This general advice applies where you have a choice of subjects. If you are to choose among "The Value of Fraternities" and "My Favorite High School Teacher" and "What I Think About Beetles," by all means plump for the beetles. By the time the instructor gets to your paper, he will be up to his ears in tedious tales about the French teacher at Bloombury High and assertions about how fraternities build character and prepare one for life. Your views on beetles, whatever they are, are bound to be a refreshing change. 20

Don't worry too much about figuring out what the instructor thinks about the subject so that you can cuddle up with him. Chances are his views are no stronger than yours. If he does have convictions and you oppose them, his problem is to keep from grading you higher than you deserve in order to show he is not biased. This doesn't mean that you should always cantankerously dissent from what the instructor says; that gets tiresome too. And if the subject assigned is "My Pet Peeve," do not begin, "My pet peeve is the English instructor who assigns papers on 'my pet peeve.'" This was still funny during the War of 1812, but it has sort of lost its edge since then. It is in general good manners to avoid personalities. 21

Slip Out of Abstraction

If you will study the essay on college football...you will perceive that one reason for its appalling dullness is that it never gets down to particulars. It is just a series of not very glittering generalities: "football is bad for the colleges," "it has become too commercial," "football is a big business," "it is bad for the players," and so on. Such round phrases thudding against the reader's brain are unlikely to convince him, though they may well render him unconscious. 22

If you want the reader to believe that college football is bad for the players, you have to do more than say so. You have to display the evil. Take your roommate, Alfred Simkins, the second-string center. Picture poor old Alfy coming home from football practice every evening, bruised and aching, agonizingly tired, scarcely able to shovel the mashed potatoes into his mouth. Let us see him staggering up to the room, getting out his econ textbook, 23 peering desperately at it with his good eye, falling asleep and failing the test in the morning. Let us share his unbearable tension as Saturday draws near. Will he fail, be demoted, lose his monthly allowance, be forced to return to the coal mines? And if he succeeds, what will be his reward? Perhaps a slight ripple of applause when the third-string center replaces him, a moment of elation in the locker room if the team wins, of despair if it loses. What will he look back on when he graduates from college? Toil and torn ligaments. And what will be his future? He is not good enough for pro football, and he is too obscure and weak in econ to succeed in stocks and bonds. College football is tearing the heart from Alfy Simkins and, when it finishes with him, will callously toss aside the shattered hulk.

This is no doubt a weak enough argument for the abolition of college football, but it is a sight better than saying, in three or four variations, that college football (in your opinion) is bad for the players. 24

Look at the work of any professional writer and notice how constantly he is moving from the generality, the abstract statement, to the concrete example, the facts and figures, the illustration. If he is writing on juvenile delinquency, he does not just tell you that juveniles are (it seems to him) delinquent and that (in his opinion) something should be done about it. He shows you juveniles being delinquent, tearing up movie theatres in Buffalo, stabbing high school principals in Dallas, smoking marijuana in Palo Alto. And more than likely he is moving toward some specific remedy, not just a general wringing of the hands. 25

It is no doubt possible to be *too* concrete, too illustrative or anecdotal, but few inexperienced writers err this way. For most the soundest advice is to be seeking always for the picture, to be always turning general remarks into seeable examples. Don't say, "Sororities teach girls the social graces." Say "Sorority life teaches a girl how to carry on a conversation while pouring tea, without sloshing the tea into the saucer." Don't say, "I like certain kinds of popular music very much." Say, "Whenever I hear Gerber Spinklittle play 'Mississippi Man' on the trombone, my socks creep up my ankles." 26

Get Rid of Obvious Padding

The student toiling away at his weekly English theme is too often tormented by a figure: five hundred words. How, he asks himself, is he to achieve this staggering total? Obviously by never using one word when he can somehow work in ten. 27

He is therefore seldom content with a plain statement like "Fast driving is dangerous." This has only four words in it. He takes thought, and the sentence becomes: 28

In my opinion, fast driving is dangerous.

Better, but he can do better still:

> In my opinion, fast driving would seem to be rather dangerous.

If he is really adept, it may come out:

> In my humble opinion, though I do not claim to be an expert on this complicated subject, fast driving, in most circumstances, would seem to be rather dangerous in many respects, or at least so it would seem to me.

Thus four words have been turned into forty, and not an iota of content has been added.

Now this is a way to go about reaching five hundred words, and if you are content with a "D" grade, it is as good a way as any. But if you aim higher, you must work differently. Instead of stuffing your sentences with straw, you must try steadily to get rid of the padding, to make your sentences lean and tough. If you are really working at it, your first draft will greatly exceed the required total, and then you will work it down, thus: 29

> It is thought in some quarters that fraternities do not contribute as much as might be expected to campus life.
>
> Some people think that fraternities contribute little to campus life.

> The average doctor who practices in small towns or in the country must toil night and day to heal the sick.
>
> Most country doctors work long hours.

> When I was a little girl, I suffered from shyness and embarrassment in the presence of others.
>
> I was a shy little girl.

> It is absolutely necessary for the person employed as a marine fireman to give the matter of steam pressure his undivided attention at all times.
>
> The fireman has to keep his eye on the steam gauge.

You may ask how you can arrive at five hundred words at this rate. Simply. You dig up more real content. Instead of taking a couple of obvious points off the surface of the topic and then circling warily around them for six paragraphs, you work in and explore, figure out the details. You illustrate. You say that fast driving is dangerous, and then you prove 30 it. How long does it take to stop a car at forty and at eighty? How far can you see at night? What happens when a tire blows? What happens in a head-on collision at fifty miles an hour? Pretty soon your paper will be full of broken glass and blood and headless torsos, and reaching five hundred words will not really be a problem.

Call a Fool a Fool

Some of the padding in freshman themes is to be blamed not on anxiety about the word minimum but on excessive timidity. The student writes, "In my opinion, the principal of my high school acted in ways that I believe every unbiased person would have to call foolish." This isn't exactly what he means. What he means is, "My high school principal was a fool." If he was a fool, call him a fool. Hedging the thing about with "in-my-opinion's" and "it-seems-to-me's" and "as-I-see-it's" and "at-least-from-my-point-of-view's" gains you nothing. Delete these phrases whenever they creep into your paper. 31

The student's tendency to hedge stems from a modesty that in other circumstances would be commendable. He is, he realizes, young and inexperienced, and he half suspects that he is dopey and fuzzy-minded beyond the average. Probably only too true. But it doesn't help to announce your incompetence six times in every paragraph. Decide what you want to say and say it as vigorously as possible, without apology and in plain words. 32

Linguistic diffidence can take various forms. One is what we call *euphemism.* This is the tendency to call a spade "a certain garden implement" or women's underwear "unmentionables." It is stronger in some eras than others and in some people than others but it always operates more or less in subjects that are touchy or taboo: death, sex, madness, and so on. Thus we shrink from saying "He died last night" but say instead "passed away," "left us," "joined his Maker," "went to his reward." Or we try to take off the tension with a lighter cliché: "kicked the bucket," "cashed in his chips," "handed in his dinner pail." We have found all sorts of ways to avoid saying *mad:* "mentally ill," "touched," "not quite right upstairs," "feeble-minded," "innocent," "simple," "off his trolley," "not in his right mind." Even such a now plain word as *insane* began as a euphemism with the meaning "not healthy." 33

Modern science, particularly psychology, contributes many polysyllables in which we can wrap our thoughts and blunt their force. To many writers there is no such thing as a bad schoolboy. Schoolboys are maladjusted or unoriented or misunderstood or in need of guidance or lacking in continued success toward satisfactory integration of the personality as a social unit, but they are never bad. Psychology no doubt makes us better men or women, more sympathetic and tolerant, but it doesn't make writing any easier. Had Shakespeare been confronted with psychology, "To be or not to be" might 34 have come out, "To continue as a social unit or not to do so. That is the personality problem. Whether 'tis a better sign of integration at the conscious level to display a psychic tolerance toward the maladjustments and repressions induced by one's lack of orientation in one's environment or—" But Hamlet would never have finished the soliloquy.

Writing in the modern world, you cannot altogether avoid modern jargon. Nor, in an effort to get away from euphemism, should you salt your paper with four-letter words. But you can do much if you will mount guard against those roundabout phrases, those echoing polysyllables that tend to slip into your writing to rob it of its crispness and force. 35

Beware of the Pat Expression

Other things being equal, avoid phrases like "other things being equal." Those sentences that come to you whole, or in two or three doughy lumps, are sure to be bad sentences. They are no creation of yours but pieces of common thought floating in the community soup. 36

Pat expressions are hard, often impossible, to avoid, because they come too easily to be noticed and seem too necessary to be dispensed with. No writer avoids them altogether, but good writers avoid them more often than poor writers. 37

By "pat expressions" we mean such tags as "to all practical intents and purposes," "the pure and simple truth," "from where I sit," "the time of his life," "to the ends of the earth," "in the twinkling of an eye," "as sure as you're born," "over my dead body," "under cover of darkness," "took the easy way out," "when all is said and done," "told him time and time again," "parted the best of friends," "stand up and be counted," "gave him the best years of her life," "worked her fingers to the bone." Like other clichés, these expressions were once forceful. Now we should use them only when we can't possibly think of anything else. 38

Some pat expressions stand like a wall between the writer and thought. Such a one is "the American way of life." Many student writers feel that when they have said that something accords with the American way of life or does not they have exhausted the subject. Actually, they have stopped at the highest level of abstraction. The American way of life is the complicated set of bonds between a hundred and eighty million ways. All of us know this when we think about it, but the tag phrase too often keeps us from thinking about it. 39

So with many another phrase dear to the politician: "this great land of ours," "the man in the street," "our national heritage." These may prove our patriotism or give a clue to our political beliefs, but otherwise they add nothing to the paper except words. 40

Colorful Words

The writer builds with words, and no builder uses a raw material more slippery and elusive and treacherous. A writer's work is a constant struggle to get the right word in the right place, to find that particular word that will convey his meaning exactly, that will persuade the reader or soothe him or startle or amuse him. He never succeeds altogether—sometimes he feels that he scarcely succeeds at all—but such successes as he has are what make the thing worth doing. 41

There is no book of rules for this game. One progresses through ever-lasting experiment on the basis of ever-widening experience. There are few useful generalizations that one can make about words as words, but there are perhaps a few. 42

Some words are what we call "colorful." By this we mean that they are calculated to produce a picture or induce an emotion. They are dressy instead of plain, specific instead of general, loud instead of soft. Thus, in place of "Her heart beat," we may write "Her heart *pounded, throbbed, fluttered, danced.*" Instead of "He sat in his chair," we may say, "He *lounged, sprawled, coiled.*" Instead of "It was hot," we may say, "It was *blistering, sultry, muggy, suffocating, steamy, wilting.*" 43

However, it should not be supposed that the fancy word is always better. Often it is as well to write "Her heart beat" or "It was hot" if that is all it did or all it was. Ages differ in how they like their prose. The nineteenth century liked it rich and smoky. The twentieth has usually preferred it lean and cool. The twentieth-century writer, like all writers, is forever seeking the exact word, but he is wary of sounding feverish. He tends to pitch it low, to understate it, to throw it away. He knows that if he gets too colorful, the audience is likely to giggle. 44

See how this strikes you: "As the rich, golden glow of the sunset died away along the eternal western hills, Angela's limpid blue eyes looked softly and trustingly into Montague's flashing brown ones, and her heart pounded like a drum in time with the joyous song surging in her soul." Some people like that sort of thing, but most modern readers would say, "Good grief," and turn on the television. 45

Colored Words

Some words we would call not so much colorful as colored—that is, loaded with associations, good or bad. All words—except perhaps structure words—have associations of some sort. We have said that the meaning of a word is the sum of the contexts in which it occurs. When we hear a word, we hear with it an echo of all the situations in which we have heard it before. 46

In some words, these echoes are obvious and discussable. The word *mother*, for example, has, for most people, agreeable associations. When you 47 hear *mother* you probably think of home, safety, love, food, and various other pleasant things. If one writes, "She was like a mother to me," he gets an effect which he would not get in "She was like an aunt to me." The advertiser makes use of the associations of *mother* by working it in when he talks about his product. The politician works it in when he talks about himself.

So also with such words as *home, liberty, fireside, contentment, patriot, tenderness, sacrifice, childlike, manly, bluff, limpid.* All of these words are loaded with favorable associations that would be rather hard to indicate in a straightforward definition. There is more than a literal difference between "They sat around the fireside" and "They sat around the stove." They might have been equally warm and happy around the stove, but *fireside* suggests leisure, grace, quiet tradition, congenial company, and *stove* does not. 48

Conversely, some words have bad associations. *Mother* suggests pleasant things, but *mother-in-law* does not. Many mothers-in-law are heroically lovable and some mothers drink gin all day and beat their children insensible, but these facts of life are beside the point. The thing is that *mother* sounds good and *mother-in-law* does not. 49

Or consider the word *intellectual.* This would seem to be a complimentary term, but in point of fact it is not, for it has picked up associations of impracticality and ineffectuality and general dopiness. So also with such words as *liberal, reactionary, Communist, socialist, capitalist, radical, schoolteacher, truck driver, undertaker, operator, salesman, huckster, speculator.* These convey meanings on the literal level, but beyond that—sometimes, in some places—they convey contempt on the part of the speaker. 50

The question of whether to use loaded words or not depends on what is being written. The scientist, the scholar, try to avoid them; for the poet, the advertising writer, the public speaker, they are standard equipment. But every writer should take care that they do not substitute for thought. If you write, "Anyone who thinks that is nothing but a Socialist (or Communist or capitalist)," you have said nothing except that you don't like people who think that, and such remarks are effective only with the most naïve readers. It is always a bad mistake to think your readers more naïve than they really are. 51

Colorless Words

But probably most student writers come to grief not with words that are colorful or those that are colored but with those that have no color at all. A pet example is *nice,* a word we would find it hard to dispense with in casual conversation but which is no longer capable of adding much to a description. Colorless words are those of such general meaning that in a particular sentence they mean nothing. Slang adjectives, like *cool* ("That's real cool") tend to explode all over the language. They are applied to everything, lose their original force, and quickly die. 52

Beware also of nouns of very general meaning, like *circumstances, cases,* 53
instances, aspects, factors, relationships, attitudes, eventualities, etc. In most circumstances you will find that those cases of writing which contain too many instances of words like these will in this and other aspects have factors leading to unsatisfactory relationships with the reader resulting in unfavorable attitudes on his part and perhaps other eventualities, like a grade of "D." Notice also what "etc." means. It means "I'd like to make this list longer, but I can't think of any more examples."

Questions for Close Reading

1. What is the selection's thesis? Locate the sentence(s) in which Roberts states his main idea. If he doesn't state the thesis explicitly, express it in your own words.
2. According to Roberts, what do students assume they have to do to get a good grade on an English composition?
3. How do "colorful words," "colored words," and "colorless words" differ? Which should be used in essay writing? Why?
4. What are Roberts's most important pieces of advice for the student writer?
5. Refer to the dictionary as needed to define the following words used in the selection: *bromides* (paragraph 13), *insufferably* (13), *inexorably* (14), *dissent* (21), *abolition* (24), *adept* (28), *euphemism* (33), and *insensible* (49)

Questions About the Writer's Craft

1. **The pattern.** What two processes does Roberts analyze in this essay? Is each process informational, directional, or a combination of the two?
2. Why do you think Roberts uses the second person "you" throughout the essay? How does this choice of point of view affect your response to the essay?
3. What is Roberts's tone in the essay? Find some typical examples of his tone. How does Roberts achieve this tone? Considering the author's intended audience, is this tone a good choice? Explain.
4. Does Roberts "practice what he preaches" about writing? Review the section headings of the essay and find examples of each piece of advice in the essay.

Writing Assignments Using Process Analysis as a Pattern of Development

1. Write a humorous essay showing how to avoid doing schoolwork, household chores, or anything else most people tend to put off. You may use the second person as Roberts does. Or you may use the first person and describe your typical method of avoidance. Before writing, read Ann Sutherland's "What Shamu Taught Me About a Happy Marriage" (page 308), a humorous model for how-to guides.
2. Borrowing some of Roberts's lively techniques, make a routine, predictable process interesting to read about. You might choose an activity such as how to register to vote, apply for a driver's license, sign up for college courses, take care

of laundry, play a simple game, study for an exam, or execute some other familiar process. Caroline Rego's "The Fine Art of Complaining" (page 327) may give you some ideas on how to explain a process in a helpful yet entertaining way.

Writing Assignments Combining Patterns of Development

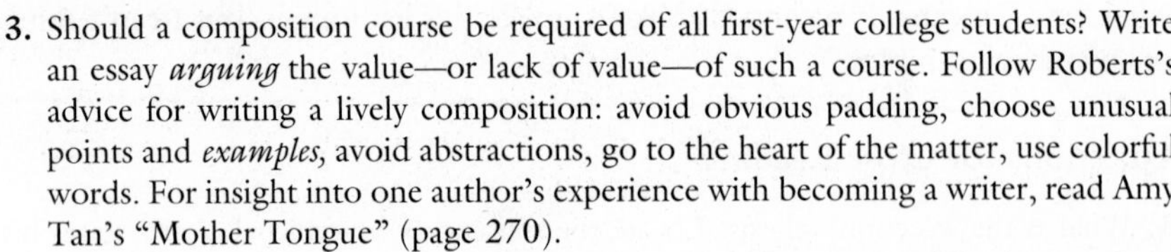

3. Should a composition course be required of all first-year college students? Write an essay *arguing* the value—or lack of value—of such a course. Follow Roberts's advice for writing a lively composition: avoid obvious padding, choose unusual points and *examples,* avoid abstractions, go to the heart of the matter, use colorful words. For insight into one author's experience with becoming a writer, read Amy Tan's "Mother Tongue" (page 270).
4. Write a paper detailing your experiences as a student in English classes—from elementary school up to now. Using several *examples, describe* how successfully or unsuccessfully English has been taught, and recommend any specific reforms or changes you feel are needed.

Writing Assignment Using a Journal Entry as a Starting Point

5. Write an essay describing an ideal high school English class. What kind of teacher would be at the helm? What kind of learning atmosphere would prevail? What sorts of skills would be covered? How? To formulate your position, review your pre-reading journal entry, drawing upon your experiences as a guide. End the essay by briefly discussing the factors that might prevent English classes from being like the ideal one you've described. To broaden your perspective on the issues involved, consider discussing the topic with friends and classmates.

Caroline Rego

Caroline Rego was born in 1950 in Edmond, Oklahoma. A graduate of the University of Oklahoma, she began her journalistic career as a police reporter for a daily newspaper in Montana. Later, while filling in for a vacationing colleague in the features section of another newspaper, she found her true calling: writing consumer-affairs articles that teach readers how to protect themselves against shoddy service, dangerous products, and inefficiency. A sought-after public speaker, Rego talks frequently to students and community groups on strategies for becoming an informed consumer. The following selection is part of a work in progress on consumer empowerment.

Pre-Reading Journal Entry

When you're disappointed with someone or something, how do you typically react—passively, assertively, or in some other way? In your journal, list a few disappointments you've experienced. How did you respond on each occasion? In retrospect, are you happy with your responses? Why or why not?

The Fine Art of Complaining

You waited forty-five minutes for your dinner, and when it came it was cold—and not what you ordered in the first place. You washed your supposedly machine-washable, preshrunk T-shirt (the one the catalogue claimed was "indestructible"), and now it's the size of a napkin. Your new car broke down a month after you bought it, and the dealer says the warranty doesn't apply. 1

Life's annoyances descend on all of us—some pattering down like gentle raindrops, others striking with the bruising force of hailstones. We dodge the ones we can, but inevitably, plenty of them make contact. And when they do, we react fairly predictably. Many of us—most of us, probably—grumble to ourselves and take it. We scowl at our unappetizing food but choke it down. We stash the shrunken T-shirt in a drawer, vowing never again to order from a catalogue. We glare fiercely at our checkbooks as we pay for repairs that should have been free. 2

A few of us go to the other extreme. Taking our cue from the crazed newscaster in the 1976 movie *Network,* we go through life mad as hell and unwilling to take it anymore. In offices, we shout at hapless receptionists when we're kept waiting for appointments. In restaurants, we make scenes that have fellow patrons craning their necks to get a look at us. In stores, we argue with salespeople for not waiting on us. We may notice after a while that our friends seem reluctant to venture into public with us, but hey—we're just standing up for our rights. Being a patsy doesn't get you anywhere in life. 3

It's true—milquetoasts live unsatisfying lives. However, people who go through the day in an eye-popping, vein-throbbing state of apoplectic rage don't win any prizes either. What persons at both ends of the scale need—what could empower the silent sufferer and civilize the Neanderthal—is a course in the gentle art of *effective* complaining. 4

Effective complaining is not apologetic and half-hearted. It's not making one awkward attempt at protest—"Uh, excuse me, I don't think I ordered the squid and onions"—and then slinking away in defeat. But neither is it roaring away indiscriminately, attempting to get satisfaction through the sheer volume of our complaint. 5

Effective complainers are people who act businesslike and important. Acting important doesn't mean puffing up your chest and saying, "Do you know who I am?"—an approach that would tempt anyone to take you down a peg or two. It doesn't mean shouting and threatening—techniques that will only antagonize the person whose help you need. It *does* mean making it clear that you know your request is reasonable and that you are confident it will be taken care of. People are generally treated the way they expect to be treated. If you act like someone making a fair request, chances are that request will be granted. Don't beg, don't explain. Just state your name, the problem, and what you expect to have done. Remain polite. But be firm. "My car has been in your garage for three days, and a mechanic hasn't even looked at it yet," you might say. "I want to know when it is going to be worked on." Period. Now it is up to them to give you a satisfactory response. Don't say, "Sorry to bother you about this, but..." or "I, uh, was sort of expecting...." You're only asking people to remedy a problem, after all; that is not grounds for apology. 6

If your problem requires an immediate response, try to make your complaint in person; a real, live, in-the-flesh individual has to be dealt with in some way. Complaining over the telephone, by contrast, is much less effective. When you speak to a disembodied voice, when the person at the other end of the line doesn't have to face you, you're more likely to get a runaround. 7

Most importantly, complain to the right person. One of the greatest frustrations in complaining is talking to a clerk or receptionist who cannot solve your problem and whose only purpose seems to be to drive you crazy. Getting mad doesn't help; the person you're mad at probably had nothing to do with your actual problem. And you'll have to repeat everything you've said to the clerk once you're passed along to the appropriate person. So make sure from the start that you're talking to someone who can help—a manager or supervisor. 8

If your problem doesn't require an immediate response, complaining by letter is probably the most effective way to get what you want. A letter of complaint should be brief, businesslike, and to the point. If you have a new vacuum cleaner that doesn't work, don't spend a paragraph describing how your Uncle Joe tried to fix the problem and couldn't. As when complaining 9 in person, be sure you address someone in a position of real authority. Here's an example of an effective letter of complaint.

Ms. Anne Lublin 10
Manager
Mitchell Appliances
80 Front Street
Newton, MA 02159

Dear Ms. Lublin: 11

First section: Explain the problem. Include facts to back up your story. 12

On August 6, I purchased a new Perma-Kool freezer from your store (a copy of 13
my sales receipt is enclosed). In the two weeks I have owned the freezer, I have had to call your repair department three times in an attempt to get it running properly. The freezer ran normally when it was installed, but since then it has repeatedly turned off, causing the food inside to spoil. My calls to your repair department have not been responded to promptly. After I called the first time, on August 10, I waited two days for the repair person to show up. It took three days to get a repair person here after my second call, on August 15. The freezer stopped yet again on August 20. I called to discuss this recent problem, but no one has responded to my call.

Second section: Tell how you trust the company and are confident that your reader 14
will fix the problem. This is to "soften up" the reader a bit.

I am surprised to receive such unprofessional service and poor quality from 15
Mitchell Appliances since I have been one of your satisfied customers for fifteen years. In the past, I have purchased a television, air conditioner, and washing machine from your company. I know that you value good relations with your customers, and I'm sure you want to see me pleased with my most recent purchase.

Third section: Explain exactly what you want to be done—repair, replacement, 16
refund, etc.

Although your repair department initially thought that the freezer needed only 17
some minor adjustments, the fact that no one has been able to permanently fix the problem convinces me that the freezer has some serious defect. I am understandably unwilling to spend any more time having repairs made. Therefore, I expect you to exchange the freezer for an identical model by the end of this week (August 30). Please call me to arrange for the removal of the defective freezer and the delivery of the new one.

Sincerely, 18

Janice Becker

P.S. (Readers always notice a P.S.) State again when you expect the problem to be taken care of, and what you will do if it isn't. 19

P.S. I am confident that we can resolve this problem by August 30. If the defective freezer is not replaced by then, however, I will report this incident to the Better Business Bureau. 20

Notice that the P.S. says what you'll do if your problem isn't solved. In other words, you make a threat—a polite threat. Your threat must be reasonable and believable. A threat to burn down the store if your purchase price isn't refunded is neither reasonable nor believable—or if it *were* believed, you could end up in jail. A threat to report the store to a consumer-protection agency, such as the Better Business Bureau, however, is credible. 21

Don't be too quick to make one of the most common—and commonly empty—threats: "I'll sue!" A full-blown lawsuit is more trouble, and more expensive, than most problems are worth. On the other hand, most areas have a small-claims court where suits involving modest amounts of money are heard. These courts don't use complex legal language or procedures, and you don't need a lawyer to use them. A store or company will often settle with you—if your claim is fair—rather than go to small-claims court. 22

Whether you complain over the phone, in person, or by letter, be persistent. One complaint may not get results. In that case, keep on complaining, and make sure you keep complaining to the same person. Chances are he or she will get worn out and take care of the situation, if only to be rid of you. 23

Someday, perhaps, the world will be free of the petty annoyances that plague us all from time to time. Until then, however, toasters will break down, stores will refuse to honor rainchecks, and bills will include items that were never purchased. You can depend upon it—there will be grounds for complaint. You might as well learn to be good at it. 24

Questions for Close Reading

1. What is the selection's thesis? Locate the sentence(s) in which Rego states her main idea. If she doesn't state the thesis explicitly, express it in your own words.
2. In Rego's opinion, what types of actions and statements are *not* helpful when making a complaint?
3. What should be included in a letter of complaint? What should be omitted?
4. What does Rego suggest doing if a complaint is ignored?
5. Refer to your dictionary as needed to define the following words used in the selection: *hapless* (paragraph 3), *venture* (3), *patsy* (3), *milquetoasts* (4), *apoplectic* (4), *Neanderthal* (4), *indiscriminately* (5), *disembodied* (7), and *credible* (21).

Questions About the Writer's Craft

1. **The pattern.** Is Rego's process analysis primarily directional or primarily informational? Explain. To what extent does Rego try to persuade readers to follow her process?
2. **Other patterns.** Where does Rego include *narrative* elements in her essay? What do these brief narratives add to the piece?
3. **Other patterns.** Numerous oppositions occur throughout the essay. How do these *contrasts* enliven the essay and help Rego persuade readers to adopt her suggestions?
4. Reread the essay, noting where Rego shifts point of view. Where does she use the second-person (*you*), the first-person-plural (*we*), and the third-person-plural (*they*) points of view? How does her use of multiple points of view add to the essay's effectiveness?

Writing Assignments Using Process Analysis as a Pattern of Development

1. Write an essay explaining to college students how to register—with someone in a position of authority—an effective complaint about a campus problem. You could show, for example, how to complain to a professor about a course's grading policy, to the bookstore manager about the markup on textbooks, to security about the poorly maintained college parking lots. Feel free to adapt some of Rego's recommendations, but be sure to invent several strategies of your own. In either case, provide—as Rego does—lively examples to illustrate the step-by-step procedure for registering an effective complaint with a specific authority figure on campus.
2. Rego argues that "people who go through the day in an eye-popping, vein-throbbing state of apoplectic rage don't win any prizes." But sometimes, getting mad can be appropriate—even productive. Write an essay explaining the best process for expressing anger effectively. Explain how to vent emotion safely, communicate the complaint in a nonthreatening way, encourage more honest interaction, and prompt change for the better. Illustrate the process by drawing upon your own experiences and observations. Consider reading James Gleick's "Life As Type A" (page 455), which addresses the origins of high-intensity behavior.

Writing Assignments Combining Patterns of Development

3. Think about a service or product that failed to live up to your expectations. Perhaps you were disgruntled about your mechanic's car repair, a store's return policy, or a hotel's accommodations. Using Rego's suggestions, write a letter of complaint in which you *describe* the problem, convey confidence in the reader's ability to resolve the problem, and state your request for specific action. Remember that a firm but cordial tone will *persuade* your reader that you have legitimate grounds for seeking the resolution you propose.

4. Rego shows that events often don't turn out as we had hoped. In an essay, *contrast* how you thought a specific situation would be with the way it actually turned out. Was the unexpected outcome better or worse than what you had expected? Did you have trouble adjusting, or did you adapt with surprising ease? Provide vivid *specifics* about the unforeseen turn of events and your *reaction* to it. Before writing, you might read Audre Lorde's "The Fourth of July" (page 140) and Richard Rodriguez's "Workers" (page 361), two professional writers' accounts of experiences that dramatically departed from their expectations.

Writing Assignment Using a Journal Entry as a Starting Point

5. Write an essay contrasting the way you reacted to a specific disappointment with the way you wish you had reacted. Reread your pre-reading journal entry, and select *one* incident that illustrates this discrepancy most dramatically. Use vigorous narrative details to make the contrast vivid and real. In your conclusion, indicate what you've learned in hindsight. Before writing, consider reading three other essays that document personal reactions to life's minor—and major—calamities: Langston Hughes's "Salvation" (page 158), Barbara Ehrenreich's "Serving in Florida" (page 162), and Beth Johnson's "Bombs Bursting in Air" (page 211).

Additional Writing Topics

PROCESS ANALYSIS

General Assignments

Develop one of the following topics through process analysis. Explain the process one step at a time, organizing the steps chronologically. If there's no agreed-on sequence, design your own series of steps. Use transitions to ease the audience through the steps in the process. You may use any tone you wish, from serious to light.

Directional: How to Do Something

1. How to improve a course you have taken
2. How to drive defensively
3. How to get away with ___________
4. How to succeed at a job interview
5. How to relax
6. How to show appreciation to others
7. How to get through school despite personal problems
8. How to be a responsible pet owner
9. How to conduct a garage or yard sale
10. How to look fashionable on a limited budget
11. How to protect a home from burglars
12. How to meet more people
13. How to improve the place where you work
14. How to gain or lose weight
15. How to get over a disappointment

Informational: How Something Happens

1. How a student becomes burned out
2. How a library's computerized catalog organizes books
3. How a dead thing decays (or how some other natural process works)
4. How the college registration process works
5. How *Homo sapiens* chooses a mate
6. How a DVD player (or some other machine) works
7. How a bad habit develops
8. How people fall into debt
9. How someone becomes an Internet addict/junkie
10. How a child develops a love of reading

Assignments with a Specific Purpose, Audience, and Point of View

On Campus

1. As an experienced campus tour guide for prospective students, you've been asked by your school's Admissions Office to write a pamphlet explaining to new tour guides how to conduct a tour of your school's campus. When explaining the process, keep in mind that tour guides need to portray the school in its best light.
2. You write an "advice to the lovelorn" column for the campus newspaper. A correspondent writes saying that he or she wants to break up with a steady girlfriend/boyfriend but doesn't know how to do this without hurting the person. Give the writer guidance on how to end a meaningful relationship with a minimal amount of pain.

At Home or in the Community

3. To help a sixteen-year-old friend learn how to drive, explain a specific driving maneuver one step at a time. You might, for example, describe how to make a three-point turn, parallel park, or handle a skid. Remember, your friend lacks self-confidence and experience.
4. Your best friend plans to move into his or her own apartment but doesn't know the first thing about how to choose one. Explain the process of selecting an apartment—where to look, what to investigate, what questions to ask before signing a lease.

On the Job

5. As a staff writer for a consumer magazine, you've been asked to write an article on how to shop for a certain product. Give specific steps explaining how to save money, buy a quality product, and the like.
6. An author of books for elementary school children, you want to show children how to do something—take care of a pet, get along with siblings, keep a room clean. Explain the process in terms a child would understand yet not find condescending.

Percy Ryall/Alamy

8

COMPARISON-CONTRAST

WHAT IS COMPARISON-CONTRAST?

Seeing how things are alike (comparing) and how they are different (contrasting) helps us impose meaning on experiences that otherwise might remain fragmented and disconnected. Barely aware that we're comparing and contrasting, we may think, "I woke up in a great mood this morning, but now I feel uneasy and anxious. I wonder why I feel so different." This inner questioning, which may occur in a flash, is just one example of how we use comparison and contrast to understand ourselves and our world.

Comparing and contrasting also help us make choices. We compare and contrast everything—from two brands of soap we might buy to two colleges we might attend. We listen to a favorite radio station, watch a preferred nightly news show, select a particular dessert from a menu—all because we have done some degree of comparing and contrasting. We often weigh these alternatives in an unstudied, casual manner, as when we flip from one radio station to another. But when we have to make important decisions, we tend to think rigorously about how things are alike or different: Should I live in a dorm or rent an apartment? Should I accept the higher-paying job or the lower-paying one that offers more challenges? Such a deliberate approach to comparison-contrast may also provide us with needed insight into complex contemporary issues: Is television's coverage of political campaigns more or less objective than it used to be? What are the merits of the various positions on abortion?

HOW COMPARISON-CONTRAST FITS YOUR PURPOSE AND AUDIENCE

Comparison-contrast works well if you want to demonstrate any of the following: (1) that one thing is better than another (the first example below); (2) that things which seem different are actually alike (the second example below); (3) that things which seem alike are actually different (the third example below).

> Compare and contrast the way male and female relationships are depicted in *Cosmopolitan, Ms., Playboy,* and *Esquire.* Which publication has the most limited view of men and women? Which has the broadest perspective?
>
> Football, basketball, and baseball differ in how they appeal to fans. Describe the unique drawing power of each sport, but also reach some conclusions about the appeals the three sports have in common.
>
> Studies show that both college students and their parents feel that post-secondary education should equip young people to succeed in the marketplace. Yet the same studies report that the two groups have a very different understanding of what it means to succeed. What differences do you think the studies identify?

Other assignments will, in less obvious ways, lend themselves to comparison-contrast. For instance, although terms like *compare, contrast, differ,* and *have in common* don't appear in the following assignments, essay responses could be organized around the comparison-contrast format:

> The emergence of the two-career family is one of the major phenomena of our culture. Discuss the advantages and disadvantages of having both parents work, showing how you feel about such two-career households.
>
> Some people believe that the 1950s, often called the golden age of television, produced several never-to-be-equaled comedy classics. Do you agree that such shows as *I Love Lucy* and *The Honeymooners* are superior to the situation comedies aired on television today?
>
> There has been considerable criticism recently of the news coverage by the city's two leading newspapers, *The Herald* and *The Beacon.* Indicate whether you think the criticism is valid by discussing the similarities and differences in the two papers' news coverage.

Note: The last assignment shows that a comparison-contrast essay may cover similarities *and* differences, not just one or the other.

As you have seen, comparison-contrast can be the key strategy for achieving an essay's purpose. But comparison-contrast can also be a supplemental method used to help make a point in an essay organized chiefly around another pattern of development. A serious, informative essay intended for laypeople might *define* clinical depression by contrasting that state of mind with ordinary run-of-the-mill blues. Writing humorously about the exhausting *effects* of trying to get in shape, you might dramatize your plight for readers by contrasting the leisurely way you used to spend your day with your current rigidly compulsive exercise regimen. Or, in an urgent *argumentation-persuasion* essay on the need for stricter controls over drug abuse in the workplace, you might provide readers with background by comparing several companies' approaches to the problem.

At this point, you have a good sense of the way writers use comparison-contrast to achieve their purpose and to connect with their readers. Now take a moment to look closely at the photograph at the beginning of this chapter. Imagine you're writing a blog entry for a consumer advocacy website. Jot down some phrases you might use when *comparing* and/or *contrasting* the vehicles in this picture, with the end of recommending one over the other.

SUGGESTIONS FOR USING COMPARISON-CONTRAST IN AN ESSAY

The suggestions here and in Figure 8.1 (page 338) will be helpful whether you use comparison-contrast as a dominant or a supportive pattern of development.

1. Be sure your subjects are at least somewhat alike. Unless you plan to develop an *analogy* (see below), the subjects you choose to compare or contrast should share some obvious characteristics or qualities. It makes sense to compare different parts of the country, two comedians, or several college teachers. But a reasonable paper wouldn't result from, let's say, a comparison of a television game show with a soap opera. Your subjects must belong

FIGURE 8.1
Development Diagram: Writing a Comparison-Contrast Essay

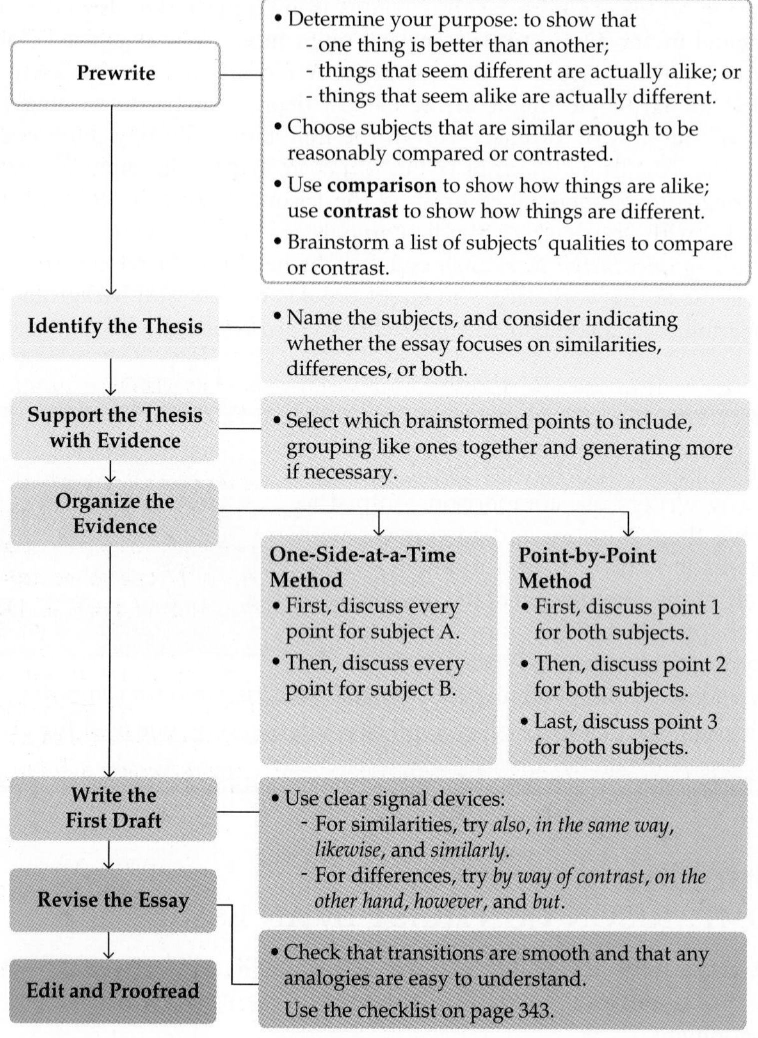

to the same general group so that your comparison-contrast stays within good logical bounds and doesn't veer off into pointlessness.

Prewrite
• Determine your purpose: to show that
- one thing is better than another;
- things that seem different are actually alike; or
- things that seem alike are actually different.
• Choose subjects that are similar enough to be reasonably compared or contrasted.
• Use comparison to show how things are alike; use contrast to show how things are different.
• Brainstorm a list of subjects' qualities to compare or contrast.
Identify the Thesis
• Name the subjects, and consider indicating whether the essay focuses on similarities, differences, or both.
Support the Thesis with Evidence
• Select which brainstormed points to include, grouping like ones together and generating more if necessary.
Organize the Evidence
One-Side-at-a-Time Method
• First, discuss every point for subject A.
• Then, discuss every point for subject B.
Point-by-Point Method
• First, discuss point 1 for both subjects.
• Then, discuss point 2 for both subjects.
• Last, discuss point 3 for both subjects.
Write the First Draft
• Use clear signal devices:
- For similarities, try also, in the same way, likewise, and similarly.
- For differences, try by way of contrast, on the other hand, however, and but.
Revise the Essay
Edit and Proofread
• Check that transitions are smooth and that any analogies are easy to understand.
Use the checklist on page 343.

2. Stay focused on your purpose. When writing, remember that comparison-contrast isn't an end in itself. That is, your objective isn't to turn an essay into a mechanical list of "how A differs from B" or "how A is like B." Like the other patterns of development discussed in this book, comparison-contrast is a strategy for making a point or meeting a larger purpose.

Consider the assignment on page 336 about the two newspapers. Your purpose here might be simply to *inform,* to present information as objectively as possible: "This is what *The Herald*'s news coverage is like. This is what *The Beacon*'s news coverage is like."

More frequently, though, you'll use comparison-contrast to *evaluate* your subjects' pros and cons, your goal being to reach a conclusion or make a judgment: "Both *The Herald* and *The Beacon* spend too much time reporting local news," or "*The Herald*'s analysis of the recent hostage crisis was more insightful than *The Beacon*'s." Comparison-contrast can also be used to *persuade* readers to take action: "People interested in thorough coverage of international events should read *The Herald* rather than *The Beacon.*" Persuasive essays may also propose a change, contrasting what now exists with a more ideal situation: "For *The Beacon* to compete with *The Herald,* it must assign more reporters to international stories."

Yet another purpose you might have is to *clear up misconceptions* by revealing previously hidden similarities or differences. For example, perhaps your town's two newspapers are thought to be sharply different. A comparison-contrast analysis might reveal that—although one paper specializes in sensationalized stories while the other adopts a more muted approach—both resort to biased, emotionally charged analyses of local politics.

Comparing and contrasting also make it possible to *draw an analogy* between two seemingly unrelated subjects. An analogy is an imaginative comparison that delves beneath the surface differences of subjects in order to expose their significant and often unsuspected similarities or differences. Your purpose may be to show that singles bars and zoos share a number of striking similarities. The analogical approach can make a complex subject easier to understand—as when the national deficit is compared to a household budget gone awry.

3. Formulate a strong thesis. Your essay should be focused by a solid thesis. Besides revealing your attitude, the thesis may do the following:

- Name the subjects being compared and contrasted.
- Indicate whether the essay focuses on the subjects' similarities, differences, or both.
- State the essay's main point of comparison or contrast.

Not all comparison-contrast essays need thesis statements as structured as those that follow. Even so, these examples can serve as models of clarity.

Note that the first thesis statement signals similarities, the second differences, and the last both similarities and differences:

Middle-aged parents are often in a good position to empathize with adolescent children because the emotional upheavals experienced by the two age groups are much the same.

The priorities of most retired people are more conducive to health and happiness than the priorities of most young professionals.

College students in their thirties and forties face many of the same pressures as younger students, but they are better equipped to withstand these pressures.

4. Select the points to be discussed. Once you have identified the essay's subjects, purpose, and thesis, you need to decide which aspects of the subjects to compare or contrast. College professors, for instance, could be compared and contrasted on the basis of their testing methods, ability to motivate students, confidence in front of a classroom, personalities, level of enthusiasm, and so forth.

Brainstorming, freewriting, and mapping are valuable for gathering possible points to cover. Whichever prewriting technique you use, try to produce more raw material than you'll need, so that you have the luxury of narrowing the material down to the most significant points.

When selecting points to cover, be sure to consider your audience. Ask yourself: "Will my readers be familiar with this item? Will I need it to get my message across? Will my audience find this item interesting or convincing?" What your readers know, what they don't know, and what you can predict about their reactions should influence your choices. And, of course, you need to select points that support your thesis. If your essay explains the differences between healthy, sensible diets and dangerous crash diets, it wouldn't be appropriate to talk about aerobic exercise.

5. Organize the points to be discussed. There are two common ways to organize an essay developed wholly or in part by comparison-contrast: the one-side-at-a-time method and the point-by-point method. Although both strategies may be used in a paper, one method usually predominates.

In the *one-side-at-a-time method* of organization, you discuss everything relevant about one subject before moving to another subject. For example, responding to the earlier assignment that asked you to analyze the news coverage in two local papers, you might first talk about *The Herald*'s coverage of international, national, and local news; then you would discuss *The Beacon*'s coverage of the same categories. Note that the areas discussed should be the same for both newspapers. Moreover, the areas compared and contrasted should be presented in the same order.

This is how you would organize the essay using the one-side-at-a-time method.

Everything about A	*The Herald*'s news coverage • International • National • Local
Everything about B	*The Beacon*'s news coverage • International • National • Local

In the *point-by-point method* of organization, you alternate from one aspect of the first subject to the same aspect of your other subject(s). For example, you would first discuss *The Herald*'s international coverage, then *The Beacon*'s international coverage; next *The Herald*'s national coverage, then *The Beacon*'s; and finally, *The Herald*'s local coverage, then *The Beacon*'s.

Using the point-by-point method, this is how the essay would be organized.

First aspect of A and B	*The Herald:* International coverage *The Beacon:* International coverage
Second aspect of A and B	*The Herald:* National coverage *The Beacon:* National coverage
Third aspect of A and B	*The Herald:* Local coverage *The Beacon:* Local coverage

Deciding which of these two methods of organization to use is largely a personal choice, though there are several factors to consider. The one-side-at-a-time method tends to convey a more unified feeling because it highlights broad similarities and differences. It is, therefore, an effective approach for subjects that are fairly uncomplicated. This strategy also works well when essays are brief; the reader won't find it difficult to remember what has been said about subject A when reading about subject B.

Because the point-by-point method permits more extensive coverage of similarities and differences, it is often a wise choice when subjects are complex. This pattern is also useful for lengthy essays since readers would probably find it difficult to remember, let's say, ten pages of information about subject A while reading the next ten pages about subject B. The point-by-point approach, however, may cause readers to lose sight of the broader picture, so remember to keep them focused on your central point.

6. Supply the reader with clear transitions. Although a well-organized comparison-contrast format is important, it doesn't guarantee that readers will be able to follow your line of thought easily. *Transitions*—especially those signaling similarities or differences—are needed to show readers where they have been and where they are going. Such cues are essential in all writing, but they're especially crucial in a paper using comparison-contrast. By indicating clearly when subjects are being compared or contrasted, the transitions help weave the discussion into a coherent whole.

The transitions (in boldface) in the following examples would *signal similarities* in an essay on the news coverage in *The Herald* and *The Beacon:*

- *The Beacon* **also** allots only a small portion of the front page to global news.
- **In the same way,** *The Herald* tries to include at least three local stories on the first page.
- **Likewise,** *The Beacon* emphasizes the importance of up-to-date reporting of town meetings.
- *The Herald* is **similarly** committed to extensive coverage of high school and college sports.

The transitions (in boldface) in the following examples would *signal differences:*

- **By way of contrast,** *The Herald's* editorial page deals with national matters on the average of three times a week.
- **On the other hand,** *The Beacon* does not share *The Herald's* enthusiasm for interviews with national figures.
- *The Beacon,* **however,** does not encourage its reporters to tackle national stories the way *The Herald* does.
- **But** *The Herald's* coverage of the Washington scene is much more comprehensive than its competitor's.

REVISION STRATEGIES

Once you have a draft of the essay, you're ready to revise. The following checklist will help you and those giving you feedback apply to comparison-contrast some of the revision techniques discussed on pages 60–62.

☑ COMPARISON-CONTRAST: A REVISION/PEER REVIEW CHECKLIST

Revise Overall Meaning and Structure

- ❑ Are the subjects sufficiently alike for the comparison-contrast to be logical and meaningful?
- ❑ What purpose does the essay serve—to inform, to evaluate, to persuade readers to accept a viewpoint, to eliminate misconceptions, or to draw a surprising analogy?
- ❑ What is the essay's thesis? How could the thesis be stated more effectively?
- ❑ Is the overall essay organized primarily by the one-side-at-a-time method or by the point-by-point method? Why is that the best strategy for this essay?
- ❑ Are the same features discussed for each subject? Are they discussed in the same order?
- ❑ Which points of comparison and/or contrast need further development? Which points should be deleted? Where do significant points seem to be missing? How has the most important similarity or difference been emphasized?

Revise Paragraph Development

- ❑ If the essay uses the one-side-at-a-time method, which paragraph marks the switch from one subject to another?
- ❑ If the essay uses the point-by-point method, do paragraphs consistently alternate between subjects? If this alternation becomes too elaborate or predictable, what could be done to eliminate the problem?
- ❑ If the essay uses both methods, which paragraph marks the switch from one method to the other? If the switch is confusing, how could it be made less so?
- ❑ Where would signal devices make it easier to see similarities and differences between the subjects being discussed?

Revise Sentences and Words

- ❑ Where do too many signal devices make sentences awkward and mechanical?
- ❑ Which sentences and words fail to convey the intended tone?

STUDENT ESSAY

The following student essay was written by Carol Siskin in response to this assignment:

> In "Beauty and the Beast," Dave Barry humorously contrasts two attitudes toward personal appearance, finding merit in the one normally considered less praiseworthy. In an essay of your own, contrast two personality types, lifestyles, or stages of life, showing that the one most people consider inferior is actually superior.

While reading Carol's paper, try to determine how well it applies the principles of comparison-contrast. The annotations on Carol's paper and the commentary following it will help you look at the essay more closely.

The Virtues of Growing Older
by Carol Siskin

The first of a two-paragraph introduction

1 Our society worships youth. Advertisements convince us to buy Grecian Formula and Oil of Olay so we can hide the gray in our hair and smooth the lines on our face. Television shows feature attractive young stars with firm bodies, perfect complexions, and thick manes of hair. Middle-aged folks work out in gyms and jog down the street, trying to delay the effects of age.

The second introductory paragraph

Thesis

2 Wouldn't any person over thirty gladly sign with the devil just to be young again? Isn't aging an experience to be dreaded? Perhaps it is un-American to say so, but I believe the answer is "No." Being young is often pleasant, but being older has distinct advantages.

First half of topic sentence for point 1: Appearance

Start of what it's like being young

Second half of topic sentence for point 1

3 When young, you are apt to be obsessed with your appearance. When my brother Dave and I were teens, we worked feverishly to perfect the bodies we had. Dave lifted weights, took megadoses of vitamins, and drank a half-dozen milkshakes a day in order to turn his wiry adolescent frame into some muscular ideal. And as a teenager, I dieted constantly. No matter what I weighed, though, I was never satisfied with the way I looked. My legs were too heavy, my shoulders too broad, my waist too big. When Dave and I were young, we begged and pleaded for the "right" clothes. If our parents didn't get them for us, we felt our world would fall apart. How could we go to school wearing loose-fitting overcoats when everyone else would be wearing fitted leather jackets? We would be considered freaks. I often wonder how my parents, and parents in general, manage to tolerate their children during the adolescent years. Now, however, Dave and I are

Start of what it's like being older

beyond such adolescent agonies. My rounded figure seems fine, and I don't deny myself a slice of pecan pie if I feel in the mood. Dave still works out, but he has actually become fond of his tall, lanky frame. The two of us enjoy wearing fashionable clothes, but we are no longer slaves to style. And women, I'm embarrassed to admit, even more than men, have always seemed to be at the mercy of fashion. Now my clothes—and my brother's—are attractive yet easy to wear. We no longer feel anxious about what others will think. As long as we feel good about how we look, we are happy.

First half of topic sentence for point 2: Life choices

Start of what it's like being older

Second half of topic sentence for point 2

Start of what it's like being younger

4 Being older is preferable to being younger in another way. Obviously, I still have important choices to make about my life, but I have already made many of the critical decisions that confront those just starting out. I chose the man I wanted to marry. I decided to have children. I elected to return to college to complete my education. But when you are young, major decisions await you at every turn. "What college should I attend? What career should I pursue? Should I get married? Should I have children?" These are just a few of the issues facing young people. It's no wonder that, despite their carefree facade, they are often confused, uncertain, and troubled by all the unknowns in their future.

Topic sentence for point 3: Self-concept

Start of what it's like being younger

Start of what it's like being older

5 But the greatest benefit of being forty is knowing who I am. The most unsettling aspect of youth is the uncertainty you feel about your values, goals, and dreams. Being young means wondering what is worth working for. Being young means feeling happy with yourself one day and wishing you were never born the next. It means trying on new selves by taking up with different crowds. It means resenting your parents and their way of life one minute and then feeling you will never be as good or as accomplished as they are. By way of contrast, forty is sanity. I have a surer self-concept now. I don't laugh at jokes I don't think are funny. I can make a speech in front of a town meeting or complain in a store because I am no longer terrified that people will laugh at me; I am no longer anxious that everyone must like me. I no longer blame my parents for my every personality quirk or keep a running score of everything they did wrong raising me. Life has taught me that I, not they, am responsible for who I am. We are all human beings—neither saints nor devils.

Conclusion

6 Most Americans blindly accept the idea that newer is automatically better. But a human life contradicts this premise. There is a great deal of happiness to be found as we grow older. My own parents, now in their sixties, recently told me that they are happier now than they have ever been. They would not want to be my age. Did this surprise me? At first, yes. Then it gladdened me. Their contentment holds out great promise for me as I move into the next—perhaps even better—phase of my life.

COMMENTARY

Purpose and thesis. In her essay, Carol disproves the widespread belief that being young is preferable to being old. The *comparison-contrast* pattern allows her to analyze the drawbacks of one and the merits of the other, thus providing the essay with an *evaluative purpose.* Using the title to indicate her point of view, Carol places the *thesis* at the end of her two-paragraph introduction: "Being young is often pleasant, but being older has distinct advantages." Note that the thesis accomplishes several things. It names the two subjects to be discussed and clarifies Carol's point of view about her subjects. The thesis also implies that the essay will focus on the contrasts between these two periods of life.

Points of support and overall organization. To support her assertion that older is better, Carol supplies examples from her own life and organizes the examples around three main points: attitudes about appearance, decisions about life choices, and questions of self-concept. Using the *point-by-point method* to organize the overall essay, she explores each of these key ideas in a separate paragraph. Each paragraph is further focused by one or two sentences that serve as a topic sentence.

Sequence of points, organizational cues, and paragraph development. Let's look more closely at the way Carol presents her three central points in the essay. She obviously considers appearance the least important of a person's worries, life choices more important, and self-concept the most critical. So she uses *emphatic order* to sequence the supporting paragraphs, with the phrase "But the greatest benefit" signaling the special significance of the last issue. Carol is also careful to use *transitions* to help readers follow her line of thinking: "*Now, however,* Dave and I are beyond such adolescent agonies" (paragraph 3); "*But* when you are young, major decisions await you at every turn" (4); and "*By way of contrast,* forty is sanity" (5).

Although Carol has worked hard to write a well-organized paper—and has on the whole been successful—she doesn't feel compelled to make the paper fit a rigid format. As you've seen, the essay as a whole uses the point-by-point method, but each supporting paragraph uses the *one-side-at-a-time* method—that is, everything about one age group is discussed before there is a shift to the other age group. Notice too that the third and fifth paragraphs start with young people and then move to adults, whereas the fourth paragraph reverses the sequence by starting with older people.

Combining patterns of development. To illustrate her points, Carol makes extensive use of *exemplification,* and her discussion also has elements typical of *causal analysis.* Throughout the essay, for instance, she traces the effect of being a certain age on her brother, herself, and her parents.

A problem with unity. As you read the third paragraph, you might have noted that Carol's essay runs into a problem. Two sentences in the paragraph disrupt the *unity* of Carol's discussion: "I often wonder how my parents, and parents in general, manage to tolerate their children during the adolescent years," and "women, I'm embarrassed to admit... have always seemed to be at the mercy of fashion." These sentences should be deleted because they don't develop the idea that adolescents are overly concerned with appearance.

Conclusion. Carol's final paragraph brings the essay to a pleasing and interesting close. The conclusion recalls the point made in the introduction: Americans overvalue youth. Carol also uses the conclusion to broaden the scope of her discussion. Rather than continuing to focus on herself, she briefly mentions her parents and the pleasure they take in life. By bringing her parents into the essay, Carol is able to make a gently philosophical observation about the promise that awaits her as she grows older. The implication is that a similarly positive future awaits us, too.

Revising the first draft. To help guide her revision, Carol asked her husband to read her first draft aloud. As he did, Carol took notes on what she sensed were the paper's strengths and weaknesses. She then jotted down her observations, as well as her husband's, on the draft. Keeping these comments in mind, Carol made a number of changes in her paper. You'll get a good sense of how she proceeded if you compare the original introduction printed here with the final version in the full essay.

Original Version of the Introduction

America is a land filled with people who worship youth. We admire dynamic young achievers; our middle-aged citizens work out in gyms; all of us wear tight tops and colorful sneakers—clothes that look fine on the young but ridiculous on aging bodies. Television shows revolve around perfect-looking young stars, while commercials entice us with products that will keep us young.

Wouldn't every older person want to be young again? Isn't aging to be avoided? It may be slightly unpatriotic to say so, but I believe the answer is "No." Being young may be pleasant at times, but I would rather be my forty-year-old self. I no longer have to agonize about my physical appearance, I have already made many of my crucial life decisions, and I am much less confused about who I am.

After hearing her original two-paragraph introduction read aloud, Carol was dissatisfied with what she had written. Although she wasn't quite sure how to proceed, she knew that the paragraphs were flat and that they failed to open the essay on a strong note. She decided to start by whittling down the opening sentence, making it crisper and more powerful: "Our society worships youth." That done, she eliminated two bland statements ("We admire dynamic young achievers" and "all of us wear tight tops and colorful sneakers") and made several vague references more concrete and interesting. For example, "Commercials entice us with products that will keep us young" became "Grecian Formula and Oil of Olay...hide the gray in our hair and smooth the lines on our face"; "perfect-looking young stars" became "attractive young stars with firm bodies, perfect complexions, and thick manes of hair." With the addition of these specifics, the first paragraph became more vigorous and interesting.

Carol next made some subtle changes in the two questions that opened the second paragraph of the original introduction. She replaced "Wouldn't every older person want to be young again?" and "Isn't aging to be avoided?" with two more emphatic questions: "Wouldn't any person over thirty gladly sign with the devil just to be young again?" and "Isn't aging an experience to be dreaded?" Carol also made some changes at the end of the original second paragraph. Because the paper is relatively short and the subject matter easy to understand, she decided to omit her somewhat awkward *plan of development* ("I no longer have to agonize about my physical appearance, I have already made many of my crucial life decisions, and I am much less confused about who I am"). This deletion made it possible to end the introduction with a clear statement of the essay's thesis.

Once these revisions were made, Carol was confident that her essay got off to a stronger start. Feeling reassured, she moved ahead and made changes in other sections of her paper. Such work enabled her to prepare a solid piece of writing that offers food for thought.

Activities: Comparison-Contrast

Prewriting Activities

1. Imagine you're writing two essays: One explores the *effects* of holding a job while in college; the other explains a *process* for budgeting money wisely. Jot down ways you might use comparison-contrast in each essay.

2. Using your journal or freewriting, jot down the advantages and disadvantages of two ways of doing something (for example, watching movies in the theater versus watching them on a DVD player at home; following trends versus ignoring them; dating one person versus playing the field; and so on). Reread your prewriting and determine what your thesis, purpose, audience, tone, and point of view might be if you were to write an essay. Make a scratch list of the main ideas you would cover. Would a point-by-point or a one-side-at-a-time method of organization work more effectively?

Revising Activities

1. Of the statements that follow, which would *not* make effective thesis statements for comparison-contrast essays? Identify the problem(s) in the faulty statements and revise them accordingly.

   a. Although their classroom duties often overlap, teacher aides are not as equipped as teachers to handle disciplinary problems.
   b. This college provides more assistance to its students than most schools.
   c. During the state's last congressional election, both candidates relied heavily on television to communicate their messages.
   d. There are many differences between American and foreign cars.

2. The following paragraph is from the draft of an essay detailing the qualities of a skillful manager. How effective is this comparison-contrast paragraph? What revisions would help focus the paragraph on the point made in the topic sentence? Where should details be added or deleted? Rewrite the paragraph, providing necessary transitions and details.

   A manager encourages creativity and treats employees courteously, while a boss discourages staff resourcefulness and views it as a threat. At the hardware store where I work, I got my boss's approval to develop a system for organizing excess stock in the storeroom. I shelved items in roughly the same order as they were displayed in the store. The system was helpful to all the salespeople, not just to me, since everyone was stymied by the boss's helter-skelter system. What he did was store overstocked items according to each wholesaler, even though most of us weren't there long enough to know which items came from which wholesaler. His supposed system created chaos. When he saw what I had done, he was furious and insisted that we continue to follow the old slapdash system. I had assumed he would welcome my ideas the way my manager did last summer when I worked in a drugstore. But he didn't and I had to scrap my work and go back to his eccentric system. He certainly could learn something about employee relations from the drugstore manager.

Eric Weiner

Eric Weiner (1963–) is a national correspondent for NPR.org, part of National Public Radio. He began his journalism career by reporting on business issues for *The New York Times* and NPR's Washington, D.C., bureau and then spent most of the 1990s reporting on wars and world events from South Asia and the Middle East. A licensed pilot who loves to eat sushi, Weiner occasionally writes lighter pieces drawing on his experience with other cultures. He is the author of *The Geography of Bliss: One Grump's Search for the Happiest Places in the World* (2008). A short version of this piece about e-mail was broadcast on *Day to Day,* a National Public Radio magazine show, on March 24, 2005; the full version, which appears here, was posted on Slate.com the next day.

For ideas about how this comparison-contrast essay is organized, see Figure 8.2 on page 353.

Pre-Reading Journal Entry

Just one hundred years ago, people communicated only by speaking face to face or by writing a letter—with an occasional brief telegram in emergencies. Today, technology has given us many ways to communicate. Think over all the different ways you communicate with your family, friends, classmates, instructors, coworkers, and others. What methods of communication do you use with each of these groups? Which forms do you prefer, and why? Use your journal to answer these questions.

Euromail and Amerimail

North America and Europe are two continents divided by a common technology: e-mail. Techno-optimists assure us that e-mail—along with the Internet and satellite TV—make the world smaller. That may be true in a technical sense. I can send a message from my home in Miami to a German friend in Berlin and it will arrive almost instantly. But somewhere over the Atlantic, the messages get garbled. In fact, two distinct forms of e-mail have emerged: Euromail and Amerimail. 1

Amerimail is informal and chatty. It's likely to begin with a breezy "Hi" and end with a "Bye." The chances of Amerimail containing a smiley face or an "xoxo" are disturbingly high. We Americans are reluctant to dive into the meat of an e-mail; we feel compelled to first inform hapless recipients about our vacation on the Cape which was really excellent except the jellyfish were biting and the kids caught this nasty bug so we had to skip the whale watching trip but about that investors' meeting in New York... Amerimail is a bundle of contradictions: rambling and yet direct; deferential, yet arrogant. In other words, Amerimail *is* America. 2

Euromail is stiff and cold, often beginning with a formal "Dear Mr. X" and ending with a brusque "Sincerely." You won't find any mention of kids 3 or the weather or jellyfish in Euromail. It's also business. It's also slow. Your correspondent might take days, even weeks, to answer a message. Euromail is also less confrontational in tone, rarely filled with the overt nastiness that characterizes American e-mail disagreements. In other words, Euromail is exactly like the Europeans themselves. (I am, of course, generalizing. German e-mail style is not exactly the same as Italian or Greek, but they have more in common with each other than they do with American mail.)

These are more than mere stylistic differences. Communication matters. Which model should the rest of the world adopt: Euromail or Amerimail? 4

A California-based e-mail consulting firm called People-onthego sheds some light on the e-mail divide. It recently asked about 100 executives on both sides of the Atlantic whether they noticed differences in e-mail styles. Most said yes. Here are a few of their observations: 5

> "Americans tend to write (e-mails) exactly as they speak."
> "Europeans are less obsessive about checking e-mail."
> "In general, Americans are much more responsive to email—they respond faster and provide more information."

One respondent noted that Europeans tend to segregate their e-mail accounts. Rarely do they send personal messages on their business accounts, or vice versa. These differences can't be explained merely by differing comfort levels with technology. Other forms of electronic communication, such as SMS text messaging, are more popular in Europe than in the United States.

The fact is, Europeans and Americans approach e-mail in a fundamentally different way. Here is the key point: For Europeans, e-mail has replaced the business letter. For Americans, it has replaced the telephone. That's why we tend to unleash what e-mail consultant Tim Burress calls a "brain dump": unloading the content of our cerebral cortex onto the screen and hitting the send button. "It makes Europeans go ballistic," he says. 6

Susanne Khawand, a German high-tech executive, has been on the receiving end of American brain dumps, and she says it's not pretty. "I feel like saying, 'Why don't you just call me instead of writing five e-mails back and forth,'" she says. Americans are so overwhelmed by their bulging inboxes that "you can't rely on getting an answer. You don't even know if they read it." In Germany, she says, it might take a few days, or even weeks, for an answer, but one always arrives. 7

Maybe that's because, on average, Europeans receive fewer e-mails and spend less time tending their inboxes. An international survey of business owners in 24 countries (conducted by the accounting firm Grant Thornton) found that people in Greece and Russia spend the least amount of time dealing with e-mail every day: 48 minutes on average. Americans, by comparison, spend two hours per day, among the highest in the world. 8

(Only Filipinos spend more time on e-mail, 2.1 hours.) The survey also found that European executives are skeptical of e-mail's ability to boost their bottom line.

It's not clear why European and American e-mail styles have evolved separately, but I suspect the reasons lie within deep cultural differences. Americans tend to be impulsive and crave instant gratification. So we send e-mails rapid-fire and get antsy if we don't receive a reply quickly. Europeans tend to be more methodical and plodding. They send (and reply to) e-mails only after great deliberation. 9

For all their Continental fastidiousness, Europeans can be remarkably lax about e-mail security, says Bill Young, an executive vice president with the Strickland Group. Europeans are more likely to include trade secrets and business strategies in e-mails, he says, much to the frustration of their American colleagues. This is probably because identity theft—and other types of backing—are much less of a problem in Europe than in the United States. Privacy laws are much stricter in Europe. 10

So, which is better: Euromail or Amerimail? Personally, I'm a convert—or a defector, if you prefer—to the former. I realize it's not popular these days to suggest we have anything to learn from Europeans, but I'm fed up with an inbox cluttered with rambling, barely cogent missives from friends and colleagues. If the alternative is a few stiffly written, politely worded bits of Euromail, then I say... bring it on. 11

Questions for Close Reading

1. What is the selection's thesis? Locate the sentence(s) in which Weiner states his main idea. If he doesn't state his thesis explicitly, express it in your own words.
2. According to Weiner, what are the main characteristics of American e-mail? What are the main characteristics of European e-mail?
3. When Americans and Europeans e-mail one another for business reasons, frustration often ensues. Why, according to Weiner, is this so? What are some examples of e-mail differences that cause frustration?
4. Which type of e-mail does Weiner favor? Why?
5. Refer to your dictionary as needed to define the following words used in the selection: *hapless* (paragraph 2), *deferential* (2), *brusque* (3), *confrontational* (3), *overt* (3), *bottom line* (8), *fastidiousness* (10), *lax* (10), *cogent* (11), and *missives* (11).

Questions About the Writer's Craft

1. The opening paragraph of this essay is full of technology-related words: *technology, e-mail, techno-optimists, Internet, Satellite TV, technical sense, Euromail,* and *Amerimail.* What is the effect of using all these "techno-terms"? How does the remainder of the essay contrast with the dominant impression of the first paragraph?

FIGURE 8.2
Essay Structure Diagram: "Euromail and Amerimail" by Eric Weiner

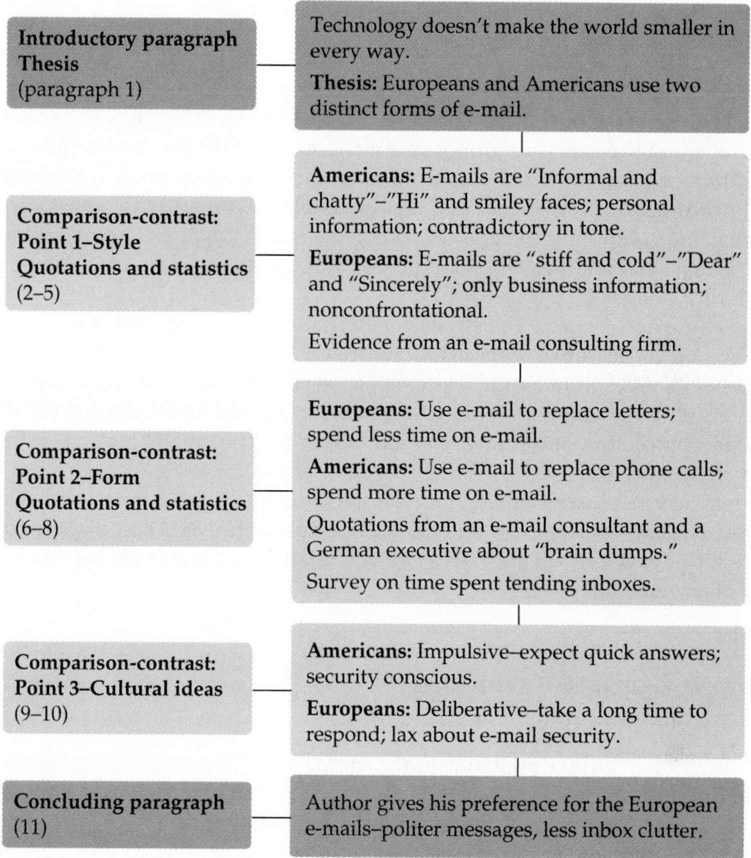

Introductory paragraph
Thesis
(paragraph 1)
Technology doesn't make the world smaller in every way.
Thesis: Europeans and Americans use two distinct forms of e-mail.
Comparison-contrast:
Point 1–Style
Quotations and statistics
(2–5)
Americans: E-mails are "Informal and chatty"–"Hi" and smiley faces; personal information; contradictory in tone.
Europeans: E-mails are "stiff and cold"–"Dear" and "Sincerely"; only business information; nonconfrontational.
Evidence from an e-mail consulting firm.
Comparison-contrast:
Point 2–Form
Quotations and statistics
(6–8)
Europeans: Use e-mail to replace letters; spend less time on e-mail.
Americans: Use e-mail to replace phone calls; spend more time on e-mail.
Quotations from an e-mail consultant and a German executive about "brain dumps."
Survey on time spent tending inboxes.
Comparison-contrast:
Point 3–Cultural ideas
(9–10)
Americans: Impulsive–expect quick answers; security conscious.
Europeans: Deliberative–take a long time to respond; lax about e-mail security.
Concluding paragraph
(11)
Author gives his preference for the European e-mails–politer messages, less inbox clutter.

2. **The Pattern.** What type of organization does Weiner use for the essay? How else could he have organized the points he makes? Which method of organization do you think is more effective for this essay?
3. **Other patterns.** Identify the transitional expressions that Weiner uses to signal similarities and differences. Why do you think there are so few of these expressions? How might the fact that this essay was meant to be read aloud affect Weiner's transitions between Amerimail and Euromail? (You can listen to the short version of the essay at www.npr.org; search using the key term "Euromail.") Do you think the essay would be better if Weiner had used more transitional expressions? Explain.

4. What type of conclusion does Weiner use? (To review strategies for conclusions, see pages 55–56). What is his concluding point? Were you surprised by this conclusion? Why or why not?

Writing Assignments Using Comparison-Contrast as a Pattern of Development

1. Weiner attributes differences between Americans and Europeans in the use of e-mail to underlying cultural differences. Consider the differences in the use of e-mail among specific sub-groups of Americans, for example, among Americans of different generations, different genders, or different ethnic groups. Drawing on your own personal experience and that of people you know, write an essay comparing and contrasting some of the ways these two different groups of Americans use e-mail. For another take on differences in communication, read Amy Tan's "Mother Tongue" (page 270).
2. The etiquette of e-mail correspondence certainly is not the only way in which Americans differ from Europeans. Consider some additional ways that Americans as a whole differ from another specific nationality or ethnic group, European or otherwise. Write an essay in which you *contrast* the way Americans and the other group approach at least three cultural practices. You might look at attitudes toward gender roles, child-rearing, personal fitness, treatment of the ill or the elderly, leisure to work ratios, the environment, and so on. Before you begin to write, consider what sort of tone might best suit your essay. You might adopt a straightforward tone (like Weiner's), or you might find a humorous approach better suits your material.

Writing Assignments Combining Patterns of Development

3. Weiner's essay focuses primarily on the business use of e-mail among Americans and Europeans. Do some research on the Internet about the various uses of e-mail that have developed. Write an essay identifying how e-mail has *affected* our personal lives, our academic lives, and our business lives. Be sure to provide specific examples and data, where possible, to support the claims you make about these areas of change. Consider concluding your essay by summarizing whether e-mail has been beneficial, harmful, or both.
4. Weiner's preference for Euromail indicates that he longs for a more formal approach to communication. Over time, several other types of behaviors have evolved to be less formal than they once were. Select another aspect of behavior that has acquired a more casual mode; examples include dining etiquette, forms of address, dress codes, classroom protocol or student-teacher dynamics, and so on. Write an essay in which you explore at least two to three *causes* for the shift from more formal to more casual expressions of this behavior. As you examine the causes, you'll probably find yourself *contrasting* former and current practices. And your conclusion should *argue* for the superiority of either the casual or the formal approach.

Writing Assignment Using a Journal Entry as a Starting Point

5. Review your pre-reading journal entry about the different communication methods you use. Select three of your favorite methods, and write an essay dividing and classifying each of these methods, analyzing how you use it to communicate, and with whom. What are each method's advantages and disadvantages? Be sure to provide specific examples along the way. For additional perspectives on modern communication, read Stephanie Ericsson's "The Ways We Lie" (page 247) and David Shipley's "Talk About Editing" (page 303). 

Alex Wright

As director of User Experience and Product Research at *The New York Times*, Alex Wright (1966–) worked on creating the *Times's* iPod app as well as on other interactive projects. He is the author of *Glut: Mastering Information Through the Ages* (2007) and of articles appearing in numerous publications, including *Salon.com, The Christian Science Monitor,* and *Utne Reader*. The following article appeared in the "Week in Review" section of *The New York Times* on December 2, 2007.

Pre-Reading Journal Entry

Most of us would say that making and keeping friends is an essential part of life. Think about your friends and others with whom you have relationships. How did you meet them? When and how did you realize that these specific relationships were important to you? How do you keep those relationships meaningful? Use your journal to answer these questions.

Friending, Ancient or Otherwise

The growing popularity of social networking sites like Facebook, MySpace and Second Life has thrust many of us into a new world where we make "friends" with people we barely know, scrawl messages on each other's walls and project our identities using totem-like visual symbols. 1

We're making up the rules as we go. But is this world as new as it seems? 2

Academic researchers are starting to examine that question by taking an unusual tack: exploring the parallels between online social networks and tribal societies. In the collective patter of profile-surfing, messaging and "friending," they see the resurgence of ancient patterns of oral communication. 3

"Orality is the base of all human experience," says Lance Strate, a communications professor at Fordham University and devoted MySpace user. He says he is convinced that the popularity of social networks stems from their appeal to deep-seated, prehistoric patterns of human communication. "We evolved with speech," he says. "We didn't evolve with writing." 4

The growth of social networks—and the Internet as a whole—stems largely from an outpouring of expression that often feels more like "talking" than writing: blog posts, comments, homemade videos and, lately, an outpouring of epigrammatic one-liners broadcast using services like Twitter and Facebook status updates (usually proving Gertrude Stein's[1] maxim that "literature is not remarks"). 5

[1]Gertrude Stein (1874–1946), an American author who lived primarily in Paris, was known for her interest in Modernist art and writing (editors' note).

"If you examine the Web through the lens of orality, you can't help but see it everywhere," says Irwin Chen, a design instructor at Parsons who is developing a new course to explore the emergence of oral culture online. "Orality is participatory, interactive, communal and focused on the present. The Web is all of these things." 6

An early student of electronic orality was the Rev. Walter J. Ong, a professor at St. Louis University and student of Marshall McLuhan[2] who coined the term "secondary orality" in 1982 to describe the tendency of electronic media to echo the cadences of earlier oral cultures. The work of Father Ong, who died in 2003, seems especially prescient in light of the social-networking phenomenon. "Oral communication," as he put it, "unites people in groups." 7

In other words, oral culture means more than just talking. There are subtler—and perhaps more important—social dynamics at work. 8

Michael Wesch, who teaches cultural anthropology at Kansas State University, spent two years living with a tribe in Papua New Guinea, studying how people forge social relationships in a purely oral culture. Now he applies the same ethnographic research methods to the rites and rituals of Facebook users. 9

"In tribal cultures, your identity is completely wrapped up in the question of how people know you," he says. "When you look at Facebook, you can see the same pattern at work: people projecting their identities by demonstrating their relationships to each other. You define yourself in terms of who your friends are." 10

In tribal societies, people routinely give each other jewelry, weapons and ritual objects to cement their social ties. On Facebook, people accomplish the same thing by trading symbolic sock monkeys, disco balls and hula girls. 11

"It's reminiscent of how people exchange gifts in tribal cultures," says Dr. Strate, whose MySpace page lists his 1,335 "friends" along with his academic credentials and his predilection for "Battlestar Galactica." 12

As intriguing as these parallels may be, they only stretch so far. There are big differences between real oral cultures and the virtual kind. In tribal societies, forging social bonds is a matter of survival; on the Internet, far less so. There is presumably no tribal antecedent for popular Facebook rituals like "poking," virtual sheep-tossing or drunk-dialing your friends. 13

Then there's the question of who really counts as a "friend." In tribal societies, people develop bonds through direct, ongoing face-to-face contact. The Web eliminates that need for physical proximity, enabling people to declare friendships on the basis of otherwise flimsy connections. 14

[2]The Canadian philosopher Herbert Marshall McLuhan (1911–1980), a pioneer in the field of communication theory, coined the phrase "The medium is the message" (editors' note).

"With social networks, there's a fascination with intimacy because it simulates face-to-face communication," Dr. Wesch says. "But there's also this fundamental distance. That distance makes it safe for people to connect through weak ties where they can have the appearance of a connection because it's safe." 15

And while tribal cultures typically engage in highly formalized rituals, social networks seem to encourage a level of casualness and familiarity that would be unthinkable in traditional oral cultures. "Secondary orality has a leveling effect," Dr. Strate says. "In a primary oral culture, you would probably refer to me as 'Dr. Strate,' but on MySpace, everyone calls me 'Lance.' " 16

As more of us shepherd our social relationships online, will this leveling effect begin to shape the way we relate to each other in the offline world as well? Dr. Wesch, for one, says he worries that the rise of secondary orality may have a paradoxical consequence: "It may be gobbling up what's left of our real oral culture." 17

The more time we spend "talking" online, the less time we spend, well, talking. And as we stretch the definition of a friend to encompass people we may never actually meet, will the strength of our real-world friendships grow diluted as we immerse ourselves in a lattice of hyperlinked "friends"? 18

Still, the sheer popularity of social networking seems to suggest that for many, these environments strike a deep, perhaps even primal chord. "They fulfill our need to be recognized as human beings, and as members of a community," Dr. Strate says. "We all want to be told: You exist." 19

Questions for Close Reading

1. What is the selection's thesis? Locate the sentence(s) in which Wright states his main idea. If he doesn't state his thesis explicitly, express it in your own words.
2. What fundamental need, in Wright's view, do social networks seem designed to satisfy? How successful are they in meeting this need?
3. To what other type of human community are academics comparing online social networks, according to Wright? Why? According to researchers, what is the importance of oral communication in any human group?
4. Why should we be concerned about the "growing popularity" of social networking sites, according to Wright's article?
5. Refer to your dictionary as needed to define the following words used in the selection: *resurgence* (paragraph 3), *epigrammatic* (5), *participatory* (6), *interactive* (6), *cadences* (7), *prescient* (7), *ethnographic* (9), *antecedent* (13), *proximity* (14), *simulates* (15), and *formalized* (16).

Questions About the Writer's Craft

1. **The pattern.** Does Wright use the one-side-at-a-time or the point-by-point method to compare and contrast the two communities he is discussing? What specific points does he discuss in his analysis? How does he say the groups are similar? How does he say they are different?

2. Throughout his article, Wright relies on outside sources for evidence. What is the primary type of outside evidence that he uses? Give at least two examples. How effective is this evidence in supporting his thesis?
3. **Other patterns.** Wright uses the term *friend* seven times in the article. How does he *define* this term? How important is the use of definition in the essay? Why? Wright also uses *cause-effect* (17 and 18). What key term signals this pattern of development? What cause(s) and effect(s) does he discuss?
4. What strategy does Wright use to conclude his article? (To review strategies for conclusions, see pages 55–56.) How does the conclusion relate to his thesis?

Writing Assignments Using Comparison-Contrast as a Pattern of Development

1. Wright sees social networking sites as ways to communicate. Think of some other ways in which people communicate and the different kinds of communications for which these methods might be suited. For example, how would you suggest vacation plans to a friend? Make an appointment to see an instructor? End a romantic relationship? Choose three communication methods, and write an essay comparing and contrasting how effective they are for conveying information, ideas, and feelings to other people. Your essay can be serious or light in tone. For an example of the use of communication technology in different cultures, read Eric Weiner's "Euromail and Amerimail" (page 350), and for a humorous view of interpersonal communication, you might read Amy Sutherland's "What Shamu Taught Me About a Happy Marriage" (page 308).
2. Online social networks have made it possible for us to have "friendships" with people we never, or hardly ever, see. In the same way, the Internet has made it easy for us to engage in other kinds of long-distance activities—buying items from stores we never enter, taking classes with instructors we never meet, even consulting with attorneys we never see in person. Write an essay in which you compare and contrast the advantages and disadvantages of engaging in a specific online activity with those of pursuing the same activity in a more traditional way.

Writing Assignments Combining Patterns of Development

3. Wright's essay focuses on the purely social functions of networks like Facebook and Twitter. Social network sites collect a lot of personal information about their subscribers, however, and some companies have sought ways to use that information for commercial purposes—to sell products and services. Some social network subscribers welcome the opportunity to learn about specific products matched to their tastes. Others argue that a network's commercial use of subscribers' personal data amounts to an unacceptable invasion of privacy. Do some online research on this subject. Then write an essay in which you *argue* one side of the issue, giving *examples* from personal experience or evidence from experts to support your arguments.

4. Maintaining participation in a social network entails effort. Subscribers may spend a lot of time updating their Facebook page, for example. Wright expresses the concern that "the more time we spend 'talking' online, the less time we spend, well, talking." Write an essay in which you analyze the *effects* of social networking on other activities, especially face-to-face communication. Do you think social networking leads to more face-to-face interaction with friends? More meaningful friendships? A wider circle of friends? Include *narrations* of your own or your friends' personal experiences with social networking as support for your ideas.

Writing Assignment Using A Journal Entry as a Starting Point

5. Review what you wrote in your pre-reading journal entry. Write an essay about the attributes you consider important in a friend. *Compare* your requirements today with requirements you might have had at other times in your life. For example, did you look for different qualities in a friend when you were a child or an adolescent? Or possibly when you were single or before you had children? Remember to include examples to *illustrate* the qualities you are comparing.

Richard Rodriguez

In his autobiographical work *Hunger of Memory* (1981), from which the following selection is taken, Richard Rodriguez describes his experiences growing up in America as a first-generation Mexican-American. Born in 1944 in San Francisco, Rodriguez spoke only Spanish for the first six years of his life. After winning a scholarship to a private high school, Rodriguez attended Stanford, Columbia, and the University of California at Berkeley, where he earned a doctorate in English literature. Rodriguez now writes for a variety of publications (*The Wall Street Journal* and *Time,* to name just two), serves as an editor at Pacific News Service in San Francisco, and regularly appears on PBS's *NewsHour.* In 1997, he won the Peabody Award for achievement in broadcasting. His books include *Mexico's Children* (1991), *Movements* (1996), and *Brown* (2002), about what it means to be Hispanic in America. The critically acclaimed *Days of Obligation: An Argument With My Mexican Father* (1992) is Rodriguez's second autobiographical book.

Pre-Reading Journal Entry

Young people often find themselves being lectured by adults claiming that kids nowadays want it easy and aren't willing to do unglamorous "real work." Do you agree with these claims? Why or why not? Drawing upon your experiences and observations, respond to these questions in your journal.

Workers

It was at Stanford, one day near the end of my senior year, that a friend told me about a summer construction job he knew was available. I was quickly alert. Desire uncoiled within me. My friend said that he knew I had been looking for summer employment. He knew I needed some money. Almost apologetically he explained: It was something I probably wouldn't be interested in, but a friend of his, a contractor, needed someone for the summer to do menial jobs. There would be lots of shoveling and raking and sweeping. Nothing too hard. But nothing more interesting either. Still, the pay would be good. Did I want it? Or did I know someone who did? 1

I did. Yes, I said, surprised to hear myself say it. 2

In the weeks following, friends cautioned that I had no idea how hard physical labor really is. ("You only *think* you know what it is like to shovel for eight hours straight.") Their objections seemed to me challenges. They resolved the issue. I became happy with my plan. I decided, however, not to tell my parents. I wouldn't tell my mother because I could guess her worried reaction. I would tell my father only after the summer was over, when I could announce that, after all, I did know what "real work" is like. 3

The day I met the contractor (a Princeton graduate, it turned out), he asked me whether I had done any physical labor before. "In high school, 4 during the summer," I lied. And although he seemed to regard me with skepticism, he decided to give me a try. Several days later, expectant, I arrived at my first construction site. I would take off my shirt to the sun. And at last grasp desired sensation. No longer afraid. At last become like a *bracero.* "We need those tree stumps out of here by tomorrow," the contractor said. I started to work.

I labored with excitement that first morning—and all the days after. 5
The work was harder than I could have expected. But it was never as tedious as my friends had warned me it would be. There was too much physical pleasure in the labor. Especially early in the day, I would be most alert to the sensations of movement and straining. Beginning around seven each morning (when the air was still damp but the scent of weeds and dry earth anticipated the heat of the sun), I would feel my body resist the first thrusts of the shovel. My arms, tightened by sleep, would gradually loosen; after only several minutes, sweat would gather in beads on my forehead and then—a short while later—I would feel my chest silky with sweat in the breeze. I would return to my work. A nervous spark of pain would fly up my arm and settle to burn like an ember in the thick of my shoulder. An hour, two passed. Three. My whole body would assume regular movements; my shoveling would be described by identical, even movements. Even later in the day, my enthusiasm for primitive sensation would survive the heat and the dust and the insects pricking my back. I would strain wildly for sensation as the day came to a close. At three-thirty, quitting time, I would stand upright and slowly let my head fall back, luxuriating in the feeling of tightness relieved.

Some of the men working nearby would watch me and laugh. Two or 6
three of the older men took the trouble to teach me the right way to use a pick, the correct way to shovel. "You're doing it wrong, too fucking hard," one man scolded. Then proceeded to show me—what persons who work with their bodies all their lives quickly learn—the most economical way to use one's body in labor.

"Don't make your back do so much work," he instructed. I stood im- 7
patiently listening, half listening, vaguely watching, then noticed his work-thickened fingers clutching the shovel. I was annoyed. I wanted to tell him that I enjoyed shoveling the wrong way. And I didn't want to learn the right way. I wasn't afraid of back pain. I liked the way my body felt sore at the end of the day.

I was about to, but, as it turned out, I didn't say a thing. Rather it was at 8
that moment I realized that I was fooling myself if I expected a few weeks of labor to gain me admission to the world of the laborer. I would not learn in three months what my father had meant by "real work." I was not bound to this job; I could imagine its rapid conclusion. For me the sensations were to be feared. Fatigue took a different toll on their bodies—and minds.

It was, I know, a simple insight. But it was with this realization that I took my first step that summer toward realizing something even more important about the "worker." In the company of carpenters, electricians, plumbers, and painters at lunch, I would often sit quietly, observant. I was not shy in such company. I felt easy, pleased by the knowledge that I was casually accepted, my presence taken for granted by men (exotics) who worked with their hands. Some days the younger men would talk and talk about sex, and they would howl at women who drove by in cars. Other days the talk at lunchtime was subdued; men gathered in separate groups. It depended on who was around. There were rough, good-natured workers. Others were quiet. The more I remember that summer, the more I realize that there was no single *type* of worker. I am embarrassed to say I had not expected such diversity. I certainly had not expected to meet, for example, a plumber who was an abstract painter in his off hours and admired the work of Mark Rothko. Nor did I expect to meet so many workers with college diplomas. (They were the ones who were not surprised that I intended to enter graduate school in the fall.) I suppose what I really want to say here is painfully obvious, but I must say it nevertheless: The men of that summer were middle-class Americans. They certainly didn't constitute an oppressed society. Carefully completing their work sheets; talking about the fortunes of local football teams; planning Las Vegas vacations; comparing the gas mileage of various makes of campers—they were not *los pobres* my mother had spoken about. 9

On two occasions, the contractor hired a group of Mexican aliens. They were employed to cut down some trees and haul off debris. In all, there were six men of varying age. The youngest in his late twenties; the oldest (his father?) perhaps sixty years old. They came and they left in a single old truck. Anonymous men. They were never introduced to the other men at the site. Immediately upon their arrival, they would follow the contractor's directions, start working—rarely resting—seemingly driven by a fatalistic sense that work which had to be done was best done as quickly as possible. 10

I watched them sometimes. Perhaps they watched me. The only time I saw them pay me much notice was one day at lunchtime when I was laughing with the other men. The Mexicans sat apart when they ate, just as they worked by themselves. Quiet. I rarely heard them say much to each other. All I could hear were their voices calling out sharply to one another, giving directions. Otherwise, when they stood briefly resting, they talked among themselves in voices too hard to overhear. 11

The contractor knew enough Spanish, and the Mexicans—or at least the oldest of them, their spokesman—seemed to know enough English to communicate. But because I was around, the contractor decided one day to make me his translator. (He assumed I could speak Spanish.) I did what I was told. Shyly I went over to tell the Mexicans that the *patrón* wanted them 12 to do something else before they left for the day. As I started to speak, I was afraid with my old fear that I would be unable to pronounce the Spanish words. But it was a simple instruction I had to convey. I could say it in phrases.

The dark sweating faces turned toward me as I spoke. They stopped their work to hear me. Each nodded in response. I stood there. I wanted to say something more. But what could I say in Spanish, even if I could have pronounced the words right? Perhaps I just wanted to engage them in small talk, to be assured of their confidence, our familiarity. I thought for a moment to ask them where in Mexico they were from. Something like that. And maybe I wanted to tell them (a lie, if need be) that my parents were from the same part of Mexico. 13

I stood there. 14

Their faces watched me. The eyes of the man directly in front of me moved slowly over my shoulder, and I turned to follow his glance toward *el patrón* some distance away. For a moment I felt swept up by that glance into the Mexicans' company. But then I heard one of them returning to work. And then the others went back to work. I left them without saying anything more. 15

When they had finished, the contractor went over to pay them in cash. (He later told me that he paid them collectively—"for the job," though he wouldn't tell me their wages. He said something quickly about the good rate of exchange "in their own country.") I can still hear the loudly confident voice he used with the Mexicans. It was the sound of the *gringo* I had heard as a very young boy. And I can still hear the quiet, indistinct sounds of the Mexican, the oldest, who replied. At hearing that voice I was sad for the Mexicans. Depressed by their vulnerability. Angry at myself. The adventure of the summer seemed suddenly ludicrous. I would not shorten the distance I felt from *los pobres* with a few weeks of physical labor. I would not become like them. They were different from me. 16

After that summer, a great deal—and not very much really—changed in my life. The curse of physical shame was broken by the sun; I was no longer ashamed of my body. No longer would I deny myself the pleasing sensations of my maleness. During those years when middle-class black Americans began to assert with pride, "Black is beautiful," I was able to regard my complexion without shame. I am today darker than I ever was as a boy. I have taken up the middle-class sport of long-distance running. Nearly every day now I run ten or fifteen miles, barely clothed, my skin exposed to the California winter rain and wind or the summer sun of late afternoon. The torso, the soccer player's calves and thighs, the arms of the twenty-year-old I never was, I possess now in my thirties. I study the youthful parody shape in the mirror: the stomach lipped tight by muscle; the shoulders rounded by chin-ups; the arms veined strong. This man. A man. I meet him. He laughs to see me, what I have become. 17

The dandy. I wear double-breasted Italian suits and custom-made English shoes. I resemble no one so much as my father—the man pictured in those honeymoon photos. At that point in life when he abandoned the dandy's posture, I assume it. At the point when my parents would not consider going on vacation, I register at the Hotel Carlyle in New York and the Plaza Athenée in Paris. I am as taken by the symbols of leisure and wealth as they were. For my parents, however, those symbols became taunts, reminders of all they could not achieve in one lifetime. For me those same symbols are reassuring reminders of public success. I tempt vulgarity to be reassured. I am filled with the gaudy delight, the monstrous grace of the nouveau riche. 18

In recent years I have had occasion to lecture in ghetto high schools. There I see students of remarkable style and physical grace. (One can see more dandies in such schools than one ever will find in middle-class high schools.) There is not the look of casual assurance I saw students at Stanford display. Ghetto girls mimic high-fashion models. Their dresses are of bold, forceful color; their figures elegant, long; the stance theatrical. Boys wear shirts that grip at their overdeveloped muscular bodies. (Against a powerless future, they engage images of strength.) Bad nutrition does not yet tell. Great disappointment, fatal to youth, awaits them still. For the moment, movements in school hallways are dancelike, a procession of postures in a sexual masque. Watching them, I feel a kind of envy. I wonder how different my adolescence would have been had I been free.... But no, it is my parents I see—their optimism during those years when they were entertained by Italian grand opera. 19

The registration clerk in London wonders if I have just been to Switzerland. And the man who carries my luggage in New York guesses the Caribbean. My complexion becomes a mark of my leisure. Yet no one would regard my complexion the same way if I entered such hotels through the service entrance. That is only to say that my complexion assumes its significance from the context of my life. My skin, in itself, means nothing. I stress the point because I know there are people who would label me "disadvantaged" because of my color. They make the same mistake I made as a boy, when I thought a disadvantaged life was circumscribed by particular occupations. That summer I worked in the sun may have made me physically indistinguishable from the Mexicans working nearby. (My skin was actually darker because, unlike them, I worked without wearing a shirt. By late August my hands were probably as tough as theirs.) But I was not one of *los pobres*. What made me different from them was an attitude of *mind*, my imagination of myself. 20

I do not blame my mother for warning me away from the sun when I was young. In a world where her brother had become an old man in his twenties because he was dark, my complexion was something to worry about. "Don't run in the sun," she warns me today. I run. In the end, my 21 father was right—though perhaps he did not know how right or why—to say that I would never know what real work is. I will never know what he felt at his last factory job. If tomorrow I worked at some kind of factory, it would go differently for me. My long education would favor me. I could act as a public person—able to defend my interests, to unionize, to petition, to speak up—to challenge and demand. (I will never know what real work is.) I will never know what the Mexicans knew, gathering their shovels and ladders and saws.

Their silence stays with me now. The wages those Mexicans received for their labor were only a measure of their disadvantaged condition. Their silence is more telling. They lack a public identity. They remain profoundly alien. Persons apart. People lacking a union obviously, people without grounds. They depend upon the relative good will or fairness of their employers each day. For such people, lacking a better alternative, it is not such an unreasonable risk. 22

Their silence stays with me. I have taken these many words to describe its impact. Only: the quiet. Something uncanny about it. Its compliance. Vulnerability. Pathos. As I heard their truck rumbling away, I shuddered, my face mirrored with sweat. I had finally come face to face with *los pobres.* 23

Questions for Close Reading

1. What is the selection's thesis? Locate the sentence(s) in which Rodriguez states his main idea. If he doesn't state the thesis explicitly, express it in your own words.
2. What does Rodriguez find appealing about the construction job when his friend first offers it to him?
3. Once on the job, how long does it take Rodriguez to realize he will never be a "laborer"? Why does he feel this way?
4. According to Rodriguez, what makes him different from *los pobres?* Is poverty the only thing that makes them distinctive?
5. Refer to your dictionary as needed to define the following words used in the selection: *menial* (paragraph 1), *skepticism* (4), *luxuriating* (5), *diversity* (9), *ludicrous* (16), *nouveau riche* (18), and *pathos* (23).

Questions About the Writer's Craft

1. **The pattern.** One way Rodriguez develops his essay is by comparing and contrasting himself to the two groups of workers. Which group is he more like? What specifics does Rodriguez provide to show his similarity to this group and his dissimilarity to the other?
2. **Other patterns.** Rodriguez uses narration to develop his comparison-contrast of the two groups of workers. How many *narrative* segments appear in the essay? Why do you think Rodriguez puts the story about the Mexican workers last?
3. **Other patterns.** Rodriguez uses especially vivid language to *describe* the sun, his sweat, and the sensation of digging. Locate some examples of these descriptions. Which ones particularly stand out? Why?
4. Why does Rodriguez include some Spanish words in his essay? How is the use of these words related to the essay's overall theme?

Writing Assignments Using Comparison-Contrast as a Pattern of Development

1. Write an essay comparing and/or contrasting a part-time or summer job you've had with your (or someone else's) full-time or "real" job. Use examples, description, anecdotes, and illustrations to clarify the points of comparison or contrast.
2. Write an essay in which you compare and/or contrast the job you hope to have after graduation with a job you now have or have had in the past. Your analysis should reach conclusions about your interests, skills, and values.

Writing Assignments Combining Patterns of Development

3. In an essay, *define* what you mean by the term *real work.* Support your definition by citing *examples* of experiences you have had or have heard about. Barbara Ehrenreich's "Serving in Florida" (page 162), David Brooks's "Psst! Human Capital" (page 266), and Jacques D'Amboise's "Showing What Is Possible" (page 402) should prompt some interesting thoughts about work.
4. Episodes of the TV show *Dirty Jobs* highlight jobs that are dangerous, physically demanding, or messy. Featured jobs include those of sewer inspector, alligator farmer, garbage pit technician, and coal miner. Write an essay *illustrating* what would be a "dirty" job for you. It might be one of the jobs shown on *Dirty Jobs* or some other type of job, such as that of IRS auditor or car repossessor. You might even find being a doctor, lawyer, or college professor unappealing! Provide abundant reasons, including detailed *descriptions,* why you would never want to do such work. You might wrap up your essay by reaching some conclusions about your priorities.

Writing Assignment Using a Journal Entry as a Starting Point

5. Write an essay comparing and/or contrasting the work habits of earlier generations with those of the current generation. Consider kinds of work, working conditions, benefits, hours on the job, and so on. In addition to drawing upon ideas from your pre-reading journal entry, interview an equal number of people of both generations to get their opinions. Where appropriate, include their views in your essay. Begin or end the essay with a statement indicating which generation's work habits you respect more. For additional insight into generational differences, read Ann Hulbert's "Beyond the Pleasure Principle" (page 444).

Dave Barry

Pulitzer Prize–winning humorist Dave Barry (1947–) began his writing career covering—as he puts it—"incredibly dull municipal meetings" for the *Daily Local News* of West Chester, Pennsylvania. Next came an eight-year stint trying to teach businesspeople not to write sentences like "Enclosed please find the enclosed enclosures." In 1983, Barry joined the staff of the *The Miami Herald,* where his rib-tickling commentary on the absurdities of everyday life quickly brought him a legion of devoted fans. Barry's column is now syndicated in more than 150 newspapers. A popular guest on television and radio, Barry has written dozens of books, including *Dave Barry's Complete Guide to Guys* (1995), *Dave Barry in Cyberspace* (1996), *Dave Barry Hits Below the Beltway* (2001), *Boogers Are My Beat* (2003), *Dave Barry's Money Secrets* (2006), and most recently *I'll Mature When I'm Dead* (2010). He has also written the the comic mystery novels *Big Trouble* (1999) and *Tricky Business* (2002). The father of two, Barry lives in Miami with his wife. The following essay, published also under the title "The Ugly Truth About Beauty," first appeared in *The Miami Herald* in 1998.

Pre-Reading Journal Entry

To what extent would you say our images of personal attractiveness are influenced by TV commercials and magazine advertisements? Think of commercials and ads you've seen recently. What physical traits are typically identified as attractive in women? In men? List as many as you can. What assumptions does each trait suggest? Use your journal to respond to these questions.

Beauty and the Beast

If you're a man, at some point a woman will ask you how she looks. 1

"How do I look?" she'll ask. 2

You must be careful how you answer this question. The best technique is to form an honest yet sensitive opinion, then collapse on the floor with some kind of fatal seizure. Trust me, this is the easiest way out. Because you will never come up with the right answer. 3

The problem is that women generally do not think of their looks in the same way that men do. Most men form an opinion of how they look in the seventh grade, and they stick to it for the rest of their lives. Some men form the opinion that they are irresistible stud muffins, and they do not change this opinion even when their faces sag and their noses bloat to the size of eggplants and their eyebrows grow together to form what appears to be a giant forehead-dwelling tropical caterpillar. 4

Most men, I believe, think of themselves as average-looking. Men will think this even if their faces cause heart failure in cattle at a range of 300 yards. Being average does not bother them; average is fine, for men. This is 5 why men never ask anybody how they look. Their primary form of beauty care is to shave themselves, which is essentially the same form of beauty care that they give to their lawns. If, at the end of his four-minute daily beauty regimen, a man has managed to wipe most of the shaving cream out of his hair and is not bleeding too badly, he feels that he has done all he can, so he stops thinking about his appearance and devotes his mind to more critical issues, such as the Super Bowl.

Women do not look at themselves this way. If I had to express, in three words, what I believe most women think about their appearance, those words would be: "not good enough." No matter how attractive a woman may appear to be to others, when she looks at herself in the mirror, she thinks: woof. She thinks that at any moment a municipal animal-control officer is going to throw a net over her and haul her off to the shelter. 6

Why do women have such low self-esteem? There are many complex psychological and societal reasons, by which I mean Barbie. Girls grow up playing with a doll proportioned such that, if it were human, it would be seven feet tall and weigh 81 pounds, of which 53 pounds would be bosoms. This is a difficult appearance standard to live up to, especially when you contrast it with the standard set for little boys by their dolls... excuse me, by their action figures. Most of the action figures that my son played with when he was little were hideous-looking. For example, he was very fond of an action figure (part of the He-Man series) called "Buzz-Off," who was part human, part flying insect. Buzz-Off was not a looker. But he was extremely self-confident. You could not imagine Buzz-Off saying to the other action figures: "Do you think these wings make my hips look big?" 7

But women grow up thinking they need to look like Barbie, which for most women is impossible, although there is a multibillion-dollar beauty industry devoted to convincing women that they must try. I once saw an Oprah show wherein supermodel Cindy Crawford dispensed makeup tips to the studio audience. Cindy had all these middle-aged women applying beauty products to their faces; she stressed how important it was to apply them in a certain way, using the tips of their fingers. All the women dutifully did this, even though it was obvious to any sane observer that, no matter how carefully they applied these products, they would never look remotely like Cindy Crawford, who is some kind of genetic mutation. 8

I'm not saying that men are superior. I'm just saying that you're not going to get a group of middle-aged men to sit in a room and apply cosmetics to themselves under the instruction of Brad Pitt, in hopes of looking more like him. Men would realize that this task was pointless and demeaning. They would find some way to bolster their self-esteem that did not require looking like Brad Pitt. They would say to Brad: "Oh YEAH? Well what do you know about LAWN CARE, pretty boy?" 9

Of course many women will argue that the reason they become obsessed with trying to look like Cindy Crawford is that men, being as shallow as a drop of spit, WANT women to look that way. To which I have two responses: 10

1. Hey, just because WE'RE idiots, that does not mean you have to be; and 11

2. Men don't even notice 97 percent of the beauty efforts you make anyway. Take fingernails. The average woman spends 5,000 hours per year worrying about her fingernails; I have never once, in more than 40 years of listening to men talk about women, heard a man say, "She has a nice set of fingernails!" Many men would not notice if a woman had upward of four hands. 12

Anyway, to get back to my original point: If you're a man, and a woman asks you how she looks, you're in big trouble. Obviously, you can't say she looks bad. But you also can't say that she looks great, because she'll think you're lying, because she has spent countless hours, with the help of the multibillion-dollar beauty industry, obsessing about the differences between herself and Cindy Crawford. Also, she suspects that you're not qualified to judge anybody's appearance. This is because you have shaving cream in your hair. 13

Questions for Close Reading

1. What is the selection's thesis? Locate the sentence(s) in which Barry states his main idea. If he doesn't state the thesis explicitly, express it in your own words.
2. Barry tells us that most men consider themselves to be "average-looking" (paragraph 5). Why, according to Barry, do men feel this way?
3. When Barry writes that most women think of themselves as "not good enough" (6), what does he mean? What, according to Barry, causes women to develop low opinions of themselves?
4. Barry implies that women could have a more rational response to the "difficult appearance standard" that pervades society (7). What would that response be?
5. Refer to your dictionary as needed to define the following words used in the selection: *regimen* (paragraph 5), *municipal* (6), *societal* (7), *dispensed* (8), *genetic* (8), *mutation* (8), *demeaning* (9), and *bolster* (9).

Questions About the Writer's Craft

1. **The pattern.** Which comparison-contrast method of organization (point-by-point or one-side-at-a-time) does Barry use to develop his essay? Why might he have chosen this pattern?
2. Barry uses exaggeration, a strategy typically associated with humorous writing. Locate instances of exaggeration in the selection. Why do you think he uses this strategy?
3. **Other patterns.** Barry demonstrates a series of *cause-effect* chains in his essay. Locate some of the cause-effect series. How do they help Barry reinforce his thesis?
4. How does the essay's title foreshadow the essay's ideas?

Writing Assignments Using Comparison-Contrast as a Pattern of Development

1. Examine the pitches made in magazines and on TV for the male and female versions of *one* kind of grooming product. Possibilities include deodorant, hair dye, soap, and so on. Then write an essay contrasting the persuasive appeals that the product makes to men with those it makes to women. (Don't forget to examine the assumptions behind the appeals.) To gain insight into advertising techniques, you'll find it helpful to read Ann McClintock's "Propaganda Techniques in Today's Advertising" (page 239). For useful perspectives on gender issues, consider reading Amy Sutherland's "What Shamu Taught Me About a Happy Marriage" (page 308). For more insight into how we judge beauty, read Natalie Angier's "The Cute Factor" (page 461).
2. Barry contrasts women's preoccupation with looking good to men's lack of concern about their appearance. Now consider the flip side—something men care about deeply that women virtually ignore. Write an essay contrasting men's stereotypical fascination with *one* area to women's indifference. You might, for example, examine male and female attitudes toward sports, cars, tools, even lawn care. Following Barry's example, adopt a playful tone in your essay, illustrating the absurdity of the obsession you discuss.

Writing Assignments Combining Patterns of Development

3. Barry implies that most men, unaffected by the "multibillion-dollar beauty industry," are content to "think of themselves as average looking." Do you agree? Conduct your own research into whether or not Barry's assertions about men are true. Begin by interviewing several male friends, family members, and classmates to see how these men feel about their physical appearance. In addition, in the library or online, research magazines such as *People, GQ,* or *Men's Health* for articles describing how everyday men as well as male celebrities view their looks. Then write an essay *refuting* or *defending* the view that being average-looking doesn't bother most men. Start by acknowledging the opposing view; then support your assertion with convincing *examples* and other evidence drawn from your research.
4. Barry blames Barbie dolls for setting up "a difficult appearance standard" for girls to emulate. Many would *argue* that the toys that *boys* play with also teach negative, ultimately damaging values. Write an essay exploring the values that are conveyed to boys through their toys. Brainstorm with others, especially males, about the toys of their youth or the toys that boys have today. Identify two to three key negative values to write about, *illustrating* each with several examples of toys.

Writing Assignment Using a Journal Entry as a Starting Point

5. Review your pre-reading journal entry. Focusing on the characteristics of male *or* female attractiveness conveyed by the mass media, identify two to three assumptions suggested by these standards. Illustrate each assumption with examples from TV commercials and/or magazine advertisements. Be sure to make clear how you feel about these assumptions.

Stephen Chapman

Stephen Chapman was an associate editor for *The New Republic,* the publication for which he wrote "The Prisoner's Dilemma" in 1980. Since then, he has joined the staff of the *Chicago Tribune,* where his twice-weekly syndicated column on national and international affairs originates. Born in Texas in 1954, Chapman graduated *cum laude* from Harvard University in 1976 and did graduate work in business administration at the University of Chicago. He has contributed articles to national magazines including *The Atlantic, Harper's, Reason,* and *The American Spectator.* Chapman lives with his family outside Chicago.

Pre-Reading Journal Entry

Should wrongdoing be punished in public? Why or why not? Use your journal to consider the pros and cons of public punishment for illegal actions. Think of three or four wrongdoings (from lesser offenses like shoplifting to serious crimes like armed robbery). For each offense, list possible forms of public punishment as well as the advantages and disadvantages of each form.

The Prisoner's Dilemma

One of the amusements of life in the modern West is the opportunity to observe the barbaric rituals of countries that are attached to the customs of the dark ages. Take Pakistan, for example.... President Zia, in harmony with the Islamic fervor that is sweeping his part of the world, revived the traditional Moslem practice of flogging lawbreakers in public. In Pakistan, this qualified as mass entertainment, and no fewer than 10,000 law-abiding Pakistanis turned out to see justice done to 26 convicts. To Western sensibilities the spectacle seemed barbaric—both in the sense of cruel and in the sense of pre-civilized. In keeping with Islamic custom each of the unfortunates—who had been caught in prostitution raids the previous night and summarily convicted and sentenced—was stripped down to a pair of white shorts, which were painted with a red stripe across the buttocks (the target). Then he was shackled against an easel, with pads thoughtfully placed over the kidneys to prevent injury. The floggers were muscular, fierce-looking sorts—convicted murderers, as it happens—who paraded around the flogging platform in colorful loincloths. When the time for the ceremony began, one of the floggers took a running start and brought a five-foot stave down across the first victim's buttocks, eliciting screams from the convict and murmurs from the audience. Each of the 26 received from five to 15 lashes. One had to be carried from the stage unconscious. 1

Flogging is one of the punishments stipulated by Koranic law, which has made it a popular penological device in several Moslem countries, including 2

Pakistan, Saudi Arabia, and, most recently, the ayatollah's Iran. Flogging, or *ta'zir,* is the general punishment prescribed for offenses that don't carry an explicit Koranic penalty. Some crimes carry automatic *hadd* punishments—stoning or scourging (a severe whipping) for illicit sex, scourging for drinking alcoholic beverages, amputation of the hands for theft. Other crimes—as varied as murder and abandoning Islam—carry the death penalty (usually carried out in public). Colorful practices like these have given the Islamic world an image in the West, as described by historian G. H. Jansen, "of blood dripping from the stumps of amputated hands and from the striped backs of malefactors, and piles of stones barely concealing the battered bodies of adulterous couples." Jansen, whose book *Militant Islam* is generally effusive in its praise of Islamic practices, grows squeamish when considering devices like flogging, amputation, and stoning. But they are given enthusiastic endorsement by the Koran itself.

Such traditions, we all must agree, are no sign of an advanced civilization. In the West, we have replaced these various punishments (including the death penalty in most cases) with a single device. Our custom is to confine criminals in prison for varying lengths of time. In Illinois, a reasonably typical state, grand theft carries a punishment of three to five years; armed robbery can get you from six to 30. The lowest form of felony theft is punishable by one to three years in prison. Most states impose longer sentences on habitual offenders. In Kentucky, for example, habitual offenders can be sentenced to life in prison. Other states are less brazen, preferring the more genteel sounding "indeterminate sentence," which allows parole boards to keep inmates locked up for as long as life. It was under an indeterminate sentence of one to 14 years that George Jackson served 12 years in California prisons for committing a $70 armed robbery. Under a Texas law imposing an automatic life sentence for a third felony conviction, a man was sent to jail for life last year because of three thefts adding up to less than $300 in property value. Texas also is famous for occasionally imposing extravagantly long sentences, often running into hundreds or thousands of years. This gives Texas a leg up on Maryland, which used to sentence some criminals to life plus a day—a distinctive if superfluous flourish.... 3

What are the advantages of being a convicted criminal in an advanced culture? First there is the overcrowding in prisons. One Tennessee prison, for example, has a capacity of 806, according to accepted space standards, but it houses 2300 inmates. One Louisiana facility has confined four and five prisoners in a single six-foot-by-six-foot cell. Then there is the disease caused by overcrowding, unsanitary conditions, and poor or inadequate medical care. A federal appeals court noted that the Tennessee prison had suffered frequent outbreaks of infectious diseases like hepatitis and tuberculosis. But the most distinctive element of American prison life is its constant violence. In his book *Criminal Violence, Criminal Justice,* Charles Silberman 4 noted that in one Louisiana prison, there were 211 stabbings in only three years, 11 of them fatal. There were 15 slayings in a prison in Massachusetts between 1972 and 1975. According to a federal court, in Alabama's penitentiaries (as in many others), "robbery, rape, extortion, theft and assault are everyday occurrences."

At least in regard to cruelty, it's not at all clear that the system of punishment that has evolved in the West is less barbaric than the grotesque practices of Islam. Skeptical? Ask yourself: would you rather be subjected to a few minutes of intense pain and considerable public humiliation, or be locked away for two or three years in a prison cell crowded with ill-tempered sociopaths? Would you rather lose a hand or spend 10 years or more in a typical state prison? I have taken my own survey on this matter. I have found no one who does not find the Islamic system hideous. And I have found no one who *given the choices* mentioned above, would not prefer its penalties to our own.... 5

Imprisonment is now the universal method of punishing criminals in the United States. It is thought to perform five functions, each of which has been given a label by criminologists. First, there is simple *retribution:* punishing the lawbreaker to serve society's sense of justice and to satisfy the victims' desire for revenge. Second, there is *specific deterrence:* discouraging the offender from misbehaving in the future. Third, *general deterrence:* using the offender as an example to discourage others from turning to crime. Fourth, *prevention:* at least during the time he is kept off the streets, the criminal cannot victimize other members of society. Finally, and most important, there is *rehabilitation:* reforming the criminal so that when he returns to society he will be inclined to obey the laws and able to make an honest living. 6

How satisfactorily do American prisons perform by these criteria? Well, of course, they do punish. But on the other scores they don't do so well. Their effect in discouraging future criminality by the prisoner or others is the subject of much debate, but the soaring rates of the last 20 years suggest that prisons are not a dramatically effective deterrent to criminal behavior. Prisons do isolate convicted criminals, but only to divert crime from ordinary citizens to prison guards and fellow inmates. Almost no one contends any more that prisons rehabilitate their inmates. If anything, they probably impede rehabilitation by forcing inmates into prolonged and almost exclusive association with other criminals. And prisons cost a lot of money. Housing a typical prisoner in a typical prison costs far more than a stint at a top university. This cost would be justified if prisons did the job they were intended for. But it is clear to all that prisons fail on the very grounds—humanity and hope of rehabilitation—that caused them to replace earlier, cheaper forms of punishment.... 7

So the debate continues to rage in all the same old ruts. No one, of course, would think of copying the medieval practices of Islamic nations and 8 experimenting with punishments such as flogging and amputation. But let us consider them anyway. How do they compare with our American prison system in achieving the ostensible objectives of punishment? First, do they punish? Obviously they do, and in a uniquely painful and memorable way. Of course any sensible person, given the choice, would prefer suffering these punishments to years of incarceration in a typical American prison. But presumably no Western penologist would criticize Islamic punishments on the grounds that they are not barbaric enough. Do they deter crime? Yes, and probably more effectively than sending convicts off to prison. Now we read about a prison sentence in the newspaper, then think no more about the criminal's payment for his crimes until, perhaps, years later we read a small item reporting his release. By contrast, one can easily imagine the vivid impression it would leave to be wandering through a local shopping center and to stumble onto the scene of some poor wretch being lustily flogged. And the occasional sight of an habitual offender walking around with a bloody stump at the end of his arm no doubt also would serve as a forceful reminder that crime does not pay.

Do flogging and amputation discourage recidivism? No one knows 9
whether the scars on his back would dissuade a criminal from risking another crime, but it is hard to imagine that corporal measures could stimulate a higher rate of recidivism than already exists. Islamic forms of punishment do not serve the favorite new right goal of simply isolating criminals from the rest of society, but they may achieve the same purpose of making further crimes impossible. In the movie *Bonnie and Clyde,* Warren Beatty successfully robs a bank with his arm in a sling, but this must be dismissed as artistic license. It must be extraordinarily difficult, at the very least, to perform much violent crime with only one hand.

Do these medieval forms of punishment rehabilitate the criminal? Plainly 10
not. But long prison terms do not rehabilitate either. And it is just as plain that typical Islamic punishments are no crueler to the convict than incarceration in the typical American state prison.

Of course there are other reasons besides its bizarre forms of punishment 11
that the Islamic system of justice seems uncivilized to the Western mind. One is the absence of due process. Another is the long list of offenses—such as drinking, adultery, blasphemy, "profiteering," and so on—that can bring on conviction and punishment. A third is all the ritualistic mumbo-jumbo in pronouncements of Islamic law.... Even in these matters, however, a little cultural modesty is called for. The vast majority of American criminals are convicted and sentenced as a result of plea bargaining, in which due process plays almost no role. It has been only half a century since a wave of religious fundamentalism stirred this country to outlaw the consumption of alcoholic beverages. Most states also still have laws imposing austere constraints on sexual conduct. The *Washington Post* reported that the FBI had spent two

and a half years and untold amounts of money to break up a nationwide pornography ring. Flogging the clients of prostitutes, as the Pakistanis did, does seem silly. But only a few months ago Mayor Koch of New York was proposing that clients caught in his own city have their names broadcast by radio stations. We are not so far advanced on such matters as we often like to think. Finally, my lawyer friends assure me that the rules of jurisdiction for American courts contain plenty of petty requirements and bizarre distinctions that would sound silly enough to foreign ears.

Perhaps it sounds barbaric to talk of flogging and amputation, and perhaps it is. But our system of punishment also is barbaric, and probably more so. Only cultural smugness about their system and willful ignorance about our own make it easy to regard the one as cruel and the other as civilized. We inflict our cruelties away from public view, while nations like Pakistan stage them in front of 10,000 onlookers. Their outrages are visible; ours are not. Most Americans can live their lives for years without having their peace of mind disturbed by the knowledge of what goes on in our prisons. To choose imprisonment over flogging and amputation is not to choose human kindness over cruelty, but merely to prefer that our cruelties be kept out of sight, and out of mind. 12

Public flogging and amputation may be more barbaric forms of punishment than imprisonment, even if they are not more cruel. Society may pay a higher price for them, even if the particular criminal does not. Revulsion against officially sanctioned violence and infliction of pain derives from something deeply ingrained in the Western conscience, and clearly it is something admirable. Grotesque displays of the sort that occur in Islamic countries probably breed a greater tolerance for physical cruelty, for example, which prisons do not do precisely because they conceal their cruelties. In fact it is our admirable intolerance for calculated violence that makes it necessary for us to conceal what we have not been able to do away with. In a way this is a good thing, since it holds out the hope that we may eventually find a way to do away with it. But in another way it is a bad thing, since it permits us to congratulate ourselves on our civilized humanitarianism while violating its norms in this one area of our national life. 13

Questions for Close Reading

1. What is the selection's thesis? Locate the sentence(s) in which Chapman states his main idea. If he doesn't state the thesis explicitly, express it in your own words.
2. Chapman calls Islamic punishment practices "barbaric." What are some of these practices? Why would they seem barbaric to most Americans?
3. According to our society's philosophy of punishment, what goals is imprisonment supposed to accomplish? How successful, in Chapman's view, are U.S. prisons in meeting these goals?

4. For Chapman, what is the core difference between the U.S. punishment system and that of Islamic nations like Pakistan? Which system does he find preferable? Why?
5. Refer to your dictionary as needed to define the following words used in the selection: *barbaric* (paragraph 1), *stipulated* (2), *penological* (2), *malefactors* (2), *effusive* (2), *brazen* (3), *genteel* (3), *indeterminate* (3), *superfluous* (3), *extortion* (4), *criteria* (7), *ostensible* (8), *recidivism* (9), *corporal* (9), *blasphemy* (11), and *sanctioned* (13).

Questions About the Writer's Craft

1. **The pattern.** In paragraphs 7 through 10, Chapman contrasts the success of the American and Islamic systems in meeting the five goals of punishment cited in paragraph 6. How does Chapman help readers keep those goals in mind as he develops his contrast?
2. **Other patterns.** In paragraphs 1, 2, and 6, Chapman provides a number of *definitions.* How do these definitions help him convince readers to accept key points in his argument?
3. **Other patterns.** Examine the *examples* that Chapman provides in paragraphs 3 and 4. Why do you think he sequences each set of examples as he does?
4. Examine Chapman's tone, especially in paragraphs 3, 4, 5, and 8 to 9. Where does he shift from a fairly neutral tone to a more sarcastic and mocking one? How does this change help Chapman convince readers of the seriousness of the problems in U.S. justice?

Writing Assignments Using Comparison-Contrast as a Pattern of Development

1. Select one situation in which people are, in your opinion, ineffectively punished for violating a law or regulation. For example, you might focus on the punishment typically imposed for driving while intoxicated, plagiarizing a school paper, or habitually coming to work late. Write an essay describing the violation and its customary punishment. Then contrast this punishment with a more effective way of correcting the offending behavior. Whether you choose the one-side-at-a-time or the point-by-point method, be sure to provide clear signals, as Chapman does, to help readers follow your ideas.
2. Chapman contrasts two cultures' approaches to criminal punishment. Write an essay comparing and/or contrasting two cultures' approaches to another aspect of life. To structure your paper, use either the one-side-at-a-time or point-by-point method of development. The cultures you discuss need not be nationalities or ethnicities. You might, for example, focus on parents' and teenagers' preferences in music, male and female expectations in a relationship, or high school teachers' and college professors' attitudes toward student responsibility. If appropriate, consider using a humorous tone to make fun of both sides—or to convey which side's approach you find preferable.

Writing Assignments Combining Patterns of Development

3. Chapman states that there is "universal acknowledgment that prisons do not rehabilitate." Conduct research in the library and/or on the Internet on recent developments in criminal rehabilitation. Bibliographic sources like EBSCOhost, the *Social Sciences Index*, and *Criminal Justice Abstracts* will help you locate relevant information. Then write an essay *refuting* or *defending* the common view that the rehabilitation of prisoners is a futile goal. Start by acknowledging the opposing view, and then support your argument with convincing *examples* and other evidence drawn from your research.
4. Chapman describes people in Islamic cultures flocking to gawk at the misfortunes of others. People in our country are also fascinated, even entertained, by others' problems. They slow down to inspect traffic accidents, follow celebrities' troubles in tabloid publications, and glue themselves to the television when a natural disaster strikes. Write an essay in which you account for the *causes* of our fascination with others' misfortunes. Begin with one or two dramatic *examples* of this phenomenon, and then explain why you think people are so attracted to the troubles of others. Consider reading Stephen King's "Why We Crave Horror Movies" (page 397) and Mark Twain's "The Damned Human Race" (page 525) for some helpful insights into this morbid human tendency.

Writing Assignment Using a Journal Entry as a Starting Point

5. Write an essay arguing that public punishment would *or* would not be appropriate for a specific transgression. From your pre-reading journal entry, select *one* crime and its most realistic form of public punishment. Supplement the material in your journal by interviewing friends, classmates, and family members. Be sure to seek out and acknowledge the views of those who don't agree with the position you take.

Additional Writing Topics

COMPARISON-CONTRAST

General Assignments

Using comparison-contrast, write an essay on one of the following topics. Your thesis should indicate whether the two subjects are being compared, contrasted, or both. Organize the paper by arranging the details in a one-side-at-a-time or point-by-point pattern. Remember to use organizational cues to help the audience follow your analysis.

1. Living at home versus living in an apartment or dorm
2. Two-career family versus one-career family
3. Two approaches for dealing with problems
4. Children's pastimes today and yesterday
5. Life before the Internet versus after the Internet
6. Neighborhood stores versus shopping malls
7. Two characters in a novel or other literary work
8. Two attitudes toward money
9. A sports team then and now
10. Watching a movie on television versus viewing it in a theater
11. Two attitudes about a controversial subject
12. Two approaches to parenting
13. A typical fan of one type of music versus another
14. Marriage versus living together
15. The atmosphere in two classes
16. Two approaches to studying
17. The place where you live and the place where you would like to live
18. Two comedians
19. The coverage of an event on television versus the coverage in a newspaper
20. Significant trend versus passing fad
21. Two horror or adventure movies
22. Handwriting a letter versus sending an e-mail message
23. Two candidates for an office
24. Your attitude before and after getting to know someone
25. Two friends with different lifestyles

Assignments with a Specific Purpose, Audience, and Point of View

On Campus

1. You would like to change your campus living arrangements. Perhaps you want to move from a dormitory to an off-campus apartment or from home to a dorm.

Before you do, though, you'll have to convince your parents (who are paying most of your college costs) that the move will be beneficial. Write out what you would say to your parents. Contrast your current situation with your proposed one, explaining why the new arrangement would be better.

2. Write a guide on "Passing Exams" for first-year college students, contrasting the right and wrong ways to prepare for and take exams. Although your purpose is basically serious, write the section on how not to approach exams with some humor.

At Home or in the Community

3. As president of your local Neighbors' Association, you're concerned about the way your local government is dealing with a particular situation (for example, an increase in robberies, muggings, graffiti, and so on). Write a letter to your mayor contrasting the way your local government handles the situation with another city or town's approach. In your conclusion, point out the advantages of adopting the other neighborhood's strategy.
4. Your old high school has invited you back to make a speech before an audience of seniors. The topic will be "how to choose the college that is right for you." Write your speech in the form of a comparison-contrast analysis. Focus on the choices available (two-year versus four-year schools, large versus small, local versus faraway, and so on), showing the advantages and/or disadvantages of each.

On the Job

5. As store manager, you decide to write a memo to all sales personnel explaining how to keep customers happy. Compare and/or contrast the needs and shopping habits of several different consumer groups (by age, spending ability, or sex), and show how to make each group comfortable in your store.
6. You work as a volunteer for a mental health hot line. Many people call simply because they feel "stressed out." Do some research on the subject of stress management, and prepare a brochure for these people, recommending a "Type B" approach to stressful situations. Focus the brochure on the contrast between "Type A" and "Type B" personalities: the former is nervous, hard-driving, competitive; the latter is relaxed and noncompetitive. Give specific examples of how each type tends to act in stressful situations.

9

CAUSE-EFFECT

WHAT IS CAUSE-EFFECT?

All of us think in terms of cause and effect, sometimes consciously, sometimes unconsciously: "Why did they give me such an odd look?" we wonder, or "How would I do at another college?" we speculate. This exploration of reasons and results is also at the heart of most professions: "What led to our involvement in Vietnam?" historians question; "What will happen if we administer this experimental drug?" scientists ask.

Cause-effect writing, often called *causal analysis,* is rooted in this elemental need to make connections. Because the drive to understand reasons and results is so fundamental, causal analysis is a common kind of writing. An article analyzing the unexpected outcome of an election, a report linking poor nutrition to low academic achievement, an editorial analyzing the impact of a proposed tax cut—all are examples of cause-effect writing.

Done well, cause-effect pieces can uncover the subtle and often surprising connections between events or phenomena. By rooting out causes and projecting effects, causal analysis enables us to make sense of our experiences, revealing a universe that is somewhat less arbitrary and chaotic.

HOW CAUSE-EFFECT FITS YOUR PURPOSE AND AUDIENCE

Many assignments and exam questions in college involve writing essays that analyze causes, effects, or both. Sometimes, as in the following examples, you'll be asked to write an essay developed primarily through the cause-effect pattern:

> Although divorces have leveled off in the last few years, the number of marriages ending in divorce is still greater than it was a generation ago. What do you think are the causes of this phenomenon?
>
> Political commentators were surprised that so few people voted in the last election. Discuss the probable causes of this weak voter turnout.
>
> Americans never seem to tire of gossip about the rich and famous. What effect has this fascination with celebrities had on U.S. culture?
>
> The federal government is expected to pass legislation that will significantly reduce the funding of student loans. Analyze the possible effects of such a cutback.

Other assignments and exam questions may not explicitly ask you to address causes and effects, but they may use words that suggest causal analysis would be appropriate. Consider these examples, paying special attention to the words in boldface:

> In contrast to the socially involved youth of the 1960s, many young people today tend to remove themselves from political issues. What do you think are the **sources** of the political apathy found among 18- to 25-year-olds? (*cause*)
>
> A number of experts forecast that drug abuse will be the most significant factor affecting U.S. productivity in the coming decade. Evaluate the validity of this observation by discussing the **impact** of drugs in the workplace. (*effect*)
>
> According to school officials, a predictable percentage of entering students drop out of college at some point during their first year. What **motivates** students to drop out? What **happens** to them once they leave? (*cause and effect*)

In addition to serving as the primary strategy for achieving an essay's purpose, causal analysis can also be a supplemental method used to help make a point in an essay developed chiefly through another pattern of development. Assume, for example, that you want to write an essay *defining* the term *the homeless.* To help readers see that unfavorable circumstances can result in nearly anyone becoming homeless, you might discuss some of the unavoidable, everyday factors causing people to live on streets and in subway stations. Similarly, in a *persuasive* proposal urging your college administration to institute an honors program, you would probably spend some time analyzing the positive effect of such a program on students and faculty.

At this point, you have a good sense of the way writers use cause-effect to achieve their purpose and to connect with their readers. Now take a moment to look closely at the photograph at the beginning of this chapter. Imagine you're writing a column, accompanied by the photo, for the website of a local environmental organization. Your purpose is to prevent further development of nearby wilderness areas. Jot down ideas you might include when discussing the *effects* of such development.

SUGGESTIONS FOR USING CAUSE-EFFECT IN AN ESSAY

The suggestions here and in Figure 9.1 (page 384) will be helpful whether you use causal analysis as a dominant or a supportive pattern of development.

1. Stay focused on the purpose of your analysis. When writing a causal analysis, don't lose sight of your overall purpose. Consider, for example, an essay on the causes of widespread child abuse. If you're concerned primarily with explaining the problem of child abuse to your readers, you might take a purely *informative* approach:

> Although parental stress is the immediate cause of child abuse, the more compelling reason for such behavior lies in the way parents were themselves mistreated in their own families.

Or you might want to *persuade* the audience about some point or idea concerning child abuse:

> The tragic consequences of child abuse provide strong support for more aggressive handling of such cases by social workers and judges.

Then again, you could choose a *speculative* approach, your main purpose being to suggest possibilities:

> Psychologists disagree about the potential effect on youngsters of all the media attention to child abuse. Will children exposed to this media coverage grow up assertive, self-confident, and able to protect themselves? Or will they become fearful and distrustful?

These examples illustrate that an essay's causal analysis may have more than one purpose.

FIGURE 9.1
Development Diagram: Writing a Cause-Effect Essay

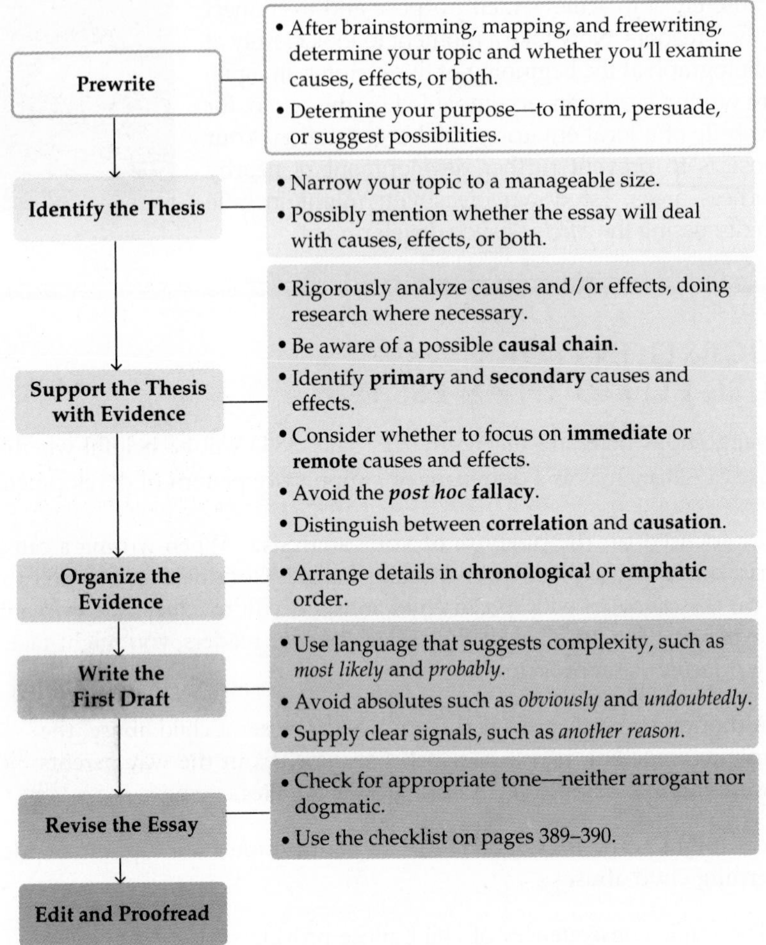

Prewrite
• After brainstorming, mapping, and freewriting, determine your topic and whether you'll examine causes, effects, or both.
• Determine your purpose—to inform, persuade, or suggest possibilities.
Identify the Thesis
• Narrow your topic to a manageable size.
• Possibly mention whether the essay will deal with causes, effects, or both.
Support the Thesis with Evidence
• Rigorously analyze causes and/or effects, doing research where necessary.
• Be aware of a possible causal chain.
• Identify primary and secondary causes and effects.
• Consider whether to focus on immediate or remote causes and effects.
• Avoid the post hoc fallacy.
• Distinguish between correlation and causation.
Organize the Evidence
• Arrange details in chronological or emphatic order.
Write the First Draft
• Use language that suggests complexity, such as most likely and probably.
• Avoid absolutes such as obviously and undoubtedly.
• Supply clear signals, such as another reason.
Revise the Essay
• Check for appropriate tone—neither arrogant nor dogmatic.
• Use the checklist on pages 389–390.
Edit and Proofread

2. Adapt content and tone to your purpose and readers. Your purpose and audience determine what supporting material and what tone will be most effective in a cause-effect essay. Assume you want to direct your essay on child abuse to general readers who know little about the subject. To *inform* readers, you might use facts, statistics, and expert opinion to provide an objective discussion of the causes of child abuse. Your analysis might show the following: (1) adults who were themselves mistreated as children tend to abuse their own offspring; (2) marital stress contributes to the mistreatment of children; and (3) certain personality disorders increase the likelihood of child abuse. Sensitive to what your readers would and wouldn't understand, you would stay away from a technical or formal tone. Rather than writing "Pathological preabuse symptomatology predicts adult transference of high aggressivity," you would say "Psychologists can often predict, on the basis of family histories, who will abuse children."

Now imagine that your purpose is to *convince* future social workers that the failure of social service agencies to act authoritatively in child-abuse cases often has tragic consequences. Hoping to encourage more responsible behavior in the prospective social workers, you would adopt a more emotional tone in the essay, perhaps citing wrenching case histories that dramatize what happens when child abuse isn't taken seriously.

3. Think rigorously about causes and effects. To write a meaningful causal analysis, you should do some careful thinking about the often complex relationship between causes and effects. Imprecise thinking has no place in essay writing. You should be willing to dig for causes, to think creatively about effects. You should examine your subject in depth, looking beyond the obvious and superficial.

Brainstorming, freewriting, and mapping will help you explore causes and effects thoroughly. No matter which prewriting technique you use, generate as many explanations as possible by asking yourself questions like these:

> *Causes:* What happened? What are the possible reasons? Which are most likely? Who was involved? Why?
>
> *Effects:* What happened? Who was involved? What were the observable results? What are some possible future consequences? Which consequences are negative? Which are positive?

If you remain open and look beyond the obvious, you'll discover that a cause may have many effects. Imagine that you're writing a paper on the effects of cigarette smoking. Prewriting would probably generate a number of consequences that could be discussed, some less obvious but perhaps more interesting than others: increased risk of lung cancer and heart disease, harm traced to secondhand smoke, legal battles regarding the rights of smokers and nonsmokers, lower birth weights in babies of mothers who smoke, and developmental problems experienced by such underweight infants.

In the same way, prewriting will help you see that an effect may have multiple causes. An essay analyzing the reasons for world hunger could discuss many causes, again some less evident but perhaps more thought-provoking than others: climatic changes, inefficient use of land, cultural predispositions for large families, and poor management of international relief funds.

Your analysis may also uncover a *causal chain* in which one cause (or effect) brings about another, which, in turn, brings about another, and so on. Here's an example of a causal chain: The Prohibition Amendment to the U.S. Constitution went into effect on January 29, 1920; bootleggers and organized crime stepped in to supply public demand for alcoholic beverages; ordinary citizens began breaking the law by buying illegal alcohol and patronizing speakeasies; disrespect for legal authority became widespread and acceptable. As you can see, a causal chain often leads to interesting points. In this case, the subject of Prohibition leads not just to the obvious (illegal consumption of alcohol) but also to the more complex issue of society's decreasing respect for legal authority.

If your subject involves multiple causes and effects, limit what you'll discuss. Identify which causes and effects are *primary* and which are *secondary*. How extensively you cover secondary factors will depend on your purpose and audience. In an essay intended to inform a general audience about the harmful effects of pesticides, you would most likely focus on everyday dangers—polluted drinking water, residues in food, and the like. You probably wouldn't include a discussion of more long-range consequences (evolution of resistant insects, disruption of the soil's acid-alkaline balance).

Similarly, decide whether to focus on *immediate,* more obvious causes and effects, or on less obvious, more *remote* ones. Or perhaps you need to focus on both. In an essay about a faculty strike at your college, should you attribute the strike simply to the faculty's failure to receive a salary increase? Or should you also examine other factors: the union's failure to accept a salary package that satisfied most professors; the administration's inability to coordinate its negotiating efforts? It may be more difficult to explore more remote causes and effects, but it can also lead to more original and revealing essays.

When developing a causal analysis, be careful to avoid the *post hoc fallacy.* Named after the Latin phrase *post hoc, ergo propter hoc,* meaning "after this, therefore because of this," this kind of faulty thinking occurs when you assume that simply because one event *followed* another, the first event *caused* the second. For example, if the Republicans win a majority of seats in Congress and, several months later, the economy collapses, can you conclude that the Republicans caused the collapse? A quick assumption of "Yes" fails the test of logic, for the timing of events could be coincidental and not indicative of any cause-effect relationship. The collapse may have been triggered by uncontrolled inflation that began well before the congressional elections. (For more information on the *post hoc* fallacy, see page 493.)

Also, be careful not to mistake *correlation* for *causation*. Two events correlate when they occur at about the same time. Such co-occurrence, however, doesn't guarantee a cause-effect relationship. For instance, while the number of ice cream cones eaten and the instances of heat prostration both increase during the summer months, this doesn't mean that eating ice-cream causes heat prostration! A third factor—in this case, summer heat—is the actual cause.

4. Write a thesis that focuses the paper on causes, effects, or both. The thesis in an essay developed through causal analysis often indicates whether the essay will deal with mostly causes, effects, or both causes and effects. Here, for example, are three thesis statements for causal analyses dealing with the public school system. You'll see that each thesis signals that essay's particular emphasis:

> Our school system has been weakened by an overemphasis on trendy electives. (*causes*)
>
> An ineffectual school system has led to crippling teachers' strikes and widespread disrespect for the teaching profession. *(effects)*
>
> Bureaucratic inefficiency has created a school system unresponsive to children's emotional, physical, and intellectual needs. (*causes and effects*)

Note that the thesis statement—in addition to signaling whether the paper will discuss causes or effects or both—may also point to the essay's plan of development. Consider the last thesis statement; it makes clear that the paper will discuss children's emotional needs first, their physical needs second, and their intellectual needs last.

The thesis statement in a causal analysis doesn't have to specify whether the essay will discuss causes, effects, or both. Nor does the thesis have to be worded in such a way that the essay's plan of development is apparent. But when first writing cause-effect essays, you may find that a highly focused thesis will keep your analysis on track.

5. Choose an organizational pattern. There are two basic ways to organize the points in a cause-effect essay: You may use a chronological or an emphatic sequence. If you select a *chronological order,* you discuss causes and effects in the order in which they occur or will occur. Suppose you're writing an essay on the causes for the popularity of imported cars. These causes might be discussed in chronological sequence: American plant workers became frustrated and dissatisfied on the job; some workers got careless while others deliberately sabotaged the production of sound cars; a growing number of defective cars hit the market; consumers grew dissatisfied with American cars and switched to imports.

Chronology might also be used to organize a discussion about effects. Imagine you want to write an essay about the need to guard against disrupting delicate balances in the country's wildlife. You might start the essay by discussing what happened when the starling, a non-native bird, was introduced into the American environment. Because the starling had few natural predators, the starling population soared out of control; starlings took over the food sources and habitats of native species; the bluebird, a native species, declined and is now threatened with extinction.

Although a chronological pattern can be an effective way to organize material, a strict time sequence can present a problem if your primary cause or effect ends up buried in the middle of the sequence. In such a case, you might use *emphatic order,* reserving the most significant cause or effect for the end. Emphatic order is an especially effective way to sequence cause-effect points when readers hold what, in your opinion, are mistaken or narrow views about a subject. To encourage readers to look more closely at the issues, you present what you consider the erroneous or obvious views first, show why they are unsound or limited, and then present what you feel to be the actual causes and effects. Such a sequence nudges the audience into giving further thought to the causes and effects you have discovered. Here is an informal outline for a causal analysis using this approach.

Subject: The causes of the riot at the rock concert

1. Some commentators blame the excessively hot weather.
2. Others cite drug use among the concertgoers.
3. Still others blame the beer sold at the concessions.
4. But the real cause of the disaster was poor planning by the concert promoters.

When using emphatic order in a causal analysis, you might want to word the thesis in such a way that it signals which point your essay will stress. Look at the following thesis statements:

Although many immigrants arrive in this country without marketable skills, their most pressing problem is learning how to make their way in a society whose language they don't know.

The space program has led to dramatic advances in computer technology and medical science. Even more important, though, the program has helped change many people's attitudes toward the planet we live on.

These thesis statements reflect an awareness of the complex nature of cause-effect relationships. While not dismissing secondary issues, the statements establish which points the writer considers most noteworthy.

Whether you use a chronological or emphatic pattern to organize your essay, you'll need to provide clear *signals* to identify when you're discussing causes and when you're discussing effects. Expressions such as "Another reason" and "A final outcome" help readers follow your line of thought.

6. Use language that hints at the complexity of cause-effect relationships. Because it's difficult—if not impossible—to identify causes and effects with certainty, you should avoid such absolutes as "It must be obvious" and "There is no doubt." Instead, try phrases like "Most likely" or "It's probable that." Using such language is not indecisive; rather, it reflects your understanding of the often tangled nature of causes and effects. Be careful, though, of going to the other extreme and being reluctant to take a stand on the issues. If you've thought carefully about causes and effects, you have a right to state your analysis with conviction. Don't undercut the hard work you've done by writing as if your ideas were unworthy of your reader's attention.

REVISION STRATEGIES

Once you have a draft of the essay, you're ready to revise. The following checklist will help you and those giving you feedback apply to cause-effect some of the revision techniques discussed on pages 60–62.

☑ CAUSE-EFFECT: A REVISION/PEER REVIEW CHECKLIST

Revise Overall Meaning and Structure

- ❑ Is the essay's purpose informative, persuasive, speculative, or a combination of these?
- ❑ What is the essay's thesis? Is it stated specifically or implied? Where? Could it be made any clearer? How?
- ❑ Does the essay focus on causes, effects, or both? How do you know?
- ❑ Where has correlation been mistaken for causation? Where is the essay weakened by *post hoc* thinking?
- ❑ Where does the essay distinguish between primary and secondary causes and effects? Do the most critical causes and effects receive special attention?
- ❑ Where does the essay dwell on the obvious?

Revise Paragraph Development

- ❑ Are the essay's paragraphs sequenced chronologically or emphatically? Could they be sequenced more effectively? How?

- ❑ Where would signal devices make it easier to follow the progression of thought within and between paragraphs?
- ❑ Which paragraphs would be strengthened by vivid examples (such as statistics, facts, anecdotes, or personal observations) that support the causal analysis?

Revise Sentences and Words

- ❑ Where do expressions like *as a result, because,* and *therefore* mislead the reader by implying a cause-effect relationship? Would words such as *following* and *previously* eliminate the problem?
- ❑ Do any words or phrases convey an arrogant or dogmatic tone (*there is no question, undoubtedly, always, never*)? What other expressions (*most likely, probably*) would improve credibility?

STUDENT ESSAY

The following student essay was written by Carl Novack in response to this assignment:

> In "Nature in the Suburbs," Jane S. Shaw explores the way suburban sprawl is affecting wildlife. Think of another aspect of everyday life that has changed recently, and discuss those factors that you believe are responsible for the change.

While reading Carl's paper, try to determine how well it applies the principles of causal analysis. The annotations on Carl's paper and the commentary following it will help you look at the essay more closely.

Americans and Food
by Carl Novack

Introduction

1 An offbeat but timely cartoon recently appeared in the local newspaper. The single panel showed a gravel-pit operation with piles of raw earth and large cranes. Next to one of the cranes stood the owner of the gravel pit—a grizzled, tough-looking character, hammer in hand, pointing proudly to the new sign he had just tacked up. The sign read, "Fred's Fill Dirt and Croissants." The cartoon illustrates an interesting phenomenon: the changing food habits of Americans. Our meals used to consist of something like home-cooked pot roast, mashed potatoes laced with butter and salt, a thick

Thesis

slice of apple pie topped with a healthy scoop of vanilla ice cream—plain, heavy meals, cooked from scratch, and eaten leisurely at home. But America has changed, and as it has, so have what we Americans eat and how we eat it.

Topic sentence: Background paragraph

We used to have simple, unsophisticated tastes and 2
looked with suspicion at anything more exotic than hamburger. Admittedly, we did adopt some foods from the various immigrant groups who flocked to our shores. We learned to eat Chinese food, pizza, and bagels. But in the last few years, the international character of our diet has grown tremendously. We can walk into any mall in Middle America and buy pita sandwiches, quiche, and tacos. Such foods are often changed on their journey from exotic imports to ordinary "American" meals (no Pakistani, for example, eats frozen-on-a-stick boysenberry-flavored yogurt), but the imports are still a long way from hamburger on a bun.

Topic sentence: Three causes answer the question

First cause

Why have we become more worldly in our tastes? For one 3
thing, television blankets the country with information about new food products and trends. Viewers in rural Montana know that the latest craving in Washington, D.C., is Cajun cooking or that something called tofu is now available in the local supermarket. Another reason for the growing international flavor of our food is that many young Americans have traveled abroad and gotten hooked on new tastes and flavors. Backpacking students and young professionals vacationing in Europe come home with cravings for authentic French bread or German beer. Finally, continuing waves of immigrants settle in the cities where many of us live, causing significant changes in what we eat. Vietnamese, Haitians, and Thais, for instance, bring their native foods and cooking styles with them and eventually open small markets or restaurants. In time, the new food will become Americanized enough to take its place in our national diet.

Second cause

Third cause

Topic sentence: Another cause

Our growing concern with health has also affected the 4
way we eat. For the last few years, the media have warned us about the dangers of our traditional diet, high in salt and fat, low in fiber. The media also began to educate us about the dangers of processed foods pumped full of chemical additives. As a result, consumers began to demand healthier foods, and manufacturers started to change some of their products. Many foods, such as lunch meat, canned vegetables, and soups, were made available in low-fat, low-sodium versions. Whole-grain cereals and higher-fiber breads also began to appear on the grocery shelves. Moreover, the food industry started to produce all-natural products—everything from potato chips to ice cream—without additives and preservatives. Not surprisingly, the restaurant industry responded to this switch to

Start of a causal chain

healthier foods, luring customers with salad bars, broiled fish, and steamed vegetables.

Topic sentence: Another cause

Our food habits are being affected, too, by the rapid increase in the number of women working outside the home. Sociologists and other experts believe that two important factors triggered this phenomenon: the women's movement and a changing economic climate. Women were assured that it was acceptable, even rewarding, to work outside the home; many women also discovered that they had to work just to keep up with the cost of living. As the traditional role of homemaker changed, so did the way families ate. With Mom working, there wasn't time for her to prepare the traditional three square meals a day. Instead, families began looking for alternatives to provide quick meals. What was the result? For one thing, there was a boom in fast-food restaurants. The suburban or downtown strip that once contained a lone McDonald's now features Wendy's, Roy Rogers, Taco Bell, Burger King, and Pizza Hut. Families also began to depend on frozen foods as another time-saving alternative. Once again, though, demand changed the kind of frozen food available. Frozen foods no longer consist of foil trays divided into greasy fried chicken, watery corn niblets, and lumpy mashed potatoes. Supermarkets now stock a range of supposedly gourmet frozen dinners—from fettucini in cream sauce to braised beef en brochette. 5

Start of a causal chain

Conclusion

It may not be possible to pick up a ton of fill dirt and a half-dozen croissants at the same place, but America's food habits are definitely changing. If it is true that "you are what you eat," then America's identity is evolving along with its diet. 6

COMMENTARY

Title and introduction. Asked to prepare a paper analyzing the reasons behind a change in our lives, Carl decided to write about a shift he had noticed in Americans' eating habits. The title of the essay, "Americans and Food," identifies Carl's subject but could be livelier and more interesting.

Despite his rather uninspired title, Carl starts his *causal analysis* in an engaging way—with the vivid description of a cartoon. He then connects the cartoon to his subject with the following sentence: "The cartoon illustrates an interesting phenomenon: the changing food habits of Americans." To back up his belief that there has been a revolution in our eating habits, Carl uses the first paragraph to summarize the kind of meal that people used to eat. He then moves into his *thesis:* "But America has changed, and as it has, so have what Americans eat and how we eat it." The thesis implies that Carl's paper will focus on both causes and effects.

Purpose. Carl's *purpose* was to write an *informative* causal analysis. But before he could present the causes of the change in eating habits, he needed to show that such a change had, in fact, taken place. He therefore uses the second paragraph to document one aspect of this change—the internationalization of our eating habits.

Topic sentences. At the beginning of the third paragraph, Carl uses a question—"Why have we become more worldly in our tastes?"—to signal that his discussion of causes is about to begin. This question also serves as the paragraph's *topic sentence,* indicating that the paragraph will focus on reasons for the increasingly international flavor of our food. The next two paragraphs, also focused by topic sentences, identify two other major reasons for the change in eating habits: "Our growing concern with health has also affected the way we eat" (paragraph 4), and "Our food habits are being affected, too, by the rapid increase in the number of women working outside the home" (5).

Combining patterns of development. Carl draws on two patterns—comparison-contrast and exemplification—to develop his causal analysis. At the heart of the essay is a basic *contrast* between the way we used to eat and the way we eat now. And throughout his essay, Carl provides convincing *examples* to demonstrate the validity of his points. Consider for a moment the third paragraph. Here Carl asserts that one reason for our new eating habits is our growing exposure to international foods. He then presents concrete evidence to show that we have indeed become more familiar with international cuisine: Television exposes rural Montana to Cajun cooking; students traveling abroad take a liking to French bread; urban dwellers enjoy the exotic fare served by numerous immigrant groups. The fourth and fifth paragraphs use similarly specific evidence (for example, "low-fat, low-sodium versions" of "lunch meat, canned vegetables, and soups") to illustrate the soundness of key ideas.

Causal chains. Let's look more closely at the evidence in the essay. Not satisfied with obvious explanations, Carl thought through his ideas carefully and even brainstormed with friends to arrive at as comprehensive an analysis as possible. Not surprisingly, much of the evidence Carl uncovered took the form of *causal chains.* In the fourth paragraph, Carl writes, "The media also began to educate us about the dangers of processed foods pumped full of chemical additives. As a result, consumers began to demand healthier foods, and manufacturers started to change some of their products." And the next paragraph shows how the changing role of American women caused families to search for alternative ways of eating. This shift, in turn, caused the restaurant and food industries to respond with a wide range of food alternatives.

Making the paper easy to follow. Although Carl's analysis digs beneath the surface and reveals complex cause-effect relationships, he wisely limits his pursuit of causal chains to *primary causes and effects.* He doesn't let the complexities distract him from his main purpose: to show why and how the American diet is changing. Carl is also careful to provide his essay with abundant *connecting devices,* making it easy for readers to see the links between points. Consider the use of *transitions* (signaled by italics) in the following sentences: "*Another* reason for the growing international flavor of our food is that many young Americans have traveled abroad" (paragraph 3); "*As a result,* consumers began to demand healthier foods" (4); and "*As* the traditional role of homemaker changed, so did the way families ate" (5).

A problem with the essay's close. When reading the essay, you probably noticed that Carl's conclusion is a bit weak. Although his reference to the cartoon works well, the rest of the paragraph limps to a tired close. Ending an otherwise vigorous essay with such a slight conclusion undercuts the effectiveness of the whole paper. Carl spent so much energy developing the body of his essay that he ran out of the stamina needed to conclude the piece more forcefully. Careful budgeting of his time would have allowed him to prepare a stronger concluding paragraph.

Revising the first draft. When Carl was ready to revise, he showed the first draft of his essay to several classmates during a peer review session. Listening carefully to what they said, he jotted down their most helpful comments and eventually transferred them, numbered in order of importance, to his draft. Comparing Carl's original version of his fourth paragraph (shown here) with his final version in the essay will show you how he went about revising.

Original Version of the Fourth Paragraph

A growing concern with health has also affected the way we eat, especially because the media have sent us warnings the last few years about the dangers of salt, sugar, food additives, high-fat and low-fiber diets. We have started to worry that our traditional meals may have been shortening our lives. As a result, consumers demanded healthier foods and manufacturers started taking some of the salt and sugar out of canned foods. "All-natural" became an effective selling point, leading to many preservative-free products. Restaurants, too, adapted their menus, luring customers with light meals. Because we now know about the link between overweight and a variety of health problems, including heart attacks, we are counting calories. In turn, food companies made fortunes on diet beer and diet cola. Sometimes, though, we seem a bit confused about the health issue; we drink soda that is sugar-free but loaded with chemical sweeteners. Still, we believe we are lengthening our lives through changing our diets.

On the advice of his classmates, Carl decided to omit all references to the way our concern with weight has affected our eating habits. It's true, of course, that calorie-counting has changed how we eat. But as soon as Carl started to discuss this point, he got involved in a causal chain that undercut the paragraph's unity. He ended up describing the paradoxical situation in which we find ourselves. In an attempt to eat healthy, we stay away from sugar and use instead artificial sweeteners that probably aren't very good for us. This is an interesting issue, but it detracts from the point Carl wants to make: that our concern with health has affected our eating habits in a *positive* way.

Carl's peer reviewers also pointed out that the fourth paragraph's first sentence contained too much material to be an effective topic sentence. Carl corrected the problem by breaking the overlong sentence into two short ones: "Our growing concern with health has also affected the way we eat. For the last few years, the media have warned us about the dangers of our traditional diet, high in salt and fat, low in fiber." The first of these sentences serves as a crisp topic sentence that focuses the rest of the paragraph.

Finally, Carl agreed with his classmates that the fourth paragraph lacked convincing specifics. When revising, he changed "manufacturers started taking some of the salt and sugar out of canned foods" to the more specific "Many foods, such as lunch meats, canned vegetables, and soups, were made available in low-fat, low-sodium versions." Similarly, generalizations about "light meals" and "all-natural products" gained life through the addition of concrete examples: restaurants lured "customers with salad bars, broiled fish, and steamed vegetables," and the food industry produced "everything from potato chips to ice cream—without additives and preservatives."

Carl did an equally good job revising other sections of his paper. With the exception of the weak spots already discussed, he made the changes needed to craft a well-reasoned essay, one that demonstrates his ability to analyze a complex phenomenon.

Activities: Cause-Effect

Prewriting Activities

1. Imagine you're writing two essays: One *argues* the need for high school courses in personal finance (how to budget money, balance a checkbook, and the like); the other explains a *process* for showing appreciation. Jot down ways you might use cause-effect in each essay.

2. Use mapping, collaborative brainstorming, or another prewriting technique to generate possible causes and/or effects for *one* of the topics below. Be sure to keep in mind the audience indicated in parentheses. Next, devise a thesis and decide whether your purpose would be informative, persuasive, speculative, or some

combination of these. Finally, organize your raw material into a brief outline, with related causes and effects grouped in the same section.

a. Pressure on students to do well (*high school students*)
b. Children's access to pornography on the Internet (*parents*)
c. Being physically fit (*those who are out of shape*)
d. Spiraling costs of a college education (*college officials*)

Revising Activities

3. Explain how the following statements demonstrate *post hoc* thinking and confuse correlation and cause-effect.

   a. Our city now has many immigrants from Latin American countries. The crime rate in our city has increased. Latin American immigrants are the cause of the crime wave.
   b. The divorce rate has skyrocketed. More women are working outside the home than ever before. Working outside the home destroys marriages.
   c. A high percentage of people in Dixville have developed cancer. The landfill, used by XYZ Industries, has been located in Dixville for twenty years. The XYZ landfill has caused cancer in Dixville residents.

4. The following paragraph is from the first draft of an essay arguing that technological advances can diminish the quality of life. How solid is the paragraph's causal analysis? Which causes and/or effects should be eliminated? Where is the analysis simplistic? Where does the writer make absolute claims even though cause-effect relationships are no more than a possibility? Keeping these questions in mind, revise the paragraph.

   How did the banking industry respond to inflation? It simply introduced a new technology—the automated teller machine (ATM). By making money more available to the average person, the ATM gives people the cash to buy inflated goods—whether or not they can afford them. Not surprisingly, ATMs have had a number of negative consequences for the average individual. Since people know they can get cash at any time, they use their lunch hours for something other than going to the bank. How do they spend this newfound time? They go shopping, and machine-vended money means more impulse buying, even more than with a credit card. Also, because people don't need their checkbooks to withdraw money, they can't keep track of their accounts and therefore develop a casual attitude toward financial matters. It's no wonder children don't appreciate the value of money. Another problem is that people who would never dream of robbing a bank try to trick the machine into dispensing money "for free." There's no doubt that this kind of fraud contributes to the immoral climate in the country.

Stephen King

Probably the best-known living horror writer, Stephen King (1947–) is the author of more than thirty books. Before earning fame through his vastly popular books, including *Carrie* (1974), *The Shining* (1977), *Cujo* (1981), and *Tommyknockers* (1987), King worked as a high school English teacher and an industrial laundry worker. Much of King's prolific output has been adapted for the screen; movies based on King's work include *Misery* (1990), *Stand By Me* (1986), and *The Green Mile* (1999). More recent works include *Dreamcatcher* (2001); *Everything's Eventual* (2002); *From a Buick 8* (2002); Volumes V, VI, and VII in the *Dark Tower* series (published in 2003, 2004, and 2004, respectively); *Cell* (2006); and *Duma Key* (2008). His most recent novel is *Under The Dome* (2009). King's book *On Writing: A Memoir of the Craft* (2000) offers insight into the writing process and examines the role that writing has played in his own life—especially following a near-fatal accident in 1999. King lives with his wife in Bangor, Maine, and has three adult children. The following essay first appeared in *Playboy* in 1982.

For ideas about how this cause-effect essay is organized, see Figure 9.2 on page 400.

Pre-Reading Journal Entry

Several forms of entertainment, besides horror movies, are highly popular despite what many consider a low level of quality. In your journal, list as many "low-brow" forms of entertainment as you can. Possibilities include professional wrestling, aggressive video games, Internet chat rooms, and so on. Review your list, and respond to the following question in your journal: What is it about each form of entertainment that attracts such popularity—and inspires such criticism?

Why We Crave Horror Movies

I think that we're all mentally ill: those of us outside the asylums only hide it a little better—and maybe not all that much better, after all. We've all known people who talk to themselves, people who sometimes squinch their faces into horrible grimaces when they believe no one is watching, people who have some hysterical fear—of snakes, the dark, the tight place, the long drop...and, of course, those final worms and grubs that are waiting so patiently underground. 1

When we pay our four or five bucks and seat ourselves at tenth-row center in a theater showing a horror movie, we are daring the nightmare. 2

Why? Some of the reasons are simple and obvious. To show that we can, that we are not afraid, that we can ride this roller coaster. Which is not to say that a really good horror movie may not surprise a scream out of us at some point, the way we may scream when the roller coaster twists through a complete 360 or plows through a lake at the bottom of the drop. And horror 3 movies, like roller coasters, have always been the special province of the young; by the time one turns 40 or 50, one's appetite for double twists or 360-degree loops may be considerably depleted.

We also go to re-establish our feelings of essential normality; the horror movie is innately conservative, even reactionary. Freda Jackson as the horrible melting woman in *Die, Monster, Die!* confirms for us that no matter how far we may be removed from the beauty of a Robert Redford or a Diana Ross, we are still light-years from true ugliness. 4

And we go to have fun. 5

Ah, but this is where the ground starts to slope away, isn't it? Because this is a very peculiar sort of fun indeed. The fun comes from seeing others menaced—sometimes killed. One critic has suggested that if pro football has become the voyeur's version of combat, then the horror film has become the modern version of the public lynching. 6

It is true that the mythic, "fairytale" horror film intends to take away the shades of gray.... It urges us to put away our more civilized and adult penchant for analysis and to become children again, seeing things in pure blacks and whites. It may be that horror movies provide psychic relief on this level because this invitation to lapse into simplicity, irrationality and even outright madness is extended so rarely. We are told we may allow our emotions a free rein...or no rein at all. 7

If we are all insane, then sanity becomes a matter of degree. If your insanity leads you to carve up women like Jack the Ripper or the Cleveland Torso Murderer, we clap you away in the funny farm (but neither of those two amateur-night surgeons was ever caught, heh-heh-heh); if, on the other hand your insanity leads you only to talk to yourself when you're under stress or to pick your nose on the morning bus, then you are left alone to go about your business...though it is doubtful that you will ever be invited to the best parties. 8

The potential lyncher is in almost all of us (excluding saints, past and present; but then, most saints have been crazy in their own ways), and every now and then, he has to be let loose to scream and roll around in the grass. Our emotions and our fears form their own body, and we recognize that it demands its own exercise to maintain proper muscle tone. Certain of these emotional muscles are accepted—even exalted—in civilized society; they are, of course, the emotions that tend to maintain the status quo of civilization itself. Love, friendship, loyalty, kindness—these are all the emotions that we applaud, emotions that have been immortalized in the couplets of Hallmark cards.... 9

When we exhibit these emotions, society showers us with positive reinforcement; we learn this even before we get out of diapers. When, as children, we hug our rotten little puke of a sister and give her a kiss, all the aunts 10 and uncles smile and twit and cry, "Isn't he the sweetest little thing?" Such coveted treats as chocolate-covered graham crackers often follow. But if we deliberately slam the rotten little puke of a sister's fingers in the door, sanctions follow—angry remonstrance from parents, aunts and uncles; instead of a chocolate-covered graham cracker, a spanking.

But anticivilization emotions don't go away, and they demand periodic exercise. We have such "sick" jokes as, "What's the difference between a truckload of bowling balls and a truckload of dead babies?" (You can't unload a truckload of bowling balls with a pitchfork... a joke, by the way, that I heard originally from a ten-year-old.) Such a joke may surprise a laugh or a grin out of us even as we recoil, a possibility that confirms the thesis: If we share a brotherhood of man, then we also share an insanity of man. None of which is intended as a defense of either the sick joke or insanity but merely as an explanation of why the best horror films, like the best fairy tales, manage to be reactionary, anarchistic, and revolutionary all at the same time. 11

The mythic horror movie, like the sick joke, has a dirty job to do. It deliberately appeals to all that is worst in us. It is morbidity unchained, our most base instincts let free, our nastiest fantasies realized... and it all happens, fittingly enough, in the dark. For those reasons, good liberals often shy away from horror films. For myself, I like to see the most aggressive of them—*Dawn of the Dead*, for instance—as lifting a trap door in the civilized forebrain and throwing a basket of raw meat to the hungry alligators swimming around in that subterranean river beneath. 12

Why bother? Because it keeps them from getting out, man. It keeps them down there and me up here. It was Lennon and McCartney who said that all you need is love, and I would agree with that. 13

As long as you keep the gators fed. 14

Questions for Close Reading

1. What is the selection's thesis? Locate the sentence(s) in which King states his main idea. If he doesn't state the thesis explicitly, express it in your own words.
2. In what ways do King's references to "Jack the Ripper" and the "Cleveland Torso Murderer" (paragraph 8) support his thesis?
3. What does King mean in paragraph 4 when he says that horror movies are "innately conservative, even reactionary"? What does he mean in paragraph 11 when he calls them "anarchistic, and revolutionary"?
4. In paragraphs 12 and 14, King refers to "alligators" and "gators." What does the alligator represent? What does King mean when he says that all the world needs is love—"[a]s long as you keep the gators fed"?
5. Refer to your dictionary as needed to define the following words used in the selection: *hysterical* (paragraph 1), *reactionary* (4), *voyeur's* (6), *lynching* (6), *penchant* (7), *immortalized* (9), *anarchistic* (11), and *morbidity* (12).

FIGURE 9.2
Essay Structure Diagram: "Why We Crave Horror Movies" by Stephen King

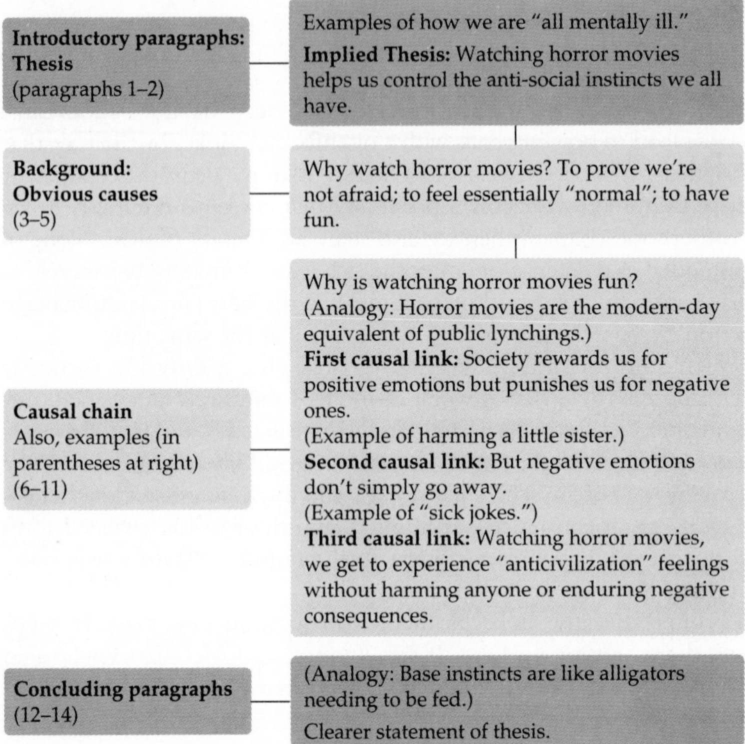

Questions About the Writer's Craft

1. **The pattern.** Does King's causal analysis have an essentially informative, speculative, or persuasive (see page 383) purpose? What makes you think so? How might King's profession as a horror writer have influenced his purpose?
2. **Other patterns.** King *compares* and *contrasts* horror movies to roller coasters (paragraph 3), public lynchings (6), and sick jokes (11–12). How do these comparisons and contrasts reinforce King's thesis about horror movies?
3. **Other patterns.** Throughout the essay, King uses several *examples* involving children. Identify these instances. How do these examples help King develop his thesis?
4. What is unusual about paragraphs 2, 5, and 14? Why do you think King might have designed these paragraphs in this way?

Writing Assignments Using Cause-Effect as a Pattern of Development

1. King argues that horror movies have "a dirty job to do": they feed the hungry monsters in our psyche. Write an essay in which you put King's thesis to the test. Briefly describe the first horror movie you ever saw; then explain its effect on you. Like King, speculate about the nature of your response—your feelings and fantasies—while watching the movie.
2. Many movie critics claim that horror movies nowadays are more violent and bloody than they used to be. Write an essay about *one* other medium of popular culture that you think has changed for the worse. You might consider action movies, televised coverage of sports, men's or women's magazines, radio talk shows, blogs, and so on. Briefly describe key differences between the medium's past and present forms. Analyze the reasons for the change, and, at the end of the essay, examine the effects of the change. For reflections on another questionable cultural practice, read Joan Didion's "Marrying Absurd" (page 604).

Writing Assignments Combining Patterns of Development

3. King advocates the horror movie precisely because "[i]t deliberately appeals to all that is worst in us." Write an essay in which you rebut King. *Argue* instead that horror movies should be avoided precisely *because* they satisfy monstrous feelings in us. To refute King, provide strong *examples* drawn from your own and other people's experience. Consider supplementing your informal research with material gathered in the library and/or on the Internet.
4. Write an essay in which you *argue,* contrary to King, that humans are by nature essentially benevolent and kind. Brainstorm with others to generate vivid *examples* in support of your thesis.

Writing Assignment Using a Journal Entry as a Starting Point

5. King believes that horror movies involve "a very peculiar sort of fun." Review your pre-reading journal entry, and select *one* other form of popular entertainment that you think provides its own strange kind of enjoyment. Like King, write an essay in which you analyze the causes of people's enjoyment of this type of entertainment. Brainstorm with others to identify convincing examples. You may, like King, endorse the phenomenon you examine—or you may condemn it. For discussion of other strange sources of people's enjoyment, read Stephen Chapman's "The Prisoner's Dilemma" (page 372) and Joan Didion's "Marrying Absurd" (page 604).

Jacques D'Amboise

When Jacques D'Amboise (1934–) was growing up in a tough, gang-infested New York City neighborhood, his French-Canadian mother wanted to give her children a glimpse into a world of beauty. She enrolled D'Amboise's sister in a ballet class and, hoping to protect her son from the dangers of street life, insisted that her son take the class, too. It was there that D'Amboise discovered his love of dance. While still in his teens, D'Amboise joined the New York City Ballet and became one of the foremost dancers of his day. He appeared in several films, including *Seven Brides for Seven Brothers* (1954) and *Carousel* (1956). In 1976, he founded the National Dance Institute (NDI), which offers dance classes to public school students, most from underprivileged backgrounds. Through NDI, hundreds of children have experienced the joy and discipline of dance. D'Amboise's NDI experience provided the basis of a book he coauthored, *Teaching the Magic of Dance* (1983), and his contributions to the arts led to his being honored at the Kennedy Center in 1995. In 2011, he published his memoir, *I Was a Dancer*. The following selection originally appeared in *Parade* magazine in 1989.

Pre-Reading Journal Entry

While you were growing up, to what extent were you exposed to the arts: music, dance, drawing, painting, and so forth? Looking back, do you think that this exposure—or lack of exposure—worked to your advantage or to your disadvantage? Use your journal to respond to these questions.

Showing What Is Possible

When I was 7 years old, I was forced to watch my sister's ballet classes. 1
This was to keep me off the street and away from my pals, who ran with gangs like the ones in *West Side Story*. The class was taught by Madame Seda, a Georgian-Armenian[1] who had a school at 181st Street and St. Nicholas Avenue in New York City. As she taught the little girls, I would sit, fidget and diabolically try to disrupt the class by making irritating little noises.

But she was very wise, Madame Seda. She let me get away with it, ignor- 2
ing me until the end of the class, when everybody did the big jumps, a series of leaps in place, called *changements*.

At that point, Madame Seda turned and, stabbing a finger at me, said, 3
"All right, little brother, if you've got so much energy, get up and do these jumps. See if you can jump as high as the girls." So I jumped. And loved it. I felt like I was flying. And she said, "Oh, that was wonderful! From now on, if you are quiet during the class, I'll let you join in the *changements*."

[1]A person from the neighboring republics of Georgia and Armenia, formerly of the Soviet Union (editors' note).

After that, I'd sit quietly in the class and wait for the jumps. A few classes later, she said, "You've got to learn how to jump and not make any noise when you come down. You should learn to do the *pliés* [graceful knee bends] that come at the beginning of the class." So I would do *pliés,* then wait respectfully for the end of class to do the jumps. 4

Finally she said, "You jump high, and you are landing beautifully, but you look awful in the air, flaying your arms about. You've got to take the rest of the class and learn how to do beautiful hands and arms." 5

I was hooked. 6

An exceptional teacher got a bored little kid, me, interested in ballet. How? She challenged me to a test, complimented me on my effort and then immediately gave me a new challenge. She set up an environment for the achievement of excellence and cared enough to invite me to be part of it. And, without realizing it fully at the time, I made an important discovery. 7

Dance is the most immediate and accessible of the arts because it involves your own body. When you learn to move your body on a note of music, it's exciting. You have taken control of your body and, by learning to do that, you discover that you can take control of your life. 8

I took classes with Madame Seda for six months, once a week, but at the end of spring, in June 1942, she called over my mother, my sister and me and did an unbelievably modest and generous thing. She said, "You and your sister are very talented. You should go to a better teacher." She sent us to George Balanchine's school—the School of American Ballet. 9

Within a few years, I was performing children's roles. At 15, I became part of a classical ballet company. What an extraordinary thing for a street boy from Washington Heights, with friends in gangs. Half grew up to become policemen and the other half gangsters—and I became a ballet dancer! 10

I had dreamed of being a doctor or an archaeologist or a priest. But by the time I was 17, I was a principal dancer performing major roles in the ballets, and by the time I was 21, I was doing movies, Broadway shows and choreography. I then married a ballerina from New York City Ballet, Carolyn George, and we were (and still are) blessed with two boys and twin daughters. 11

It was a joyful career that lasted four decades. That's a long time to be dancing and, inevitably, a time came when I realized that there were not many years left for me as a performer. I wasn't sure what to do next, but then I thought about how I had become a dancer, and the teachers who had graced my life. Perhaps I could engage young children, especially boys, in the magic of the arts—in dance in particular. Not necessarily to prepare them to be professional performers, but to create an awareness by giving them a chance to experience the arts. So I started National Dance Institute. 12

That was 13 years ago. Since then, with the help of fellow teachers and staff at NDI, I have taught dance to thousands of inner-city children. And in each class, I rediscover why teaching dance to children is so important. 13

Each time I can use dance to help a child discover that he can control the way he moves, I am filled with joy. At a class I recently taught at P.S. 59 in Brooklyn, there was one boy who couldn't get from his right foot to his left. He was terrified. Everyone was watching. And what he had to do was so simple: take a step with his left foot on a note of music. All his classmates could do it, but he couldn't. 14

He kept trying, but he kept doing it wrong until finally he was frozen, unable to move at all. I put my arm around him and said, "Let's do it together. We'll do it in slow motion." We did it. I stepped back and said, "Now do it alone, and fast." With his face twisted in concentration, he slammed his left foot down correctly on the note. He did it! 15

The whole class applauded. He was so excited. But I think I was even happier, because I knew what had taken place. He had discovered he could take control of his body, and from that he can learn to take control of his life. If I can open the door to show a child that that is possible, it is wonderful. 16

Dance is the art to express time and space. That is what our universe is about. We can hardly make a sentence without signifying some expression of distance, place or time: "See you later." "Meet you at the corner in five minutes." 17

Dance is the art that human beings have developed to express that we live, right now, in a world of movement and varying tempos. 18

Dance, as an art, has to be taught. However, when teaching, it's important to set up an environment where both the student and teacher can discover together. Never teach something you don't love and believe in. But how to set up that environment? 19

When I have a new group of young students and I'm starting a class, I use Madame Seda's technique. I say, "Can you do this test? I'm going to give all 100 of you exactly 10 seconds to get off your seats and be standing and spread out all over the stage floor. And do it silently. Go!" And I start a countdown. Naturally, they run, yelling and screaming, and somehow arrive with several seconds to spare. I say, "Freeze. You all failed. You made noise, and you got there too soon. I said 'exactly 10 seconds'—not 6 or 8 or 11. Go back to your seats, and we'll do it again. And if you don't get it, we'll go back and do it again until you do. And if, at the end of the hour, you still haven't gotten it, I'm not going to teach you." 20

They usually get it the second time. Never have I had to do it more than three. 21

Demand precision, be clear and absolutely truthful. When they respond—and they will—congratulate them on the extraordinary control they have just exhibited. Why is that important? Because it's the beginning of knowing yourself, knowing that you can manage yourself if you want. And it's the beginning of dance. Once the children see that we are 22 having a class of precision, order and respect, they are relieved, and we have a great class.

I've taught dance to Russian children, Australian children, Indian children, Chinese children, fat children, skinny children, handicapped children, groups of Australian triathletes, New York City police, senior citizens and 3-year-olds. The technique is the same everywhere, although there are cultural differences. 23

For example, when I was in China, I would say to the children, "I want everybody to come close and watch what I am going to do." But in China they have had to deal with following a teacher when there are masses of them. And they discovered that the way to see what the teacher does is not to move close but to move away. So 100 people moved back to watch the one—me. 24

I realized they were right. How did they learn that? Thousands of years of masses of people having to follow one teacher. 25

There are cultural differences and there are differences among people. In any group of dancers, there are some who are ready and excel more than others. There are many reasons—genetic, environment, the teachers they had. People blossom at different times. 26

But whatever the differences, someone admiring you, encouraging you works so much better than the reverse. "You can do it, you are wonderful," works so much better than, "You're no good, the others are better than you, you've got to try harder." That never works. 27

I don't think there are any untalented children. But I think there are those whose talents never get the chance to flower. Perhaps they were never encouraged. Perhaps no one took the time to find out how to teach them. That is a tragedy. 28

However, the single most terrible thing we are doing to our children, I believe, is polluting them. I don't mean just with smog and crack, but by not teaching them the civilizing things we have taken millions of years to develop. But you cannot have a dance class without having good manners, without having respect. Dance can teach those things. 29

I think of each person as a trunk that's up in the attic. What are you going to put in the trunk? Are you going to put in machine guns, loud noises, foul language, dirty books and ignorance? Because if you do, that's what is going to be left after you, that's what your children are going to have, and that will determine the world of the future. Or are you going to fill that trunk with music, dance, poetry, literature, good manners and loving friends? 30

I say, fill your trunk with the best that is available to you from the wealth of human culture. Those things will nourish you and your children. You can clean up your own environment and pass it on to the next generation. That's why I teach dance. 31

Questions for Close Reading

1. What is the selection's thesis? Locate the sentence(s) in which D'Amboise states his main idea. If he doesn't state the thesis explicitly, express it in your own words.
2. In paragraph 2, D'Amboise says that Madame Seda "was very wise." In what ways was she wise?
3. D'Amboise believes that dance has to be taught in a particular kind of environment. What, according to D'Amboise, are the most important qualities of that environment?
4. What does D'Amboise mean in paragraph 29 when he says that we pollute our children? What does D'Amboise consider the possible consequences of such pollution?
5. Refer to your dictionary as needed to define the following words used in the selection: *diabolically* (paragraph 1), *flaying* (5), *accessible* (8), *choreography* (11), *inevitably* (12), and *triathletes* (23).

Questions About the Writer's Craft

1. **The pattern.** Writers often organize cause-effect pieces using either a chronological or an emphatic sequence—or perhaps a combination of the two. Identify the organizational pattern that D'Amboise uses.
2. **Other patterns.** D'Amboise begins his essay with a *narrative* that tells the story of his first experience with Madame Seda. What is the purpose of this opening narrative? How does it prepare readers for what follows?
3. Reread paragraphs 20–21. The two short sentences in paragraph 21 could have concluded paragraph 20. Why do you think D'Amboise placed these two sentences in a separate paragraph?
4. In the last two paragraphs, D'Amboise uses an *analogy* (a comparison between two objects or people that seem to have little in common). Identify the analogy, and explain its relevance to the essay's central idea.

Writing Assignments Using Cause-Effect as a Pattern of Development

1. According to D'Amboise, a good teacher is one who provides a classroom of precision and order. Without structure and clear expectations, D'Amboise suggests, children will not flourish in the classroom. Do you think the same might be said of children in the home? Write a paper analyzing the effect on children of *one* of the following: a parenting style that imposes a reasonable number of boundaries, one that imposes too many limits, one that imposes too few restrictions. When writing, draw upon your own experiences and observations as well as those of friends, classmates, and family members. The following essays provide insight into different parenting styles: Judith Ortiz Cofer's "A Partial Remembrance of a Puerto Rican Childhood" (page 117), Audre Lorde's "The Fourth of July" (page 140), and Kay S. Hymowitz's "Tweens: Ten Going On Sixteen" (page 190).
2. D'Amboise asserts that "the single most terrible thing we are doing to our children…is polluting them…by not teaching them the civilizing things we have

taken millions of years to develop." Among the pollutants he lists are drugs, violence, and pornography. Select one of these negative influences (or another you consider important), and write an essay analyzing how it pollutes children. You might show how this factor affects children's behavior, self-concept, and attitudes toward others. Before preparing your paper, interview classmates, friends, and family members to learn in what ways they think this factor influences children.

Writing Assignments Combining Patterns of Development

3. D'Amboise attributes his love of dance to Madame Seda, whom he calls an "exceptional teacher." Very likely, you too at some point in your life experienced the influence of a special adult—perhaps a teacher, coach, parent, grandparent, neighbor, or religious instructor. Using one extended *example* or a series of shorter examples, write an essay showing how your interaction with this person taught you important lessons that had a larger *impact* on your life. Before you begin writing, consider reading Maya Angelou's "Sister Flowers" (page 87), a loving portrait of a childhood mentor.

4. D'Amboise's opening narrative *illustrates* how he became interested in dance. Consider the career path you have chosen or are thinking about choosing. What experiences pointed you in that direction? Write an essay in which you explain why you are interested in that particular career. *Recount* at least two experiences that helped you feel this work would be interesting and rewarding. Use vivid dialogue to dramatize the intensity of the experiences.

Writing Assignment Using a Journal Entry as a Starting Point

5. Write an essay arguing that it is *or* is not important for schools to expose children to the arts. The material you generated in your pre-reading journal entry will help you develop your position. You'll probably also find it helpful to talk to others about their experiences with the arts. Since the issue of arts-education funding is currently being debated, you should have little trouble researching this topic in the library and/or on the Internet. No matter which position you take, be sure to acknowledge opposing viewpoints, such as those in Gerry Garibaldi's "How the Schools Shortchange Boys" (page 536) and Michael Kimmel's "A War Against Boys?" (page 543).

Juan Williams

Juan Williams was born in 1954, the year of the historic U.S. Supreme Court decision in *Brown* v. *Board of Education*. Williams and his family emigrated to the United States from Panama in 1958, and Willliams, who attended New York City public schools for many years, went on to earn a B.A. in philosophy from Haverford College. During the course of his career, Williams has written for many prominent media outlets, including *The New York Times, The Washington Post,* and National Public Radio. In addition, he is the author of a number of books, including *Eyes on the Prize: America's Civil Rights Years, 1954–1965.* He currently works for Fox News Channel. The following selection was first published in the April 2004 issue of the *American School Board Journal.*

Pre-Reading Journal Entry

Like legal rulings, personal decisions can have far-reaching or unintended consequences. Think of decisions you have made, for example, deciding where to go to college, whom to have as a roommate, or whether to take (or quit) a job. Were the results of those decisions what you expected? Jot down some notes in your journal about those decisions.

The Ruling That Changed America

Fifty years later, the *Brown*[1] decision looks different. At a distance from the volcanic heat of May 17, 1954, the real impact of the legal, political, and cultural eruption that changed America is not exactly what it first appeared to be. 1

On that Monday in May, the high court's ruling outlawing school segregation in the United States generated urgent news flashes on the radio and frenzied black headlines in special editions of afternoon newspapers. One swift and unanimous decision by the top judges in the land was going to end segregation in public schools. Southern politicians reacted with such fury and fear that they immediately called the day "Black Monday." 2

South Carolina Gov. James Byrnes, who rose to political power with passionate advocacy of segregation, said the decision was "the end of civilization in the South as we have known it." Georgia Gov. Herman Talmadge struck an angry tone. He said Georgia had no intention of allowing "mixed race" schools as long as he was governor. And he touched on Confederate pride from the days when the South went to war with the federal government over slavery by telling supporters that the Supreme Court's ruling 3

[1]In the legal case *Brown* v. *Board of Education*, the U.S. Supreme Court ruled that separation of schools and other public facilities by race (known as the "separate but equal" doctrine) violated the Constitution (editors' note).

was not law in his state; he said it was "the first step toward national suicide." The *Brown* decision should be regarded, he said, as nothing but a "mere scrap of paper."

Meanwhile, newspapers for black readers reacted with exultation. 4
"The Supreme Court decision is the greatest victory for the Negro people since the Emancipation Proclamation,"[2] said Harlem's *Amsterdam News.* A writer in the *Chicago Defender* explained, "neither the atomic bomb nor the hydrogen bomb will ever be as meaningful to our democracy." And Thurgood Marshall,[3] the NAACP lawyer who directed the legal fight that led to *Brown,* predicted the end of segregation in all American public schools by the fall of 1955.

Slow Progress, Backward Steps

Ten years later, however, very little school integration had taken place. 5
True to the defiant words of segregationist governors, the Southern states had hunkered down in a massive resistance campaign against school integration. Some Southern counties closed their schools instead of allowing blacks and whites into the same classrooms. In other towns, segregationist academies opened, and most if not all of the white children left the public schools for the racially exclusive alternatives. And in most places, the governors, mayors, and school boards found it easy enough to just ask for more time before integrating schools.

That slow-as-molasses approach worked. In 1957. President Eisenhower 6
had to send troops from the 101st Airborne into Little Rock just to get nine black children safely into Central High School. Only in the late '60s, under the threat of losing federal funding, did large-scale school integration begin in Southern public schools. And in many places, in both the North and the South, black and white students did not go to school together until a federal court ordered schoolchildren to ride buses across town to bring the races together. 7

Today, 50 years later, a study by the Civil Rights Project at Harvard University finds that the percentage of white students attending public schools with Hispanic or black students has steadily declined since 1988. In fact, the report concludes that school integration in the United States is "lower in 2000 than in 1970, before busing for racial balance began." In the South, home to the majority of America's black population, there is now less school integration than there was in 1970. The Harvard report concluded, "At the beginning of the 21st century, American schools are now 12 years into the process of continuous resegregation."

[2]On January 1, 1863, President Abraham Lincoln issued an executive order, known as the Emancipation Proclamation, freeing most slaves in the states and territories (editors' note).
[3]Thurgood Marshall went on to become the first African-American Supreme Court justice, serving from 1967 to 1991 (editors' note).

Today, America's schools are so heavily segregated that more than two-thirds of black and Hispanic students are in schools where a majority of the students are not white. And today, most of the nation's white children attend a school that is almost 80 percent white. Hispanics are now the most segregated group of students in the nation because they live in highly concentrated clusters. 8

At the start of the new century, 50 years after *Brown* shook the nation, segregated housing patterns and an increase in the number of black and brown immigrants have concentrated minorities in impoverished big cities and created a new reality of public schools segregated by race and class. 9

The Real Impact of *Brown*

So, if *Brown* didn't break apart school segregation, was it really the earth-quake that it first appeared to be? 10

Yes. Today, it is hard to even remember America before *Brown* because the ruling completely changed the nation. It still stands as the laser beam that first signaled that the federal government no longer gave its support to racial segregation among Americans. 11

Before *Brown*, the federal government lent its power to enforcing the laws of segregation under an 1896 Supreme Court ruling that permitted "separate but equal" treatment of blacks and whites. Blacks and whites who tried to integrate factories, unions, public buses and trains, parks, the military, restaurants, department stores, and more found that the power of the federal government was with the segregationists. 12

Before *Brown*, the federal government had struggled even to pass a law banning lynching. 13

But after the Supreme Court ruled that segregation in public schools was a violation of the Constitution, the federal attitude toward enforcing second-class citizenship for blacks shifted on the scale of a change in the ocean's tide or a movement in the plates of the continents. Once the highest court in the land said equal treatment for all did not allow for segregation, then the lower courts, the Justice Department, and federal prosecutors, as well as the FBI, all switched sides They didn't always act to promote integration, but they no longer used their power to stop it. 14

An irreversible shift had begun, and it was the direct result of the *Brown* decision. 15

The change in the attitude of federal officials created a wave of anticipation among black people, who became alert to the possibility of achieving the long-desired goal of racial equality. There is no way to offer a hard measure of a change in attitude. But the year after *Brown*, Rosa Parks refused to give up her seat to a white man on a racially segregated bus in Montgomery, Ala. That led to a yearlong bus boycott and the emergence of massive, nonviolent 16 protests for equal rights. That same year, Martin Luther King Jr. emerged as the nation's prophet of civil rights for all Americans.

Even when a black 14-year-old, Emmit Till, was killed in Mississippi for supposedly whistling at a white woman, there was a new reaction to old racial brutality. One of Till's elderly relatives broke with small-town Southern tradition and dared to take the witness stand and testify against the white men he saw abduct the boy. Until *Brown,* the simple act of a black man standing up to speak against a white man in Mississippi was viewed as futile and likely to result in more white-on-black violence. 17

The sense among black people—and many whites as well—that a new era had opened created a new boldness. Most black parents in Little Rock did not want to risk harm to their children by allowing them to join in efforts to integrate Central High. But working with local NAACP officials, the parents of nine children decided it was a new day and time to make history. That same spirit of new horizons was at work in 1962 when James Meredith became the first black student to enroll at the University of Mississippi. And in another lurch away from the traditional support of segregation, the federal government sent troops as well as Justice Department officials to the university to protect Meredith's rights. 18

The next year, when Alabama Gov. George Wallace felt the political necessity of making a public stand against integration at the University of Alabama, he stood only briefly in the door to block black students and then stepped aside in the face of federal authority. That was another shift toward a world of high hopes for racial equality; again, from the perspective of the 21st century, it looks like another aftershock of the *Brown* decision. 19

The same psychology of hope infected young people, black and white, nationwide in the early '60s. The Freedom Rides, lunch-counter sit-ins, and protest marches for voting rights all find their roots in *Brown.* So, too, did the racially integrated 1963 March on Washington at which Martin Luther King Jr. famously said he had a vision of a promised land where the sons of slaves and the sons of slave owners could finally join together in peace. The desire for change became a demand for change in the impatient voice of Malcolm X, the militant Black Muslim who called for immediate change by violent means if necessary. 20

In 1964, a decade after *Brown*, the Civil Rights Act[4] was passed by a Congress beginning to respond to the changing politics brought about by the landmark decision. The next year, 1965, the wave of change had swelled to the point that Congress passed the Voting Rights Act[5]. 21

[4]Civil Rights Act of 1964 essentially prohibits discrimination against people on the basis of race, color, religion, sex, or national origin (editors' note).

[5]The National Voting Rights Act of 1965 outlaws any voting requirements, such as literacy tests, that have the effect of preventing people, especially minorities, from exercising their right to vote (editors' note).

Closer to the Mountaintop

This sea change in black and white attitudes toward race also had an impact on culture. Churches began to grapple with the Christian and Jewish principles of loving thy neighbor, even if thy neighbor had a different color skin. Major league baseball teams no longer feared a fan revolt if they allowed more than one black player on a team. Black writers, actors, athletes, and musicians—ranging from James Baldwin to the Supremes and Muhammad Ali—began to cross over into the mainstream of American culture. 22

The other side of the change in racial attitudes was white support for equal rights College-educated young white people in the '60s often defined themselves by their willingness to embrace racial equality. Bob Dylan sang about the changing times as answers "blowing in the wind." Movies like "Guess Who's Coming to Dinner"[6] found major audiences among all races. And previously all white private colleges and universities began opening their doors to black students. The resulting arguments over affirmative action in college admissions led to the Supreme Court's 1978 decision in the *Bakke*[7] case, which outlawed the use of quotas, and its recent ruling that the University of Michigan can take race into account as one factor in admitting students to its law school. The court has also had to deal with affirmative action in the business world, in both hiring and contracts—again as a result of questions of equality under the Constitution raised by *Brown*. 23

But the most important legacy of the *Brown* decision, by far, is the growth of an educated black middle class. The number of black people graduating from high school and college has soared since *Brown*, and the incomes of blacks have climbed steadily as a result. Home ownership and investment in the stock market among black Americans have rocketed since the 1980s. The political and economic clout of that black middle class continues to bring America closer to the mountaintop vision of racial equality that Dr. King might have dreamed of 50 years ago. 24

The Supreme Court's May 17, 1954, ruling in *Brown* remains a landmark legal decision. But it is much more than that. It is the "Big Bang" of all American history in the 20th century. 25

[6]In the movie, which stars Sidney Poitier, a young white woman from a liberal family brings her black fiancé home to introduce to her parents (editors' note).

[7]The U.S. Supreme Court decided, in the case *Regents of the University of California* v. *Bakke*, that racial quotas were illegal in college admissions, but that race could be used as one factor in deciding on an applicant's admission (editors' note).

Questions for Close Reading

1. What is the selection's thesis? Locate the sentence(s) in which Williams states his main idea. If he doesn't state his thesis explicitly, express it in your own words.
2. According to Williams, what were the two contrasting types of reactions to the Supreme Court decision in the *Brown* case?
3. What does Williams say about the ultimate effect of the *Brown* decision on school integration? What evidence does he provide to support his point of view?
4. What other impact does Williams think *Brown* had in the decade following the decision? What are some examples he uses to make his point?
5. How does Williams characterize the effect of the *Brown* decision on American culture? What examples does he use to support his view?
6. Refer to your dictionary as needed to define the following words used in the selection: *segregation* (paragraph 2), *defiant* (5), *hunkered down* (5), *clusters* (8), *plates* (14), *affirmative action* (23), and *Big Bang* (25).

Questions About the Writer's Craft

1. **The pattern.** In the section headed "The Real Impact of *Brown*," the author establishes a causal chain. Identify the components of the chain. Does the author's analysis seem well supported?
2. The author uses section headings in his essay. What effect does this have? What do the headings reflect about the essay's organization? How is information organized within each section?
3. **Other patterns.** Williams uses illustration and comparison to educate readers about the realities of segregation. Where is comparison used most effectively in the essay? What are some metaphors Williams uses to describe the *Brown* decision?
4. Williams gives many examples and quotations to support his thesis. He also cites a study. What study is this? How is the study used? Do you think the study offers reliable proof?

Writing Assignments Using Cause-Effect as a Pattern of Development

1. Williams asserts that the *Brown* decision eventually led to the passage of important federal civil rights legislation. Think of a federal law that has had a big impact on Americans' civil liberties. Some possibilities are the Americans with Disabilities Act, the Individuals with Disabilities Education Act, Title IX (sports education for girls and women), and the Indian Civil Rights Act. Do some research and write an essay explaining the effects of the law. Include any relevant personal examples.
2. The author ascribes much of the progress in civil rights to a "change in racial attitudes." Think of a law, custom, or societal attitude that you feel should be changed. For example, you might think that attitudes toward consumerism need to change. Brainstorm a list of possible actions that could cause the attitude change and possible consequences of a successful attitude change. Write an essay in which you focus on causes, effects, or both. Remember to use specific examples to support your points.

Writing Assignments Combining Patterns of Development

3. The author mentions two examples of art that express changed racial attitudes: Bob Dylan's song "Blowin' in the Wind" and the movie *Guess Who's Coming to Dinner*, starring Sidney Poitier. Identify two other works of art—movies, books, plays, and so on—that express a change in cultural attitudes. For example, the movies *Philadelphia* and *Brokeback Mountain* might reflect a change in attitudes toward homosexuality. *Describe* the works and explain how they *illustrate* cultural change. "Mother Tongue" (page 270) by Amy Tan, "Why We Crave Horror Movies" (page 397) by Stephen King, and "Showing What Is Possible" (page 402) by Jacques D'Amboise all have some ideas about how art works in society.
4. The term *segregation*, used throughout Williams's essay, is not defined, but it is illustrated with many examples. Choose another similar term, such as *discrimination, bias, prejudice, anti-Semitism, racism, intolerance,* or *bigotry*. Write an essay in which you *define* the term, saying what it is and is not. Give examples to *illustrate* your ideas. To see how other authors write about these ideas, read "The Fourth of July" (page 140) by Audre Lorde, "Black Men and Public Space" (page 207) by Brent Staples, "Mother Tongue" (page 270) by Amy Tan, "The Handicap of Definition" (page 468) by William Raspberry, "Free-Speech Follies" (page 509) by Stanley Fish, or "The World House" (page 597) by Martin Luther King, Jr.

Writing Assignment Using a Journal Entry as a Starting Point

From your journal entry, select one decision that you made. What effect did you anticipate from that decision? How did the actual consequences compare with your expectations? Write an essay in which you explore the reasons you think your decision had particular results.

John M. Darley and Bibb Latané

Harvard graduate John M. Darley (1938–) is professor of psychology at Princeton University, where he studies the principles of moral judgment in children and adults. Bibb Latané (1937–) has been chair of the Psychology Department at Florida Atlantic University, director of the Institute for Research in Social Science at the University of North Carolina, and director of the Behavioral Science Laboratory at Ohio State University. Currently head of the Center for Human Science in Chapel Hill, North Carolina, Latané is interested in how groups of people change and interact. Darley and Latané are coauthors of *The Unresponsive Bystander: Why Doesn't He Help?* (1970) and *Help in a Crisis: Bystander Response to an Emergency* (1976). Based on their research into the origins of noninvolvement, "When Will People Help in a Crisis?" (1968) was awarded an essay prize from the American Association for the Advancement of Science.

Pre-Reading Journal Entry

Faced with a challenging or difficult situation, people sometimes choose *not* to get involved—and then later regret this decision. Such situations might include, for example, helping an injured stranger, standing up for someone being bullied, and letting in a stray animal on a cold day. In your journal, write about one or more times when you faced a difficult situation and failed to respond in a way that you now believe you should have.

When Will People Help in a Crisis?

Kitty Genovese is set upon by a maniac as she returns home from work at 3 A.M. Thirty-eight of her neighbors in Kew Gardens, N.Y., come to their windows when she cries out in terror; not one comes to her assistance, even though her assailant takes half an hour to murder her. No one so much as calls the police. She dies. 1

Andrew Mormille is stabbed in the head and neck as he rides in a New York City subway train. Eleven other riders flee to another car as the 17-year-old boy bleeds to death; not one comes to his assistance, even though his attackers have left the car. He dies. 2

Eleanor Bradley trips and breaks her leg while shopping on New York City's Fifth Avenue. Dazed and in shock, she calls for help, but the hurrying stream of people simply parts and flows past. Finally, after 40 minutes, a taxi driver stops and helps her to a doctor. 3

How can so many people watch another human being in distress and do nothing? Why don't they help? 4

Since we started research on bystander responses to emergencies, we have heard many explanations for the lack of intervention in such cases. 5

"The megalopolis in which we live makes closeness difficult and leads to the alienation of the individual from the group," says the psychoanalyst. "This sort of disaster," says the sociologist, "shakes the sense of safety and sureness of the individuals involved and causes psychological withdrawal." "Apathy," says others. "Indifference."

All of these analyses share one characteristic: they set the indifferent witness apart from the rest of us. Certainly not one of us who reads about these incidents in horror is apathetic, alienated or depersonalized. Certainly these terrifying cases have no personal implications for us. We needn't feel guilty, or re-examine ourselves, or anything like that. Or should we? 6

If we look closely at the behavior of witnesses to these incidents, the people involved begin to seem less inhuman and a lot more like the rest of us. They were not indifferent. The 38 witnesses of Kitty Genovese's murder, for example, did not merely look at the scene once and then ignore it. They continued to stare out of their windows, caught, fascinated, distressed, unwilling to act but unable to turn away. 7

Why, then, didn't they act? 8

There are three things the bystander must do if he is to intervene in an emergency: *notice* that something is happening; *interpret* that event as an emergency; and decide that he has *personal responsibility* for intervention. As we shall show, the presence of other bystanders may at each stage inhibit his action. 9

The Unseeing Eye

Suppose that a man has a heart attack. He clutches his chest, staggers to the nearest building and slumps sitting to the sidewalk. Will a passerby come to his assistance? First, the bystander has to notice that something is happening. He must tear himself away from his private thoughts and pay attention. But Americans consider it bad manners to look closely at other people in public. We are taught to respect the privacy of others, and when among strangers we close our ears and avoid staring. In a crowd, then, each person is less likely to notice a potential emergency than when alone. 10

Experimental evidence corroborates this. We asked college students to an interview about their reactions to urban living. As the students waited to see the interviewer, either by themselves or with two other students, they filled out a questionnaire. Solitary students often glanced idly about while filling out their questionnaires: those in groups kept their eyes on their own papers. 11

As part of the study, we staged an emergency: smoke was released into the waiting room through a vent. Two thirds of the subjects who were alone noticed the smoke immediately, but only 25 percent of those waiting in groups saw it as quickly. Although eventually all the subjects did become aware of the smoke—when the atmosphere grew so smoky as to make them 12 cough and rub their eyes—this study indicates that the more people present, the slower an individual may be to perceive an emergency and the more likely he is not to see it at all.

Seeing Is Not Necessarily Believing

Once an event is noticed, an onlooker must decide if it is truly an emergency. Emergencies are not always clearly labeled as such; "smoke" pouring into a waiting room may be caused by fire, or it may merely indicate a leak in a steam pipe. Screams in the street may signal an assault or a family quarrel. A man lying in a doorway may be having a coronary—or he may simply be sleeping off a drunk. 13

A person trying to interpret a situation often looks at those around him to see how he should react. If everyone else is calm and indifferent, he will tend to remain so; if everyone else is reacting strongly, he is likely to become aroused. This tendency is not merely slavish conformity; ordinarily we derive much valuable information about new situations from how others around us behave. It's a rare traveler who, in picking a roadside restaurant, chooses to stop at one where no other cars appear in the parking lot. 14

But occasionally the reactions of others provide false information. The studied nonchalance of patients in a dentist's waiting room is a poor indication of their inner anxiety. It is considered embarrassing to "lose your cool" in public. In a potentially acute situation, then, everyone present will appear more unconcerned that he is in fact. A crowd can thus force inaction on its members by implying, through its passivity, that an event is not an emergency. Any individual in such a crowd fears that he may appear a fool if he behaves as though it were. 15

To determine how the presence of other people affects a person's interpretation of an emergency, Latané and Judith Rodin set up another experiment. Subjects were paid $2 to participate in a survey of game and puzzle preferences conducted at Columbia University by the Consumer Testing Bureau. An attractive young market researcher met them at the door and took them to the testing room, where they were given questionnaires to fill out. Before leaving, she told them that she would be working next door in her office, which was separated from the room by a folding room-divider. She then entered her office, where she shuffled papers, opened drawers and made enough noise to remind the subjects of her presence. After four minutes she turned on a high-fidelity tape recorder. 16

On it, the subjects heard the researcher climb up on a chair, perhaps to reach for a stack of papers on the bookcase. They heard a loud crash and a scream as the chair collapsed and she fell, and they heard her moan, "Oh, my foot... I... I... can't move it Oh, I... can't get this... thing off me." Her cries gradually got more subdued and controlled. 17

Twenty-six people were alone in the waiting room when the "accident" occurred. Seventy percent of them offered to help the victim. Many pushed back the divider to offer their assistance; others called out to offer their help. 18

Among those waiting in pairs, only 20 percent—8 out of 40—offered to help. The other 32 remained unresponsive. In defining the situation as a nonemergency, they explained to themselves why the other member of the pair did not leave the room; they also removed any reason for action themselves. Whatever had happened, it was believed to be not serious. "A mild sprain," some said. "I didn't want to embarrass her." In a "real" emergency, they assured us, they would be among the first to help. 19

The Lonely Crowd

Even if a person defines an event as an emergency, the presence of other bystanders may still make him less likely to intervene. He feels that his responsibility is diffused and diluted. Thus, if your car breaks down on a busy highway, hundreds of drivers whiz by without anyone's stopping to help—but if you are stuck on a nearly deserted country road, whoever passes you first is likely to stop. 20

To test this diffusion-of-responsibility theory, we simulated an emergency in which people overheard a victim calling for help. Some thought they were the only person to hear the cries; the rest believed that others heard them, too. As with the witnesses to Kitty Genovese's murder, the subjects could not *see* one another or know what others were doing. The kind of direct group inhibition found in the other two studies could not operate. 21

For the simulation, we recruited 72 students at New York University to participate in what was referred to as a "group discussion" of personal problems in an urban university. Each student was put in an individual room equipped with a set of headphones and a microphone. It was explained that this precaution had been taken because participants might feel embarrassed about discussing their problems publicly. Also, the experimenter said that he would not listen to the initial discussion, but would only ask for reactions later. Each person was to talk in turn. 22

The first to talk reported that he found it difficult to adjust to New York and his studies. Then, hesitantly and with obvious embarrassment, he mentioned that he was prone to nervous seizures when he was under stress. Other students then talked about their own problems in turn. The number of people in the "discussion" varied. But whatever the apparent size of the group—two, three or six people—only the subject was actually present; the others, as well as the instructions and the speeches of the victim-to-be, were present only on a pre-recorded tape. 23

When it was the first person's turn to talk again, he launched into the following performance, becoming louder and having increasing speech 24 difficulties: "I can see a lot of er of er how other people's problems are similar to mine because er I mean er they're not er e-easy to handle sometimes and er I er um I think I I need er if if could er er somebody er er er give me give me a little er give me a little help here because er I er *uh* I've got a a one of the er seiz-er er things coming *on* and and er uh uh (choking sounds)..."

Eighty-five percent of the people who believed themselves to be alone with the victim came out of their room to help. Sixty-two percent of the people who believed there was *one* other bystander did so. Of those who believed there were four other bystanders, only 31 percent reported the fit. The responsibility-diluting effect of other people was so strong that single individuals were more than twice as likely to report the emergency as those who thought other people also knew about it. 25

The Lesson Learned

People who failed to report the emergency showed few signs of the apathy and indifference thought to characterize "unresponsive bystanders." When the experimenter entered the room to end the situation, the subject often asked if the victim was "all right." Many of them showed physical signs of nervousness; they often had trembling hands and sweating palms. If anything, they seemed more emotionally aroused than did those who reported the emergency. Their emotional behavior was a sign of their continuing conflict concerning whether to respond or not. 26

Thus, the stereotype of the unconcerned, depersonalized *homo urbanus,* blandly watching the misfortunes of others, proves inaccurate. Instead, we find that a bystander to an emergency is an anguished individual in genuine doubt, wanting to do the right thing but compelled to make complex decisions under pressure of stress and fear. His reactions are shaped by the actions of others—all too frequently by their inaction. 27

And we are that bystander. Caught up by the apparent indifference of others, we may pass by an emergency without helping or even realizing that help is needed. Once we are aware of the influence of those around us, however, we can resist it. We can choose to see distress and step forward to relieve it. 28

Questions for Close Reading

1. What is the selection's thesis? Locate the sentence(s) in which Darley and Latané state their main idea. If they don't state the thesis explicitly, express it in your own words.
2. According to the authors, what three factors prevent people in a crowd from helping victims during an emergency?
3. Why did Darley and Latané isolate the subjects in separate rooms during the staged emergency described in paragraphs 21–26?

4. What kind of person, according to the authors, would tend to ignore or bypass a person experiencing a problem? What might encourage this person to act more responsibly?
5. Refer to your dictionary as needed to define the following words used in the selection: *megalopolis* (paragraph 5), *apathy* (5), *indifference* (5), *alienated* (6), *depersonalized* (6), *inhibit* (9), *corroborates* (11), *coronary* (13), *slavish* (14), *nonchalance* (15), *diffused* (20), and *blandly* (27).

Questions About the Writer's Craft

1. **The pattern.** What techniques do Darley and Latané use to help readers focus on the causes of people's inaction during an emergency?
2. **Other patterns.** The three brief *narratives* that open the essay depict events that happened well before Darley and Latané wrote their essay. Why might the authors have chosen to recount these events in the present tense rather than in the past tense?
3. Locate places where Darley and Latané describe the experiments investigating bystander behavior. How do the authors show readers the steps—and the implications—of each experiment?
4. What purpose do you think the authors had in mind when writing the selection? How do you know?

Writing Assignments Using Cause-Effect as a Pattern of Development

1. Write an essay showing the "responsibility-diluting effect" that can occur when several people witness a critical event. Brainstorm with others to gather examples of this effect; then select two or three dramatic situations as the basis of your essay. Be sure to acknowledge other factors that may have played a role in inhibiting people's ability to act responsibly.
2. Although Darley and Latané focus on times when individuals fail to act responsibly, people often respond with moral heroism during difficult situations. Brainstorm with others to identify occasions in which people have taken the initiative to avert a crisis. Focusing on two or three compelling instances, write an essay in which you analyze the possible motives for people's responsible behavior. Also show how their actions affected the other individuals involved. To gain additional insight, read "Where Do We Go from Here: Chaos or Community?" by Martin Luther King, Jr. (page 593).

Writing Assignments Combining Patterns of Development

3. How could families or schools or communities or religious organizations encourage children to act rather than withdraw when confronted by someone in difficulty? Focusing on *one* of these situations, talk with friends, classmates, and family members to gather their experiences and recommendations. Then consider doing some research on this subject in the library and/or on the Internet. Select the most provocative ideas, and write an essay explaining the *steps* that this particular institution

could take to help develop children's sense of responsibility to others. Develop your points with specific *examples* of what has been done and what could be done.

4. Darley and Latané cite social critics who believe that the United States has become a nation of strangers, alienated and withdrawn from one another. Write an essay *refuting* this claim by presenting several vivid *instances* of small acts of everyday kindness—examples in which people demonstrate their sense of connectedness to those around them. Generate examples by drawing on your own and other people's experiences. Before writing, you might want to read Maya Angelou's "Sister Flowers" (page 87) for a portrait of an individual who shows—in small, quiet ways—that she cares for others.

Writing Assignment Using a Journal Entry as a Starting Point

5. Though the authors don't state so directly, they suggest that unresponsive bystanders often may regret their inaction later on. Reviewing the material you generated in your journal entry, select the most compelling or profound of the incidents you described. Then write an essay in which you narrate *one* situation in which you chose not to get involved but now realize you should have. Be sure to provide dialogue and vivid descriptive details to bring the incident to life for your readers. Conclude your essay with a brief reflection on what you wish you had done and how your failure to respond properly has affected you. You might also begin by reading Gordon Parks's "Flavio's Home" (page 95), which conveys the author's impulse to get involved when he witnesses the desperate circumstances of another, and Joan Murray's "Someone's Mother" (page 154), which gives one person's response to a stranger in distress.

Jane S. Shaw

Jane S. Shaw, born in 1944, received a B.A. in English from Wellesley College and was an associate economics editor at *Business Week*. Currently president of the Pope Center for Higher Education Policy, Shaw was formerly a senior fellow at the Property and Environment Research Center, a nonprofit organization that advocates improving the environment by means of property rights and market forces, rather than by government regulation. Shaw's articles have appeared in publications such as *The Wall Street Journal, The Washington Times, USA Today, Liberty, Public Choice,* and *The Cato Journal*. She is coeditor with Ronald D. Utt of *A Guide to Smart Growth: Shattering Myths and Providing Solutions* (2000). The following selection, adapted from *A Guide to Smart Growth*, was published separately by The Heritage Foundation in 2004. The footnotes are all the author's.

Pre-Reading Journal Entry

Encounters with wildlife and other animals can inspire a range of responses. Think of several encounters you have had with animals, for example, spying a deer in your backyard, purchasing a canary as pet, or catching a fish. How did you feel about these encounters? In your journal make some notes about your experiences.

Nature in the Suburbs

A decade ago, who would have thought that New Jersey would host a black bear hunt—the first in 33 years? Or that Virginia, whose population of bald eagles was once down to 32 breeding pairs, would have 329 known active bald eagle nests? Who would have expected *Metropolitan Home* magazine to be advising its readers about ornamental grasses to keep away white-tailed deer, now found in the millions around the country? 1

Such incidents illustrate a transformed America. This nation, often condemned for being crowded, paved over, and studded with nature-strangling shopping malls, is proving to be a haven for wild animals. 2

It is difficult to ignore this upsurge of wildlife, because stories about bears raiding trashcans and mountain lions sighted in subdivisions frequently turn up in the press or on television. Featured in these stories are animals as large as moose, as well as once-threatened birds such as eagles and falcons and smaller animals like wolverines and coyotes. 3

One interpretation of these events is that people are moving closer to wilderness and invading the territory of wild animals. But this is only a small part of the story. As this essay will show, wild animals increasingly find suburban life in the United States to be attractive. 4

The stories, while fascinating, are not all upbeat. Americans are grappling with new problems—the growing hazard of automobile collisions with deer, debates over the role of hunting, the disappearance of fragile wild 5 plants gobbled up by hungry ruminants, and even occasional human deaths caused by these animals.

At the same time, the proliferation of wildlife should assure Americans that the claim that urban sprawl is wiping out wildlife is simply poppycock. Human settlement in the early 21st century may be sprawling and suburban—about half the people in this country live in suburbs—but it is more compatible with wildlife than most people think. There may be reasons to decry urban sprawl or the suburbanization of America, but the loss of wildlife is not one of them. 6

Why So Many Wild Animals?

Two phenomena are fueling this increase in wild animals. One is natural reforestation, especially in the eastern United States. This is largely a result of the steady decline in farming, including cotton farming, a decline that allows forests to retake territory they lost centuries ago. The other is suburbanization, the expansion of low-density development outside cities, which provides a variety of landscapes and vegetation that attract animals. Both trends undermine the claim that wild open spaces are being strangled and that habitat for wild animals is shrinking. 7

The trend toward regrowth of forest has been well-documented. The percent of forested land in New Hampshire increased from 50 percent in the 1880s to 86 percent 100 years later. Forested land in Connecticut, Massachusetts, and Rhode Island increased from 35 percent to 59 percent over that same period. "The same story has been repeated in other places in the East, the South, and the Lake States," writes forestry expert Roger Sedjo.[1] 8

Environmentalist Bill McKibben exulted in this "unintentional and mostly unnoticed renewal of the rural and mountainous East" in a 1995 article in the *Atlantic Monthly.* Calling the change "the great environmental story of the United States, and in some ways of the whole world," he added, "Here, where 'suburb' and 'megalopolis' were added to the world's vocabulary, an explosion of green is under way."[2] Along with the reforestation come the animals; McKibben cites a moose "ten miles from Boston," as well as an eastern United States full of black bears, deer, alligators, and perhaps even mountain lions. 9

This re-greening of the eastern United States explains why some large wild animals are thriving, but much of the wildlife Americans are seeing today is a direct result of the suburbs. Clearly, suburban habitat is not sterile. 10

[1]Roger A. Sedjo, "Forest Resources," in Kenneth D. Frederick and Roger A. Sedjo, eds., *America's Renewable Resources: Historical Trends and Current Challenges* (Washington, D.C.: Resources for the Future, 1991), p. 109.

[2]Bill McKibben, "An Explosion of Green," *Atlantic Monthly*, April 1995, p. 64.

Habitat for Wildlife

11 When people move onto what once was rural land, they modify the landscape. Yes, they build more streets, more parking lots, and more buildings. Wetlands may be drained, hayfields may disappear, trees may be cut down, and pets may proliferate. At the same time, however, the new residents will create habitat for wildlife. They will create ponds, establish gardens, plant trees, and set up bird nesting-boxes. Ornamental nurseries and truck farms may replace cropland, and parks may replace hedgerows.

12 This new ecology is different, but it is often friendly to animals, especially those that University of Florida biologist Larry Harris calls "meso-mammals," or mammals of medium size.[3] They do not need broad territory for roaming to find food, as moose and grizzly bears do. They can find places in the suburbs to feed, nest, and thrive, especially where gardens flourish.

13 One example of the positive impact of growth is the rebound of the endangered Key deer, a small white-tailed deer found only in Florida and named for the Florida Keys. According to *Audubon* magazine, the Key deer is experiencing a "remarkable recovery."[4] The news report continues: "Paradoxically, part of the reason for the deer's comeback may lie in the increasing development of the area." Paraphrasing the remarks of a university researcher, the reporter says that human development "tends to open up overgrown forested areas and provide vegetation at deer level—the same factors fueling deer population booms in suburbs all over the country."

14 Indeed, white-tailed deer of normal size are the most prominent species proliferating in the suburbs. In *The New York Times*, reporter Andrew C. Revkin has commented that "suburbanization created a browser's paradise: a vast patchwork of well-watered, fertilizer-fattened plantings to feed on and vest-pocket forests to hide in, with hunters banished to more distant woods."[5]

15 The increase in the number of deer in the United States is so great that many people, especially wildlife professionals, are trying to figure out what to do about them. In 1997, the Wildlife Society, a professional association of wildlife biologists, devoted a special 600-page issue of its *Bulletin* to "deer overabundance." The lead article noted, "We hear more each year about the high costs of crop and tree-seedling damage, deer-vehicle collisions, and nuisance deer in suburban locales."[6] Insurance companies are worried about the increase in damage from automobile collisions with deer and similar-sized animals. And there are fears that the increase in deer in populated areas means that the deer tick could be causing the increased number of reported cases of Lyme disease.

[3]Larry D. Harris, in e-mail communication with the author, January 16, 2000.

[4]Nancy Klingener, "Doe, Re, Key Deer," *Audubon*, January-February 2000, p. 17.

[5]Andrew C. Revkin, "Out of Control: Deer Send Ecosystem into Chaos," *The New York Times*, November 12, 2002.

[6]Donald M. Waller and William S. Alverson, "The White-Tailed Deer: A Keystone Herbivore," *Wildlife Society Bulletin*, Vol. 25, No. 2 (Summer 1997), p. 217.

Yes, the proliferation of deer poses problems, as do geese, whose flocks can foul ponds and lawns and are notorious nuisances on golf courses, and beaver, which can cut down groves of trees. Yet the proliferation of deer is also a wildlife success story. At least that is the view of Robert J. Warren, editor of the *Bulletin*, who calls the resurgence of deer "one of the premier examples of successful wildlife management."[7] Today's deer population in the United States may be as high as 25 million, says Richard Nelson, writing in *Sports Afield*.[8] 16

People have mixed feelings about deer. In the *Wildlife Society Bulletin*, Dale R. McCullough and his colleagues reported on a survey of households in El Cerrito and Kensington, two communities near Berkeley, California. Twenty-eight percent of those who responded reported severe damage to vegetation by the deer, and 25 percent reported moderate damage. Forty-two percent liked having the deer around, while 35 percent disliked them and 24 percent were indifferent. The authors summarized the findings by saying: "As expected, some residents loved deer, whereas others considered them 'hoofed rats.'"[9] 17

James Dunn, a geologist who has studied wildlife in New York State, believes that suburban habitat fosters deer more than forests do. Dunn cites statistics on the harvest of buck deer reported by the New York State government. Since 1970 the deer population has multiplied 7.1 times in suburban areas (an increase of 610 percent), but only 3.4 times (an increase of 240 percent) in the state overall.[10] 18

Dunn explains that the forests have been allowed to regrow without logging or burning, so they lack the "edge" that allows sunlight in and encourages vegetation suitable for deer. In his view, that explains why counties with big cities (and therefore with suburbs) have seen a greater increase in deer populations than have the isolated, forested rural counties. Supporting this point, Andrew Revkin quotes a wildlife biologist at the National Zoo in Washington, D.C. "Deer are an edge species," he says, "and the world is one big edge now."[11] 19

Deer are not the only wild animals that turn up on lawns and doorsteps, however. James Dunn lists species in the Albany, New York, suburbs in addition to deer: birds such as robins, woodpeckers, chickadees, grouse, finches, hawks, crows, and nuthatches, as well as squirrels, chipmunks, opossums, raccoons, foxes, and rabbits.[12] Deer attract coyotes 20

[7]Robert J. Warren, "The Challenge of Deer Overabundance in the 21st Century," *Wildlife Society Bulletin*, Vol. 25, No. 2 (Summer 1997), p. 213.

[8]Richard Nelson, "Deer Nation," *Sports Afield*, September 1998, p. 40.

[9]Dale R. McCullough, Kathleen W. Jennings, Natalie B. Gates, Bruce G. Elliott, and Joseph E. DiDonato, "Overabundant Deer Populations in California," *Wildlife Society Bulletin*, Vol. 25, No. 2 (1997), p. 481.

[10]James R. Dunn, "Wildlife in the Suburbs," Political Economy Research Center, PERC Reports, September 1999, pp. 3-5. See also James R. Dunn and John E. Kinney, *Conservative Environmentalism: Reassessing the Means, Redefining the Ends* (Westport, Conn.: Quorum Books, 1996).

[11]Revkin, "Out of Control."

[12]Dunn, "Wildlife in the Suburbs," p. 3.

too. According to a 1999 article in *Audubon*, biologists estimate that the coyote population (observed in all states except Hawaii) is about double what it was in 1850.[13]

Joel Garreau, author of *Edge City*, includes black bears, red-tailed hawks, peregrine falcons, and beaver on his list of animals that find suburban niches. Garreau still considers these distant "edge city" towns a "far less diverse ecology than what was there before." However, he writes, "if you measure it by the standard of city, it is a far more diverse ecology than anything humans have built in centuries, if not millennia."[14] 21

For one reason or another, some environmental activists tend to dismiss the resurgence of deer and other wildlife. In an article criticizing suburban sprawl, Carl Pope, executive director of the Sierra Club, says that the suburbs are "very good for the most adaptable and common creatures—raccoons, deer, sparrows, starlings, and sea gulls" but "devastating for wildlife that is more dependent upon privacy, seclusion, and protection from such predators as dogs and cats."[15] 22

Yet the suburbs attract animals larger than meso-mammals, and the suburban habitat may be richer than what they replace. In many regions, suburban growth comes at the expense of agricultural land that was cultivated for decades, even centuries. Cropland doesn't necessarily provide abundant habitat. Environmental essayist Donald Worster, for example, has little favorable to say about land cultivated for crops or used for livestock grazing. In Worster's view, there was a time when agriculture was diversified, with small patches of different crops and a variety of animals affecting the landscape. Not now. "[T]he trend over the past two hundred years or so," he writes, "has been toward the establishment of monocultures on every continent."[16] In contrast, suburbs are not monocultures. 23

Even large animals can be found at the edges of metropolitan areas. Early in 2004, a mountain lion attacked a woman riding a bicycle in the Whiting Ranch Wilderness Park in the foothills above populous Orange County, and the same animal may have killed a man who was found dead nearby. According to the *Los Angeles Times*, if the man's death is confirmed as caused by the mountain lion, it would be the first death by a mountain lion in Orange County. The *Times* added, however, that "[m]ountain lions are no strangers in Orange County's canyons and wilderness parks."[17] Indeed, in 1994, mountain lions killed two women in state parks near San Diego and 24

[13]Mike Finkel, "The Ultimate Survivor," *Audubon*, May-June 1999, p. 58.

[14]Joel Garreau, *Edge City: Life on the New Frontier* (New York: Random House, 1991), p. 57.

[15]Carl Pope, "Americans Are Saying No to Sprawl," Political Economy Research Center, PERC Reports, February 1999, p. 6.

[16]Donald Worster, *The Wealth of Nature: Environmental History and the Ecological Imagination.* (New York: Oxford University Press, 1993), p. 59.

[17]Kimi Yoshino, David Haldane, and Daniel Yi, "Lion Attacks O.C. Biker; Man Found Dead Nearby," *Los Angeles Times*, January 9, 2004.

Sacramento. Deer may be attracting the cats, suggests Paul Beier, a professor at the University of California at Berkeley.[18]...

Sharing Our Turf

The fact that wildlife finds a home in suburban settings does not mean that all wildlife will do so. The greening of the suburbs is no substitute for big stretches of land—both public and private—that allow large mammals such as grizzly bears, elk, antelope, and caribou to roam. The point of this essay is that the suburbs offer an environment that is appealing to many wild animal species. 25

If the United States continues to prosper, the 21st century is likely to be an environmental century. Affluent people will seek to maintain or, in some cases, restore an environment that is attractive to wildlife, and more parks will likely be nestled within suburban developments, along with gardens, arboreta, and environmentally compatible golf courses. As wildlife proliferates, Americans will learn to live harmoniously with more birds and meso-mammals. New organizations and entrepreneurs will help integrate nature into the human landscape. There is no reason to be pessimistic about the ability of wildlife to survive and thrive in the suburbs. 26

---

[18]McCullough et al., "Overabundant Deer Populations in California," p. 479.

Questions for Close Reading

1. What is the selection's thesis? Locate the sentence(s) in which Shaw states her main idea. If she doesn't state her thesis explicitly, express it in your own words.
2. What evidence does Shaw give to support her assertion, at the beginning of the article and then later on, about an "upsurge in wildlife"?
3. Shaw gives two causes for the increase in wildlife—reforestation and suburbanization. How have these two trends brought about an increase in wildlife? Why does she believe that suburbanization may promote more wildlife than either thick forest growth or cropland?
4. An increase in wildlife, Shaw says, has its negative side. Give at least two examples she uses to prove this point Why do you think Shaw includes these?
5. Refer to your dictionary as needed to define the following words used in the selection: *haven* (paragraph 2), *upsurge* (3), *proliferation* (6), *decry* (6), *megalopolis* (9), *ecology* (12), *paradoxically* (13), *notorious* (16), *resurgence* (16), and *monocultures* (23).

Questions About the Writer's Craft

1. **The pattern.** To what extent does the author focus on causes, on effects, or on both causes and effects? Identify at least one causal chain.
2. Is Shaw's purpose to inform, entertain, or persuade? How effective is the author's use of research in achieving this purpose? Identify at least three kinds of sources the author uses, and give an example of each. How credible are the sources (see "Evaluating Source Materials" on pages 607–610 in Appendix A)?

3. **Other patterns.** At different points, Shaw states objections to her main ideas and then refutes those objections. Find at least two instances of this *argument* technique.
4. The selection opens with a series of questions. What do you think is the author's purpose in posing these questions? How effective do you think the questions are?

Writing Assignments Using Cause-Effect as a Pattern of Development

1. Just as cropland can become suburbs, other environments can also change. Think of a place you know that has been changed by human activity. Maybe a polluted stream has been cleaned up and filled with fish, or an abandoned lot has become a vibrant neighborhood park. In an essay, show either what *caused* the change or what *effects* the change has had. Use your personal experiences as examples to support your ideas. Read Wendell Berry's "Farming and the Global Economy" (page 520) for insights into how people can affect the land.
2. Like environmental changes made by people, human inventions can also have unintended consequences. Write an essay showing how an innovation may have had unintended *effects*. For example, the automobile makes travel easy, but it may also lead to a sedentary lifestyle. If possible, include a relevant causal chain. Be sure to add specific details to support your ideas.

Writing Assignments Combining Patterns of Development

3. Wild animals can be dangerous. Yet many people acquire animals such as tigers, cobras, and chimpanzees as pets. In an essay, *define* what "pet" means to you. Then *compare* the pros and cons of wild animals and domestic animals as pets. Include examples to *illustrate* your ideas. For some insights into dealing with animals, read Amy Sutherland's "What Shamu Taught Me About a Happy Marriage" (page 308) or Natalie Angier's "The Cute Factor" (page 461).
4. Shaw argues that suburbanization has benefited wildlife. Research some evidence that suburbanization can have a negative or neutral impact on wildlife. You might ask, for example, how it has affected migrating birds. Use some of Shaw's sources, and develop new sources. Write an essay *arguing* a different point of view from Shaw's. Make sure to use *examples* and to document your sources.

Writing Assignment Using a Journal Entry as a Starting Point

Choose an experience with animals that you wrote about in your journal. Write an essay in which you narrate your encounter and describe your ideas and feelings about it. What did you learn about the animal? About yourself? To see how others have written about animals and our relationships with them, read George Orwell's "Shooting an Elephant" (page 146), Amy Sutherland's "What Shamu Taught Me About a Happy Marriage" (page 308), Natalie Angier's "The Cute Factor" (page 461), or Mark Twain's "The Damned Human Race" (page 525).

Additional Writing Topics

CAUSE-EFFECT

General Assignments

Write an essay that analyzes the causes and/or effects of one of the following topics. Determine your purpose before beginning to write: Will the essay be informative, persuasive, or speculative? As you prewrite, think rigorously about causes and effects; try to identify causal chains. Provide solid evidence for the thesis and use either chronological or emphatic order to organize your supporting points.

1. Sleep deprivation
2. Having the parents you have
3. Lack of communication in a relationship
4. Overexercising or not exercising
5. A particular TV or rock star's popularity
6. Skill or ineptitude in sports
7. A major life decision
8. Stiffer legal penalties for drunken driving
9. Changing attitudes toward protecting the environment
10. A particular national crisis
11. The mass movement of women into the workforce
12. Choosing to attend this college
13. "Back to basics" movement in schools
14. Headaches
15. An act of violence
16. A natural event: leaves turning, birds migrating, animals hibernating, an eclipse occurring
17. Text-messaging
18. Use of computers in the classroom
19. Banning disposable cans and bottles
20. A bad habit
21. A fear of ________
22. Legalizing drugs
23. Abolishing the F grade
24. Joining a particular organization
25. Owning a pet

Assignments with a Specific Purpose, Audience, and Point of View

On Campus

1. A debate about the prominence of athletics at colleges and universities is going to be broadcast on the local cable station. For this debate, prepare a speech

pointing out either the harmful or the beneficial effects of "big-time" college athletic programs.

2. Why do students "flunk out" of college? Write an article for the campus newspaper outlining the main causes of failure. Your goal is to steer students away from dangerous habits and situations that lead to poor grades or dropping out.

At Home or in the Community

3. Write a letter to the editor of your favorite newspaper analyzing the causes of the country's current "trash crisis." Be sure to mention the nationwide love affair with disposable items and the general disregard of the idea of thrift. Conclude by offering brief suggestions for how people in your community can begin to remedy this problem.
4. Write a letter to the head of your religious congregation or a civic organization that you belong to suggesting ways, such as installing solar panels, that the group can become more energy efficient. Discuss the positive impact that energy conservation can have on efforts to stop global warming.

On the Job

5. As the manager of a store or office, you've noticed that a number of employees have negative workplace habits and/or attitudes. Write a memo for your employees in which you identify these negative behaviors and show how they affect the workplace environment. Be sure to adopt a tone that will sound neither patronizing nor overly harsh.
6. Why do you think teenage suicide is on the rise? You're a respected psychologist. Write a fact sheet for parents of teenagers and for high school guidance counselors describing the factors that could make a young person desperate enough to attempt suicide. At the end, suggest what parents and counselors can do to help confused, unhappy young people.

DEFINITION

WHAT IS DEFINITION?

For language to communicate, words must have accepted *definitions.* Dictionaries, the sourcebooks for accepted definitions, are compilations of current word meanings, enabling speakers of a language to understand one another. But as you might suspect, things are not as simple as they first appear. We all know that a word like *discipline* has a standard dictionary definition. We also know, though, that parents argue over what constitutes "discipline" and that controversies about the meaning of "discipline" rage within school systems year after year. Moreover, many of the wrenching moral debates of our time also boil down to questions of definition. Much of the controversy over abortion, for instance, centers on what is meant by "life" and when it "begins."

Words can, in short, be slippery. Each of us has unique experiences, attitudes, and values that influence the way we use words and the way we interpret the words of others. In addition, some words may shift in meaning over time. The word *pedagogue,* for instance, originally meant "a teacher or leader of children." However, with time, *pedagogue* has come to mean "a dogmatic, pedantic teacher." And, of course, we invent other words (*modem, byte, e-mail*) as the need arises.

Writing a definition, then, is no simple task. Primarily, the writer tries to answer basic questions: "What does ______ mean?" and "What is the special or true nature of ______?" As you will see, there are various strategies for expanding definitions far beyond the single-word synonyms or brief phrases that dictionaries provide.

HOW DEFINITION FITS YOUR PURPOSE AND AUDIENCE

Many times, short-answer exam questions call for definitions. Consider the following examples:

> Define the term *mob psychology*.
>
> What is the difference between a metaphor and a simile?
>
> How would you explain what a religious cult is?

In such cases, a good response might involve a definition of several sentences or several paragraphs.

Other times, definition may be used in an essay organized mainly around another pattern of development. In this situation, all that's needed is a brief formal definition or a short definition given in your own words. For instance, a *process analysis* showing readers how computers have revolutionized the typical business office might start with a textbook definition of the term *artificial intelligence*. In an *argumentation-persuasion* paper urging students to support recent efforts to abolish fraternities and sororities, you could refer to the definitions of *blackballing* and *hazing* found in the university handbook. Or your personal definition of *hero* could be the starting point for a *causal analysis* that explains to readers why there are few real heroes in today's world.

But the most complex use of definition, and the one we are primarily concerned with in this chapter, involves exploring a subject through an *extended definition*. Extended definition allows you to apply a personal interpretation to a word, to make a case for a revisionist view of a commonly accepted meaning, to analyze words representing complex or controversial issues. "Pornography," "gun control," "secular humanism," and "right-to-life" would be excellent subjects for extended definition—each is multifaceted, often misunderstood, and fraught with emotional meaning.

At this point, you have a good sense of the way writers use definition to achieve their purpose and to connect with their readers. Now take a moment to look closely at the photograph at the beginning of this chapter. Imagine you're writing an essay, accompanied by the photo, for publication in your campus newspaper. Your purpose is to explain what it means to be an American in the twenty-first century. Jot down some ideas you might include in your *definition*.

SUGGESTIONS FOR USING DEFINITION IN AN ESSAY

The suggestions here and in Figure 10.1 will be helpful whether you use definition as a dominant or a supportive pattern of development.

1. Stay focused on the essay's purpose, audience, and tone. Since your purpose for writing an extended definition shapes the entire paper, you need to keep that objective in mind when developing your definition. Suppose you decide to write an essay defining *jazz.* The essay could be purely *informative* and discuss the origins of jazz, its characteristic tonal patterns, and some of the great jazz musicians of the past. Or the essay could move beyond pure information and take on a *persuasive* edge.

FIGURE 10.1
Development Diagram: Writing a Definition Essay

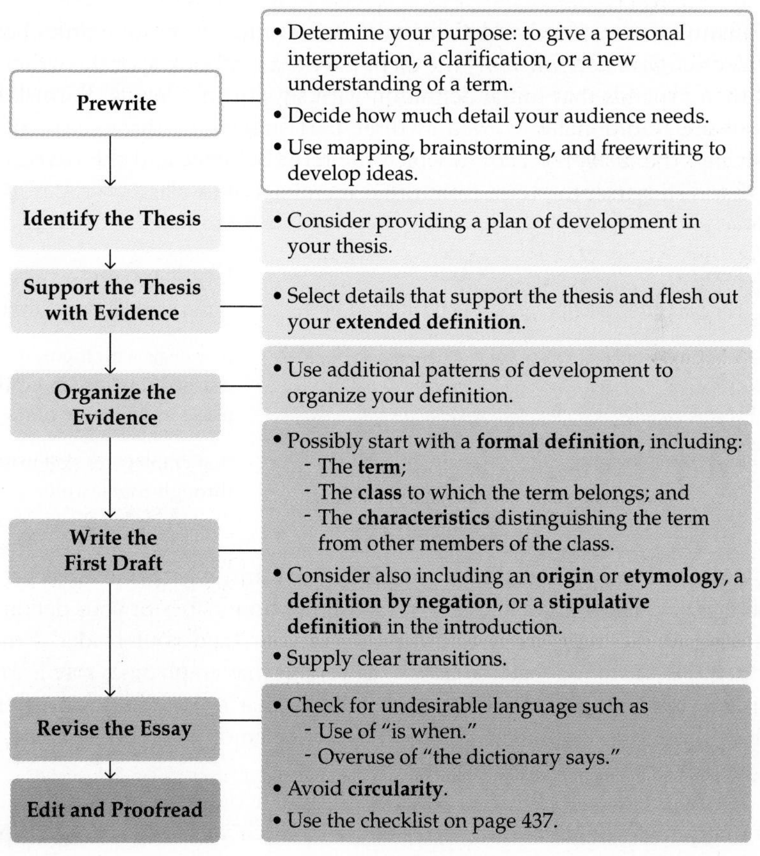

Prewrite
• Determine your purpose: to give a personal interpretation, a clarification, or a new understanding of a term.
• Decide how much detail your audience needs.
• Use mapping, brainstorming, and freewriting to develop ideas.
Identify the Thesis
• Consider providing a plan of development in your thesis.
Support the Thesis with Evidence
• Select details that support the thesis and flesh out your extended definition.
Organize the Evidence
• Use additional patterns of development to organize your definition.
Write the First Draft
• Possibly start with a formal definition, including:
- The term;
- The class to which the term belongs; and
- The characteristics distinguishing the term from other members of the class.
• Consider also including an origin or etymology, a definition by negation, or a stipulative definition in the introduction.
• Supply clear transitions.
Revise the Essay
• Check for undesirable language such as
- Use of "is when."
- Overuse of "the dictionary says."
• Avoid circularity.
• Use the checklist on page 437.
Edit and Proofread

It might, for example, argue that jazz is the only contemporary form of music worth considering seriously.

Just as your purpose in writing will vary, so will your tone. A strictly informative definition will generally assume a detached, objective tone ("Apathy is an emotional state characterized by listlessness and indifference"). By way of contrast, a definition essay with a persuasive slant might be urgent in tone ("To combat student apathy, we must design programs that engage students in campus life"), or it might take a satiric approach ("An apathetic stance is a wise choice for any thinking student").

As you write, keep thinking about your audience as well. Not only do your readers determine what terms need to be defined (and in how much detail), but they also keep you focused on the essay's purpose and tone. For instance, you probably wouldn't write a serious, informative piece for the college newspaper about the "mystery meat" served in the campus cafeteria. Instead, you would adopt a light tone as you defined the culinary horror and might even make a persuasive pitch about improving the food prepared on campus.

2. Formulate an effective definition. A definition essay sometimes begins with a brief *formal definition*—the dictionary's, a textbook's, or the writer's—and then expands that initial definition with supporting details. Formal definitions are traditionally worded as three-part statements that consist of the following: the *term,* the *class* to which the term belongs, and the *characteristics* that distinguish the term from other members of its class.

Term	Class	Characteristics
The peregrine falcon,	an endangered bird,	is the world's fastest flyer.
A bodice-ripper	is a paperback book	that deals with highly charged romance in exotic places and faraway times.
Back to basics	is a trend in education	that emphasizes skill mastery through rote learning.

A definition that meets these guidelines will clarify what your subject *is* and what it *is not.* These guidelines also establish the boundaries of your definition, removing unlike items from consideration in your (and your reader's) mind. For example, defining "back to basics" as a trend that emphasizes rote learning signals a certain boundary; it lets readers know that other educational trends, such as those that emphasize children's social or emotional development, will not be part of the essay's definition.

If you decide to include a formal definition, avoid tired openers like "the dictionary says" or "according to *Webster's.*" Such weak starts are just plain boring and often herald an unimaginative essay. You should also keep in mind that a strict dictionary definition may actually confuse readers.

You should also stay clear of ungrammatical "is when" definitions: "Blind ambition is when you want to get ahead, no matter how much other people are hurt." Instead, write "Blind ambition is wanting to get ahead, no matter how much other people are hurt." A final pitfall to avoid in writing formal definitions is *circularity,* saying the same thing twice and therefore defining nothing: "A campus tribunal is a tribunal composed of various members of the university community." Circular definitions like this often repeat the term being defined (*tribunal*) or use words having the same meaning (*campus; university community*).

3. Develop the extended definition. You can choose from a variety of patterns when formulating an extended definition. Description, narration, process analysis, and comparison-contrast can be used—alone or in combination. Imagine that you're planning to write an extended definition of "robotics." You might develop the term by providing *examples* of the ways robots are currently being used in scientific research; by *comparing* and *contrasting* human and robot capabilities; or by *classifying* robots, starting with the most basic and moving to the most advanced or futuristic models.

Which patterns of development to use will often become apparent during the prewriting stage. Here is a list of prewriting questions as well as the pattern of development implied by each question.

Question	Pattern of Development
How does X look, taste, smell, feel, and sound?	Description
What does X do? When? Where?	Narration
What are some typical instances of X?	Exemplification
What are X's component parts? What different forms can X take?	Division-classification
How does X work?	Process analysis
What is X like or unlike?	Comparison-contrast
What leads to X? What are X's consequences?	Cause-effect

Those questions yielding the most material often suggest the effective pattern(s) for developing an extended definition.

4. Organize the material that develops the definition. If you use a single pattern to develop the extended definition, apply the principles of organization suited to that pattern, as described in the appropriate chapter of this book. Assume that you're defining "fad" by means of *process analysis.* You might organize your paragraphs according to the steps in the process: a fad's slow start as something avant-garde or eccentric; its wildfire acceptance by the general public; the fad's demise as it becomes familiar or tiresome. If you want to define "character" by means of a single *narration,* you would probably organize paragraphs chronologically.

5. Write an effective introduction. It can be helpful to provide—near the beginning of a definition essay—a brief formal definition of the term you're going to develop in the rest of the paper. You might explain the *origin* of the term being defined: "Acid rock is a term first coined in the 1960s to describe music that was written or listened to under the influence of the drug LSD." Similarly, you could explain the *etymology,* or linguistic origin, of the key word that focuses the paper.

You may also use the introduction to clarify what the subject is *not.* Such *definition by negation* can be an effective strategy at the beginning of a paper, especially if readers don't share your view of the subject. In such a case, you might write something like this: "The gorilla, far from being the vicious killer of jungle movies and popular imagination, is a sedentary, gentle creature living in a closely knit family group." Such a statement provides the special focus of your essay and signals some of the misconceptions or fallacies soon to be discussed.

In addition, you may include in the introduction a *stipulative definition,* one that puts special restrictions on a term: "Strictly defined, a mall refers to a one- or two-story enclosed building containing a variety of retail shops and at least two large anchor stores. Highway-strip shopping centers or downtown centers cannot be considered true malls." When a term has multiple meanings, or when its meaning has become fuzzy through misuse, a stipulative definition sets the record straight right at the start, so that readers know exactly what is, and is not, being defined.

Finally, the introduction may end with a *plan of development* that indicates how the definition essay will unfold. A student who returned to school after having raised a family decided to write a paper defining the *midlife crisis* that led to her enrollment in college. After providing a brief formal definition of "midlife crisis," the student rounded off her introduction with this sentence: "Such a midlife crisis starts with vague misgivings, turns into depression, and ends with a significant change in lifestyle."

REVISION STRATEGIES

Once you have a draft of the essay, you're ready to revise. The following checklist will help you and those giving you feedback apply to definition some of the revision techniques discussed on pages 60–62.

☑ DEFINITION: A REVISION/PEER REVIEW CHECKLIST

Revise Overall Meaning and Structure

- ❑ Is the essay's purpose informative, persuasive, or both?
- ❑ Is the term being defined clearly distinguished from similar terms?
- ❑ Where does a circular definition cloud meaning? Where are technical, nonstandard, or ambiguous terms a source of confusion?
- ❑ Where would a word's historical or linguistic origin clarify meaning? Where would a formal definition, stipulative definition, or definition by negation help?
- ❑ Which patterns of development are used to develop the definition? How do these help the essay achieve its purpose?
- ❑ If the essay uses only one pattern, is the essay's method of organization suited to that pattern (step-by-step for process analysis, chronological for narration, and so on)?
- ❑ Where could a dry formal definition be deleted without sacrificing overall clarity?

Revise Paragraph Development

- ❑ If the essay uses several patterns of development, where would separate paragraphs for different patterns be appropriate?
- ❑ Which paragraphs are flat or unconvincing? How could they be made more compelling?

Revise Sentences and Words

- ❑ Which sentences and words are inconsistent with the essay's tone?
- ❑ Where should overused phrases like "the dictionary says" and "according to *Webster's*" be replaced by more original wording?
- ❑ Have "is when" definitions been avoided?

STUDENT ESSAY

The following student essay was written by Laura Chen in response to this assignment:

> In "Who's a Pirate? In Court, a Duel over Definitions," Keith Johnson tries defining an old term for a new context. Choose a specialized term and define it in such a way that you reveal something significant about contemporary life.

While reading Laura's paper, try to determine how well it applies the principles of definition. The annotations on Laura's paper and the commentary following it will help you look at the essay more closely.

Physics in Everyday Life
by Laura Chen

Introduction

A boulder sits on a mountainside for a thousand years. 1
The boulder will remain there forever unless an outside force intervenes. Suppose a force does affect the boulder—an earthquake, for instance. Once the boulder begins to thunder down the mountain, it will remain in motion and head in one direction only—downhill—until another force interrupts its progress. If the boulder tumbles into a gorge, it will finally come to rest as gravity anchors it to the earth once more. In both cases, the boulder is exhibiting the physical principle of inertia: the tendency of matter to remain at rest or, if moving, to keep moving in one direction unless affected by an outside force. Inertia, an important factor in the world of physics, also plays a crucial role in the human world. Inertia affects our individual lives as well as the direction taken by society as a whole.

Formal definition

Thesis

Plan of development

Topic sentence

Inertia often influences our value systems and personal 2
growth. Inertia is at work, for example, when people cling to certain behaviors and views. Like the boulder firmly fixed to the mountain, most people are set in their ways. Without thinking, they vote Republican or Democratic because they have always voted that way. They regard with suspicion a couple having no children, simply because everyone else in the neighborhood has a large family. It is only when an outside force—a jolt of some sort—occurs that people change their views. A white American couple may think little about racial discrimination, for instance, until they adopt an Asian child and must comfort her when classmates tease her because she looks different. Parents may consider promiscuous any unmarried teenage girl who has a baby until their seventeen-year-old honor student confesses that she is pregnant. Personal jolts like these force people to think, perhaps for the first time, about issues that now affect them directly.

Start of a series of causes and effects

Topic sentence

To illustrate how inertia governs our lives, it is helpful to 3
compare the world of television with real life. On TV, inertia does not exist. Television shows and commercials show people making all kinds of drastic changes. They switch brands of coffee or try a new hair color with no hesitation. In one car commercial, an ambitious young accountant abandons her career with a flourish and is seen driving off into the sunset as she heads for a small cabin by the sea to write poetry. In a soap

Start of a series of contrasts

opera, a character may progress from homemaker to hooker to nun in a single year. But in real life, inertia rules. People tend to stay where they are, to keep their jobs, to be loyal to products. A second major difference between television and real life is that, on television, everyone takes prompt and dramatic action to solve problems. The construction worker with a thudding headache is pain-free at the end of the sixty-second commercial; the police catch the murderer within an hour; the family learns to cope with their son's life-threatening drug addiction by the time the made-for-TV movie ends at eleven. But in the real world, inertia persists, so that few problems are solved neatly or quickly. Illnesses drag on, few crimes are solved, and family conflicts last for years.

Topic sentence

4 Inertia is, most importantly, a force at work in the life of our nation. Again, inertia is two-sided. It keeps us from moving and, once we move, it keeps us pointed in one direction. We find ourselves mired in a certain path, accepting the inferior, even the dangerous. We settle for toys that break, winter coats with no warmth, and rivers clogged with pollution. Inertia also compels our nation to keep moving in one direction—despite the uncomfortable suspicion that it is the wrong direction. We are not sure if manipulating genes is a good idea, yet we continue to fund scientific projects in genetic engineering. More than sixty years ago, we were shaken when we saw the devastation caused by an atomic bomb. But we went on to develop weapons hundreds of times more destructive. Although warned that excessive television viewing may be harmful, we continue to watch hours of television each day.

Start of a series of examples

Conclusion

5 We have learned to defy gravity, one of the basic laws of physics; we fly high above the earth, even float in outer space. But most of us have not learned to defy inertia. Those special individuals who are able to act when everyone else seems paralyzed are rare. But the fact that such people do exist means that inertia is not all-powerful. If we use our reasoning ability and our creativity, we can conquer inertia, just as we have conquered gravity.

COMMENTARY

Introduction. As the title of her essay suggests, Laura has taken a scientific term (*inertia*) from a specialized field and drawn on the term to help explain some everyday phenomena. Using the *simple-to-complex* approach to structure the introduction, she opens with a vivid *descriptive* example of inertia. This description is then followed by a *formal definition* of inertia: "the tendency of matter to remain at rest or, if moving, to keep moving in one direction unless affected by an outside force." Laura wisely begins the paper with the easy-to-understand description rather than with the more-difficult-to-grasp scientific definition. Had the order been reversed, the essay would not have gotten off to nearly as effective a start. She then ends her introductory paragraph with a *thesis,* "Inertia, an important factor in the world of physics, also plays a crucial role in the human world," and with a *plan of development,* "Inertia affects our individual lives as well as the direction taken by society as a whole."

Organization. To support her definition of inertia and her belief that it can rule our lives, Laura generates a number of compelling examples. She organizes these examples by grouping them into three major points, each point signaled by a *topic sentence* that opens each of the essay's three supporting paragraphs (2–4).

A definite organizational strategy determines the sequence of Laura's three central points. The essay moves from the way inertia affects the individual to the way it affects the nation. The phrase "most importantly" at the beginning of the fourth paragraph shows that Laura has arranged her points emphatically, believing that inertia's impact on society is most critical.

A weak example. When reading the fourth paragraph, you might have noticed that Laura's examples aren't sequenced as effectively as they could be. To show that we, as a nation, tend to keep moving in the same direction, Laura discusses our ongoing uneasiness about genetic engineering, nuclear arms, and excessive television viewing. The point about nuclear weapons is most significant, yet it gets lost because it's sandwiched in the middle. The paragraph would be stronger if it ended with the point about nuclear arms. Moreover, the example about excessive television viewing doesn't belong in this paragraph since, at best, it has limited bearing on the issue being discussed.

Combining patterns of development. In addition to using numerous *examples* to illustrate her points, Laura draws on several other patterns of development to show that inertia can be a powerful force. In the second and fourth paragraphs, she uses *causal analysis* to explain how inertia can paralyze people and nations. The second paragraph indicates that only "an outside force—a jolt of some sort—" can motivate inert people to change. To support this view, Laura provides two examples of parents who experience such jolts. Similarly, in the fourth paragraph, she contends that inertia causes the persistence of specific national problems: shoddy consumer goods and environmental pollution.

Another pattern, *comparison-contrast,* is used in the third paragraph to highlight the differences between television and real life: on television, people zoom into action, but in everyday life, people tend to stay put and muddle through. The essay also contains a distinct element of *argumentation-persuasion,* since Laura clearly wants readers to accept her definition of inertia and her view that it often governs human behavior.

Conclusion. Laura's *conclusion* rounds off the essay nicely and brings it to a satisfying close. Laura refers to another law of physics, one with which we are all familiar—gravity. By creating an *analogy* between gravity and inertia, she suggests that our ability to defy gravity should encourage us to defy inertia. The analogy enlarges the scope of the essay; it allows Laura to reach out to her readers by challenging them to action. Such a challenge is, of course, appropriate in a definition essay having a persuasive bent.

Revising the first draft. When it was time to rework her essay, Laura began by reading her paper aloud. She noted in the margin of her draft the problems she detected, numbering them in order of importance. After reviewing her notes, she started to revise in earnest, paying special attention to her third paragraph. The first draft of that paragraph is reprinted here:

Original Version of the Third Paragraph

The ordinary actions of daily life are, in part, determined by inertia. To understand this, it is helpful to compare the world of television with real life, for, in the TV-land of ads and entertainment, inertia does not exist. For example, on television, people are often shown making all kinds of drastic changes. They switch brands of coffee or try a new hair color with no hesitation. In one car commercial, a young accountant leaves her career and sets off for a cabin by the sea to write poetry. In a soap opera, a character may progress from homemaker to hooker to nun in a single year. In contrast, inertia rules in real life. People tend to stay where they are, to keep their jobs, to be loyal to products (wives get annoyed if a husband brings home the wrong brand or color of bathroom tissue from the market). Middle-aged people wear the hairstyles or makeup that suited them in high school. A second major difference between television and real life is that, on TV, everyone takes prompt and dramatic action to solve problems. A woman finds the solution to dull clothes at the end of a commercial; the police catch the murderer within an hour; the family learns to cope with a son's disturbing lifestyle by the time the movie is over. In contrast, the law of real-life inertia means that few problems are solved neatly or quickly. Things, once started, tend to stay as they are. Few crimes are actually solved. Medical problems are not easily diagnosed. Messy wars in foreign countries seem endless. National problems are identified, but Congress does not pass legislation to solve them.

After rereading what she had written, Laura realized that her third paragraph rambled. To give it more focus, she removed the last two sentences ("Messy wars in foreign countries seem endless" and "National problems are identified, but Congress does not pass legislation. . . .") because they referred to national affairs but were located in a section focusing on the individual. Then, she eliminated two flat, unconvincing examples: wives who get annoyed when their husbands bring home the wrong brand of bathroom tissue and middle-aged people whose hairstyles and makeup are outdated. Condensing the two disjointed sentences that originally opened the paragraph also helped tighten this section of the essay. Note how much crisper the revised sentences are: "To illustrate how inertia rules our lives, it is helpful to compare the world of television with real life. On TV, inertia does not exist."

Laura also worked to make the details and the language in the paragraph more specific and vigorous. The vague sentence "A woman finds the solution to dull clothes at the end of the commercial" is replaced by the more dramatic "The construction worker with a thudding headache is pain-free at the end of the sixty-second commercial." Similarly, Laura changed a "son's disturbing lifestyle" to a "son's life-threatening drug addiction"; "by the time the movie is over" became "by the time the made-for-TV movie ends at eleven"; and "a young accountant leaves her career and sets off for a cabin by the sea to write poetry" was changed to "an ambitious young accountant abandons her career with a flourish and is seen driving off into the sunset as she heads for a small cabin by the sea to write poetry."

After making these changes, Laura decided to round off the paragraph with a powerful summary statement highlighting how real life differs from television: "Illnesses drag on, few crimes are solved, and family conflicts last for years."

These third-paragraph revisions are similar to those that Laura made elsewhere in her first draft. Her astute changes enabled her to turn an already effective paper into an especially thoughtful analysis of human behavior.

Activities: Definition

Prewriting Activities

1. Imagine you're writing two essays: one explains the *process* for registering a complaint that gets results; the other *contrasts* the styles of two stand-up comics. Jot down ways you might use definition in each essay.

2. Select a term whose meaning varies from person to person or one for which you have a personal definition. Some possibilities include:

success	femininity	a liberal
patriotism	affirmative action	a housewife
individuality	pornography	intelligence

   Brainstorm with others to identify variations in the term's meaning. Then examine your prewriting material. What thesis comes to mind? If you were writing an essay, would your purpose be informative, persuasive, or both? Finally, prepare a scratch list of the points you might cover.

Revising Activities

3. Explain why each of the following is an effective or ineffective definition. Rewrite those you consider ineffective.
   a. *Passive aggression* is when people show their aggression passively.
   b. A *terrorist* tries to terrorize people.
   c. *Being assertive* means knowing how to express your wishes and goals in a positive, noncombative way.
   d. *Pop music* refers to music that is popular.
   e. *Loyalty* is when someone stays by another person during difficult times.

4. The following introductory paragraph is from the first draft of an essay contrasting walking and running as techniques for reducing tension. Although intended to be a definition paragraph, it actually doesn't tell us anything we don't already know. It also relies on the old-hat "*Webster's* says." Rewrite the paragraph so it is more imaginative. You might use a series of anecdotes or one extended example to define *tension* and introduce the essay's thesis more gracefully.

   According to *Webster's, tension* is "mental or nervous strain, often accompanied by muscular tightness or tautness." Everyone feels tense at one time or another. It may occur when there's a deadline to meet. Or it could be caused by the stress of trying to fulfill academic, athletic, or social goals. Sometimes it comes from criticism by family, bosses, or teachers. Such tension puts wear and tear on our bodies and on our emotional well-being. Although some people run to relieve tension, research has found that walking is a more effective tension reducer.

Ann Hulbert

Writer Ann Hulbert was born in 1956 and attended Harvard College and Cambridge University. Her work has appeared in many publications, including *Slate, The New York Times Book Review, The New York Review of Books,* and *The New Republic.* Hulbert is the author of *The Interior Castle: The Art and Life of Jean Stafford* and *Raising America: Experts, Parents, and a Century of Advice About Children.* This article was published on March 11, 2007, in *The New York Times Magazine.*

Pre-Reading Journal Entry

One of the benefits of family life is getting to know people of other generations. What generations are represented by the people in your extended family? What generation do you belong to? What generation do your parents and your children, if any, belong to? How do the generations in your family differ? Use your journal to answer these questions.

Beyond the Pleasure Principle

1 It is a point of pride among baby boomers that after our kids leave home, we enjoy a continuing closeness with them that our parents rarely had with us. We certainly do keep in touch: 80 percent of 18- to 25-year-olds had talked to their parents in the past day, according to "A Portrait of Generation Next," a recent study conducted by the Pew Research Center in tandem with MacNeil/Lehrer Productions. Yet if the survey is any guide, Gen Nexters aren't getting the credit they deserve for being—as many of them told pollsters they felt they were—"unique and distinct." It is not easy carving out your niche in the shadow of parents who still can't get over what an exceptional generation they belong to.

2 So what is special about Gen Nexters? Don't count on them to capture their own quintessence. "The words and phrases they used varied widely," the Pew researchers noted, "ranging from 'lazy' to 'crazy' to 'fun.'" But if you look closely, what makes Gen Nexters *sui generis*—and perhaps more mysterious than their elders appreciate—are their views on two divisive social topics, abortion and gay marriage. On the by-now-familiar red-and-blue map of the culture wars, positions on those issues are presumed to go hand in hand: those on the right oppose both as evidence of a promiscuous society and those on the left embrace them as rights that guarantee privacy and dignity. Yet as a group, Gen Nexters seem to challenge the package deals.

3 Young Americans, it turns out, are unexpectedly conservative on abortion but notably liberal on gay marriage. Given that 18- to 25-year-olds are the least Republican generation (35 percent) and less religious than their elders (with 20 percent of them professing no religion or atheism or

agnosticism), it is curious that on abortion they are slightly to the right of the general public. Roughly a third of Gen Nexters endorse making abortion generally available, half support limits and 15 percent favor an outright ban. By contrast, 35 percent of 50- to 64-year-olds support readily available abortions. On gay marriage, there was not much of a generation gap in the 1980s, but now Gen Nexters stand out as more favorably disposed than the rest of the country. Almost half of them approve, compared with under a third of those over 25.

It could simply be, of course, that some young people are pro-gay marriage 4
and others are pro-life and that we can expect more of the same old polarized culture warfare ahead of us. But what if Gen Nexters, rather than being so, well, lazy, are forging their own new crossover path? When I contacted John Green, an expert on religious voters who is currently working at the Pew Forum on Religion and Public Life, he said that pollsters hadn't tackled that question. But after crunching some numbers, he suggested that there might indeed be a middle way in the making. Many individual Gen Nexters hold what seem like divergent views on homosexuality and government involvement with morality—either liberal on one while being conservative on the other or else confirmed in their views on one question while ambivalent on the other.

Oh, how these young people can confound us! All this could amount to 5
no more than what the experts call a "life-cycle effect": Gen Nexters may hold heterogeneous views now because they are exploring diverse values that may congeal in more conventional ways as they get older. But a more intriguing possibility is that it is a "cohort effect," a distinctive orientation that will stick with them. Liberals could take heart that perhaps homosexual marriage has replaced abortion as the new "equality issue" for Gen Nexters, suggested John Russonello, a Washington pollster whose firm is especially interested in social values; Gen Nexters may have grown up after the back-alley abortion era, but they haven't become complacent about sexual rights. Conservatives might take comfort from a different hypothesis that Green tried out: maybe Gen Nexters have been listening to their parents' lectures about responsibility. Don't do things that make you have an abortion, young people may have concluded, and do welcome everyone into the social bulwark of family responsibility.

Put the two perspectives together, and an ethos emerges that looks at 6
once refreshingly pragmatic and yet still idealistic. On one level, Gen Nexters sound impatient with a strident stalemate between entrenched judgments of behavior; after all, experience tells them that in the case of both abortion and gay rights, life is complicated and intransigence has only impeded useful social and political compromises. At the same time, Gen Nexters give every indication of being attentive to the moral issues at stake: they aren't willing to ignore what is troubling about abortion and what is equally troubling about intolerant exclusion. A hardheadedness, but also a high-mindedness and softheartedness, seems to be at work.

7 And to risk what might be truly wishful thinking, maybe there are signs here that Gen Nexters are primed to do in the years ahead what their elders have so signally failed to manage: actually think beyond their own welfare to worry about—of all things—the next generation. For when you stop to consider it, at the core of Gen Nexters' seemingly discordant views on these hot-button issues could be an insistence on giving priority to children's interests. Take seriously the lives you could be creating: the Gen Next wariness of abortion sends that message. Don't rule out for any kid who is born the advantage of being reared by two legally wedded parents: that is at least one way to read the endorsement of gay marriage. However you end up sorting out the data, fun or crazy wouldn't be how I would describe the Gen Next mix. Judged against the boomers' own past or present, though, the outlook definitely looks unique.

Questions for Close Reading

1. What is the selection's thesis? Locate the sentence(s) in which Hulbert states her main idea. If she doesn't state her thesis explicitly, express it in your own words.
2. What statistics about Gen Nexters are the basis for much of the extended definition in this article?
3. What is the difference between a "life-cycle effect" and a "cohort effect"? Which type of effect does Hulbert claim her essay is about?
4. According to Hulbert, what has the elder generation—the baby boomers—failed to do?
5. Refer to your dictionary as needed to define the following words used in the selection: *tandem* (paragraph 1), *quintessence* (2), *sui generis* (2), *promiscuous* (2), *agnosticism* (3), *heterogeneous* (5), *congeal* (5), *bulwark* (5), *ethos* (6), *intransigence* (6), *impeded* (6), and *discordant* (7).

Questions About the Writer's Craft

1. What is Hulbert's underlying purpose in defining the characteristics of Gen Nexters? Is her purpose mainly informative, speculative, or persuasive? How can you tell?
2. **The pattern.** Hulbert uses the "definition by negation" strategy throughout this essay. Identify examples of this strategy in the article and evaluate how well it works.
3. **Other patterns.** Hulbert also uses the compare-contrast strategy at many points in her article. What signal devices does she use to signal when she is comparing and contrasting?
4. What is the effect of the delayed thesis on the reader's experience of this article? Is the delayed thesis effective? Do you think Hulbert should have stated her thesis at the beginning of the essay?

Writing Assignments Using Definition as a Pattern of Development

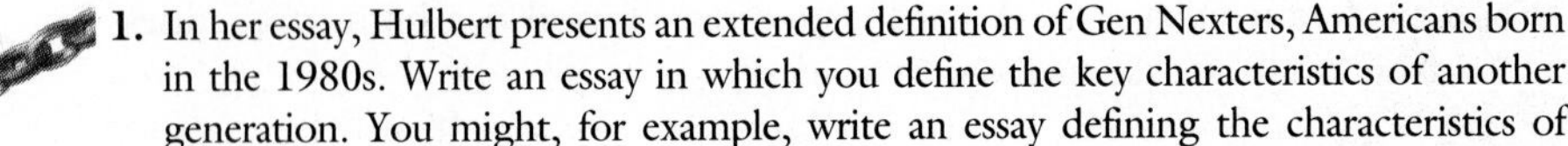

1. In her essay, Hulbert presents an extended definition of Gen Nexters, Americans born in the 1980s. Write an essay in which you define the key characteristics of another generation. You might, for example, write an essay defining the characteristics of

FIGURE 10.2
Essay Structure: "Beyond the Pleasure Principle" by Ann Hulbert

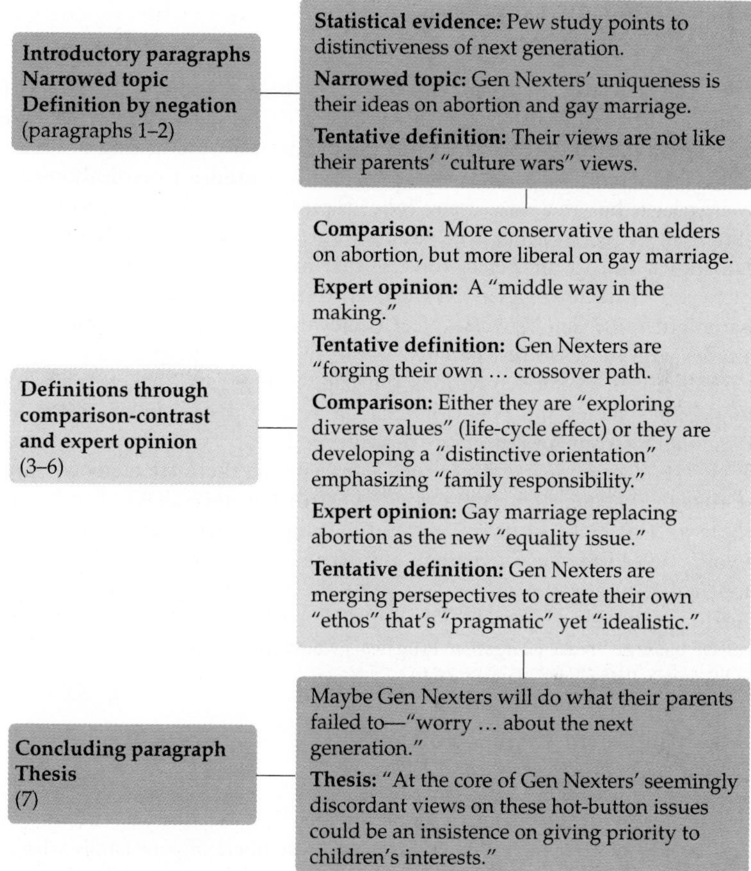

baby boomers (born from 1946 through the early 1960s), Generation Xers (born from 1965 to 1980), or the as-yet-unnamed youngest generation of those under 18 (born in the 1990s or later). If you choose to define the youngest generation, be sure to give it an "official" name. Before you write, decide whether your tone will be serious or humorous. For an essay written by a member of one generation about an encounter with a member of another generation, see Joan Murray's "Someone's Mother" (page 154).

Introductory paragraphs
Narrowed topic
Definition by negation
(paragraphs 1–2)
Statistical evidence: Pew study points to distinctiveness of next generation.
Narrowed topic: Gen Nexters' uniqueness is their ideas on abortion and gay marriage.
Tentative definition: Their views are not like their parents' "culture wars" views.
Definitions through comparison-contrast and expert opinion
(3–6)
Comparison: More conservative than elders on abortion, but more liberal on gay marriage.
Expert opinion: A "middle way in the making."
Tentative definition: Gen Nexters are "forging their own ... crossover path.
Comparison: Either they are "exploring diverse values" (life-cycle effect) or they are developing a "distinctive orientation" emphasizing "family responsibility."
Expert opinion: Gay marriage replacing abortion as the new "equality issue."
Tentative definition: Gen Nexters are merging persepectives to create their own "ethos" that's "pragmatic" yet "idealistic."
Concluding paragraph
Thesis
(7)
Maybe Gen Nexters will do what their parents failed to—"worry ... about the next generation."
Thesis: "At the core of Gen Nexters' seemingly discordant views on these hot-button issues could be an insistence on giving priority to children's interests."

2. In her article, Hulbert mentions the current polarization of Americans—liberals versus conservatives and blue states versus red states. The meanings of these four terms can vary widely, however, often depending on the viewpoint of the writer. Write an essay in which you define what you think it means to be a liberal or a conservative, or to live in a red state or a blue state. What are the key characteristics

of the term you chose? What are the values and attitudes associated with the term? Discussing these issues with friends and family might help you clarify your ideas before you write.

Writing Assignments Combining Patterns of Development

3. Go to the Pew Research Center website (http://pewresearch.org) and read *A Portrait of "Generation Next": How Young People View Their Lives, Futures, and Politics,* the 2007 report that was the occasion for the writing of Hulbert's article. Hulbert focused on Generation Next's attitudes toward abortion and gay marriage, but there are many other topics covered by this report, such as political affiliation, violence, sex, the future, technology and the Internet, body decorations, and so on. Select topic(s) that interest you and write an essay in which you characterize Gen Nexters' attitudes toward those topics. Explain what might *cause* Gen Nexters to feel as they do, and *compare and contrast* their attitudes with those of their parents.
4. In paragraph 5, Hulbert mentions the "life-cycle effect," which refers to the way people's values and behaviors change as they pass from one stage of life to the next—from adolescence to adulthood, for example. Some of these life-cycle effects are marked by ritual. For example, there are many coming-of-age rites of passage, such as graduation, bar or bat mitzvah, confirmation, the debutante's ball, the *quinceañera,* and getting a driver's license. Choose one of your own life's rites of passage and write an essay about it. Narrate what happened, describe the *process* you went through, and give *examples* of how your life changed as a result. For insight into how two authors experienced rites of passage, read Langston Hughes's "Salvation" (page 158) and Richard Rodriguez's "Workers" (page 361).

Writing Assignment Using a Journal Entry as a Starting Point

5. Review your pre-reading journal entry in which you describe the various generations represented by your relatives. Select two members of your family who come from different generations, and write an essay in which you describe them. What are their similarities and differences? What aspects of their attitudes and behaviors are generational, and what aspects are unique to them as individuals? Why is each of these people important to you? What roles do they play in your life?

Keith Johnson

Keith Johnson, born in 1972, was educated at the University of Georgia, where he earned a B.A. in history and an M.A. in Spanish literature. Early in his career, he joined *The Wall Street Journal*, where he continues to work as a journalist. Between 1998 and 2001, as a news assistant, Johnson mostly reported on technology and politics. Then, as a staff reporter from 2001 to 2007, he covered Spain, terrorism, airlines, and energy, including reporting on the Iraqi oil industry in the summer of 2003. Johnson went on to run the *Journal*'s blog *Environmental Capital*, which focuses on energy and the environment, from 2008 to early 2010. Currently, he is part of the newspaper's national security team, for which he reports on areas such as homeland security, domestic and transnational terrorism, piracy, and energy security, as well as on some Latin American issues. The following article was published in *The Wall Street Journal* on August 20, 2010.

Pre-Reading Journal Entry

Pirates have been romanticized in movies such as *Pirates of the Caribbean* and *The Sea Hawk* and in novels such as *Treasure Island*. Why do you think pirates are such glamorous figures? What other kinds of villains have been treated similarly? Do some freewriting in your journal on this subject.

Who's a Pirate? In Court, A Duel over Definitions

Not since Lt. Robert Maynard of the Royal Navy sailed back triumphantly to nearby Hampton Roads in 1718 with the severed head of Blackbeard[1] swinging from his bowsprit has this Navy town been so embroiled in the fight against piracy. 1

Prosecuting pirates, rather than hanging them from the yardarm, is the modern world's approach to the scourge of Somali piracy that has turned huge swathes of the Indian Ocean into a no-go zone for commercial vessels. 2

But there's a problem: Some 2,000 years after Cicero[2] defined pirates as the "common enemy of all," nobody seems able to say, legally, exactly what a pirate is. 3

U.S. law long ago made piracy a crime but didn't define it. International law contains differing, even contradictory, definitions. The confusion threatens to hamstring U.S. efforts to crack down on modern-day Blackbeards. 4

The central issue in Norfolk: If you try to waylay and rob a ship at sea—but you don't succeed—are you still a pirate? 5

[1]Blackbeard is the pseudonym of an infamous British pirate who operated off the Eastern Coast of the United States (editors' note).
[2]Cicero (106–43 BCE) was a philosopher and statesman in ancient Rome (editors' note).

It may seem strange there should be doubt about an offense as old as this one. Piracy was the world's first crime with universal jurisdiction, meaning that any country had the right to apprehend pirates on the high seas. 6

The Romans took piracy so seriously they overrode a cautious Senate and gave near-dictatorial powers to an up-and-coming general named Pompey,[3] who soon swept away piracy in the Mediterranean. 7

In more recent centuries, European countries such as Britain cracked down on pirates—except when busy enlisting certain ones, dubbed "privateers," to help them fight their wars by raiding enemy ships. 8

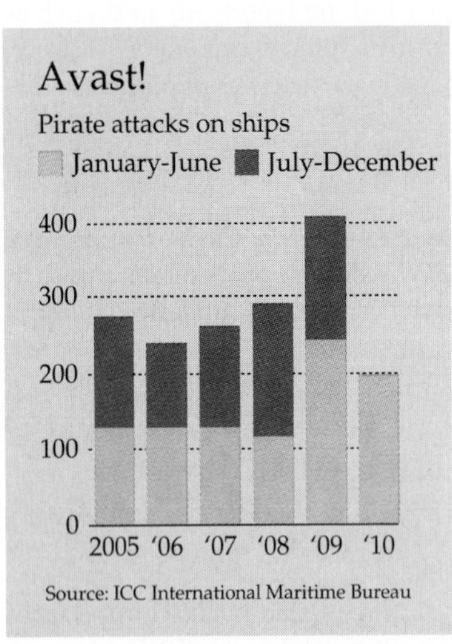

Pirates even spurred the creation of the U.S. Navy, after Thomas Jefferson erupted over the cost of paying tribute to the Barbary Corsairs[4] for safe passage of U.S. merchant ships. At the time, the U.S. was paying about one-tenth of the federal budget to the pirates. Supplied with warships, President Jefferson waged war on the Barbary pirates (whence the line "to the shores of Tripoli" in the Marines' Hymn). By 1815, the North African pirate kingdoms had been subdued. 9

When Congress dealt with piracy in a statute four years later, the crime was so easy to recognize that legislators didn't bother to describe it, just the punishment. The 1819 statute that made piracy a capital offense (since changed to mandatory life in prison) simply deferred to "the law of nations." That legal punt has kept American jurists scrambling ever since. 10

The stage was set for the Norfolk trial on April 10 of this year [2010] when the USS Ashland, cruising in the Gulf of Aden about 330 miles off Djibouti, was fired upon at 5 a.m. by Somali men in a small skiff. The Navy vessel, an amphibious dock landing ship, returned fire with 25-mm cannon, wrecking the 18-foot skiff and sending its six occupants overboard. 11

The Ashland sent a search boat to recover the Somalis and photograph the smoking hulk of the skiff, which contained at least one weapon and what looked like a grappling hook or anchor. Though that boat was blasted to pieces, even when pirate skiffs survive, the ships they target are often loath to 12

[3]Pompey (106–48 BCE) was a statesman and great military leader in ancient Rome (editors' note).
[4]The Barbary Corsairs were Muslim pirates or privateers who operated out of North Africa (editors' note).

bring the skiffs aboard. One captured by a Navy force in 2006, according to the judge advocate's testimony in a subsequent trial in Kenya, was crawling with "roaches the size of leopards."

In Norfolk, the prosecution has begun its effort to convince the U.S. District Court for the Eastern District of Virginia that the quickly foiled Somalis are guilty not just of lesser charges they face but of the main charge of piracy. 13

"Violent attacks on the high seas without lawful authority have always been piracy under the law of nations, in 1819 and today," said the lead prosecutor, Benjamin Hatch, at a pretrial hearing last month [July 2010]. 14

"So if one ship fires a bow-and-arrow," asked Judge Raymond Jackson, rubbing his brow, "or a slingshot, or a rock, those are all acts of violence, and thus piracy?" The prosecutor nodded. 15

The public defender, Geremy Kamens, weighed in. "That a slingshot fired upon another ship would expose the defendant to a mandatory life sentence shows the absurd result of this reading," he said. The defense added that under this broad definition, Greenpeace[5] activists could be considered pirates for their anti-whaling antics on the seas. 16

The defense lawyers trawled through history books, coming to rest upon an obscure 1820 Supreme Court ruling. 17

"We have, therefore, no hesitation in declaring that piracy, by the law of nations, is robbery upon the sea," Justice Joseph Story wrote for the majority in the case of United States v. Smith. 18

That gave the defense lawyers their main argument: Piracy is robbery on the high seas; it isn't merely attempted robbery at sea, which is covered by a separate statute that the Somalis are charged with as well. 19

Since the attack on the Ashland clearly failed, it wasn't piracy, the defense argues, and therefore, the most serious charge should be dropped. 20

But the prosecutors, too, have probed early sources—17th-century Dutch jurists, 18th-century British writers, 19th-century maritime cases, an 1800 speech by then-congressman John Marshall, and a slew of international treaties. 21

The prosecution has leaned heavily on a 1934 ruling by Britain's Privy Council,[6] which pondered the case of a similarly failed attack at sea, near Hong Kong. In that case, the jury found the defendants guilty, but said its verdict was subject to the question of whether it's really piracy if no actual robbery occurs. The court in Hong Kong said it isn't, and acquitted the attackers. 22

The Privy Council members, however, after hacking through thickets of legal technicalities, ultimately reached a different conclusion. "Actual robbery is not an essential element in the crime of piracy," they said; "A frustrated attempt to commit piratical robbery is equally piracy." 23

[5]Greenpeace, an activist environmental organization, is known for putting its ships between "whales and harpoons," as its website notes, on the high seas to deter whaling (editors' note).

[6]The Privy Council, formerly very powerful, is a group of advisors to the British sovereign (editors' note).

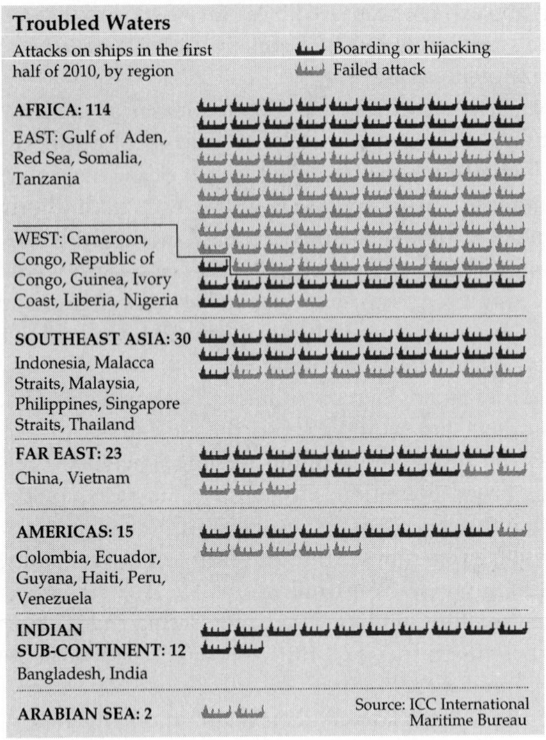

Troubled Waters

Attacks on ships in the first half of 2010, by region

Boarding or hijacking
Failed attack

AFRICA: 114
EAST: Gulf of Aden, Red Sea, Somalia, Tanzania
WEST: Cameroon, Congo, Republic of Congo, Guinea, Ivory Coast, Liberia, Nigeria

SOUTHEAST ASIA: 30
Indonesia, Malacca Straits, Malaysia, Philippines, Singapore Straits, Thailand

FAR EAST: 23
China, Vietnam

AMERICAS: 15
Colombia, Ecuador, Guyana, Haiti, Peru, Venezuela

INDIAN SUB-CONTINENT: 12
Bangladesh, India

ARABIAN SEA: 2

Source: ICC International Maritime Bureau

They added, with more than a hint of exasperation: "Their Lordships 24
are almost tempted to say that a little common sense is a valuable quality in the interpretation of international law."

Beyond the legal wrangling and obscure historical references, the implications 25
of the case in Norfolk are serious. Piracy's golden age may have passed two centuries ago, but it remains a scourge in places like the Strait of Malacca in Indonesia and Malaysia, off the coast of Nigeria, and above all off the east coast of Africa, where the disintegration of Somalia has led to a major resurgence.

The first half of 2010 saw about 200 raids and unsuccessful attacks on 26
ships at sea worldwide, the bulk of them off Somalia. In early August, two cargo ships were hijacked. In all, an estimated 18 ships and their crews are currently [as of August 2010] being held for ransom.

To fight the problem, the U.S. and the United Nations are counting on 27
prosecuting pirates. Some U.N. officials dream of establishing an international piracy tribunal, similar to the one for war crimes in The Hague.

In the meantime, the U.S. and other countries have helped Kenya, the 28
closest stable country to the source, to put scores of pirates on trial. But Kenyan law is cumbersome, requiring witnesses to testify on three separate occasions, a tough order logistically for merchant sailors. The European Union is now trying to jump-start Kenya's pirate prosecutions—the first sentence will come later this month—but progress is slow.

As a result, attackers captured by European warships in the Indian Ocean often are let go for lack of any real legal recourse. A Spanish warship caught seven Somali pirates red-handed in early August, men who had been trying to waylay a Norwegian chemical tanker. The Spanish frigate immediately released them because it would have been difficult to prosecute them, the EU naval force off Somalia said. 29

That leaves courtrooms like the one in Norfolk as among the best hopes for bringing pirates to justice and deterring future ones. But even seemingly clear-cut cases don't necessarily pass muster in court. 30

After a celebrated incident in April 2009, when U.S. Navy Seals snipers killed three Somali men holding an American captain hostage on a small boat after a raid, rescuing him, the lone Somali survivor of that attack on the Maersk Alabama pleaded guilty to lesser charges in New York, not to piracy. 31

Indeed, the last U.S. piracy conviction was in 1861, of a Confederate blockade runner. 32

Now the court in Norfolk must contend with the defense motion to dismiss the piracy charge, which would leaving only such lesser charges as attempted plunder. 33

The prosecution argues that U.S. courts should defer to international law, especially an 1982 U.N. Law of the Sea treaty the U.S. never ratified. Aping the 1958 Geneva Convention,[7] it offers an expansive definition of piracy as any illegal acts of violence, detention or depredation committed for private ends on the high seas. 34

Defense lawyers balk at that suggestion. "We do not interpret U.S. law based on U.N. resolutions, but rather what Congress meant at the time," says the public defender, Mr. Kamens. 35

Judge Jackson is expected to rule soon.[8] 36

---

[7]The Geneva Convention of April 29, 1958, sets forth internationally agreed-upon rules for conduct on the high seas, for example, fishing rights (editors' note).

[8]The Norfolk court ultimately ruled against trying the men on the charge of piracy.

Questions for Close Reading

1. What is the selection's thesis? Locate the sentence(s) in which Johnson states his main idea. If he doesn't state his thesis explicitly, express it in your own words.
2. What, according to the author, is the essential issue with defining *piracy*? What does the author have to say about the history of piracy before this century?
3. What were the prosecution's arguments in favor of trying the defendants for piracy? What arguments did the defense put forth?
4. Two graphs accompany the article. What information do the graphs supply? How do they support Johnson's point that it is important to resolve the definition of piracy at this time?
5. Refer to your dictionary as needed to define the following words used in the selection: *bowsprit* (paragraph 1), *yardarm* (2), *hamstring* (4), *jurisdiction* (6), *privateers* (8), *tribute* (9), *jurists* (10), *skiff* (11), *grappling hook* (12), *loath* (12), *foiled* (13), *slew* (21), *tribunal* (27), *recourse* (29), and *frigate* (29).

Questions About the Writer's Craft

1. **The pattern.** What are the term, class, and characteristics involved in the definition of *piracy*? In what way does the selection focus on definition by negation? (See page 436.)
2. Does the author intend to inform, entertain, or persuade the reader? What is the selection's tone? Is it suitable to his purpose? How are the two graphs relevant, or not relevant, to the author's purpose?
3. What historical anecdote does Johnson use to open his article? What is the effect of this opening? Describe the two current-day piracy anecdotes, besides that of the Norfolk trial, that the author relates.
4. The author refers to a number of legal rulings and often gives technical terms for parts of ships. What language techniques does he use to keep the selection interesting and accessible to the average reader? Give some examples.

Writing Assignments Using Definition as a Pattern of Development

1. The Geneva Convention sets forth rules for treating noncombatants during wartime. One major controversy today concerns how to treat captured terrorists. Do some research, and write an essay in which you define *terrorism*. In your definition include your view of whether a non-U.S. citizen on trial for terrorism should be treated as a civilian or an enemy combatant.
2. Recently, *piracy* has come to mean acts such as downloading music from the Internet without permission, knocking off designer handbags, or bootlegging copies of movies. Write an essay in which you establish a definition of *piracy* that focuses on these kinds of acts. Decide whether these acts should be considered theft. For some ways to write about ethics, read Charles Sykes's "The 'Values' Wasteland" (page 198) or Stephanie Ericsson's "The Ways We Lie" (page 247).

Writing Assignments Combining Patterns of Development

3. As with romantic images of pirates, our feelings about something can change radically when we actually experience it. Write an essay in which you describe how your ideas on a subject changed as you got to know it better. For example, you might *compare* how boring you thought camping would be until you went on a camping trip in a national park, or how cool you thought getting drunk would be until you tried it yourself. Use examples from your own experience to *illustrate* your ideas.
4. Should crimes against humanity have universal jurisdiction, as piracy does? For example, in 1998 the Chilean dictator Augusto Pinochet was indicted by a magistrate in Spain for human rights violations committed in Chile. He was arrested in London, but then ultimately released and allowed to return to Chile. Do some research on how human rights crimes are prosecuted internationally. Write an essay in which you *describe* and *compare* the possibilities for prosecution of human rights violations.

Writing Assignment Using a Journal Entry as a Starting Point

Using the material in your journal, write an essay in which you *illustrate* the appeal of a particular kind of villain—pirates, outlaws, organized crime figures, and so on. What *causes* us to enjoy watching these characters in movies or reading about them in books?

James Gleick

After graduating from Harvard College in 1976, James Gleick helped found *Metropolis,* an alternative newspaper in Minneapolis. He then spent ten years as a reporter and editor with *The New York Times,* where he wrote a column about the impact of science and technology on modern life. His earlier books, *Chaos: Making a New Science* (1987) and *Genius: The Life and Science of Richard Feynman* (1992), were both finalists for the National Book Award and Pulitzer Prize. Most recently, he has written *What Just Happened: A Chronicle From the Information Frontier* (2002), the biography *Isaac Newton* (2003), and *The Information: A History, a Theory, a Flood,* (2011). Formerly McGraw Distinguished Lecturer at Princeton University, Gleick lives with his wife, writer Cynthia Crossen, in New York. The following piece is taken from *Faster: The Acceleration of Just About Everything* (1999).

Pre-Reading Journal Entry

Like many people, you may feel harried and under pressure at least some of the time. Use your journal to reflect on the sources of stress in your everyday life. List several examples. For each, consider the factors leading to this frenzied feeling.

Life As Type A

Everyone knows about Type A. This magnificently bland coinage, put forward by a pair of California cardiologists in 1959, struck a collective nerve and entered the language. It is a token of our confusion: are we victims or perpetrators of the crime of haste? Are we living at high speed with athleticism and vigor, or are we stricken by hurry sickness? 1

The cardiologists, Meyer Friedman and Ray Rosenman, listed a set of personality traits which, they claimed, tend to go hand in hand with one another and also with heart disease. They described these traits rather unappealingly, as characteristics about and around the theme of impatience. Excessive competitiveness. Aggressiveness. "A harrying sense of time urgency." The Type A idea emerged in technical papers and then formed the basis of a popular book and made its way into dictionaries. The canonical Type A, as these doctors portrayed him, was "Paul": 2

> A very disproportionate amount of his emotional energy is consumed in struggling against the normal constraints of time. "How can I move faster, and do more and more things in less and less time?" is the question that never ceases to torment him.
>
> Paul hurries his thinking, his speech and his movements. He also strives to hurry the thinking, speech, and movements of those about him; they must communicate rapidly and relevantly if they

wish to avoid creating impatience in him. Planes must arrive and depart precisely on time for Paul, cars ahead of him on the highway must maintain a speed he approves of, and there must never be a queue of persons standing between him and a bank clerk, a restaurant table, or the interior of a theater. In fact, he is infuriated whenever people talk slowly or circuitously, when planes are late, cars dawdle on the highway, and queues form.

Let's think... Do we know anyone like "Paul"?

This was the first clear declaration of *hurry sickness*—another coinage of Friedman's. It inspired new businesses: mind-body workshops; videotapes demonstrating deep breathing; anxiety-management retreats; seminars on and even institutes of stress medicine. "I drove all the way in the right-hand lane," a Pacific Gas and Electric Company executive said proudly one morning in 1987 to a group of self-confessed hurriers, led by Friedman himself, by then seventy-six years old. In the battle against Type A jitters, patients tried anything and everything—the slow lane, yoga, meditation, visualization: "Direct your attention to your feet on the floor.... Be aware of the air going in your nostrils cool and going out warm.... Visualize a place you like to be.... Experience it and see the objects there, the forms and shadows. Take another deep breath and experience the sounds, the surf, the wind, leaves, a babbling brook." Some hospital television systems now feature a "relaxation channel," with hour after hour of surf, wind, leaves, and babbling brooks. 3

We believe in Type A—a triumph for a notion with no particular scientific validity. The Friedman-Rosenman claim has turned out to be both obvious and false. Clearly some heart ailments do result from, or at least go along with, stress (itself an ill-defined term), both chronic and acute. Behavior surely affects physiology, at least once in a while. Sudden dashes for the train, laptop computer in one hand and takeout coffee in the other, can accelerate heartbeats and raise blood pressure. That haste makes coronaries was already a kind of folk wisdom—that is, standard medical knowledge untainted by research. "Hurry has a clearly debilitating effect upon the tissues and may in time injure the heart," admonished Dr. Cecil Webb-Johnson in *Nerve Troubles,* an English monograph of the early 1900s. "The great men of the centuries past were never in a hurry," he added sanctimoniously, "and that is why the world will never forget them in a hurry." It might be natural—even appealing—to expect certain less-great people to receive their cardiovascular comeuppance. But in reality, three decades of attention from cardiologists and psychologists have failed to produce any carefully specified and measurable set of character traits that predict heart disease—or to demonstrate that people who change their Type A behavior will actually lower their risk of heart disease. 4

Indeed, the study that started it all—Friedman and Rosenman's "Association of Specific Overt Behavior Pattern with Blood and Cardiovascular Findings"—appears to have been a wildly flawed piece of research. It used a small sample—eighty-three people (all men) in what was then called "Group A." The selection process was neither random nor blind. White-collar male employees of large businesses were rounded up by acquaintances of Friedman and Rosenman on a subjective basis—they fit the type. The doctors further sorted the subjects by interviewing them personally and observing their appearance and behavior. Did a man gesture rapidly, clench his teeth, or exhibit a "general air of impatience"? If so, he was chosen. It seems never to have occurred to these experienced cardiologists that they might have been consciously or unconsciously selecting people whose physique indicated excess weight or other markers for incipient heart disease. The doctors' own data show that the final Group A drank more, smoked more, and weighed more than Group B. But the authors dismissed these factors, asserting, astonishingly, that there was no association between heart disease and cigarette smoking. 5

In the years since, researchers have never settled on a reliable method for identifying Type A people, though not for want of trying. Humans are not reliable witnesses to their own impatience. Researchers have employed questionnaires like the Jenkins Activity Survey, and they have used catalogues of grimaces and frowns—Ekman and Friesen's Facial Action Coding System, for example, or the Cook-Medley Hostility Inventory. In the end, nothing conclusive emerges. Some studies have found Type A people to have *lower* blood pressure. The sedentary and obese have cardiac difficulties of their own. 6

The notion of Type A has expanded, shifted, and flexed to suit the varying needs of different researchers. V. A. Price adds *hypervigilance* to the list of traits. Some doctors lose patience with the inconclusive results and shift their focus to anger and hostility—mere subsets of the original Type A grab-bag. Cynthia Perry finds that Type A people have fewer daydreams. How does she know? She asks them to monitor lines flashing across a computer screen for forty painfully boring minutes and finds that, when interrupted by a beep (1000 hertz at 53 decibels), they are less likely to press a black button to confess that irrelevant thoughts had strayed into their minds. Studies have labeled as Type A not only children (those with a tendency to interrupt and to play competitively at games) but even babies (those who cry more). Meanwhile, researchers interested in pets link the Type A personality to petlessness; a National Institutes of Health panel reports: "The description of a 'coronary-prone behavior pattern,' or Type A behavior, and its link to the probability of developing overt disease provided hope that, with careful training, individuals could exercise additional control over somatic illness by altering their lifestyle.... Relaxation, meditation, and stress management 7 have become recognized therapies.... It therefore seems reasonable that pets, who provide faithful companionship to many people, also might promote greater psychosocial stability for their owners, and thus a measure of protection from heart disease." This is sweet, but it is not science.

Typically a Type A study will begin with researchers who assume that there are some correlations to be found, look for a wide variety of associations, fail to find some and succeed in finding others. For example, a few dozen preschool children are sorted according to their game-playing styles and tested for blood pressure. No correlation is found. Later, however, when performing a certain "memory game," the supposed Type A children rank somewhat higher in, specifically, systolic pressure. Interesting? The authors of various published papers evidently think so, but they are wrong, because if their technique is to keep looking until they find some correlation, somewhere, they are bound to succeed. Such results are meaningless. 8

The categorizations are too variable and the prophecies too self-fulfilling. It is never quite clear which traits *define* Type A and which are fellow travelers. The "free-floating, but well-rationalized form of hostility"? The "deep-seated insecurity"? "Their restlessness, their tense facial muscles, their tics, or their strident-staccato manner of speaking"? If you are hard-driving yet friendly, chafing yet self-assured—if you race for the airport gate and then settle *happily* into your seat—are you Type A or not? If you are driven to walk briskly, briskly, all the time, isn't that good for your heart? 9

Most forget that there is also supposed to be a Type B, defined not by the personality traits its members possess but by the traits they lack. Type B people are the shadowy opposites of Type A people. They are those who are not so very Type A. They do *not* wear out their fingers punching that elevator button. They do *not* allow a slow car in the fast lane to drive their hearts to fatal distraction; in fact, they are at the wheel of that slow car. Type B played no real part in that mass societal gasp of recognition in the 1970's. Type B-ness was just a foil. Doctors Friedman and Rosenman actually claimed to have had trouble finding eighty men in all San Francisco who were not under any time pressure. They finally came up with a few, they wrote solemnly, "in the municipal clerks' and the embalmers' unions." 10

Even more bizarrely, that first Friedman-Rosenman study also included a Group C, comprising forty-six unemployed blind men. Not much haste in Group C. "The primary reason men of Group C exhibited little ambition, drive, or desire to compete," the doctors wrote, "was the presence of total blindness for ten or more years and the lack of occupational deadlines because none was gainfully employed." No wonder they omitted Type C from the subsequent publicity. 11

If the Type A phenomenon made for poor medical research, it stands nonetheless as a triumph of social criticism. Some of us yield more willingly to impatience than others, but on the whole Type A is who we are—not just 12 the coronary-prone among us, but all of us, as a society and as an age. No wonder the concept has proven too rich a cultural totem to be dismissed.

Questions for Close Reading

1. What is the selection's thesis? Locate the sentence(s) in which Gleick states his main idea. If he doesn't state the thesis explicitly, express it in your own words.
2. What is Gleick's opinion of the study Friedman and Rosenman conducted? List at least two elements of the study that Gleick uses to support his assessment.
3. In paragraph 7, Gleick observes that the concept of Type A has changed since Friedman and Rosenman's study first chronicled it. How has it changed? What accounts for this change?
4. According to Gleick, how do Friedman and Rosenman define the Type B personality? Why does Gleick find fault with their definition of this personality type?
5. Refer to your dictionary as needed to define the following words used in the selection: *coinage* (paragraph 1), *harrying* (2), *canonical* (2), *circuitously* (2), *sanctimoniously* (4), *overt* (5), *incipient* (5), *sedentary* (6), *hypervigilance* (7), *correlations* (8), *strident* (9), *staccato* (9), *foil* (10), and *totem* (12).

Questions About the Writer's Craft

1. **The pattern and other patterns.** In their work, Friedman and Rosenman use a *description* of Paul to *define* "canonical Type A" behavior (paragraph 2). Why do you suppose that Gleick, who criticizes Friedman and Rosenman's research, quotes their portrait of Paul at such length?
2. **The pattern.** Gleick uses a sequence of three fragments when discussing (in paragraph 2) how Type A has been defined. Identify these fragments. What effect do you think Gleick wanted the fragments to have?
3. Locate places where Gleick uses the first-person pronouns "we," "us," and "our." What do you think Gleick's purpose is in using these pronouns?
4. In paragraph 1, Gleick sarcastically refers to the phrase *Type A* as "magnificently bland." Find other places in the essay where he uses sarcasm. Why might he have chosen to employ such language?

Writing Assignments Using Definition as a Pattern of Development

1. Write an essay offering a fuller definition of the Type B personality than Gleick's essay provides. Rather than defining Type B through negation, as Friedman and Rosenman do, marshal convincing evidence that illustrates the validity of the Type B phenomenon. Brainstorming with friends, family, and classmates will help you generate strong examples of this personality type. At some point in the essay, you might offer a brief personality sketch of the "canonical" Type B as well as discuss the factors that shape the Type B personality as you define it.
2. Gleick notes that, like *Type A*, *stress* is an ill-defined term. Brainstorm with others to identify as many examples of different kinds of stress as you can. Review the brainstormed material, and select a specific type of stress to focus on. Then write

an essay providing a *clear* definition of that particular stress. Possibilities include "dating stress," "workplace stress," "online stress," "fitness stress." Near the end of the essay, you might provide concise hints for managing the stress you define. Your essay may have a humorous or a serious tone—whichever seems appropriate to your subject. Reading William Zinsser's "College Pressures" (page 257) might help you generate ideas.

Writing Assignments Combining Patterns of Development

3. Write an essay *contrasting* situations in which being Type A would be beneficial with situations in which it would be counterproductive. Under what circumstances would Type A characteristics be desirable? Under what circumstances would they be undesirable? Drawing upon your own experiences and observations, reach some conclusions about the advantages and/or limitations of the Type A personality. Along the way, you should explore the *effects* of Type A behavior in the circumstances you're addressing.
4. Gleick observes that "hurry sickness" is a trait induced by society at large. Identify a trait of yours that you think is also a reflection or *effect* of the society in which you live. You might discuss your tendency to be aggressive or nonassertive, materialistic or idealistic, studious or fun-loving. Write an essay *illustrating* this character trait at work in your everyday behavior. Explain whether you think this trait works to your advantage or disadvantage. For additional insight into how personal traits can affect one's daily life, read Barbara Ehrenreich's "Serving in Florida" (page 162).

Writing Assignment Using a Journal Entry as a Starting Point

5. Gleick claims that the Type A phenomenon is pervasive in our society. Write an essay of your own illustrating the extent to which your life reflects this phenomenon. Draw upon the most dramatic examples in your pre-reading journal entry. At the end of the essay, describe steps that you or anyone with similar pressures could take to slow down the frenetic pace of everyday life. Gathering information in the library and/or on the Internet might be helpful when you develop the final section of your paper.

Natalie Angier

Natalie Angier was born in 1958 and was raised in the Bronx, New York, and in Michigan. She attended Barnard College, where she studied literature, astronomy, and physics. After working for *Discover* magazine, she became a reporter for the science section of *The New York Times* in 1990. The following year she won a Pulitzer Prize for her science reporting. In addition to reporting, Angier has written several books, including *The Beauty of the Beastly* (1995), *Natural Obsessions: Striving to Unlock the Deepest Secret of the Cancer Cell* (1999), *Woman: An Intimate Geography* (1999), and *The Canon: A Whirligig Tour of the Beautiful Basics of Science* (2008). Angier has always been interested in bridging the gap between science and the humanities. This article, about the scientific basis of cuteness, was published in *The New York Times* on January 3, 2006.

Pre-Reading Journal Entry

Some concepts—like beauty, elegance, and cuteness—are hard to explain, although people usually believe they understand what those concepts are. Take a moment to reflect in your journal on what *you* mean when you say something is "cute." What qualities come to mind? Consider the kinds of things that you would deem cute, and list as many as you can think of in your journal.

The Cute Factor

If the mere sight of Tai Shan, the roly-poly, goofily gamboling masked bandit of a panda cub now on view at the National Zoo isn't enough to make you melt, then maybe the crush of his human onlookers, the furious flashing of their cameras and the heated gasps of their mass rapture will do the trick. 1

Awww.... Scientists who study the evolution of visual signaling have identified a wide and still-expanding assortment of features and behaviors that make something look cute. 2

Cute cues are those that indicate extreme youth, vulnerability, harmlessness and need, scientists say. 3

"Omigosh, look at him! He is too cute!" 4

"How adorable! I wish I could just reach in there and give him a big squeeze!" 5

"He's so fuzzy! I've never seen anything so cute in my life!" 6

A guard's sonorous voice rises above the burble. "OK, folks, five oohs and aahs per person, then it's time to let someone else step up front." 7

The 6-month-old, 25-pound Tai Shan—whose name is pronounced tie-SHON and means, for no obvious reason, "peaceful mountain"—is the first surviving giant panda cub ever born at the Smithsonian's zoo. And though the zoo's adult pandas have long been among Washington's top 8 tourist attractions, the public debut of the baby in December has unleashed an almost bestial frenzy here. Some 13,000 timed tickets to see the cub were snapped up within two hours of being released, and almost immediately began trading on eBay for up to $200 a pair.

Panda mania is not the only reason that 2005 proved an exceptionally cute year. Last summer, a movie about another black-and-white charmer, the emperor penguin, became one of the highest-grossing documentaries of all time.[1] Sales of petite, willfully cute cars like the Toyota Prius and the Mini Cooper soared, while those of noncute sport utility vehicles tanked. 9

Women's fashions opted for the cute over the sensible or glamorous, with low-slung slacks and skirts and abbreviated blouses contriving to present a customer's midriff as an adorable preschool bulge. Even the too big could be too cute. King Kong's newly reissued face has a squashed baby-doll appeal, and his passion for Naomi Watts ultimately feels like a serious case of puppy love—hopeless, heartbreaking, cute.[2] 10

Scientists who study the evolution of visual signaling have identified a wide and still expanding assortment of features and behaviors that make something look cute: bright forward-facing eyes set low on a big round face, a pair of big round ears, floppy limbs and a side-to-side, teeter-totter gait, among many others. 11

Cute cues are those that indicate extreme youth, vulnerability, harmlessness and need, scientists say, and attending to them closely makes good Darwinian sense. As a species whose youngest members are so pathetically helpless they can't lift their heads to suckle without adult supervision, human beings must be wired to respond quickly and gamely to any and all signs of infantile desire. 12

The human cuteness detector is set at such a low bar, researchers said, that it sweeps in and deems cute practically anything remotely resembling a human baby or a part thereof, and so ends up including the young of virtually every mammalian species, fuzzy-headed birds like Japanese cranes, woolly bear caterpillars, a bobbing balloon, a big round rock stacked on a smaller rock, a colon, a hyphen and a close parenthesis typed in succession. 13

The greater the number of cute cues that an animal or object happens to possess, or the more exaggerated the signals may be, the louder and more italicized are the squeals provoked. 14

Cuteness is distinct from beauty, researchers say, emphasizing rounded over sculptured, soft over refined, clumsy over quick. Beauty attracts admiration and demands a pedestal; cuteness attracts affection and demands a lap. Beauty is rare and brutal, despoiled by a single pimple. Cuteness 15

[1]A reference to *March of the Penguins* (2005), directed by Luc Jacquet (editors' note).

[2]A reference to the 2005 version of *King Kong*, directed by Peter Jackson and starring Naomi Watts as Ann Darrow, the oversized ape's female human ally (editors' note).

is commonplace and generous, content on occasion to cosegregate with homeliness.

Observing that many Floridians have an enormous affection for the manatee, which looks like an overfertilized potato with a sock puppet's face, Roger L. Reep of the University of Florida said it shone by grace of contrast. "People live hectic lives, and they may be feeling overwhelmed, but then they watch this soft and slow-moving animal, this gentle giant, and they see it turn on its back to get its belly scratched," said Dr. Reep, author with Robert K. Bonde of *The Florida Manatee: Biology and Conservation.* 16

"That's very endearing," said Dr. Reep. "So even though a manatee is 3 times your size and 20 times your weight, you want to get into the water beside it." 17

Even as they say a cute tooth has rational roots, scientists admit they are just beginning to map its subtleties and source. New studies suggest that cute images stimulate the same pleasure centers of the brain aroused by sex, a good meal or psychoactive drugs like cocaine, which could explain why everybody in the panda house wore a big grin. 18

At the same time, said Denis Dutton, a philosopher of art at the University of Canterbury in New Zealand, the rapidity and promiscuity of the cute response makes the impulse suspect, readily overridden by the angry sense that one is being exploited or deceived. 19

"Cute cuts through all layers of meaning and says, Let's not worry about complexities, just love me," said Dr. Dutton, who is writing a book about Darwinian aesthetics. "That's where the sense of cheapness can come from, and the feeling of being manipulated or taken for a sucker that leads many to reject cuteness as low or shallow." 20

Quick and cheap make cute appealing to those who want to catch the eye and please the crowd. Advertisers and product designers are forever toying with cute cues to lend their merchandise instant appeal, mixing and monkeying with the vocabulary of cute to keep the message fresh and fetching. 21

That market-driven exercise in cultural evolution can yield bizarre if endearing results, like the blatantly ugly Cabbage Patch dolls, Furbies, the figgy face of E.T., the froggy one of Yoda. As though the original Volkswagen Beetle wasn't considered cute enough, the updated edition was made rounder and shinier still. 22

"The new Beetle looks like a smiley face," said Miles Orvell, professor of American studies at Temple University in Philadelphia. "By this point its origins in Hitler's regime, and its intended resemblance to a German helmet, is totally forgotten." 23

Whatever needs pitching, cute can help. A recent study at the Veterans Affairs Medical Center at the University of Michigan showed that high 24 school students were far more likely to believe antismoking messages accompanied by cute cartoon characters like a penguin in a red jacket or a smirking polar bear than when the warnings were delivered unadorned.

"It made a huge difference," said Sonia A. Duffy, the lead author of the report, which was published in *The Archives of Pediatrics and Adolescent Medicine.* "The kids expressed more confidence in the cartoons than in the warnings themselves." 25

Primal and widespread though the taste for cute may be, researchers say it varies in strength and significance across cultures and eras. They compare the cute response to the love of sugar: everybody has sweetness receptors on the tongue, but some people, and some countries, eat a lot more candy than others. 26

Experts point out that the cuteness craze is particularly acute in Japan, where it goes by the name "kawaii" and has infiltrated the most masculine of redoubts. Truck drivers display Hello Kitty–style figurines on their dashboards. The police enliven safety billboards and wanted posters with two perky mouselike mascots, Pipo kun and Pipo chan. 27

Behind the kawaii phenomenon, according to Brian J. McVeigh, a scholar of East Asian studies at the University of Arizona, is the strongly hierarchical nature of Japanese culture. "Cuteness is used to soften up the vertical society," he said, "to soften power relations and present authority without being threatening." 28

In this country, the use of cute imagery is geared less toward blurring the line of command than toward celebrating America's favorite demographic: the young. Dr. Orvell traces contemporary cute chic to the 1960's, with its celebration of a perennial childhood, a refusal to dress in adult clothes, an inversion of adult values, a love of bright colors and bloopy, cartoony patterns, the Lava Lamp. 29

Today, it's not enough for a company to use cute graphics in its advertisements. It must have a really cute name as well. "Companies like Google and Yahoo leave no question in your mind about the youthfulness of their founders," said Dr. Orvell. 30

Madison Avenue may adapt its strategies for maximal tweaking of our inherent baby radar, but babies themselves, evolutionary scientists say, did not really evolve to be cute. Instead, most of their salient qualities stem from the demands of human anatomy and the human brain, and became appealing to a potential caretaker's eye only because infants wouldn't survive otherwise. 31

Human babies have unusually large heads because humans have unusually large brains. Their heads are round because their brains continue to grow throughout the first months of life, and the plates of the skull stay flexible and unfused to accommodate the development. Baby eyes and ears are situated comparatively far down the face and skull, and only later 32 migrate upward in proportion to the development of bones in the cheek and jaw areas.

Baby eyes are also notably forward-facing, the binocular vision a likely legacy of our tree-dwelling ancestry, and all our favorite Disney characters also sport forward-facing eyes, including the ducks and mice, species that in reality have eyes on the sides of their heads. 33

The cartilage tissue in an infant's nose is comparatively soft and undeveloped, which is why most babies have button noses. Baby skin sits relatively loose on the body, rather than being taut, the better to stretch for growth spurts to come, said Paul H. Morris, an evolutionary scientist at the University of Portsmouth in England; that lax packaging accentuates the overall roundness of form. 34

Baby movements are notably clumsy, an amusing combination of jerky and delayed, because learning to coordinate the body's many bilateral sets of large and fine muscle groups requires years of practice. On starting to walk, toddlers struggle continuously to balance themselves between left foot and right, and so the toddler gait consists as much of lateral movement as of any forward momentum. 35

Researchers who study animals beloved by the public appreciate the human impulse to nurture anything even remotely babylike, though they are at times taken aback by people's efforts to identify with their preferred species.... 36

The giant panda offers... [a] case study in accidental cuteness. Although it is a member of the bear family, a highly carnivorous clan, the giant panda specializes in eating bamboo. 37

As it happens, many of the adaptations that allow it to get by on such a tough diet contribute to the panda's cute form, even in adulthood. Inside the bear's large, rounded head, said Lisa Stevens, assistant panda curator at the National Zoo, are the highly developed jaw muscles and the set of broad, grinding molars it needs to crush its way through some 40 pounds of fibrous bamboo plant a day. 38

When it sits up against a tree and starts picking apart a bamboo stalk with its distinguishing pseudo-thumb, a panda looks like nothing so much like Huckleberry Finn shucking corn. Yet the humanesque posture and paws again are adaptations to its menu. The bear must have its "hands" free and able to shred the bamboo leaves from their stalks. 39

The panda's distinctive markings further add to its appeal: the black patches around the eyes make them seem winsomely low on its face, while the black ears pop out cutely against the white fur of its temples. 40

As with the penguin's tuxedo, the panda's two-toned coat very likely serves a twofold purpose. On the one hand, it helps a feeding bear blend peacefully into the dappled backdrop of bamboo. On the other, the sharp contrast between light and dark may serve as a social signal, helping the solitary bears locate each other when the time has come to find the perfect, too-cute mate. 41

Questions for Close Reading

1. What is the selection's thesis? Locate the sentence(s) in which Angier states her main idea. If she doesn't state her thesis explicitly, express it in your own words.
2. Angier uses the scientific term *visual signaling* (paragraphs 2, 11). What is visual signaling? Give some examples from the article of the visual signaling of "cute."
3. In paragraph 13, Angier quotes researchers as saying that the "human cuteness detector is set at...a low bar." What does Angier assert is the underlying reason that people respond so strongly to cuteness?
4. In paragraph 26, Angier indicates that cute varies from culture to culture. How does the significance of cute in Japan differ from its significance in the United States? Give some examples of the differences between the two cultures.
5. Refer to your dictionary as needed to define the following words used in the selection: *gamboling* (paragraph 1), *rapture* (1), *sonorous* (7), *despoiled* (15), *cosegregate* (15), *homeliness* (15), *aesthetics* (20), *blatantly* (22), *unadorned* (24), *primal* (26), *redoubts* (27), *hierarchical* (28), *inherent* (31), *salient* (31), and *winsomely* (40).

Questions About the Writer's Craft

1. The opening of a newspaper article is called a *lead*, and its purpose is to hook the reader and set up a framework for the story. Analyze the lead of Angier's article (paragraphs 1–3). How does she try to engage your interest (the hook)? How does this lead frame the contents of the remainder of the article? How are the lead and the thesis statement related in this article?
2. **The pattern.** What is the tone of Angier's article? Why did she adopt this tone? Do you think her tone is appropriate given her objective of defining the term *cuteness*? Explain your answer.
3. **Other patterns.** In paragraph 15, Angier contrasts cuteness with beauty. What are some transitional words and phrases that help sharpen this contrast?
4. **Other patterns.** Paragraphs 32 through 35 contain a lengthy description of a baby's appearance. What is the purpose of this description? Is the description mostly objective or subjective? Support your answer with examples.

Writing Assignments Using Definition as a Pattern of Development

1. In paragraph 15, Angier briefly characterizes beauty as sculptured, refined, and quick. She also contrasts beauty with cuteness. Do you agree with Angier's characterization of beauty? What are some words you would use to characterize beauty? Using Angier's characterization of beauty as a starting point, write an extended definition of beauty. Your essay can be serious, lighthearted, humorous, or satiric. For a humorous treatment of beauty, read Dave Barry's "Beauty and the Beast" (page 368).
2. Angier indicates that the American view of cuteness is closely related to our celebration of youth (paragraph 29). Write an extended definition of youth in American culture. Consider actual youthfulness (children), the effort of mature adults to appear younger than they are, the efforts of young people to appear

older than they are, youthful fashions, and other cultural manifestations of youth in America. For a view of changing youth culture, you might read Kay S. Hymowitz's "Tweens: Ten Going On Sixteen" (page 190).

Writing Assignments Combining Patterns of Development

3. Angier gives examples of cuteness in movies (*March of the Penguins,* the 2005 version of *King Kong,* the characters E.T. and Yoda), product design (the VW Beetle), and advertising (an antismoking campaign aimed at teens). Select one of these examples of cuteness—or another of your own choosing—and do some research on it. For example, if you choose a character in a movie or TV show, watch the movie or show; if you choose a product, do research on it and use it if possible; and if you choose an ad campaign, collect examples of the ads. Then write an essay in which you *describe* the item, explain how it is an *example* of cuteness, and recount the *effect* it has on you.

4. Angier's article suggests that all humans respond to cuteness, although there are cultural differences in these responses. Are there other differences as well? For example, do men and women respond differently to cuteness? Teenagers and senior citizens? Parents and nonparents? Reflect on your own experiences with cuteness, and inquire into the experiences of your friends, family members, and others. Then write an essay *comparing* and *contrasting* your responses with those of someone who differs from you in gender, age, or parental status. Explain the possible *causes* and *effects* of your different responses to cuteness. For one man's take on some differences between men and women, read Dave Barry's "Beauty and the Beast" (page 368). For additional views on our responses to the natural world, read Jane S. Shaw's "Nature in the Suburbs" (page 422).

Writing Assignment Using a Journal Entry as a Starting Point

5. Review the cute things you listed in your pre-reading journal. Do these things fall into categories, such as toys, cartoons, or animals? Which of them, if any, are cute according to the extended definition in Angier's article? Write an essay in which you *classify* your cute things and explain how they *exemplify* (or do not exemplify) Angier's definition of cute. If your items present different characteristics from those outlined by Angier, offer your own definition of cuteness.

William Raspberry

Journalist William Raspberry was born in 1935 in Okolona, Mississippi. From his mother, an English teacher and poet, Raspberry learned to care "about the rhythm and grace of words." His father, a shop teacher, taught him "that neither end tables nor arguments are worthwhile unless they stand solidly on all four legs." Raspberry graduated from Indiana Central College and later joined the staff of the Indianapolis *Recorder* as a reporter and editor. Following a two-year stint in the army, he was hired by *The Washington Post,* where his nationally syndicated column ran from 1971 to 2005. His coverage of the Watts race riots in 1965 won him the Capital Press Club Journalist of the Year award, and he later went on to win the Pulitzer Prize for commentary in 1994. *Looking Backward at Us,* a collection of Raspberry's columns, was published in 1991. He currently teaches Communication and Journalism at Duke University. He and his wife live in Washington, D.C., and have three children. The following selection appeared in Raspberry's *Washington Post* column in 1982.

Pre-Reading Journal Entry

Which do you think plays a more important role in determining what a person accomplishes: innate talent or belief in oneself? Take a few minutes to respond to this question in your journal, jotting down examples drawn from your experiences and observations.

The Handicap of Definition

I know all about bad schools, mean politicians, economic deprivation and racism. Still, it occurs to me that one of the heaviest burdens black Americans—and black children in particular—have to bear is the handicap of definition: the question of what it means to be black. 1

Let me explain quickly what I mean. If a basketball fan says that the Boston Celtics' Larry Bird plays "black," the fan intends it—and Bird probably accepts it—as a compliment. Tell pop singer Tom Jones he moves "black" and he might grin in appreciation. Say to Teena Marie or the Average White Band that they sound "black" and they'll thank you. 2

But name one pursuit, aside from athletics, entertainment or sexual performance, in which a white practitioner will feel complimented to be told he does it "black." Tell a white broadcaster he talks "black" and he'll sign up for diction lessons. Tell a white reporter he writes "black" and he'll take a writing course. Tell a white lawyer he reasons "black" and he might sue you for slander. 3

What we have here is a tragically limited definition of blackness, and it isn't only white people who buy it. 4

Think of all the ways black children can put one another down with charges of "whiteness." For many of these children, hard study and hard 5 work are "white." Trying to please a teacher might be criticized as acting "white." Speaking correct English is "white." Scrimping today in the interest of tomorrow's goals is "white." Educational toys and games are "white."

An incredible array of habits and attitudes that are conducive to success in business, in academia, in the nonentertainment professions are likely to be thought of as somehow "white." Even economic success, unless it involves such "black" undertakings as numbers banking, is defined as "white." 6

And the results are devastating. I wouldn't deny that blacks often are better entertainers and athletes. My point is the harm that comes from too narrow a definition of what is black. 7

One reason black youngsters tend to do better at basketball, for instance, is that they assume they can learn to do it well, and so they practice constantly to prove themselves right. 8

Wouldn't it be wonderful if we could infect black children with the notion that excellence in math is "black" rather than white, or possibly Chinese? Wouldn't it be of enormous value if we could create the myth that morality, strong families, determination, courage and love of learning are traits brought by slaves from Mother Africa and therefore quintessentially black? 9

There is no doubt in my mind that most black youngsters could develop their mathematical reasoning, their elocution and their attitudes, the way they develop their jump shots and their dance steps: by the combination of sustained, enthusiastic practice and the unquestioned belief that they can do it. 10

In one sense, what I am talking about is the importance of developing positive ethnic traditions. Maybe Jews have an innate talent for communication; maybe the Chinese are born with a gift for mathematical reasoning; maybe blacks are naturally blessed with athletic grace. I doubt it. What is at work, I suspect, is assumption, inculcated early in their lives, that this is a thing our people do well. 11

Unfortunately, many of the things about which blacks make this assumption are things that do not contribute to their career success—except for that handful of the truly gifted who can make it as entertainers and athletes. And many of the things we concede to whites are the things that are essential to economic security. 12

So it is with a number of assumptions black youngsters make about what it is to be a "man": physical aggressiveness, sexual prowess, the refusal to submit to authority. The prisons are full of people who, by this perverted definition, are unmistakably men. 13

But the real problem is not so much that the things defined as "black" are negative. The problem is that the definition is much too narrow. 14

Somehow, we have to make our children understand that they are intelligent, competent people, capable of doing whatever they put their minds to and making it in the American mainstream, not just in a black subculture. 15

What we seem to be doing, instead, is raising up yet another generation of young blacks who will be failures—by definition. 16

Questions for Close Reading

1. What is the selection's thesis? Locate the sentence(s) in which Raspberry states his main idea. If he doesn't state the thesis explicitly, express it in your own words.
2. In paragraph 14, Raspberry emphasizes that the word *black* presents a problem not because it's negative but because it has become "much too narrow." According to Raspberry, what limitations have become associated with the term *black*? What negative consequences does he see resulting from these limitations?
3. In paragraph 11, Raspberry talks about "positive ethnic traditions." What does he mean by this term? What examples does he provide?
4. In Raspberry's opinion, what needs to be done to ensure the future success of African-American children?
5. Refer to your dictionary as needed to define the following words used in the selection: *diction* (paragraph 3), *scrimping* (5), *array* (6), *quintessentially* (9), *elocution* (10), *inculcated* (11), and *concede* (12).

Questions About the Writer's Craft

1. **The pattern.** Raspberry is primarily concerned with showing how limited the definition of *black* has come to be in our society. In the course of the essay, though, he also defines three other terms. Locate these terms and their definitions. How do the definitions and the effects of the definitions help Raspberry make his point about the narrowness of the term *black*?
2. **Other patterns.** In his opening paragraph, Raspberry uses the *argumentation* technique of refutation. What does he refute? What does he achieve by using this strategy at the very beginning of the essay?
3. A black journalist, Raspberry wrote, for many years, a nationally syndicated column that originated in *The Washington Post*, a major newspaper serving the nation's capital and the nation as a whole. Consider these facts when examining Raspberry's use of the pronouns *I, we,* and *our* in the essay. What do these pronouns seem to imply about Raspberry's intended audience? What is the effect of these pronouns?
4. Raspberry has chosen a relatively abstract topic to write about—the meaning of the term *black*. What techniques does he use to draw in readers and keep them engaged? Consider his overall tone, choice of examples, and use of balanced sentence structure.

Writing Assignments Using Definition as a Pattern of Development

1. Raspberry points out how restrictive the definitions of *black* and *white* can be. Do you think that the definitions of *male* and *female* can be equally restrictive? Focusing on the term *male* or *female,* write an essay showing how the term was defined as you were growing up. Considering the messages conveyed by your

family, the educational system, and society at large, indicate whether you came to perceive the term as limiting or liberating. Before planning your paper, you may want to read one of these essays, which deal with the way gender roles influence behavior: Amy Sutherland's "What Shamu Taught Me About a Happy Marriage" (page 308) or Dave Barry's "Beauty and the Beast" (page 368).

2. In paragraph 15, Raspberry seems to define *success* as "making it in the American mainstream," but not everyone would agree that this is what constitutes success. Write an essay in which you offer your personal definition of *success*. You might contrast what you consider success with what you consider failure. Or you might narrate the success story of a person you respect highly. No matter how you proceed, be sure to provide telling specifics that support your definition.

Writing Assignments Combining Patterns of Development

3. Like most people, you've probably had a "defining" term applied to you at one time or another. Perhaps you've been called "shy" or "stubborn" or "the class clown" or "the athlete in the family." Focusing on one such label that's been applied to you, write an essay showing the *effect* of this term on your life. Be sure to explain why you got the label and how you felt about it. The following essays will give you additional perspectives on the ways that labels and names affect people's lives and self-image: Audre Lorde's "The Fourth of July" (page 140) and Roberto Rodriguez's "The Border on Our Backs" (page 559).
4. In his conclusion, Raspberry makes a plea for providing the younger generation with a more positive, more expansive definition of *black*. Consider the beliefs and principles that today's older generation seems to impart to the younger generation. Write an essay *arguing* which aspects of this value system seem helpful and valid and which do not. Also explain what additional values and convictions the older generation should be passing on, providing *examples* along the way. How should parents, teachers, and others convey these precepts? For a discussion of some obstacles to children's moral instruction, read Ellen Goodman's "Family Counterculture" (page 7), Kay S. Hymowitz's "Tweens: Ten Going On Sixteen (page 190), and Charles Sykes's "The 'Values' Wasteland" (page 198).

Writing Assignment Using a Journal Entry as a Starting Point

5. Developing the material in your pre-reading journal entry, write an essay arguing that an individual's innate talent *or* self-confidence is the critical factor in determining achievement. Consider brainstorming with others to generate examples in support of your contention. At some point in the essay, you should acknowledge the opposing viewpoint, dismantling as much of it as you can. For an inspirational account of personal achievement despite the odds, read Jacques D'Amboise's "Showing What Is Possible" (page 402).

Additional Writing Topics

DEFINITION

General Assignments

Use definition to develop any of the following topics. Once you fix on a limited subject, decide if the essay has an informative or a persuasive purpose. The paper might begin with the etymology of the term, a stipulative definition, or a definition by negation. You may want to use a number of writing patterns—such as description, comparison, narration, process analysis—to develop the definition. Remember, too, that the paper doesn't have to be scholarly and serious. There is no reason it can't be a lighthearted discussion of the meaning of a term.

1. Fads
2. A family fight
3. Helplessness
4. An epiphany
5. A workaholic
6. A Pollyanna
7. A con artist
8. A stingy person
9. A team player
10. A Yiddish term like *mensch, klutz,* or *chutzpah,* or a term from some other ethnic group
11. Adolescence
12. Fast food
13. A perfect day
14. Hypocrisy
15. Inner peace
16. Obsession
17. Generosity
18. Exploitation
19. Depression
20. A double bind

Assignments with a Specific Purpose, Audience, and Point of View

On Campus

1. You've been asked to write part of a pamphlet for students who come to the college health clinic. For this pamphlet, define *one* of the following conditions and its symptoms: *depression, stress, burnout, test anxiety, addiction* (to alcohol, drugs,

TV, or computer games), *workaholism.* Part of the pamphlet should describe ways to cope with the condition described.

2. One of your responsibilities as a peer counselor in the student counseling center involves helping students communicate more effectively. To assist students, write a definition of some term that you think represents an essential component of a strong interpersonal relationship. You might, for example, define *respect, sharing, equality,* or *trust.* Part of the definition should employ definition by negation, a discussion of what the term is *not.*

At Home or in the Community

3. *Newsweek* magazine runs a popular column called "My Turn," consisting of readers' opinions on subjects of general interest. Write a piece for this column defining *today's college students.* Use the piece to dispel some negative stereotypes (for example, that college students are apathetic, ill-informed, self-centered, and materialistic).
4. In your apartment building, several residents have complained about their neighbors' inconsiderate and rude behavior. You're president of the Residents' Association, and it's your responsibility to address this problem at your next meeting. Prepare a talk in which you define *courtesy,* the quality you consider most essential to neighborly relations. Use specific examples of what courtesy is and isn't to illustrate your definition.

On the Job

5. You're an attorney arguing a case of sexual harassment—a charge your client has leveled against an employer. To win the case, you must present to the jury a clear definition of exactly what *sexual harassment* is and isn't. Write such a definition for your opening remarks in court.
6. A new position has opened in your company. Write a job description to be sent to employment agencies that will screen candidates. Your description should define the job's purpose, state the duties involved, and outline essential qualifications.

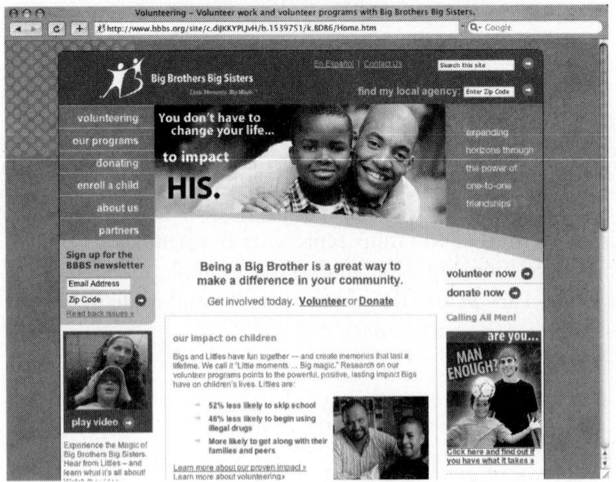

ARGUMENTATION-PERSUASION

WHAT IS ARGUMENTATION-PERSUASION?

"You can't possibly believe what you're saying."
"Look, I know what I'm talking about, and that's that."

Does this heated exchange sound familiar? Probably. When we hear the word *argument,* most of us think of a verbal battle propelled by stubbornness and irrational thought, with one person pitted against the other.

Argumentation in writing, though, is a different matter. Using clear thinking and logic, the writer tries to convince readers of the soundness of a particular opinion on a controversial issue. If, while trying to convince, the writer uses emotional language and dramatic appeals to readers' concerns, beliefs, and values, then the piece is called *persuasion.* Besides encouraging acceptance of an opinion, persuasion often urges readers (or another group) to commit themselves to a course of action. Assume you're writing an essay protesting the federal government's policy of offering aid to those suffering from hunger in other countries while many Americans go hungry. If your purpose is to document, coolly and objectively, the presence of hunger in the United States, you would prepare an argumentation essay. Such an essay would be filled with statistics, report findings, and expert opinion to demonstrate how widespread hunger is nationwide. If, however, your purpose is to shake up readers, even motivate them to write letters to their congressional representatives and push for a change in policy, you would write a persuasive essay. In this case, your essay might contain emotional accounts of undernourished children, ill-fed pregnant women, and nearly starving elderly people.

Because people respond rationally *and* emotionally to situations, argumentation and persuasion are usually *combined.* Suppose you decide to write an article for the campus newspaper advocating a pre-Labor Day start for the school year. Your audience includes the college administration, students, and faculty. The article might begin by *arguing* that several schools starting the academic year earlier were able to close for the month of January and thus reduce heating and other maintenance expenses. Such an argument, supported by documented facts and figures, would help convince the administration. To gain student and faculty support for your idea, you might argue further that the proposed change would mean that students and faculty could leave for winter break with the semester behind them—papers written, exams taken, grades calculated and recorded. To make this part of your argument especially compelling, you could adopt a *persuasive* strategy by using emotional appeals and positively charged language.

When argumentation and persuasion blend in this way, emotion *supports* rather than *replaces* logic and sound reasoning. Although some writers resort to emotional appeals to the exclusion of rational thought, when you prepare argumentation-persuasion essays, you should advance your position through a balanced appeal to reason and emotion.

HOW ARGUMENTATION-PERSUASION FITS YOUR PURPOSE AND AUDIENCE

Your own writing involves argumentation-persuasion. When you prepare a *causal analysis, descriptive piece, narrative,* or *definition essay,* you advance a specific point of view: MTV has a negative influence on teens' view of sex; Cape Cod in winter is imbued with a special kind of magic; a disillusioning experience can teach people much about themselves; *character* can be defined as the willingness to take unpopular positions on difficult issues. Indeed, an essay organized around any of the patterns of development described in this book may have a persuasive intent. You might, for example, encourage readers to try out a *process* you've explained, or to see one of the two movies you've *compared.*

Argumentation-persuasion, however, involves more than presenting a point of view and providing evidence. Unlike other forms of writing, it assumes controversy and addresses opposing viewpoints. Consider the following assignments, all of which require the writer to take a position on a controversial issue:

> In parts of the country, communities established for older citizens or childless couples have refused to rent to families with children.

> How do you feel about this situation? What do you think are the rights of the parties involved?
>
> Citing the fact that the highest percentage of automobile accidents involve young men, insurance companies consistently charge their highest rates to young males. Is this policy fair? Why or why not?
>
> Some colleges and universities have instituted a "no pass, no play" policy for athletes. Explain why this practice is or is not appropriate.

It's impossible to predict with absolute certainty what will make readers accept the view you advance or take the action you propose. But the ancient Greeks, who formulated our basic concepts of logic, isolated three factors crucial to the effectiveness of argumentation-persuasion: *logos, pathos,* and *ethos.*

Your main concern in an argumentation-persuasion essay should be with the *logos,* or soundness, of your argument: the facts, statistics, examples, and authoritative statements you gather to support your viewpoint. This supporting evidence must be unified, specific, adequate, accurate, and representative (see pages 34–36). Imagine, for instance, you want to convince people that a popular charity misappropriates the money it receives from the public. Your readers, inclined to believe in the good works of the charity, will probably dismiss your argument unless you can substantiate your claim with valid, well-documented evidence that enhances the *logos* of your position.

Sensitivity to *pathos,* or the emotional power of language, is another key consideration for writers of argumentation-persuasion essays. *Pathos* appeals to readers' needs, values, and attitudes, encouraging them to commit themselves to a viewpoint or course of action. The *pathos* of a piece derives partly from the writer's language. *Connotative* language—words with strong emotional overtones—can move readers to accept a point of view and may even spur them to act.

Advertising and propaganda generally rely on *pathos* to the exclusion of logic, using emotion to influence and manipulate. Consider the following pitches for a man's cologne and a woman's perfume. The language—and the attitudes to which it appeals—is different in each case:

> Brawn: Experience the power. Bold. Yet subtle. Clean. Masculine. The scent for the man who's in charge.
>
> Black Lace is for you—the woman who dresses for success but who dares to be provocative, slightly naughty. Black Lace. Perfect with pearls by day and with diamonds by night.

The appeal to men plays on the impact that terms like *Brawn, bold, power,* and *in charge* may have for some males. Similarly, the charged words *Black Lace, provocative, naughty,* and *diamonds* are intended to appeal to business women who—in the advertiser's mind, at least—may be looking for ways to reconcile sensuality and professionalism. (For more on slanted language, read Ann McClintock's "Propaganda Techniques in Today's Advertising," page 239.)

Like an advertising copywriter, you must select language that reinforces your message. In a paper supporting an expanded immigration policy, you might use evocative phrases like "land of liberty," "a nation of immigrants," and "America's open-door policy." However, if you were arguing for strict immigration quotas, you might use language like "save jobs for unemployed Americans," "flood of unskilled labor," and "illegal aliens." Remember, though: Such language should support, not supplant, clear thinking.

Finally, whenever you write an argumentation-persuasion essay, you should establish your *ethos,* or credibility and integrity. You cannot expect readers to accept or act on your viewpoint unless you convince them that you know what you're talking about and that you're worth listening to. Be sure, then, to tell readers about any experiences you've had that make you knowledgeable about the issue being discussed. You will also come across as knowledgeable and trustworthy if you present a logical, reasoned argument that takes opposing views into account. And make sure that your appeals to emotion aren't excessive. Overwrought emotionalism undercuts credibility. Remember, too, that *ethos* isn't constant. A writer may have credibility on one subject but not on another: An army general might be a reliable source for information on military preparedness but not for information on federal funding of day care.

Writing an effective argumentation-persuasion essay involves an interplay of *logos, pathos,* and *ethos.* The exact balance among these factors is determined by your audience and purpose (that is, whether you want the audience simply to agree with your view or whether you also want them to take action). More than any other kind of writing, argumentation-persuasion requires that you *analyze your readers* and tailor your approach to them. You need to determine how much they know about the issue, how they feel about you and your position, what their values and attitudes are, what motivates them.

In general, most readers will fall into one of three broad categories: supportive, wavering, or hostile. Each type of audience requires a different blend of *logos, pathos,* and *ethos* in an argumentation-persuasion essay.

1. A supportive audience. If your audience agrees with your position and trusts your credibility, you don't need a highly reasoned argument dense with facts, examples, and statistics. Although you may want to solidify support by providing additional information (*logos*), you can rely primarily on *pathos*—a strong emotional appeal—to reinforce readers' commitment to your shared viewpoint. Assume that you belong to a local fishing club and have volunteered to write an article encouraging members to support threatened fishing rights in state parks. You might begin by stating that fishing strengthens the fish population by thinning out overcrowded streams. Since your audience would certainly be familiar with this idea, you wouldn't need to devote much discussion to it. Instead, you would attempt to move them emotionally. You might evoke the camaraderie in the sport, the pleasure of a perfect cast, the beauty of the outdoors, and perhaps conclude with "If you want these enjoyments to continue, please make a generous contribution to our fund."

2. A wavering audience. At times, readers may be open to what you have to say but may not be committed fully to your viewpoint. Or perhaps they're not as informed about the subject as they should be. In either case, you don't want to risk alienating them with a heavy-handed emotional appeal. Concentrate instead on *ethos* and *logos,* bolstering your image as a reliable source and providing the evidence needed to advance your position. If you want to convince an audience of high school seniors to take a year off to work between high school and college, you might establish your credibility by recounting the year you spent working and by showing the positive effects it had on your life (*ethos*). In addition, you could cite studies indicating that delayed entry into college is related to higher grade point averages. A year's savings, you would explain, allows students to study when they might otherwise need to hold down a job to earn money for tuition (*logos*).

3. A hostile audience. An apathetic, skeptical, or hostile audience is obviously most difficult to convince. With such an audience, you should avoid emotional appeals because they might seem irrational, sentimental, or even comical. Instead, weigh the essay heavily in favor of logical reasoning and hard-to-dispute facts (*logos*). Assume your college administration is working to ban liquor from the student pub. You plan to submit to the campus newspaper an open letter supporting this generally unpopular effort. To sway other students, you cite the positive experiences of schools that have gone dry. Many colleges, you explain, have found their tavern revenues actually increase because all students—not just those of drinking age—can now support the pub. With the greater revenues, some schools have upgraded the food served in the pubs and have hired disc jockeys or musical groups to provide entertainment. Many schools have also seen a sharp reduction in alcohol-related vandalism. Readers may not be won over to your side, but your sound, logical argument may encourage them to be more tolerant of your viewpoint. Indeed, such increased receptivity may be all you can reasonably expect from a hostile audience. (For more help in analyzing your audience, see pages 18–19.)

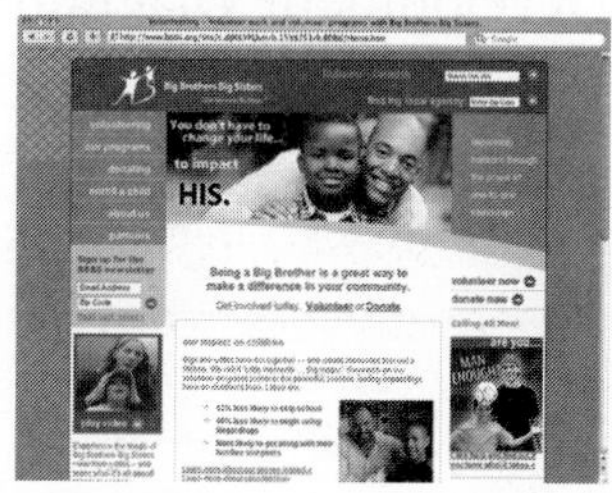

At this point, you have a good sense of the way writers use argumentation-persuasion to achieve their purpose and to connect with their readers. Take a moment to look closely at the website screen shot at the beginning of this chapter. The sponsoring organization is Big Brothers, Big Sisters, a mentoring organization for young people. Imagine you're writing an article, linked to this website, about the benefits of mentoring young people today. Jot down some ideas you might cover when *arguing* that this organization offers young people more than a place to hang out.

SUGGESTIONS FOR USING ARGUMENTATION-PERSUASION IN AN ESSAY

The suggestions here and in Figure 11.1 on page 480 will be helpful for writing an argument-persuasion essay.

1. At the beginning of the paper, identify the controversy surrounding the issue and state your position in the thesis. Your introduction should clarify the controversy about the issue. In addition, it should provide as much background information as your readers are likely to need.

The thesis of an argumentation-persuasion paper is often called the *assertion* or *proposition*. Occasionally, the proposition appears at the paper's end, but it is usually stated at the beginning. If you state the thesis right away, your audience knows where you stand and is better able to evaluate the evidence presented.

Be sure your proposition focuses on a controversial issue and indicates your view. Avoid a proposition that is merely factual; what is demonstrably true allows little room for debate. To see the difference between a factual statement and an effective thesis, examine the two statements that follow:

Fact: In the past decade, the nation's small farmers have suffered financial hardships.

Thesis: Inefficient management, rather than competition from agricultural conglomerates, is responsible for the financial plight of the nation's small farmers.

FIGURE 11.1
Development Diagram: Writing an Argumentation-Persuasion Essay

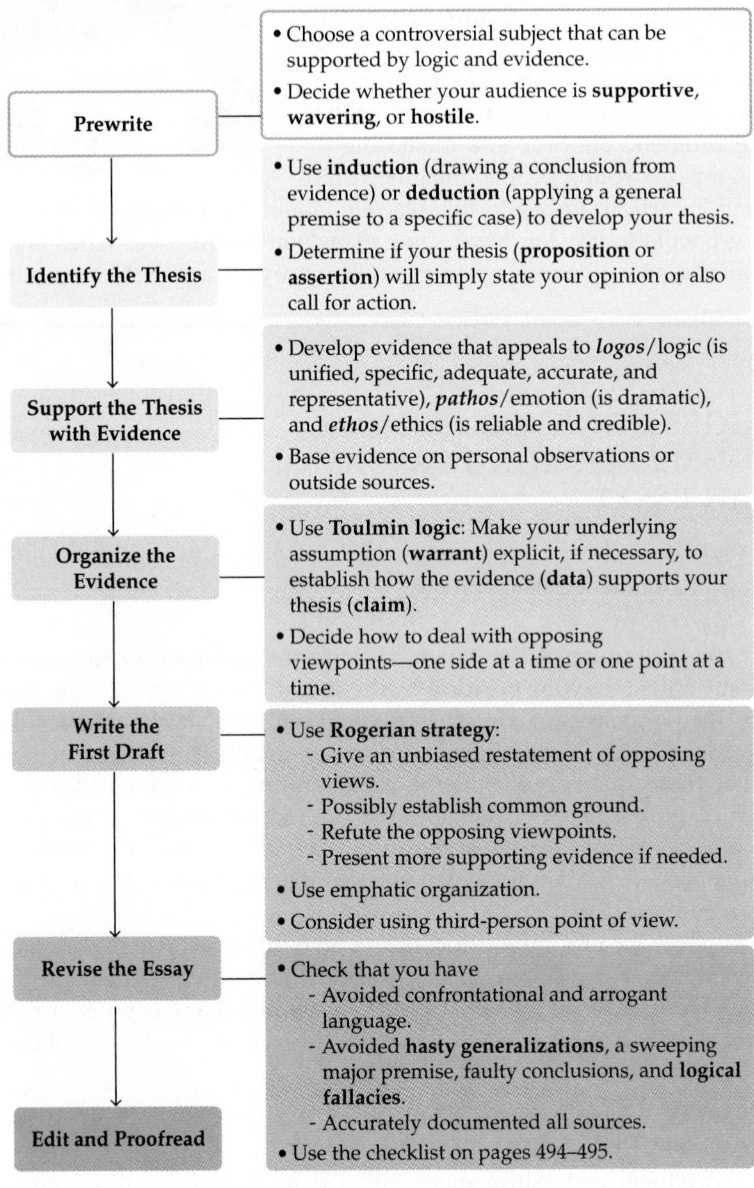

Prewrite
• Choose a controversial subject that can be supported by logic and evidence.
• Decide whether your audience is supportive, wavering, or hostile.
Identify the Thesis
• Use induction (drawing a conclusion from evidence) or deduction (applying a general premise to a specific case) to develop your thesis.
• Determine if your thesis (proposition or assertion) will simply state your opinion or also call for action.
Support the Thesis with Evidence
• Develop evidence that appeals to logos/logic (is unified, specific, adequate, accurate, and representative), pathos/emotion (is dramatic), and ethos/ethics (is reliable and credible).
• Base evidence on personal observations or outside sources.
Organize the Evidence
• Use Toulmin logic: Make your underlying assumption (warrant) explicit, if necessary, to establish how the evidence (data) supports your thesis (claim).
• Decide how to deal with opposing viewpoints—one side at a time or one point at a time.
Write the First Draft
• Use Rogerian strategy:
- Give an unbiased restatement of opposing views.
- Possibly establish common ground.
- Refute the opposing viewpoints.
- Present more supporting evidence if needed.
• Use emphatic organization.
• Consider using third-person point of view.
Revise the Essay
• Check that you have
- Avoided confrontational and arrogant language.
- Avoided hasty generalizations, a sweeping major premise, faulty conclusions, and logical fallacies.
- Accurately documented all sources.
• Use the checklist on pages 494–495.
Edit and Proofread

The first statement is certainly true. It would be difficult to find anyone who believes that these are easy times for small farmers. Because the statement invites little opposition, it can't serve as the focus of an argumentation-persuasion essay. The second statement, though, takes a controversial stance on a complex issue. Such a proposition is a valid starting point for a paper intended to argue and persuade.

Remember also to keep the proposition narrow and specific, so you can focus your thoughts in a purposeful way. Consider the following statements:

Broad thesis: The welfare system has been abused over the years.

Narrow thesis: Welfare payments should be denied to unmarried teenage girls who have more than one child out of wedlock.

If you tried to write a paper based on the first statement, you would face an unmanageable task—showing all the ways that welfare has been abused. Your readers would also be confused about what to expect in the paper: Will it discuss unscrupulous bureaucrats, fraudulent bookkeeping, dishonest recipients? In contrast, the revised thesis is limited and specific. It signals that the paper will propose severe restrictions on welfare payments. Such a proposal will surely have opponents and is thus appropriate for argumentation-persuasion.

The thesis in an argumentation-persuasion essay can simply state your opinion about an issue, or it can go a step further and call for some action:

Opinion: The lack of affordable day-care centers discriminates against lower-income families.

Call for action: The federal government should support the creation of more day-care centers in low-income neighborhoods.

In either case, your stand on the issue must be clear to your readers.

2. Provide readers with strong support for the thesis. Finding evidence that relates to the readers' needs, values, and experience is a crucial part of writing an effective argumentation-persuasion essay. Readers will be responsive to evidence that is *unified, adequate, specific, accurate,* and *representative* (see pages 34–38). It might consist of personal experiences or observations. Or it could be gathered from outside sources—statistics; facts; examples; or expert authority taken from books, articles, reports, interviews, and documentaries. A paper arguing that elderly Americans are better off than they used to be might incorporate the following kinds of evidence:

- *Personal observation or experience:* A description of the writer's grandparents who are living comfortably on Social Security and pensions.

- *Statistics from a report:* A statement that the per capita after-tax income of older Americans is $335 greater than the national average.
- *Fact from a newspaper article:* The point that the majority of elderly Americans do not live in nursing homes or on the streets; rather, they have their own houses or apartments.
- *Examples from interviews:* Accounts of several elderly couples living comfortably in well-managed retirement villages in Florida.
- *Expert opinion cited in a documentary:* A statement by Dr. Marie Sanchez, a specialist in geriatrics: "An over-sixty-five American today is likely to be healthier, and have a longer life expectancy, than a fifty-year-old living only a decade ago."

As you seek outside evidence, you may—perhaps to your dismay—come across information that undercuts your argument. Resist the temptation to ignore such material; instead, use the evidence to arrive at a more balanced, perhaps somewhat qualified viewpoint. Conversely, don't blindly accept points made by sources agreeing with you. Retain a healthy skepticism, analyzing the material as rigorously as if it were advanced by the opposing side.

Also, keep in mind that outside sources aren't infallible. They may have biases that cause them to skew evidence. So be sure to evaluate your sources. If you're writing an essay supporting a woman's right to abortion, the National Abortion Rights Action League (NARAL) can supply abundant statistics, case studies, and reports. But realize that NARAL most likely won't give you the complete picture; it will probably present evidence that supports its "pro-choice" position only. To counteract such bias, you should review what those with differing opinions have to say. You should, for example, examine material published by such "pro-life" organizations as the National Right-to-Life Committee—keeping in mind, of course, that this material is also bound to present support for its viewpoint only. Remember, too, that there are more than two sides to a complex issue. To get as broad a perspective as possible, you should also track down sources that have no axe to grind—that is, sources that make a deliberate effort to examine all sides of the issue.

Whatever sources you use, be sure to *document* (give credit to) that material. Otherwise, readers may dismiss your evidence as nothing more than your subjective opinion, or they may conclude that you have *plagiarized*—tried to pass off someone else's ideas as your own. (Documentation isn't necessary when material is commonly known or is a matter of historical or scientific record.) In brief informal papers, documentation may consist of simple citations like "Psychologist Aaron Beck believes depression is the result of distorted thoughts" or "*Newsweek* (July 27, 2009) observes that teens have embraced new technologies in their everyday lives." In longer, more formal papers, documentation is more detailed (see Appendix A, "A Guide to Using Sources").

3. Seek to create goodwill. To avoid alienating readers with views different from your own, stay away from condescending expressions like "Anyone can see that..." or "It's obvious that..." Also, guard against personalizing the debate and being confrontational: "*My opponents* find the law ineffective" sounds adversarial, whereas "*Those opposed* to the law find it ineffective" or "*Opponents* of the law find it ineffective" is more evenhanded. The last two statements also focus—as they should—on the issue, not on the people involved in the debate.

Goodwill can also be established by finding a *common ground*—some points on which all sides can agree, despite their differences. Assume a township council has voted to raise property taxes. The additional revenues will be used to preserve, as parkland, a wooded area that would otherwise be sold to developers. Before introducing its tax-hike proposal, the council would do well to remind homeowners of everyone's shared goals: maintaining the town's beauty and preventing the community's overdevelopment. This reminder of the common values shared by the town council and homeowners will probably make residents more receptive to the tax hike. (For more on establishing common ground, see pages 484–486.)

4. Organize the supporting evidence. The support for an argumentation-persuasion paper can be organized in a variety of ways. Any of the patterns of development described in this book (description, narration, definition, causal analysis, and so on) may be used—singly or in combination—to develop the essay's proposition. Imagine you're writing a paper arguing that car racing should be banned from television. Your essay might contain a *description* of a horrifying accident that was televised in graphic detail; you might devote part of the paper to a *causal analysis* showing that the broadcast of such races encourages teens to drive carelessly; you could include a *process analysis* to explain how young drivers "soup up" their cars in a dangerous attempt to imitate the racers seen on television. If your essay includes several patterns, you may need a separate paragraph for each.

When presenting evidence, arrange it so you create the strongest possible effect. In general, you should end with your most compelling point, leaving readers with dramatic evidence that underscores your proposition's validity.

5. Use Rogerian strategy to acknowledge differing viewpoints. A good argument seeks out and acknowledges conflicting viewpoints. Such a strategy strengthens your argument in several ways. It helps you anticipate objections, alerts you to flaws in your own position, and makes you more aware of the other sides' weaknesses. Further, by acknowledging dissenting views, you come across as reasonable and thorough—qualities that may disarm readers and leave them more receptive to your argument. You may not convince them to surrender their views, but you can enlarge their perspectives and encourage them to think about your position.

Psychologist Carl Rogers took the idea of acknowledging contrary viewpoints a step further. He believed that argumentation's goal should be to *reduce conflict,* rather than to produce a "winner" and a "loser." But he recognized that people identify so strongly with their opinions that they experience any challenge to those opinions as an attack on their very identity. And what's the characteristic response to such a perceived attack? People become defensive; they dig in their heels and become more adamant than ever about their position. Indeed, when confronted with solid information that calls their opinion into question, they devalue that evidence rather than allow themselves to be persuaded. Experiments show that after people form a first impression of another person, they are unlikely to let future conflicting information affect that impression. If, for example, they initially perceive someone to be unpleasant and disagreeable, they tend to reject subsequent evidence that casts the person in a more favorable light.

For these reasons, Rogerian strategy rejects any adversarial approach and adopts, instead, a respectful, conciliatory posture that demonstrates a real understanding of opposing views and emphasizes shared interests and values. The ideal is to negotiate differences and arrive at a synthesis: a new position that both parties find at least as acceptable as their original positions. What follows are three basic Rogerian strategies to keep in mind as you write.

First, you may acknowledge the opposing viewpoint in a two-part proposition consisting of a subordinate clause followed by a main clause. The *first part of the proposition* (the subordinate clause) *acknowledges opposing opinions;* the *second part* (the main clause) *states your opinion* and implies that your view stands on more solid ground. The following thesis illustrates this strategy (the opposing viewpoint is underlined once; the writer's position is underlined twice):

Although some instructors think that standardized finals restrict academic freedom, such exams are preferable to those prepared by individual professors.

Second, *in the introduction,* you may provide—separate from the proposition—a *one- or two-sentence summary of the opposing viewpoint.* Suppose you're writing an essay advocating a ten-day waiting period before an individual can purchase a handgun. Before presenting your proposition at the end of the introductory paragraph, you might include sentences like these: "Opponents of the waiting period argue that the ten-day delay is worthless without a nationwide computer network that can perform background checks. Those opposed also point out that only a percentage of states with a waiting period have seen a reduction in gun-related crime."

Third, you can take *one or two body paragraphs* near the beginning of the essay to *present in greater detail arguments raised by opposing viewpoints.* After that, you *grant* (when appropriate) the validity of some of those points

("It may be true that...," "Granted,..."). Then you go on to *present evidence* for your position ("Even so...," "Nevertheless..."). Imagine you're preparing an editorial for your student newspaper arguing that fraternities and sororities on your campus should be banned. You "research" the opposing viewpoint by seeking out supporters of Greek organizations and listening respectfully to the points they raise. When it comes time to write the editorial, you start by summarizing the points made by those supporting fraternities and sororities. You might, for example, mention their argument that Greek organizations build college spirit, contribute to worthy community causes, and provide valuable contacts for entry into the business world. Following this summary of the opposing viewpoint, you might concede that the point about the Greeks' contributions to community causes is especially valid; you could then reinforce this conciliatory stance by stressing some common ground you share—perhaps that enjoyable social activities with like-minded people are an important part of campus life. Having done all that, you would be in a good position to present arguments why you nevertheless think fraternities and sororities should be banned.

6. Refute differing viewpoints. There will be times, though, that acknowledging opposing viewpoints and presenting your own case won't be enough. Particularly when an issue is complex and when readers strongly disagree with your position, you may have to refute all or part of the *dissenting views. Refutation* means pointing out the problems with opposing viewpoints, thereby highlighting your own position's superiority. You may focus on the opposing sides' inaccurate or inadequate evidence, or you may point to their faulty logic. (Some common types of illogical thinking are discussed on pages 487–490, and 492–494.)

Let's consider how you could refute a competing position in an essay you're writing that supports sex education in public schools. Adapting the Rogerian approach to suit your purposes, you might start by acknowledging the opposing viewpoint's key argument: "Sex education should be the prerogative of parents." After granting the validity of this view in an ideal world, you might show that many parents don't provide such education. You could present statistics on the number of parents who avoid discussing sex with their children because the subject makes them uncomfortable; you could cite studies revealing that children in single-parent homes are apt to receive even less parental guidance about sex; and you could give examples of young people whose parents provided sketchy, even misleading information.

You may refute opposing views *one side at a time* or *one point at a time*. When using the one-side-at-a-time approach, you cite all the points raised by the opposing side and then present your counterargument to each point. When using the one-point-at-a-time strategy, you mention the first point made by the opposing side, refute that point, then move on to the second point and refute that, and so on. (For more on comparing and contrasting the sides of an issue, see pages 337–342.)

Throughout the essay, be sure to provide clear signals so that readers can distinguish your arguments from the other side's: "Despite the claims of those opposed to the plan, many think that..." and "Those not in agreement think that...."

7. Use induction or deduction to think logically about your argument. There are two basic ways to think about a subject: *inductively* and *deductively.* Though the following discussion treats induction and deduction as separate processes, the two often overlap and complement each other.

Inductive reasoning involves examination of specific cases, facts, or examples. Based on these specifics, you then draw a conclusion or make a generalization. This is the kind of thinking scientists use when they examine evidence (the results of experiments, for example) and then draw a *conclusion:* "Smoking increases the risk of cancer." All of us use inductive reasoning in everyday life. We might think the following: "My head is aching" (evidence); "My nose is stuffy" (evidence); "I'm coming down with a cold" (conclusion). Based on the conclusion, we might go a step further and take some action: "I'll take a cold remedy."

Let's suppose that you're writing a paper about a crime wave in the small town where you live. You might use inductive thinking to structure the essay's argument:

> Several people were mugged last month while shopping in the center of town. (*evidence*)
>
> Several homes and apartments were burglarized in the past few weeks. (*evidence*)
>
> Several cars were stolen from people's driveways over the weekend. (*evidence*)
>
> The police force hasn't adequately protected town residents. (*conclusion, or proposition, for an argumentation essay with probable elements of persuasion*)
>
> The police force should take steps to upgrade its protection of town residents. (*conclusion, or proposition, for an argumentation essay with a clearly persuasive intent*)

This inductive sequence highlights a possible structure for the essay. After providing a clear statement of your proposition, you might detail recent muggings, burglaries, and car thefts. Then you could move to the opposing viewpoint: a description of the steps the police say they have taken to protect town residents. At that point, you would refute the police's claim, citing additional evidence that shows the measures taken have not been sufficient. Finally, if you wanted your essay to have a decidedly persuasive purpose, you could end by recommending specific action the police department should take to improve its protection of the community.

As in all essays, your evidence should be *specific, unified, adequate,* and *representative* (see pages 34–38). These last two characteristics are critical when you think inductively; they guarantee that your conclusion would be equally valid even if other evidence were presented. Insufficient or atypical evidence often leads to *hasty generalizations* that mar the essay's logic. For example, you might think the following: "Some elderly people are very wealthy and do not need Social Security checks" (evidence), and "Some Social Security recipients illegally collect several checks" (evidence). If you then conclude "Social Security is a waste of taxpayers' money," your conclusion is invalid and hasty because it's based on only a few atypical examples. Millions of Social Security recipients aren't wealthy and don't abuse the system. If you've failed to consider the full range of evidence, any action you propose ("The Social Security system should be disbanded") will probably be considered suspect by thoughtful readers. It's possible, of course, that Social Security should be disbanded, but the evidence leading to such a conclusion must be sufficient and representative.

When reasoning inductively, you should also be careful that the evidence you collect is both *recent* and *accurate.* No valid conclusion can result from dated or erroneous evidence. To ensure that your evidence is sound, you also need to evaluate the reliability of your sources. When a person who is legally drunk claims to have seen a flying saucer, the evidence is shaky, to say the least. But if two respected scientists, both with 20/20 vision, saw the saucer, their evidence is worth considering.

Finally, it's important to realize that there's always an element of uncertainty in inductive reasoning. The conclusion can never be more than an *inference,* involving what logicians call an *inductive leap.* There could be other explanations for the evidence cited and thus other positions to take and actions to advocate. For example, given a small town's crime wave, you might conclude not that the police force has been remiss but that residents are careless about protecting themselves and their property. In turn, you might call for a different kind of action—perhaps that the police conduct public workshops in self-defense and home security. In an inductive argument, your task is to weigh the evidence, consider alternative explanations, then choose the conclusion and course of action that seem most valid.

Unlike inductive reasoning, which starts with a specific case and moves toward a generalization or conclusion, *deductive reasoning* begins with a generalization that is then applied to a specific case. This movement from general to specific involves a three-step form of reasoning called a *syllogism.* The first part of a syllogism is called the *major premise,* a general statement about an entire group. The second part is the *minor premise,* a statement about an individual within that group. The syllogism ends with a *conclusion* about that individual.

Just as you use inductive thinking in everyday life, you use deductive thinking—often without being aware of it—to sort out your experiences. When trying to decide which car to buy, you might think as follows:

Major premise:	In an accident, large cars are safer than small cars.
Minor premise:	The Turbo Titan is a large car.
Conclusion:	In an accident, the Turbo Titan will be safer than a small car.

Based on your conclusion, you might decide to take a specific action, buying the Turbo Titan rather than the smaller car you had first considered.

To create a valid syllogism and thus arrive at a sound conclusion, you need to avoid two major pitfalls of deductive reasoning. First, be sure not to start with a *hasty generalization* (see page 487) as your *major premise.* Second, don't accept as truth a *faulty conclusion.* Let's look at each problem.

Sweeping major premise. Perhaps you're concerned about a trash-to-steam incinerator scheduled to open near your home. Your thinking about the situation might follow these lines:

Major premise:	Trash-to-steam incinerators have had serious problems and pose significant threats to the well-being of people living near the plants.
Minor premise:	The proposed incinerator in my neighborhood will be a trash-to-steam plant.
Conclusion:	The proposed trash-to-steam incinerator in my neighborhood will have serious problems and pose significant threats to the well-being of people living near the plant.

Having arrived at this conclusion, you might decide to join organized protests against the opening of the incinerator. But your thinking is somewhat illogical. Your *major premise* is a *sweeping* one because it indiscriminately groups all trash-to-steam plants into a single category. It's unlikely that you're familiar with the operations of all trash-to-steam incinerators in this country and abroad; it's probably not true that *all* such plants have had serious difficulties that endangered the public. For your argument to reach a valid conclusion, the major premise must be based on repeated observations or verifiable facts. You would have a better argument, and thus reach a more valid conclusion, if you restricted or qualified the major premise, applying it to some, not all, of the group.

Major premise: A number of trash-to-steam incinerators have had serious problems and posed significant threats to the well-being of people living near the plants.

Minor premise: The proposed incinerator in my neighborhood will be a trash-to-steam plant.

Conclusion: It's possible that the proposed trash-to-steam incinerator in my neighborhood will run into serious problems and pose significant threats to the well-being of people living near the plant.

This new conclusion, the result of more careful reasoning, would probably encourage you to learn more about trash-to-steam incinerators in general and about the proposed plant in particular. If further research still left you feeling uncomfortable about the plant, you would probably decide to join the protest. On the other hand, your research might convince you that the plant has incorporated into its design a number of safeguards that have been successful at other plants. This added information could reassure you that your original fears were unfounded. In either case, the revised deductive process would lead to a more informed conclusion and course of action.

Faulty conclusion. Your syllogism—and thus your reasoning—would also be invalid if your *conclusion reverses the "if...then" relationship implied in the major premise.* Assume you plan to write a letter to the college newspaper urging the resignation of the student government president. Perhaps you pursue a line of reasoning that goes like this:

Major premise: Students who plagiarize papers must appear before the Faculty Committee on Academic Policies and Procedures.

Minor premise: Yesterday, Jennifer Kramer, president of the student government, appeared before the Faculty Committee on Academic Policies and Procedures.

Conclusion: Jennifer must have plagiarized a paper.

Action: Jennifer should resign her position as president of the student government.

Such a chain of reasoning is illogical and unfair. Here's why. *If* students plagiarize their papers and are caught, *then* they must appear before the committee. However, the converse isn't necessarily true—that *if* students appear before the committee, *then* they must have plagiarized. In other words, not *all* students appearing before the committee have been called up on plagiarism charges. For example, Jennifer could have been speaking on behalf of another student; she could have been protesting some action taken by the committee; she could have been seeking the committee's help on an article she plans to write about academic honesty. The conclusion doesn't allow for other possible explanations.

Now that you're aware of potential problems associated with deductive reasoning, let's look at the way you can use a syllogism to structure an argumentation-persuasion essay. Suppose you decide to write a paper advocating support for a projected space mission. You know that controversy surrounds the manned space program, especially since seven astronauts died in a 1986 launch and another crew of seven died in a shuttle reentry accident in 2003. Confident that these tragedies have led to more rigorous controls, you want to argue that the benefits of an upcoming mission outweigh its risks. A deductive pattern could be used to develop your argument. In fact, outlining your thinking as a syllogism might help you formulate a proposition, organize your evidence, deal with opposing viewpoints, and—if appropriate—propose a course of action:

Major premise:	Space programs in the past have led to important developments in technology, especially in medical science.
Minor premise:	The Cosmos Mission is the newest space program.
Proposition (essay might be persuasive):	The Cosmos Mission will most likely lead to important developments in technology, especially in medical science.
Proposition (essay clearly is persuasive):	Congress should continue its funding of the Cosmos Mission.

Having outlined the deductive pattern of your thinking, you might begin by stating your proposition and then discuss some new procedures developed to protect the astronauts and the rocket system's structural integrity. With that background established, you could detail the opposing claim that little of value has been produced by the space program so far. You could then move to your refutation, citing significant medical advances derived from former space missions. Finally, the paper might conclude on a persuasive note, with a plea to Congress to continue funding the latest space mission.

8. Use Toulmin logic to establish a strong connection between your evidence and your thesis. Whether you use an essentially inductive or deductive approach, your argument depends on strong evidence. In *The Uses of Argument,* Stephen Toulmin describes a useful approach for strengthening the connection between evidence and thesis. Toulmin divides a typical argument into three parts:

- **Claim**—The thesis, proposition, or conclusion.
- **Data**—The evidence (facts, statistics, examples, observations, expert opinion) used to convince readers of the claim's validity.

- **Warrant**—The underlying assumption that justifies moving from evidence to claim.

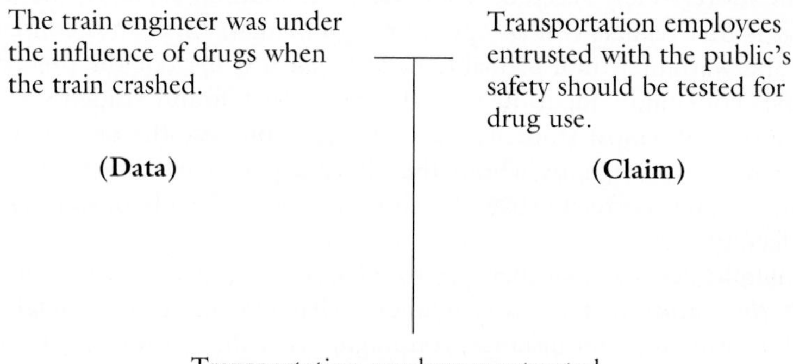
The train engineer was under the influence of drugs when the train crashed.
(Data)
Transportation employees entrusted with the public's safety should be tested for drug use.
(Claim)
Transportation employees entrusted with the public's safety should not be allowed on the job if they use drugs.
(Warrant)

As Toulmin explains in his book, readers are more apt to consider your argument valid if they know what your warrant is. Sometimes your warrant will be so obvious that you won't need to state it explicitly; an *implicit warrant* will be sufficient. Assume you want to argue that the use of live animals to test product toxicity should be outlawed. To support your claim, you cite the following evidence: first, current animal tests are painful and usually result in the animal's death; second, human cell cultures frequently offer more reliable information on how harmful a product may be to human tissue; and third, computer simulations often can more accurately rate a substance's toxicity. Your warrant, although not explicit, is nonetheless clear: "It is wrong to continue product testing on animals when more humane and valid test methods are available."

Other times, you'll do best to make your warrant *explicit.* Suppose you plan to argue that students should be involved in deciding which faculty members are granted tenure. To develop your claim, you present some evidence. You begin by noting that, currently, only faculty members and administrators review candidates for tenure. Next, you call attention to the controversy surrounding two professors, widely known by students to be poor teachers, who were nonetheless granted tenure. Finally, you cite a decision, made several years ago, to discontinue using student evaluations as part of the tenure process; you emphasize that since that time complaints about teachers' incompetence have risen dramatically. Some readers, though, still might wonder how you got from your evidence to your claim. In this case, your argument could be made stronger by stating your warrant explicitly: "Since students are as knowledgeable as the faculty and administrators about which professors are competent, they should be involved in the tenure process."

The more widely accepted your warrant, Toulmin explains, the more likely it is that readers will accept your argument. If there's no consensus about the warrant, you'll probably need to *back it up*. For the preceding example, you might mention several reports that found students evaluate faculty fairly (most students don't, for example, use the ratings to get back at professors against whom they have a personal grudge); further, students' ratings correlate strongly with those given by administrators and other faculty.

Toulmin describes another way to increase receptivity to an argument: *qualify the claim*—that is, explain under what circumstances it might be invalid or restricted. For instance, you might grant that most students know little about their instructors' research activities, scholarly publications, or participation in professional committees. You could, then, qualify your claim this way: "Because students don't have a comprehensive view of their instructors' professional activities, they should be involved in the tenure process but play a less prominent role than faculty and administrators."

As you can see, Toulmin's approach provides strategies for strengthening an argument. So, when prewriting or revising, take a few minutes to ask yourself the questions listed below.

☑ QUESTIONS FOR USING TOULMIN LOGIC: A CHECKLIST

- ❑ What data (*evidence*) should I provide to support my claim (*thesis*)?
- ❑ Is my warrant clear? Should I state it explicitly? What backup can I provide to justify my warrant?
- ❑ Would qualifying my claim make my argument more convincing?

Your responses to these questions will help you structure a convincing and logical argument.

9. Recognize logical fallacies. When writing an argumentation-persuasion essay, you need to recognize *logical fallacies* both in your own argument and in points raised by opposing sides. Work to eliminate such gaps in logic from your own writing and, when they appear in opposing arguments, try to expose them in your refutation. Logicians have identified many logical fallacies—including the sweeping or hasty generalization and the faulty conclusion discussed on pages 487 and 489. Other logical fallacies are described in Ann McClintock's "Propaganda Techniques in Today's Advertising" (page 239) and in the paragraphs that follow.

The *post hoc fallacy* (short for a Latin phrase meaning "after this, therefore because of this") occurs when you conclude that a cause-effect relationship exists simply because one event preceded another. Let's say you note the growing number of immigrants settling in a nearby city, observe the city's economic decline, and conclude that the immigrants' arrival caused the decline. Such a chain of thinking is faulty because it assumes a cause-effect relationship based purely on co-occurrence. Perhaps the immigrants' arrival was a factor in the economic slump, but there could also be other reasons: the lack of financial incentives to attract business to the city, restrictions on the size of the city's manufacturing facilities, citywide labor disputes that make companies leery of settling in the area. Your argument should also consider these possibilities. (For more on the *post hoc* fallacy, see page 386.)

The *non sequitur fallacy* (Latin for "it does not follow") is an even more blatant muddying of cause-effect relationships. In this case, a conclusion is drawn that has no logical connection to the evidence cited: "Millions of Americans own cars, so there is no need to fund public transportation." The faulty conclusion disregards the millions of Americans who don't own cars; it also ignores pollution and road congestion, both of which could be reduced if people had access to safe, reliable public transportation.

An *ad hominem argument* (from the Latin meaning "to the man") occurs when someone attacks a person rather than a point of view. Suppose your college plans to sponsor a physicians' symposium on the abortion controversy. You decide to write a letter to the school paper opposing the symposium. Taking swipes at two of the invited doctors who disapprove of abortion, you mention that one was recently involved in a messy divorce and that the other is alleged to have a drinking problem. By hurling personal invective, you avoid discussing the issue. Mudslinging is a poor substitute for reasoned argument.

Appeals to questionable or faulty authority also weaken an argument. Most of us have developed a healthy suspicion of phrases like *sources close to, an unidentified spokesperson states, experts claim,* and *studies show.* If these people and reports are so reliable, they should be clearly identified.

Begging the question involves failure to establish proof for a debatable point. The writer expects readers to accept as given a premise that's actually controversial. For instance, you would have trouble convincing readers that prayer should be banned from public schools if you based your argument on the premise that school prayer violates the U.S. Constitution. If the Constitution does, either explicitly or implicitly, prohibit prayer in public education, your essay must demonstrate that fact. You can't build a strong argument if you pretend there's no controversy surrounding your premise.

A *false analogy* wrongly implies that because two things share *some* characteristics, they are therefore *alike in all respects.* You might, for example, compare nicotine and marijuana. Both, you could mention, involve health risks and have addictive properties. If, however, you go on to conclude, "Driving while smoking a cigarette isn't illegal, so driving while smoking marijuana shouldn't be illegal either," you're employing a false analogy. You've overlooked a major difference between nicotine and marijuana: Marijuana impairs perception and coordination—important aspects of driving—while there's no evidence that nicotine does the same.

The *either/or fallacy* occurs when you assume that a particular viewpoint or course of action can have only one of two diametrically opposed outcomes—either totally this or totally that. Say you argue as follows: "Unless colleges continue to offer scholarships based solely on financial need, no one who is underprivileged will be able to attend college." Such a statement ignores the fact that bright, underprivileged students could receive scholarships based on their potential or their demonstrated academic excellence.

Finally, a *red herring argument* is an intentional digression from the issue—a ploy to deflect attention from the matter being discussed. Imagine that you're arguing that condoms shouldn't be dispensed to high school students. You would introduce a red herring if you began to rail against parents who fail to provide their children with any information about sex. Most people would agree that parents *should* provide such information. However, the issue being discussed is not parents' irresponsibility but the pros and cons of schools' distributing condoms to students.

REVISION STRATEGIES

Once you have a draft of the essay, you're ready to revise. The following checklist will help you and those giving you feedback apply to argumentation-persuasion some of the revision techniques discussed on pages 60–62.

☑ ARGUMENTATION-PERSUASION: A REVISION/PEER REVIEW CHECKLIST

Revise Overall Meaning and Structure

- ❑ What issue is being discussed? What is controversial about it?
- ❑ What is the essay's thesis? How does it differ from a generalization or mere statement of fact?
- ❑ What is the essay's purpose—to win readers over to a point of view, to spur readers to some type of action?
- ❑ For what audience is the essay written? What strategies are used to make readers receptive to the essay's thesis?

- ❑ What tone does the essay project? Is the tone likely to win readers over?
- ❑ If the essay's argument is essentially deductive, is the major premise sufficiently restricted? What evidence is the premise based on? Are the minor premise and conclusion valid? If not, how could these problems be corrected?
- ❑ Where is the essay weakened by hasty generalizations, a failure to weigh evidence honestly, or a failure to draw the most valid conclusion?
- ❑ Where does the essay commit any of the following logical fallacies: Concluding that a cause-effect relationship exists simply because one event preceded another? Attacking a person rather than an issue? Drawing a conclusion that isn't logically related to the evidence? Failing to establish proof for a debatable point? Relying on questionable or vaguely specified authority? Drawing a false analogy? Resorting to *either/or* thinking? Using a *red herring* argument?

Revise Paragraph Development

- ❑ How apparent is the link between the evidence (data) and the thesis (claim)? How could an explicit warrant clarify the connection? How would supporting the warrant or qualifying the claim strengthen the argument?
- ❑ Which paragraphs lack sufficient evidence (facts, examples, statistics, and expert opinion)?
- ❑ Which paragraphs lack unity? How could they be made more focused? In which paragraph(s) does evidence seem bland, overly general, unrepresentative, or inaccurate?
- ❑ Which paragraphs take opposing views into account? Are these views refuted? How? Which counterarguments are ineffective?
- ❑ Where do outside sources require documentation?

Revise Sentences and Words

- ❑ What words and phrases help readers distinguish the essay's arguments from those advanced by the opposing side?
- ❑ Which words carry strong emotional overtones? Is this connotative language excessive? Where does emotional language replace rather than reinforce clear thinking?
- ❑ Where might dogmatic language ("Anyone can see that..." and "Obviously,...") alienate readers?

STUDENT ESSAY

The following student essay was written by Mark Simmons in response to this assignment:

> Mary Sherry's "In Praise of the 'F' Word" invites controversy by attacking the popular notion that failing students is a harmful practice. Select another controversial issue, one that you feel strongly about. Conduct library research to gather evidence in support of your position, and brainstorm with others to identify some points that might be raised by those who oppose your view. Then, using logic and formal, documented evidence, convince readers that your viewpoint is valid.

Your instructor may not ask you to include research in your essay. But, if you're asked—as Mark was—to research your paper and to provide *formal documentation,* you'll want to pay special attention to the way Mark credits his sources. (In *your* paper, the Works Cited list should be double-spaced—along with the rest of the paper—and placed at the end on a separate page.) You'll also find it helpful to refer to Appendix A, "A Guide to Using Sources" (page 607). If your instructor wants you to research your paper but will accept *informal documentation,* the material on pages 481–482 should come in handy.

Whether or not you include research in your paper, the annotations on Mark's essay and the comments following it will help you determine how well it applies the principles of argumentation-persuasion.

Simmons 1

Mark Simmons

Professor Chen

English 102

17 November 2011

Compulsory National Service

Center title and double-space all text.

Beginning of two-paragraph introduction

1 Our high school history class spent several weeks studying the events of the 1960s. The most interesting thing about that decade was the spirit of service and social commitment among young people. In the '60s, young people thought about issues beyond themselves; they joined the Peace Corps, worked in poverty-stricken Appalachian communities, and participated in freedom marches against segregation. Most young people today, despite their concern with careers and getting ahead, would also like an opportunity to make a worthwhile contribution to society.

Common knowledge: No need to document

Parenthetical citation of unpaged anonymous material. Use abbreviated title.

2 Convinced that many young adults are indeed eager for such an opportunity, President Bill Clinton implemented in 1994 a pilot program of voluntary national service. The following year, the program was formalized, placed under the management of the Corporation for National Service (CNS), and given the name AmeriCorps. In the years 1994–2007, approximately 400,000 AmeriCorps volunteers provided varied assistance in communities across the country ("About AmeriCorps"). Such voluntary national service was also endorsed by President George W. Bush. Following the devastating terrorist attacks on September 11, 2001, President Bush urged Americans to volunteer as a way of assisting in the nation's recovery and of demonstrating a spirit of national unity. He issued an executive order in early 2002 establishing USA Freedom Corps, an organization seeking to persuade Americans to perform 4,000 hours of volunteer service over a lifetime (Hutcheson). In general, programs such as USA Freedom Corps and the more established AmeriCorps hold out so much promise that it seems only natural to go one step further and make young

Simmons 2

Start of two-sentence thesis

people's participation in these programs or some kind of national service mandatory. By instituting a program of compulsory national service, the country could tap youth's idealistic desire to make a difference. Such a system would yield significant benefits.

Definition paragraph

Beginning of summary of a source's ideas

3 What exactly is meant by compulsory national service? Traditionally, it has tended to mean that everyone between the ages of seventeen and twenty-five would serve the country for two years. These young people could choose between two major options: military service or a public-service corps. They could serve their time at any point within an eight-year span. The unemployed or the uncertain could join immediately after high school; college-bound students could complete their education before joining the national service. Years ago, Senator Sam Nunn and Representative Dave McCurdy gave a new twist to the definition of compulsory national service. They proposed a plan that would require all high school graduates applying for federal aid for college tuition to serve either in the military or in a Citizens Corps. Anyone in the Citizens Corps would be required to work full-time at public-service duties for one or two years. During that time, participants would receive a weekly stipend and, at the end, be given a voucher worth $10,000 for each year of civilian service. The voucher could then be applied toward college credit, employment training, or a down payment on a house (Sudo).

No page number needed for a one-page source.

Topic sentence

Beginning of summary of three points made by the opposing viewpoint

4 The traditional plan for compulsory national service and the one proposed by Nunn and McCurdy are just two of many variations that have been discussed over the years. While this country debates the concept, some nations such as France have gone ahead and accepted it enthusiastically. The idea could be workable in this country too. Unfortunately, opponents are doing all they can to prevent the idea from taking hold. They contend, first of all, that the program would cost too much. A great deal of money, they argue, would be spent administering the program, paying young people's wages, and providing housing for participants. Another

Simmons 3

argument against compulsory national service is that it would demoralize young people; supposedly, the plan would prevent the young from moving ahead with their careers and would make them feel as though they were engaged in work that offered no personal satisfaction. A third argument is that compulsory service would lay the groundwork for a dictatorship. The picture is painted of an army of young people, controlled by the government, much like the Hitler Youth of World War II.

Topic sentence: Refutation of first point

5 Despite opponents' claims that compulsory national service would involve exorbitant costs, the program would not have to be that expensive to run. AmeriCorps has already provided an excellent model for achieving substantial benefits at reasonable cost. For example, a study conducted by universities in Iowa and Michigan showed that each dollar spent on AmeriCorps programs yielded $2.60 in reduced welfare costs, increased earnings, and other benefits (Garland 120). Also, the sums required for wages and housing could be reduced considerably through payments made by the towns, cities, and states using the corps's services. And the economic benefits of the program could be significant. AmeriCorps's official website gives an idea of the current scope of the program's activities. Volunteers provide crucial services including building affordable homes for families, improving health services, responding to natural disasters, and tutoring children. A compulsory national corps could also clean up litter, provide day care services, staff libraries, immunize children, and care for the country's growing elderly population ("About AmeriCorps"; Clinton). All these projects would help solve many of the problems that plague our nation, and they would probably cost less than if they were handled by often inefficient government bureaucracies.

Parenthetical citation of a specific page of a source

Information from two sources. Sources, separated by a semicolon, are given in the order in which they appear in the Works Cited list.

Topic sentence: Refutation of second point

6 Also, rather than undermining the spirit of young people, as opponents contend, the program would probably boost their morale. Many young people feel enormous pressure and uncertainty; they are not sure whether they want to find a job or further their

Simmons 4

Attribution giving author's full name and area of expertise

Full-sentence quotation is preceded by a comma and begins with a capital letter.

Quotation with ellipsis

Parenthetical citation for source having two authors. No page given since electronic text is unpaged.

Where secondary source was quoted

Quotation is blended into the sentence (no comma and the quotation begins with a lowercased word).

Just the page number is provided because the author's name is cited in the preceding attribution.

education. Compulsory national service could give these young people much-needed breathing space. As Edward Lewis, president of St. Mary's College, says, "Many students are not ready for college at seventeen or eighteen. This kind of program responds to that need" (qtd. in Fowler). Robert Coles, psychiatrist and social activist, argues that a public service stint enriches participants' lives in yet another way. Coles points out that young people often have little sense of the job market. When they get involved in community service, though, they frequently "discover an area of interest...that launches them on a career" (93). Equally important, compulsory national service can provide an emotional boost for the young; all of them would experience the pride that comes from working hard, reaching goals, acquiring skills, and handling responsibilities (Wofford and Waldman). A positive mind-set would also result from the sense of community that would be created by serving in the national service. All young people—rich or poor, educated or not, regardless of sex and social class—would come together and perceive not their differences but their common interests and similarities (Wofford and Waldman). As President Clinton proclaimed at the Year 2000 swearing-in of AmeriCorps's recruits in Philadelphia, AmeriCorps gives volunteers a chance "to tear down barriers of distrust and misunderstanding and old-fashioned ignorance, and build a genuine American community" (Clinton).

Topic sentence: Refutation of third point

Finally, in contrast to what opponents claim, compulsory 7
national service would not signal the start of a dictatorship. Although the service would be required, young people would have complete freedom to choose any two years between the ages of seventeen and twenty-five. They would also have complete freedom to choose the branch of the military or public service corps that suits them best. And the corps would not need to be outfitted in military uniforms or to live in barrack-like camps. It could be set up like a regular job, with young people living at home as much as possible, following a nine-to-five schedule, enjoying all the personal

Simmons 5

freedoms that would ordinarily be theirs. Also, a dictatorship would no more likely emerge from compulsory national service than it has from our present military system. We would still have a series of checks and balances to prohibit the taking of power by one group or individual. We should also keep in mind that our system is different from that of fascist regimes; our long tradition of personal liberty makes improbable the seizing of absolute power by one person or faction. A related but even more important point to remember is that freedom does not mean people are guaranteed the right to pursue only their individual needs. That is mistaking selfishness for freedom. And, as everyone knows, selfishness leads only to misery. The national service would not take away freedom. On the contrary, serving in the corps would help young people grasp this larger concept of freedom, a concept that is badly needed to counteract the deadly "look out for number one" attitude that is spreading like a poison across the nation. "We think that there's an inherent idealism in every person, especially young people, that if we give them the right structure and opportunity, we can call it out," says John Sarvey, who trains AmeriCorps participants for work in City Year San Jose, the program he directs ("Helping").

Parenthetical citation uses abbreviated title.

Beginning of two-paragraph conclusion

Perhaps there will never be a time like the 1960s when so many young people were concerned with remaking the world. Still, a good many of today's young people want meaningful work. They want to feel that what they do makes a difference. A program of compulsory national service would harness this idealism and help young people realize the best in themselves. Such a program would also help resolve some of the country's most critical social problems.

Attribution leading to a long quotation. Attribution is followed by a colon since the lead-in is a full sentence. If the lead-in isn't a full sentence, use a comma after the attribution.

Almost two decades ago, political commentator Donald Eberly expressed his belief in the power of national service. Urging the inauguration of such a program, Eberly wrote the following: 8

Long quotation is indented one inch. Don't leave any extra space within, above, or below the quotation.

> The promise of national service can be manifested in many ways: in cleaner air and fewer forest fires; in

Simmons 6

For an indented quotation, the period is placed *before* the parenthetical citation.

> well-cared-for infants and old folks; in a better-educated citizenry and better-satisfied work force; perhaps in a more peaceful world. National service has a lot of promise. It's a promise well worth keeping. (561)

Several years later, President Clinton took office, gave his support 9
to the concept, and AmeriCorps was born. This advocacy of public service was then championed, at least in word, by President Bush. During his administration, however, AmeriCorps was threatened by deep budget cuts advocated by opponents of the program and its Clintonian legacy. Fortunately, despite these measures, Congress voted in 2003 with overwhelming bipartisan support to save AmeriCorps and salvage a portion of its budget ("Timely Help"). In the words of a *Philadelphia Inquirer* editorial, "The civic yield from that investment is incalculable" ("Ill Served"). An efficient and successful program of voluntary service, AmeriCorps has paved the way. Now seems to be the perfect time to expand the concept and make compulsory national service a reality.

Start list on a new page, double-spaced, no extra space after heading or between entries. Each entry begins flush left; Indent successive lines half an inch.

Simmons 7

Works Cited

"About AmeriCorps: What Is AmeriCorps?" *AmeriCorps.* Corporation for National and Community Service, 3 Nov. 2008. Web. 3 Nov. 2008.

Clinton, William J. "Remarks by the President to AmeriCorps." Memorial Hall, Philadelphia. 11 Oct. 2000. Transcript. *Clinton Presidential Materials Project.* National Archives and Records Administration. Web. 6 Nov. 2008. Transcript. <http://clinton6.nara.gov/2000/10/2000-10-11-remarks-by-the-president-to-americorps.html>.

For anonymous Internet material, start with title, give website (italicized) and sponsoring organization, followed by publication date. Give page numbers if available. State medium consulted ("Web") and date of access.

Transcript of a speech found online. Give URL *only* for hard-to-retrieve sources.

Book by a single author. Give medium ("Print") at the end of the citation.

Article from weekly magazine

TV show transcript found online

Newspaper editorial found online

Newspaper article whose text is only one page

Scholarly journal article, by two authors, found in a database ("*EBSCOhost*"). Give issue number (or volume and issue number, if available) and year, followed by pages or "n. pag." if no page numbers are given in the source.

Coles, Robert. *The Call of Service.* Boston: Houghton, 1993. Print.

Eberly, Donald. "What the President Should Do about National Service." *Vital Speeches of the Day.* 15 Aug. 1989: 561-63. Print.

Fowler, Margaret. "New Interest in National Youth Corps." *New York Times* 16 May 1989, natl. ed.: A25. Print.

Garland, Susan B. "A Social Program CEOs Want to Save." *Business Week* 19 June 1996: 120-21. Print.

"Helping Hands." *Online NewsHour.* Public Broadcasting Service, 19 July 2000. Web. 11 Nov. 2008. Transcript.

Hutcheson, Ron. "Bush Moves to Establish His New Volunteer Program." *Philadelphia Inquirer* 31 Jan. 2002: A2. Print.

"Ill Served." Editorial. *Philadelphia Inquirer Online.* Philly.com, 27 June 2003. Web. 8 Nov. 2008.

Sudo, Phil. "Mandatory National Service?" *Scholastic Update* 23 Feb. 1990. Print.

"Timely Help for AmeriCorps." Editorial. *New York Times.* New York Times, 17 July 2003. Web. 11 Nov. 2008.

Wofford, Harris, and Steven Waldman. "AmeriCorps the Beautiful? Habitat for Conservative Values." *Policy Review* 79 (1996): n. pag. *EBSCOhost.* Web. 11 Nov. 2008.

COMMENTARY

Blend of argumentation and persuasion. In his essay, Mark tackles a controversial issue. He takes the position that compulsory national service would benefit both the country as a whole and its young people in particular. Mark's essay is a good example of the way argumentation and persuasion often mix: Although the paper presents Mark's position in a logical, well-reasoned manner (argumentation), it also appeals to readers' personal values and suggests a course of action (persuasion).

Audience analysis. When planning the essay, Mark realized that his audience—his composition class—would consist largely of two kinds of readers. Some, not sure of their views, would be inclined to agree with him if he presented his case well. Others would probably be reluctant to accept his view. Because of this mixed audience, Mark knew he couldn't depend on *pathos* (an appeal to emotion) to convince readers. Rather, his argument had to rely mainly on *logos* (reason) and *ethos* (credibility). So Mark organized his essay around a series of logical arguments—many of them backed by expert opinion—and he evoked his own authority by drawing on his knowledge of history and his "inside" knowledge of young people.

Introduction and thesis. Mark introduces his subject by discussing an earlier decade when large numbers of young people worked for social change. Mark's references to the Peace Corps, community work, and freedom marches reinforce his image as a knowledgeable source and establish a context for his position. These historical references, combined with the comments about AmeriCorps, the program of voluntary national service, lead into the two-sentence thesis at the end of the two-paragraph introduction: "By instituting a program of compulsory national service, the country could tap youth's idealistic desire to make a difference. Such a system would yield significant benefits."

The second paragraph in the introduction also illustrates Mark's first use of outside sources. Because the assignment called for research in support of an argument, Mark went to the library and online and identified sources that helped him defend his position. If Mark's instructor had required extensive investigation of an issue, Mark would have been obligated both to dig more deeply into his subject and to use more scholarly and specialized sources. But given the instructor's requirements, Mark proceeded just as he should have: He searched out expert opinion that supported his viewpoint; he presented that evidence clearly; he documented his sources carefully.

Background paragraph and use of outside sources. The third paragraph provides a working *definition* of compulsory national service by presenting two common interpretations of the concept. Such background information guarantees that Mark's readers will share his understanding of the essay's central concept.

Acknowledging the opposing viewpoint. Having explained the meaning of compulsory national service, Mark is now in a good position to launch his argument. Even though he wasn't required to research the opposing viewpoint, Mark wisely decided to get together with some friends to brainstorm some issues that might be raised by the dissenting view. He acknowledges this position in the *topic sentence* of the essay's fourth paragraph: "Unfortunately, opponents are doing all they can to prevent the idea from taking hold." Next he summarizes the main points the dissenting opinion might advance: compulsory national service would be expensive, demoralizing to young people, and dangerously authoritarian. Mark uses the rest of the essay to counter these criticisms.

Refutation. The next three paragraphs (5–7) *refute* the opposing stance and present Mark's evidence for his position. Mark structures the essay so that readers can follow his *counterargument* with ease. Each paragraph argues against one opposing point and begins with a *topic sentence* that serves as Mark's response to the dissenting view. Note the way the italicized portion of each topic sentence recalls a dissenting point cited earlier: "Despite opponents' claims that *compulsory national service would involve exorbitant costs,* the program would not have to be that expensive to run" (paragraph 5); "Also, rather than *undermining the spirit of young people,* as opponents contend, the program would probably boost their morale" (6); "Finally, in contrast to what opponents claim, *compulsory national service would not signal the start of a dictatorship*" (7). Mark also guides the reader through the various points in the refutation by using *transitions* within paragraphs: "*And* the economic benefits... could be significant" (5); "*Equally important,* compulsory national service could provide an emotional boost..." (6); "*Also,* a dictatorship would no more likely emerge..." (7).

Throughout the three-paragraph refutation, Mark uses outside sources to lend power to his argument. If the assignment had called for in-depth research, he would have cited facts, statistics, and case studies to develop this section of his essay. Given the nature of the assignment, though, Mark's reliance on expert opinion is perfectly acceptable.

Mark successfully incorporates material from these outside sources into his refutation. He doesn't, for example, string one quotation numbingly after another; instead he usually develops his refutation by *summarizing* expert opinion and saves *direct quotations* for points that deserve emphasis. Moreover, whenever Mark quotes or summarizes a source, he provides clear signals to indicate that the material is indeed borrowed. (If you'd like some suggestions for citing outside sources in an essay of your own, see pages 481–482 and 607–638.)

Some problems with the refutation. Overall, Mark's three-paragraph refutation is strong, but it would have been even more effective if the paragraphs had been resequenced. As it now stands, the last paragraph in the refutation (7) seems anticlimactic. Unlike the preceding two paragraphs, which are developed through fairly extensive reference to outside sources, paragraph 7 depends entirely on Mark's personal feelings and interpretations for its support. Of course, Mark was under no obligation to provide research in all sections of the paper. Even so, the refutation would have been more persuasive if Mark had placed the final paragraph in the refutation in a less emphatic position. He could, for example, have put it first or second in the sequence, saving for last either of the other two more convincing paragraphs.

You may also have felt that there's another problem with the third paragraph in the refutation. Here, Mark seems to lose control of his counterargument. Beginning with "And, as everyone knows…," Mark falls into the *logical fallacy* called *begging the question*. He shouldn't assume that everyone agrees that a selfish life inevitably brings misery. He also indulges in charged emotionalism when he refers—somewhat melodramatically—to the "deadly 'look out for number one' attitude that is spreading like a poison across the nation."

Inductive reasoning. In part, Mark arrived at his position *inductively*, through a series of *inferences* or *inductive leaps*. He started with some personal *observations* about the nation and its young people. Then, to support those observations, he added his friends' insights as well as information gathered through research. Combined, all this material led him to the general *conclusion* that compulsory national service would be both workable and beneficial.

Combining patterns of development. To develop his argument, Mark draws on several patterns of development. The third paragraph relies on *definition* to clarify what is meant by compulsory national service. The first paragraph of both the introduction and conclusion *compares* and *contrasts* young people of the 1960s with those of today. And, to support his position, Mark uses a kind of *causal analysis*; he both speculates on the likely consequences of compulsory national service and cites expert opinion to illustrate the validity of some of those speculations.

Conclusion. Despite some problems in the final section of his refutation, Mark comes up with an effective two-paragraph conclusion for his essay. In the first closing paragraph, he echoes the point made in the introduction about the 1960s and restates his thesis. That done, he moves to the second paragraph of his conclusion. There, he quotes a dramatic statement from a knowledgeable source, cites efforts to undermine AmeriCorps, and ends by pointing out that AmeriCorps has earned the respect of some unlikely supporters. All that Mark does in this final paragraph lends credibility to the crisp assertion and suggested course of action at the very end of his essay.

Revising the first draft. Given the complex nature of his argument, Mark found that he had to revise his essay several times. One way to illustrate some of the changes he made is to compare his final introduction with the original draft printed here:

Original Version of the Introduction

"There's no free lunch." "You can't get something for nothing." "You have to earn your way." In America, these sayings are not really true. In America, we gladly take but give back little. In America, we receive economic opportunity, legal protection, the right to vote, and, most of all, a personal freedom unequaled throughout the world. How do we repay our country for such gifts? In most cases, we don't. This unfair relationship must be changed. The best way to make a start is to institute a system of national compulsory service for young people. This system would be of real benefit to the country and its citizens.

When Mark met with a classmate for a peer review session, he found that his partner had a number of helpful suggestions for revising various sections of the essay. But Mark's partner focused most of her comments on the essay's introduction because she felt it needed special attention. Following his classmate's suggestion, Mark deleted the original introduction's references to Americans in general. He made this change because he wanted readers to know—from the very start of the essay—that the paper would focus not on all Americans but on American youth. To reinforce this emphasis, he also added the point about the social commitment characteristic of young people in the 1960s. This reference to an earlier period gave the discussion an important historical perspective and lent a note of authority to Mark's argument. The decision to mention the '60s also helped Mark realize that his introduction should point out more recent developments—specifically, the promise of AmeriCorps. Mark was pleased to see that adding this new material not only gave the introduction a sharper focus, but it also provided a smoother lead-in to his thesis.

These are just a few of the many changes Mark made while reworking his essay. Because he budgeted his time carefully, he was able to revise thoroughly. With the exception of some weak spots in the refutation, Mark's essay is well-reasoned and convincing.

MLA format. Mark followed the style given in the MLA Handbook for Writers of Research Papers to format his paper. For more guidance on styling in-text references and Works Cited lists, see pages 625–638.

ACTIVITIES: ARGUMENTATION-PERSUASION

Prewriting Activities

1. Following are several thesis statements for argumentation-persuasion essays. For each thesis, determine whether the three audiences indicated in parentheses are apt to be supportive, wavering, or hostile. Then select *one* thesis and use group brainstorming to identify, for each audience, specific points you would make to persuade each group.

   a. Students should not graduate from college until they have passed a comprehensive exam in their majors (*college students, their parents, college officials*).

b. Abandoned homes owned by the city should be sold to low-income residents for a nominal fee (*city officials, low-income residents, general citizens*).
c. The town should pass a law prohibiting residents who live near the reservoir from using pesticides on their lawns (*environmentalists, homeowners, members of the town council*).
d. Faculty advisors to college newspapers should have the authority to prohibit the publication of articles that reflect negatively on the school (*alumni, college officials, student journalists*).

Revising Activities

2. Following is the introduction from the first draft of an essay advocating the elimination of mandatory dress codes in public schools. Revise the paragraph, being sure to consider these questions: How effectively does the writer deal with the opposing viewpoint? Does the paragraph encourage those who might disagree with the writer to read on? Why or why not? Do you see any logical fallacies in the writer's thinking? Where? Does the writer introduce anything that veers away from the point being discussed? Where? Before revising, you may find it helpful to do some brainstorming—individually or in a group—to find ways to strengthen the paragraph.

   After reworking the paragraph, take a few minutes to consider how the rest of the essay might unfold. What persuasive strategies could be used? How could Rogerian argument win over readers? What points could be made? What action could be urged in the effort to build a convincing argument?

   In three nearby towns recently, high school administrators joined forces to take an outrageously strong stand against students' constitutional rights. Acting like fascists, they issued an edict in the form of a preposterous dress code that prohibits students from wearing expensive jewelry, designer jeans, leather jackets—anything that the administrators, in their supposed wisdom, consider ostentatious. Perhaps the next thing they'll want to do is forbid students to play rock music at school dances. What prompted the administrators' dictatorial prohibition against certain kinds of clothing? Somehow or other, they got it into their heads that having no restrictions on the way students dress creates an unhealthy environment, where students vie with each other for the flashiest attire. Students and parents alike should protest this and any other dress code. If such codes go into effect, we might as well throw out the Constitution.

Stanley Fish

Stanley Fish is best known as a scholar of the English poet John Milton and as a literary theorist. He was born in Providence, Rhode Island, in 1938. Fish has taught English at the University of California at Berkeley, Johns Hopkins University, and Duke University. From 1999 to 2004 he was dean of the College of Liberal Arts and Sciences at the University of Illinois at Chicago, and in 2005 he became a professor of humanities and law at Florida International University. His best-known work on Milton is *Surprised by Sin: The Reader in* Paradise Lost (1967). In addition to his distinguished academic career and many scholarly publications, Fish has also had a career as a public intellectual. He has written and lectured about many issues, including the politics of the university. His books on current political and cultural issues include *There's No Such Thing as Free Speech...and It's a Good Thing, Too* (1994) and *The Trouble with Principle* (1999). This article was published in *The Chronicle of Higher Education,* for which Fish writes a regular column on campus politics and academic careers, on June 13, 2003.

For ideas about how this argumentation-persuasion essay is organized, see Figure 11.2 on page 513.

Pre-Reading Journal Entry

How do you feel about freedom of speech on campus? In your journal, list several controversial issues that might be debated in a college setting. For each issue, indicate whether you feel that divergent, even inflammatory views should have an opportunity to be heard on campus—for example, in class, in the college newspaper, or in a lecture series. Reflect in your journal on why you feel as you do.

Free-Speech Follies

The modern American version of crying wolf is crying First Amendment.[1] If you want to burn a cross on a black family's lawn or buy an election by contributing millions to a candidate or vilify Jerry Falwell and his mother in a scurrilous "parody," and someone or some government agency tries to stop you, just yell "First Amendment rights" and you will stand a good chance of getting to do what you want to do. 1

In the academy,[2] the case is even worse: Not only is the First Amendment pressed into service at the drop of a hat (especially whenever anyone is disciplined for anything), it is invoked ritually when there are no First Amendment issues in sight. 2

[1]The relevant part of the First Amendment of the U.S. Constitution reads: "Congress shall make no law... abridging the freedom of speech, or of the press; or the right of the people peaceably to assemble, and to petition the Government for a redress of grievances" (editors' note).
[2]Refers to institutions of higher learning (editors' note).

Take the case of the editors of college newspapers who will always cry First Amendment when something they've published turns out to be the cause of outrage and controversy. These days the offending piece or editorial or advertisement usually involves (what is at least perceived to be) an attack on Jews. In January of this year, the *Daily Illini,* a student newspaper at the University of Illinois at Urbana-Champaign, printed a letter from a resident of Seattle with no university affiliation. The letter ran under the headline "Jews Manipulate America" and argued that because their true allegiance is to the state of Israel, the president should "separate Jews from all government advisory positions"; otherwise, the writer warned, "the Jews might face another Holocaust." 3

When the predictable firestorm of outrage erupted, the newspaper's editor responded by declaring, first, that "we are committed to giving all people a voice"; second, that, given this commitment, "we print the opinions of others with whom we do not agree"; third, that to do otherwise would involve the newspaper in the dangerous acts of "silencing" and "self-censorship"; and, fourth, that "what is hate speech to one member of a society is free speech to another." 4

Wrong four times. 5

I'll bet the *Daily Illini* is not committed to giving all people a voice—the KKK? man-boy love? advocates of slavery? would-be Unabombers? Nor do I believe that the editors sift through submissions looking for the ones they disagree with and then print those. No doubt they apply some principles of selection, asking questions like, Is it relevant, or Is it timely, or Does it get the facts right, or Does it present a coherent argument? 6

That is, they exercise judgment, which is quite a different thing from silencing or self-censorship. No one is silenced because a single outlet declines to publish him; silencing occurs when that outlet (or any other) is forbidden by the state to publish him on pain of legal action; and that is also what censorship is. 7

As for self-censoring, if it is anything, it is what we all do whenever we decide it would be better not to say something or cut a sentence that went just a little bit too far or leave a manuscript in the bottom drawer because it is not yet ready. Self-censorship, in short, is not a crime or a moral failing; it is a responsibility. 8

And, finally, whatever the merits of the argument by which all assertions are relativised—your hate speech is my free speech—this incident has nothing to do with either hate speech or free speech and everything to do with whether the editors are discharging or defaulting on their obligations when they foist them off on an inapplicable doctrine, saying in effect, "The First Amendment made us do it." 9

More recently, the same scenario played itself out at Santa Rosa Junior College. This time it was a student who wrote the offending article. Titled "Is Anti-Semitism Ever the Result of Jewish Behavior?" it answered the question in the affirmative, creating an uproar that included death threats, an avalanche of hate mail, and demands for just about everyone's resignation. 10

The faculty adviser who had approved the piece said, "The First Amendment isn't there to protect agreeable stories."

He was alluding to the old saw that the First Amendment protects unpopular as well as popular speech. But what it protects unpopular speech *from* is abridgment by the government of its free expression; it does not protect unpopular speech from being rejected by a newspaper, and it confers no positive obligation to give your pages over to unpopular speech, or popular speech, or any speech. 11

Once again, there is no First Amendment issue here, just an issue of editorial judgment and the consequences of exercising it. (You can print anything you like; but if the heat comes, it's yours, not the Constitution's.) 12

In these controversies, student editors are sometimes portrayed, or portray themselves, as First Amendment heroes who bravely risk criticism and censure in order to uphold a cherished American value. But they are not heroes; they are merely confused and, in terms of their understanding of the doctrine they invoke, rather hapless. 13

Not as hapless, however, as the Harvard English department, which made a collective fool of itself three times when it invited, disinvited and then reinvited poet Tom Paulin to be the Morris Gray lecturer. Again the flash point was anti-Semitism. In his poetry and in public comments, Paulin had said that Israel had no right to exist, that settlers on the West Bank "should be shot dead," and that Israeli police and military forces were the equivalent of the Nazi SS. When these and other statements came to light shortly before Paulin was to give his lecture, the department voted to rescind the invitation. When the inevitable cry of "censorship, censorship" was heard in the land, the department flip-flopped again, and a professor-spokesman declared, "This was a clear affirmation that the department stood strongly by the First Amendment." 14

It was of course nothing of the kind; it was a transparent effort of a bunch that had already put its foot in its mouth twice to wriggle out of trouble and regain the moral high ground by striking the pose of First Amendment defender. But, in fact, the department and its members were not First Amendment defenders (a religion they converted to a little late), but serial bunglers. 15

What should they have done? Well, it depends on what they wanted to do. If they wanted to invite this particular poet because they admired his poetry, they had a perfect right to do so. If they were aware ahead of time of Paulin's public pronouncements, they could have chosen either to say something by way of explanation or to remain silent and let the event speak for itself; either course of action would have been at once defensible and productive of risk. If they knew nothing of Paulin's anti-Israel sentiments (difficult to believe of a gang of world-class researchers) but found out about them after the fact, they might have said, "Oops, never mind" or toughed it out—again alternatives not without risk. But at each stage, whatever they did or didn't do would have had no relationship whatsoever to any First Amendment right—Paulin had no right to be invited—or obligation—there 16 was no obligation either to invite or disinvite him, and certainly no obligation to reinvite him, unless you count the obligations imposed on yourself by a succession of ill-thought-through decisions. Whatever the successes or failures here, they were once again failures of judgment, not doctrine.

In another case, it looked for a moment that judgment of an appropriate kind was in fact being exercised. The University of California at Berkeley houses the Emma Goldman Papers Project, and each year the director sends out a fund-raising mailer that always features quotations from Goldman's work. But this January an associate vice chancellor edited the mailer and removed two quotations that in context read as a criticism of the Bush administration's plans for a war in Iraq. He explained that the quotations were not randomly chosen and were clearly intended to make a "political point, and that is inappropriate in an official university situation." 17

The project director (who acknowledged that the quotes were selected for their contemporary relevance) objected to what she saw as an act of censorship and a particularly egregious one given Goldman's strong advocacy of free expression. 18

But no one's expression was being censored. The Goldman quotations are readily available and had they appeared in the project's literature in a setting that did not mark them as political, no concerns would have been raised. It is just, said the associate vice chancellor, that they are inappropriate in this context, and, he added, "It is not a matter of the First Amendment." 19

Right, it's a matter of whether or not there is even the appearance of the university's taking sides on a partisan issue; that is, it is an empirical matter that requires just the exercise of judgment that associate vice chancellors are paid to perform. Of course he was pilloried by members of the Berkeley faculty and others who saw First Amendment violations everywhere. 20

But there were none. Goldman still speaks freely through her words. The project director can still make her political opinions known by writing letters to the editor or to everyone in the country, even if she cannot use the vehicle of a university flier to do so. Everyone's integrity is preserved. The project goes on unimpeded, and the university goes about its proper academic business. Or so it would have been had the administration stayed firm. But it folded and countermanded the associate vice chancellor's decision. 21

At least the chancellor had sense enough to acknowledge that no one's speech had been abridged. It was just, he said, an "error in judgment." Aren't they all? 22

Are there then no free-speech issues on campuses? Sure there are; there just aren't very many. When Toni Smith, a basketball player at Manhattanville College, turned her back to the flag during the playing of the national anthem in protest against her government's policies, she was truly exercising her First Amendment rights, rights that ensure that she cannot be compelled to an affirmation she does not endorse.... And as she stood by her principles 23 in the face of hostility, she truly was (and is) a First Amendment hero, as the college newspaper editors, the members of the Harvard English department, and the head of the Emma Goldman Project are not. The category is a real one, and it would be good if it were occupied only by those who belong in it.

FIGURE 11.2
Essay Structure Diagram: "Free-Speech Follies" by Stanley Fish

Introductory paragraphs: Thesis (paragraphs 1–2)	Invoking the First Amendment has become a way of "crying wolf." **Thesis:** In the academy, the First Amendment is invoked often in situations that don't really concern free speech.
Opposing and supporting arguments illustrated by examples (3–22)	**Example:** Anti-Semitic letter in University of Illinois newspaper. **Opposing arguments:** (1) Editors have an obligation to give all people a voice. (2) Editors have an obligation to print views they don't agree with. (3) Not to publish is "silencing" and self-censorship. (4) Hate speech to one person is free speech to another. First Amendment protects all speech, not just agreeable speech. **Supporting arguments:** (1) Editors must use some selection criteria—for writing quality and content. (2) Exercising judgment is not the same as silencing because writers are free to publish elsewhere. (3) Self-censorship is not a crime; it's a responsibility. (4) The incident did not concern hate speech vs. free speech, but rather whether editors discharged their responsibilities. **Example:** Anti-Semitic article in a Santa Rosa Junior College newspaper. (Opposing and supporting arguments given.) **Example:** Harvard English department invites, then uninvites, then reinvites a poet who had expressed anti-Semitic views. (Opposing and supporting arguments given.) **Example:** Quotations critical of the Bush administration deleted from a University of California at Berkeley exhibit flyer. (Opposing and supporting arguments given.)
Concluding paragraph (23)	Example of a true First Amendment hero: College basketball player turning her back on the flag during the national anthem to protest government policies.

Questions for Close Reading

1. What is the selection's thesis? Locate the sentence(s) in which Fish states his main idea. If he doesn't state his thesis explicitly, express it in your own words.
2. What does Fish mean by "Self-censorship, in short, is not a crime or a moral failing; it is a responsibility" (paragraph 8)?
3. In paragraph 15, Fish refers to the Harvard English department as "serial bunglers." What does he mean by this?
4. According to Fish, why aren't the editors of student newspapers that publish inflammatory material First Amendment heroes? Who does he believe are the true First Amendment heroes?
5. Refer to your dictionary as needed to define the following words used in the selection: *vilify* (paragraph 1), *scurrilous* (1), *firestorm* (4), *coherent* (6), *abridgment* (11), *hapless* (13), *rescind* (14), *chancellor* (17), *egregious* (18), *partisan* (20), *empirical* (20), *pilloried* (20), and *countermanded* (21).

Questions About the Writer's Craft

1. **The pattern.** Fish presents the viewpoint that self-censorship is not a violation of the First Amendment. What strategies does Fish use to deal with this view and to present his own argument?
2. **Other patterns.** All the examples that Fish uses to support his argument are related to anti-Semitism. If Fish had broadened the examples to include instances of speech that defamed groups other than Jews, would the essay have been more or less effective? Support your answer.
3. Paragraph 5 is just "Wrong four times." What is the effect of this brevity?
4. Most readers of *The Chronicle of Higher Education*, where this essay was first published, are academics—administrators, faculty, and graduate students—or those with a professional interest in higher education. They are likely to know Fish by reputation, especially since he publishes a regular column. Given this, how would you assess Fish's *ethos*? How effective is his use of *logos* in this argument? How effective is his use of *pathos*?

Writing Assignments Using Argumentation-Persuasion as a Pattern of Development

1. Fish gives an example of a controversy surrounding an anti-Semitic letter to the editor published in a campus student newspaper. Since publications print letters to the editor to open up their pages to public opinion and dissent, one might argue that the criteria for printing letters to the editor should be quite broad—much broader than the criteria the publication uses for its own articles—in order to give members of the public an opportunity to air their views. Write an essay in which you *argue* that letters to the editor should (or should not) be printed with the aim of giving all readers an opportunity to state their opinions. Don't forget to acknowledge (and, if possible, to refute) opposing viewpoints.
2. Many colleges and universities have limited controversial speech to designated "free-speech zones," areas on campus where speeches, rallies, and pamphleteering

are permitted. Elsewhere free speech is subject to tight administration control. Proponents argue that universities have a right to control activities that interfere with their operation; opponents argue that free-speech zones are unconstitutional. Do some research about free-speech zones on the Internet or in the library. Write an essay *arguing* that free-speech zones are (or are not) a legitimate way to manage free-speech issues on campus. If your own campus has free-speech zones, use it as an example to support your argument. Use other colleges and universities as examples as well. Conclude your essay with a call to action.

Writing Assignments Combining Patterns of Development

3. What procedures has your college or university established so that people can file grievances if they feel they have been the targets of hate speech or have been discriminated against in some way? In an essay, describe this *process* and indicate whether you feel it is adequate and appropriate. If it isn't, explain what steps need to be taken to improve the procedures. Provide *examples* to illustrate your point of view.

4. Stereotyping isn't restricted to minorities. Most of us have felt unfairly stereotyped at some time or another, perhaps because of gender, physical or intellectual abilities, or even a hobby or interest. Write an essay *recounting* a time you were treated unfairly or cruelly because of some personal characteristic. Be sure to show how the event *affected* you. The following essays will provide insight into the potentially corrosive effect of labels and stereotypes: Audre Lorde's "The Fourth of July" (page 140), William Raspberry's "The Handicap of Definition" (page 468), and Roberto Rodriguez's "The Border on Our Backs" (page 559).

Writing Assignment Using a Journal Entry as a Starting Point

5. Write an editorial for your college newspaper arguing that a college campus is *or* is not the place to air conflicting, even inflammatory views about *one* of the controversial issues listed in your pre-reading journal entry. Perhaps you feel that the issue warrants a public forum in one campus setting but not another. If so, explain why. To lend authority to your position, interview students who don't share your point of view. Be sure to acknowledge their position in your editorial.

Mary Sherry

Following her graduation from Dominican University in 1962 with a degree in English, Mary Sherry (1940–) wrote freelance articles and advertising copy while raising her family. Over the years, a love of writing and an interest in education have been integral to all that Sherry does professionally. Founder and owner of a small research and publishing firm in Minnesota, she has taught creative and remedial writing to adults for more than twenty years. The following selection first appeared as a 1991 "My Turn" column in *Newsweek*.

Pre-Reading Journal Entry

Imagine you had a son or daughter who didn't take school seriously. How would you go about motivating the child to value academic success? Would your strategies differ depending on the age and gender of the child? If so, how and why? What other factors might influence your approach? Use your journal to respond to these questions.

In Praise of the "F" Word

Tens of thousands of 18-year-olds will graduate this year and be handed meaningless diplomas. These diplomas won't look any different from those awarded their luckier classmates. Their validity will be questioned only when their employers discover that these graduates are semiliterate. 1

Eventually a fortunate few will find their way into educational repair shops—adult-literacy programs, such as the one where I teach basic grammar and writing. There, high-school graduates and high-school dropouts pursuing graduate-equivalency certificates will learn the skills they should have learned in school. They will also discover they have been cheated by our educational system. 2

As I teach, I learn a lot about our schools. Early in each session I ask my students to write about an unpleasant experience they had in school. No writers' block here! "I wish someone would have had made me stop doing drugs and made me study." "I liked to party and no one seemed to care." "I was a good kid and didn't cause any trouble, so they just passed me along even though I didn't read well and couldn't write." And so on. 3

I am your basic do-gooder, and prior to teaching this class I blamed the poor academic skills our kids have today on drugs, divorce and other impediments to concentration necessary for doing well in school. But, as I rediscover each time I walk into the classroom, before a teacher can expect students to concentrate, he has to get their attention, no matter what distractions may be at hand. There are many ways to do this, and they have much to do with teaching style. However, if style alone won't do it, there is another way to show who holds the winning hand in the classroom. That is to reveal the trump card[1] of failure. 4

[1]In cards, an advantage held in reserve until it's needed (editors' note).

I will never forget a teacher who played that card to get the attention of one of my children. Our youngest, a world-class charmer, did little to develop his intellectual talents but always got by. Until Mrs. Stifter. 5

Our son was a high-school senior when he had her for English. "He sits in the back of the room talking to his friends," she told me. "Why don't you move him to the front row?" I urged, believing the embarrassment would get him to settle down. Mrs. Stifter looked at me steely-eyed over her glasses. "I don't move seniors," she said. "I flunk them." I was flustered. Our son's academic life flashed before my eyes. No teacher had ever threatened him with that before. I regained my composure and managed to say that I thought she was right. By the time I got home I was feeling pretty good about this. It was a radical approach for these times, but, well, why not? "She's going to flunk you," I told my son. I did not discuss it any further. Suddenly English became a priority in his life. He finished out the semester with an A. 6

I know one example doesn't make a case, but at night I see a parade of students who are angry and resentful for having been passed along until they could no longer even pretend to keep up. Of average intelligence or better, they eventually quit school, concluding they were too dumb to finish. "I should have been held back" is a comment I hear frequently. Even sadder are those students who are high-school graduates who say to me after a few weeks of class, "I don't know how I ever got a high-school diploma." 7

Passing students who have not mastered the work cheats them and the employers who expect graduates to have basic skills. We excuse this dishonest behavior by saying kids can't learn if they come from terrible environments. No one seems to stop to think that—no matter what environments they come from—most kids don't put school first on their list unless they perceive something is at stake. They'd rather be sailing. 8

Many students I see at night could give expert testimony on unemployment, chemical dependency, abusive relationships. In spite of these difficulties, they have decided to make education a priority. They are motivated by the desire for a better job or the need to hang on to the one they've got. They have a healthy fear of failure. 9

People of all ages can rise above their problems, but they need to have a reason to do so. Young people generally don't have the maturity to value education in the same way my adult students value it. But fear of failure, whether economic or academic, can motivate both. 10

Flunking as a regular policy has just as much merit today as it did two generations ago. We must review the threat of flunking and see it as it really is—a positive teaching tool. It is an expression of confidence by both teachers and parents that the students have the ability to learn the material presented to them. However, making it work again would take a dedicated, caring conspiracy between teachers and parents. It would mean facing the 11 tough reality that passing kids who haven't learned the material—while it might save them grief for the short term—dooms them to long-term illiteracy. It would mean that teachers would have to follow through on their threats, and parents would have to stand behind them, knowing their children's best interests are indeed at stake. This means no more doing Scott's assignments for him because he might fail. No more passing Jodi because she's such a nice kid.

This is a policy that worked in the past and can work today. A wise teacher, with the support of his parents, gave our son the opportunity to succeed—or fail. It's time we return this choice to all students. 12

Questions for Close Reading

1. What is the selection's thesis? Locate the sentence(s) in which Sherry states her main idea. If she doesn't state the thesis explicitly, express it in your own words.
2. Sherry opens her essay with these words: "Tens of thousands of 18-year-olds will graduate this year and be handed meaningless diplomas." Why does Sherry consider these diplomas meaningless?
3. According to Sherry, what justification do many teachers give for "passing students who have not mastered the work" (paragraph 8)? Why does Sherry think that it is wrong to pass such students?
4. What does Sherry think teachers should do to motivate students to focus on school despite the many "distractions...at hand" (4)?
5. Refer to your dictionary as needed to define the following words used in the selection: *validity* (paragraph 1), *semiliterate* (1), *equivalency* (2), *impediments* (4), *composure* (6), *radical* (6), *priority* (6), *resentful* (7), *testimony* (9), *motivate* (10), *merit* (11), *conspiracy* (11), and *illiteracy* (11).

Questions About the Writer's Craft

1. **The pattern.** To write an effective argumentation-persuasion essay, writers need to establish their credibility. How does Sherry convince readers that she is qualified to write about her subject? What does this attempt to establish credibility say about Sherry's perception of her audience's point of view?
2. Sherry's title is deliberately misleading. What does her title lead you to believe the essay will be about? Why do you think Sherry chose this title?
3. Why do you suppose Sherry quotes her students rather than summarizing what they had to say? What effect do you think Sherry hopes the quotations will have on readers?
4. **Other patterns.** What *example* does Sherry provide to show that the threat of failure can work? How does this example reinforce her case?

Writing Assignments Using Argumentation-Persuasion as a Pattern of Development

1. Like Sherry, write an essay arguing your position on a controversial school-related issue. Possibilities include but need not be limited to the following: College students should *or* should not have to fulfill a physical education requirement; high school students should *or* should not have to demonstrate computer proficiency

before graduating; elementary school students should *or* should not be grouped according to ability; a course in parenting should *or* should not be a required part of the high school curriculum. Once you select a topic, brainstorm with others to gather insight into varying points of view. When you write, restrict your argument to one level of education, and refute as many opposing arguments as you can. The following essays will help you identify educational issues worth writing about: Charles Sykes's "The 'Values' Wasteland" (page 198), William Zinsser's "College Pressures" (page 257), Paul Roberts's "How to Say Nothing in 500 Words" (page 314), Jacques D'Amboise's "Showing What Is Possible" (page 402), and William Raspberry's "The Handicap of Definition" (page 468).

2. Sherry acknowledges that she used to blame students' poor academic skills on "drugs, divorce and other impediments." To what extent should teachers take these and similar "impediments" into account when grading students? Are there certain situations that call for leniency, or should out-of-school forces affecting students not be considered? To gain perspective on this issue, interview several friends, classmates, and instructors. Then write an essay in which you argue your position. Provide specific examples to support your argument, being sure to acknowledge and—when possible—to refute opposing viewpoints.

Writing Assignments Combining Patterns of Development

3. You probably feel, as Sherry does, that Mrs. Stifter is a strong, committed professional. Write an essay *illustrating* the qualities you think a teacher needs to have to be effective. Ask friends, classmates, family members, and instructors for their opinions; however, in your paper, focus on only those attributes you believe are most critical. To highlight the importance of these qualities, begin with a dramatic *contrasting* example of an ineffective teacher—someone who lacks the attributes you consider most important. To gain insight into some of the factors that make teachers effective or ineffective, read Jacques D'Amboise's "Showing What Is Possible" (page 402).
4. Where else, besides in the classroom, do you see people acting irresponsibly, expending little effort, and taking the easy way out? You might consider the workplace, a school-related club or activity, family life, or interpersonal relationships. Select *one* area and write an essay *illustrating* the *effects* of this behavior on everyone concerned. For a broader perspective on the issue of personal responsibility, read Joan Murray's "Someone's Mother" (page 154), Charles Sykes's "The 'Values' Wasteland" (page 198), John M. Darley and Bibb Latané's "When Will People Help in a Crisis?" (page 415), William Raspberry's "The Handicap of Definition" (page 468), and Star Parker's "*Se Habla* Entitlement" (page 564).

Writing Assignment Using a Journal Entry as a Starting Point

5. Write the text for a brochure presenting parents with a step-by-step guide for dealing with academically unmotivated students. Focus your discussion on a specific level of schooling. From your pre-reading journal entry, select those strategies you consider most realistic and productive. When presenting your ideas, take into account children's likely resistance to the strategies described, and instruct parents how to deal with this resistance. Interviewing others (especially parents) and doing some research in the library and/or on the Internet will broaden your understanding of the issues involved.

Wendell Berry

A widely respected American writer, Wendell Berry, born in 1934, earned a B.A. and an M.S. in English from the University of Kentucky, where he returned to teach creative writing for extended periods between 1964 and 1993. In 1965, Berry purchased a farm, Lane's Landing, where he continues to farm to this day. He has published numerous books of poetry and fiction, as well as many essays, primarily on approaches to agriculture, and has won numerous awards for his writing. The following essay is from his collection *Another Turn of the Crank* (1996).

Pre-Reading Journal Entry

Think of areas—for example, education, communications, transportation, and medicine—in which technology has brought about major change. Was the change ultimately positive or negative? In your journal, take some notes on your ideas.

Farming and the Global Economy

We have been repeatedly warned that we cannot know where we wish to go if we do not know where we have been. And so let us start by remembering a little history. 1

As late as World War II, our farms were predominantly solar powered. That is, the work was accomplished principally by human beings and horses and mules. These creatures were empowered by solar energy, which was collected, for the most part, on the farms where they worked and so was pretty cheaply available to the farmer. 2

However, American farms had not become as self-sufficient in fertility as they should have been—or many of them had not. They were still drawing, without sufficient repayment, against an account of natural fertility accumulated over thousands of years beneath the native forest trees and prairie grasses. 3

The agriculture we had at the time of World War II was nevertheless often pretty good, and it was promising. In many parts of our country we had begun to have established agricultural communities, each with its own local knowledge, memory, and tradition. Some of our farming practices had become well adapted to local conditions. The best traditional practices of the Midwest, for example, are still used by the Amish[1] with considerable success in terms of both economy and ecology. 4

Now that the issue of sustainability has arisen so urgently, and in fact so transformingly, we can see that the correct agricultural agenda following World War II would have been to continue and refine the already established connection between our farms and the sun and to correct, where necessary, 5

[1]Members of the Amish Church, a Christian denomination, believe in living simply and avoiding modern technology; Amish farmers typically use horses, rather than tractors, and cow manure, rather than synthetic fertilizers, for farm work (editors' note).

the fertility deficit. There can be no question, now, that that is what we should have done.

It was, notoriously, not what we did. Instead, the adopted agenda called for a shift from the cheap, clean, and, for all practical purposes, limitless energy of the sun to the expensive, filthy, and limited energy of the fossil fuels. It called for the massive use of chemical fertilizers to offset the destruction of topsoil and the depletion of natural fertility. It called also for the displacement of nearly the entire farming population and the replacement of their labor and good farming practices by machines and toxic chemicals. This agenda has succeeded in its aims, but to the benefit of no one and nothing except the corporations that have supplied the necessary machines, fuels, and chemicals—and the corporations that have bought cheap and sold high the products that, as a result of this agenda, have been increasingly expensive for farmers to produce. 6

The farmers have not benefited—not, at least, as a class—for as a result of this agenda they have become one of the smallest and most threatened of all our minorities. Many farmers, sad to say, have subscribed to this agenda and its economic assumptions, believing that they would not be its victims. But millions, in fact, have been its victims—not farmers alone but also their supporters and dependents in our rural communities. 7

The people who benefit from this state of affairs have been at pains to convince us that the agricultural practices and policies that have almost annihilated the farming population have greatly benefited the population of food consumers. But more and more consumers are now becoming aware that our supposed abundance of cheap and healthful food is to a considerable extent illusory. They are beginning to see that the social, ecological, and even the economic costs of such "cheap food" are, in fact, great. They are beginning to see that a system of food production that is dependent on massive applications of drugs and chemicals cannot, by definition, produce "pure food." And they are beginning to see that a kind of agriculture that involves unprecedented erosion and depletion of soil, unprecedented waste of water, and unprecedented destruction of the farm population cannot by any accommodation of sense or fantasy be called "sustainable." 8

From the point of view, then, of the farmer, the ecologist, and the consumer, the need to reform our ways of farming is now both obvious and imperative. We need to adapt our farming much more sensitively to the nature of the places where the farming is done. We need to make our farming practices and our food economy subject to standards set not by the industrial system but by the health of ecosystems and of human communities. 9

The immediate difficulty in even thinking about agricultural reform is that we are rapidly running out of farmers. The tragedy of this decline is not just in its numbers; it is also in the fact that these farming people, assuming we will ever recognize our need to replace them, cannot be replaced anything like as quickly or easily as they have been dispensed with. Contrary to popular assumption, good farmers are not in any simple way part of the "labor force." Good farmers, like good musicians, must be raised to the trade. 10

The severe reduction of our farming population may signify nothing to our national government, but the members of country communities feel the significance of it—and the threat of it—every day. Eventually urban consumers will feel these things, too. Every day farmers feel the oppression of their long-standing problems: overproduction, low prices, and high costs. Farmers sell on a market that because of overproduction is characteristically depressed, and they buy their supplies on a market that is characteristically inflated—which is necessarily a recipe for failure, because farmers do not control either market. If they will not control production and if they will not reduce their dependence on purchased supplies, then they will keep on failing. 11

The survival of farmers, then, requires two complementary efforts. The first is entirely up to the farmers, who must learn—or learn again—to farm in ways that minimize their dependence on industrial supplies. They must diversify, using both plants and animals. They must produce, on their farms, as much of the required fertility and energy as they can. So far as they can, they must replace purchased goods and services with natural health and diversity and with their own intelligence. To increase production by increasing costs, as farmers have been doing for the last half century, is not only unintelligent; it is crazy. If farmers do not wish to cooperate any longer in their own destruction, then they will have to reduce their dependence on those global economic forces that intend and approve and profit from the destruction of farmers, and they will have to increase their dependence on local nature and local intelligence. 12

The second effort involves cooperation between local farmers and local consumers. If farmers hope to exercise any control over their markets, in a time when a global economy and global transportation make it possible for the products of any region to be undersold by the products of any other region, then they will have to look to local markets. The long-broken connections between towns and cities and their surrounding landscapes will have to be restored. There is much promise and much hope in such a restoration. But farmers must understand that this requires an economics of cooperation rather than competition. They must understand also that such an economy sooner or later will require some rational means of production control. 13

If communities of farmers and consumers wish to promote a sustainable, safe, reasonably inexpensive supply of good food, then they must see that the best, the safest, and most dependable source of food for a city is not the global economy, with its extreme vulnerabilities and extravagant transportation costs, but its own surrounding countryside. It is, in every way, in the best interest of urban consumers to be surrounded by productive land, well farmed and well maintained by thriving farm families in thriving farm communities. 14

If a safe, sustainable local food economy appeals to some of us as a goal that we would like to work for, then we must be careful to recognize not only the great power of the interests arrayed against us but also our own weakness. The hope for such a food economy as we desire is represented by no political party and is spoken for by no national public officials of any 15 consequence. Our national political leaders do not know what we are talking about, and they are without the local affections and allegiances that would permit them to learn what we are talking about.

But we should also understand that our predicament is not without precedent; it is approximately the same as that of the proponents of American independence at the time of the Stamp Act—and with one difference in our favor: in order to do the work that we must do, we do not need a national organization. What we must do is simple: we must shorten the distance that our food is transported so that we are eating more and more from local supplies, more and more to the benefit of local farmers, and more and more to the satisfaction of local consumers. This can be done by cooperation among small organizations: conservation groups, churches, neighborhood associations, consumer co-ops, local merchants, local independent banks, and organizations of small farmers. It also can be done by cooperation between individual producers and consumers. We should not be discouraged to find that local food economies can grow only gradually; it is better that they should grow gradually. But as they grow they will bring about a significant return of power, wealth, and health to the people. 16

One thing at least should be obvious to us all: the whole human population of the world cannot live on imported food. Some people somewhere are going to have to grow the food. And wherever food is grown, the growing of it will raise the same two questions: How do you preserve the land in use? And how do you preserve the people who use the land? 17

The farther the food is transported, the harder it will be to answer those questions correctly. The correct answers will not come as the inevitable by-products of the aims, policies, and procedures of international trade, free or unfree. They cannot be legislated or imposed by international or national or state agencies. They can only be supplied locally, by skilled and highly motivated local farmers meeting as directly as possible the needs of informed local consumers. 18

Questions for Close Reading

1. What is the selection's thesis? Locate the sentence(s) in which Berry states his main idea. If he doesn't state his thesis explicitly, express it in your own words.
2. What does Berry think of farming practices up until the first half of the twentieth century? What changes have happened to farming since World War II? What does he say are the negative effects of those changes? How are consumers responding?
3. What does Berry see as the major immediate obstacle to changing the food production system? What two solutions does he offer for overcoming this obstacle?
4. How does Berry suggest his solutions can be implemented? Ultimately, who can supply the correct answers to questions about land use?
5. Refer to your dictionary as needed to define the following words used in the selection: *solar energy* (paragraph 2), *economy* (4), *ecology* (4), *agenda* (5), *sustainability* (5), *fossil fuels* (6), *topsoil* (6), *depletion* (6), *annihilated* (8), *illusory* (8), *erosion* (8), *imperative* (9), *ecosystems* (9), *complementary* (12), *diversify* (12), and *arrayed* (15).

Questions About the Writer's Craft

1. **The pattern.** Do you think the audience for this essay is supportive, wavering, or hostile (see pages 477–478)? What makes you say so? What is the author's purpose?
2. Berry uses two analogies to communicate ideas about farmers and about changing the current food production system. What are those analogies? What do they imply? How valid are they? How effective?
3. **Other patterns.** The author uses comparison-contrast at the beginning of the essay. What does he compare? Give some details of the comparison.
4. The very first word of the essay is "We," and Berry continues to use the third-person plural throughout. Who is "we"? What does Berry accomplish by writing from this point of view? Give some examples of how Berry uses "we."

Writing Assignments Using Argumentation-Persuasion as a Pattern of Development

1. Berry argues that the growth of local food economies will ultimately bring "power, wealth, and health to the people." Think of foods you like that do not grow in your region. Write an essay in which you *argue* that the global food marketplace enhances quality of life by making a wide variety of foods available at low prices. You might visit your local supermarket for examples to support your ideas.
2. The author opposes large agricultural corporations. Yet he also seems against asking "national political leaders" for help. Do some research on the federal regulation of agriculture. Write an essay in which you *argue* for or against additional federal regulation. For what purpose? Include examples to illustrate your points.

Writing Assignments Combining Patterns of Development

3. Some advocates of large-scale mechanized farming say that it enables the production of surplus food that can be sent to poor countries. Do some research about food aid at organizations like the United Nations and the U.S. Department of Agriculture. Write an essay in which you *describe* efforts to relieve hunger worldwide and *categorize* the types of aid programs available. Include statistics and other facts that you uncover.
4. According to the author, good farmers are in short supply. Think of another kind of worker that society could use more of. Write an essay in which you *define* a particular job and explain the *process* involved in training for and becoming good at the job. To see how others have written about work and workers, read Barbara Ehrenreich's "Serving in Florida" (page 162), David Brooks's "Psst! Human Capital" (page 266), or Richard Rodriguez's "Workers" (page 361).

Writing Assignment Using a Journal Entry as a Starting Point

5. Choose one example of major technological change from your journal notes. Write an essay in which you argue for the positive or negative impact of that technology on human society and the environment. Assume that your audience is supportive of your point of view, and end by recommending a course of action.

Mark Twain

Mark Twain is a central figure in American literature. Published in 1884, *The Adventures of Huckleberry Finn,* Twain's finest work, recounts a journey down the Mississippi by two memorable figures: a white boy and a black slave. Twain was born Samuel Langhorne Clemens in 1835 and was raised in Hannibal, Missouri. During his early years, he worked as a riverboat pilot, newspaper reporter, printer, and gold prospector. Although his popular image is as the author of such comic works as *The Adventures of Tom Sawyer* (1876), *Life on the Mississippi* (1883), and *The Prince and the Pauper* (1882), Twain had a darker side that may have resulted from the bitter experiences of his life: financial failure and the deaths of his wife and daughter. His last writings are savage, satiric, and pessimistic. The following selection is taken from *Letters From the Earth,* one of Twain's later works.

Pre-Reading Journal Entry

What would you identify as the major differences between human beings and other animals? What are the similarities? In your journal, list as many items for each as you can, from the obvious to the subtle. Be as specific as you can.

The Damned Human Race

I have been studying the traits and dispositions of the "lower animals" (so-called), and contrasting them with the traits and dispositions of man. I find the result humiliating to me. For it obliges me to renounce my allegiance to the Darwinian theory of the Ascent of Man from the Lower Animals; since it now seems plain to me that the theory ought to be vacated in favor of a new and truer one, this new and truer one to be named the *Descent* of Man from the Higher Animals. 1

In proceeding toward this unpleasant conclusion I have not guessed or speculated or conjectured, but have used what is commonly called the scientific method. That is to say, I have subjected every postulate that presented itself to the crucial test of actual experiment, and have adopted it or rejected it according to the result. Thus I verified and established each step of my course in its turn before advancing to the next. These experiments were made in the London Zoological Gardens, and covered many months of painstaking and fatiguing work. 2

Before particularizing any of the experiments, I wish to state one or two things which seem to more properly belong in this place than further along. This in the interest of clearness. The massed experiments established to my satisfaction certain generalizations, to wit: 3

1. That the human race is of one distinct species. It exhibits slight variations—in color, stature, mental caliber, and so on—due to climate,

environment, and so forth; but it is a species by itself, and not to be confounded with any other.

2. That the quadrupeds are a distinct family, also. This family exhibits variations—in color, size, food preferences and so on; but it is a family by itself.
3. That the other families—the birds, the fishes, the insects, the reptiles, etc.—are more or less distinct, also. They are in the procession. They are links in the chain which stretches down from the higher animals to man at the bottom.

Some of my experiments were quite curious. In the course of my reading I had come across a case where, many years ago, some hunters on our Great Plains organized a buffalo hunt for the entertainment of an English earl—that, and to provide some fresh meat for his larder. They had charming sport. They killed seventy-two of those great animals; and ate part of one of them and left the seventy-one to rot. In order to determine the difference between an anaconda and an earl—if any—I caused seven young calves to be turned into the anaconda's cage. The grateful reptile immediately crushed one of them and swallowed it, then lay back satisfied. It showed no further interest in the calves, and no disposition to harm them. I tried this experiment with other anacondas; always with the same result. The fact stood proven that the difference between an earl and an anaconda is that the earl is cruel and the anaconda isn't; and that the earl wantonly destroys what he has no use for, but the anaconda doesn't. This seemed to suggest that the anaconda was not descended from the earl. It also seemed to suggest that the earl was descended from the anaconda, and had lost a good deal in the transition. 4

I was aware that many men who have accumulated more millions of money than they can ever use have shown a rabid hunger for more, and have not scrupled to cheat the ignorant and the helpless out of their poor servings in order to partially appease that appetite. I furnished a hundred different kinds of wild and tame animals the opportunity to accumulate vast stores of food, but none of them would do it. The squirrels and bees and certain birds made accumulations, but stopped when they had gathered a winter's supply, and could not be persuaded to add to it either honestly or by chicanery. In order to bolster up a tottering reputation the ant pretended to store up supplies, but I was not deceived. I know the ant. These experiments convinced me that there is this difference between man and the higher animals: he is avaricious and miserly, they are not. 5

In the course of my experiments I convinced myself that among the animals man is the only one that harbors insults and injuries, broods over them, waits till a chance offers, then takes revenge. The passion of revenge is unknown to the higher animals. 6

Roosters keep harems, but it is by consent of their concubines; therefore no wrong is done. Men keep harems, but it is by brute force, privileged by atrocious laws which the other sex were allowed no hand in making. In this matter man occupies a far lower place than the rooster. 7

Cats are loose in their morals, but not consciously so. Man, in his descent from the cat, has brought the cat's looseness with him but has left the unconsciousness behind—the saving grace which excuses the cat. The cat is innocent, man is not. 8

Indecency, vulgarity, obscenity—these are strictly confined to man; he invented them. Among the higher animals there is no trace of them. They hide nothing; they are not ashamed. Man, with his soiled mind, covers himself. He will not even enter a drawing room with his breast and back naked, so alive are he and his mates to indecent suggestion. Man is "The Animal that Laughs." But so does the monkey, as Mr. Darwin pointed out; and so does the Australian bird that is called the laughing jackass. No—Man is the Animal that Blushes. He is the only one that does it—or has occasion to. 9

At the head of this article[1] we see how "three monks were burnt to death" a few days ago, and a prior "put to death with atrocious cruelty." Do we inquire into the details? No; or we should find out that the prior was subjected to unprintable mutilations. Man—when he is a North American Indian—gouges out his prisoner's eyes; when he is King John, with a nephew to render untroublesome, he uses a red-hot iron; when he is a religious zealot dealing with heretics in the Middle Ages, he skins his captive alive and scatters salt on his back; in the first Richard's time he shuts up a multitude of Jew families in a tower and sets fire to it; in Columbus's time he captures a family of Spanish Jews and—but *that* is not printable; in our day in England a man is fined ten shillings for beating his mother nearly to death with a chair, and another man is fined forty shillings for having four pheasant eggs in his possession without being able to satisfactorily explain how he got them. Of all the animals, man is the only one that is cruel. He is the only one that inflicts pain for the pleasure of doing it. It is a trait that is not known to the higher animals. The cat plays with the frightened mouse; but she has this excuse, that she does not know that the mouse is suffering. The cat is moderate—unhumanly moderate: she only scares the mouse, she does not hurt it; she doesn't dig out its eyes, or tear off its skin, or drive splinters under its nails—man-fashion; when she is done playing with it she makes a sudden meal of it and puts it out of its trouble. Man is the Cruel Animal. He is alone in that distinction. 10

The higher animals engage in individual fights, but never in organized masses. Man is the only animal that deals in that atrocity of atrocities, 11

[1]Twain originally began his article with newspaper clippings containing telegrams that reported atrocities in Crete (editors' note).

War. He is the only one that gathers his brethren about him and goes forth in cold blood and with calm pulse to exterminate his kind. He is the only animal that for sordid wages will march out, as the Hessians did in our Revolution, and as the boyish Prince Napoleon did in the Zulu war, and help to slaughter strangers of his own species who have done him no harm and with whom he has no quarrel.

Man is the only animal that robs his helpless fellow of his country—takes possession of it and drives him out of it or destroys him. Man has done this in all the ages. There is not an acre of ground on the globe that is in possession of its rightful owner, or that has not been taken away from owner after owner, cycle after cycle, by force and bloodshed. 12

Man is the only Slave. And he is the only animal who enslaves. He has always been a slave in one form or another, and has always held other slaves in bondage under him in one way or another. In our day he is always some man's slave for wages, and does that man's work; and this slave has other slaves under him for minor wages, and they do *his* work. The higher animals are the only ones who exclusively do their own work and provide their own living. 13

Man is the only Patriot. He sets himself apart in his own country, under his own flag, and sneers at the other nations, and keeps multitudinous uniformed assassins on hand at heavy expense to grab slices of other people's countries, and keep *them* from grabbing slices of *his*. And in the intervals between campaigns he washes the blood off his hands and works for "the universal brotherhood of man"—with his mouth. 14

Man is the Religious Animal. He is the only Religious Animal. He is the only animal that has the True Religion—several of them. He is the only animal that loves his neighbor as himself, and cuts his throat if his theology isn't straight. He has made a graveyard of the globe in trying his honest best to smooth his brother's path to happiness and heaven. He was at it in the time of the Caesars, he was at it in Mahomet's time, he was at it in the time of the Inquisition, he was at it in France a couple of centuries, he was at it in England in Mary's day, he has been at it ever since he first saw the light, he is at it today in Crete—as per the telegrams quoted above[2]—he will be at it somewhere else tomorrow. The higher animals have no religion. And we are told that they are going to be left out, in the Hereafter. I wonder why? It seems questionable taste. 15

Man is the Reasoning Animal. Such is the claim. I think it is open to dispute. Indeed, my experiments have proven to me that he is the Unreasoning Animal. Note his history, as sketched above. It seems plain to me that whatever he is he is *not* a reasoning animal. His record is the fantastic record of a maniac. I consider that the strongest count against his intelligence is the 16

[2]See note, page 527 (editors' note).

fact that with that record back of him he blandly sets himself up as the head animal of the lot: whereas by his own standards he is the bottom one.

In truth, man is incurably foolish. Simple things which the other animals easily learn, he is incapable of learning. Among my experiments was this. In an hour I taught a cat and a dog to be friends. I put them in a cage. In another hour I taught them to be friends with a rabbit. In the course of two days I was able to add a fox, a goose, a squirrel and some doves. Finally a monkey. They lived together in peace; even affectionately. 17

Next, in another cage I confined an Irish Catholic from Tipperary, and as soon as he seemed tame I added a Scotch Presbyterian from Aberdeen. Next a Turk from Constantinople; a Greek Christian from Crete; an Armenian; a Methodist from the wilds of Arkansas; a Buddhist from China; a Brahman from Benares. Finally, a Salvation Army Colonel from Wapping. Then I stayed away two whole days. When I came back to note results, the cage of Higher Animals was all right, but in the other, there was but a chaos of gory odds and ends of turbans and fezzes and plaids and bones and flesh—not a specimen left alive. These Reasoning Animals had disagreed on a theological detail and carried the matter to a Higher Court. 18

One is obliged to concede that in true loftiness of character, Man cannot claim to approach even the meanest of the Higher Animals. It is plain that he is constitutionally incapable of approaching that altitude; that he is constitutionally afflicted with a Defect which must make such approach forever impossible, for it is manifest that this defect is permanent in him, indestructible, ineradicable. 19

I find this Defect to be *the Moral Sense.* He is the only animal that has it. It is the secret of his degradation. It is the quality *which enables him to do wrong.* It has no other office. It is incapable of performing any other function. It could never have been intended to perform any other. Without it, man could do no wrong. He would rise at once to the level of the Higher Animals. 20

Since the Moral Sense has but the one office, the one capacity—to enable man to do wrong—it is plainly without value to him. It is as valueless to him as is disease. In fact, it manifestly *is* a disease. *Rabies* is bad, but it is not so bad as this disease. Rabies enables a man to do a thing which he could not do when in a healthy state: kill his neighbor with a poisonous bite. No one is the better man for having rabies: The Moral Sense enables a man to do wrong. It enables him to do wrong in a thousand ways. Rabies is an innocent disease, compared to the Moral Sense. No one, then, can be the better man for having the Moral Sense. What, now, do we find the Primal Curse to have been? Plainly what it was in the beginning: the infliction upon man of the Moral Sense; the ability to distinguish good from evil; and with it, necessarily, the ability to *do* evil; for there can be no evil act without the presence of consciousness of it in the doer of it. 21

And so I find that we have descended and degenerated, from some far ancestor—some microscopic atom wandering at its pleasure between the mighty horizons of a drop of water perchance—insect by insect, animal by animal, reptile by reptile, down the long highway of smirchless innocence, till we have reached the bottom stage of development—namable as the Human Being. Below us—nothing. 22

Questions for Close Reading

1. What is the selection's thesis? Locate the sentence(s) in which Twain states his main idea. If he doesn't state the thesis explicitly, express it in your own words.
2. Because of their intelligence, humans are usually called the highest animal. What, according to Twain, are the specific traits that make humans the lowest animal?
3. How does the story of the earl who hunted down seventy-two buffalo show that an anaconda is superior to an earl?
4. What does Twain mean when he points out that humankind is the only animal that "has occasion to" blush? What are some of the occasions for blushing that he highlights in the essay?
5. Refer to your dictionary as needed to define the following words used in the selection: *confounded* (paragraph 3), *anaconda* (4), *wantonly* (4), *chicanery* (5), *heretics* (10), *constitutionally* (19), *ineradicable* (19), and *smirchless* (22).

Questions About the Writer's Craft

1. **The pattern.** Most writers don't tell the reader outright the reasoning process they used to arrive at their essay's proposition. But Twain claims that he reached his conclusion about human beings inductively—through the use of the "scientific method." Why does Twain make this claim?
2. Where in the essay does Twain try to shock the audience? Why do you think he adopts this technique?
3. **Other patterns.** In some paragraphs, Twain provides numerous *examples* of political and religious atrocities. Why do you suppose he supplies so many examples?
4. Black humor is defined as "the use of the morbid and the absurd for comic purposes." What elements of the morbid and the absurd do you find in Twain's essay? Would you say "The Damned Human Race" is an example of black humor? Explain.

Writing Assignments Using Argumentation-Persuasion as a Pattern of Development

1. In an essay, argue that human beings are worthy of being considered the "highest animal." The paper should acknowledge and then refute Twain's charges that people are miserly, vengeful, foolish, and so on. To support your proposition, use specific examples of how human beings can be kind, caring, generous, and peace-loving.
2. Write an essay agreeing with Twain that it is our everyday meannesses, unkindnesses, and cruelties that make us the "lowest animal." Use compelling examples

to support your argument, including description and dialogue whenever appropriate. You might focus on one of the following topics:

Violence toward children
Abuse of animals
Hurtful sarcasm
Insults of a racial, sexist, or religious nature
Indifference to the unfortunate

Somewhere in the essay, you should acknowledge the view that humans are capable of considerable kindness and compassion. For more perspectives like Twain's, read Stephanie Ericsson's "The Ways We Lie" (page 247) and Stephen King's "Why We Crave Horror Movies" (page 397).

Writing Assignments Combining Patterns of Development

3. What failings of human decency do you see around you every day in your town, on your campus, or at your job? Write an essay *arguing* that inhumanity resides not just in atrocities but also in ordinary acts of indifference. Providing compelling *examples* or *anecdotes* will be crucial as you make your argument. In your essay, you may use Twain's kind of bitter sarcasm, or you may adopt a more objective, less vitriolic tone. You might also read John M. Darley and Bibb Latané's "When Will People Help in a Crisis?" (page 415), another essay specifically exploring the causes of inhumanity.
4. How could humans become less cruel? Write an essay outlining a new *process* for raising children or "re-civilizing" adults—a process that, if instituted, would have a clearly beneficial *effect* on human morality.

Writing Assignment Using a Journal Entry as a Starting Point

5. Write an essay in which, unlike Twain, you illustrate the *similarities* between human beings and other species of animals. Using your pre-reading journal entry, select the most compelling similarities. Try to explore likenesses that go beyond such obvious ones as eating, sleeping, reproduction, etc.; focus instead on behaviors and traits that are elusive but telling. Your essay, which may be humorous or serious, should reveal your attitude toward the similarities you discuss. Do they reflect favorably or negatively on the human species?

Anna Quindlen

Writer Anna Quindlen was born in Philadelphia, Pennsylvania, in 1952, and now lives in New York City. While attending Barnard College, she worked as a copy girl at *The New York Times.* After graduating, Quindlen was a reporter for *The New York Post* before returning to the *Times* in 1977. At the *Times* she eventually became a regular op-ed columnist, winning the Pulitzer Prize for Commentary in 1992. In 1995 Quindlen left newspaper work and devoted herself primarily to fiction. She has written novels, nonfiction, self-help books, and children's books. Quindlen also wrote regularly for *Newsweek,* where this article appeared on June 11, 2007.

Pre-Reading Journal Entry

Getting a driver's license is an important rite of passage for young people in the United States. It's often preceded by a highly stressful process of learning to drive. Recall your own driving lessons and licensing tests. Who taught you to drive? What were the lessons like? What emotions did you experience while learning to drive and taking your driving test? If you do not know how to drive, why not? How do you feel about not having a driver's license? Use your journal to answer these questions.

Driving to the Funeral

The four years of high school grind inexorably to a close, the milestones passed. The sports contests, the SATs, the exams, the elections, the dances, the proms. And too often, the funerals. It's become a sad rite of passage in many American communities, the services held for teenagers killed in auto accidents before they've even scored a tassel to hang from the rearview mirror. The hearse moves in procession followed by the late-model compact cars of young people, boys trying to control trembling lower lips and girls sobbing into one another's shoulders. The yearbook has a picture or two with a black border. A mom and dad rise from their seats on the athletic field or in the gym to accept a diploma posthumously. 1

It's simple and inarguable: car crashes are the No. 1 cause of death among 15- to 20-year-olds in this country. What's so peculiar about that fact is that so few adults focus on it until they are planning an untimely funeral. Put it this way: if someone told you that there was one single behavior that would be most likely to lead to the premature death of your kid, wouldn't you try to do something about that? Yet parents seem to treat the right of a 16-year-old to drive as an inalienable one, something to be neither questioned nor abridged. 2

This makes no sense unless the argument is convenience, and often it is. In a nation that developed mass-transit amnesia and traded the exurb for the small town, a licensed son or daughter relieves parents of a relentless 3 roundelay of driving. Soccer field, Mickey Ds, mall, movies. Of course, if that's the rationale, why not let 13-year-olds drive? Any reasonable person would respond that a 13-year-old is too young. But statistics suggest that that's true of 16-year-olds as well. The National Highway Traffic Safety Administration has found that neophyte drivers of 17 have about a third as many accidents as their counterparts only a year younger.

In 1984 a solution was devised for the problem of teenage auto accidents that lulled many parents into a false sense of security. The drinking age was raised from 18 to 21. It's become gospel that this has saved thousands of lives, although no one actually knows if that's the case; fatalities fell, but the use of seat belts and airbags may have as much to do with that as penalties for alcohol use. And there has been a pronounced negative effect on college campuses, where administrators describe a forbidden-fruit climate that encourages binge drinking. The pitchers of sangria and kegs of beer that offered legal refreshment for 18-year-olds at sanctioned campus events 30 years ago have given way to a new tradition called "pre-gaming," in which dry college activities are preceded by manic alcohol consumption at frats, dorms and bars. 4

Given the incidence of auto-accident deaths among teenagers despite the higher drinking age, you have to ask whether the powerful lobby Mothers Against Drunk Driving simply targeted the wrong D. In a survey of young drivers, only half said they had seen a peer drive after drinking. Nearly all, however, said they had witnessed speeding, which is the leading factor in fatal crashes by teenagers today. In Europe, governments are relaxed about the drinking age but tough on driving regulations and licensing provisions; in most countries, the driving age is 18. 5

In America some states have taken a tough-love position and bumped up the requirements for young drivers: longer permit periods, restrictions or bans on night driving. Since the greatest danger to a teenage driver is another teenager in the car—the chance of having an accident doubles with two teenage passengers and skyrockets with three or more—some new rules forbid novice drivers from transporting their peers. 6

In theory this sounds like a good idea; in fact it's toothless. New Jersey has some of the most demanding regulations for new drivers in the nation, including a provision that until they are 18 they cannot have more than one nonfamily member in the car. Yet in early January three students leaving school in Freehold Township died in a horrific accident in which the car's 17-year-old driver was violating that regulation by carrying two friends. No wonder he took the chance: between July 2004 and November 2006, only 12 provisional drivers were ticketed for carrying too many passengers. Good law, bad enforcement. 7

States might make it easier on themselves, on police officers and on teenagers, too, if instead of chipping away at the right to drive they merely raised the legal driving age wholesale. There are dozens of statistics to back up such a change: in Massachusetts alone, one third of 16-year-old drivers 8 have been involved in serious accidents. Lots and lots of parents will tell you that raising the driving age is untenable, that the kids need their freedom and their mobility. Perhaps the only ones who wouldn't make a fuss are those parents who have accepted diplomas at graduation because their children were no longer alive to do so themselves, whose children traded freedom and mobility for their lives. They might think it was worth the wait.

Questions for Close Reading

1. What is the selection's thesis? Locate the sentence(s) in which Quindlen states her main idea. If she doesn't state her thesis explicitly, express it in your own words.
2. According to Quindlen, what solutions to the problem of teenage auto accidents have not worked over the last twenty five years?
3. What approach to young adults' drinking and driving do European nations take?
4. According to Quindlen, what would be a more effective solution to the problem of teen auto accidents?
5. Refer to your dictionary as needed to define the following words used in the selection: *inexorably* (paragraph 1), *posthumously* (1), *inalienable* (2), *exurb* (3), *roundelay* (3), *neophyte* (3), *sanctioned* (4), *provisional* (7), and *untenable* (8).

Questions About the Writer's Craft

1. **The pattern.** What type of audience—supportive, wavering, or hostile (see page 477–478)—does Quindlen seem to be addressing? How can you tell?
2. **The pattern.** How effective are the statistics in this essay? Use the criteria for sound evidence on pages 32–38 to evaluate Quindlen's use of statistics.
3. **Other patterns.** What other patterns does Quindlen use in this essay? Where? What purpose do these passages serve?
4. **The pattern.** What appeals to *pathos* (see pages 476–478) does Quindlen use? How effective are they?

Writing Assignments Using Argumentation-Persuasion as a Pattern of Development

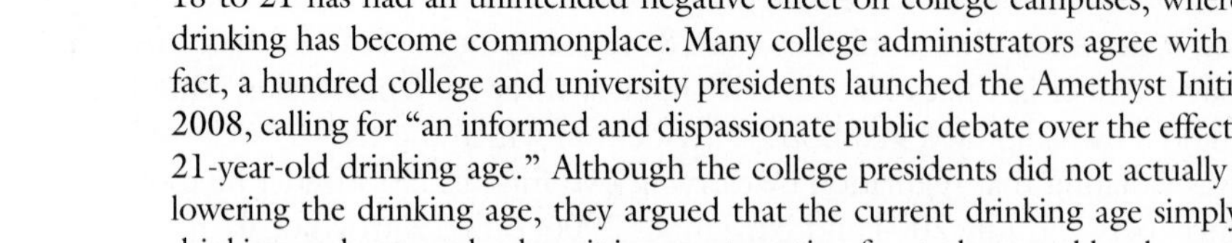

1. In paragraph 4 of her essay, Quindlen claims that raising the drinking age from 18 to 21 has had an unintended negative effect on college campuses, where binge drinking has become commonplace. Many college administrators agree with her. In fact, a hundred college and university presidents launched the Amethyst Initiative in 2008, calling for "an informed and dispassionate public debate over the effects of the 21-year-old drinking age." Although the college presidents did not actually call for lowering the drinking age, they argued that the current drinking age simply drives drinking underground, where it is more tempting for students and harder to control. Do you agree with the college presidents that the current drinking age of 21 should be reexamined and possibly lowered? Or do you disagree? Do some research on the Amethyst Initiative and the drinking age issue, and then write an essay in which you argue that the current drinking age should be lowered or should remain the same. Be sure to support your position with sound evidence (see pages 32–38).

2. Quindlen supports raising the legal driving age in order to decrease teen auto accidents, indicating that the main arguments for a low legal driving age are that it "relieves parents of an endless roundelay of driving" (paragraph 3) and that "the kids need their freedom and their mobility" (paragraph 8). Are there any other reasons that might support a low legal driving age? Write an essay opposing Quindlen's argument for a higher driving age and supporting a legal driving age of 16, with or without restrictions, depending on your view. Be sure to support your argument with reasons and examples.

Writing Assignments Combining Patterns of Development

3. Provisional driver's licenses vary from state to state, but all are designed to decrease teen auto accidents by restricting driving privileges among the youngest drivers and gradually allowing them more freedom as they get older and remain accident-free. Develop your own rules for a fair and effective provisional driver's license, and write a *process analysis* essay explaining your system. Indicate what drivers are allowed to do at various ages until they are granted full driving privileges as well as the penalties you would impose for infractions and accidents, and give *examples* to illustrate the provisions. In support of your plan, explain the beneficial *effects* that your provisional license would have on teen driving.
4. Roadside memorials that mark the sites of fatal auto accidents have become commonplace, as well as controversial, in the last twenty years. Often carefully tended by family and friends of the victim for months or years, the shrines usually consist of flowers, religious symbols, and personal mementos. Some people oppose the memorials, claiming they are dangerous distractions for drivers, obstacles for road crews, or simply illegal displays of religious symbols on public property. Look at the roadside memorials in your area, or do an image search on the Internet. What do the shrines look like? What effect do these shrines have on the victim's family? on strangers? Should they be regulated? Write an essay in which you *describe* the shrines and their effects. In your essay take a position on the memorials and argue that they should be allowed, regulated, or banned. For insights into how people deal with grief and loss, you might read Riverbend's "Bloggers Without Borders" (page 111) or Beth Johnson's "Bombs Bursting in Air" (page 211).

Writing Assignment Using a Journal Entry as a Starting Point

5. Review your pre-reading journal entry in which you describe the people, events, and emotions involved in learning to drive and getting a driver's license—or in *not* learning to drive and *not* getting a driver's license. Write an essay about experiencing—or skipping—this rite of passage. You can write a process analysis essay describing how you got a license, or a cause-effect essay explaining why you didn't get a license, or an exemplification essay in which you describe your best or worst driving lessons. Since this subject has so many possibilities, you should first narrow the focus of the essay and then decide whether you are going to inform, entertain, or persuade your audience and whether your experiences lend themselves to a serious or a humorous tone.

Gerry Garibaldi

Writer and teacher Gerry Garibaldi was born in 1951, grew up in San Francisco, and attended San Francisco State University. Following college, he worked for Paramount Pictures first as a reader and eventually as a vice president of production, which involved working with writers and directors. For the next twenty-five years he worked as an executive, a freelance writer for film studios, and a journalist. Then Garibaldi changed careers, moving to Connecticut, with his wife and children, to teach high school English. This article was published in *City Journal*, an urban policy quarterly, in summer 2006.

Pre-Reading Journal Entry

Think back to your own high school days. Recall how boys and girls were treated in school and how they behaved. Did you notice any differences in the way boys and girls were treated by teachers? In the way they behaved in class? In your journal, record some of the differences between the sexes that you noted. To what extent was your own behavior as a high school student influenced by your gender?

How the Schools Shortchange Boys

In the newly feminized classroom, boys tune out. 1

Since I started teaching several years ago, after 25 years in the movie business, I've come to learn firsthand that everything I'd heard about the feminization of our schools is real—and far more pernicious to boys than I had imagined. Christina Hoff Sommers was absolutely accurate in describing, in her 2000 bestseller, *The War Against Boys*, how feminist complaints that girls were "losing their voice" in a male-oriented classroom have prompted the educational establishment to turn the schools upside down to make them more girl-friendly, to the detriment of males. 2

As a result, boys have become increasingly disengaged. Only 65 percent earned high school diplomas in the class of 2003, compared with 72 percent of girls, education researcher Jay Greene recently documented. Girls now so outnumber boys on most university campuses across the country that some schools, like Kenyon College, have even begun to practice affirmative action for boys in admissions. And as in high school, girls are getting better grades and graduating at a higher rate. 3

As Sommers understood, it is boys' aggressive and rationalist nature—redefined by educators as a behavioral disorder—that's getting so many of them in trouble in the feminized schools. Their problem: they don't want to be girls. 4

Take my tenth-grade student Brandon. I noted that he was on the no-pass list again, after three consecutive days in detention for being disruptive. "Who gave it to you this time?" I asked, passing him on my way out. 5

"Waverly," he muttered into the long folding table. 6

"What for?" 7

"Just asking a question," he replied. 8

"No," I corrected him. "You said"—and here I mimicked his voice—" 'Why do we have to do this crap anyway?' Right?" 9

Brandon recalls one of those sweet, ruby-cheeked boys you often see depicted on English porcelain. 10

He's smart, precocious, and—according to his special-education profile—has been "behaviorally challenged" since fifth grade. The special-ed classification is the bane of the modern boy. To teachers, it's a yellow flag that snaps out at you the moment you open a student's folder. More than any other factor, it has determined Brandon's and legions of other boys' troubled tenures as students. 11

Brandon's current problem began because Ms. Waverly, his social studies teacher, failed to answer one critical question: What was the point of the lesson she was teaching? One of the first observations I made as a teacher was that boys invariably ask this question, while girls seldom do. When a teacher assigns a paper or a project, girls will obediently flip their notebooks open and jot down the due date. Teachers love them. God loves them. Girls are calm and pleasant. They succeed through cooperation. 12

Boys will pin you to the wall like a moth. They want a rational explanation for everything. If unconvinced by your reasons—or if you don't bother to offer any—they slouch contemptuously in their chairs, beat their pencils, or watch the squirrels outside the window. Two days before the paper is due, girls are handing in the finished product in neat vinyl folders with colorful clip-art title pages. It isn't until the boys notice this that the alarm sounds. "Hey, you never told us 'bout a paper! What paper?! I want to see my fucking counselor!" 13

A female teacher, especially if she has no male children of her own, I've noticed, will tend to view boys' penchant for challenging classroom assignments as disruptive, disrespectful—rude. In my experience, notes home and parent-teacher conferences almost always concern a boy's behavior in class, usually centering on this kind of conflict. In today's feminized classroom, with its "cooperative learning" and "inclusiveness," a student's demand for assurance of a worthwhile outcome for his effort isn't met with a reasonable explanation but is considered inimical to the educational process. Yet it's this very trait, innate to boys and men, that helps explain male success in the hard sciences, math, and business. 14

The difference between the male and female predilection for hard proof shows up among the teachers, too. In my second year of teaching, I attended a required seminar on "differentiated instruction," a teaching model that is the current rage in the fickle world of pop education theory. The method addresses the need to teach all students in a classroom where academic abilities vary greatly—where there is "heterogeneous grouping," to use the ed-school jargon—meaning kids with IQs of 55 sit side by side with the gifted. The theory goes that the "least restrictive environment" is best for helping the intellectually 15 challenged. The teacher's job is to figure out how to dice up his daily lessons to address every perceived shortcoming and disability in the classroom.

After the lecture, we broke into groups of five, with instructions to work cooperatively to come up with a model lesson plan for just such a classroom situation. My group had two men and three women. The women immediately set to work; my seasoned male cohort and I reclined sullenly in our chairs. 16

"Are the women going to do all the work?" one of the women inquired brightly after about ten minutes. 17

"This is baloney," my friend declared, yawning, as he chucked the seminar handout into a row of empty plastic juice bottles. "We wouldn't have this problem if we grouped kids by ability, like we used to." 18

The women, all dedicated teachers, understood this, too. But that wasn't the point. Treating people as equals was a social goal well worth pursuing. And we contentious boys were just too dumb to get it. 19

Female approval has a powerful effect on the male psyche. Kindness, consideration, and elevated moral purpose have nothing to do with an irreducible proof, of course. Yet we male teachers squirm when women point out our moral failings—and our boy students do, too. This is the virtue that has helped women redefine the mission of education. 20

The notion of male ethical inferiority first arises in grammar school, where women make up the overwhelming majority of teachers. It's here that the alphabet soup of supposed male dysfunctions begins. And make no mistake: while girls occasionally exhibit symptoms of male-related disorders in this world, females diagnosed with learning disabilities simply don't exist. 21

For a generation now, many well-meaning parents, worn down by their boy's failure to flourish in school, his poor self-esteem and unhappiness, his discipline problems, decide to accept administration recommendations to have him tested for disabilities. The pitch sounds reasonable: admission into special ed qualifies him for tutoring, modified lessons, extra time on tests (including the SAT), and other supposed benefits. It's all a hustle, Mom and Dad privately advise their boy. Don't worry about it. We know there's nothing wrong with you. 22

To get into special ed, however, administrators must find something wrong. In my four years of teaching, I've never seen them fail. In the first IEP (Individualized Educational Program) meeting, the boy and his parents learn the results of disability testing. When the boy hears from three smiling adults that he does indeed have a learning disability, his young face quivers like Jell-O. For him, it was never a hustle. From then on, however, his expectations of himself—and those of his teachers—plummet. 23

Special ed is the great spangled elephant in the education parade. Each year, it grows larger and more lumbering, drawing more and more boys into the procession. Since the publication of Sommers's book, it has grown tenfold. Special ed now is the single largest budget item, outside of basic operations, in most school districts across the country. 24

Special-ed boosters like to point to the success that boys enjoy after they begin the program. Their grades rise, and the phone calls home cease. Anxious parents feel reassured that progress is happening. In truth, I have rarely seen any real improvement in a student's performance after he's become a special-ed kid. On my first day of teaching, I received manila folders for all five of my special-ed students—boys all—with a score of modifications that I had to make in each day's lesson plan. 25

I noticed early on that my special-ed boys often sat at their desks with their heads down or casually staring off into space, as if tracking motes in their eyes, while I proceeded with my lesson. A special-ed caseworker would arrive, take their assignments, and disappear with the boys into the resource room. The students would return the next day with completed assignments. 26

"Did you do this yourself?" I'd ask, dubious. 27

They assured me that they did. I became suspicious, however, when I noticed that they couldn't perform the same work on their own, away from the resource room. A special-ed caseworker's job is to keep her charges from failing. A failure invites scrutiny and reams of paperwork. The caseworkers do their jobs. 28

Brandon has been on the special-ed track since he was nine. He knows his legal rights as well as his caseworkers do. And he plays them ruthlessly. In every debate I have with him about his low performance, Brandon delicately threads his response with the very sinews that bind him. After a particularly easy midterm, I made him stay after class to explain his failure. 29

"An 'F'?!" I said, holding the test under his nose. 30

"You were supposed to modify that test," he countered coolly. "I only had to answer nine of the 27 questions. The nine I did are all right." 31

His argument is like a piece of fine crystal that he rolls admiringly in his hand. He demands that I appreciate the elegance of his position. I do, particularly because my own is so weak. 32

Yet while the process of education may be deeply absorbing to Brandon, he long ago came to dismiss the content entirely. For several decades, white Anglo-Saxon males—Brandon's ancestors—have faced withering assault from feminism- and multiculturalism-inspired education specialists. Armed with a spiteful moral rectitude, their goal is to sever his historical reach, to defame, cover over, dilute . . . and then reconstruct. 33

In today's politically correct textbooks, Nikki Giovanni and Toni Morrison stand shoulder-to-shoulder with Mark Twain, William Faulkner, and Charles Dickens, even though both women are second-raters at best. But even in their superficial aspects, the textbooks advertise publishers' intent to pander to the prevailing PC[1] attitudes. The books feature page after page of healthy, exuberant young girls in winning portraits. Boys (white 34

[1]Short for "politically correct," usually used pejoratively (editors' note).

boys in particular) will more often than not be shunted to the background in photos or be absent entirely or appear sitting in wheelchairs.

35 The underlying message isn't lost on Brandon. His keen young mind reads between the lines and perceives the folly of all that he's told to accept. Because he lacks an adult perspective, however, what he cannot grasp is the ruthlessness of the war that the education reformers have waged. Often when he provokes, it's simple boyish tit for tat.

36 A week ago, I dispatched Brandon to the library with directions to choose a book for his novel assignment. He returned minutes later with his choice and a twinkling smile.

37 "I got a grreat book, Mr. Garibaldi!" he said, holding up an old, bleary, clothbound item. "Can I read the first page aloud, pahlease?"

38 My mind buzzed like a fly, trying to discover some hint of mischief.

39 "Who's the author?"

40 "Ah, Joseph Conrad," he replied, consulting the frontispiece. "Can I? Huh, huh, huh?"

41 "I guess so."

42 Brandon eagerly stood up before the now-alert class of mostly black and Puerto Rican faces, adjusted his shoulders as if straightening a prep-school blazer, then intoned solemnly: "*The Nigger of the 'Narcissus'*"—twinkle, twinkle, twinkle. "Chapter one...."

43 Merry mayhem ensued. Brandon had one of his best days of the year.

44 Boys today feel isolated and outgunned, but many, like Brandon, don't lack pluck and courage. They often seem to have more of it than their parents, who writhe uncomfortably before a system steeled in the armor of "social conscience." The game, parents whisper to themselves, is to play along, to maneuver, to outdistance your rival. Brandon's struggle is an honest one: to preserve truth and his own integrity.

45 Boys who get a compartment on the special-ed train take the ride to its end without looking out the window. They wait for the moment when they can step out and scorn the rattletrap that took them nowhere. At the end of the line, some, like Brandon, may have forged the resiliency of survival. But that's not what school is for.

Questions for Close Reading

1. What is the selection's thesis? Locate the sentence(s) in which Garibaldi states his main idea. If he doesn't state his thesis explicitly, express it in your own words.
2. According to Garibaldi, how do boys and girls—and men and women—react to being given an assignment?

3. Why are so many boys tested for disabilities, according to Garibaldi?
4. How does Garibaldi's student Brandon take advantage of his special education designation?
5. Refer to your dictionary as needed to define the following words used in the selection: *pernicious* (paragraph 1), *disengaged* (2), *rationalist* (4), *precocious* (11), *bane* (11), *penchant* (14), *inimical* (14), *predilection* (15), *heterogeneous* (15), *cohort* (16), *contentious* (19), *irreducible* (20), *plummet* (23), *motes* (26), *withering* (33), *rectitude* (33), *pander* (34), *resiliency* (45).

Questions About the Writer's Craft

1. **The pattern.** What types of evidence does Garibaldi use in this essay? How effective is his evidence in supporting his argument?
2. **Other patterns.** Garibaldi uses a lot of cause-effect, comparison-contrast, and process analysis in this essay. Identify passages in which these patterns are used.
3. The first sentence in the essay is a strongly worded declaration: "In the newly feminized classroom, boys tune out." Where else does Garibaldi use such strongly worded statements? What is the effect of this style?
4. Where does Garibaldi use vulgar or offensive language? What effect, if any, does this have on his argument?

Writing Assignments Using Argumentation-Persuasion as a Pattern of Development

1. Read Michael Kimmel's "A War Against Boys?" (page 543), an essay that takes exception to Garibaldi's view of boys' education. Decide which writer presents his case more convincingly. Then write an essay arguing that the *other writer* has trouble making a strong case for his position. Consider the merits and flaws (including any logical fallacies) in the argument, plus such issues as the writer's credibility, strategies for dealing with the opposing view, and use of emotional appeals. Throughout, support your opinion with specific examples drawn from the selection. Keep in mind that you are critiquing the effectiveness of the writer's argument. It's not appropriate, then, simply to explain why you agree or disagree with the writer's position or merely to summarize what the writer says.
2. Although Garibaldi argues forcefully that boys are shortchanged by the "feminization" of education and the special education system, he does not propose any changes to improve the way boys are educated. How might public elementary, middle, and high school education be changed so that boys flourish? What activities or subjects would help boys in school? Using Garibaldi's essay as a take-off point, write an essay in which you argue for changes in education that would benefit boys.

Writing Assignments Combining Patterns of Development

3. As Garibaldi puts it, "Special ed is the great spangled elephant in the education parade." He is correct in asserting that the number of children in special education, and the amount spent to educate them, have increased dramatically in recent

years. Brainstorm with others to identify *factors* that might be contributing to this growth; then do some research on the history of special education and current trends. Focusing on several related factors, write an essay showing how these factors contribute to the problem. Possible factors include the following: increases in the number of diagnoses of learning disabilities and autism; lack of standards for determining who needs special education; assigning all low-achieving students to special education whether or not they have a disability; racism; financial incentives for school districts to increase special education enrollment. At the end of the essay, offer some recommendations about *steps* that can be taken to ensure that only children who need it are assigned to special education.

4. In paragraph 34, Garibaldi refers to "politically correct textbooks" and "PC attitudes." What does the phrase "politically correct" mean to you? What are its connotations? Write an essay in which you *define* "political correctness." Be sure to give examples to support your definition. Before you start, decide whether the purpose of your essay is to inform, persuade, or entertain, and approach your definition accordingly. You might find that Amy Tan's "Mother Tongue" (page 270) has interesting insights about how we use language.

Writing Assignment Using a Journal Entry as a Starting Point

5. Review your pre-reading journal entry about differences between how boys and girls were treated in high school, and how they behaved. How do your recollections compare with Garibaldi's observations? Do they support his position, or undermine it? Write an essay in which you summarize and respond to Garibaldi's argument based on your own experiences and observations of high school. Be sure to give specific examples of your points.

Michael Kimmel

Michael Kimmel is a professor of sociology at State University of New York at Stonybrook and one of the world's leading researchers in gender studies. Born in New York City in 1951, he attended Vassar College and received a master's degree from Brown University and a Ph.D. from the University of California at Berkeley. He is the author or editor of more than twenty volumes on men and masculinity, including *Manhood in America: A Cultural History* (1996) and his latest work, *Guyland: The Perilous World Where Boys Become Men* (2008). His articles appear in dozens of magazines, newspapers, and scholarly journals, and he lectures extensively. The following piece was excerpted from an article published in the Fall 2006 issue of *Dissent Magazine*.

Pre-Reading Journal Entry

The phrase "boys will be boys" is often cited to explain certain types of male behavior. What kinds of actions typically fall in this category? List a few of them in your journal. Which behaviors are positive? Why? Which are negative? Why?

A War Against Boys?

Doug Anglin isn't likely to flash across the radar screen at an Ivy League admissions office. A seventeen-year-old senior at Milton High School, a suburb outside Boston, Anglin has a B-minus average and plays soccer and baseball. But he's done something that millions of other teenagers haven't: he's sued his school district for sex discrimination. 1

Anglin's lawsuit, brought with the aid of his father, a Boston lawyer, claims that schools routinely discriminate against males. "From the elementary level, they establish a philosophy that if you sit down, follow orders, and listen to what they say, you'll do well and get good grades," he told a journalist. "Men naturally rebel against this." He may have a point: overworked teachers might well look more kindly on classroom docility and decorum. But his proposed remedies—such as raising boys' grades retroactively—are laughable. 2

And though it's tempting to parse the statements of a mediocre high school senior—what's so "natural" about rebelling against blindly following orders, a military tactician might ask—Anglin's apparent admissions angle is but the latest skirmish of a much bigger battle in the culture wars. The current salvos concern boys. The "trouble with boys" has become a staple on talk-radio, the cover story in *Newsweek*, and the subject of dozens of columns in newspapers and magazines. And when the First Lady offers a helping hand to boys, you know something political is in the works. "Rescuing" boys actually translates into bashing feminism. 3

There is no doubt that boys are not faring well in school. From elementary schools to high schools they have lower grades, lower class rank, and 4 fewer honors than girls. They're 50 percent more likely to repeat a grade in elementary school, one-third more likely to drop out of high school, and about six times more likely to be diagnosed with attention deficit and hyperactivity disorder (ADHD).

College statistics are similar—if the boys get there at all. Women now constitute the majority of students on college campuses, having passed men in 1982, so that in eight years women will earn 58 percent of bachelor's degrees in U.S. colleges. One expert, Tom Mortensen, warns that if current trends continue, "the graduation line in 2068 will be all females." Mortensen may be a competent higher education policy analyst, but he's a lousy statistician. His dire prediction is analogous to predicting forty years ago that, if the enrollment of black students at Ol' Miss was one in 1964, and, say, two hundred in 1968 and one thousand in 1976, then "if present trends continue" there would be no white students on campus by 1982. Doomsayers lament that women now outnumber men in the social and behavioral sciences by about three to one, and that they've invaded such traditionally male bastions as engineering (where they now make up 20 percent) and biology and business (virtually par). 5

These three issues—declining numbers, declining achievement, and increasingly problematic behavior—form the empirical basis of the current debate. But its political origins are significantly older and ominously more familiar. Peeking underneath the empirical façade helps explain much of the current lineup. 6

Why now? 7

If boys are doing worse, whose fault is it? To many of the current critics, it's women's fault, either as feminists, as mothers, or as both. Feminists, we read, have been so successful that the earlier "chilly classroom climate" has now become overheated to the detriment of boys. Feminist-inspired programs have enabled a whole generation of girls to enter the sciences, medicine, law, and the professions; to continue their education; to imagine careers outside the home. But in so doing, these same feminists have pathologized boyhood. Elementary schools are, we read, "anti-boy"—emphasizing reading and restricting the movements of young boys. They "feminize" boys, forcing active, healthy, and naturally exuberant boys to conform to a regime of obedience, "pathologizing what is simply normal for boys," as one psychologist puts it. Schools are an "inhospitable" environment for boys, writes Christina Hoff Sommers, where their natural propensities for rough-and-tumble play, competition, aggression, and rambunctious violence are cast as social problems in the making. Michael Gurian argues in *The Wonder of Boys,* that, with testosterone surging through their little limbs, we demand that they sit still, raise their hands, and take naps. We're giving them the message, he says, that "boyhood is defective." By the time they get to college, they've been steeped in anti-male propaganda. "Why would any 8 self-respecting boy want to attend one of America's increasingly feminized universities?" asks George Gilder in *National Review*. The American university is now a "fluffy pink playpen of feminist studies and agitprop 'herstory,' taught amid a green goo of eco-motherism..." [author's ellipsis].

Such claims sound tinnily familiar. At the turn of the last century, cultural critics were concerned that the rise of white-collar businesses meant increasing indolence for men, whose sons were being feminized by mothers and female teachers. Then, as now, the solutions were to find arenas in which boys could simply be boys, and where men could be men as well. So fraternal lodges offered men a homo-social sanctuary, and dude ranches and sports provided a place where these sedentary men could experience what Theodore Roosevelt called the strenuous life. Boys could troop off with the Boy Scouts, designed as a fin-de-siècle "boys' liberation movement." Modern society was turning hardy, robust boys, as Boy Scouts' founder Ernest Thompson Seton put it, into "a lot of flat chested cigarette smokers with shaky nerves and doubtful vitality." Today, women teachers are once again to blame for boys' feminization. "It's the teacher's job to create a classroom environment that accommodates both male and female energy, not just mainly female energy," explains Gurian. 9

What's wrong with this picture? Well, for one thing, it creates a false opposition between girls and boys, assuming that educational reforms undertaken to enable girls to perform better hinder boys' educational development. But these reforms—new classroom arrangements, teacher training, increased attentiveness to individual learning styles—actually enable larger numbers of boys to get a better education. Though the current boy advocates claim that schools used to be more "boy friendly" before all these "feminist" reforms, they obviously didn't go to school in those halcyon days, the 1950s, say, when the classroom was far more regimented, corporal punishment common, and teachers far more authoritarian; they even gave grades for "deportment." Rambunctious boys were simply not tolerated; they dropped out. 10

Gender stereotyping hurts both boys and girls. If there is a zero-sum game, it's not because of some putative feminization of the classroom. The net effect of the No Child Left Behind Act has been zero-sum competition, as school districts scramble to stretch inadequate funding, leaving them little choice but to cut noncurricular programs so as to ensure that curricular mandates are followed. This disadvantages "rambunctious" boys, because many of these programs are after-school athletics, gym, and recess. And cutting "unnecessary" school counselors and other remedial programs also disadvantages boys, who compose the majority of children in behavioral and remedial educational programs. The problem of inadequate school funding lies not at feminists' door, but in the halls of Congress. This is further compounded by changes in the insurance industry, which often pressure therapists to put children on medication for ADHD rather than pay for expensive therapy. 11

Another problem is that the frequently cited numbers are misleading. More people—that is, males and females—are going to college than ever before. In 1960, 54 percent of boys and 38 percent of girls went directly to college; today the numbers are 64 percent of boys and 70 percent of girls. It is true that the rate of increase among girls is higher than the rate of increase among boys, but the numbers are increasing for both. 12

The gender imbalance does not obtain at the nation's most elite colleges and universities, where percentages for men and women are, and have remained, similar. Of the top colleges and universities in the nation, only Stanford sports a fifty-fifty gender balance. Harvard[1] and Amherst enroll 56 percent men, Princeton and Chicago 54 percent men, Duke and Berkeley 52 percent, and Yale 51 percent. In science and engineering, the gender imbalance still tilts decidedly toward men: Cal Tech is 65 percent male and 35 percent female; MIT is 62 percent male, 38 percent female. 13

And the imbalance is not uniform across class and race. It remains the case that far more working-class women—of all races—go to college than do working-class men. Part of this is a seemingly rational individual decision: a college-educated woman still earns about the same as a high-school educated man, \$35,000 to \$31,000. By race, the disparities are more starkly drawn. Among middle-class, white, high school graduates going to college this year, half are male and half are female. But only 37 percent of black college students and 45 percent of Hispanic students are male. The numerical imbalance turns out to be more a problem of race and class than gender. It is what Cynthia Fuchs Epstein calls a "deceptive distinction"—a difference that appears to be about gender, but is actually about something else. 14

Why don't the critics acknowledge these race and class differences? To many who now propose to "rescue" boys, such differences are incidental because, in their eyes, all boys are the same aggressive, competitive, rambunctious little devils. They operate from a facile, and inaccurate, essentialist dichotomy between males and females. Boys must be allowed to be boys—so that they grow up to be men. 15

This facile biologism leads the critics to propose some distasteful remedies to allow these testosterone-juiced boys to express themselves. Gurian, for example, celebrates all masculine rites of passage, "like military boot camp, fraternity hazings, graduation day, and bar mitzvah" as "essential parts of every boy's life." He also suggests reviving corporal punishment, both at home and at school—but only when administered privately with cool indifference and never in the heat of adult anger. He calls it "spanking responsibly," though I suspect school boards and child welfare agencies might have another term for it. 16

[1]Harvard University now enrolls more women than men (author's note).

But what boys need turns out to be pretty much what girls need. In their best-selling *Raising Cain,* Michael Thompson and Dan Kindlon describe boys' needs: to be loved, get sex, and not be hurt. Parents are counseled to allow boys their emotions; accept a high level of activity; speak their language; and treat them with respect. They are to teach the many ways a boy can be a man, use discipline to guide and build, and model manhood as emotionally attached. Aside from the obvious tautologies, what they advocate is exactly what feminists have been advocating for girls for some time.... 17

How does a focus on the ideology of masculinity explain what is happening to boys in school? Consider the parallel for girls. Carol Gilligan's work on adolescent girls describes how these assertive, confident, and proud young girls "lose their voices" when they hit adolescence. At that same moment, Pollack[2] notes, boys become more confident, even beyond their abilities. You might even say that boys find their voices, but it is the inauthentic voice of bravado, posturing, foolish risk-taking, and gratuitous violence. He calls it "the boy code." The boy code teaches them that they are supposed to be in power, and so they begin to act as if they are. They "ruffle in a manly pose," as William Butler Yeats[3] once put it, "for all their timid heart." 18

In adolescence, both boys and girls get their first real dose of gender inequality: girls suppress ambition, boys inflate it. Recent research on the gender gap in school achievement bears this out. Girls are more likely to undervalue their abilities, especially in the more traditionally "masculine" educational arenas such as math and science. Only the most able and most secure girls take courses in those fields. Thus, their numbers tend to be few, and their mean test scores high. Boys, however, possessed of this false voice of bravado (and facing strong family pressure) are likely to overvalue their abilities, to remain in programs though they are less capable of succeeding. 19

This difference, and not some putative discrimination against boys, is the reason that girls' mean test scores in math and science are now, on average, approaching that of boys. Too many boys remain in difficult math and science courses longer than they should; they pull the boys' mean scores down. By contrast, the smaller number of girls, whose abilities and self-esteem are sufficient to enable them to "trespass" into a male domain, skew female data upward. 20

A parallel process is at work in the humanities and social sciences. Girls' mean test scores in English and foreign languages, for example, outpace those of boys. But this is not the result of "reverse discrimination"; it is because the boys bump up against the norms of masculinity. Boys regard English as a "feminine" subject. Pioneering research by Wayne Martino in Australia and Britain found that boys avoid English because of what it might 21

[2]William Pollack, author of *Real Boys* (editors' note).

[3]Yeats (1865–1939) was a major Irish poet and playwright (editors' note).

say about their (inauthentic) masculine pose. "Reading is lame, sitting down and looking at words is pathetic," commented one boy. "Most guys who like English are faggots." The traditional liberal arts curriculum, as it was before feminism, is seen as feminizing. As Catharine Stimpson[4] recently put it, "Real men don't speak French."

Boys tend to hate English and foreign languages for the same reasons that girls love them. In English, they observe, there are no hard-and-fast rules, one expresses one's opinion about the topic and everyone's opinion is equally valued. "The answer can be a variety of things, you're never really wrong," observed one boy. "It's not like maths and science where there is one set answer to everything." Another boy noted: 22

> I find English hard. It's because there are no set rules for reading texts . . . [author's ellipsis]. English isn't like maths where you have rules on how to do things and where there are right and wrong answers. In English you have to write down how you feel and that's what I don't like. 23

Compare this to the comments of girls in the same study: 24

> I feel motivated to study English because . . . [author's ellipsis] you have freedom in English—unlike subjects such as maths and science—and your view isn't necessarily wrong. There is no definite right or wrong answer, and you have the freedom to say what you feel is right without it being rejected as a wrong answer. 25

It is not the school experience that "feminizes" boys, but rather the ideology of traditional masculinity that keeps boys from wanting to succeed. "The work you do here is girls' work," one boy commented to a researcher. "It's not real work." 26

"Real work" involves a confrontation—not with feminist women, whose sensible educational reforms have opened countless doors to women while closing off none to men—but with an anachronistic definition of masculinity that stresses many of its vices (anti-intellectualism, entitlement, arrogance, and aggression) but few of its virtues. When the self-appointed rescuers demand that we accept boys' "hardwiring," could they possibly have such a monochromatic and relentlessly negative view of male biology? Maybe they do. But simply shrugging our collective shoulders in resignation and saying "boys will be boys" sets the bar much too low. Boys can do better than that. They can be men. 27

[4]Stimpson, a professor of English at New York University, has written about women in culture and society (editors' note).

Perhaps the real "male bashers" are those who promise to rescue boys from the clutches of feminists. Are males not also "hardwired" toward compassion, nurturing, and love? If not, would we allow males to be parents? It is never a biological question of whether we are "hardwired" for some behavior; it is, rather, a political question of which "hardwiring" we choose to respect and which we choose to challenge.... 28

Questions for Close Reading

1. What is the selection's thesis? Locate the sentence(s) in which Kimmel states his main idea. If he doesn't state his thesis explicitly, express it in your own words.
2. How does Kimmel interpret the statistics that show that more girls than boys go to college?
3. According to Kimmel, how do girls and boys change when they reach adolescence?
4. What does Kimmel mean by the phrase " 'the boy code' " (paragraph 18)?
5. Refer to your dictionary as needed to define the following words used in the selection: *docility* (paragraph 2), *parse* (3), *bastions* (5), *par* (5), *pathologized* (8), *indolence* (9), *sedentary* (9), *halcyon* (10), *deportment* (10), *rambunctious* (10), *zero-sum* (11), *putative* (11), *facile* (15), *biologism* (16), *tautologies* (17), and *anachronistic* (27).

Questions About the Writer's Craft

1. **The pattern.** What strategy does Kimmel use in the opening paragraphs of his essay? Is it effective?
2. **The pattern.** What is the purpose of paragraphs 4–6? Paragraphs 7–9? Where does Kimmel start presenting his own view of the causes of boys' difficulty in school?
3. **Other patterns.** What is the main pattern, other than argumentation-persuasion, that is used in this essay? Give specific examples.
4. Reread the biographical sketch of Kimmel on page 543. How does Kimmel's background contribute to the *ethos* of this argument? Does it influence your response to his claims?

Writing Assignments Using Argumentation-Persuasion as a Pattern of Development

1. Both Garibaldi and Kimmel focus primarily on how gender inequality affects boys, but gender inequality affects girls as well (see Kimmel, paragraphs 19 and following). Write an essay in which you argue that gender roles and norms limit (or do not limit) what women can accomplish in school and in their careers. For some perspective on the role of women in society, read Barbara Ehrenreich's "Serving in Florida" (page 162).
2. Kimmel criticizes those who claim that biology, or inborn traits, are primarily responsible for shaping gender differences. He believes that biological differences may exist, but that the environment, including political and cultural forces, have

a strong influence. Write an essay arguing your own position about the role that biology and environment play in determining sex-role attitudes and behaviors. Remember to acknowledge opposing views and to defend your own position with examples based on your experiences and observations. Amy Sutherland's "What Shamu Taught Me About a Happy Marriage" (page 308) and Dave Barry's "Beauty and the Beast" (page 368) may give you some humorous insights on this subject.

Writing Assignments Combining Patterns of Development

3. Feminism is mentioned throughout Garibaldi's and Kimmel's essays, but neither of them defines the term. Do some research in the library and/or on the Internet about the history of feminism. Brainstorm with others—both men and women—about the topic, and write an essay in which you *define* feminism. Be sure to give *examples* of what you mean by feminism, either from your own experience or from history.
4. According to Kimmel, gender differences become more defined during adolescence, when the "boy code"—and, correspondingly, the "girl code"—begin to influence attitudes and behaviors. Look back on your own adolescence and your experiences of gender differences, and write an essay in which you *describe* the "boy code" and the "girl code" and how they affected you and your friends. *Compare and contrast* boys' and girls' attitudes and behaviors, and give *examples* to support your points.

Writing Assignment Using a Journal Entry as a Starting Point

5. In paragraph 27, Kimmel says, "Saying 'boys will be boys' sets the bar much too low. Boys can do better than that. They can be men." Kimmel clearly believes that "boys will be boys" behavior should be discouraged; yet others believe such behavior is natural and therefore acceptable. What do you think? Drawing upon your pre-reading journal entry, write an essay taking a position on this issue. Provide persuasive examples to support your viewpoint, refuting as much of the opposing argument as you can. Discussing this type of gendered behavior with others and doing some research in the library and/or on the Internet will broaden your understanding of this issue.

Alexander T. Tabarrok

Canadian economist Alexander Tabarrok, born in 1966, received his Ph.D. from George Mason University. He is an associate professor of economics at George Mason University and holds the Bartley J. Madden Chair in Economics at the Mercatus Center. He has also taught at the University of Virginia and Ball State University. Tabarrok's writings on a range of economic issues have appeared in the *Journal of Law and Economics, Public Choice, Economic Inquiry, Journal of Health Economics, Journal of Theoretical Politics, The American Law and Economics Review,* and *Kyklos* as well as in magazines and newspapers. He is research director for The Independent Institute, a public policy research group, and assistant editor of the organization's *Independent Review*. The following selection appeared as a *Newsroom* article on the Independent Institute's website on February 19, 2001.

Pre-Reading Journal Entry

How persuasive do you find economic principles? In your own life, do you tend to make decisions on a financial basis or do you have other criteria for making decisions? What kinds of decisions are these? Jot down some notes in your journal on these ideas.

A Moral Solution to the Organ Shortage

Thousands of people will die this year while they wait helplessly for an organ transplant. Tragically, these deaths could be avoided if only more people signed their organ donor cards. Yet every year the organ shortage tends to become worse as medical technology increases the number of potential beneficiaries while social apathy and fear keep the number of donors relatively constant. Today, roughly 60,000 people are waiting for organ transplants, while less than 10,000 will become donors. Despite a prominent advertising campaign with Michael Jordan as spokesperson, and a national campaign of pastors, rabbis and other clergy supporting donation, the supply of donors remains far below that necessary to save everyone on the waiting list. 1

Nobel Prize–winning economist Gary Becker has suggested that one possible solution to the crisis is to increase the incentive to donate organs by paying donors. One system, for example, would let organ procurement organizations pay the funeral expenses of organ donors. 2

Economists argue that anytime the price of a good or service is held below its market demand, a shortage develops. Just as government-mandated rent controls imposed in New York and other cities have led to a shortage of housing, government rules that outlaw buying or selling organs on the open market hold the price of organs at zero and make an organ shortage inevitable. Lift the restrictions, Becker and others say, and the shortage will end. 3

To some, this analysis may sound shocking, but these ideas are now so familiar to economists that at least one well-known textbook—Pindyck and Rubinfeld's *Microeconomics*—uses the organ shortage to illustrate the effect of price controls more generally. Nonetheless, many people may still be uncomfortable with the idea of human organs for sale. And for better or worse, few politicians are likely to take up the banner of laissez-faire when it comes to human organs. Fortunately, there is another possible solution. 4

I propose that the United Network for Organ Sharing (UNOS) consider restricting organ transplants to those who previously agreed to be organ donors; in short, a "no-give no-take" rule. While it is understandable that some people may have misgivings about becoming donors for personal or religious reasons, why should someone who was not willing to give an organ be allowed to take an organ? 5

Signing your organ donor card should be thought of as entry into a club, the club of potential organ recipients. Current UNOS policy is that organs are a "national resource." This is wrong. Organs should be the resource of potential organ donors, and signing an organ donor card should be tantamount to buying insurance. Being willing to give up an organ, should it no longer be of use to you, is the premium to be paid for the right to receive someone else's organ if one of yours fails. 6

How would the "no-give no-take" rule work in practice? Anyone could sign an organ donor card at any time and be registered as a potential donor. Most people would sign their cards when they receive their driver's license, as occurs today. Children would be automatically eligible to receive organs until the age of 16, when they would have the option of signing their card. To prevent someone from signing after learning they were in need, there would be a mandatory waiting period of at least one year before the right to receive an organ took effect. 7

Organs are now allocated on the basis of a point system in which medical need, the probability that the transplant would be effective, and the length of time already spent on the waiting list all play a role. A modest version of the "no-give no-take" rule could be implemented by stating that, henceforth, points should also be awarded for previously having signed one's organ donor card. 8

While this change may result in some people losing the chance to receive a transplant, far more people will be able to be served because there will be many more potential organ donors. If enough people sign their donor cards, this plan could even produce a surplus of organs. 9

What is needed to end the shortage of human organs, and to save the thousands of individuals who die because of the shortage, is a rethinking of the moral basis of organ collection and donation. Organs should not be owned by the nation as a whole, but rather by you and I and every other potential organ donor. We may still disagree on whether organs should be 10 commodities traded on the open market, but few could argue with the notion that those who are willing to give should be the first to receive.

Questions for Close Reading

1. What is the selection's thesis? Locate the sentence(s) in which Tabarrok states his main idea. If he doesn't state his thesis explicitly, express it in your own words.
2. What problem does the author see in the current procedures for obtaining organ transplants? What evidence does he give for his view?
3. The author suggests that one way of bettering the organ shortage is to allow donors to be paid. What arguments does he offer in support of this view? What arguments does he give in opposition to it?
4. What solution does Tabarrok advocate? Why does he say his solution is fair? What essential premise is his solution based on?
5. Refer to your dictionary as needed to define the following words used in the selection: *transplant* (paragraph 1), *apathy* (1), *incentive* (2), *procurement* (2), *mandated* (3), *laissez-faire* (4), *tantamount* (6), *premium* (6), *allocated* (8), *implemented* (8), and *commodities* (10).

Questions About the Writer's Craft

1. **The pattern.** What types of evidence does Tabarrok use? Why or why not is the evidence persuasive?
2. **Other patterns.** The author uses exemplification throughout the essay. Give two instances of exemplification. How effective are these?
3. What is the metaphor that Tabarrok uses to describe his proposal? Is the metaphor effective? Why or why not?
4. Who is the audience for this essay? Do you think it is aimed at medical personnel? People waiting on transplant lists? Politicians? The general public?

Writing Assignments Using Argumentation-Persuasion as a Pattern of Development

1. Tabarrok's thesis requires society to change how we view organs—from seeing them as a "national resource" to thinking of them as "the resource of potential organ donors." How would making such a change in our basic assumption about organ donation affect our feelings about the sale of organs? Formulate a thesis in response to that question, and write an essay in which you support your thesis. For evidence, draw on Tabarrok's essay and also on "Need Transplant Donors? Pay Them" (page 555), by Virginia Postrel, which also advocates a change in the organ donation system.
2. Tabarrok argues in favor of an economic solution to the inadequacy of the organ donation system. Think of another societal issue—for example, our dependency on imported oil—that might benefit from an economic approach. You may wish to do some research on your subject. Then write an essay in which you suggest a possible economic action. Make sure to give both the pros and cons in your argument.

Writing Assignments Combining Patterns of Development

3. Health care reform is a serious concern today. Do you know someone who needs an organ transplant or who has had a serious illness or injury? Was the person's experience with medical professionals and institutions mostly positive or mostly negative? Write an essay in which you *narrate* the person's story, including *descriptive* details and *examples* to support your ideas.

4. By far, the organ most commonly donated is the kidney. Kidneys from deceased donors are offered on a first-come, first-served basis, but one proposal suggests that kidneys be matched to recipients whose age is within fifteen years of the donor's age. This procedure would favor young people, who would get kidneys with a long life expectancy and perhaps not need future transplants. However, many older people waiting a long time for kidneys would be unlikely ever to receive them. Write an essay in which you *compare* the ethics of this proposal with the ethics of Tabarrok's proposal. Discuss the possible *effects* of putting either proposal into action. For insight into how other authors have written about ethics and morals, read Joan Murray's "Someone's Mother" (page 154), Charles Sykes's "The 'Values' Wasteland" (page 198), Beth Johnson's "Bombs Bursting in Air" (page 211), Stephanie Ericsson's "The Ways We Lie" (page 247), Stephan Chapman's "The Prisoner's Dilemma" (page 372), John M. Darley and Bibb Latané's "When Will People Help in a Crisis?" (page 415), or Stanley Fish's "Free-Speech Follies" (page 509).

Writing Assignment Using a Journal Entry as a Starting Point

5. Reread your journal notes. Write a short essay in which you argue for or against using economics as a basis for decision making for individuals. For example, how important are economic or financial considerations in deciding where to live, what job to take, where to go to college, and so on? Illustrate your position with examples from your own experience and the experiences of people you know.

Virginia Postrel

Virginia Postrel (1960–) graduated Phi Beta Kappa from Princeton University with a degree in English literature. She worked as a reporter for *The Wall Street Journal* and as a columnist for *Forbes*. Postrel was an economics columnist for *The New York Times* business section for six years before working as a columnist for *The Atlantic* from 2006 to 2009. An award-winning writer, Postrel writes on cultural and economic subjects and has published articles in a wide range of publications. Her work has been featured in *The Best American Science and Nature Writing 2004* and *The Best American Science and Nature Writing 2009*. Postrel is the author of two books—*The Future and Its Enemies* (1999) and *The Substance of Style* (2004). The following selection is excerpted from an article published in the *Los Angeles Times* on June 10, 2006.

Pre-Reading Journal Entry

Like the author of this essay, many of us have performed a selfless act for the benefit of others, whether it was to save a life as Postrel did or simply to volunteer at a local charity or help a neighbor. Think about altruistic acts you have performed. What motivated you? How did you feel afterward? If you had received payment or a reward for the action, would your feelings and behavior have been different? Take notes on your ideas.

Need Transplant Donors? Pay Them

...Our national transplant system is broken: it spends too much time coping with an ever-growing, life-threatening organ shortage rather than finding ways to reduce or end it. More than 66,000 Americans are languishing on the national waiting list for kidneys—10 times the number of kidneys transplanted from deceased donors each year. And the list keeps growing, with a queue of more than 100,000 expected by 2010. 1

Kidney patients literally live or die by where they are on the waiting list. While getting progressively sicker, they must spend several hours at least three times a week hooked up to a dialysis machine,[1] the kidney-disease equivalent of an iron lung[2] (it prolongs your life but imposes a physically debilitating prison sentence). 2

Increasing the supply of deceased donors, while desirable, is difficult—organ donors have to die healthy and in exactly the right circumstances. But even if every eligible cadaver were harvested, it wouldn't fill the gap. We need more kidney donors, lots more. And they need to be alive. 3

Unfortunately, our laws and culture discourage healthy people from donating organs, as I learned this spring when I gave a kidney to a friend. 4

[1]A dialysis machine filters a person's blood to cleanse it of waste (editors' note).

[2]The iron lung, used mainly in the first half of the twentieth century, is a metal machine that helps people to breathe when their chest muscles are paralyzed; most of the person's body is placed in the machine, with only the head and neck remaining free (editors' note).

My parents were appalled. My doctor told me, "You know you can change your mind." Many people couldn't understand why I didn't at least wait until my friend had been on dialysis for a while. 5

This pervasive attitude not only pressures donors to back out, it shapes policies that deter them. Some transplant centers require intrusive, demeaning psychological probes that scare people off. Some bioethicists suspect that donors suffer from a mental disorder, as opposed to being motivated by benevolence or religious conviction. 6

The scrutiny is particularly nasty when healthy people want to give their organs to strangers—not truly unknown people, mind you, but patients they have gotten to know through Internet sites or press coverage. 7

Many transplant centers flatly refuse "directed donations" to specific strangers. Some argue that it's "unfair" for patients to jump the queue with personal initiative and an appealing story; others insist that such donors aren't to be trusted (they must be either criminal or crazy). Posters at living-donorsonline.org warn givers to never even mention the Internet, lest their good intentions be thwarted. 8

Sandra Grijalva, a San Francisco woman with polycystic kidney disease,[3] asked Kaiser[4] officials if she could find a donor online—after having one of her friends disqualified because of high blood pressure. "They said absolutely not," she says. The donor, Kaiser maintained, might someday try to extort money. (So might your cousin, but at least you'd be alive.) 9

Instead of dire possibilities, consider a cold reality: Without tens of thousands of new living donors, most of the people on that very long waiting list are going to suffer and die on dialysis. The transplant community's top priority should be increasing the supply of willing donors. 10

The most obvious way to increase the supply of any scarce commodity—paying more for it—is illegal. Federal law blocks transplant centers, patients and insurers from compensating donors in an above-board process, with full legal and medical protections. The growing and inevitable "transplant tourism" industry, and even shadier organ brokers, are the kidney equivalents of back-alley abortionists. 11

Legalized financial incentives would encourage more people to volunteer their organs. Donors would probably still be relatively rare, just as surrogate mothers[5] are. Many, like me, would still help out without payment, just as some people get paid for giving blood or fighting fires while others do it for free. 12

Paying donors need not hurt the poor, any more than paying dialysis centers does. Compensation could, in fact, help low-income Americans, 13

[3]Polycystic kidney disease is a genetic disease that leads to kidney failure; the disease affects nearly 1 in 1,000 Americans (editors' note).

[4]Kaiser Permanente is a major health management organization based in California but operating in regions throughout the United States (editors' note).

[5]A surrogate mother is a woman who agrees to become pregnant and give birth to a child for a couple to adopt and raise; the surrogate may or may not be the genetic mother of the child (editors' note).

who are disproportionately likely to suffer from kidney disease. A one-year tax holiday for donors would nudge rich people to help. A pool to make up for lost wages (legal, but rare today) would enable many otherwise willing friends and relatives to contribute.

But even talking about incentives is taboo to some self-styled patient advocates. 14

In 2006, the American Enterprise Institute held a conference in Washington on incentive-based transplant reforms. (It was organized by my kidney recipient, a physician and health-policy scholar at the institute.) When the National Kidney Foundation heard about the conference, its chief executive, John Davis, complained to the institute's president, "We don't see how an AEI forum would contribute substantively to debate on this issue." 15

Davis' group adamantly opposes donor compensation, lobbying against even experimental programs and small tax credits. It's as though the National Parkinson Foundation opposed stem cell research, or thought researchers should work for free. 16

Even a limited market in kidneys would transfer power from the rationing establishment to kidney patients and supportive communities. It would give patients more options. Grijalva, who works with developmentally disabled seniors, would welcome the shift. 17

"My biggest fear and my biggest feeling," she says, "is that I'm totally out of control, that these people have the control and they are making all the decisions, and I have absolutely no input whatsoever." 18

Questions for Close Reading

1. What is the selection's thesis? Locate the sentence(s) in which Postrel states her main idea. If she doesn't state her thesis explicitly, express it in your own words.
2. What does the author tell us about the state of kidney donations? What evidence does she use to support her assertion?
3. What is the author's personal experience with kidney transplants? What does she say is society's view of living donors? Identify at least three examples the author gives to support her assessment.
4. What consequences will result if donors are paid for their kidney donations, in the author's view? Do her conclusions about consequences make her argument more or less convincing? Why?
5. Refer to your dictionary as needed to define the following words used in the selection: *queue* (paragraph 1), *literally* (2), *dialysis* (2), *debilitating* (2), *bioethicists* (6), *extort* (9), *above-board* (11), and *substantively* (15).

Questions About the Writer's Craft

1. **The pattern.** What claim about the transplant community's obligations does the author ask us to accept? What does she say about other claims that might be the reasons for readers' hesitation to accept her proposal?

2. **The pattern.** Is the essay based primarily on the appeal of *ethos*, *pathos*, or *logos* (see pages 476–477)? In what ways?
3. **Other patterns.** The author makes a number of comparisons throughout the essay. Identify at least two comparisons. What do you think is the intended effect? Are the comparisons convincing?
4. Who do you think is the audience for this essay—the general public? Medical professionals? Patients? Possible voluntary donors? Why?

Writing Assignments Using Argumentation-Persuasion as a Pattern of Development

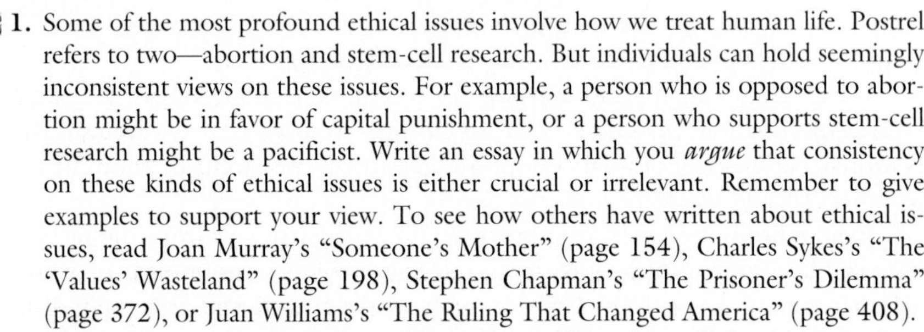

1. Some of the most profound ethical issues involve how we treat human life. Postrel refers to two—abortion and stem-cell research. But individuals can hold seemingly inconsistent views on these issues. For example, a person who is opposed to abortion might be in favor of capital punishment, or a person who supports stem-cell research might be a pacifist. Write an essay in which you *argue* that consistency on these kinds of ethical issues is either crucial or irrelevant. Remember to give examples to support your view. To see how others have written about ethical issues, read Joan Murray's "Someone's Mother" (page 154), Charles Sykes's "The 'Values' Wasteland" (page 198), Stephen Chapman's "The Prisoner's Dilemma" (page 372), or Juan Williams's "The Ruling That Changed America" (page 408).
2. The author says that "increasing the supply of willing donors" should be the "top priority" of the organ transplant community. Do you agree? Or do you think that another goal—for example, ensuring the fair distribution of organs or preventing the exploitation of living donors—should be the highest priority? Do some research on the bioethics of organ donation. Then write an essay in which you *argue* a position on this issue, using expert opinion to support your own views.

Writing Assignments Combining Patterns of Development

3. Read Alexander Tabarrok's essay "A Moral Solution to the Organ Shortage" (page 551). In what ways is the concept of compensation the same or different in these two selections? Write an essay in which you *compare* Tabarrok's idea of rewarding people who sign organ donor cards with Postrel's idea of allowing "[e]ven a limited market in kidneys." Support your argument with examples from the readings.
4. Postrel uses economic theory to reinforce her conclusions about the positive consequences of offering donors compensation. Could compensating donors also lead to negative consequences? Write an essay in which you suggest possible negative *effects* from compensating donors, *arguing* either that the positive outweighs the negative or vice versa. Use examples from the essay and from your own experiences of buying and selling to support your ideas.

Writing Assignment Using a Journal Entry as a Starting Point

5. Look over your journal notes. Write an essay in which you *relate* a personal experience you had as the doer of a good deed. Discuss what you think the *effect* of being paid for your actions would have had on you. Using your own experience, draw some conclusions about the best ways to motivate people to perform altruistic acts.

Roberto Rodriguez

Roberto Rodriguez was born in 1954 in Aguacalientes, Mexico, and raised in East Los Angeles. In 1972, he began his journalism career at *La Gente,* a newspaper at the University of California, Los Angeles. He has written for many publications, including *Black Issues in Higher Education, Lowrider* magazine, the *Eastside Sun* (Los Angeles), and *La Opinion,* the largest Spanish-language daily newspaper in the United States. In addition, Rodriguez's columns have been syndicated in *The Washington Post,* the *Los Angeles Times,* and *USA Today.* Since 1994, he and his wife, Patrisia Gonzales, have written *Column of the Americas,* a blog that focuses on current issues from the perspective of indigenous peoples. Two books he wrote about police brutality were published under one title, *Justice: A Question of Race* (1997). In 2002, Rodriguez and Gonzales were named Distinguished Community Scholars at the Cesar Chavez Center at UCLA, where they are establishing the discipline of indigenous studies. The following article was posted on the *Column of the Americas* website, www.voznuestra.com/Americas, on April 17, 2006.

Pre-Reading Journal Entry

Do you think that schools should engage in discussions of immigration, ethnicity, and racism, which can be sensitive and painful topics? Why do you feel as you do? Would such discussions be appropriate at some levels of school but not at others? Take some time to explore these questions in your journal.

The Border on Our Backs

Look up the word *Mexican* or *Central American* in any U.S. political dictionary and you will find these definitions: 1

> 1) people who are illegal, or are treated as such, no matter how long they've been living in this country; 2) the nation's number one threat to homeland security; 3) people who do the jobs no Americans want and who threaten the American Way of Life; 4) as a result of extremist politicians, the nation's favorite scapegoats; and 5) people, who due to vicious anti-immigrant hysteria, are prone to become Democrats.

By next year, there may be two new entries: 6) Peoples who carry the border on their backs, and 7) peoples not afraid to stand up for their rights. 2

Who could have predicted that millions of peoples would be taking to the streets nationwide to protest draconian immigration bills that call for the building of Berlin-style walls, more *migra,*[1] massive repatriations, 3

[1]Mexican term for "immigration police" (editors' note).

the criminalization of human beings and the creation of a new anti-family apartheid-style Bracero[2] or Guest Worker program? Beyond the bills, the protests are actually about asserting the right—virtually a cry—to be treated as full human beings.

How long was this community supposed to remain in silence? 4

Perhaps it is racial/cultural fatigue. 5

Let's not pretend that this hysteria is not about race, color and dehumanization. It's not even anti-immigrant or even anti-Latino/Hispanic bigotry. It's the exploitation of a deep-seated fear and loathing of Mexicans and Central Americans by shameless politicians. Why? Because of what our color represents. Otherwise, how and why do government agents single us out at lines, borders and internal checkpoints? Otherwise, why do dragnet immigrant raids always target brown peoples? Why is all the hate and vilification directed at brown peoples and the southern border? Otherwise, why are these politicians also not bothered by the millions of Canadians, Europeans or Russians who overstay their visas? (No one should hate them either.) 6

Just what does brown represent in this country? Shall we delude ourselves like the Census Bureau and pretend that we're actually White? 7

Or should we simply stop speaking our languages, stop eating our own foods . . . and stop identifying with our home countries of Mexico, El Salvador, Guatemala, Peru, Colombia, etc. In other words, we're OK if we stop being who we are—if we culturally deport ourselves and conduct auto ethnic cleansing campaigns (we're also OK if we fight their illegal permanent wars). 8

And yet, there's that small matter of our red-brown skin. Just what could it possibly represent? A reminder? Memory? Might it be our thousands-of-years old Indigenous cultures—the ones that were supposedly obliterated—the ones we were supposed to reject? 9

We deny the nopal[3] no longer. We know full well we're not on foreign soil, but on Indian lands. (Were we supposed to forget that too?) So there's no going back. If anything, we are back. The whole continent, the whole earth—which our ancestors have traversed for thousands of years—is our mother. Meanwhile, we watch Congress and the president do a dance about not pardoning or not granting amnesty to those who've been remanded to live in shadows. Sinverguenzas![4] Just who precisely needs to be pardoned? Those who are exploited and who've been here forever . . . or those who've been complicit in our dehumanization? 10

Through all this, we've been baited into fighting with African Americans, American Indians, Asians, Mexican Americans, and poor and white middle 11

[2]Latin American migrant worker (editors' note).

[3]Literally, "prickly pear." There is a common Mexican expression, "Pareces que tienes el nopal en la frente," which literally translated means "It appears you have a prickly pear on your forehead." Idiomatically, the meaning is "You appear to be Indian, yet you deny it" (editors' note).

[4]Mexican expression meaning "Scoundrels!" (editors' note).

class workers—because Mexicans supposedly steal their jobs and are ruining the quality of life.

The truth is, American Indians, African Americans and Asians should be at the head of our protests—for it is they and their struggles against dehumanization that we draw inspiration from. But in the end, it is those who allow extremists to speak in their name, who must also step forward and tell their representatives that a society divided into legal and illegal human beings is no longer acceptable. 12

Every cell in our bodies tells us this. And the unprecedented protests have created the consciousness that a two-tiered society—the definition of apartheid—is intolerable. 13

A flawed bill will pass—many bills will pass—yet some sectors of the population will continue to view and treat Mexicans/Central Americans as illegal, unwanted and subhuman. 14

But enough. Ya Basta! IKUALI![5] As is said at the rallies: Nosotros no somos ilegales ni inmigrantes. Somos de este continente.[6] We are neither illegal nor even immigrants. Tojuan Titehuaxkalo Panin Pacha Mama.[7] 15

---

[5] *Ya basta* is Spanish and *ikuali* is Nahuatl (the Aztec language) for "enough" (editors' note).
[6] Spanish for "We are neither illegal nor immigrants. We are from this continent" (editors' note).
[7] Nahuatl for "We are from this earth" (editors' note).

Questions for Close Reading

1. What is the selection's thesis? Locate the sentence(s) in which Rodriguez states his main idea. If he doesn't state his thesis explicitly, express it in your own words.
2. What is the meaning of the essay's title, "The Border on Our Backs"?
3. According to Rodriguez, how are American policies on illegal immigrants similar to apartheid?
4. According to Rodriguez, who should be the inspiration for illegal Mexican and Central American immigrants in the United States? Why?
5. Refer to your dictionary as needed to define the following words used in the selection: *scapegoats* (paragraph 1), *draconian* (3), *repatriations* (3), *apartheid* (3), *bigotry* (6), *dragnet* (6), *vilification* (6), *delude* (7), *indigenous* (9), *obliterated* (9), *traversed* (10), *amnesty* (10), *remanded* (10), and *complicit* (10).

Questions About the Writer's Craft

1. Rodriguez opens his essay with some definitions of *Mexican* and *Central American* that he claims can be found in any U.S. political dictionary. How effective is this opening? What tone does it set for the remainder of the essay?
2. **The pattern.** What evidence does Rodriguez cite to support his claim that American attitudes toward immigrants from Mexico and Central America are

fundamentally racist? How effective is this evidence and the way it is presented? What is the balance between *logos* and *pathos* here?

3. Rodriguez uses many words and phrases in Spanish and Nahuatl throughout the essay without translating them. How effective is this use of language? What does it suggest about the audience for which he is writing?
4. **The pattern.** What fallacies, if any, are in this argument? Explain the nature of the fallacy or fallacies.

Writing Assignments Using Argumentation-Persuasion as a Pattern of Development

1. Rodriguez argues that the struggle of illegal immigrants is similar to the struggle of American Indians, African Americans, Mexican Americans, and other American groups who have fought against dehumanization (paragraphs 11 and 12). Do you agree? Focusing on a specific group of disadvantaged Americans, write an essay in which you support or challenge Rodriguez's argument. To ensure that your position is more than a reflexive opinion, conduct some library research on the group in question, and read Star Parker's "*Se Habla* Entitlement" (page 564), an essay that is in sharp opposition to Rodriguez's. No matter which side you take, assume that some readers are opposed to your point of view. Acknowledge and try to dismantle as many of their objections as possible. Refer, whenever it's relevant, to Parker's argument in your paper.
2. Rodriguez suggests that racial profiling at the U.S. borders unfairly targets people of color and is used by politicians to exploit whites' fears (paragraph 6). In recent years, racial profiling has been used by many law enforcement agencies to identify suspected criminals and terrorists as well as illegal immigrants, although many people dispute both the fairness and the effectiveness of the technique. Do some research on racial profiling and then write an essay arguing that racial profiling is (or is not) a fair and effective method of identifying people who are likely to be criminals. Your essay can focus on the issue of racial profiling in general, or it can focus on a particular use of racial profiling. In your essay, you should acknowledge and refute as many opposing arguments as possible.

Writing Assignments Combining Patterns of Development

3. Rodriguez believes that illegal immigrants should stand up for their right to be treated as "full human beings." Select a group that you believe is disadvantaged and should stand up for its rights. Possibilities include a specific racial, ethnic, or religious group; the disabled; the overweight; those in abusive relationships. Write an essay explaining some specific *steps* these groups could take to secure their rights. Conclude your paper by discussing the *effects* of winning such rights. What would be gained? What, if anything, would be lost? Before writing, read one or more of the following essays to sharpen your understanding of disadvantaged people and the struggle for human rights: Riverbend's "Bloggers Without Borders" (page 111) Audre Lorde's "The Fourth of July" (page 140), Richard Rodriguez's "Workers" (page 361), and William Raspberry's "The Handicap of Definition" (page 468).

4. Rodriguez refers to Mexicans and Central Americans as threatening the American Way of Life (paragraph 1). Write an essay in which you *define* what the American Way of Life means to you. Along the way, *compare* and/or *contrast* your definition with what you think is the prevailing definition of this term. To illustrate your definition, provide *examples* and/or *stories.* Your essay can be serious, humorous, or satiric in tone.

Writing Assignment Using a Journal Entry as a Starting Point

5. Write an essay arguing that schools should or should not encourage students to discuss immigration, ethnicity, and racism. Review your pre-reading journal entry, and select a specific level of schooling to focus on before taking a position. Supplement the material in your journal by gathering the opinions, experiences, and observations of friends, family, and classmates. No matter which position you take, remember to cite opposing arguments, refuting as many of them as you can.

Star Parker

Star Parker, born in 1957, is the founder and leader of the Coalition on Urban Renewal and Education, a nonprofit organization that advocates on issues of race, poverty, education, and inner-city neighborhoods. At one time a single mother living on welfare in Los Angeles, Parker eventually returned to college for a bachelor's degree in marketing. She went on to establish an urban Christian magazine and become a strong advocate for conservative Christian political views. In 1992, her business was destroyed in the Los Angeles riots. This experience intensified her focus on faith-based and free-market approaches to solving the problems of poverty. As a social policy consultant, Parker frequently appears on national television and radio stations, including CNN, MSNBC, and Fox, and she often testifies before Congress. Parker has published three books: *Pimps, Whores, and Welfare Brats: From Welfare Cheat to Conservative Messenger* (1998), *Uncle Sam's Plantation: How Big Government Enslaves American's Poor and What We Can Do About It* (2003), and *White Ghetto: How Middle Class America Reflects Inner City Decay* (2006). This opinion piece was published on WorldNetDaily.com, an independent news website, on April 18, 2006.

Pre-Reading Journal Entry

The issue of immigration—especially questions of who should be permitted into the country and who should be permitted to stay—has recently been hotly debated both by politicians and pundits and by everyday people. What do you think would happen if U.S. immigration laws were strictly enforced and those who were here illegally were sent back to their home countries? What positive effects would there be? What negative effects would there be? What do you think would happen if all immigrants who were here illegally were allowed to stay and start the process of becoming citizens? Take some time to respond to these questions in your journal.

Se Habla[1] Entitlement

When it comes to matters of economy, I think of myself as libertarian. I believe in free markets, free trade and limited government. But I must confess, our Latino neighbors are challenging my libertarian instincts regarding our immigration conundrum. 1

The recent pro-immigration demonstrations around the country have been a major turnoff. 2

There is something not convincing about illegal immigrants demonstrating to claim they have inalienable rights to come here, be here, work here, become citizens here—and make all these claims in Spanish. 3

Hearing "We Shall Overcome" in Spanish just doesn't provoke my sympathies. I don't buy that, along with life, liberty and the pursuit of happiness, 4

[1]Spanish for "is spoken" (editors' note).

our Creator endowed anyone with the right to sneak into the United States, bypass our laws and set up shop. Maybe our immigration laws do need fixing. But this is a discussion for American citizens. In English.

This could be the finest hour for the political left if we really can be 5
convinced that illegal immigration is a right, that those here illegally are innocent victims, and that the real guilt lies with U.S. citizens who believe our laws mean something and should be enforced.

Draping these bogus claims in the garb of the civil-rights movement is 6
particularly annoying.

The civil-rights movement was about enforcing the law, not breaking 7
it. The Civil War amendments to the Constitution were not getting the job done in what has been a long struggle in this country to treat blacks as human beings. If Americans were kidnapping Mexicans and selling them into slavery here, I might see the equivalence. But these are free people, who chose to come here and chose to do so illegally.

Just considering Mexicans, how can we understand their taking to the 8
streets of our country to demand rights and freedom when they seem to have little interest in doing this where they do have rights, which is in Mexico? There is no reason why Mexico, a country rich in beauty and natural resources, cannot be every bit as prosperous as the United States.

It's not happening because of a long history of mismanagement, corrup- 9
tion and excessive government. Although Mexico is a democracy, for some reason Mexicans seem to need to be north of the Rio Grande to get politically active and demand the benefits of a free society.

Last year the Pew Hispanic Center surveyed adults in Mexico and asked 10
them if they would come to the United States if they had the means and opportunity to do so. Forty-six percent responded yes. Almost half of Mexican adults said they'd rather live here! When asked if they would do it illegally, more than 20 percent said yes.

Yet in the contest for the Mexican presidency, the leading candidate is a 11
leftist former mayor of Mexico City who is polling in the high 30s.[2]

Maybe you can figure out why almost half of Mexican adults say they 12
would rather live in the United States, presumably because of the opportunities our free society affords, yet vote for a leftist candidate who will continue policies in Mexico that choke off any prospect for growth, prosperity and opportunity.

So forgive me for being a little suspicious of the wholesome picture be- 13
ing painted of these folks who are pouring across our border allegedly just to be free, work and maintain traditional families.

Anyone who lives in Southern California, as I do, knows that the 14
Latino-immigrant community is far from the paragon of virtue that the

[2]With a very narrow margin, the more conservative Felipe Calderón ultimately defeated the leftist Andrés Manuel López Obrador in the Mexican presidential election of 2006.

forces who want to encourage open borders would have us believe. I see much of the same troubling behavior that blacks get tarred with. Much of the gang behavior in Los Angeles, unfortunately, is Latino-related. The L.A. Unified School District is over three-quarters Latino, who drop out at the same alarming 50 percent rate as inner-city blacks. Out-of-wedlock births among Hispanic women approach 50 percent.

Those who want to hoist the banner of the Statue of Liberty, Ellis Island and the American tradition of immigration should remember that when immigrants were passing through Ellis Island at the early part of the last century, the federal government accounted for about 3 percent of the American economy. Today it is 25 percent. 15

Part of the package deal that comes with showing up in the United States today is our welfare state as well as our free economy. Illegal status is really a temporary situation, anyway. Illegal immigrants' children who are born here are U.S. citizens. Significant demands are being made on our tax dollars in the way of schools, health care and government services, including law enforcement. 16

Yes, let's encourage freedom. But freedom is a privilege and a responsibility. 17

We have enough people already here who think it's all about entitlement. 18

Questions for Close Reading

1. What is the selection's thesis? Locate the sentence(s) in which Parker states her main idea. If she doesn't state her thesis explicitly, express it in your own words.
2. Why does Parker object to pro-immigration demonstrators adopting the strategies of the American civil rights movement?
3. In paragraph 15, Parker contrasts the size of the federal government a hundred years ago with its size now. To what does she attribute its increase?
4. Why does Parker object to the feeling of entitlement that she claims immigrants have?
5. Refer to your dictionary as needed to define the following words used in the selection: *entitlement* (title), *libertarian* (paragraph 1), *conundrum* (1), *inalienable* (3), *provoke* (4), *bogus* (6), *garb* (6), and *paragon* (14).

Questions About the Writer's Craft

1. **The pattern.** Which of the two possible strategies for organizing a refutation (see pages 485–486) does Parker use in her essay? Do you consider the points she makes in the refutation sufficiently persuasive? Explain.
2. **Other patterns.** In paragraph 14, Parker compares and contrasts the Latino and African American communities of southern California. What is the purpose of this comparison? How effective is it?
3. The second paragraph of the Declaration of Independence begins: "We hold these truths to be self-evident, that all men are created equal, that they are endowed by their Creator with certain unalienable Rights, that among these are Life, Liberty

and the pursuit of Happiness." There are echoes of this sentence in paragraphs 3 and 4 of Parker's essay. What is the effect of her adopting this vocabulary?

4. Throughout the essay, Parker uses language that describes her reactions to pro-immigration demonstrations and arguments: "a major turnoff" (paragraph 2), "not convincing" (3), "doesn't provoke my sympathies" (4), "particularly annoying" (6), and "a little suspicious" (13). What do these phrases contribute to the tone of the essay? How do they help Parker communicate her argument more convincingly?

Writing Assignments Using Argumentation-Persuasion as a Pattern of Development

1. Parker, an African American, claims to have been "turned off" by the pro-immigration demonstrations that took place in spring of 2006 in an attempt to influence immigration legislation pending in Congress. She objects to the pro-immigration movement's adoption of the strategies of the American civil rights movement—the language, the demonstrations, and the songs sung in Spanish. In contrast, in "The Border on Our Backs" (page 559), Roberto Rodriguez, a Mexican American, is elated by these demonstrations, claiming that immigrants are finally asserting their human rights in the great tradition of the civil rights movement. What do you think of demonstrations in the United States by illegal immigrants? Do you sympathize with the immigrants' arguments? Do you think their demonstrations further the immigrants' cause, or set it back? Write an essay in which you argue that demonstrations by illegal immigrants are (or are not) justified and appropriate, citing at least two or three reasons for your position. Be sure to support your reasons with *examples* wherever possible.
2. Parker characterizes herself as a libertarian in matters of economics. Libertarians advocate that individuals should be free to do whatever they wish with themselves and their property, as long as they do not infringe on the liberty of others. Libertarians also believe that people are responsible for their own actions. They strongly oppose welfare programs, which they believe force taxpayers to provide aid to others. In fact, Parker's final reason for opposing illegal immigrants is that they contribute to the growth of the welfare state (paragraph 15 and 16). Write an essay supporting or opposing the libertarian position on the welfare state. Argue that government does (or does not) have the responsibility to help individuals in times of need (poor economic conditions, disability, and natural disasters, for example). Be sure to address whether the effect on individuals of such government assistance is empowering—or whether it perpetuates dependence. Use specific examples to support your position.

Writing Assignments Combining Patterns of Development

3. Imagine what your life would be like if you moved to another state or country alone or just with your immediate family. Then write an essay in which you provide *examples* showing how your life would or would not change if you moved to a strange place. Consider the language barrier, if any, in your education, your

work, your friendships, and your family life. Reach some conclusions about the overall *effect* of making this move, including whether life would be easier or more difficult.

4. Choose a social program or common practice that involves the concept of entitlement. For example, among social programs you could choose affirmative action, Medicaid, Medicare, welfare, or unemployment insurance. Among common practices you might select nepotism (favoring relatives or friends when hiring), legacy admissions to colleges (admitting the children of alumni), or illegal campaign contributions. Research the program or practice on the Internet or in the library. Write an essay in which you explain the *effects* of such a program or practice on recipients. *Compare* and *contrast* the benefits and drawbacks of receiving such an entitlement. Finally, *argue* that the program or practice should be continued or abolished.

Writing Assignment Using a Journal Entry as a Starting Point

5. Review your journal entries about the possible effects of deporting illegal immigrants or allowing them to stay, also called *amnesty*. The last amnesty in the United States took place in 1986 and was granted to immigrants who could prove they had resided here for five years or more. Amnesty is always controversial. Some argue that granting amnesty rewards illegal behavior and encourages more illegal immigration. Others argue that regularizing the status of long-time illegal residents simply provides them with a path for becoming full citizens, upholding the ideals of an open and democratic society. Write an essay in which you *argue* either in favor of or against an amnesty for current illegal immigrants who have resided in the United States for at least five years. In addition to discussing the *effects* of allowing immigrants to stay that you outlined in your journal entry, do some research on the 1986 amnesty to understand its *effects*. If they are still relevant today, use them to support your point of view about amnesty.

Additional Writing Topics

ARGUMENTATION-PERSUASION

General Assignments

Using argumentation-persuasion, develop one of the topics below in an essay. After choosing a topic, think about your purpose and audience. Remember that the paper's thesis should state the issue under discussion as well as your position on the issue. As you work on developing evidence, you might want to do some outside research. Keep in mind that effective argumentation-persuasion usually means that some time should be spent acknowledging and perhaps refuting opposing points of view. Be careful not to sabotage your argument by basing your case on a logical fallacy.

1. Euthanasia
2. Hiring or college-admissions quotas
3. Giving birth control devices to teenagers
4. Prayer in the schools
5. Torturing suspected terrorists
6. The drinking age
7. Spouses sharing housework equally
8. Smoking in public places
9. Big-time sports in college
10. Pornography on the Internet
11. Single parents with young children
12. Global warming
13. Legalizing marijuana
14. Political campaigns
15. Requiring college students to pass a comprehensive exam in their majors before graduating
16. Reinstating the military draft
17. Putting elderly parents in nursing homes
18. An optional pass-fail system for courses
19. The homeless
20. Nonconformity in a neighborhood: allowing a lawn to go wild, keeping many pets, painting a house an odd color, or some other atypical behavior

Assignments with a Specific Purpose, Audience, and Point of View

On Campus

1. Your college's Financial Aid Department has decided not to renew your scholarship for next year, citing a drop in your grades last semester and an unenthusiastic recommendation from one of your instructors. Write a letter to the director of financial aid arguing for the renewal of your scholarship.

2. You strongly believe that a particular policy or regulation on campus is unreasonable or unjust. Write a letter to the dean of students (or other appropriate administrator) arguing that the policy needs to be, if not completely revoked, amended in some way. Support your contention with specific examples showing how the regulation has gone wrong. End by providing constructive suggestions for how the policy problem can be solved.

At Home or in the Community

3. You and one or more family members don't agree on some aspect of your romantic life (you want to live with your boyfriend/girlfriend and they don't approve; you want to get married and they want you to wait; they simply don't like your partner). Write a letter explaining why your preference is reasonable. Try hard to win your family member(s) over to your side.
4. Assume you're a member of a racial, ethnic, religious, or social minority. You might, for example, be a Native American, an elderly person, a female executive. On a recent television show or in a TV commercial, you saw something that depicts your group in an offensive way. Write a letter (to the network or the advertiser) expressing your feelings and explaining why you feel the material should be taken off the air.

On the Job

5. As a staff writer for an online pop-culture magazine, you've been asked to nominate the "Most Memorable TV Moment of the Last 50 Years" to be featured as the magazine's lead article. Write a letter to your supervising editor in support of your nominee.
6. As a high school teacher, you support some additional restriction on students. The restriction might be "no cell phones in school," "no T-shirts," "no food in class," "no smoking on school grounds." Write an article for the school newspaper, justifying this new rule to the student body.

COMBINING THE PATTERNS

Throughout this book, you've studied the patterns of development—narration, process analysis, definition, and so on—in depth. You've seen how the patterns are used as strategies for generating, developing, and organizing ideas for essays. You've also learned that, in practice, most types of writing combine two or more patterns. The two sections that follow provide additional information about these important points. The rest of the chapter then gives you an opportunity to look more closely at the way several writers use the patterns of development in their work.

THE PATTERNS IN ACTION: DURING THE WRITING PROCESS

The patterns of development come into play throughout the composing process. In the prewriting stage, awareness of the patterns encourages you to think about your subject in fresh, new ways. Assume, for example, that you've been asked to write an essay about the way children are disciplined in school. However, you draw a blank as soon as you try to limit this general subject. To break the logjam, you could apply one or more patterns of development to your subject. *Comparison-contrast* might prompt you to write an essay investigating the differences between your parents' and your own feelings about school discipline. *Division-classification* might lead you to another paper—one that categorizes the kinds of discipline used in school. And *cause-effect* might point to still another essay—one that explores the way students react to being suspended.

Further along in the writing process—after you've identified your limited subject and your thesis—the patterns of development can help you generate your paper's evidence. Imagine that your thesis is "Teachers shouldn't discipline students publicly just to make an example of them." You're not sure, though, how to develop this thesis. Calling upon the patterns might spark some promising possibilities. *Narration* might encourage you to recount the disastrous time you were singled out and punished for the misdeeds of an entire class. Using *definition*, you might explain what is meant by an *autocratic* disciplinary style. *Argumentation-persuasion* might prompt you to advocate a new plan for disciplining students fairly and effectively.

The patterns of development also help you organize your ideas by pointing the way to an appropriate framework for a paper. Suppose you plan to write an essay for the campus newspaper about the disturbingly high incidence of shoplifting among college students; your purpose is to persuade young people not to get involved in this tempting, supposedly victimless crime. You believe that many readers will be deterred from shoplifting if you tell them about the harrowing *process* set in motion once a shoplifter is detected. With this step-by-step explanation in mind, you can now map out the essay's content: what happens when a shoplifter is detained by a salesperson, questioned by store security personnel, led to a police car, booked at the police station, and tried in a courtroom.

THE PATTERNS IN ACTION: IN AN ESSAY

Although this book devotes a separate chapter to each of the nine patterns of development, all chapters emphasize the same important point: Most writing consists of several patterns, with the dominant pattern providing the piece's organizational framework. To reinforce this point, each chapter contains a section, "How [the Pattern] Fits Your Purpose and Audience," that shows how a writer's purpose often leads to a blending of patterns. Also, the commentary following each student essay talks about the way the paper mixes patterns. Similarly, at least one of the questions in the "Questions About the Writer's Craft" section following each professional selection asks you to analyze the piece's combination of patterns. Further, the assignments in "Writing Assignments Combining Patterns of Development" encourage you to experiment with mixing patterns in your own writing. In short, all through *The Longman Reader* we emphasize that the patterns of development are far from being mechanical formulas. On the contrary: They are practical strategies that open up options in every stage of the composing process.

Now you'll have a chance to focus on the way student and professional writers combine patterns in their essays. In the pages ahead, you'll find one student essay and six professional selections, two by each of the following three writers: Barbara Kingsolver; Martin Luther King, Jr.; and Joan Didion. As you read each essay, ask yourself these questions:

1. What are the writer's *purpose* and *thesis*?
2. What *pattern of development dominates* the essay? How does this pattern help the writer support the essay's thesis and fulfill the essay's purpose?
3. What *other patterns appear* in the essay? How do these secondary patterns help the writer support the essay's thesis and fulfill the essay's purpose?

Your responses to these three questions will reward you with a richer understanding of the way writers work. To give you an even clearer sense of how writers mix patterns, we have annotated the student essay (Tasha Walker's "The Super-Sizing of America's Kids" below) and the first professional essay (Barbara Kingsolver's "The Good Farmer" on page 578). The preceding three questions served as our guide when we prepared the annotations. By making your own annotations on these essays and then comparing them to ours, you can measure your ability to analyze writers' use of the patterns. You can further evaluate your analysis of the pieces by answering the three questions on your own and then comparing your responses to ours on pages 576–577 and 584–586.

STUDENT ESSAY

The following student essay was written by Tasha Walker in response to this assignment:

> In the essay "Tweens: Ten Going On Sixteen," Kay S. Hymowitz explores an alarming trend among children: the tendency of preteens to act much older than they are. Write an essay analyzing the causes and effects of another significant problem among young people today. Conclude your essay by offering possible solutions for the problem you've examined.

The annotations on the essay will help you look at the way Tasha uses various patterns of development to achieve her purpose and develop her thesis.

Introduction has *narrative* and *descriptive* elements

The Super-Sizing of America's Kids
by Tasha Walker

Examples of foods *contrast* with *examples* later in ¶

Contrast between average breakfast in the 1950s and today

Picture this scene from the 1950s. A couple of kids wake 1
up, get dressed, and sit down for breakfast before leaving for school. They're greeted by an array of healthy choices: a glass of orange juice, a bowl of cornflakes or oatmeal with a healthy serving of milk, perhaps a plateful of scrambled eggs and toast. Now fast-forward a few decades to the present. The situation is very different. If kids sit down for breakfast at all, they gulp down a bowl of rainbow-colored sugary bits with a dollop of milk. Or, racing out the door, they grab a syrupy jumbo cinnamon bun or a glazed, fudge-filled toaster tart.

Exemplification in the form of facts and statistics

Causal analysis (main pattern) begins with *effects* of problem

What's the harm, you might ask, in giving kids tasty, 2
convenient food options? After all, kids burn so much energy; they shouldn't have to worry about their diet until they're adults. Right? Wrong, says the latest information on obesity in the United States. According to several recent studies cited by the magazine *Children's Health* (October 2003), the number of overweight American kids has more than doubled in the last thirty years. As many as 22 percent of today's children are considered dangerously obese. Many are developing diet-related

Statement of purpose/thesis: Need to end increasing childhood obesity; emotional language urging action reinforces essay's *persuasive* intent

diabetes, a disease that used to be seen almost exclusively in adults. When California's students (grades 5 through 12) were given a basic fitness test, almost eight out of ten failed. These statistics point to a clear conclusion: There's a growing problem of childhood obesity in this country, a dire trend that must be stopped in its tracks.

Causal analysis shifts to several *causes* of problem

Transition signals first *cause* of problem

3 Whether they're called big-boned, chubby, husky, or plus-sized, kids are becoming heavier at younger ages and less physically fit than ever before. But why? Like most serious problems, this one has a number of causes. One factor is the massive impact of electronic entertainment on kids' lives. Kids used to go outside to play because that was more fun than sitting around the house. Today, kids at home have access to cable TV channels, the Internet, DVD players, and a dizzying assortment of video games, all of which diminish the lure of outdoor play.

Transition signals second *cause* of problem

4 Another cause is the lack of parental supervision. Decades ago, most kids had an adult at home encouraging them to play outdoors. Now, a large number of American families have two working parents or a working single parent. For most of the daylight hours, parents aren't around to make sure their kids get some exercise. Parents who can't be home may feel guilty; one way to relieve this guilt is to buy kids the game system of their dreams and a nice wide-screen TV to play it on, almost guaranteeing that kids will sit idle rather than participate in vigorous physical activity.

Transition signals most important *cause* of problem

5 But more than any other factor, fast-food restaurants and other sources of calorie-laden junk have dramatically contributed to the fattening of America's kids. In *Super Size Me,* director Morgan Spurlock, dismayed by American obesity statistics (particularly among children), decided to eat nothing but McDonald's fast food for a month and film the experience. To many of today's kids, normal dinnertime equals McDonald's, Domino's, Taco Bell, or Kentucky Fried Chicken. And increasingly, lunchtime at school means those foods too since a good number of schools have sold chain restaurants the right to put their food items on the lunch line. Many schools also allow candy and soft-drink vending machines on their campuses. Given the choice between an apple and a candy bar, how many kids would choose the apple?

Start of *secondary causal analysis* (*effects* of fast food on kids)

Exemplification in the form of facts and statistics

6 Whether for breakfast, lunch, or dinner, when fast food becomes the staple of young people's diets, it's the kids who become Whoppers. And it has become the staple for many. *Children's Health* reports that nationwide, kids get 40 percent of their meals from fast-food chains and convenience stores. And what makes the situation even worse is the increasingly huge portions sold by fast-food restaurants. In the 1950s, the

standard meal at McDonald's consisted of a hamburger, two ounces of French fries, and a 12-ounce Coke. That meal provided 590 calories. But today's customers are encouraged to say "Super-size that!" For very little extra money, diners end up with a quarter-pound burger, extra-large fries, and a gigantic cup of Coke, all adding up to 1,550 calories. A whole generation of kids is growing up believing that this massive shot of fat, sugar, and sodium equals a "normal portion." Kids' perception of what's normal is also distorted by the size of the drinks sold by fast-food and convenience stores. The drinks, often sporting names like the "Big Gulp" or "Super Thirst Quencher," are huge in both size and popularity. Every day, the average adolescent chugs enough soda and fruit beverages to equal the sugar content of fifty chocolate-chip cookies. No wonder kids are becoming "super-sized" themselves.

Emotional language reinforces essay's *persuasive* intent

7 The fast-food franchises push youngsters to overeat in other ways too. Plunking themselves down in front of the TV to watch after-school and Saturday-morning cartoons, children see at least an hour of commercials for every five hours of programming. On Saturday mornings, nine out of ten of those TV ads are for sugary cereals, fast foods, and other non-nutritious junk. Watching those commercials makes the kids hungry—or at least makes them think they are. So they snack as they sit in front of the TV set. Then at mealtime, they beg for the junk food they've seen televised all day long. The result? Kids get bigger, and bigger, and bigger.

Exemplification in the form of facts and statistics

End of secondary causal analysis

Emotional language reinforces essay's *persuasive* intent

8 There's no overnight solution to the problem of American children's increasing weight. But there are some remedies that could be put into place easily. To begin, fast-food meals and junk-food vending machines should be banned from schools, as some states have started to do. Second, food companies should reduce serving sizes and lower the fat and sugar content of the snack items that children eat most often. (Kraft Foods has recently begun to take such steps.) Third, commercials for junk food should be prohibited from being aired on TV during children's viewing time, specifically Saturday mornings. Fourth, parents and schools need to educate kids about the benefits of healthy foods and moderate portion size—and about the drawback of huge meals of junk food. Schools could, for example, mount an educational effort equivalent to the school-based anti-smoking campaign of the 1980s and 1990s. Fifth, fast-food restaurants should be required to do something like what tobacco companies have to do: clearly display health warnings on their products. If young people learned in school and at home about healthy eating, they might think twice about ordering a Double Whopper

Argumentation presents several possible solutions to problem

Transitions signal several solutions

Exemplification in the form of hypothetical situation

with cheese, an extra-large order of fries and a king-sized Dr. Pepper, especially if they read something like this:

- *Your meal provides 2030 calories, 860 of those calories from fat.*
- *Your recommended daily intake is 2000 calories, with no more than 600 of those calories coming from fat.*

At a glance, they could see that in one fast-food meal, they would be taking in more calories and fat than they should consume in an entire day.

Transition signals last solution

Finally, parents need to curb their reliance on fast food to nourish their children. Making fast food an occasional treat rather than an everyday habit can make a significant difference. Parents may argue that they simply don't have time to cook healthy, well-balanced meals, particularly during the week. The answer may be to get the whole family involved in preparing meals ahead of time. (Younger kids, whose attitudes are still in the formative stage, love helping out in the kitchen.) Letting kids assist in preparing, packaging, and freezing their own nutritious, reasonably sized individual servings for later use can go a long way toward helping youngsters develop more healthy attitudes toward food. 9

Restatement of purpose/thesis; emotional language urging action reinforces essay's *persuasive* intent

Such efforts, challenging as they may be, are well worth the trouble. Why? Because overweight kids today become overweight adults tomorrow. Overweight adults are at increased risk for heart disease, diabetes, stroke, and cancer. Schools, fast-food restaurants, and the media are contributing to a public-health disaster in the making. Anything that decreases the role that super-sized junk food plays in kids' lives needs to be done, and done quickly. 10

The following answers to the questions on page 572 ill help you analyze Tasha Walker's use of the patterns of development in her essay "The Super-Sizing of America's Kids."

1. *What are the writer's purpose and thesis?*

Tasha's general purpose, clearly indicated in the assignment, is to explore the causes and effects of a significant problem among young people today. Tasha chooses to address the problem of increasing obesity among children. She expresses her thesis in the final sentence of paragraph 2: "There's a growing problem of childhood obesity in this country, a dire trend that must be stopped in its tracks." Over the course of her essay, Tasha marshals compelling evidence of the obesity problem, explores its causes and effects, and concludes with thoughts on how this problem might be rectified.

2. *What pattern of development dominates the essay? How does this pattern help the writer support the essay's thesis and fulfill the essay's purpose?*

As the assignment required, Tasha uses *causal analysis* as her essay's principal pattern of development. To establish the severity of the childhood obesity problem,

Tasha presents, in paragraph 2, a battery of statistics pointing to obesity's dire and pervasive *effects*. She then shifts gears in paragraph 3 to consider the *causes* of this obesity. The phrase "Like most serious problems, this one has a number of causes" announces that Tasha will discuss a series of causes. She uses various signal phrases, including "One factor" (3), "Another cause" (4), and "But more than any other factor" (5), to direct readers' attention to each factor under consideration. This clear, easy-to-follow presentation—first of effects and then of causes—allows Tasha to develop her thesis and meet her writing objectives. Along the way, several *secondary causal analyses* buttress her overarching examination of causes and effects. Consider paragraphs 5–7. There, Tasha begins by citing fast-food restaurants as the most significant cause of kids' poor eating habits; that done, she examines how the fast-food industry affects kids—how it distorts their perception of portion size and uses enticing commercials to increase their reliance on "calorie-laden junk" (5).

3. *What other patterns appear in the essay? How do these secondary patterns help the writer support the essay's thesis and fulfill the essay's purpose?*

Although Tasha's essay is primarily a causal analysis, it contains a strong element of *argumentation-persuasion*. For one thing, Tasha's thesis takes the form of an *argument:* The "dire trend [of childhood obesity] ... must be stopped in its tracks" (paragraph 2). Careful to support her argument with solid reasoning, Tasha uses facts and statistics throughout the essay. She also employs strong language to enhance the argument's *persuasiveness*. Note, for example, the way she's worded her thesis to convey a sense of urgency. Note, too, the way she forcefully restates her core argument at various points in the essay. In paragraph 3, she asserts that "kids are becoming heavier at younger ages and less physically fit than ever before," and later she argues, "No wonder kids are becoming 'super-sized' themselves" (6) and "Kids get bigger, and bigger, and bigger" (7). The essay's last sentence ("Anything that decreases the role that super-sized junk food plays in kids' lives needs to be done, and done quickly") echoes the feeling of urgency expressed in the thesis.

Tasha's essay draws upon other patterns of development as well. The introductory anecdote, *narrative* and *descriptive* in structure, *contrasts* kids' waking up to breakfast in the 1950s with what happens nowadays. Vivid contrasting *examples* ("a bowl of ... oatmeal" versus a "bowl of rainbow-colored sugary bits") help Tasha establish her key point: that childhood obesity is a contemporary trend that didn't exist in the past. Tasha continues to use exemplification in the form of facts (6 and 8), statistics (2 and 7), and hypothetical situations (8 and 9). Taken together, all these patterns help Tasha make her point about the importance of reversing the dangerous trend of childhood obesity.

Now that you've seen the way one student writer brings together several patterns of development in an essay, it will be helpful to look at the way a renowned prose stylist, Barbara Kingsolver, does the same in her essay "The Good Farmer."

Barbara Kingsolver

Barbara Kingsolver was born in Maryland in 1955. Though she grew up in rural Kentucky, her family often relocated to areas in underdeveloped countries, where her father would donate his expertise as a medical doctor. She studied science, as well as anthropology, music theory, creative writing, and other liberal arts subjects, and received a B.A. in biology from DePauw University. After graduation, Kingsolver traveled around Europe, earning her way at various jobs. Returning to the States, she eventually took a master's degree at the University of Arizona and settled in the area. She and her first husband were involved with organizations that focused on human rights violations involving the border with Mexico. Early in her career, Kingsolver wrote science articles; she then expanded her range of subjects and, in 1985, became a full-time freelance writer. She eventually moved into fiction writing with the publication of her very successful first novel, *The Bean Trees*, in 1988. Over the ensuing years, she endured family hardships, including serious illness and a divorce, but continued writing and earning critical acclaim as well as awards. Teaching on a Lila Wallace fellowship, she met her second husband, a biology professor, and remarried in 1994. Together, they honed an interest in ecology and farming, moving in 2004 into a renovated, hundred-year-old farmhouse, on a working farm in Virginia. Kingsolver's other novels include *Animal Dreams* (1990), *Pigs in Heaven* (1993), *The Poisonwood Bible* (1998), *Prodigal Summer* (2000), and *The Lacuna* (2009). She has also published a collection of short stories, *Homeland and Other Stories* (1989), and a book of poetry, *Another America* (1992). Her collections of essays and other nonfiction include *Holding the Line: Women in the Great Arizona Mine Strike* (1989), *High Tide in Tucson: Essays from Now or Never* (1995), *Small Wonder* (2002), and *Last Stand: America's Virgin Lands* (2002) with photographer Annie Griffiths Belt. Her most recent nonfiction book, *Animal, Vegetable, Miracle: A Year of Food Life* (2007), features a memoir of a year in which she and her family lived on food they had produced or obtained locally. "The Good Farmer" was published in the anthology *The Essential Agrarian Reader: The Future of Culture, Community and the Land* (2003), edited by Norman Wirzba. The second essay, "Stone Soup," appeared in *High Tide in Tucson: Essays from Now or Never* (1995).

The Good Farmer

Introduction: poses a statement opposite to the author's thesis

1 Sometime around my 40th birthday I began an earnest study of agriculture. I worked quietly on this project, speaking of my new interest to almost no one because of what they might think. Specifically, they might think I was out of my mind.

Cause and effect: four reasons people might agree with statement in introduction

2 Why? Because at this moment in history it's considered smart to get out of agriculture. And because I was already embarked on a career as a writer, doing work that many people might consider intellectual and therefore superior

to anything involving the risk of dirty fingernails. Also, as a woman in my early 40s, I conformed to no right-minded picture of an apprentice farmer. And finally, with some chagrin I'll admit that I grew up among farmers and spent the first decades of my life plotting my escape from a place that seemed to offer me almost no potential for economic, intellectual, or spiritual satisfaction.

Description: start of "treasure" metaphor for good-farming values

3 It took nigh onto half a lifetime before the valuables I'd casually left behind turned up in the lost and found.

Continuation of "treasure" metaphor

Exemplification: personal anecdote about interest in gardening

Comparison-contrast: thesis background—not logical that different fields don't communicate

4 The truth, though, is that I'd kept some of that treasure jingling in my pockets all along: I'd maintained an interest in gardening always, dragging it with me wherever I went, even into a city backyard where a neighbor who worked the night shift insisted that her numerous nocturnal cats had every right to use my raised vegetable beds for their litter box. (I retaliated, in my way, by getting a rooster who indulged his right to use the hour of 6 a.m. for his personal compunctions.) In graduate school I studied ecology and evolutionary biology, but the complex mathematical models of predator-prey cycles only made sense to me when I converted them in my mind to farmstead analogies—even though, in those days, the Ecology Department and the College of Agriculture weren't on speaking terms. In my 20s, when I was trying hard to reinvent myself as a person without a Kentucky accent, I often found myself nevertheless the lone argumentative voice in social circles where "farmers" were lumped with political troglodytes and devotees of All-Star wrestling.

Narration: personal anecdote about tobacco farming

5 Once in the early 1980s, when cigarette smoking had newly and drastically fallen from fashion, I stood in someone's kitchen at a party and listened to something like a Greek chorus chanting out the reasons why tobacco should be eliminated from the face of the earth, like smallpox. Some wild tug on my heart made me blurt out, "But what about the tobacco farmers?"

Narration: use of dialogue

6 "Why," someone asked, glaring, "should I care about tobacco farmers?"

7 I was dumbstruck. I couldn't form the words to answer: Yes, it is carcinogenic, and generally grown with too many inputs, but tobacco is the last big commodity in America that's still mostly grown on family farms, in an economy that won't let these farmers shift to another crop. If it goes extinct, so do they.

Narration and description: personal account of childhood memories on a farm

8 I couldn't speak because my mind was flooded with memory, pictures, scents, secret thrills. Childhood afternoons spent reading Louisa May Alcott in a barn loft suffused with the sweet smell of aged burley. The bright, warm days in late spring and early fall when school was functionally closed because whole extended families were drafted to the cooperative work of setting, cutting, stripping, or hanging tobacco. The incalculable fellowship measured out in funerals, family reunions, even bad storms or late-night calvings. The hard-muscled pride of showing I could finally throw a bale of hay onto the truck bed myself. (The year before, when I was 11, I'd had the less honorable job of driving the truck.) The satisfaction of walking across the stage at high school graduation in a county where my name and my relationship to the land were both common knowledge.

Resumption of anecdote about tobacco farmers

9 But when I was pressed, that evening in the kitchen, I didn't try to defend the poor tobacco farmer. As if the deck were not already stacked against his little family enterprise, he was now tarred with the brush of evil along with the companies that bought his product, amplified its toxicity, and attempted to sell it to children. In most cases it's just the more ordinary difficulty of the small family enterprise failing to measure up to the requisite standards of profitability and efficiency. And in every case the rational arguments I might frame in its favor will carry no weight without the attendant silk purse full of memories and sighs and songs of what family farming is worth. Those values are an old currency now, accepted as legal tender almost nowhere.

Return to "treasure" metaphor about farming values

Contrast: writing about "human conventions" vs. writing about the "land"

10 I found myself that day in the jaws of an impossible argument, and I find I am there still. In my professional life I've learned that as long as I write novels and nonfiction books about strictly human conventions and constructions, I'm taken seriously. But when my writing strays into that muddy territory where humans are forced to own up to our dependence on the land, I'm apt to be declared quaintly irrelevant by the small, acutely urban clique that decides in this country what will be called worthy literature. (That clique does not, fortunately, hold much sway over what people actually read.) I understand their purview, I think. I realize I'm beholden to people working in urban centers for many things I love: They publish books, invent theater, produce films and music. But if I had not been raised such a polite Southern girl, I'd offer these critics a blunt proposition: I'll go a week without attending a movie or concert,

Contrast: urban products vs. rural products

you go a week without eating food, and at the end of it we'll sit down together and renegotiate "quaintly irrelevant."

Part of purpose/thesis: need for society to deal with issue of food production

Exemplification: written source

11 This is a conversation that needs to happen. Increasingly I feel sure of it; I just don't know how to go about it when so many have completely forgotten the genuine terms of human survival. Many adults, I'm convinced, believe that food comes from grocery stores. In Wendell Berry's novel *Jayber Crow*, a farmer coming to the failing end of his long economic struggle despaired aloud, "I've wished sometimes that the sons of bitches would starve. And now I'm getting afraid they actually will."

Part of purpose/thesis: rejection of idea that urban and rural people share "no common ground"

Exemplification: personal anecdote about the red-blue electoral divide on TV

12 Like that farmer, I am frustrated with the imposed acrimony between producers and consumers of food, as if this were a conflict in which one could possibly choose sides. I'm tired of the presumption of a nation divided between rural and urban populations whose interests are permanently at odds, whose votes will always be cast different ways, whose hearts and minds share no common ground. This is as wrong as blight, a useless way of thinking, similar to the propaganda warning us that any environmentalist program will necessarily be anti-human. Recently a national magazine asked me to write a commentary on the great divide between "the red and the blue"—imagery taken from election-night TV coverage that colored a map according to the party each state elected, suggesting a clear political difference between the rural heartland and urban coasts. Sorry, I replied to the magazine editors, but I'm the wrong person to ask: I live in red, tend to think blue, and mostly vote green. If you're looking for oversimplification, skip the likes of me.

Part of purpose/thesis: rejection of red-blue division

Comparison: what farmers, hunters, and environmentalists have in common

Comparison: what all people have in common

13 Better yet, skip the whole idea. Recall that in every one of those red states, just a razor's edge under half the voters likely pulled the blue lever, and vice versa—not to mention the greater numbers everywhere who didn't even show up at the polls, so far did they feel from affectionate toward any of the available options. Recall that farmers and hunters, historically, are more active environmentalists than many progressive, city-dwelling vegetarians. (And, conversely, that some of the strongest land-conservation movements on the planet were born in the midst of cities.) Recall that we all have the same requirements for oxygen and drinking water, and that we all like them clean but relentlessly pollute them. Recall that whatever lofty things you might accomplish today, you will do them only because you first ate something that grew out of dirt.

Part of purpose/thesis: survival depends on a good relationship with the land

14 We don't much care to think of ourselves that way—as creatures whose cleanest aspirations depend ultimately on the health of our dirt. But our survival as a species depends on our coming to grips with that, along with some other corollary notions, and when I entered a comfortable midlife I began to see that my kids would get to do the same someday, or not, depending on how well our species could start owning up to its habitat and its food chain. As we faced one environmental crisis after another, did our species seem to be making this connection? As we say back home, not so's you'd notice.

Description: simile comparing food products to "celebrities"

Contrast continues the simile: celebrity foods vs. "gal-next-door" foods

15 Our gustatory industries treat food items like spoiled little celebrities, zipping them around the globe in luxurious air-conditioned cabins, dressing them up in gaudy outfits, spritzing them with makeup, and breaking the bank on advertising, for heaven's sake. My farm-girl heritage makes me blush and turn down tickets to that particular circus. I'd rather wed my fortunes to the sturdy gal-next-door kind of food, growing what I need or getting it from local "you-pick" orchards and our farmers' market.

Description: specific details about the author's farm

Statement of personal values

16 It has come to pass that my husband and I, in what we hope is the middle of our lives, are in possession of a farm. It's not a hobby homestead, it is a farm, somewhat derelict but with good potential. It came to us with some 20 acres of good, tillable bottomland, plus timbered slopes and all the pasture we can ever use, if we're willing to claim it back from the brambles. A similar arrangement is available with the 75-year-old apple orchard. The rest of the inventory includes a hundred-year-old clapboard house, a fine old barn that smells of aged burley, a granary, poultry coops, a root cellar, and a century's store of family legends. No poisons have been applied to this land for years, and we vow none ever will be.

Narration: raising children on a farm, with specific examples, as proof of personal values

17 Our agrarian education has come in as a slow undercurrent beneath our workaday lives and the rearing of our children. Only our closest friends, probably, have taken real notice of the changes in our household: that nearly all the food we put on our table, in every season, was grown in our garden or very nearby. That the animals we eat took no more from the land than they gave back to it, and led sunlit, contentedly grassy lives. Our children know how to bake bread, stretch mozzarella cheese, ride a horse, keep a flock of hens laying, help a neighbor, pack a healthy lunch, and politely decline the world's less wholesome offerings. They know the first fresh garden tomato tastes as good as it does, partly, because you've waited

Metaphor: waiting for home-grown tomatoes likened to self-restraint

for it since last Thanksgiving, and that the awful ones you could have bought at the grocery in between would only subtract from this equation. This rule applies to many things beyond tomatoes. I have noticed that the very politicians who support purely market-driven economics, which favor immediate corporate gratification over long-term responsibility, also express loud concern about the morals of our nation's children and their poor capacity for self-restraint. I wonder what kind of tomatoes those men feed their kids.

Exemplification: Netherlands as a place where freedom and respect for land co-exist

Exemplification: rhetorical questions as illustrations

Statement of personal values

I have heard people of this same political ilk declare that it is perhaps sad but surely inevitable that our farms are being cut up and sold to make nice-sized lawns for suburban folks to mow, because the most immediately profitable land use must prevail in a free country. And yet I have visited countries where people are perfectly free, such as the Netherlands, where this sort of disregard for farmland is both illegal and unthinkable. Plenty of people in this country, too, seem to share a respect for land that gives us food; why else did so many friends of my youth continue farming even while the economic prospects grew doubtful? And why is it that more of them each year are following sustainable practices that defer some immediate profits in favor of the long-term health of their fields, crops, animals, and watercourses? Who are the legions of Americans who now allocate more of their household budgets to food that is organically, sustainably, and locally grown, rather than buying the cheapest products they can find? My husband and I, bearing these trends in mind, did not contemplate the profitable option of subdividing our farm and changing its use. Frankly, that seemed wrong. 18

Comparison: money and morality

Definition by negation: avarice is not the work ethic

Exemplification: religious reasons not to maximize money

It's an interesting question, how to navigate this tangled path between money and morality: not a new question by any means, but one that has taken strange turns in modern times. In our nation's prevailing culture there exists right now a considerable confusion between prosperity and success—so much so that avarice is frequently confused with a work ethic. One's patriotism and good sense may be called into doubt if one elects to earn less money or own fewer possessions than is humanly possible. The notable exception is that a person may do so for religious reasons: Christians are asked by conscience to tithe or assist the poor; Muslims do not collect interest; Catholics may respectably choose a monastic life of 19 communal poverty; and any of us may opt out of a scheme that we feel to be discomforting to our faith. It is in this spirit that we, like you perhaps and so many others before us, have worked to rein in the free market's tyranny over our family's tiny portion of America and install values that override the profit motive. Upon doing so, we receive a greater confidence in our children's future safety and happiness. I believe we are also happier souls in the present, for what that is worth. In the darkest months I look for solace in seed catalogs and articles on pasture rotation. I sleep better at night, feeling safely connected to the things that help make a person whole. It is fair to say that this has been, in some sense, a spiritual conversion.

20 Modern American culture is fairly empty of any suggestion that one's relationship to the land, to consumption and food, is a religious matter. But it's true; the decision to attend to the health of one's habitat and food chain is a spiritual choice. It's also a political choice, a scientific one, a personal and a convivial one. It's not a choice between living in the country or the town; it is about understanding that every one of us, at the level of our cells and respiration, lives in the country and is thus obliged to be mindful of the distance between ourselves and our sustenance.

Thesis statement

Conclusion: summarizes author's outlook and convictions

21 I have worlds to learn about being a good farmer. Last spring when a hard frost fell upon our orchards on May 21, I felt despair at ever getting there at all. But in any weather, I may hope to carry a good agrarian frame of mind into my orchards and fields, my kitchen, my children's schools, my writing life, my friendships, my grocery shopping, and the county landfill. That's the point: It goes everywhere. It may or may not be a movement—I'll leave that to others to say. But it does move, and it works for us.

The following answers to the questions on page 572 will help you analyze Barbara Kingsolver's use of the patterns of development in the essay "The Good Farmer."

1. *What are the writer's purpose and thesis?*

Kingsolver's *purpose* is to persuade us that we all—whether we live in rural or urban areas, vote "blue" or "red," or identify ourselves as conservationists or free-market capitalists—have a profound stake in supporting sustainable agriculture and traditional small farms. Unless our society takes steps to support small family farms and practices that renew the land—especially by buying locally and organically produced foods in preference to foods shipped from far away—we will end up with profoundly negative consequences to our health and ultimately to our economic and spiritual lives.

The author expresses her thesis near the end of the essay: "[T]he decision to attend to the health of one's habitat and food chain is . . . not a choice between living in the country or the town; it is about understanding that every one of us, at the level of our cells and respiration, lives in the country and is thus obliged to be mindful of the distance between ourselves and our sustenance" (paragraph 20).

2. *What pattern of development dominates the essay? How does this pattern help the writer support the essay's thesis and fulfill the essay's purpose?*

Although Kingsolver uses narration, description, and even definition to prove her points, she relies primarily on comparison-contrast to illuminate her thesis. We get a hint of conflict between what the author sees as important and what society sees as important in the first two paragraphs. She is reluctant to tell others about her interest in farming because they might think she "was out of [her] mind" (1). And she understands this attitude, confiding to us that she also had at one time thought of the farm as "a place that seemed to offer . . . almost no potential for economic, intellectual, or spiritual satisfaction" (2). We get a stronger intimation of this conflict in societal values in paragraph 4, where Kingsolver tells us that in graduate school "the Ecology Department and the College of Agriculture weren't on speaking terms" (4).

The author goes on to reinforce the contrast, drawing a distinction between "urban" intellectuals' positive responses to her "novels and nonfiction books about strictly human conventions and constructions" and their dismissive reactions when she "strays into that muddy territory where humans are forced to own up to our dependence on the land" (10). She then offers a dramatic and concrete contrast between urban and rural products: "I'll go a week without attending a movie or concert, you go a week without eating food, and at the end of it we'll sit down together and renegotiate 'quaintly irrelevant'" (10).

After pointing out this "acrimony between producers and consumers of food," Kingsolver says she is "tired of the presumption" that "rural and urban populations" must be "permanently at odds" and she begins to emphasize the ways in which they share "common ground" (12). Even though "the red and the blue [of election-night coverage]" (13) implies "a clear political difference between the rural heartland and urban coasts," in reality, "farmers and hunters . . . are more active environmentalists than many progressive, city-dwelling vegetarians" and "some of the strongest land-conservation movements . . . were born in the . . . cities" (13). In the end, we all have a common interest because we all have "the same requirements for [clean] oxygen and drinking water" (13).

The author also refutes the idea that as a society we must choose between "money and morality" (19) in the uses of land, especially regarding the practice of breaking up farms to create "nice-sized lawns for suburban folks to mow" (18). She argues, using the Netherlands as an example, that it's possible to have a country "where people are perfectly free" (18), but where agricultural land is protected from such devastation. Earning less money by keeping one's farm intact does not reflect badly on "one's patriotism and good sense" (19). She concludes with a series of rhetorical questions promoting the idea that many Americans have worked and continue to work together to "rein in the free market's tyranny over our family's tiny portion of America and install values that override the profit motive" (19).

3. *What other patterns appear in the essay? How do these secondary patterns help the writer support the essay's thesis and fulfill the essay's purpose?*

In addition to comparison-contrast, the author also uses *cause and effect, description, narration, exemplification*, and *definition* to get her points across. In paragraph 2, Kingsolver gives four reasons that might *cause* people to think she is "out of [her] mind" to be interested in farming: most people think it's "smart to get out of agriculture"; she has a successful "career as a writer"; she's not the "picture of an apprentice farmer"; and she herself had sought as a young woman to escape farming because it "seemed to offer...almost no potential" for personal growth.

In paragraph 3, she begins a *descriptive* metaphor, in which she likens farming and farming values to "treasures," that reappears in paragraphs 4 and 9. Kingsolver employs a simile in paragraph 15 to illustrate how our society treats food products "like spoiled little celebrities, zipping them around the globe in luxurious air-conditioned cabins, dressing them up in gaudy outfits, spritzing them with makeup, and breaking the bank on advertising, for heaven's sake." One of the best uses of description is in paragraph 16, where details about the author's current farm—"some 20 acres of good, tillable bottomland, plus timbered slopes and all the pasture we can ever use," "75-year-old apple orchard," and "a hundred-year-old clapboard house, a fine old barn that smells of aged burley, a granary, poultry coops, a root cellar, and a century's store of family legends"—really help the reader visualize and appreciate the farm life.

In paragraphs 5 through 9, Kingsolver *narrates* a personal anecdote to show how farming—even tobacco farming—is misunderstood as a way of life. She dramatizes the narrative with dialogue: "'Why,' someone asked, glaring, 'should I care about tobacco farmers?'" (6). And she includes a detailed reminiscence of her childhood spent on a tobacco farm, including "the bright, warm days in late spring and early fall when school was functionally closed because whole extended families were drafted to the cooperative work of setting, cutting, stripping, or hanging tobacco" (8).

Exemplification appears throughout the essay. A personal example in paragraph 4 highlights how the author had maintained an interest in farming wherever she lived, even in "a city backyard" where she planted "raised vegetable beds." She also cites a book—Wendell Berry's novel *Jayber Crow* (15). She also relates a personal anecdote about turning down a request from "a national magazine" to write about "the great divide between...the rural heartland and urban coasts" (12). As a proof that a free-market economy and respect for the land can co-exist, Kingsolver refers to "the Netherlands, where this sort of disregard for farmland is both illegal and unthinkable" (18). In addition, to support her idea that it can be acceptable to choose "morality" over money, the author offers examples from religion: "Christians are asked by conscience to tithe or assist the poor; Muslims do not collect interest; Catholics may respectably choose a monastic life of communal poverty; and any of us may opt out of a scheme that we feel to be discomforting to our faith" (19).

Finally, Kingsolver introduces *definition by negation* near the end of the essay as a way to explore the supposed conflict between "money and morality": In our nation's prevailing culture...avarice is frequently confused with a work ethic. One's patriotism and good sense may be called into doubt if one elects to earn less money or own fewer possessions than is humanly possible" (19).

Barbara Kingsolver

Stone Soup[1]

In the catalog of family values, where do we rank an occasion like this? A curly-haired boy who wanted to run before he walked, age seven now, a soccer player scoring a winning goal. He turns to the bleachers with his fists in the air and a smile wide as a gap-toothed galaxy. His own cheering section of grown-ups and kids all leap to their feet and hug each other, delirious with love for this boy. He's Andy, my best friend's son. The cheering section includes his mother and her friends, his brother, his father and stepmother, a stepbrother and stepsister, and a grandparent. Lucky is the child with this many relatives on hand to hail a proud accomplishment. I'm there too, witnessing a family fortune. But in spite of myself, defensive words take shape in my head. I am thinking: I dare *anybody* to call this a broken home. 1

Families change, and remain the same. Why are our names for home so slow to catch up to the truth of where we live? 2

When I was a child, I had two parents who loved me without cease. One of them attended every excuse for attention I ever contrived, and the other made it to the ones with higher production values, like piano recitals and appendicitis. So I was a lucky child too. I played with a set of paper dolls called "The Family of Dolls," four in number, who came with the factory-assigned names of Dad, Mom, Sis, and Junior. I think you know what they looked like, at least before I loved them to death and their heads fell off. 3

Now I've replaced the dolls with a life. I knit my days around my daughter's survival and happiness, and am proud to say her head is still on. But we aren't the Family of Dolls. Maybe you're not, either. And if not, even though you are statistically no oddity, it's probably been suggested to you in a hundred ways that yours isn't exactly a real family, but an impostor family, a harbinger of cultural ruin, a slapdash substitute—something like counterfeit money. Here at the tail end of our century, most of us are up to our ears in the noisy business of trying to support and love a thing called family. But there's a current in the air with ferocious moral force that finds its way even into political campaigns, claiming there is only one right way to do it, the Way It Has Always Been. 4

In the face of a thriving, particolored world, this narrow view is so pickled and absurd I'm astonished that it gets airplay. And I'm astonished that it still stings. 5

Every parent has endured the arrogance of a child-unfriendly grump sitting in judgment, explaining what those kids of ours really need (for example, 6

[1]"Stone Soup" is reprinted with permission from *High Tide In Tucson: Essays from Now or Never*, published by HarperCollins.

"a good licking"). If we're polite, we move our crew to another bench in the park. If we're forthright (as I am in my mind, only, for the rest of the day), we fix them with a sweet imperious stare and say, "Come back and let's talk about it after you've changed a thousand diapers."

But it's harder somehow to shrug off the Family-of-Dolls Family Values 7
crew when they judge (from their safe distance) that divorced people, blended families, gay families and single parents are failures. That our children are at risk, and the whole arrangement is messy and embarrassing. A marriage that ends is not called "finished," it's called *failed*. The children of this family may have been born to a happy union, but now they are called *the children of divorce.*

I had no idea how thoroughly these assumptions overlaid my culture 8
until I went through divorce myself. I wrote to a friend: "This might be worse than being widowed. Overnight I've suffered the same losses—companionship, financial and practical support, my identity as a wife and partner, the future I'd taken for granted. I am lonely, grieving, and hard-pressed to take care of my household alone. But instead of bringing casseroles, people are acting like I had a fit and broke up the family china."

Once upon a time I held these beliefs about divorce: that everyone who 9
does it could have chosen not to do it. That it's a lazy way out of marital problems. That it selfishly puts personal happiness ahead of family integrity. Now I tremble for my ignorance. It's easy, in fortunate times, to forget about the ambush that could leave your head reeling: serious mental or physical illness, death in the family, abandonment, financial calamity, humiliation, violence, despair.

I started out like any child, intent on being the Family of Dolls. I set 10
upon young womanhood believing in most of the doctrines of my generation: I wore my skirts four inches above the knee. I had that Barbie with her zebra-striped swimsuit and a figure unlike anything found in nature. And I understood the Prince Charming Theory of Marriage, a quest for Mr. Right that ends smack dab where you find him. I did not completely understand that another whole story *begins* there, and no fairy tale prepared me for the combination of bad luck and persistent hope that would interrupt my dream and lead me to other arrangements.

Like a cancer diagnosis, a dying marriage is a thing to fight, to deny, and 11
finally, when there's no choice left, to dig in and survive. Casseroles would help. Likewise, I imagine it must be a painful reckoning in adolescence (or later on) to realize true love will never look like the soft-focus fragrance ads because Prince Charming (surprise!) is a princess. Or vice versa. Or has skin the color your parents didn't want you messing with, except in the Crayola box.

It's awfully easy to hold in contempt the straw broken home, and that 12
mythical category of persons who toss away nuclear family for the sheer fun of it. Even the legal terms we use have a suggestion of caprice. I resent the phrase "irreconcilable differences," which suggests a stubborn refusal to accept a spouse's little quirks. This is specious. Every happily married couple I know

has loads of irreconcilable differences. Negotiating where to set the thermostat is not the point. A nonfunctioning marriage is a slow asphyxiation. It is waking up despised each morning, listening to the pulse of your own loneliness before the radio begins to blare its raucous gospel that you're nothing if you aren't loved. It is sharing your airless house with the threat of suicide or other kinds of violence, while the ghost that whispers, "Leave here and destroy your children," has passed over every door and nailed it shut. Disassembling a marriage in these circumstances is as much *fun* as amputating your own gangrenous leg. You do it, if you can, to save a life—or two, or more.

I know of no one who really went looking to hoe the harder row, especially the daunting one of single parenthood. Yet it seems to be the most American of customs to blame the burdened for their destiny. We'd like so desperately to believe in freedom and justice for all, we can hardly name that rogue bad luck, even when he's a close enough snake to bite us. In the wake of my divorce, some friends (even a few close ones) chose to vanish, rather than linger within striking distance of misfortune. 13

But most stuck around, bless their hearts, and if I'm any the wiser for my trials, it's from having learned the worth of steadfast friendship. And also, what not to say. The least helpful question is: "Did you want the divorce, or didn't you?" Did I want to keep that gangrenous leg, or not? How to explain, in a culture that venerates choice: two terrifying options are much worse than none at all. Give me any day the quick hand of cruel fate that will leave me scarred but blameless. As it was, I kept thinking of that wicked third-grade joke in which some boy comes up behind you and grabs your ear, starts in with a prolonged tug, and asks, "Do you want this ear any longer?" 14

Still, the friend who holds your hand and says the wrong thing is made of dearer stuff than the one who stays away. And generally, through all of it, you live. My favorite fictional character, Kate Vaiden (in the novel by Reynolds Price), advises: "Strength just comes in one brand—you stand up at sunrise and meet what they send you and keep your hair combed." 15

Once you've weathered the straits, you get to cross the tricky juncture from casualty to survivor. If you're on your feet at the end of a year or two, and have begun putting together a happy new existence, those friends who were kind enough to feel sorry for you when you needed it must now accept you back to the ranks of the living. If you're truly blessed, they will dance at your second wedding. Everybody else, for heaven's sake, should stop throwing stones. 16

Arguing about whether nontraditional families deserve pity or tolerance is a little like the medieval debate about left-handedness as a mark of the devil. Divorce, remarriage, single parenthood, gay parents, and blended families simply are. They're facts of our time. Some of the reasons listed by sociologists for these family reconstructions are: the idea of marriage as a romantic partnership rather than a pragmatic one; a shift in women's expectations, from servility to self-respect and independence; and longevity (prior to antibiotics no marriage 17 was expected to last many decades—in Colonial days the average couple lived to be married less than twelve years). Add to all this our growing sense of entitlement to happiness and safety from abuse. Most would agree these are all good things. Yet their result—a culture in which serial monogamy and the consequent reshaping of families are the norm—gets diagnosed as "failing."

For many of us, once we have put ourselves Humpty-Dumpty-wise back together again, the main problem with our reorganized family is that other people think we have a problem. My daughter tells me the only time she's uncomfortable about being the child of divorced parents is when her friends say they feel sorry for her. It's a bizarre sympathy, given that half the kids in her school and nation are in the same boat, pursuing childish happiness with the same energy as their married-parent peers. When anyone asks how *she* feels about it, she spontaneously lists the benefits: our house is in the country and we have a dog, but she can go to her dad's neighborhood for the urban thrills of a pool and sidewalks for roller-skating. What's more, she has three sets of grandparents! 18

Why is it surprising that a child would revel in a widened family and the right to feel at home in more than one house? Isn't it the opposite that should worry us—a child with no home at all, or too few resources to feel safe? The child at risk is the one whose parents are too immature themselves to guide wisely; too diminished by poverty to nurture; too far from opportunity to offer hope. The number of children in the U.S. living in poverty at this moment is almost unfathomably large: twenty percent. There are families among us that need help all right, and by no means are they new on the landscape. The rate at which teenage girls had babies in 1957 (ninety-six per thousand) was twice what it is now. That remarkable statistic is ignored by the religious right—probably because the teen birth rate was cut in half mainly by legalized abortion. In fact, the policy gatekeepers who coined the phrase "family values" have steadfastly ignored the desperation of too-small families, and since 1979 have steadily reduced the amount of financial support available to a single parent. But, this camp's most outspoken attacks seem aimed at the notion of families getting too complex, with add-ons and extras such as a gay parent's partner, or a remarried mother's new husband and his children. 19

To judge a family's value by its tidy symmetry is to purchase a book for its cover. There's no moral authority there. The famous family comprised of Dad, Mom, Sis, and Junior living as an isolated economic unit is not built on historical bedrock. In *The Way We Never Were*, Stephanie Coontz writes, "Whenever people propose that we go back to the traditional family, I always suggest that they pick a ballpark date for the family they have in mind." Colonial families were tidily disciplined, but their members (meaning everyone but infants) labored incessantly and died young. Then the Victorian family adopted a new division of labor, in which women's role was domestic and allowed time for study and play, but this was an upper-class construct supported by myriad slaves. Coontz writes, "For every nineteenth-century 20 middle-class family that protected its wife and child within the family circle, there was an Irish or German girl scrubbing floors...a Welsh boy mining coal to keep the home-baked goodies warm, a black girl doing the family laundry, a black mother and child picking cotton to be made into clothes for the family, and a Jewish or an Italian daughter in a sweatshop making 'ladies' dresses or artificial flowers for the family to purchase."

The abolition of slavery brought slightly more democratic arrangements, in which extended families were harnessed together in cottage industries; at the turn of the century came a steep rise in child labor in mines and sweatshops. Twenty percent of American children lived in orphanages at the time; their parents were not necessarily dead, but couldn't afford to keep them. 21

During the Depression and up to the end of World War II, many millions of U.S. households were more multigenerational than nuclear. Women my grandmother's age were likely to live with a fluid assortment of elderly relatives, in-laws, siblings, and children. In many cases they spent virtually every waking hour working in the company of other women—a companionable scenario in which it would be easier, I imagine, to tolerate an estranged or difficult spouse. I'm reluctant to idealize a life of so much hard work and so little spousal intimacy, but its advantage may have been resilience. A family so large and varied would not easily be brought down by a single blow: it could absorb a death, long illness, an abandonment here or there, and any number of irreconcilable differences. 22

The Family of Dolls came along midcentury as a great American experiment. A booming economy required a mobile labor force and demanded that women surrender jobs to returning soldiers. Families came to be defined by a single breadwinner. They struck out for single-family homes at an earlier age than ever before, and in unprecedented numbers they raised children in urban isolation. The nuclear family was launched to sink or swim. 23

More than a few sank. Social historians corroborate that the suburban family of the postwar economic boom, which we have recently selected as our definition of "traditional," was no panacea. Twenty-five percent of Americans were poor in the mid-1950s, and as yet there were no food stamps. Sixty percent of the elderly lived on less than $1,000 a year, and most had no medical insurance. In the sequestered suburbs, alcoholism and sexual abuse of children were far more widespread than anyone imagined. 24

Expectations soared, and the economy sagged. It's hard to depend on one other adult for everything, come what may. In the last three decades, that amorphous, adaptable structure we call "family" has been reshaped once more by economic tides. Compared with fifties families, mothers are far more likely now to be employed. We are statistically more likely to divorce, and to live in blended families or other extranuclear arrangements. We are also more likely to plan and space our children, and to rate our marriages as "happy." We are less likely to suffer abuse without recourse or to stare out at our lives through a glaze of prescription tranquilizers. Our aged parents are less likely 25 to be destitute, and we're half as likely to have a teenage daughter turn up a mother herself. All in all, I would say that if "intact" in modern family-values jargon means living quietly desperate in the bell jar, then hip-hip-hooray for "broken." A neat family model constructed to service the Baby Boom economy seems to be returning gradually to a grand, lumpy shape that human families apparently have tended toward since they first took root in Olduvai Gorge. We're social animals, deeply fond of companionship, and children love best to run in packs. If there is a *normal* for humans, at all, I expect it looks like two or three Families of Dolls, connected variously by kinship and passion, shuffled like cards and strewn over several shoeboxes.

The sooner we can let go the fairy tale of families functioning perfectly in isolation, the better we might embrace the relief of community. Even the admirable parents who've stayed married through thick and thin are very likely, at present, to incorporate other adults into their families—household help and baby-sitters if they can afford them, or neighbors and grandparents if they can't. For single parents, this support is the rock-bottom definition of family. And most parents who have split apart, however painfully, still manage to maintain family continuity for their children, creating in many cases a boisterous phenomenon that Constance Ahrons in her book *The Good Divorce* calls the "binuclear family." Call it what you will—when ex-spouses beat swords into plowshares and jump up and down at a soccer game together, it makes for happy kids. 26

Cinderella, look, who needs her? All those evil stepsisters? That story always seemed like too much cotton-picking fuss over clothes. A childhood tale that fascinated me more was the one called "Stone Soup," and the gist of it is this: Once upon a time, a pair of beleaguered soldiers straggled home to a village empty-handed, in a land ruined by war. They were famished, but the villagers had so little they shouted evil words and slammed their doors. So the soldiers dragged out a big kettle, filled it with water, and put it on a fire to boil. They rolled a clean round stone into the pot, while the villagers peered through their curtains in amazement. 27

"What kind of soup is that?" they hooted. 28

"Stone soup," the soldiers replied. "Everybody can have some when it's done." 29

"Well, thanks," one matron grumbled, coming out with a shriveled carrot. "But it'd be better if you threw this in." 30

And so on, of course, a vegetable at a time, until the whole suspicious village managed to feed itself grandly. 31

Any family is a big empty pot, save for what gets thrown in. Each stew turns out different. Generosity, a resolve to turn bad luck into good, and respect for variety—these things will nourish a nation of children. Name-calling and suspicion will not. My soup contains a rock or two of hard times, and maybe yours does too. I expect it's a heck of a bouillabaise. 32

Martin Luther King, Jr.

More than forty years after his assassination, Martin Luther King, Jr. (1929–68), is still recognized as the towering figure in the struggle for civil rights in the United States. Born in Atlanta, Georgia, King earned doctorates from Boston University and Chicago Theological Seminary and served as pastor of a Baptist congregation in Montgomery, Alabama. Advocating a philosophy of nonviolent resistance to racial injustice, he led bus boycotts, marches, and sit-ins that brought about passage of the 1964 Civil Rights Act and the Voting Rights Act of 1965. Dr. King was awarded the Nobel Peace Prize in 1964. The following two selections by King are taken from *Where Do We Go from Here: Chaos or Community?* (1967).

Where Do We Go from Here: Chaos or Community?

1 A final problem that mankind must solve in order to survive in the world house that we have inherited is finding an alternative to war and human destruction. Recent events have vividly reminded us that nations are not reducing but rather increasing their arsenals of weapons of mass destruction. The best brains in the highly developed nations of the world are devoted to military technology. The proliferation of nuclear weapons has not been halted, in spite of the limited-test-ban treaty.

2 In this day of man's highest technical achievement, in this day of dazzling discovery, of novel opportunities, loftier dignities and fuller freedoms for all, there is no excuse for the kind of blind craving for power and resources that provoked the wars of previous generations. There is no need to fight for food and land. Science has provided us with adequate means of survival and transportation, which make it possible to enjoy the fullness of this great earth. The question now is, do we have the morality and courage required to live together as brothers and not be afraid?

3 One of the most persistent ambiguities we face is that everybody talks about peace as a goal, but among the wielders of power peace is practically nobody's business. Many men cry "Peace! Peace!" but they refuse to do the things that make for peace.

4 The large power blocs talk passionately of pursuing peace while expanding defense budgets that already bulge, enlarging already awesome armies and devising ever more devastating weapons. Call the roll of those who sing the glad tidings of peace and one's ears will be surprised by the responding sounds. The heads of all the nations issue clarion calls for peace, yet they come to the peace table accompanied by bands of brigands each bearing unsheathed swords.

5 The stages of history are replete with the chants and choruses of the conquerors of old who came killing in pursuit of peace. Alexander, Genghis

Khan, Julius Caesar, Charlemagne and Napoleon were akin in seeking a peaceful world order, a world fashioned after their selfish conceptions of an ideal existence. Each sought a world at peace which would personify his egotistic dreams. Even within the life span of most of us, another megalomaniac strode across the world stage. He sent his blitzkrieg-bent legions blazing across Europe, bringing havoc and holocaust in his wake. There is grave irony in the fact that Hitler could come forth, following nakedly aggressive expansionist theories, and do it all in the name of peace.

So when in this day I see the leaders of nations again talking peace while preparing for war, I take fearful pause. When I see our country today intervening in what is basically a civil war, mutilating hundreds of thousands of Vietnamese children with napalm, burning villages and rice fields at random, painting the valleys of that small Asian country red with human blood, leaving broken bodies in countless ditches and sending home half-men, mutilated mentally and physically; when I see the unwillingness of our government to create the atmosphere for a negotiated settlement of this awful conflict by halting bombings in the North and agreeing unequivocally to talk with the Vietcong—and all this in the name of pursuing the goal of peace—I tremble for our world.[1] I do so not only from dire recall of the nightmares wreaked in the wars of yesterday, but also from dreadful realization of today's possible nuclear destructiveness and tomorrow's even more calamitous prospects. 6

Before it is too late, we must narrow the gaping chasm between our proclamations of peace and our lowly deeds which precipitate and perpetuate war. We are called upon to look up from the quagmire of military programs and defense commitments and read the warnings on history's signposts. 7

One day we must come to see that peace is not merely a distant goal that we seek but a means by which we arrive at that goal. We must pursue peaceful ends through peaceful means. How much longer must we play at deadly war games before we heed the plaintive pleas of the unnumbered dead and maimed of past wars? 8

President John F. Kennedy said on one occasion, "Mankind must put an end to war or war will put an end to mankind." Wisdom born of experience should tell us that war is obsolete. There may have been a time when war served as a negative good by preventing the spread and growth of an evil force, but the destructive power of modern weapons eliminates even the possibility that war may serve any good at all. If we assume that life is worth living and that man has a right to survive, then we must find an alternative to 9

[1]Only after more than 58,000 Americans had been killed did the United States withdraw from Vietnam. The war then continued until the North Vietnamese, aided by the Vietcong, took over all of Vietnam (editors' note).

war. In a day when vehicles hurtle through outer space and guided ballistic missiles carve highways of death through the stratosphere, no nation can claim victory in war. A so-called limited war will leave little more than a calamitous legacy of human suffering, political turmoil and spiritual disillusionment. A world war will leave only smoldering ashes as mute testimony of a human race whose folly led inexorably to ultimate death. If modern man continues to flirt unhesitatingly with war, he will transform his earthly habitat into an inferno such as even the mind of Dante[2] could not imagine.

Therefore I suggest that the philosophy and strategy of nonviolence become immediately a subject for study and for serious experimentation in every field of human conflict, by no means excluding the relations between nations. It is, after all, nation-states which make war, which have produced the weapons that threaten the survival of mankind and which are both genocidal and suicidal in character. 10

We have ancient habits to deal with, vast structures of power, indescribably complicated problems to solve. But unless we abdicate our humanity altogether and succumb to fear and impotence in the presence of the weapons we have ourselves created, it is as possible and as urgent to put an end to war and violence between nations as it is to put an end to poverty and racial injustice. 11

The United Nations is a gesture in the direction of nonviolence on a world scale. There, at least, states that oppose one another have sought to do so with words instead of with weapons. But true nonviolence is more than the absence of violence. It is the persistent and determined application of peaceable power to offenses against the community—in this case the world community. As the United Nations moves ahead with the giant tasks confronting it, I would hope that it would earnestly examine the uses of nonviolent direct action. 12

I do not minimize the complexity of the problems that need to be faced in achieving disarmament and peace. But I am convinced that we shall not have the will, the courage and the insight to deal with such matters unless in this field we are prepared to undergo a mental and spiritual re-evaluation, a change of focus which will enable us to see that the things that seem most real and powerful are indeed now unreal and have come under sentence of death. We need to make a supreme effort to generate the readiness, indeed the eagerness, to enter into the new world which is now possible, "the city which hath foundation, whose Building and Maker is God." 13

It is not enough to say, "We must not wage war." It is necessary to love peace and sacrifice for it. We must concentrate not merely on the eradication 14

[2]In The *Divine Comedy* (1321), Italian poet Dante depicts the burning torments of hell endured by a lost soul before it can attain salvation (editors' note).

of war but on the affirmation of peace. A fascinating story about Ulysses and the Sirens[3] is preserved for us in Greek literature. The Sirens had the ability to sing so sweetly that sailors could not resist steering toward their island. Many ships were lured upon the rocks, and men forgot home, duty and honor as they flung themselves into the sea to be embraced by arms that drew them down to death. Ulysses, determined not to succumb to the Sirens, first decided to tie himself tightly to the mast of his boat and his crew stuffed their ears with wax. But finally he and his crew learned a better way to save themselves: They took on board the beautiful singer Orpheus, whose melodies were sweeter than the music of the Sirens. When Orpheus sang, who would bother to listen to the Sirens?

So we must see that peace represents a sweeter music, a cosmic melody 15
that is far superior to the discords of war. Somehow we must transform the dynamics of the world power struggle from the nuclear arms race, which no one can win, to a creative contest to harness man's genius for the purpose of making peace and prosperity a reality for all the nations of the world. In short, we must shift the arms race into a "peace race." If we have the will and determination to mount such a peace offensive, we will unlock hitherto tightly sealed doors of hope and bring new light into the dark chambers of pessimism.

[3]Ulysses and the Sirens, as well as Orpheus (mentioned later in the paragraph), are all figures in Greek mythology (editors' note).

Martin Luther King, Jr.

The World House

Some years ago a famous novelist died. Among his papers was found a list of suggested plots for future stories, the most prominently underscored being this one: "A widely separated family inherits a house in which they have to live together." This is the great new problem of mankind. We have inherited a large house, a great "world house" in which we have to live together—black and white, Easterner and Westerner, Gentile and Jew, Catholic and Protestant, Moslem and Hindu—a family unduly separated in ideas, culture and interest, who, because we can never again live apart, must learn somehow to live with each other in peace. 1

However deeply American Negroes are caught in the struggle to be at last at home in our homeland of the United States, we cannot ignore the larger world house in which we are also dwellers. Equality with whites will not solve the problems of either whites or Negroes if it means equality in a world society stricken by poverty and in a universe doomed to extinction by war. 2

All inhabitants of the globe are now neighbors. This worldwide neighborhood has been brought into being largely as a result of the modern scientific and technological revolutions. The world of today is vastly different from the world of just one hundred years ago. A century ago Thomas Edison had not yet invented the incandescent lamp to bring light to many dark places of the earth. The Wright brothers had not yet invented that fascinating mechanical bird that would spread its gigantic wings across the skies and soon dwarf distance and place time in the service of man. Einstein had not yet challenged an axiom and the theory of relativity had not yet been posited. 3

Human beings, searching a century ago as now for better understanding, had no television, no radios, no telephones and no motion pictures through which to communicate. Medical science had not yet discovered the wonder drugs to end many dread plagues and diseases. One hundred years ago military men had not yet developed the terrifying weapons of warfare that we know today—not the bomber, an airborne fortress raining down death; nor napalm, that burner of all things and flesh in its path. A century ago there were no skyscraping buildings to kiss the stars and no gargantuan bridges to span the waters. Science had not yet peered into the unfathomable ranges of interstellar space, nor had it penetrated oceanic depths. All these new inventions, these new ideas, these sometimes fascinating and sometimes frightening developments came later. Most of them have come within the past sixty years, sometimes with agonizing slowness, more characteristically with bewildering speed, but always with enormous significance for our future. 4

The years ahead will see a continuation of the same dramatic developments. Physical science will carve new highways through the stratosphere. In a few years astronauts and cosmonauts will probably walk comfortably across the uncertain pathways of the moon. In two or three years it will be possible, because of the new supersonic jets, to fly from New York to London in two and one-half hours. In the years ahead medical science will greatly prolong the lives of men by finding a cure for cancer and deadly heart ailments. Automation and cybernation will make it possible for working people to have undreamed-of amounts of leisure time. All this is a dazzling picture of the furniture, the workshop, the spacious rooms, the new decorations and the architectural pattern of the large world house in which we are living. 5

Along with the scientific and technological revolution, we have also witnessed a worldwide freedom revolution over the last few decades. The present upsurge of the Negro people of the United States grows out of a deep and passionate determination to make freedom and equality a reality "here" and "now." In one sense the civil rights movement in the United States is a special American phenomenon which must be understood in the light of American history and dealt with in terms of the American situation. But on another and more important level, what is happening in the United States today is a significant part of a world development. 6

We live in a day, said the philosopher Alfred North Whitehead, "when civilization is shifting its basic outlook; a major turning point in history where the presuppositions on which society is structured are being analyzed, sharply challenged, and profoundly changed." What we are seeing now is a freedom explosion, the realization of "an idea whose time has come," to use Victor Hugo's[1] phrase. The deep rumbling of discontent that we hear today is the thunder of disinherited masses, rising from dungeons of oppression to the bright hills of freedom. In one majestic chorus the rising masses are singing, in the words of our freedom song, "Ain't gonna let nobody turn us around." All over the world like a fever, freedom is spreading in the widest liberation movement in history. The great masses of people are determined to end the exploitation of their races and lands. They are awake and moving toward their goal like a tidal wave. You can hear them rumbling in every village street, on the docks, in the houses, among the students, in the churches and at political meetings. For several centuries the direction of history flowed from the nations and societies of Western Europe out into the rest of the world in "conquests" of various sorts. That period, the era of colonialism, is at an end. East is moving West. The earth is being redistributed. Yes, we are "shifting our basic outlooks." 7

These developments should not surprise any student of history. Oppressed people cannot remain oppressed forever. The yearning for freedom 8

[1]Victor Hugo (1802–85) was a French poet, dramatist, and novelist (editors' note).

eventually manifests itself. The Bible tells the thrilling story of how Moses stood in Pharaoh's court centuries ago and cried, "Let my people go." This was an opening chapter in a continuing story. The present struggle in the United States is a later chapter in the same story. Something within has reminded the Negro of his birthright of freedom, and something without has reminded him that it can be gained. Consciously or unconsciously, he has been caught up by the spirit of the times, and with his black brothers of Africa and his brown and yellow brothers in Asia, South America and the Caribbean, the United States Negro is moving with a sense of great urgency toward the promised land of racial justice.

Nothing could be more tragic than for men to live in these revolutionary times and fail to achieve the new attitudes and the new mental outlooks that the new situation demands. In Washington Irving's familiar story of Rip Van Winkle, the one thing that we usually remember is that Rip slept twenty years. There is another important point, however, that is almost always overlooked. It was the sign on the inn in the little town on the Hudson from which Rip departed and scaled the mountain for his long sleep. When he went up, the sign had a picture of King George III of England. When he came down, twenty years later, the sign had a picture of George Washington. As he looked at the picture of the first President of the United States, Rip was confused, flustered and lost. He knew not who Washington was. The most striking thing about this story is not that Rip slept twenty years, but that he slept through a revolution that would alter the course of human history. 9

One of the great liabilities of history is that all too many people fail to remain awake through great periods of social change. Every society has its protectors of the status quo and its fraternities of the indifferent who are notorious for sleeping through revolutions. But today our very survival depends on our ability to stay awake, to adjust to new ideas, to remain vigilant and to face the challenge of change. The large house in which we live demands that we transform this worldwide neighborhood into a worldwide brotherhood. Together we must learn to live as brothers or together we will be forced to perish as fools. 10

We must work passionately and indefatigably to bridge the gulf between our scientific progress and our moral progress. One of the great problems of mankind is that we suffer from a poverty of the spirit which stands in glaring contrast to our scientific and technological abundance. The richer we have become materially, the poorer we have become morally and spiritually. 11

Every man lives in two realms, the internal and the external. The internal is that realm of spiritual ends expressed in art, literature, morals, and religion. The external is that complex of devices, techniques, mechanisms, and instrumentalities by means of which we live. Our problem today is that we have allowed the internal to become lost in the external. We have 12 allowed the means by which we live to outdistance the ends for which we live. So much of modern life can be summarized in that suggestive phrase of Thoreau:[2] "Improved means to an unimproved end." This is the serious predicament, the deep and haunting problem, confronting modern man. Enlarged material powers spell enlarged peril if there is not proportionate growth of the soul. When the external of man's nature subjugates the internal, dark storm clouds begin to form.

Western civilization is particularly vulnerable at this moment, for our material abundance has brought us neither peace of mind nor serenity of spirit. An Asian writer has portrayed our dilemma in candid terms: 13

> You call your thousand material devices "labor-saving machinery," yet you are forever "busy." With the multiplying of your machinery you grow increasingly fatigued, anxious, nervous, dissatisfied. Whatever you have, you want more; and wherever you are you want to go somewhere else... your devices are neither time-saving nor soul-saving machinery. They are so many sharp spurs which urge you on to invent more machinery and to do more business.

This tells us something about our civilization that cannot be cast aside as a prejudiced charge by an Eastern thinker who is jealous of Western prosperity. We cannot escape the indictment. 14

This does not mean that we must turn back the clock of scientific progress. No one can overlook the wonders that science has wrought for our lives. The automobile will not abdicate in favor of the horse and buggy, or the train in favor of the stagecoach, or the tractor in favor of the hand plow, or the scientific method in favor of ignorance and superstition. But our moral and spiritual "lag" must be redeemed. When scientific power outruns moral power, we end up with guided missiles and misguided men. When we foolishly minimize the internal of our lives and maximize the external, we sign the warrant for our own day of doom. 15

Our hope for creative living in this world house that we have inherited lies in our ability to reestablish the moral ends of our lives in personal character and social justice. Without this spiritual and moral reawakening we shall destroy ourselves in the misuse of our own instruments. 16

[2]Henry David Thoreau (1817–62) was an American philosopher and essayist (editors' note).

Joan Didion

Known for her taut prose style and sharp social commentary, Joan Didion (1934–) graduated from the University of California at Berkeley. Her essays have appeared in *The Saturday Evening Post, The American Scholar,* and the *National Review,* as well as in three collections: *Slouching Towards Bethlehem* (1969), *The White Album* (1979), and *After Henry* (1992). *Salvador* (1983) is a book-length essay about a 1982 visit to Central America. The coauthor of several screenplays (including *A Star Is Born* in 1976 and *Up Close and Personal* in 1996), Didion has also written novels, including *Run River* (1963), *A Book of Common Prayer* (1977), *Democracy* (1984), *The Last Thing He Wanted* (1996), and *Where I Was From* (2003), as well as *Fixed Ideas: America Since 9.11* (2003), a book of political commentary. In 2005, Didion published *The Year of Magical Thinking,* a memoir. "The Santa Ana" and "Marrying Absurd" are both from *Slouching Towards Bethlehem.*

The Santa Ana

There is something uneasy in the Los Angeles air this afternoon, some unnatural stillness, some tension. What it means is that tonight a Santa Ana will begin to blow, a hot wind from the northeast whining down through the Cajon and San Gorgonio Passes, blowing up sandstorms out along Route 66, drying the hills and the nerves to the flash point. For a few days now we will see smoke back in the canyons, and hear sirens in the night. I have neither heard nor read that a Santa Ana is due, but I know it, and almost everyone I have seen today knows it too. We know it because we feel it. The baby frets. The maid sulks. I rekindle a waning argument with the telephone company, then cut my losses and lie down, given over to whatever is in the air. To live with the Santa Ana is to accept, consciously or unconsciously, a deeply mechanistic view of human behavior. 1

I recall being told, when I first moved to Los Angeles and was living on an isolated beach, that the Indians would throw themselves into the sea when the bad wind blew. I could see why. The Pacific turned ominously glossy during a Santa Ana period, and one woke in the night troubled not only by the peacocks screaming in the olive trees but by the eerie absence of surf. The heat was surreal. The sky had a yellow cast, the kind of light sometimes called "earthquake weather." My only neighbor would not come out of her house for days, and there were no lights at night, and her husband roamed the place with a machete. One day he would tell me that he had heard a trespasser, the next a rattlesnake. 2

"On nights like that," Raymond Chandler[1] once wrote about the Santa Ana, "every booze party ends in a fight. Meek little wives feel the edge of the 3

[1]Raymond Chandler (1888–1959) was an American novelist, best known for his detective novels featuring the character of Philip Marlowe (editors' note).

carving knife and study their husbands' necks. Anything can happen." That was the kind of wind it was. I did not know then that there was any basis for the effect it had on all of us, but it turns out to be another of those cases in which science bears out folk wisdom. The Santa Ana, which is named for one of the canyons it rushes through, is a *foehn* wind, like the *foehn* of Austria and Switzerland and the *hamsin* of Israel. There are a number of persistent malevolent winds, perhaps the best known of which are the mistral of France and the Mediterranean sirocco, but a *foehn* wind has distinct characteristics: it occurs on the leeward slope of a mountain range and, although the air begins as a cold mass, it is warmed as it comes down the mountain and appears finally as a hot dry wind. Whenever and wherever a *foehn* blows, doctors hear about headaches and nausea and allergies, about "nervousness," about "depression." In Los Angeles some teachers do not attempt to conduct formal classes during a Santa Ana, because the children become unmanageable. In Switzerland the suicide rate goes up during the *foehn,* and in the courts of some Swiss cantons the wind is considered a mitigating circumstance for crime. Surgeons are said to watch the wind, because blood does not clot normally during a *foehn.* A few years ago an Israeli physicist discovered that not only during such winds, but for the ten or twelve hours which precede them, the air carries an unusually high ratio of positive to negative ions. No one seems to know exactly why that should be; some talk about friction and others suggest solar disturbances. In any case the positive ions are there, and what an excess of positive ions does, in the simplest terms, is make people unhappy. One cannot get much more mechanistic than that.

Easterners commonly complain that there is no "weather" at all in 4
Southern California, that the days and the seasons slip by relentlessly, numbingly bland. That is quite misleading. In fact the climate is characterized by infrequent but violent extremes: two periods of torrential subtropical rains which continue for weeks and wash out the hills and send subdivisions sliding toward the sea; about twenty scattered days a year of the Santa Ana, which, with its incendiary dryness, invariably means fire. At the first prediction of a Santa Ana, the Forest Service flies men and equipment from northern California into the southern forests, and the Los Angeles Fire Department cancels its ordinary non-firefighting routines. The Santa Ana caused Malibu to burn the way it did in 1956, and Bel Air in 1961, and Santa Barbara in 1964. In the winter of 1966–67 eleven men were killed fighting a Santa Ana fire that spread through the San Gabriel Mountains.

Just to watch the front-page news out of Los Angeles during a Santa 5
Ana is to get very close to what it is about the place. The longest single Santa Ana period in recent years was in 1957, and it lasted not the usual three or four days but fourteen days, from November 21 until December 4. On the first day 25,000 acres of the San Gabriel Mountains were burning, with gusts reaching 100 miles an hour. In town, the wind reached Force 12, or

hurricane force, on the Beaufort Scale; oil derricks were toppled and people ordered off the downtown streets to avoid injury from flying objects. On November 22 the fire in the San Gabriels was out of control. On November 24 six people were killed in automobile accidents, and by the end of the week the Los Angeles *Times* was keeping a box score of traffic deaths. On November 26 a prominent Pasadena attorney, depressed about money, shot and killed his wife, their two sons, and himself. On November 27 a South Gate divorcée, twenty-two, was murdered and thrown from a moving car. On November 30 the San Gabriel fire was still out of control, and the wind in town was blowing eighty miles an hour. On the first day of December four people died violently, and on the third the wind began to break.

It is hard for people who have not lived in Los Angeles to realize how 6
radically the Santa Ana figures in the local imagination. The city burning is Los Angeles's deepest image of itself: Nathanael West perceived that, in *The Day of the Locust;* and at the time of the 1965 Watts riots what struck the imagination most indelibly were the fires.[2] For days one could drive the Harbor Freeway and see the city on fire, just as we had always known it would be in the end. Los Angeles weather is the weather of catastrophe, of apocalypse, and, just as the reliably long and bitter winters of New England determine the way life is lived there, so the violence and the unpredictability of the Santa Ana affect the entire quality of life in Los Angeles, accentuate its impermanence, its unreliability. The wind shows us how close to the edge we are.

[2]Set in Hollywood, West's 1939 novel, *The Day of the Locust,* ends with a description of Los Angeles engulfed in flames. In 1965, the Watts section of Los Angeles experienced widespread riots, leaving much of the area devastated by fire (editors' note).

Joan Didion

Marrying Absurd

To be married in Las Vegas, Clark County, Nevada, a bride must swear that she is eighteen or has parental permission and a bridegroom that he is twenty-one or has parental permission. Someone must put up five dollars for the license. (On Sundays and holidays, fifteen dollars. The Clark County Courthouse issues marriage licenses at any time of the day or night except between noon and one in the afternoon, between eight and nine in the evening, and between four and five in the morning.) Nothing else is required. The State of Nevada, alone among these United States, demands neither a premarital blood test nor a waiting period before or after the issuance of a marriage license. Driving in across the Mojave from Los Angeles, one sees the signs way out on the desert, looming up from that moonscape of rattle-snakes and mesquite, even before the Las Vegas lights appear like a mirage on the horizon: "GETTING MARRIED? Free License Information First Strip Exit." Perhaps the Las Vegas wedding industry achieved its peak operational efficiency between 9:00 P.M. and midnight of August 26, 1965, an otherwise unremarkable Thursday which happened to be, by Presidential order,[1] the last day on which anyone could improve his draft status merely by getting married. One hundred and seventy-one couples were pronounced man and wife in the name of Clark County and the State of Nevada that night, sixty-seven of them by a single justice of the peace, Mr. James A. Brennan. Mr. Brennan did one wedding at the Dunes and the other sixty-six in his office, and charged each couple eight dollars. One bride lent her veil to six others. "I got it down from five to three minutes," Mr. Brennan said later of his feat. "I could've married them *en masse,* but they're people, not cattle. People expect more when they get married." 1

What people who get married in Las Vegas actually do expect—what, in the largest sense, their "expectations" are—strikes one as a curious and self-contradictory business. Las Vegas is the most extreme and allegorical of American settlements, bizarre and beautiful in its venality and in its devotion to immediate gratification, a place the tone of which is set by mobsters and call girls and ladies' room attendants with amyl nitrite poppers[2] in their uniform pockets. Almost everyone notes that there is no "time" in Las 2

[1]Refers to a declaration made by President Lyndon Johnson regarding the draft for the Vietnam conflict (editors' note).

[2]An illegal liquid drug, inhaled through the nose, that originally came in small capsules that would "pop" upon opening. Known for heightening sexual arousal, it also causes dizziness and sometimes a blackout (editors' note).

Vegas, no night and no day and no past and no future (no Las Vegas casino, however, has taken the obliteration of the ordinary time sense quite so far as Harold's Club in Reno, which for a while issued, at odd intervals in the day and night, mimeographed "bulletins" carrying news from the world outside); neither is there any logical sense of where one is. One is standing on a highway in the middle of a vast hostile desert looking at an eighty-foot sign which blinks "STARDUST" or "CAESAR'S PALACE." Yes, but what does that explain? This geographical implausibility reinforces the sense that what happens there has no connection with "real" life; Nevada cities like Reno and Carson City are ranch towns, Western towns, places behind which there is some historical imperative. But Las Vegas seems to exist only in the eye of the beholder. All of which makes it an extraordinarily stimulating and interesting place, but an odd one in which to want to wear a candlelight satin Priscilla of Boston wedding dress with Chantilly lace insets, tapered sleeves and a detachable modified train.

And yet the Las Vegas wedding business seems to appeal to precisely 3
that impulse. "Sincere and Dignified Since 1954," one wedding chapel advertises. There are nineteen such wedding chapels in Las Vegas, intensely competitive, each offering better, faster, and, by implication, more sincere services than the next: Our Photos Best Anywhere, Your Wedding on A Phonograph Record, Candlelight with Your Ceremony, Honeymoon Accommodations, Free Transportation from Your Motel to Courthouse to Chapel and Return to Motel, Religious or Civil Ceremonies, Dressing Rooms, Flowers, Rings, Announcements, Witnesses Available, and Ample Parking. All of these services, like most others in Las Vegas (sauna baths, payroll-check cashing, chinchilla coats for sale or rent) are offered twenty-four hours a day, seven days a week, presumably on the premise that marriage, like craps, is a game to be played when the table seems hot.

But what strikes one most about the Strip chapels, with their wishing 4
wells and stained-glass paper windows and their artificial bouvardia, is that so much of their business is by no means a matter of simple convenience, of late-night liaisons between show girls and baby Crosbys. Of course there is some of that. (One night about eleven o'clock in Las Vegas I watched a bride in an orange minidress and masses of flame-colored hair stumble from a Strip chapel on the arm of her bridegroom, who looked the part of the expendable nephew in the movies like *Miami Syndicate*.[3] "I gotta get the kids," the bride whimpered. "I gotta pick up the sitter, I gotta get to the midnight show." "What you gotta get," the bridegroom said, opening the door of a Cadillac Coupe de Ville and watching her crumple on the seat, "is sober.") But Las Vegas seems to offer something other than "convenience"; it is merchandising

[3]The actual title is *The Miami Story,* a 1954 film about a group of citizens destroying a crime syndicate with the help of a reformed criminal (editors' note).

"niceness," the facsimile of proper ritual, to children who do not know how else to find it, how to make the arrangements, how to do it "right." All day and evening long on the Strip, one sees actual wedding parties, waiting under the harsh lights at a crosswalk, standing uneasily in the parking lot of the Frontier while the photographer hired by The Little Church of the West ("Wedding Place of the Stars") certifies the occasion, takes the picture: the bride in a veil and white satin pumps, the bridegroom usually in a white dinner jacket, and even an attendant or two, a sister or a best friend in hot-pink *peau de soie,* a flirtation veil, a carnation nosegay. "When I Fall in Love It Will Be Forever," the organist plays, and then a few bars of *Lohengrin.* The mother cries; the stepfather, awkward in his role, invites the chapel hostess to join them for a drink at the Sands. The hostess declines with a professional smile; she has already transferred her interest to the group waiting outside. One bride out, another in, and again the sign goes up on the chapel door: "One moment please—Wedding."

I sat next to one such wedding party in a Strip restaurant the last time 5
I was in Las Vegas. The marriage had just taken place; the bride still wore her dress, the mother her corsage. A bored waiter poured out a few swallows of pink champagne ("on the house") for everyone but the bride, who was too young to be served. "You'll need something with more kick than that," the bride's father said with heavy jocularity to his new son-in-law; the ritual jokes about the wedding night had a certain Panglossian character, since the bride was clearly several months pregnant. Another round of pink champagne, this time not on the house, and the bride began to cry. "It was just as nice," she sobbed, "as I hoped and dreamed it would be."

Appendix A

A GUIDE TO USING SOURCES

Many assignments in *The Longman Reader* suggest that you might want to do some research in the library and/or on the Internet. Such research enlarges your perspective and enables you to move beyond off-the-top-of-your-head opinions to those that are firmly supported. This appendix will be useful if you do decide to draw upon outside sources when preparing a paper. The appendix explains how to (1) evaluate articles, books, and Web sources; (2) analyze and synthesize sources you find; (3) use quotation, summary, and paraphrase correctly to avoid plagiarism; (4) integrate source material into your writing; and (5) document print, Internet, and other sources.

EVALUATING SOURCE MATERIALS

The success of your essay will depend in large part on the evidence you provide (see pages 34–38 on the characteristics of evidence). Evidence from sources, whether print or electronic, needs to be evaluated for its *relevance, timeliness, seriousness of approach*, and *objectivity*.

Relevance

Titles can be misleading. To determine if a source is relevant for your paper, review it carefully. For a book, read the preface or introduction, skim the table of contents, and check the index to see whether the book is likely to contain information that's important to your topic. If the source is an influential text in the field, you may want to read the entire book for background and specific ideas. Or if a text devotes just a few pages to your topic, you might read those pages, taking notes on important information. For an article, read the abstract of the article, if there is one. If not, read the first few paragraphs and skim the rest to determine if it might be useful. As you read a source, make use of the reading checklists on pages 2–3 to get the most from the material. If a source turns out to be irrelevant, just make a note to yourself that you consulted the source and found it didn't relate to your topic.

Timeliness

To some extent, the topic and the kind of research you're doing will determine whether a work is outdated. If you're researching a historical topic such as the internment of Japanese Americans during World War II, you would most likely consult sources published in the 1940s and 1950s, as well as more up-to-date sources. In contrast, if you're investigating a recent scientific development—cloning, for example—it would make sense to restrict your search to current material. For most college research, a source older than ten years is considered outdated unless it was the first to present key concepts in a field.

Seriousness of Approach

As you review a source, ask yourself if it is suitable for your purpose and your instructor's requirements. Articles from *general* periodicals (newspapers and widely read magazines like *Time* and *Newsweek*) and *serious* publications (such as *National Geographic* and *Scientific American*) may be sufficient to provide support in a personal essay. But an in-depth research paper in your major field of study will require material from *scholarly* journals and texts (for example, *American Journal of Public Health* and *Film Quarterly*).

Objectivity

As you examine your sources for possible bias, keep in mind that a strong conclusion or opinion is *not in itself* a sign of bias. As long as a writer doesn't ignore opposing positions or distort evidence, a source can't be considered biased. A biased source presents only those facts that fit the writer's predetermined conclusions. Such a source is often marked by emotionally charged language (see page 19). Publications sponsored by special interest groups—a particular industry, religious association, advocacy group, or political party—are usually biased. Reading such materials *does* familiarize you with a specific point of view, but remember that contrary evidence has probably been ignored or skewed.

The following checklist provides some questions to ask yourself as you evaluate print sources.

☑ EVALUATING ARTICLES AND BOOKS: A CHECKLIST

- ❑ If the work is scholarly, is the author well-known in his or her field? Is the author affiliated with an accredited college or university?

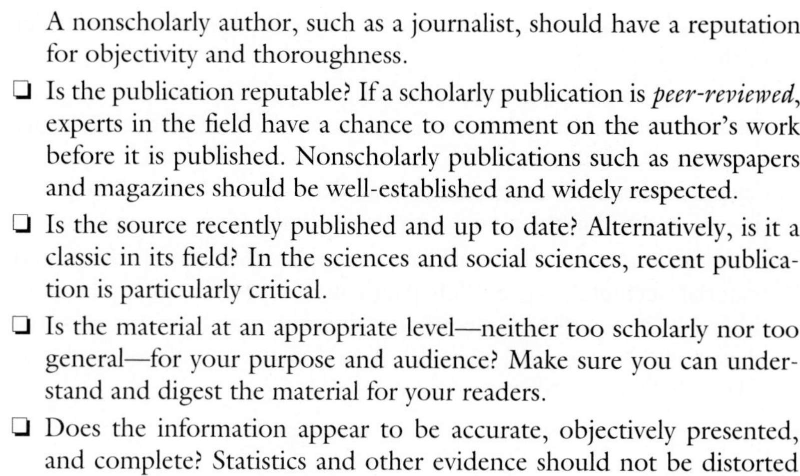
A nonscholarly author, such as a journalist, should have a reputation for objectivity and thoroughness.

- ❑ Is the publication reputable? If a scholarly publication is *peer-reviewed*, experts in the field have a chance to comment on the author's work before it is published. Nonscholarly publications such as newspapers and magazines should be well-established and widely respected.
- ❑ Is the source recently published and up to date? Alternatively, is it a classic in its field? In the sciences and social sciences, recent publication is particularly critical.
- ❑ Is the material at an appropriate level—neither too scholarly nor too general—for your purpose and audience? Make sure you can understand and digest the material for your readers.
- ❑ Does the information appear to be accurate, objectively presented, and complete? Statistics and other evidence should not be distorted or manipulated to make a point.

Special care must be taken to evaluate the worth of material found on the Web. Electronic documents often seem to appear out of nowhere and can disappear without a trace. And anyone—from scholar to con artist—can create a Web page. How, then, do you know if an Internet source is credible? The following checklist provides some questions to ask when you work with online material.

☑ EVALUATING INTERNET MATERIALS: A CHECKLIST

- ❑ Who is the author of the material? Does the author offer his or her credentials in a résumé or biographical note? Do these credentials qualify the author to provide reliable information on the topic? Does the author provide an e-mail address so you can request more information? The less you know about an author, the more suspicious you should be about using the data.
- ❑ Can you verify the accuracy of the information presented? Does the author refer to studies or to other authors you can investigate? If the author doesn't cite other works or other points of view, that may suggest the document is opinionated and one-sided. In such a case, it's important to track down material addressing alternative points of view.
- ❑ Who's sponsoring the Web site? Check for an "About Us" link on the home page, which may tell you the site's sponsorship and goals. Many sites are established by organizations—businesses, agencies, lobby groups—as well as by individuals. If a sponsor pushes a single point of view, you should use the material with great caution. Once

again, make an extra effort to locate material addressing other sides of the issue.

- ❑ Is the cited information up-to-date? Being on the Internet doesn't guarantee that information is current. To assess the timeliness of Internet materials, check at the top or bottom of the document for copyright date, publication date, and/or revision date. Those dates will help you determine whether the material is recent enough for your purposes.
- ❑ Is the information original or taken from another source? Is quoted material accurate? Some Web pages may reproduce material from other sources without identifying them. Watch out for possible plagiarism. Nonoriginal material should be accurately quoted and acknowledged on the site.

ANALYZING AND SYNTHESIZING SOURCE MATERIAL

As you read your sources and begin taking notes, you may not be able to judge immediately how helpful a source will be. At that time, you probably should take fairly detailed notes. After a while, you'll become more selective. You'll find that you are thinking more critically about the material you read, isolating information and ideas that are important to your thesis, and formulating questions about your topic.

Analyzing Source Material

To begin with, you should spend some time analyzing each source for its *central ideas, main supporting points,* and *key details.* (See Chapter 1 for tips on effective reading techniques.) As you read, keep asking yourself how the source's content meshes with your working thesis and with what you know about your subject. Does the source repeat what you already know, or does it supply new information? If a source provides detailed support for important ideas or suggests a new angle on your subject, read carefully and take full notes. If the source refers to other sources, you might decide to consult those.

Make sure you have all necessary citation information for every source you consult. (See pages 607–638 for information you will need for documenting citations.) Then, as you read relevant sources, make sure to take plenty of notes. Articles you have printed out can be highlighted and annotated with your comments. (See the checklist on pages 608–610 for annotation techniques.) In addition, you may wish to photocopy selected book pages to annotate. However, you will also have to take handwritten or typewritten notes on some material. When you do so, make sure to put quotation marks around direct quotes. Annotating and note-taking will help you think through and respond to the source's ideas. (For help with analyzing images in your sources—for example, graphs and illustrations—see pages 4–6.)

Your notes might include any of the following: facts, statistics, anecdotal accounts, expert opinion, case studies, surveys, reports, results of experiments. When you are recording data, check that you have copied the figures accurately. Also note how and by whom the statistics were gathered, as well as where and when they were first reported.

Take down your source's interpretation of the statistics, but be sure to scrutinize the interpretation for any "spin" that distorts them. For example, if 80 percent of Americans think violent crime is our number one national problem, that doesn't mean that violent crime *is* our main problem; it simply means that 80 percent of the people polled *think* it is. And if a "majority" of people think that homelessness should be among our top national priorities, it may be that a mere 51 percent—a bare majority—feel that way. In short, make sure the statistics mean what your sources say they mean. If you have any reason to suspect distortion, it's a good idea to corroborate such figures elsewhere; tracking down the original source of a statistic is the best way to ensure that numbers are being reported fairly.

Synthesizing Source Materials

As you go along, you may come across material that challenges your working thesis and forces you to think differently about your subject. Indeed, the more you learn, the more difficult it may be to state anything conclusively. This is a sign that you're synthesizing and weighing all the evidence. In time, the confusion will lessen, and you'll emerge with a clearer understanding of your subject.

Suppose you find sources that take positions contrary to the one that you had previously considered credible. When you come across such conflicting material, you can be sure you've identified a pivotal issue within your topic. To decide which position is more valid, you need to take good notes or carefully annotate your photocopies or printed documents. Then evaluate the sources for bias. On this basis alone, you might discover serious flaws in one or several sources. Also compare the key points and supporting evidence in the sources. Where do they agree? Where do they disagree? Does one source argue against another's position, perhaps even discrediting some of the opposing view's evidence? The answers to these questions may very well cause you to question the quality, completeness, or fairness of one or more sources.

To resolve such a conflict, you can also research your subject more fully. For example, if your conflicting sources are at the general or serious level, you should probably turn to more scholarly sources. By referring to more authoritative material, you may be able to determine which of the conflicting sources is more valid.

When you attempt to resolve discrepancies among sources, be sure not to let your own bias come into play. Try not to favor one position over the other simply because it supports your working thesis. Remember, your goal is to arrive at the most well-founded position you can. In fact, researching a topic may lead you to change your original viewpoint. In this case, you shouldn't hesitate to revise your working thesis to accord with the evidence you gather.

☑ ANALYZING AND SYNTHESIZING SOURCE MATERIAL: A CHECKLIST

- ❑ As you read sources, note central ideas, main supporting points, and key details.
- ❑ Make sure to record all bibliographic information carefully, identify any quotations, and copy statistical data accurately.
- ❑ Annotate or take full notes on sources that deal with ideas that are important to your topic or suggest a new angle on your subject.
- ❑ Examine statistics and other facts for any distortions.
- ❑ Read carefully material that causes you to take a different view of your subject. Keep an open mind and do additional research to confirm or change your thesis.

USING QUOTATION, SUMMARY, AND PARAPHRASE WITHOUT PLAGIARIZING

Your paper should contain your own ideas stated in your own words. To support your ideas, you can introduce evidence from sources in three ways—with direct quotations, summaries, and paraphrases. Knowing how and when to use each type is an important part of the research process.

Quotation

A *quotation* reproduces, word for word, that which is stated in a source. Although quoting can demonstrate the thoroughness with which you reviewed relevant sources, don't simply use one quotation after another without any intervening commentary or analysis. To do so would mean you hadn't evaluated and synthesized your sources sufficiently. Aim for one to three quotations from each major source; more than that can create a problem in your paper. Consider using quotations in the following situations:

- If a source's ideas are unusual or controversial, include a representative quotation in your paper to show you have accurately conveyed the source's viewpoint.

- Record a quotation if a source's wording is so eloquent or convincing that it would lose its power if you restated the material in your own words.
- Use a quotation if a source's ideas reinforce your own conclusions. If the source is a respected authority, such a quotation will lend authority to your own ideas.
- In an analysis of a literary work, use quotation from the work to support your interpretations.

Remember to clearly identify quotes in your notes so that you don't confuse the quotation with your own comments when you begin drafting your paper. Record the author's statement *exactly* as it appears in the original work, right down to the punctuation. In addition, make sure to properly document the quotation. See "How to Document: MLA In-Text References" and "How to Document: MLA List of Works Cited" on pages 626–638.

Original Passage 1

In this excerpt from *The Canon: A Whirligig Tour of the Beautiful Basics of Science*, by Natalie Angier, page 22, the author is discussing the subject of scientific reasoning.

> Much of the reason for its success is founded on another fundamental of the scientific bent. Scientists accept, quite staunchly, that there is a reality capable of being understood, and understood in a way that can be shared with and agreed upon by others. We can call this "objective" reality if we like, as opposed to subjective reality, or opinion, or "whimsical set of predilections." The concept is deceptive, however, because it implies that the two are discrete entities with remarkably little in common.

Original Passage 2

The following is the entire text of Amendment I of the Constitution of the United States.

> Congress shall make no law respecting an establishment of religion, or prohibiting the free exercise thereof; or abridging the freedom of speech, or of the press; or the right of the people peaceably to assemble, and to petition the Government for a redress of grievances.

Acceptable Uses of Quotation For a paper on society's perception of important freedoms, a student writer used this quotation in its entirety:

The First Amendment of the Constitution of the United States delineates what were thought to be society's most cherished freedoms: "Congress shall make no law respecting an establishment of religion, or prohibiting the free exercise thereof; or abridging the freedom of speech, or of the press; or the right of the people peaceably to assemble, and to petition the Government for a redress of grievances."

In a paper on science education in schools, one student writer used this quotation:

In explaining scientific reasoning, Angier says, "Scientists accept, quite staunchly, that there is a reality capable of being understood, and understood in a way that can be shared with and agreed upon by others" (22).

Notice that both quotations are reproduced exactly as they appear in the source and are enclosed in quotation marks. The parenthetical reference to the page number in the second example is a necessary part of documenting the quotation. (See pages 626–629 for more on in-text references.) The first example requires no page number because quotations from well-known sources such as the Constitution and the Bible are sufficiently identified by their own numbering systems, in this case, the text's use of "First Amendment of the Constitution."

Incorrect Use of Quotation Another student writer, attempting to provide some background on the scientific method, used the source material incorrectly.

To understand the scientific method, it is important to understand that scientists believe there is a reality capable of being understood (Angier 22).

The phrase "a reality capable of being understood," which are the source's exact words, should have quotations around it. Even though the source is identified correctly in the parenthetical reference, the lack of quotation marks actually constitutes plagiarism, the use of someone's words or ideas without proper acknowledgement (see pages 618–619).

Summary

A *summary* is a condensation of a larger work. You extract the essence of someone's ideas and restate it in your own words. The length of a summary depends on your topic and purpose, but generally a summary is *much* shorter than the item you are summarizing. For example, you may summarize the plot of a novel in a few short paragraphs, or you might summarize a reading from this book in a few sentences. You might choose to use a summary for the following reasons:

- To give a capsule presentation of the main ideas of a book or an article, use a summary.
- If the relevant information is too long to be quoted in full, use a summary.
- Use a summary to give abbreviated information about such elements such as plot, background, or history.
- To present an idea from a source without including all the supporting details, use a summary.

To summarize a source, read the material; jot down or underline the main idea, main supporting points, and key details; and then restate the information in shortened form in your own words. Your summary should follow the order of information in the original. Also, be sure to treat any original wording as quotations in your summary. *A caution:* When summarizing, don't use the ellipsis to signal that you have omitted some ideas. The ellipsis is used only when quoting.

Original Passage 3

This excerpt is from *The Homeless and History* by Julian Stamp, page 8.

> The key to any successful homeless policy requires a clear understanding of just who are the homeless. Since fifty percent of shelter residents have drug and alcohol addictions, programs need to provide not only a place to sleep but also comprehensive treatment for addicts and their families. Since roughly one-third of the homeless population is mentally ill, programs need to offer psychiatric care, perhaps even institutionalization, and not just housing subsidies. Since the typical head of a homeless family (a young woman with fewer than six months' working experience) usually lacks the know-how needed to maintain a job and a home, programs need to supply employment and life skills training; low-cost housing alone will not ensure the family's stability.
>
> However, if we switch our focus from the single person to the larger economic issues, we begin to see that homelessness cannot be resolved solely at the level of individual treatment. Beginning in the 1980s and through the 1990s, the gap between the rich and the poor has widened, buying power has stagnated, industrial jobs have fled overseas, and federal funding for low-cost housing has been almost eliminated. Given these developments, homelessness begins to look like a product of history, our recent history, and only by addressing shifts in the American economy can we begin to find effective solutions for people lacking homes. Moreover, these solutions—ranging from renewed federal spending to tax laws favoring job-creating companies—will require a sustained national commitment that transcends partisan politics.

Acceptable Use of Summary The following summary was written by a student working on a paper related to the causes of homelessness.

In his *The Homeless and History*, Stamp asserts that society must not only provide programs to help the homeless with their personal problems, it must also develop government programs to deal with the economic causes of homelessness (8).

The writer gives the gist of Stamp's argument in his own words. The parenthetical reference at the end tells the reader that the material being summarized is on page 8 of the source (see pages 626–629 for more on in-text references).

Incorrect Use of Summary The student who wrote the following has incorrectly summarized ideas from the Stamp passage.

Who are the homeless? According to Stamp, the homeless are people with big problems like addiction, mental illness, and poor job skills. Because they haven't been provided with proper treatment and training, the homeless haven't been able to adapt to a changing economy. So their numbers soared in the 1990s (8).

The writer was so determined to put things her way that she added her own ideas and ended up distorting Stamp's meaning. For instance, note the way she emphasizes personal problems over economic issues, making the former the cause of the latter. Stamp does just the opposite and highlights economic solutions rather than individual treatment.

Paraphrase

Unlike a summary, which condenses the original, a *paraphrase* recasts material by using roughly the same number of words and retaining the same level of detail as the original. The challenge with paraphrasing is to capture the information without using the original language of the material. Paraphrasing is useful in these situations:

- If you want to include specific details from a source but you want to avoid using a long quotation or string of quotations, paraphrase the material.
- To interpret or explain material as you include it, try using a paraphrase.
- Paraphrase to avoid injecting another person's style into your own writing.

One way to compose a paraphrase is to read the original passage and then set it aside while you draft your restatement. As you write, make sure to use appropriate synonyms and to vary the sentence structure from that of the original. Then compare the passages to make sure you have not used any of the original language, unless you have enclosed it in quotation marks.

Acceptable Use of Paraphrase In the following example, the student writer paraphrases the second paragraph of Stamp's original, fitting the restatement into her argument.

Can we work together as a society to eliminate homelessness? One historian urges us to look at larger economic issues, claiming that the problem cannot be solved simply by the treatment of personal problems such as substance abuse. Economic conditions for the poor have worsened in the last few decades, with fewer jobs and substantially diminished federal support for low-cost housing. To find a solution to homelessness, society must deal with these economic causes. A "sustained national commitment," regardless of political ideology, to stepped-up federal spending and tax laws that promote the creation of jobs, as well as to other initiatives, is needed (Stamp 8).

Note that the paraphrase is nearly as long as the original. Apart from the single instance of original language, enclosed in quotation marks, the writer has not used phrases or even sentence structures from the original. Notice also that it is easy to see where the paraphrase starts and ends: The phrase "One historian" begins the paraphrase, and the parenthetical reference ends it. Because the text does not identify the source by name, the source's name is included in the parenthetical reference.

Incorrect Use of Paraphrase When preparing the following paraphrase, the student stayed too close to the source and borrowed much of Stamp's language word for word (highlighted). Because the student did not enclose the original phrases in quotation marks, this paraphrase constitutes plagiarism, *even though* this student acknowledged Stamp in the paper. The lack of quotation marks implies that the language is the student's when, in fact, it is Stamp's.

Only by addressing changes in the American economy—from the gap between the wealthy and the poor to the loss of industrial jobs to overseas markets—can we begin to find solutions for the homeless. And these solutions, ranging from renewed federal spending to tax laws favoring job-creating companies, will not be easy to find or implement (Stamp 8).

As the following example shows, another student believed, erroneously, that if he changed a word here and omitted a word there, he'd be preparing an effective paraphrase. Note that the language is all Stamp's *except* for the words not highlighted, which are the student's.

Only by addressing shifts in the economy can we find solutions for the homeless. These solutions will require a sustained federal commitment that avoids partisan politics (Stamp 8).

The student in the immediately preceding example occasionally deleted a word from Stamp's original, thinking that such changes would result in a legitimate paraphrase. For example, in "Only by addressing shifts in the [American] economy can we [begin to] find [effective] solutions" the brackets show where the student has omitted Stamp's words. The student couldn't place quotation marks around these near-quotes because his wording isn't identical to that of the source. Yet the near-quotes are deceptive; the lack of quotation marks suggests that the language is the student's when actually it's substantially (but not exactly) Stamp's. Such near-quotes are also considered plagiarism, even if, when writing the paper, the student supplies a parenthetical reference citing the source.

☑ USING QUOTATION, SUMMARY, AND PARAPHRASE: A CHECKLIST

- ❑ For a *quotation*, give the statement *exactly* as it was originally written.
- ❑ Always accompany quotations with your own commentary or analysis.
- ❑ Don't string quotations together one after the other without intervening text.
- ❑ Avoid using too many quotations. One to three quotations from any major source is sufficient.
- ❑ For a *summary*, restate ideas from the source in your own words.
- ❑ Keep summaries much shorter than the original material.
- ❑ Make sure your summary does not distort the meaning or tone of the original.
- ❑ For a *paraphrase*, recast ideas with the same level of detail as the original.
- ❑ Make sure to use your own language in a paraphrase—finding appropriate synonyms and varying sentence structure from that of the original.
- ❑ Check that any original source language used in a summary or paraphrase is enclosed in quotation marks.

Avoiding Plagiarism

Plagiarism occurs when a writer borrows someone else's ideas, facts, or language but doesn't properly credit that source. Summarizing and paraphrasing, in particular, can lead to plagiarism, but improper use of quotation can also constitute plagiarism.

Copyright law and the ethics of research require that you give credit to those whose words and ideas you borrow; that is, you must represent the source's words and ideas accurately and provide full documentation (see pages 626–638). Missing or faulty documentation can constitute plagiarism and undermine your credibility. For one thing, readers may suspect that you're hiding something if you fail to identify your sources clearly. Further, readers planning follow-up research of their own will be perturbed if they have trouble locating your sources. Finally, weak documentation makes it difficult for readers to distinguish your ideas from those of your sources.

To avoid plagiarizing, you must provide proper documentation in the following situations:

- When you include a word-for-word quotation from a source.
- When you paraphrase or summarize ideas or information from a source, unless that material is commonly known and accepted

(whether or not you yourself were previously aware of it) or is a matter of historical or scientific record.
- When you combine a summary or paraphrase with a quotation.

One exception to formal documentation occurs in writing for the general public. For example, you may have noticed that while the authors of this book's essays, as well as newspaper and magazine writers, identify sources they have used, these writers don't use full documentation. Academic writers, though, must provide full documentation for all borrowed information.

INTEGRATING SOURCES INTO YOUR WRITING

On the whole, your paper should be written in your own words. As you draft your paper, indicate places where you might want to add evidence from sources to support your ideas. Depending on the source and the support you need, you may choose to use quotations, paraphrases, or summaries to present this evidence, as discussed in the preceding section.

Take care to blend the evidence seamlessly into your own writing through the use of introductions (see pages 48, 53–55, 68), transitions (see pages 51–52, 68), and conclusions (see pages 48, 55–56, 70). At a minimum, each paragraph should have a topic sentence, and it may also be useful to introduce evidence with an *attribution*, a phrase that identifies the source and forms part of the documentation you will need to use (see pages 620–621).

A quotation, by itself, won't always make your case for you. In addition, you will need to interpret quotations, showing why they are significant and explaining how they support your central points. Indeed, such commentary is often precisely what's needed to blend source material gracefully into your discussion. Also, use quotations sparingly; draw upon them only when they dramatically illustrate key points you want to make or when they lend authority to your own conclusions. A string of quotations signals that you haven't sufficiently evaluated and distilled your sources.

Awkward Use of a Quotation In the following example, note how the quotation is dropped awkwardly into the text, without any transition or commentary. (For an explanation of the parenthetical reference at the end of the quotation, see pages 626–627.)

Recent studies of parenting styles are designed to control researcher bias. "Recent studies screen out researchers whose strongly held attitudes make objectivity difficult" (Layden 10).

Effective Use of Quotation Adding brief interpretive remarks in this example provides a transition that smoothly merges the quotation with the surrounding material:

Recent studies of parenting styles are designed to control researcher bias. The psychologist Marsha Layden, a harsh critic of earlier studies, acknowledges that nowadays most investigations "screen out researchers whose strongly held beliefs make objectivity difficult" (10).

Introducing a Source

Try to avoid such awkward constructions as these: *According to Julian Stamp, he says that*...and *In the book by Julian Stamp, he argues that*...Instead, follow these hints for writing smooth, graceful attributions.

Identifying the Source An introduction to a source may specify the author's name, it may inform readers of an author's expertise, or it may refer to a source more generally. To call attention to an author who is prominent in the field, important to your argument, or referred to many times in your paper, you may give the author's full name and identifier at the first mention in the text. Then in subsequent mentions, you may give only the last name. Don't use personal titles such as *Mr.* or *Ms.* In the following two examples, language that identifies or explains the source is highlighted.

Natalie Angier, a Pulitzer Prize–winning journalist who writes about science, says that.... Angier goes on to explain....

The historian Julian Stamp argues that.... As Stamp explains....

For other sources, use a more general attribution and include the source's name (highlighted below), along with any page numbers, in the parenthetical citation.

One writer points out... (Angier 22).

According to statistics, fifty percent... (Stamp 8).

As part of an introduction, you may mention the title of the book, article, or other source.

In *The Homeless and History*, Stamp maintains that....

According to the National Aeronautics and Space Administration (NASA),...

When the author's name is provided in the text, don't repeat the name in the parenthetical reference. (See pages 626–628 for more details on parenthetical references.)

One psychologist who is a harsh critic of earlier studies acknowledges that nowadays most investigations "screen out researchers whose strongly held beliefs make objectivity difficult" (Layden 10).

The psychologist Marsha Layden acknowledges that... (10).

Using Variety in Attributions Don't always place attributions at the beginning of the sentence; experiment by placing them in the middle or at the end:

The key to any successful homeless policy, Stamp explains, "requires a clear understanding of just who are the homeless" (8).

Half of homeless individuals living in shelters are substance abusers, according to statistics (Stamp 8).

Try not to use a predictable subject-verb sequence (*Stamp argues that, Stamp explains that*) in all your attributions. Aim for variations like the following:

The information compiled by Stamp shows....

In Stamp's opinion,...

Stamp's study reveals that....

Rather than repeatedly using the verbs *says* or *writes* in your introductions, seek out more vigorous verbs, making sure the verbs you select are appropriate to the tone and content of the piece you're quoting. The list below offers a number of options.

acknowledges	demonstrates	reports
adds	endorses	responds
admits	grants	reveals
argues	implies	says
asserts	insists	shows
believes	maintains	speculates
compares	notes	states
confirms	points out	suggests
contends	questions	wonders
declares	reasons	writes

Shortening or Clarifying Quotations

To make the best use of quotations, you will often need to shorten or excerpt them. It's acceptable to omit parts of quotations as long as you do not change the wording or distort the meaning of the original.

Quoting a Single Word, a Phrase, or Part of a Sentence Put double quotation marks around a quoted element you are integrating into your own sentence. In the following examples, the quotations are highlighted.

Angier says that to speak of "objective" and "subjective" realities is to imply that these are "discrete entities" (22).

Making these changes will necessitate "a sustained national commitment that transcends partisan politics," according to Stamp (8).

Omitting Material in the Middle of the Original Sentence Insert three spaced periods, called an *ellipsis* (. . .), in place of the deleted words. Leave a space before the first period of the ellipsis and leave a space after the third period of the ellipsis before continuing with the quoted matter.

"However, if we switch our focus . . . to the larger economic issues, we begin to see that homelessness cannot be resolved solely at the level of individual treatment" (Stamp 8).

Omitting Material at the End of the Original Sentence If no parenthetical reference is needed, insert a period before the first ellipsis period and provide the closing quotation mark, as in the first example below. If a parenthetical reference is needed, use only the ellipsis and add the period after the parentheses.

The First Amendment of the Constitution of the United States lays the foundation for the doctrine of free speech: "Congress shall make no law respecting an establishment of religion, or prohibiting the free exercise thereof; or abridging the freedom of speech, or of the press. . . ."

In discussing scientific reasoning, Angier states, "We can call this 'objective' reality if we like, as opposed to subjective reality . . ." (22).

Omitting Material at the Start of a Quotation No ellipses are required. Simply place the quotation marks where you begin quoting directly. Capitalize the first word if the resulting quotation forms a complete sentence.

Simply providing housing for homeless will not suffice: "Programs need to supply employment and life skills training" (Stamp 8).

Adding Material to a Quotation If, for the sake of clarity or grammar, you need to add a word or short phrase to a quotation (for example, by changing a verb tense or replacing a vague pronoun with a noun), enclose your insertion in brackets:

Moreover, Angier discredits the concept that "the two [objective reality and subjective reality] are discrete entities with remarkably little in common" (22).

Capitalizing and Punctuating Short Quotations

The way a short quotation is used in a sentence determines whether it begins or doesn't begin with a capital letter and whether it is or isn't preceded by a comma. For the formatting and punctuation of a long (block) quotation, see page 628–629.

Introducing a Quotation That Can Stand Alone as a Sentence If a quotation can stand alone as a grammatical sentence, capitalize the quotation's first word. Also, precede the quotation with a comma:

Stamp observes, "Beginning in the 1980s and through the 1990s, the gap between the rich and the poor has widened..." (8).

According to Stamp, "Federal funding for low-cost housing has been almost eliminated" (8).

Using **That, Which,** *or* **Who** *(Stated or Implied)* If you use *that, which,* or *who* to blend a quotation into the structure of your own sentence, don't capitalize the quotation's first word and don't precede it with a comma.

Stamp observes that "beginning in the 1980s and through the 1990s, the gap between the rich and the poor has widened, buying power has stagnated, industrial jobs have fled overseas, and federal funding for low-cost housing has been almost eliminated" (8).

Angier describes scientists as firmly believing there is "a reality capable of being understood" (22).

Even if, as in the first example above, the material being quoted originally started with a capital letter, you still use lowercase when incorporating the quotation into your own sentence. Note that in the second example, the word *that* is implied (before the word *there*).

Interrupting a Full-Sentence Quotation with an Attribution Place commas on both sides of the attribution, and resume the quotation with a lowercase letter.

"The key to any successful homeless policy," Stamp comments, "requires a clear understanding of just who are the homeless" (8).

Using a Quotation with a Quoted Word or Phrase When a source you're quoting contains a quoted word or phrase, place single quotation marks around the quoted words. (See page 628 for how to treat a source that is quoting another source.)

"We can call this 'objective' reality if we like, as opposed to subjective reality, or opinion, or 'whimsical set of predilections,'" Angier posits (22).

Punctuating with a Question Mark or Exclamation Point If the question mark or exclamation point is part of the quotation, place it inside the quotation marks. If the mark is part of the structure of the framing sentence, as in the second example below, place it outside the quotation marks and after any parenthetical reference.

Discussing a child's epileptic attack, the psychoanalyst Erik Erikson asks, in *Childhood and Society*, "What was the psychic stimulus?" (26).

But what does Stamp see as the "key to any successful homeless policy" (8)?

Presenting Statistics

Citing statistics can be a successful strategy for supporting your ideas. Be careful, though, not to misinterpret the data or twist their significance, and remember to provide an attribution indicating the source. Also, be sure not to overwhelm readers with too many statistics; include only those that support your central points in compelling ways. Keep in mind, too, that statistics won't speak for themselves. You need to interpret them for readers, showing how the figures cited reinforce your key ideas.

Ineffective Use of Statistics For a paper showing that Medicare reform is needed to control increasing costs, one student writer presented the following statistics.

The Centers for Medicaid and Medicare Services reports that 1992 revenues ($185 billion) exceeded spending ($120 billion). But in 1997, revenues ($204 billion) and spending ($208 billion) were almost the same. It is projected that by the year 2010, revenues will be $310 billion and spending $410 billion (Mohr 14).

The student gave one statistic after the other, without explanatory commentary or attribution. This presentation makes it hard for the reader to understand the meaning of the statistics.

Effective Use of Statistics Instead of including so many statistics, the writer could have presented only the most telling statistics, being sure to explain their significance.

The Centers for Medicaid and Medicare Services reports that in 1992, Medicare revenues actually exceeded spending by about $65 billion. But five years later, costs had increased so much that they exceeded revenues by about $4 billion. This trend toward escalated costs is expected to continue. It's projected that by the year 2010, revenues will be only $310 billion, while spending—if not controlled—will climb to at least $410 billion (Mohr 14).

☑ INTEGRATING SOURCES INTO YOUR WRITING: A CHECKLIST

- ❑ Introduce an important or oft-used source by giving the author's full name and credentials at the first mention. Thereafter, refer to author by last name only. Don't use personal titles such as *Mr.* or *Ms.*
- ❑ Use general introductions (*One historian says...*) for less important sources.
- ❑ Vary the style of attributions by sometimes positioning them at the middle or end, using different verbs, or blending quotations into your own sentences.
- ❑ Words may be deleted from a quotation as long as the author's original meaning isn't changed. Insert an ellipsis (...) in place of the deleted words. An ellipsis is not needed when material is omitted from the start of a quotation. Use a period plus an ellipsis when the end of a sentence is deleted.
- ❑ Use brackets to add clarifying information to quotations.
- ❑ If a quotation can stand alone as a grammatical sentence, capitalize its first word and precede it with a comma. If a quotation is blended into the structure of your own sentence, don't capitalize the quotation's first word and don't precede it with a comma. If an attribution interrupts a quotation, place commas before and after the attribution and resume the quotation with a lowercase letter.
- ❑ For a quotation within a quotation, use single quotation marks.
- ❑ Place question marks and exclamation points inside quotation marks only if they belong to the quotation.
- ❑ Limit statistics and explain them fully to convey essential information.

DOCUMENTING SOURCES: MLA STYLE

In Chapter 11, you learned the importance of documentation—giving credit to the print and electronic sources whose words and ideas you borrow in an essay (see page 482). That earlier discussion showed you how to document sources in informal papers. The following pages will show you how to use the documentation system of the Modern Language Association (MLA)[1] when citing sources in more formal papers.

To avoid plagiarism, you must provide documentation when you include quotations from a source or you summarize or paraphrase in your own words ideas or information from a source. However, if the information you are including is commonly known or is a matter of historical or scientific record (the date of the Gettyburg Address or the temperature at which water boils, for example), you need not document it.

The discussion here covers key features of the MLA system. For more detailed coverage, you may want to consult a recent composition handbook or the latest edition of the *MLA Handbook for Writers of Research Papers.* For a sample paper that uses MLA documentation, turn to the student essay on pages 497–503.

HOW TO DOCUMENT: MLA IN-TEXT REFERENCES

The MLA documentation system uses the *parenthetical reference*, a brief note in parentheses inserted into the text after borrowed material. The parenthetical reference doesn't provide full bibliographic information, but it presents enough so that readers can turn to the Works Cited list (see pages 502–503) at the end of the paper for complete information.

Whenever you quote or summarize material from an outside source, you must do two things: (1) identify the source (usually an author) and (2) specify the page(s) in your source on which the material appears. The author's name may be given either in an introduction (often called the *attribution*) or in the parentheses following the borrowed material. The page number always appears in parentheses, usually at the end of the sentence just before the period. The examples below illustrate the MLA documentation style. You may also consult pages 620–624 for additional examples of attributions and parenthetical references.

In the examples below, the two parts of the reference—author's name or identifier and page number—are highlighted.

Single Source: Parentheses Only

In the following example, a complete parenthetical reference follows a summary.

[1]MLA documentation is appropriate in papers written for humanities courses, such as your composition class. If you're writing a paper for a course in the social sciences (for example, psychology, economics, or sociology), your professor will probably expect you to use the citation format developed by the American Psychological Association (APA). For information about APA documentation, consult *The Longman Writer* or the most recent edition of the *Publication Manual of the American Psychological Association.*

Counseling and support services are not enough to solve the problem of homelessness; proposed solutions must also address the complex economic issues at the heart of homelessness (Stamp 8).

If a source is alphabetized by title in your Works Cited list, use a shortened version of the title in place of the author's name in the parenthetical reference. In the following example, the full title of the source is "Supreme Court of the United States."

The U.S. Supreme Court is fundamentally an appeals court, responsible for "cases arising under the Constitution, laws, or treaties of the United States" among others ("Supreme Court").

Complete parenthetical references follow these uses of quotation. Note that the comma after "issues" in the quotation is not part of the original quotation. It has been added because the sentence grammar requires a comma.

If we look beyond the problems of homelessness, to "larger economic issues," it is clear that "homelessness cannot be resolved solely at the level of the individual" (Stamp 8).

Single Source: Parentheses and Attributions

When the attribution gives the author's name, only the page number appears in the parenthetical reference. The attribution should make it clear where the quotation, summary, or paraphrase begins.

Julian Stamp argues that homelessness must be addressed in terms of economics, not simply in terms of individual counseling, addiction therapy, or job training (8).

In *The Homeless and History*, Stamp maintains that economic issues, rather than difficulties in people's personal lives, are at the core of the homeless problem (8).

Stamp points out that "homelessness cannot be resolved solely at the level of the individual" (8), although other experts disagree.

Note that in the immediately preceding example, the parenthetical reference follows the quotation in the middle of the sentence; placing the reference at the end of the sentence would erroneously imply that the idea expressed by "although other experts disagree" is Stamp's.

More Than One Source by the Same Author

When your paper includes references to more than one work by the same author, you must specify—either in the parenthetical reference or in the attribution—the particular work being cited. You do this by providing the title, as well as the author's name and the page(s). Here are examples from a paper in which two works by the psychologist Jean Piaget were used.

In *The Language and Thought of the Child*, Jean Piaget states that "discussion forms the basis for a logical point of view" (240).

Piaget considers dialogue essential to the development of logical thinking (Language 240).

The *Child's Conception of the World* shows that young children think that the name of something can never change (Piaget 81).

Young children assume that everything has only one name and that no others are possible (Piaget, *Child's Conception* 81).

Notice that when a work is named in the attribution, the full title appears; when a title is given in the parenthetic citation, though, only the first few significant words appear. (However, don't use the ellipsis to indicate that some words have been omitted from the title; the ellipsis is used only in actual quotations.) Note also that when name, title, and page number all appear in the parenthetical reference, a comma follows the author's name.

Source Within a Source

If you quote or summarize a *secondary source* (a source whose ideas come to you only through another source), you need to make this clear. The parenthetical documentation should indicate "as quoted in" with the abbreviation *qtd. in*:

According to Sherman, "Recycling has, in several communities, created unanticipated expenses" (qtd. in Pratt 3).

Sherman explains that recycling can be surprisingly costly (qtd. in Pratt 3).

If the material you're quoting includes a quotation, place single quotation marks around the secondary quotation:

Pratt believes that "recycling efforts will be successful if, as Sherman argues, 'communities launch effective public-education campaigns' " (3).

Note: Your Works Cited list should include the source you actually read (Pratt), rather than the source you refer to secondhand (Sherman).

Long (Block) Quotations

A quotation longer than four lines starts on a new line and is indented, throughout, one inch from the left margin. Since this block format indicates a quotation, quotation marks are unnecessary. Double-space the block quotation, as you do the rest of your paper. Don't leave extra space above or below the quotation. Long quotations, always used sparingly, require a lead-in. A lead-in that isn't a full sentence is followed by a comma; a lead-in that is a full sentence (see below) is followed by a colon:

Stamp cites changing economic conditions as the key to a national homeless policy:

> Beginning in the 1980s and through the 1990s, the gap between the rich and the poor has widened, buying power has stagnated, industrial jobs have fled overseas, and federal funding for low-cost housing has been almost eliminated. Given these developments, homelessness begins to look like a product of history, our recent history, and only by addressing shifts in the American economy can we begin to find effective solutions for people lacking homes. (8)

Notice that the page number in parentheses appears *after* the period, not before as it would with a short quotation.

Key Points to Remember

Take a moment to look again at the preceding examples and note the points presented in the following checklist.

☑ USING MLA PARENTHETICAL REFERENCES: A CHECKLIST

- ❑ The parenthetical reference is usually placed immediately after the borrowed material.
- ❑ The parenthetical reference is placed before any internal punctuation (a comma or semicolon) as well as before any terminal punctuation (a period or question mark), except in a block quotation, where the reference appears after the period.
- ❑ The first time the author is referred to in an attribution, give the author's full name; afterward, give only the last name. To inform readers of an author's area of expertise, identify the author by profession (*The historian Julian Stamp argues that...*), title, or affiliation.
- ❑ When an author's name is provided in the attribution, the name is not repeated in the parentheses. When the author's name is provided in the parentheses, only the last name is given.
- ❑ If a source is cited by title rather than author, use a shortened form of the title in the parenthetical reference.
- ❑ The page number comes directly after the author's name. (If the source is only one page long, only the author's name is needed.) There is no punctuation between the author's name and the page number, and there is no *p.* or *page* preceding the page number.

HOW TO DOCUMENT: MLA LIST OF WORKS CITED

A documented paper ends with a list of Works Cited, which includes only those sources you actually acknowledge in the paper. Placed on its own page, the Works Cited list provides the reader with full bibliographic information about the sources cited in the parenthetical references (see pages 620–624). By referring to the Works Cited list that appears at the end of the student essay on pages 502–503, you will notice the following:

- The list is organized alphabetically by authors' last names. Entries without an author are alphabetized by the first major word in the title (that is, not *A, An,* or *The*).
- Entries are not numbered.
- If an entry runs longer than one line, each additional line is indented half an inch. Entries are double-spaced with no extra space between entries.
- Each entry gives the medium in which the source was found, for example, "Print" for an article found in a printed newspaper or "Web" for an article found in the online version of a newspaper.

Listed here are sample Works Cited entries for the most commonly used kinds of sources. Refer to these samples when you prepare your own Works Cited list, taking special care to reproduce the punctuation and spacing exactly. If you don't spot an entry for the kind of source you need to document, consult the latest edition of the *MLA Handbook* for more comprehensive examples.

CITING PRINT SOURCES—BOOKS

For a book, you'll need to consult (1) the title page and (2) the copyright notice on the back of the title page. You will also need to know the specific page numbers of any material you are citing.

Basic MLA Format for a Printed Book

Author's last name, Author's first name. *Book Title: Book Subtitle*. City of publication: Publisher, year of publication. Print.

- **Author.** Follow the guidelines for authors' names on page 631. If the article is unsigned, begin with its title.
- **Book title.** Give the complete book title in italics, capitalizing the major words. If the book has a subtitle, separate it from the title with a colon and a single space. End the title with a period.

- **City of publication.** Give the city of publication, followed by a colon and a space. Use the city listed first on the title page.
- **Publisher.** Supply the publisher's name, giving only key words and omitting the words *Company, Press, Publishers, Inc.,* and the like. (For example, write *Rodale for Rodale Press* and *Norton* for *W. W. Norton and Company.*) In addition, use *UP* to abbreviate the names of university presses (as in *Columbia UP* and *U of California P*). Place a comma and a space after the publisher's name.
- **Year of publication.** Supply the most recent year of copyright. Don't use the year of the most recent printing.
- **Medium.** Include *Print* at the end of the citation followed by a period.

Book by One Author

List the author's last name followed by a comma, the first name, and a period. Then give the title (italicized or underlined),[2] followed by a period. Next, give the city of publication, followed by a colon and the shortened version of the publisher's name (for example, use *UP* for "University Press" and *Norton* for "W.W. Norton & Co."), a comma, the year of publication, and a period. End with the medium of publication (*Print*) and a period.

McDonnell, Lorraine M. *Politics, Persuasion, and Educational Testing.* Cambridge: Harvard UP, 2004. Print.

Book by Two or Three Authors

Provide all the authors' names in the order in which they appear on the title page of the book, but reverse only the first author's name.

Douglas, Susan, and Meredith Michaels. *The Mommy Myth: The Idealization of Motherhood and How It Has Undermined Women.* New York: Free, 2004. Print.

Gunningham, Neil A., Robert Kagan, and Dorothy Thornton. *Shades of Green: Business, Regulation, and Environment.* Palo Alto: Stanford UP, 2003. Print.

Book by Four or More Authors

For a work by four or more authors, give only the first author's name followed by a comma and *et al.* (Latin for "and others"). Do not italicize "et al."

[2]For a review of when titles should be italicized and when they should appear in quotation marks, see pages 650–651, the "Misuse of Italics and Underlining" section of Appendix B.

Brown, Michael K., et al. *Whitewashing Race: The Myth of a Color-Blind Society.* Berkeley: U of California P, 2003. Print.

Two or More Works by the Same Author

List each book separately. Give the author's name in the first entry only; begin the entries for other books by that author with three hyphens followed by a period. Arrange the works alphabetically by title.

McChesney, Robert W. *The Problem of the Media: U.S. Communication Politics in the 21st Century.* New York: Monthly Review, 2004. Print.

---. *Rich Media, Poor Democracy: Communication Politics in Dubious Times.* Champaign: U of Illinios P, 1999. Print.

Revised Edition

Indicate a revised edition (*Rev. ed., 2nd ed., 3rd ed., 4th ed.*, and so on) after the title.

Weiss, Thomas G., David P. Forsythe, and Roger A. Coate. *The United Nations and Changing World Politics.* 3rd ed. Boulder: Westview, 2001. Print.

Zinn, Howard. *A People's History of the United States: 1492-Present.* Rev. ed. New York: Perennial, 2003. Print.

Book with an Author and Editor or Translator

Give the author's name first. Following the title, type *Ed.* or *Trans.* (for "Edited by" or "Translated by"), followed by the name of the editor or translator.

Douglass, Frederick. *My Bondage and My Freedom.* Ed. John David Smith. New York: Penguin, 2003. Print.

Anthology or Compilation of Works by Different Authors

List anthologies according to editors' names, followed by *ed.* or *eds.* (for "editor" or "editors").

Kasser, Tim, and Allen D. Kanner, eds. *Psychology and Consumer Culture: The Struggle for a Good Life in a Materialistic World.* Washington: Amer. Psychological Assn, 2004. Print.

Section of an Anthology or Compilation

Begin this entry with the author and title of the selection (in quotation marks), followed by the title of the anthology. The editors' names are listed after the anthology title and are preceded by *Ed.* (for "Edited by"). Note that the entry gives the page numbers on which the selection appears.

Levin, Diane E., and Susan Linn. "The Commercialization of Childhood: Understanding the Problem and Finding Solutions." *Psychology and Consumer Culture: The Struggle for a Good Life in a Materialistic World.* Ed. Tim Kasser and Allen D. Kanner. Washington: Amer. Psychological Assn, 2004. 212-28. Print.

Section or Chapter in a Book by One Author

Wolfson, Evan. "Is Marriage Equality a Question of Civil Rights?" *Why Marriage Matters: America, Equality, and Gay People's Right to Marry.* New York: Simon, 2004. 242-69. Print.

Reference Work

"Temperance Movements." *Columbia Encyclopedia.* 6th ed. New York: Columbia UP, 2000. Print.

Book by an Institution or Corporation

Give the name of the institution or corporation in the author position, even if the same institution is the publisher.

United Nations. Department of Economic and Social Affairs. *Human Development, Health, and Education: Dialogues at the Economic and Social Council.* New York: United Nations, 2004. Print.

CITING PRINT SOURCES—PERIODICALS

For a periodical in print form, you'll need to consult (1) the page with the journal title and copyright information and (2) all the pages on which the article appears.

Basic MLA Format for a Printed Periodical

Author's last name, Author's first name, "Article Title: Article Subtitle." *Journal Title* vol. issue (year): pages. Print.

- **Author.** Follow the guidelines for authors' names on page 631. If the article is unsigned, begin with its title.
- **Article title.** Give the article's complete title, with main words capitalized, followed by a period, all enclosed in quotation marks.
- **Periodical title.** Supply the periodical's name, with main words capitalized, in italics, without any initial *A, An* or *The.* Don't place any punctuation after the title.

- **Volume and issue numbers.** For scholarly journals, give the volume number, then a period, and then the issue number (if available), right after the period. Use arabic, not roman, numerals, without either *volume* or *vol.* Generally, a yearly *volume* consists of a number of *issues.* Most periodicals are paginated continuously; that is, the first issue of each yearly volume starts with page 1 and each subsequent issue picks up where the previous one left off. Some journals do not paginate continuously; they start each new issue in a volume with page 1.
- **Date of publication.** For scholarly publications, include the year, in parentheses, followed by a colon. For newspapers and weekly magazines, include the day, month, and year—in that order—followed by a colon.
- **Page numbers.** Do not use *p.*, *pp.*, *page*, or *pages* before the numbers. If the pages in an article are continuous, give the page range (for example, 67–72, 321–25, or 497–502). If the pages in an article aren't continuous (for example, 67–68, 70, 72), write the first page number and a plus sign (67+). End with a period.
- **Medium.** Include *Print* at the end of the citation followed by period.

Article in a Weekly or Biweekly Magazine

Provide the author's name (if the article is signed) and article title (in quotation marks). Then give the periodical name (italicized and with *no* period) and date of publication (day, month, year), followed by a colon and the page number(s) of the article. End with the medium of publication (*Print*).

Leo, John. "Campus Censors in Retreat." *U.S. News & World Report* 16 Feb. 2004: 64–65. Print.

Article in a Monthly or Bimonthly Magazine

Wheeler, Jacob. "Outsourcing the Public Good." *Utne* Sept.-Oct. 2004: 13–14. Print.

Article in a Daily Newspaper

Omit the initial *The* from newspaper names.

Doolin, Joseph. "Immigrants Deserve a Fair Deal." *Boston Globe* 19 Aug. 2003: A19+. Print.

Editorial, Letter to the Editor, or Reply to a Letter

List as you would any signed or unsigned article, but indicate the type of piece after the article's title.

Johnson, Paul. "Want to Prosper? Then Be Tolerant." Editorial. *Forbes* 21 June 2004: 41. Print.

"Playing Fair with Nuclear Cleanup." Editorial. *Seattle Times* 5 Oct. 2003: D2. Print.

Article in a Scholarly Journal

Regardless of how a journal is paginated, include *both* the issue number (if available) and the volume number. In the first example, each issue is paginated individually. In the second example, the entire volume is paginated continuously throughout the issues.

Chew, Cassie. "Achieving Unity through Diversity." *Black Issues in Higher Education* 21.5 (2004): 8-11. Print.

Manning, Wendy D. "Children and the Stability of Cohabiting Couples." *Journal of Marriage & Family* 66.3 (2004): 674-89. Print.

CITING SOURCES FOUND ON A WEBSITE

Citations for sources found on the Internet require much of the same information used in citations for print sources. Internet addresses (URLs) change so frequently that unless you judge that a source would be very difficult to find without one, do not give the URL in the citation. (See "Personal and Professional Website" for an example using a URL.)

Basic MLA Format for a Website

Author's last name, Author's first name. "Article or Item Title." *Website Title.* Version or edition, if any. Website Sponsor or Publisher, day month year of publication. Web. day month year of access.

- **Author's name.** Follow the guidelines for author's names on page 631. If the article is unsigned, begin with its title.
- **Title of the selection.** To cite a selection on the website, give the title of the selection, followed by a period, all enclosed in quotation marks. To cite the entire website, see "Source," below.
- **Source.** Give the title of the website, italicized, and followed by a period.
- **Version or edition.** List any version or edition number (for example, for an online book), if relevant.
- **Publisher or sponsor.** Cite the publisher, owner, or sponsor of the website, followed by a comma. This information is often found at the bottom of the Web page. If none is available, use *N.p.* (for "no publisher").

- **Date of publication.** Give the date of publication as day, month, year, followed by a period. If the information is not available, use *n.d.* (for "no date").
- **Medium.** Include *Web* followed by a period.
- **Access date.** End with the date you retrieved the information (day, month, year) followed by a period.

Newspaper or Magazine Article

Orecklin, Michele. "Stress and the Superdad." *Time.* Time.com, 16 Aug. 2004. Web. 2 Dec. 2008.

Nachtigal, Jeff. "We Own What You Think." *Salon.com.* Salon Media Group, 18 Aug. 2004. Web. 17 Mar. 2005.

"Restoring the Wetlands." Editorial. *Los Angeles Times.* Los Angeles Times, 26 July 2008. Web. 6 Jan. 2009.

Online Reference Work

"Salem Witch Trials." *Encyclopaedia Britannica Online.* Encyclopaedia Britannica, 2008. Web. 3 Jan. 2009.

Scholarly Journal Found on the Internet

For articles accessed from a website, follow the citation format for print articles, but specify *Web* as the medium and give the date of access. If no page numbers are available, insert *n. pag.* See also the entry for "Scholarly Journal Found in an Online Database."

Njeng, Eric Sipyinyu, "Achebe, Conrad, and the Postcolonial Strain." *CLCWeb: Comparative Literature and Culture* 10.1 (2008): *n. pag.* Web. 12 Dec. 2008.

Qin, Desiree Baolian. "The Role of Gender in Immigrant Children's Educational Adaptation." *Current Issues in Comparative Education* 9.1 (2006): 8-19. Web. 5 Jan. 2009.

Personal and Professional Website

Because the site would otherwise be difficult to access, the first entry below contains a URL, enclosed in angle brackets and followed by a period. Note that long Web addresses should be broken up only after slashes. In the second entry below, *Uncle Tom's Cabin* is *not* italicized. It's a title that would ordinarily be italicized, but since the rest of the website title is italicized, the book title is set off in regular type.

Finney, Dee. *Native American Culture.* 23 May 2008. Web. 6 June 2008. <http://www.greatdreams.com/native.htm>.

Railton, Stephen, ed. Uncle Tom's Cabin *& American Culture: A Multi-Media Archive.* Dept. of English, U of Virginia, 2007. Web. 9 Apr. 2006.

Blog

If the blog has no title, insert "Online posting" in place of the title, without quotation marks or italics.

Waldman, Deane. "'Care' Has Deserted Managed Care." *Huffington Post.* HuffingtonPost.com, 26 June 2008. Web. 18 Nov. 2008.

Podcast

Elisabeth Arnold. "Tale of Two Alaska Villages." Podcast. *NPR.org.* Natl. Public Radio. 29 July 2008. Web. 13 Dec. 2008.

CITING SOURCES FOUND THROUGH AN ONLINE DATABASE OR SCHOLARLY PROJECT

Specify the database or project, but do not include the URL or information about the library system used.

Scholarly Journal Found in an Online Database

Begin with the same information as for online periodicals. After the publication information (volume, issue, date, and page numbers), give the title of the database (italicized or underlined) and the medium of publication (*Web*). Complete the entry with the date you accessed the information. See also the entry "Scholarly Journal Found on the Internet."

Weiler, Angela M. "Using Technology to Take Down Plagiarism." *Community College Week* 16.16 (2004): 4-6. *EBSCOhost.* Web. 17 Oct. 2008.

Book Found in an Online Scholarly Project

When it's available, include the book's original publication information. Also include (when available) the name of the site's editor, its electronic publication date, its sponsoring organization, your date of access, and the Web address.

Franklin, Benjamin. *The Autobiography of Benjamin Franklin.* London, 1793. *Electronic Text Center.* Ed. Judy Boss. Web. 16 Jan. 2009.

CITING OTHER COMMON SOURCES

Include the medium through which you accessed the source, for example, *CD* for "compact disc" or *E-mail* for an e-mail message you received.

Television or Radio Program

"A Matter of Choice? Gay Life in America." Part 4 of 5. *Nightline*. Narr. Ted Koppel. ABC. WPVI-TV, Philadelphia. 23 May 2002. Television.

Movie, Recording, Videotape, DVD, Filmstrip, or Slide Program

Provide the author or composer of the piece (if appropriate); title (italicized or underlined); director, conductor, or performer; manufacturer or distributor; and year of release. Give the medium at the end of the citation.

Fahrenheit 911. Dir. Michael Moore. Sony, 2004. DVD.

CD-ROM or DVD-ROM

Cite the following information (when available): author, title (italicized or underlined), version, place of publication, publisher, year of publication, and medium (CD-ROM or DVD-ROM).

World Book Encyclopedia. 2006 Edition. Renton, WA: Topics Entertainment, 2006. CD-ROM.

Personal or Telephone Interview

Specify "Personal interview" for an interview you conducted in person and "Telephone interview" for an interview you conducted over the telephone.

Langdon, Paul. Personal interview. 26 Jan. 2008.

Lecture, Speech, Address, or Reading

Blacksmith, James. "Urban Design in the New Millennium." Cityscapes Lecture Series. Urban Studies Institute. Metropolitan College, Washington, DC. 18 Apr. 2005. Lecture.

Papa, Andrea. "Reforming the Nation's Tax Structure." Accounting 302. Cypress College, Astoria, NY. 3 Dec. 2004. Lecture.

E-mail Message

Start with the sender's name. Then give the title (from the subject line) in quotation marks, a description, the date of the message, and the medium (*E-mail*).

Mack, Lynn. "New Developments in Early Childhood Education." Message to the author. 30 Aug. 2006. E-mail.

AVOIDING TEN COMMON WRITING ERRORS

Many students consider grammar a nuisance. Taking the easy way out, they cross their fingers and hope they haven't made too many mistakes. They assume that their meaning will come across, even if their writing contains some errors—perhaps a misplaced comma here or a dangling modifier there. Not so. Surface errors annoy readers and may confuse them. Such errors also weaken a writer's credibility because they defy language conventions, customs that readers expect writers to honor. By mastering grammar, punctuation, and spelling conventions, students can increase their power and versatility as writers.

This concise appendix, "Avoiding Ten Common Writing Errors," will help you brush up on the most useful rules and conventions of writing. It's organized according to the broad skill areas, listed below, that give writers the most trouble. Throughout this appendix, grammatical terminology is kept to a minimum. Although we assume that you know the major parts of speech (noun, verb, pronoun, and so on), we do, when appropriate, provide on-the-spot definitions of more technical grammatical terms.

Here are the ten common writing errors covered:

1. Fragments
2. Comma Splices and Run-ons
3. Faulty Subject-Verb Agreement

4. Faulty Pronoun Agreement
5. Misplaced and Dangling Modifiers
6. Faulty Parallelism
7. Comma Misuse
8. Apostrophe Misuse
9. Confusing Homonyms
10. Misuse of Italics and Underlining

1 FRAGMENTS

A full *sentence* satisfies two conditions: (1) it has a subject and a verb, and (2) it can stand alone as a complete thought. Although a *fragment* is punctuated like a full sentence, it doesn't satisfy these two requirements.

NO Meteorologists predict a drought this summer. *In spite of heavy spring rains.*

NO *A victim of her own hypocrisy.* The senator lost the next election.

Some Easy Ways to Correct Fragments

A. Attach the fragment to the beginning or end of the preceding (or following) sentence, changing punctuation and capitalization as needed.

YES In spite of heavy spring rains, meteorologists predict a drought this summer.

or

Meteorologists predict a drought this summer, in spite of heavy spring rains.

B. Attach the fragment to a newly created sentence.

YES Meteorologists predict a drought this summer. *They do so* in spite of heavy spring rains.

C. Insert the fragment into the preceding (or following) sentence, adding commas as needed.

YES The senator, *a victim of her own hypocrisy,* lost the next election.

D. Supply the missing subject and/or verb, changing other words as necessary.

YES *The senator became* a victim of her own hypocrisy. *She* lost the next election.

2 COMMA SPLICES AND RUN-ONS

Consider the following faulty sentences:

NO The First Amendment cannot be taken for granted, it is the bedrock of our democracy.

NO The First Amendment cannot be taken for granted it is the bedrock of our democracy.

The first example is a *comma splice:* a comma used to join, or splice together, two complete thoughts, even though the comma alone is not strong enough to connect the two independent ideas. The second example is a *run-on,* or fused, sentence: two sentences run together without any punctuation indicating where the first sentence ends and the second begins.

Some Easy Ways to Correct Comma Splices and Run-ons

A. Place a period, question mark, or exclamation point at the end of the first sentence, and capitalize the first letter of the second sentence.

YES The First Amendment cannot be taken for *granted. It* is the bedrock of our democracy.

B. Use a semicolon to mark where the first sentence ends and the second begins.

YES The First Amendment cannot be taken for *granted; it* is the bedrock of our democracy.

C. Turn one of the sentences into a dependent phrase.

YES *Because* it is the bedrock of our democracy, the First Amendment cannot be taken for granted.

D. Keep or add a comma at the end of the first sentence, but follow the comma with a coordinating conjunction (*and, but, for, nor, or, so, yet*).

YES The First Amendment cannot be taken for granted, *for* it is the bedrock of our democracy.

3 FAULTY SUBJECT-VERB AGREEMENT

A verb should match its subject in number. If the subject is singular (one person, place, or thing), the verb should have a singular form. If the subject is plural (two or more persons, places, or things), the verb should have a plural form. Always determine the verb's subject and make sure that the verb agrees with it, rather than with some other word in the sentence.

NO The *documents* from the court case *was* unsealed for the first time in three decades.

YES The *documents* from the court case *were* unsealed for the first time in three decades.

Some Easy Ways to Correct Faulty Subject-Verb Agreement

A. When there are two or more singular subjects (joined by *and*) in a sentence, use a plural verb. (However, when the word *or* joins the subjects, use a *singular* verb.)

YES A sprawling maple *and* a lush rose bush *flank* [not *flanks*] my childhood home.

B. When the subject and verb are separated by a prepositional phrase, be sure to match the verb to its subject—not to a word in the prepositional phrase that comes between them.

YES The *quality* of student papers *has* [not *have*] been declining over the past semester.

C. When the words *either...or* or *neither...nor* connect two subjects, use the verb form (singular or plural) that agrees with the subject *closer* to the verb.

YES *Neither* the employees *nor* the store *owner was* [not *were*] aware of the theft.

YES *Neither* the store owner *nor* her *employees were* [not *was*] aware of the theft.

D. When using the indefinite pronouns *anybody, anyone, anything, each, either, everybody, everyone, everything, neither, nobody, none, no one, nothing, one, somebody, someone,* or *something,* use a *singular* verb.

YES *Neither* of the candidates *is* [not *are*] willing to address the issue.

When you use the indefinite pronouns *all, any, most, none,* or *some,* use a **singular** or a **plural** verb, depending on whether the pronoun refers to one thing or to a number of things.

YES The spokesperson announced that only *some* of the *report has* been confirmed.

In the preceding sentence, *some* refers to a single report and therefore takes a *singular* verb. In the following sentence, *some* refers to *multiple* reports and therefore takes a *plural* verb.

> **YES** The spokesperson announced that only *some* of the *reports have* been confirmed.

E. When the subject of a sentence refers to a group acting as a unit, use a *singular* verb.

> **YES** The local baseball *team is* [not *are*] boycotting the new sports stadium.

F. When words such as *here, there, how, what, when, where, which, who,* and *why* invert normal sentence order—so that the verb comes before the subject—look ahead for the subject and make sure that it and the verb agree.

> **YES** There *is* [not *are*] a *series* of things to consider before deciding on a college major.
>
> **YES** What *are* [not *is*] the *arguments* against energy conservation?

4 FAULTY PRONOUN AGREEMENT

A *pronoun* must agree in number with its *antecedent*—the noun or pronoun it replaces or refers to. If the antecedent is singular, the pronoun must be singular. If the antecedent is plural, the pronoun must be plural.

Some Easy Ways to Correct Faulty Pronoun Agreement

A. A compound subject (two or more nouns joined by *and*) requires plural pronouns.

> **YES** Both the car *manufacturers* and the tire *company* had trouble restoring *their* reputations after losing the class-action lawsuit.

However, when the nouns are joined by ***or*** or ***nor,*** the pronoun form (singular or plural) should agree with the noun that is ***closer*** to the verb.

> **YES** Neither the car manufacturers *nor* the tire *company* restored *its* reputation after losing the class-action lawsuit.
>
> **YES** Neither the tire company *nor* the car *manufacturers* restored *their* reputations after losing the class-action lawsuit.

B. A subject that is a *collective noun* (referring to a group that acts as a unit) takes a singular pronoun.

YES The *orchestra* showed *its* appreciation by playing a lengthy encore.

Or, if a singular pronoun sounds awkward, simply make the antecedent plural.

YES The orchestra *members* showed *their* appreciation by playing a lengthy encore.

C. The indefinite pronouns *anybody, anyone, anything, each, either, everybody, everyone, everything, neither, nobody, no one, nothing, one, somebody, someone,* and *something* are singular and therefore take singular pronouns.

YES *Each* of the buildings had *its* [not *their*] roof replaced.
YES *Neither* of the executives resigned *his* [not *their*] position after the revelations.

Using the singular form with indefinite pronouns can be awkward or sexist when the pronoun encompasses both male and female. To avoid these problems, you can make the antecedent plural and use a plural pronoun.

AWK *Anyone* who exhibits symptoms should see her or his doctor immediately.
YES *Individuals* who exhibit symptoms should see *their* doctor immediately.

D. Within a sentence, pronouns should be in the same *person* (point of view) as their antecedents.

NO To register to vote, *citizens* [third person] can visit the state government's website, where *you* [second person] can download the appropriate forms.
YES To register to vote, *citizens* [third person] can visit the state government's website, where *they* [third person] can download the appropriate forms.

5 MISPLACED AND DANGLING MODIFIERS

A *modifier* is a word or group of words that describes something else. Sometimes sentences are written in such a way that modifiers are misplaced. Here is an example of a *misplaced modifier:*

NO Television stations carried the story of the disastrous tornado *throughout the nation.* [The tornado was throughout the nation?]

YES Television stations *throughout the nation* carried the story of the disastrous tornado.

Modifiers are commonly misused in another way. An introductory modifier must modify the subject of the sentence. If it doesn't, it may be a *dangling modifier*. Here's an example:

NO *Faded and brittle with age,* archaeologists unearthed a painted clay pot near the riverbank. [The archaeologists were faded and brittle with age?]

YES Archaeologists unearthed a painted clay pot, *faded and brittle with age,* near the riverbank.

or

Faded and brittle with age, a painted clay pot was unearthed near the riverbank by archaeologists.

An Easy Way to Correct Misplaced Modifiers

A. Place the modifier next to the word(s) it describes.

NO Passengers complained about the flight at the customer service desk, *which was turbulent and delayed.* [The customer service desk was turbulent and delayed?]

YES Passengers complained about the flight, *which was turbulent and delayed,* at the customer service desk.

NO She *nearly* ran the marathon in four hours. [Did she or didn't she run?]

YES She ran the marathon in *nearly* four hours.

Some Easy Ways to Correct Dangling Modifiers

The following dangling modifier can be corrected in one of two ways, discussed below.

NO *Leaping gracefully across the stage,* spectators were in awe of the agile dancer.

A. Rewrite the sentence by adding to the modifying phrase the word that is being described.

YES *As the agile dancer leaped* gracefully across the stage, spectators were in awe of him.

B. Rewrite the sentence so that the word being modified becomes the subject.

YES Leaping gracefully across the stage, the agile dancer awed the spectators.

6 FAULTY PARALLELISM

Items in a pair, a series, or a list should be phrased in *parallel* (matching) grammatical structures. Otherwise, *faulty parallelism* results.

NO After hiking all day, the campers were *exhausted, hungry,* and *experienced soreness.* [Of the three items in the series, the first two are adjectives, but the last is a verb plus a noun.]

YES After hiking all day, the campers were *exhausted, hungry,* and *sore.*

Words that follow *correlative conjunctions—either... or, neither... nor, both... and, not only... but also*—should also be parallel.

NO Every road to the airport is **either** *jammed* **or** *is closed* for repairs. [The word *either* is followed by an adjective (*jammed*), but *or* is followed by a verb and adjective (*is closed*).]

YES Every road to the airport is **either** *jammed* **or** *closed* for repairs.

An Easy Way to Correct Faulty Parallelism

A. Use the *same grammatical structure* for each item in a pair or series.

NO The finalists for the sales job possess *charismatic personalities, excellent references,* and *they are extensively experienced.*

YES The finalists for the sales job possess *charismatic personalities, excellent references,* and *extensive experience.*

NO We observed *that the leaves were changing color, the sun was setting earlier,* and *that the air was becoming chillier.* [The word *that* precedes the first and last clauses, but not the second. It must be inserted before the second clause or, preferably, deleted from before the last clause.]

YES We observed *that the leaves were changing color, the sun was setting earlier,* and *the air was becoming chillier.*

NO Students go to college with many goals:

1. To become more educated.
2. Preparing for future careers.
3. They also want to meet new people.

YES Students go to college with many goals:

1. To become more educated.
2. To prepare for future careers.
3. To meet new people.

NO The romantic comedy that premiered last night was neither *romantic* nor *was it funny.*

YES The romantic comedy that premiered last night was neither *romantic* nor *funny.*

7 COMMA MISUSE

The *comma* is so frequent in writing that mastering its use is essential. By dividing a sentence into its parts, commas clarify meaning.

Most Common Uses of the Comma

A. When two complete sentences are joined with a coordinating conjunction (*and, but, for, nor, or, so, yet*), a comma is placed *before* the conjunction.

YES Many attended the political rally, *but* few demonstrated enthusiasm for the cause.

B. Introductory material, which precedes a sentence's main subject and verb, usually is followed by a comma.

YES *Like most kids,* the children in the study were powerfully influenced by TV advertisements.

Similarly, material attached to the end of a sentence may be preceded by a comma.

YES The children in the study were powerfully influenced by TV advertisements, *which peddled expensive toys and unhealthy snacks.*

C. When a word or phrase describes a noun but isn't crucial for identifying that noun, it is set off from the rest of the sentence with a comma.

YES First-year film students are required to analyze *Metropolis,* a late-1920s film that exhibited important artistic innovations.

D. When words or phrases inserted into the body of a sentence can be removed without significant loss of meaning, such elements are considered *interrupters.* Interrupters should be preceded and followed by commas when they occur midsentence.

YES Dr. Gene Nome, *a leading genetic researcher,* testified before Congress on the need for increased funding.

E. In a list of *three or more* items in a series, the items should be separated by commas.

YES The writing process usually entails *prewriting, drafting,* and *revising.*

F. A comma should be inserted between a short quotation and a phrase that indicates the quotation's source.

YES One voter commented, "This is the first candidate I've voted for enthusiastically."

or

"This is the first candidate I've voted for enthusiastically," one voter commented.

or

"This is the first candidate," one voter commented, "I've voted for enthusiastically."

G. Commas are placed between the numbers in a date and between the elements of the address with the exception that no comma precedes a zip code.

YES On November 17, 2006, the fourth graders mailed "Dear President" letters to The White House, 1600 Pennsylvania Avenue, Washington, DC 20500.

8 APOSTROPHE MISUSE

Like the comma, the *apostrophe* is a commonly used—and misused—punctuation mark.

Most Common Uses of the Apostrophe

A. In standard contractions, an apostrophe replaces any omitted letters.

YES can't, don't, I'm, she's, we've

B. The possessive form of most singular nouns requires adding *'s*.

YES Senator Ross's position is that health care is every person's right.

For ***plural nouns*** ending in *s*, an apostrophe only is added to show possession.

YES The twelve senators' position on Native Americans' rights is clear.

Plural nouns that do not end in *s* need *'s* to show possession.

YES Improvement in the children's test scores enabled the school to rise in rank.

However, an apostrophe is ***not*** used to form the simple plural of a noun.

NO The central role of *radio's* in American homes has declined in recent decades.

YES The central role of *radios* in American homes has declined in recent decades.

C. Beware of confusing possessive pronouns with contractions. The possessive forms of personal pronouns do *not* include an apostrophe. Here are the correct forms:

YES mine, yours, his, hers, its, ours, theirs

Note that *its* (*without* an apostrophe) is the possessive form of *it,* whereas *it's* (*with* an apostrophe) means "it is" or "it has."

YES The factory closed *its* [not *it's*] doors last week.

YES The company president determined that *it's* [for "it is"] time to close down the factory.

Similarly, *whose* (*without* an apostrophe) is the possessive form of *who,* whereas *who's* (*with* an apostrophe) means "who is" or "who has."

YES The sculptor *whose* [not *who's*] work is being exhibited just arrived at the gallery.

YES The sculptor *who's* [for *who is*] exhibiting his work just arrived at the gallery.

9 CONFUSING HOMONYMS

Homonyms are words that sound alike but have different spellings and meanings. Here are some of the most troublesome.

Accept means "receive" or "agree to." **Except** means "but" or "excluding."

YES *Except* for your position on mandatory school uniforms, I *accept* your ideas about changing the education system.

Affect means "influence" (verb). **Effect** means "result" (noun) or "bring about" (verb).

YES It's amazing how much a hurricane's *effects* can *affect* a region's economy.

Its means "belonging to it." **It's** means "it is" or "it has."

YES *It's* been years since the factory produced *its* last car.

Principal means either "main" (adjective) or "the person in charge of a school (noun)." **Principle** (noun) means "a law or concept."

YES The *principal* topic you should study for your midterm is the *principle* of gravity.

Than is a word used in comparisons. **Then** means "at that time."

YES The insurance agent assessed the house and *then* wrote a report stating that the damage was worse *than* expected.

Their means "belonging to them." **There** refers to a place other than "here." **They're** means "they are."

YES *They're* planning to drop off *their* donations for the food drive in the bin over *there*.

To can be part of a verb (as in *to smile* or *came to*) or a preposition meaning "toward." **Too** means "overly" (as in *too hot*) or "also." ***Two*** refers to the number 2.

YES *Two* of my coworkers go outside *to* eat lunch every day; today they invited me, *too*.

Whose means "belonging to someone or something." **Who's** means "who is" or "who has."

YES We're trying to determine *who's* going to call my aunt, *whose* son was injured in an accident.

Your means "belonging to you." **You're** means "you are."

YES When *your* mother calls you by *your* first, middle, and last name, you know *you're* in trouble.

10 MISUSE OF ITALICS AND UNDERLINING

Computers and other printing innovations have allowed italics (*slanted type*) to replace underlining (underlined type) in printed text. The following are the most common uses of italics (or of underlining, if you're writing by hand or if your instruction prefers underlining).

A. The titles of works that are published (or, in the case of visual works, displayed) individually should be italicized. Such works, which are often lengthy, include books, magazines, journals, newspapers, websites, online databases, movies (including DVDs), TV and radio programs, musical recordings (albums, CDs, audiocassettes), plays, paintings, and sculptures.

Note: The titles of shorter works—such as poems, short stories, articles, essays, songs, and TV episodes—published as part of a magazine, anthology, or other collection are not italicized; use quotation marks for such titles.

YES After reading Anne Sexton's poem "The Starry Night" from the collection *All My Pretty Ones,* the students went online to look at Van Gogh's painting *The Starry Night.*

YES The Discovery Channel program *The Beatles: The Later Years* focused primarily on the band's albums *Sgt. Pepper's Lonely Hearts Club Band* and *Abbey Road.*

B. Foreign words not fully incorporated into mainstream English should be italicized or underlined.

YES The labor union leaders sought a *tête-à-tête* with the company's executives in order to resolve a work strike.

C. Words that you wish to emphasize should be italicized or underlined. However, this should be done sparingly at the risk of actually *weakening* emphasis.

YES Users of the new computer program report that they don't like it. They *love* it.

D. When a word is being referred to *as a word* or as a *defined term,* it should be italicized or underlined. Definitions of italicized terms are often put in quotation marks.

YES When writing, avoid using a word like *conflagration* when *fire* will do.

YES The word *conflagration* actually means "fire."

GLOSSARY

Abstract and concrete language refers to two different qualities of words. Abstract words and phrases convey concepts, qualities, emotions, and ideas that we can think and talk about but not actually see or experience directly, such as *conservatism, courage, avarice, joy,* and *hatred.* Words or phrases whose meanings are directly seen or experienced by the senses are concrete terms, such as *split-level house, waddling penguin,* and *short pink waitress uniform.*

Adequate—see *Evidence.*

***Ad hominem* argument**—see *Logical fallacies.*

Analogy refers to an imaginative comparison between two subjects that seem to have little in common. Often a writer can make a complex idea or topic understandable by comparing it to a more familiar subject. For example, to explain how the economic difficulties of farmers weaken an entire nation, a writer might create an analogy between failing farms and a cancer that slowly destroys a person's life.

Argumentation-persuasion tries to encourage readers to accept a writer's point of view on some controversial issue. In *argumentation,* a writer uses objective reasoning, facts, and hard evidence to demonstrate the soundness of a position. In *persuasion,* the writer uses appeals to the emotions and value systems, often in the hope of encouraging readers to take a specific action. Argumentation and persuasion are frequently used together in an essay. For example, a writer might argue for the construction of a highway through town by pointing out that the road would bring new business, create new jobs, and lighten traffic. The writer also might try to persuade readers to vote for a highway appropriations bill by appealing to their emotions, claiming that the highway would allow people to get home faster, thus giving them more time for family life and leisure activities.

Assertion refers to the *thesis* of an *argumentation-persuasion* essay. The assertion, or *proposition,* is a point of view or opinion on a controversial issue or topic. The assertion cannot be merely a statement of a fact. Such statements as "Women still experience discrimination in the job market," "General Rabb would make an ideal mayor for our town," and "This university should devote more funds to raising the quality of the food services" are examples of assertions.

Attribution is a phrase or sentence that identifies a source and helps incorporate source material into an essay.

Audience refers to a writer's intended readers. In planning the content and tone of an essay, you should identify your audience and consider its needs. How similar are the members of your audience to you in knowledge and point of view? What will they need to know for you to achieve your *purpose?* What *tone* will make them open to receiving your message? For example, if you wrote about the high cost of clothing for an economics professor, you would choose a serious, analytic tone and supply statistical evidence for your points. If you wrote about the same topic for the college newspaper, you might use a tone tinged with humor and provide helpful hints on finding bargain clothing.

Begging the question—see *Logical fallacies.*

Brainstorming is a technique used in the *prewriting* stage. It helps you discover the limited subject you can successfully write about and also generates raw material—ideas and details—to develop that subject. In brainstorming, you allow your mind to play freely with the subject. You try to capture fleeting thoughts about it, no matter how random, minor, or tangential, and jot them down rapidly before they disappear from your mind.

Causal analysis—see *Cause-effect.*

Causal chain refers to a series of causes and effects, in which the result or effect of a cause becomes itself the cause of a further effect, and so on. For example, a person's alarm clock failing to buzz might begin a causal chain by causing the person to oversleep. Oversleeping then causes the person to miss the bus, and missing the bus causes the person to arrive late to work. Arriving late causes the person to miss an important phone call, which causes the person to lose a chance at a lucrative contract.

Cause-effect, sometimes called *causal analysis,* involves analyzing the reasons for or results of an event, action, decision, or phenomenon. Writers develop an essay through an analysis of causes whenever they attempt to answer such questions as "Why has this happened?" or "Why does this exist?" When writers explore such questions as "What happens or would happen if a certain change occurs?" or "What will happen if a condition continues?" their essays involve a discussion of effects. Some cause-effect essays concentrate on the causes of a situation, some focus on the effects, and others present both causes and effects.

Characteristics—see *Formal definition.*

Chronological sequence—see *Narrative sequence* and *Organization.*

Circularity is an error in *formal definition* resulting from using variations of the to-be-defined word in the definition. For example, "A scientific hypothesis is a hypothesis made by a scientist about the results of an experiment" is circular because the unknown term is used to explain itself.

Class—see *Formal definition.*

Coherence refers to the clear connection among the various parts of an essay. As a writer, you can draw upon two key strategies to make writing coherent. You can use a clear *organizational format* (for example, a chronological, spatial, emphatic, or simple-to-complex sequence). You can also provide *appropriate signaling* or *connecting devices* (transitions, bridging sentences, repeated words, synonyms, and pronouns).

Comparison-contrast means explaining the similarities and/or differences between events, objects, people, ideas, and so on. The comparison-contrast format can be used to meet a purely factual purpose ("This is how A and B are alike or different"). But usually writers use comparison-contrast to make a judgment about the relative merits of the subjects under discussion. Sometimes a writer will concentrate solely on similarities *or* differences. For instance, when writing about married versus single life, you would probably devote most of your time to discussing the differences between these lifestyles. Other times, comparison and contrast are found together. In an essay analyzing two approaches to U.S. foreign policy, you would probably discuss the similarities *and* the differences in the goals and methods characteristic of each approach.

Conclusion refers to the one or more paragraphs that bring an essay to an end. Effective conclusions give the reader a sense of completeness and finality. Writers often use the conclusion as a place to reaffirm the *thesis* and to express a final thought about the subject. Methods of conclusion include summarizing main points, using a quotation, predicting an outcome, and recommending an action.

Conflict creates tension in the readers of a *narration*. It is produced by the opposition of characters or other forces in a story. Conflict can occur between individuals, between a person and society or nature, or within a person. Readers wonder how a conflict will be resolved and read on to find out.

Connotative and denotative language refers to the ability of language to emphasize one or another aspect of a word's range of meaning. *Denotative language* stresses the dictionary meaning of words. *Connotative language* emphasizes the echoes of feeling that cluster around some words. For example, the terms *weep, bawl, break down,* and *sob* all denote the same thing: to cry. But they have different associations and call up different images.

Controlling idea—see *Thesis.*

Deductive reasoning is a form of logical thinking in which general statements believed to be true are applied to specific situations or cases. The result of deduction is a conclusion or prediction about the specific situation. Deduction is often expressed in a three-step pattern called a *syllogism.* The first part of the syllogism is a general statement about a large class of items or situations, the *major premise.* The second part is the *minor premise,* a more limited statement about a specific item or case. The third part is the *conclusion,* drawn from the major premise, about that specific case or item.

Definition explains the meaning of a word or concept. The brief formal definitions found in the dictionary can be useful if you need to clarify or restrict the meaning of a term used in an essay. In such cases, the definition is short and to the point. But you may also use an *extended definition* in an essay, taking several paragraphs, even the entire piece, to develop the meaning of a term. You may use extended definition to convey a personal slant on a well-known term, to refute a commonly held interpretation of a word, or to dissect a complex or controversial issue.

Definition by negation is a method of defining a term by first explaining what the term is *not,* and then going on to explain what it is. For example, you might begin a critical essay about television with a definition by negation: "Television, far from being a medium that dispenses only light, insubstantial fare, actually disseminates a dangerously distorted view of family life." Definition by negation can provide a stimulating introduction to an essay.

Denotative language—see *Connotative and denotative language.*

Description involves the use of vivid word pictures to express what the five senses have experienced. The subject of a descriptive essay can be a person, a place, an object, or an event. In an *objective description,* a writer provides details about a subject without conveying the emotions the subject arouses. For example, if you were involved in a traffic accident, your insurance agent might ask you to write an objective description of the events leading up to and during the crash. But in a *subjective description,* the writer's goal is to evoke in the reader the emotions felt during the experience. For example, in a cautionary letter to a friend who has a habit of driving dangerously, you might write a subjective description of your horrifyingly close call with death during a car accident.

Development—see *Evidence.*

Dialogue is the writer's way of directly presenting the exact words spoken by characters in a *narration.* By using dialogue, writers can convey people's individuality and also add drama and immediacy to an essay.

Directional process analysis—see *Process analysis.*

Division-classification refers to a logical method for analyzing a single subject or several related subjects. Though often used together in an essay, division and classification are separate processes. *Division* involves breaking a subject or idea into its component parts. For instance, the concept "an ideal vacation" could be divided according to its destination, accommodations, or cost. *Classification* involves organizing a number of related items into categories. For example, in an essay about the overwhelming flow of paper in our everyday lives, you might classify the typical kinds of mail most people receive: personal mail (letters, birthday cards, party invitations), business mail (bills, bank statements, charge-card receipts), and junk mail (flyers about bargain sales, solicitations to donate, contest announcements).

Dominant impression refers to the purpose of a descriptive essay. While some descriptive essays have a thesis, others do not; instead, they convey a dominant impression or main point. For example, one person writing a descriptive essay about New York City might use its architectural diversity as a focal point. Another person writing a description of Manhattan might concentrate on the overpowering sense of hustle and speed about everyone and everything in the city. Both writers would select only those details that supported their dominant impressions.

Dramatic license refers to the writer's privilege, when writing a narrative, to alter facts or details to strengthen the support of the *thesis* or *narrative point.* For example, a writer is free to flesh out the description of an event whose specific details may be partially forgotten or to modify or omit details of a narrative that do not contribute to the meaning the writer wishes to convey.

Either-or fallacy—see *Logical fallacies.*

Emphatic sequence—see *Organization.*

Ethos refers to a writer's reliability or credibility. Such an image of trustworthiness is particularly important to readers of an *argumentation-persuasion* essay or piece. Writers establish their *ethos* by using reason and logic, by being moderate in their appeals to emotions, by avoiding a hostile tone, and by demonstrating overall knowledgeability of the subject. The most effective argumentation-persuasion involves an interplay of *ethos, logos,* and *pathos.*

Etymology refers to the history of a word or term. All English words have their origins in other, often ancient, languages. Giving a brief etymology of a word can help a writer establish the context for developing an *extended definition* of the word. For example, the word *criminal* is derived from a Latin word meaning "accusation" or "accused." Today, our word *criminal* goes beyond the concept of "accused" to mean "guilty."

Evidence lends substance, or support, to a writer's main ideas and thus helps the reader to accept the writer's viewpoint. Evidence should meet several criteria. First of all, it should be *unified,* in the sense that all supporting ideas and details should relate directly to the key point the writer is making. Second, evidence should be *adequate;* there should be enough evidence to convince the reader to agree with the thesis. Third, evidence should be *specific;* that is, vivid and detailed rather than vague and general. Fourth, evidence must be *accurate* and not overstate or understate information. Fifth, evidence should be *representative,* relying on the typical rather than the atypical to make a point. The bulk of an essay is devoted to supplying evidence.

Exemplification, at the heart of all effective writing, involves using concrete specifics to support generalizations. In exemplification, writers provide examples or instances that support or clarify broader statements. You might support the thesis statement "I have a close-knit family" by using such examples as the following: "We have a regular Sunday dinner at my grandmother's house with at least ten family members present"; "My sisters and brothers visit my parents every week"; "I spend so much time on the phone talking with my sisters that sometimes I have trouble finding time for my new college friends."

Extended definition—see *Definition.*

Fallacies—see *Logical fallacies.*

False analogy—see *Logical fallacies.*

Figures of speech are imaginative comparisons between two things usually thought of as dissimilar. Some major figures of speech are *simile, metaphor,* and *personification. Similes* are comparisons that use the signal words *like* or *as:* "Superman was as powerful as a locomotive." *Metaphors,* which do not use signal words, directly equate unlike things: "The boss is a tiger when it comes to landing a contract"; "The high-powered pistons of the boxer's arms pummeled his opponent." *Personification* attributes human characteristics to inanimate things or nonhuman beings: "The angry clouds unleashed their fury on the town"; "The turtle shyly poked his head out of his shell."

First draft refers to the writer's first try at producing a basic, unpolished version of the whole essay. It is often referred to as the "rough" draft, and nothing about it is final or unchangeable. The process of writing the first draft often brings up new ideas or details. Writers sometimes break off writing the draft to *brainstorm* or *freewrite* as new ideas occur to them and then return to the draft with new inspiration. You shouldn't worry about spelling, grammar, or style in the first-draft stage; instead, you should keep focused on casting your ideas into sentence and paragraph form.

Flashback—see *Narrative sequence.*

Flashforward—see *Narrative sequence.*

Formal definition involves stating a definition in a three-part pattern of about one sentence in length. In presenting a formal definition, a writer puts the *term* in a *class* and then lists the *characteristics* that separate the term from other members of its class. For example, a formal definition of a word processor might be "A word processor (term) is an electronic machine (class) that is used to write, edit, store, and produce typewritten documents (characteristics)." Writers often use a formal definition to prepare a reader for an extended definition that follows.

Freewriting is most often used during the *prewriting* stage to help writers generate ideas about a limited topic. To use this method, write nonstop for five or ten minutes about everything your topic brings to mind. Disregard grammar, spelling, and organization as you keep your pen and mind moving. Freewriting is similar to *brainstorming,* except that the result is a rambling, detail-filled paragraph rather than a list. Freewriting can also be used to generate ideas during later stages of the writing process.

Gender-biased language gives the impression that one sex is more important, powerful, or valuable than the other. When writing, you should work to replace such sexist language with *gender-neutral* or *nonsexist* terms that convey no sexual prejudice. First of all, try to avoid *sexist vocabulary* that demeans or excludes one of the sexes: *stud, jock, chick, fox,* and so on. Also, just as adult males should be called *men,* adult females should be referred to as *women,* not *girls.* And men shouldn't be empowered with professional and honorary titles (*President* Barack Obama) while professional women—such as congressional representatives—are assigned only personal titles (*Ms.* Gwen Moore). Third, recognize that indefinite pronouns like *anyone, each,* and *everybody* may also pave the way to sexist pronoun use.

Hasty generalization—see *Logical fallacies.*

Inductive reasoning is a form of logical thinking in which specific cases and facts are examined to draw a wider-ranging conclusion. The result of inductive reasoning is a generalization that is applied to situations or cases similar to the ones examined. Induction is typical of scientific investigation and of everyday thinking. For example, on the basis of specific experiences, you may have concluded that when you feel chilly in a room where everyone else is comfortable, you are likely to develop a cold and fever in the next day or two. In an *argumentation-persuasion* essay, the conclusion reached by induction would be your *assertion* or *thesis.*

Inference is the term for a conclusion based on *inductive reasoning.* Because the reasoning behind specific cases may not be simple, there is usually an element of uncertainty in an inductive conclusion. Choosing the correct explanation for specific cases is a matter of carefully weighing and selecting alternative conclusions.

Informational process analysis—see *Process analysis.*

Introduction refers to the first paragraph or several paragraphs of an essay. The introduction serves three purposes. It informs readers of the general subject of the essay, it catches their attention, and it presents the controlling idea or thesis. The methods of introducing an essay include the use of an anecdote, a quotation or surprising statistic or fact, and questions.

Irony occurs when a writer or speaker implies (rather than states directly) a discrepancy or incongruity of some kind. *Verbal irony,* which is often tongue-in-cheek, involves a discrepancy between the literal words and what's actually meant ("I know you must be unhappy about receiving the highest grade in the course"). If the ironic comment is designed to be hurtful or insulting, it qualifies as *sarcasm* ("Congratulations! You failed the final exam"). In *situational irony,* the circumstances are themselves incongruous. For example, although their constitutional rights were violated when the federal government detained them in internment camps, Japanese-Americans nevertheless played American football, sang American songs, and saluted the American flag during their imprisonment.

Journal writing is a form of prewriting in which writers make daily entries in a private journal, much as they would in a diary. Whether they focus on one topic or wander freely, journal writers jot down striking incidents, images, and ideas encountered in the course of a day. Such journal material can produce ideas for future essays.

Logical fallacies are easily committed mistakes in reasoning that writers must avoid, especially when writing *argumentation-persuasion* essays. There are many kinds of logical fallacies. Here are several:

Ad hominem argument occurs when someone attacks another person's point of view by criticizing that person, not the issue. Often called "mudslinging," *ad hominem* arguments try to invalidate a person's ideas by revealing unrelated, past or present, personal or ethical flaws. For example, to claim that a person cannot govern the country well because it can be proven he or she has little sense of humor is to use an *ad hominem* argument.

Begging the question is a fallacy in which the writer assumes the truth of something that needs to be proven. Imagine a writer argues the following: "A law should be passed requiring dangerous pets like German shepherds and Doberman pinschers to be restrained by fences, leashes, and muzzles." Such an argument begs the question since it assumes readers will automatically accept the view that such dogs are indeed dangerous.

Either-or fallacies occur when it's argued that a complex situation can be resolved in only one of two possible ways. Here's an example: "If the administration doesn't grant striking professors more money, the college will never be able to attract outstanding teachers in years ahead." Such an argument oversimplifies matters. Excellent teachers might be attracted to a college for a variety of reasons, not just because of good salaries.

False analogy erroneously suggests that because two things are alike in some regards, they are similar in all ways. In the process, significant differences between the two are disregarded. If you argue that a woman prosecuting a rapist is subjected to a second rape in court, you're guilty of a false analogy. As embarrassing, painful, and hurtful as the court proceedings may be, the woman is not physically assaulted, as she was when she was raped. Also, as difficult as her decision to seek justice might be, she's in court by choice and not against her will.

Hasty generalizations are unsound *inductive inferences* based on too few instances of a behavior, situation, or process. For example, it would be a hasty generalization to conclude that you're allergic to a food such as curry because you once ate it and became ill. There are several other possible explanations for your illness, and only repetitions of this experience or a lab test could prove conclusively that you're allergic to this food.

Non sequiturs are faulty conclusions about cause and effect. Here's an example: "Throughout this country's history, most physicians have been male. Women apparently have little interest in becoming doctors." The faulty conclusion accords one factor—the possible vocational preferences of women—the status of sole cause. The conclusion fails to consider pressures on women to devote themselves to homemaking and to avoid an occupation sexually stereotyped as "masculine."

Post hoc thinking results when it's presumed that one event caused another just because it occurred first. For instance, if your car broke down the day after you lent it to your brother, you would be committing the *post hoc* fallacy if you blamed him, unless you knew he did something to your car's engine.

Questionable authority, revealed by such phrases as "studies show" and "experts claim," undercuts a writer's credibility. Readers become suspicious of such vague and unsubstantial appeals to authority. Writers should demonstrate the reliability of their sources by citing them specifically.

Red herring arguments are deliberate attempts to focus attention on a peripheral matter rather than examine the merits of the issue under discussion. Imagine that a local environmental group advocates stricter controls for employees at a nearby chemical plant. The group points out that plant employees are repeatedly exposed to high levels of toxic chemicals. If you respond, "Many of the employees are illegal aliens and shouldn't be allowed to take jobs from native-born townspeople," you're throwing in a red herring. By bringing in immigration policies, you sidetrack attention from the matter at hand.

Logos is a major factor in creating an effective argument. It refers to the soundness of *argumentation,* as created by the use of facts, statistics, information, and commentary by authoritative sources. The most effective arguments involve an interplay among *logos, pathos,* and *ethos.*

Major premise—see *Deductive reasoning.*

Minor premise—see *Deductive reasoning.*

MLA documentation is the system developed by the Modern Language Association for citing sources in a paper. When you quote or summarize source material, you must do two things within your paper's text: (1) identify the author and (2) specify the pages on which the material appears. You may provide the author's name in a lead-in sentence or within parentheses following the borrowed material; the page number always appears in parentheses, inserted in the text after the borrowed material. The material in the parentheses is called a *parenthetical reference.* A paper using MLA documentation ends with a *Works Cited* list, which includes only those sources actually acknowledged in the paper. Entries are organized alphabetically by authors' last names. Entries without an author are alphabetized by the first major word in the title.

Narration means recounting an event or a series of related events to make a point. Narration can be an essay's principal pattern of development, or it can be used to supplement a paper organized primarily around another pattern. For instance, to persuade readers to avoid drug use, a writer might use the narrative pattern by recounting the story of an abuser's addiction and recovery.

Narrative point refers to the meaning the writer intends to convey to a reader by telling a certain story. This narrative point might be a specific message, or it might be a feeling about the situation, people, or place of the story. This underlying meaning is achieved by presenting details that support it and eliminating any that are nonessential. For example, in an essay about friendship, a writer's point might be that friendships change when one of the friends acquires a significant partner of the opposite sex. The writer would focus on the details of how her close female friend had less time for her, changed their usual times of getting together, and confided in her less. The writer would omit judgments of the friend's choice of boyfriend and her friend's declining grades because these details would distract the reader from the essay's narrative point.

Narrative sequence refers to the order in which a writer recounts events. When you follow the order of the events as they happened, you're using *chronological sequence.* This sequence, in which you begin at the beginning and end with the last event, is the most basic and commonly used narrative sequence. If you interrupt this flow to present an event that happened before the beginning of the narrative sequence, you're employing a *flashback*. If you skip ahead to an event later than the one that comes next in your narrative, you're using the *flashforward* technique.

Non sequiturs—see *Logical fallacies.*

Objective description—see *Description.*

One-side-at-a-time method refers to one of the two techniques for organizing a *comparison-contrast* essay. In using this method, a writer discusses all the points about one of the compared and contrasted subjects before going on to the other. For example, in an essay titled "Single or Married?" a writer might first discuss single life in terms of amount of independence, freedom of career choice, and companionship. Then the writer would, within reason, discuss married life in terms of these same three subtopics. The issues the writer discusses in each half of the essay would be identical and presented in the same order. See also *Point-by-point method.*

Organization refers to the process of arranging evidence to support a thesis in the most effective way. When organizing, a writer decides what ideas come first, next, and last. In *chronological* sequence, details are arranged according to occurrence in time. In *spatial* sequence, details appear in the order in which they occur in space. In *emphatic* order, ideas are sequenced according to importance, with the most significant, outstanding, or convincing evidence being reserved for last. In *simple-to-complex* order, easy-to-grasp material is presented before more-difficult-to-comprehend information.

Outlining involves making a formal plan before writing a *first draft.* Writing an outline helps you determine whether your supporting evidence is logical and adequate. As you write, you can use the outline to keep yourself on track. Many writers use the indentation system of Roman numerals, letters, and Arabic numbers to outline; sometimes writers use a less formal system.

Paradox refers to a statement that seems impossible, contrary to common sense, or self-contradictory, yet that can—after consideration—be seen to be plausible or true. For example, Oscar Wilde produced a paradox when he wrote "When the gods wish to punish us, they answer our prayers." The statement doesn't contradict itself because often, Wilde believes, that which we wish for turns out to be the very thing that will bring us the most pain.

Parenthetical reference—see *MLA documentation.*

Pathos refers to the emotional power of an *argumentation-persuasion* essay. By appealing to the needs, values, and attitudes of readers and by using *connotative language,* writers can increase the chances that readers will come to agree with the ideas in an essay. Although *pathos* is an important element of persuasion, such emotional appeals should reinforce rather than replace reason. The most effective argumentation-persuasion involves an interplay among *pathos, logos,* and *ethos.*

Peer review is the critical reading of another person's writing with the intention of suggesting changes. To be effective, peer review calls for readers who are objective, skilled, and tactful enough to provide useful feedback. Begin by giving your readers a clear sense of what you expect from the review. To promote specific responses, ask the reviewers targeted (preferably written) questions. Following the review, rank the problems and solutions that the reviewers identified. Then enter your own notes for revising in the margins of your draft so that you'll know exactly what changes need to be made in your draft as you rework it.

Plan of development refers to a technique whereby the writer supplies the reader with a brief map of the main points to be covered in an essay. If used, the plan of development occurs as part of the *thesis* or in a sentence following the thesis. In it, the main ideas are mentioned in the order in which they'll appear in the supporting paragraphs. Longer essays and term papers usually need a plan of development to maintain unity, but shorter papers may do without one.

Point-by-point method refers to one of the two techniques for organizing a *comparison-contrast* essay. A writer using this method moves from one aspect of one subject to the same aspect of another subject before going on to the second aspect of each subject. For example, in an essay titled "Single or Married?" a writer might first discuss the amount of independence a person has when single and when married. Then, the writer might go on to discuss how much freedom of career choice a person has when single and when married. Finally, the writer might discuss, in turn, the amount of companionship available in each of the two lifestyles. See also *One-side-at-a-time method.*

Point of view refers to the perspective a writer chooses when writing about a subject. If you narrate events as you experience them, you're using the *first-person* point of view. You might say, for example, "*I* noticed jam on the child's collar and holes in her shirt." If you relate the events from a distance—as if you observed them but did not experience them personally—you're using the *third-person* point of view; for instance, "Jam splotched the child's collar, and her shirt had several holes in it." The point of view should be consistent throughout an essay.

***Post hoc* thinking**—see *Logical fallacies.*

Prewriting is the first stage of the writing process. During prewriting, you jot down rough ideas about your subject without yet moving to writing a draft of your essay. Your goals at this stage are to (1) understand the boundaries of the assignment, (2) discover the limited subject you could write about, (3) generate raw material about the limited subject, and (4) organize the raw material into a very rough *scratch outline.* If you keep in mind that prewriting is "unofficial," it can be a low-pressure, even enjoyable activity.

Process analysis refers to writing that explains the steps involved in doing something or the sequence of stages in an event or behavior. There are two types of process analysis. In *directional process analysis,* readers are shown how to do something step by step. Cookbook recipes, tax form instructions, and how-to books are some typical uses of directional process analysis. In *informational process analysis,* the writer explains how something is done or occurs, without expecting the reader to attempt the process. "A Senator's Road to Political Power," "How a Bee Makes Honey," and "How a Convict Gets Paroled" would be titles of essays developed through informational process analysis.

Proofreading involves rereading a final draft carefully to catch any errors in spelling, grammar, punctuation, or typing that have slipped by. While such errors are minor, a significant number of them can seriously weaken the effectiveness of an essay.

Proposition—see *Assertion.*

Purpose is the reason a writer has for preparing a particular essay. Usually, writers frame their purposes in terms of the effect they wish to have on their *audience*. They may wish to explore the personal meaning of a subject or experience, explain an idea or process, provide information, influence opinion, or entertain. Many essays combine purposes, with one purpose predominating and providing the essay's focus.

Red herring argument—see *Logical fallacies.*

Refutation is an important strategy in *argumentation-persuasion*. In refutation, writers acknowledge that there are opposing views on the subject under discussion and then go on to do one of two things. Sometimes they may admit that the opposing views are somewhat valid but assert that their own position has more merit and devote their essay to demonstrating that merit. For example, a writer might assert, "Business majors often find interesting and lucrative jobs. However, in the long run, liberal arts graduates have many more advantages in the job market because the breadth of their background helps them think better, learn faster, and communicate more effectively." This writer would concentrate on proving the advantages that liberal arts graduates have. At other times, writers may choose to argue actively against an opposing position by dismantling that view point by point. Such refutation of opposing views can strengthen the writer's own arguments.

Repeated words, synonyms, and pronouns—see *Signaling devices.*

Revision means, literally, "reseeing" a *first draft* with a fresh eye, as if the writer had not actually prepared the draft. When revising, you move from more global issues (like clarifying meaning and organization) to more specific matters (like fine-tuning sentences and word choice). While revising, you make whatever changes are necessary to increase the essay's effectiveness. You might strengthen your thesis, resequence paragraph order, or add more transitions. Such changes often make the difference between mediocre and superior writing.

Satire is a humorous form of social criticism usually aimed at society's institutions or human behavior. Often irreverent as well as witty, satire is serious in purpose: to point out evil, injustice, and absurdity and bring about change through an increase in awareness. Satire ranges widely in tone: it may be gentle or biting; it may sarcastically describe a real situation or use fictional characters and events to spoof reality. Satire often makes use of *irony*.

Scratch outline refers to your first informal plan for an essay, devised at the end of the *prewriting* stage. In making a scratch outline, you select ideas and details from your raw material for inclusion in your essay and discard the rest. You also arrange these ideas in an order that makes sense and that will help you achieve your *purpose*. A scratch outline is tentative and flexible, and can be reshaped as needed.

Sensory description vividly evokes the sights, smells, tastes, sounds, and physical feelings of a scene or event. For example, if a writer carefully chooses words and images, readers can see the vibrant reds and oranges of falling leaves, taste the sourness of an underripe grapefruit, hear the growling of motorcycles as a gang sweeps through a town, smell the spicy aroma of a grandmother's homemade tomato soup, and feel the pulsing pain of a jaw after Novocain wears off. Sensory description is particularly important in writing *description* or *narration*.

Sentence variety adds interest to the style of an essay or paragraph. In creating sentence variety, writers mix different kinds of sentences and sentence patterns.

For example, you might vary the way your sentences open or intersperse short sentences with long ones, simple sentences with complex ones. Repetitive sentence patterns tend to make readers lose interest.

Signaling devices indicate the relationships among ideas in an essay. They help the reader follow the train of thought from sentence to sentence and from paragraph to paragraph. There are three types of connectives. *Transitions* are words that clarify flow of meaning. They can signal an additional or contrasting point, an enumeration of ideas, the use of an example, or other movement of ideas. *Linking sentences* summarize a point just made and then introduce a follow-up point. *Repeated words, synonyms,* and *pronouns* create a sense of flow by keeping important concepts in the mind of the reader.

Spatial sequence—see *Organization.*

Specific—see *Evidence.*

Stipulative definition is a way of restricting a term for the purposes of discussion. Many words have multiple meanings that can get in the way of clarity when a writer is creating an *extended definition.* For example, you might stipulate the following definition of *foreign car:* "While many American automobiles use parts or even whole engines made by foreign car manufacturers, for the purposes of discussion, 'foreign car' refers only to those automobiles designed and manufactured wholly by a company based in another country. By this definition, a European vehicle made in Pennsylvania is *not* a foreign car."

Subjective description—see *Description.*

Support—see *Evidence.*

Syllogism—see *Deductive reasoning.*

Term—see *Formal definition.*

Thesis is the central idea in any essay, usually expressed in a one- or two-sentence *thesis statement.* Writers accomplish two things by providing a thesis statement in an essay: They indicate the essay's limited subject and express an attitude about that subject. Also called the *controlling idea,* the thesis statement consists of a particular slant, angle, or point of view about the limited subject.

Tone conveys your attitude toward yourself, your purpose, your topic, and your readers. As in speaking, tone in writing may be serious, playful, sarcastic, and so on. Generally, readers detect tone more by how you say something (that is, through your sentence structure and word choice) than by what you say.

Topic sentence is the term for the sentence(s) that convey the main idea of a paragraph. Such sentences are often, but not always, found at the start of a paragraph. They provide a statement of the subject to be discussed and an indication of the writer's attitude toward that subject. Writers usually concern themselves with topic sentences during the writing of the first draft.

Transitions—see *Signaling devices.*

Unified—see *Evidence.*

Works Cited—see *MLA documentation.*

ACKNOWLEDGMENTS

Angelou, Maya, "Sister Flowers." Copyright © 1969 and renewed 1997 by Maya Angelou, from *I Know Why the Caged Bird Sings* by Maya Angelou. Used by permission of Random House, Inc.

Angier, Natalie, "The Cute Factor." From *The New York Times*, January 3, 2006 © 2006 The New York Times. All rights reserved. Used by permission and protected by the Copyright Laws of the United States. The printing, copying, redistribution, or retransmission of this Content without express written permission is prohibited.

Barry, Dave, "Beauty and the Beast." The Miami Herald, February 1, 1998. Used by permission of Dave Barry.

Berry, Wendell, "Farming and the Global Economy." Copyright © 1995 by Wendell Berry from *Another Turn of the Crank*. Reprinted by permission of Counterpoint.

Brooks, David, "Psst! 'Human Capital.'" From *The New York Times*, November 13, 2005. © 2005 The New York Times. All rights reserved. Used by permission and protected by the Copyright Laws of the United States. The printing, copying, redistribution, or retransmission of this Content without express written permission is prohibited.

Chapman, Stephen, "The Prisoner's Dilemma." From *The New Republic*, March 8, 1980. Reprinted by permission of *The New Republic*, © 1980, The New Republic, LLC.

Cofer, Judith Ortiz, "A Partial Remembrance of a Puerto Rican Childhood." "Casa" reprinted with permission from the publisher of *Silent Dancing: A Partial Remembrance of a Puerto Rican Childhood* by Judith Ortiz Cofer (© 1990 Arte Publico Press—University of Houston).

D'Amboise, Jacques, "Showing What Is Possible." From *Parade*, August 6, 1989. Reprinted with permission of the author.

Didion, Joan, "The Santa Ana" (excerpt from "Los Angeles Notebook") and "Marrying Absurd." From *Slouching Towards Bethlehem* by Joan Didion. Copyright © 1966, 1968, renewed 1996 by Joan Didion. Reprinted by permission of Farrar, Straus and Giroux, LLC.

Divakaruni, Chitra Banerjee, "Common Scents: The Smell of Childhood Never Fades." Copyright © 1997 by Chitra Divakaruni. First appeared on Salon.com. Reprinted by permission of the author and the Sandra Dijkstra Literary Agency.

Ehrenreich, Barbara, "Serving in Florida." From the book *Nickel and Dimed: On (Not) Getting By in America* by Barbara Ehrenreich. Copyright © 2001 by Barbara Ehrenreich. Reprinted by permission of Henry Holt and Company, LLC.

Ericsson, Stephanie, "The Ways We Lie." Copyright © 1992 by Stephanie Ericsson. Reprinted by the permission of Dunham Literary as agents for the author. Originally published by *The Utne Reader*.

Fish, Stanley, "Free-Speech Follies." © 2003, Stanley Fish, Davidson-Kahn Distinguished University Professor of Humanities and Law, Florida International University, College of Law. Reprinted with permission.

Garibaldi, Gerry, "How the Schools Shortchange Boys." From *City Journal* Summer 2006, Copyright The Manhattan Institute. Reprinted with permission.

Gleick, James, "Life as Type A." From *Faster: The Acceleration of Just About Everything* by James Gleick. Copyright © 1999 by James Gleick. Used by permission of Pantheon Books, a division of Random House, Inc.

Goodman, Ellen, "Family Counterculture." From *The Boston Globe*, August 16, 1991. © 1991 The Boston Globe. All rights reserved. Used by permission and protected by the Copyright Laws of the United States. The printing, copying, redistribution, or retransmission of this Content without express written permission is prohibited.

Helvarg, David, "The Storm This Time." Originally published in *Multinational Monitor*, Sept./Oct. 2005, pp. 9–18. Reprinted with permission from Multinational Monitor.

Hughes, Langston, "Salvation." From *The Big Sea* by Langston Hughes. Copyright © 1940 by Langston Hughes. Copyright renewed 1968 by Arna Bontemps and George Houston Bass. Reprinted by permission of Hill and Wang, a Division of Farrar, Straus and Giroux, LLC.

Hulbert, Ann, "Beyond the Pleasure Principle." Originally published in *The New York Times*. Copyright © 2007 by Ann Hulbert and *The New York Times*. Used with permission of The Wylie Agency LLC.

Hymowitz, Kay S., "Tweens: Ten Going On Sixteen." From *City Journal*, Autumn 1998, Vol. 8, No. 4. Reprinted with permission of City Journal/Manhattan Institute.

Johnson, Beth, "Bombs Bursting in Air." Used by permission of the author.

Johnson, Keith, "Who's a Pirate? In Court, A Duel over Definitions." Reprinted by permission of *The Wall Street Journal*, Copyright © August 20, 2010 Dow Jones & Company, Inc. All Rights Reserved Worldwide. License number 2577751180340.

King, Martin Luther Jr., "Where Do We Go From Here: Chaos or Community?" Reprinted by arrangement with The Heirs to the Estate of Martin Luther King Jr., c/o Writers House as agent for the proprietor New York, NY. Copyright © 1964 Dr. Martin Luther King Jr; copyright renewed 1992 Coretta Scott King; Copyright © 1967 Dr. Martin Luther King Jr; copyright renewed 1995 Coretta Scott King.

King, Stephen, "Why We Crave Horror Movies." Reprinted With Permission. © Stephen King. All rights reserved. Originally appeared in *Playboy* (1982).

Kingsolver, Barbara, "Stone Soup." (pp. 135–45) From *High Tide in Tucson: Essays from Now or Never* by Barbara Kingsolver. Copyright © 1995 by Barbara Kingsolver. Reprinted by permission of HarperCollins Publishers.

Kingsolver, Barbara, "The Good Farmer." From *The Essential Agrarian Reader: The Future of Culture, Community and the Land*, University Press of Kentucky, 2003, pp. ix–xvii. Used by permission.

McClintock, Ann, "Propaganda Techniques in Today's Advertising." Reprinted by permission of the author.

Murray, Joan, "Someone's Mother." From *The New York Times*, May 13, 2007. © 2007 The New York Times. All rights reserved. Used by permission and protected by the Copyright Laws of the United States. The printing, copying, redistribution, or retransmission of this Content without express written permission is prohibited.

Parker, Star, "*Se Habla* Entitlement." Posted on worldnetdaily.com, April 18, 2006. Reprinted with permission.

Parks, Gordon, "Flavio's Home." From *Voices in the Mirror* by Gordon Parks. Copyright © 1990 by Gordon Parks. Used by permission of Doubleday, a division of Random House, Inc.

Postrel, Virginia, "Need Transplant Donors? Pay Them." © June 10, 2006 in *Los Angeles Times*.

Quindlen, Anna, "Driving to the Funeral." Reprinted by permission of International Creative Management, Inc. Copyright © 2007 by Anna Quindlen. First appeared in *Newsweek*.

Raspberry, William, "The Handicap of Definition." *The Washington Post*, 1982. All rights reserved. Used by permission and protected by the Copyright Laws of the United States. The printing, copying, redistribution, or retransmission of the Material without express written permission is prohibited.

Rego, Caroline, "The Fine Art of Complaining." Used by permission of the author.

Riverbend, "Bloggers without Borders..." (October 22, 2007) from *Baghdad Burning* blog, http://riverbendblog.blogspot.com. Reprinted by permission of The Feminist Press at the City University of New York, www.feministpress.org. All rights reserved.

Roberts, Paul, "How to Say Nothing In 500 Words." From *Understanding English* by Paul Roberts. Copyright © 1958 by Paul Roberts. Reprinted by permission of Pearson Education, Inc.

Rodriguez, Richard, "Workers." From *Hunger of Memory: The Education of Richard Rodriguez* by Richard Rodriguez. Reprinted by permission of David R. Godine, Publisher, Inc. Copyright © 1982 by Richard Rodriguez.

Rodriguez, Roberto, "The Border on Our Backs." From "Column of the Americas." Reprinted with permission of the author.

Shaw, Jane S., "Nature in the Suburbs." Heritage Foundation. Used by permission.

Sherry, Mary, "In Praise of the 'F' Word." From *Newsweek*, May 6, 1991. Reprinted with permission of the author.

Shipley, David, "Talk About Editing." From *The New York Times*, July 2005. © 2005 The New York Times. All rights reserved. Used by permission and protected by the Copyright Laws of the United States. The printing, copying, redistribution, or retransmission of this Content without express written permission is prohibited.

Staples, Brent, "Just Walk on By: A Black Man Ponders His Power to Alter Public Space." *Ms.* Magazine, 1986. Used by permission of the author.

Sutherland, Amy, "What Shamu Taught Me About a Happy Marriage." From *The New York Times*, June 25, 2006. Reprinted by permission of the author.

Sykes, Charles, "The 'Values' Wasteland," Dumbing Down Our Kids, St. Martin's Press. Copyright © 1995 by the author and reprinted by permission of St. Martin's Press, LLC.

Tabarrok, Alexander T., A" Moral Solution to the Organ Shortage." © Feb19, 2001, in *The Independent Institute*, © Feb 19, 2001, http://www.independent.org/newsroom/article.asp?id=283.

Tan, Amy, "Mother Tongue." Copyright © 1989 by Amy Tan. First appeared in Threepenny Review. Reprinted by permission of the author and the Sandra Dijkstra Literary Agency.

Twain, Mark, "The Damned Human Race." From *Letters from the Earth* by Mark Twain, edited by Bernard Devoto. Copyright © 1938, 1944, 1946, 1959, 1962 by The Mark Twain Company. Copyright © 1942 by The President and Fellows of Harvard College. Reprinted by permission of HarperCollins Publishers.

Weiner, Eric, "Euromail and Amerimail." Broadcast on NPR 3/24/05, full version published on Slate.com 3/25/05. Reprinted with permission of the author.

Williams, Juan, "The Ruling That Changed America." Reprinted with permission from American School Board Journal, April 2004. Copyright © 2004 National School Boards Association. All rights reserved.

Wright, Alex, "Friending, Ancient or Otherwise." From *The New York Times*, December 2, 2007. © 2007 The New York Times. All rights reserved. Used by permission and protected by the Copyright Laws of the United States. The printing, copying, redistribution, or retransmission of this Content without express written permission is prohibited.

Zinsser, William, "College Pressures." Copyright © 1979 by William K. Zinsser. Reprinted by permission of the author.

pp. 1, 13, 571, 607, 639: ©Don White/SuperStock

p. 5: Ricardo Arduengo/AP Images

p. 72, 75: ©Rudi Von Briel/PhotoEdit, Inc.

p. 105, 106: ©David Helvard/Blue Frontier Campaign

p. 126, 127: ©Bill Pugliano/Getty Images

p. 175, 177: ©Bill Arnon/PhotoEdit, Inc.

p. 223, 226: ©LWA-Dann Tardiff/Corbis

p. 279, 281: ©Angelo Cavalli/Getty Images

p. 335, 337: ©Percy Ryall/Alamy

p. 381, 383: ©Ken McGraw/Photolibrary

p. 431, 432: ©Donald Miralle/Getty Images

p. 450, 452: © ICC International Maritime Bureau. Used by permission.

p. 474, 479: ©Big Brothers Big Sisters of America homepage screen capture, BigBrothersBigSisters.org. Reprinted with permission.

INDEX